FIRST COMES LOVE:

The DeProgramming of An Army Wife

A *Memoir*
by
L. L. Morton

Third Millennium Publishing
A Cooperative of Writers and Resources
On the INTERNET
http://3mpub.com

ISBN 1-934805-52-1
    978-1-934805-52-7

571 pages

L. L. Morton
PO Box 3203
Ashland, OR 97520-1422
Email: LL.Morton1@gmail.com

Morton, L. L. 1936 -
First Comes Love: The DeProgramming of An Army Wife

1. Psychology - Trauma, loss, abuse 2. Family - Sibling rivalry
3. Mental illness - Addiction 4. Religion 5. US Army life -
Biography - United States

Third Millennium Publishing
PO Box 14026
Tempe, AZ 85284-0068
mccollum@3mpub.com

20120204B

INFORMATION ABOUT FIRST EDITION

First Comes Love: The DeProgramming of An Army Wife, a Memoir, an expanded and revised edition, was first published in 1993 by Independent-House Press, Dover, MA, as a fictionalized autobiography under the title: *A Make-Believe Face,* copyright 1987, 1990/Library of Congress Cataloging-in-Publication #92-74119/ISBN 0-9634673-0-1.

For information or permission to reproduce, contact:
L. L. Morton
P. O. Box 3203
Ashland, OR 97520-1422

◆

For my children,
and theirs, and theirs,
and theirs...

Table of Contents

INTRODUCTION

Life is 10% of what happens to you, and 90% of how you respond to it.

Learn from the mistakes of others, you can't live long enough to make them all yourself.

"He believed that in order to deal with the future, you have to know and understand the past."

—Ted Kennedy, Jr.,
(paraphrased, at the funeral
of his father, Senator Kennedy)

Meet the Author: May 1989

If I truly love one person I love all persons, I love the world. I love life. If I can say to somebody else, "I love you," I must be able to say, "I love in you everybody. I love through you the world, I love in you also myself."
                                          —Eric Fromm, *The Art of Loving*

Just driving through Cambridge, past Harvard that first day, was a delightful, but terrifying experience. It was hard to believe that at my age I was really going back to college, full time, without having to go to work in order to afford tuition. I was only here at the suggestion of my husband's secretary, who listened to him on a daily basis give a running commentary on whatever was my current undertaking. He would often say that one of the things that kept him coming home was that he never knew what he would find when he got there — what new hairstyle, sewing or craft project, furniture antiquing I may have begun, unannounced. Despite never having met me, his secretary recommended Lesley College as the best place for women of all ages to broaden their educational experience. Their unique Expressive Therapies Program sounded to be just what I needed. Introductory to choosing which direction I wished to go, I was allowed to observe several of the classes that were part of this curriculum.

Observing the dance therapy group, I felt the music clear to my toes, and I remembered it was the year we lived in Georgia, in the fourth grade at Annie West School in East Atlanta, where I was first asked to play for the students to march into assembly for a parent's program. Sitting near the piano, awaiting the final exit to play again, the rest of my class was exhibiting our latest square dance to the *Old Grey Mare* being heard from a portable Victrola. In the middle of this lively display up on stage, my father slipped up to the front, took me forcibly by the arm, and marched me out of the auditorium to the principle's office. With very angry words, it was made painfully clear to her, and all those within an earshot, that I was not to participate in such "ungodly doings" again. When dancing was the scheduled activity, the art teacher would discreetly request for my help on the large hall mural.

Mrs. Chamblee, not much taller than I, was one of those little, round ladies whose mere presence exuded warmth, and she had a marvelous eye for color. Letting me work with the chalk right along with her, she said I was a real artist. That Horn of

3

Plenty, displayed for weeks for the whole school to see, took away part of the sting I suffered from being otherwise excluded. What smart teachers I had!

Back at Lesley in the Art Therapy class, we were asked to draw our name without using any letters. The sound of my stodgy proper name would often elicit the scene in my mind of a lonely child. Although my sketching was amateurish, I attempted to draw her peering out one of the small panes of a Colonial style window with her nose pressed flat against the glass. It was this feeling of isolation, of such sadness that went with the sound of my name, that prompted me to change it to a nickname, when, after my teenage divorce, I applied for my first job – a break from the past in a very intended way.

Observing these different classes, their respective avenues to the subconscious, were already beginning to trigger many memories. At home, I was putting story after story on paper. So it was no surprise that when I had the mandatory interview with the Dean of this program, I had volumes of written work to show him.

He was a large man, possibly well over three-hundred pounds. It was clear he had a physical condition with which he must have struggled for years. My heart went out to him as we were just learning how food was an effective painkiller for psychic trauma. *How much pain this man must have suffered!* My thoughts were putting me at ease so that I was able to share with him my own circumstances, of learning to cope daily with our family's unusual and diverse challenges, while at the same time still operating myself from behind stubborn walls of what one doctor called "lingering repression." Still unaware, though, was I, even as the Dean scanned the many memoir pieces, the term papers and essays from past psychology and sociology courses, editorials to the Boston Globe, short stories…

The Dean flipped through several pages, reading, reading. Finally he looked up at me, and said, "I think you are in the wrong program; you need to be in Writing."

I wanted to say: There is so much missing; ignorance is *not* bliss. Instead, I said, "I don't know enough, that's why I signed up for Psychology."

The Dean wasn't really listening; he was putting all my work together and shoving it across the table towards me. Waving me out, he said, "You need to transfer to Writing, that is where your heart is. It's clear you already *are* a writer."

I t was as if I had been given a whole new way to look at myself: *A writer...*

It was then that I began to look at all the writing and recognized a pattern. They were all about some part of that little girl who had been locked away, out of consciousness.

I had written:

Remembering childhood, for most adults, is like turning on a light in a dark place: illuminating, enlightening, taking away the bogeyman. But to some, like me, the memories remain as holes in the dark, bits here and there that filter through a blanket of a void still echoing terror: Hush, don't take on so, don't tell. The windows to the world of that lively, open-minded child are clouded with fear, distorted, and stunted perceptions crystallized, fixing the evolving adult – forever a child.

"Do you remember that day?" I was often asked, even by strangers. "Where were you when it happened?" they would gently pry. I'd try to tell them, when I learned the words, but by then the feelings had gone to sleep. As in a glass globe full of snow, the white lies still around a pretty house. Then out of the blue someone shakes the heavy glass by asking, "Did your mama have little feet, too?" And the snow flies every-which-way. This blizzard of emotion complicates the already difficult task of separating fact from things imagined. However, I have found that fitting the pieces of memory correctly into stories told, though necessary, become less important than the sense of order, of wholeness, that's generated by ultimately finding a way through the storm.

M y new Writing professor was saying, "There are many other ways to heal than through psychiatry. Therapy is simply learning about *you*, and learning can take place in many kinds of settings. Besides, how can you understand your children, your family, until you understand yourself?"

Little did I know that this concentrated study would culminate years of searching and ultimately result in that long sought-for emotional awakening. Then, and only then, would I finally be able to truly know and love my family, each one for themselves alone.

G rowing up in an intellectual and social vacuum is, in itself, cause for a severe warping of the personality. To understand how this could happen to someone while being enrolled in a mid-western, considered superior, public school system where notables such as Golda Meir, Liberace, and Oprah Winfrey once attended, one would have to be submersed into the world of *us* and *them,* the *saved* and the *damned.*

If one were a part of *us*, we were praising God for His tender mercies for bringing *us* into the light of His glorious truth. If one were not, we were praying for *them*, for God to *save them* by showing them the way to *our* blessed salvation. As a child, I remember feeling so sad for *them*, believing that even though *we* constituted a very small minority at the time, *we* were of that select few who had been privileged to have found favor with the Almighty. Being on the "right" side of the "truth" can have a stymying effect upon the development of a young mind. Even though I was extremely ashamed of *us*, of being so different, I was, after all, going to heaven, and they, "poor souls without Jesus," were bound for everlasting damnation.

In my sunset years, I see that same childhood nightmare taking shape — the same intellectual vacuum reflected in our communications, the cocksureness; the name of Jesus being invoked by politicians, TV pundits, and radio talkers at every turn while at the same time ignoring the inclusion of which the life and teachings of Jesus represent. This religiosity is now dividing us, subtly turning us into an *us* and *them* society.

Compensation for this narrow and limited view of the world though, was the protection it gave me from a brutally harsh inner reality. "Losing a mother at an early age is such a catastrophic event in the development of a young child's psyche, the emotional devastation wrought can never be completely remedied as it leaves an IOU for which currency is no longer issued."[1] That void, that emptiness has driven my life. A treachery of loneliness and isolation, upon which the lives of four beautiful children have been built, has left sadness and near destruction in its wake.

Perceiving another's life through *their* lens of severe repression is rather like trying to discern the skin color of a shadow, but realizing how detrimental was the authoritarian way used in my upbringing – which was also used with my own children – I feel the need to share my family's struggle. Some names and places are changed and situation composites may condense time and events, but the basic truth of the story remains.

                                                              –L. L. Morton

---

[1] Douglas A. Col, Ph. D., Neuropsychologist

The Past as Prologue

Dorie Mae Evermardt-Tuckermoore:
1915-1939

After a long inquest which included an autopsy, my death was ruled an accident. In less than a month, soon after my twenty-fourth birthday, my third child would be due. In family-way, I was carrying another girl, a sister for Sammy Sue, almost three. A baby brother came in between there, but he only lived nine months, a "water head" we called his hydrocephalic condition. Since the doctors said Jesse Woodrow's head was so large and getting larger by the day because it was filled with water, being Southerners we called things as we saw them. There was no help for it then; now, even in the womb the fluid can be drained off. The world wasn't so sophisticated only having the radio to listen to and just the beginning of talking movies, if you could spare the nickel.

Originally, we were a farming family from West Tennessee, but after the terrible depression, people were bad off. My father, a quick witted and determined sort who sprang from a plain, gentle British mother and a staunch German father in "the old country," Calvin Evermardt was endowed with an entrepreneurial spirit which ran high in the Evermardt family's blood. When his first wife, Cornelia, up and walked out on him and left him with four children to rear, Papa was forced to search for a more predictable living.

Cornelia did not appear to have been a very able body; it was surmised that she never quite recovered from the birth of her last child. She disappeared one day on the local, weekly coach run while our Papa was on a business trip to Charleston. He came home to find his four younguns in the care of a kind neighbor, who, it was said, kept them in biscuits and strap molasses awaiting their father's return.

A practical gentleman with an eye for the future, Papa said he then needed to find a god-fearing woman to tend his brats – a formidable task in 1909.

By this time, Papa said he had lost touch with his only brother, who had taken his share of the family inheritance and gone East, forcing Papa to tighten his belt and seek his own way. Poverty was something that lurked behind every corner awaiting those not blessed with his vision. Papa always said the world was divided up into those who worked and those who didn't – it was that simple, and he believed himself to be one of those privileged few who had the intelligence and vision, the energy and gumption to carry out a plan – and great business plans Papa did have.

While on one of Papa's necessary business trips to South Carolina, he took to patronizing the services of Mrs. Cory, a widow lady who earned her living by taking in laundry. It was her daughter who caught his eye when he'd taken his shirts to be done. This wash girl was not only amiable, gentle as his deceased mother and with the same blue eyes that seemed to sparkle with the mention of her name, she appeared obedient and helpful, a prime prerequisite in his mind, for his future.

On that momentous occasion, with one eye on the petite and delicate, but lovely Samantha Sue, Papa reminisces asking, "Mrs. Cory, can I come calling on your daughter tomorrow evening?"

The woman's eyes opened wide in surprise. Papa would recall her saying, "Samantha Sue is not my daughter, only an orphaned cousin I am looking out for, but I can see no harm in your visitin'."

Mama, who had crystal clear blue eyes and dark, dark hair, liked to say that Papa came calling in his best suit. His black, bushy eyebrows had been combed and pasted to match his black mustache, the essence of "handsome" for the times. Papa would say "what a shy creature your mama was, so young — who spoke with such purity of spirit."

At this juncture, Papa made no mention of his four brats back home in West Tennessee, though *there* his predicament was common knowledge. Instead, while she giggled and smiled, and flashed those lively, blue eyes, he strummed his guitar and sang her a song:

I had a girl named cross-eyed Sue;
her eyes were red and her lips were blue;
she had rosy hair and curly cheeks;
her glass teeth rattled
and her false eye squeaked

"Saturday evening, I see there is a special church meeting with that shaggy haired Billy Sunday. Reckon you'd care to go with me, if your Cousin Ma sees fit?"

He remembered watching her eyes turn to sunshine just as they did every time she had handed him his finished laundry.

It was the lively Church of God, a new sect that had sprung up in this southern town, that they visited that week and held hands after the offering had been collected. It was a bold move, as "we hid our clasped hands under the church hymnal." Papa admitted he had little time to waste on the propriety of spooning, "my youngest nearly walking and a housekeeper hard to come by."

Papa believed Mama's youth was in her favor in dealing with his large family; her own misfortune would make her an understanding mother for his children. But what he liked most was her quickness: she could hang a line of clothes faster than three, and her adeptness with the needle made her all the more a desirable choice, her laughter an unexpected pleasure. The sound of it "warmed my sad heart," he said, and helped to heal the hurt. Surely this girl would not succumb to hardship; her strength seemed to energize the air he breathed.

Mama claimed to have "more energy than sense" when people asked her, how did she manage to tend to all of it and still find time to crochet faster than the eye could follow? Her hands were never, ever idle. She gave credit to her lineage, which was partly French and the rest was *The Duke's Mixture* (a popular brand of sweet-smelling tobacco).

Papa was aware of Mama's young girl innocence, but he did not think her scrawny build would hinder her readiness for childbearing. When he pointed out to Mrs. Cory that it would be "one less mouth to feed," she quickly replied, "Two less hands for folding and pressing, either way, it all adds up to less — worry as well."

When the depression hit the farmers, and before I was to start school, Papa said he could no longer support us on the Tennessee farmland he had purchased as the strong young men had gravitated to the cities in search for work. He was forced to follow them, and grabbed the chance to sub-let his 40-acres in exchange for a small pittance, while sharecroppers worked the fields of horseradish, already planted. Little did I imagine then, as a small child, that this small clapboard farmhouse, that had housed us for a time, would be the bridal home for me one day, down the road.

We headed north to the German settlement on the shores of Lake Michigan that fostered independence and frugality, where there were factories that paid good wages. With Papa's imagination and thrift, he knew how to utilize that money being spent.

In South Milwaukee Papa built him a store front business in a huge two-story house right on the streetcar line. Our family made, bottled, and sold horseradish. The many beer-drinking establishments also fed this "old country" community.

If you walked into Mama's house almost any time of the day you might see anywhere from two to ten younguns sitting around the living room in a circle, peeling away, often with tears running down our cheeks; we all took our turn cleaning and scraping the smelly roots. Of the sixteen children Mama raised, twelve her own, all of our hands were mighty busy.

Even though I managed to graduate high school in South Milwaukee from that little red school house still standing, a historical monument, my druthers were to become a secretary as I could take Pitman shorthand as quick as a person could talk, but I was needed to help in the grinding and bottling out in the store. Papa trusted me a great deal; I could sell, too.

One day a mean ol' man came in to buy some horseradish and accused us of watering it down with plain ol' white turnips. It got all over me, and I pulled back the wet cloth we kept over the large crock to keep it fresh, and I suggested he "come on over behind the counter and take a good whiff. See for yourself," I said. When he bent over it, I could see his eyes tearing up. He couldn't back away fast enough, nearly overcome. For a while, I was the talk of the town.

In the summers, Jenny Lou, my closest sister, and I got to go down to Tennessee with my pa and my brothers to help in the picking. That's where we met the Tuckermoore boys who were from a neighboring sharecropper's family. Jenny Lou, fourteen, took a shine to Wilbur, sixteen, and they married right off and moved in with Wilbur's mama and daddy. Orin, an older brother, had run off from home at sixteen to make his way in the world, but when he came home to visit, he swapped his mule colt for a Baby

Overland car to court me. Although Orin had to turn the crank to start it, and the brakes gave out going down a steep hill once, we had a right smart time riding in it on those winding dirt roads. By the time Orin talked me into marrying, it was 1935; I was twenty and he was twenty-five.

At first, for a spell, we lived with Orin's sister, Beulah and her husband, in a divided house on Poplar Ridge Road, in Trimble. This is the same town that a drunk lay down on the railroad tracks and was run over by a train. His brains were picked up and put into a shoe box, making this Tennessee town a bit famous.

Papa left his land in our keeping and we were privileged to work it with the help of one of my brothers. We raised horseradish, corn and beans, and we had a right healthy sow that Orin bred. Of the eight piglets, we got to keep half the litter. Orin was also right handy with a saw and a hammer and made us a couch out of Willie Knight's wagon that Papa had left on the place.

In November of 1936, Doctor Gray came to that little clapboard house and helped to bring Samantha Sue into the world. When she was eight months old, she frightened us with spells called convulsions. Doctor Gray took us in a covered surrey to the big town of Martin to see a brain specialist. On the way, Orin said he prayed to God to heal his baby girl. In Martin, the doctor told us that the ex-rays showed a scar on an artery and gave us medicine to give her, but she never had another spell. I do believe this was the beginning of Orin's newly found respect for his Maker.

Sammy Sue was walking at ten months and potty trained herself even before that. Oh mercy, how she hated wet diapers. I think I named her well, after Mama with her head full of black hair and her short little legs. A doll walking, some said. Persnickety she was, too, just like her Gramma E.

Big in family-way with Jesse Woodrow, I was going out to our storm house when I lost my footing and fell flat on my back. This bad fall, I came to believe, is what brought him too early. Times were hard, with two babies to feed. When my pa came to visit us to see about his land, he asked us to go home to Milwaukee with him. Papa needed someone to peddle his relishes in all the taverns. Beer was sold on almost every corner of town, and being that Orin was not a teetotaler, the proposition looked to be right promising. Jenny Lou, Wilbur, and their first girl, Maureen, came on up behind us to share the four-room upper-flat above Mama and Papa and the store.

There's not too much to tell about that day; it all happened so fast. Little Sammy Sue being right there in the middle of it all, I knew she was going to have a hard time as sensitive as she was about things. It has been painful, yet satisfying, to watch her growing from that little bitty thing into a right intelligent woman. Her affinity to words is how she took after me: I loved to hear them, write them, and spell them. I could spend hours on a crossword puzzle, if work be done. Jenny Lou would rather mess with her hair and work with her fingers in her leisure, like our mama.

It's funny how people's lives cross, like country roads – some coming to a dead end, and others spilling out into a grand highway. I could see how my Sammy Sue could become one of those spectacular folks, who could take the bull by the horns and drag life wherever it took a mind to lead her. But her never learning to claim her sadness at my passing had cost her in a big way. It seemed every time she would just get to the next rung in the ladder of this emotional undertaking, she would look down and lose her footing, thinking she had no one. She just didn't know I was there all the time, watching.

It was her ultimate acceptance of the different life choices made by each one of her children that would bring her to peace within herself and the world and finally let her settle the promise God made with me that last day, to help her become the grownup woman I would cease to be, *Please, God...* was my prayer those moments as I held her in my arms soothing away her overly zealous baby tears. It was as if she knew more than she should or ever could, that before her was a life filled with pain and promise played out in three-quarter rhythm with a thunderous ovation at every turn. Had there been a way to tell her, she wouldn't have believed it. She just had to live it — one excruciating juncture at a time.

◆

BOOK ONE

A Make-Believe Face

"…What is most personal and unique in each one of us is probably the very element which would, if it were shared or expressed, speak most deeply to others."

– Carl Rogers
On Becoming A Person

"It is not enough for parents to understand children. They must accord children the privilege of understanding them."

– Milton R. Sapirstein-
Paradoxes of Everyday Life

CHAPTER ONE

Not Army Issue: 1963

Rumpelstiltskin had nothing on me. I felt as though I'd slept right through my whole life and was just waking up with a bang, wham! We were in Japan, and where, in Ray's words, *all hell broke loose* in my head. At the time I thought it had something to do with the way sex was viewed there – as an art always in the making, but, actually, it was as much *the times*, it turns out. It was happening everywhere, to everyone. "Nooky," as touted by Rusty Warren's blue comedy, was becoming *in* back home; here in the Far East two unaccompanied women out at a pizza parlor could bring invitations to a brothel – "for how you want, mens or womens?" Of course, for me, breaking out was bound to happen sooner or later, *somewhere*. It just turned out that it was to Japan we were sent in July of that year — our first overseas assignment together, Ray's second as an officer, his first time since basic training in spook-dom to wear the uniform.

Japan was such a strange, faraway place then for any American, but for someone as closed-off to the world as I, Mars would have been more familiar. For Ray, though, a knowing city kid whose high school gang had mostly ended up in prison, this was just another job. What, after all, could possibly compare with the excitement of the last assignment in our nation's capital: the Cuban Crisis, its Bay of Pigs fiasco, and getting a firsthand look at Bobby Kennedy in maneuvering his brother's administration? But these kinds of things Ray couldn't really tell me about with his top, top secret clearances. To me, he was just a nervous husband getting the six of us loaded onto a plane after a cross-country drive to San Francisco, and a week's stay at a guest cottage at Traverse AFB. There we awaited space available on military transport that would take us – Sharon, then ten; Suzie, six; Kelly, four; baby Sean, and me, Sam, a starry-eyed twenty-six-year-old filled with apprehension – as part of the cargo. For that is how it felt being herded onto the rickety C-123 along with the mail. I found out later it was the final mission of this particular aircraft before being retired to the tin-can museum in Arizona; need I say more?

The flight was thirty-three hours in the air with one refueling stop at Anchorage, Alaska, where we had to use a small makeshift terminal; the regular one had been demolished in the recent earthquake. It was night and we all were half asleep. For Kelly, and me especially, sleep was a welcome relief as we shared very queasy stomachs throughout the entire trip. By the time we began the descent for landing at Tachikawa AFB, near Tokyo, poor Kelly's stomach gave out. The odors of dead fish, that greeted us as the doors of the plane opened to our new home for the next three years, mixed well with his upchucked lunch all over my lap.

This smell of fish seemed to haunt me the next months everywhere we went in country, as well as the still open sewage running alongside the roads in *benjo ditches*. Since fish was in abundance on the island, the heads were fed to the pigs and chickens. Would you believe eggs and bacon, while cooking, could smell like fish?

The nausea that stayed with me constantly, from the odors insulting my poor nose, was not eased by the unexpected earth tremors that seemed to shift the very bed under us, beginning that first night at Camp Yuhi (rhyming with loony!). The six of us shared two rooms across the wide hall from each other. Without a crib, eight-month-old Sean slept on a cot set up between our twin beds.

We were given some Army issue dishes and utensils to use during what was supposed to be a "temporary" stay at Building 650, a three-story converted Bachelor Officer's Quarters, known as the BOQ. A shared kitchen, one per floor, provided us with a stove and sink. I cooked in one place, and carried what limited selection of food I could prepare back to our rooms. The largest latrines were at each end of the floors: one large shower, several sinks, and two open toilet stalls. Hello Japan! The Army didn't exactly welcome us, but complaining was not my style. I just put on my shy smile, thankful just to be there instead of at home without my husband.

To keep busy, as if four kids weren't enough, there were many things I wanted to do: take an art class, volunteer for an Extra in Japanese film. Before I could do much of anything, I set about hiring a Japanese maid – an expected thing for an officer's wife to do to aid the Japanese economy.

To help us in interviewing, we were taught a few necessary Japanese words. For instance: *Hi* meant *Yes*. Every girl said the same thing to me at the end of the interview, *Hi, go men a sai.*

Only understanding the *Yes*, I was disappointed when nobody showed up for work. After several times, I decided to take a quick introductory language course offered on Post. There I learned that what followed *Yes*, was, *I'm sorry!* The teacher proceeded to explain to us that Buddhism taught never to say *No*. For if one said *Yes*, perhaps there may be a way to fulfill the request – but just in case that doesn't happen, an apology was given in advance. In other words, the minute any girl heard I had four children, it was *Yes, but [already] I am sorry.*

Riki was hired for 360 yen (one dollar U.S.) per day. She came several days a week and helped with laundry, ironing, and light housekeeping – no cooking. She spoke little English, smiled always, and ironed everything – even socks, and left for home in the afternoons after she set the table for dinner. Hiring her allowed me to work as an Extra in the movies as an American tourist for ten dollars per day, and I was able to spend a week up north at Hakoni's Mt. Fujiyama resort. While there, I was introduced to boys holding hands, dancing with each other (their form of birth-control until they could afford to marry, we were told), mixed bathing, toilets in the floor (that flushed), and soggy cucumber sandwiches. The highlight of the trip for me was being given a non-speaking, walking part on the tourist's bus set. Besides looking Japanese (except for my nose) with similar skin coloring and tiny bones, I inadvertently behaved as one because of my perpetually happy, geisha-like smiling face, behind which, I had up until now conducted my life. This enabled me to be used as a Dance Extra with Japanese men, as well.

Back in my new world in Building 650, Sharon was now babysitting. Other than crying and screaming in the shower that she wanted to die, which I credited to the onset of puberty, she seemed very mature. With the watchful eye of someone else living in the building who would look in on them from time to time – as we were rarely more than a block away at the Officer's Club – our night life took on greater latitude and unexpected turns, especially as we began getting more social invitations. Although popularity is not something I had consciously sought, I did want to be accepted, especially by those of higher rank — "a healthy respect," Ray called it.

Happy Hour was as strange sounding for a name of a party as was Coffee for the ladies' morning get-togethers. Before my 24th birthday, while Ray was in Korea, I didn't know the names of liquors or drinks any more than I knew the difference between a filtered and non-filtered cigarette. Since then, desperately wanting to be accepted as one of the crowd, I became intent on trying *everything*.

It wasn't that I was dumb in an intelligence sort of way. It was growing up in that religious social vacuum, by the world's standard – without books, movies, and a single friend carefully selected. This left me devoid of knowing so many ordinary things, the severe childhood repression ultimately silencing what was an otherwise curious mind. The day I married Ray, though, was like a small light being thrust into the darkness; slowly I became aware of the world around me – oh, so painfully slowly. With the birth of each of my children, another part of me had come alive. Each new place we moved to introduced me to another buried part of myself.

Still, nothing had prepared me for anything like this, even being uprooted and transplanted as a child – sometimes as often as several times in a school year and into to some very unusual living situations. Every time I had to move, I'd think, *Maybe this place will really feel like home.* Here, in a foreign country, military families were all thrown together – what better place to find it? My eagerness and enthusiasm to participate in my new surroundings was only dampened by my constant, horrendous fear that I would do or say something to reveal my ignorance. But this fear, I soon learned, began to subside somewhat after my first drink.

This particular night, Ray and I were spending another evening playing the card games he began teaching me on our honeymoon, our one free entertainment. Although we had been invited to the nightly Happy Hour at the Officer's Club and had gone a few times, our past drinking (prior to Japan) had been limited to an occasional all night party. Ever since Ray's homecoming from Korea – he'd brought home several bottles of the best that went down like buttered toffee: Crown Royal, straight, compliments of the U.S. Military at less than half stateside prices – when I'd landed smack dab in the middle of my kitchen floor before our guests even made it through the buffet line, my humiliation made me determined to never let *anyone* see me tipsy again. Besides that, we had never begun the practice of keeping booze in the house, primarily because of the cost. Drinking as an accepted part of every day was beginning to disturb to me. This was in the back of my mind when, a few evenings before, we had been invited upstairs to dinner with Major Daniels' family.

Sophie Daniels, a college graduate, ten years my senior, and my new hoped-for friend and mentor I badly needed, carried a martini around with her while she cooked dinner. To be polite, I, of course, felt I should join in, but I was a slow sipper. Plainly, I was scared of what I'd always heard about military people and their drinking, and feared we'd get like them. What especially frightened me was hearing what came after — a step beyond what I'd experienced back in Michigan, where Ray had left us during his Korean tour. There, even without my husband's presence, being married had afforded me some measure of protection, but here there seemed to be no limits. The conversation itself was frightening: what they had done at the last party, who got drunk, and who ended up in bed with whom.

These worries were on my mind this particular night. Ray and I were celebrating our getting, after three months wait, one of the new makeshift apartments the Army had created at the ends of each floor. Having our own bedroom to ourselves was a treat that allowed us the privacy to indulge in a game of Strip Poker.

Ray made anybody want to beat him, especially at cards – the way he snapped them somehow when he dealt each one, sending them gliding low across the table, hugging the wood like a flame. He was good at most things, cavalierly challenging his opponents with his cocky arrogance, a wicked and irritating burr that could dare the cleverest of games-men. So much like his father – competition, winning was his sustenance. "If Ray couldn't win, he'd quit," his brother, Rich, once said. "Ray just won't play for a losing team." His winning now in Strip Poker was apparently eminent as I had lost all but my black underwear; he had given up only his shoes. In this last hand of Showdown, the highest card I'd turned up was a ten and he already had a king and a pair of deuces showing, with two more cards to go. Stripping one piece of clothing at a time, I was down to my bikinis, garter-belt, and the new black mesh nylons they just got in at the Army PX. My bared nipples were chilled and uncomfortably protruding from my childlike breasts. The realization of what I was doing was reminiscent of tweezing my eyebrows. Initial discomfort slowly spreads into your brain making you finally wince as the message of pain filters in: the embarrassment, sitting here revealing slowly more skin, the uncovering prying open forgotten windows, the vulnerability was turning me inward. I had a vague notion of wanting to reach for my crotch and scream, run, find an escape from, again, having to open my legs, my heart... *What should come off next – the garter-belt, the sexy hose?* Just the thought of either made goose bumps swell, my blood rush; I felt heat creep into my face. Oh, God, I didn't want to blush, he *was* after all my husband! Didn't I *belong* to him, for all of seven years no less? I wasn't sinning. *Why did I cringe like this?* Did *everyone* feel so sordid? *Stoning at moments like this would be a kindness, a reprieve...* Even more disconcerting was the pulsating warmth in my groin, thighs, the feeling of wanting to open myself to him creeping into my consciousness. *Oh, to pull him into me, absorb him, until no separation was left between us, no beginning, no ending. Just the two of us fused together into one, no more that feeling of being lost, alone, desperately needy, wanting... His picture-perfect specimen of manhood... gorgeous un-circumcised...* Stop! Stop! My Victorian mind was still the warden of my soul.

Ray, still in his uniform khakis, his piercing blue eyes larger than ever and gleaming in triumph, slapped down the third deuce with a loud, gloating laugh.

The garters left little puffs in the tops of my hose as I unhooked them, and pulled the garter-belt out of my near-nothing panties. Sitting squaw-legged in the middle of the bed, the filmy net stockings stretched thinly over the shadow of bone and skin peeking through.

Smoke from the cigar butt clenched in his teeth curled upward. With his eyes squinting and never leaving his cards, Ray said ever so softly, "God, you've got the sexiest knees in the whole world."

To keep the kids from hearing, in their own rooms across the wide expanse of a hall, in between swirling his tongue, Ray was whispering into my ear, "It must be that time again; your eyes are just dancing."

"Really? Come to think of it, it is. But it's okay," I said, turning to face him so his lips would find mine. "I put the Delfin cream in before, while you were shuffling the cards."

"So you're ready, I think... I got Trojans this time, the expensive ones, so it shouldn't slide off. I'll be so glad when we don't have to use all this stuff, if that day ever comes."

Kissing me, pulling me over under him, I could tell this wasn't going to take long, and I had so much to talk to him about. During sex was the only time he seemed to hear me.

"I'm ready," he said. He'd already begun...

The strip poker had unnerved me. Being naked with the lights on, without covers to hide me, was something we had never done before. Dark, like this, was better... Still, ever since I had taken my bra off, I felt like crying. Being without clothes left me feeling embarrassed, dirty, ashamed... Right now the tears wouldn't stay back, no matter that he was *ready*. I said, "Ray I'm so scared about all the booze... these people... Please, don't let us get like they are," I begged, "drinking and carrying on like they all do, don't let's ever change."

He was biting on my tongue, sucking on my ear, and beginning to move... move...

If only he would just listen to me, try to understand. He surprised me then, with his letting me know he'd already thought about it. "We're not like they are," he said into my ear, "and we won't."

By now I was sobbing, uncertain if it was fear of our drinking, or my not ever really getting what I thought I was supposed to from sex. So many feelings lately seemed to come to a head during these very brief moments we could fit in together, without the kids... Or was his sudden, unexpected understanding flooding me with emotions? I felt certain he had to mean it though, when he stayed with me afterwards and held me close, for a very long time.

Together we would be strong, but I guess it was already too late...

His hand was on my right breast gently fingering it when I first began to come awake. I was sleeping soundly from the tranquilizer, out like a light when I hit the pillow. I didn't even get tight at the promotion party; I never did in that short a time. It took hours to get enough booze into me to even get a buzz on. That is one of the things Ray and I had begun to fight over when we were partying — when to go home. Coming from that long line of hard-drinking Irishmen, he was soon able to down three bourbons before I had even made a dent in my fancy Pink Squirrel, which tasted like a strawberry milkshake. Tonight I hadn't even finished that first drink.

The party was given by one of Ray's buddies who'd just made Captain. Ray had left me there while he got on a plane for Okinawa. A weekend night was a crazy time to leave for Temporary Duty, but when you're stationed in the Far East, just a hop-skip-and-a-jump from our only war, a lot of things are crazy.

Ray's junior rank of First Lieutenant, put us very low on the housing list. Knowing that we'd probably never make it high enough on the roster to qualify, Army housing tried to accommodate us by giving us one of the new apartments. Ours was on the second floor, nearest the road and Post exit gate. The apartment had four large rooms, and a smaller maid's room, which we gave to the boys. The huge two-stall and three-sink bathroom was a plus though, with our large family. There was ample play area in the huge bedrooms, and the small pool table we'd shipped fit easily into the end of the living room. The kitchen, also huge, had been wired for our washer and dryer, and Housing had supplied us with extra furniture.

From all appearances we had a hunky-dory set up. There was only one catch – we could not lock any of our doors, not even the outside entrance from the fire-escape, the Army was very strict on that point. Inside, two heavy fire doors separated our converted apartment from the rest of the floor. These also had to be left unlocked, and marked as such according to fire regulations. The military police routinely checked them as they walked down the very wide hall through our apartment, most of the time without even bothering to knock. Once, caught in my nightgown, I had raised my voice at the young military police. They both apologized profusely for their intrusion, but they continued to walk through at will and dared to shine flashlights into my face while I was sitting in my living room, as though inspecting something. Although relieved that they were at least Americans, they were nevertheless infuriating, so I dared never to be without a robe. At night, when Ray was gone, I was frightened. Being in a foreign country for the first time, without speaking the language, was bad enough, but we were very close to the outside, unmanned gate. Because of the kids, and not believing it right to lock them in, our own bedroom doors remained open, except for exceptionally short periods that would happen to fall in the late night hours; sex was easy for us both to make-believe didn't exist, especially to our children; we had enough trouble dealing with it ourselves. We were beginning to learn that a few drinks at a party seemed to overcome our shyness, and allow us to keep pushing back our own built-in barriers. Mostly, I would try not to think about it afterwards, what we had ventured to do, believing *it* wasn't the real me; thus sex after booze was becoming a habit... And why, when I felt his hand gently massage my nipple, I had wanted to turn right over and cooperate. In my drowsiness, I thought it was strange he was not starting right in, like he usually did.

Ray never was very devious in his approach. I told him once, "I think you consider getting undressed, foreplay!"

"Isn't it?" he said.

Since our long Korean separation, all the books we'd read or hints I'd dropped never seemed to register, to slow him: "A fighter, not a lover," he said. The hand starting at the top was definitely a switch in technique – and then I remembered Ray had left for TDY. The evenings' events flashed through my mind bringing my eyes wide open — this man in my bed was *not* my husband. Fully awake, I realized who it must be. I sat up, tore back the covers, and spoke in a very loud whisper, "What in Gods' earth do you think you are doing?"

"Awe, Baby, c'mon. Just relax," he said, trying to pull me back into the pillow.

"Don't give me any Baby crap. You get yourself out of this house, *now*! And I mean *now*, or I'll scream! And I mean I'll scream, I can promise you that. The Provost Marshall lives right downstairs, you know!" I said as mean as I knew how.

Apparently mentioning the head of the military police was the right thing to do because I never saw anyone move so fast, get his britches on so quick, or drop so much out of his pockets as he disappeared on a run through both closed doors.

My heart was thumping in my ears like a galloping horse. I got up and turned on the light. George Crocker had dropped a gold engraved Bulova watch and an assortment of change, all strewn about the floor. I had all the evidence I could ever need, I thought. *Just you wait, Mister Lieutenant Colonel! Ray will fix your little red wagon when he gets home! Messing with Ray's wife will teach you!*

Ray was as sweet as he could be. I was scared to tell him the whole story for fear he might not believe me. But he must have known about some men. He did ask me to repeat the part about the pool game.

After only a few minutes at the party, Ray had to leave and thought I should stay for awhile. "No need for you to miss a good time on my account," he had said. I was always nervous anyhow at these functions, but being there without him was worse, so I headed for the hostess to say a few words to her before discreetly slipping out.

She was a real Georgia peach, complete with a ma-arvelous southern drawl, a college graduate who had majored in art, and seemed to be especially encouraging in my attempt at oil painting. She always asked what I was doing, and, as the emotional three-year-old that I was, I loved talking about it. My latest interest was a still life of fruit set around a beautiful blue, ceramic decanter that had come filled with our latest booze. Enthusiastically, I was describing the difficulty I had when copying the scene etched in white on the decanter. "It's so neat," I said, "if I can just get it right. It is of Socrates, Aristotle, and Pluto all sitting in a circle, conversing. You know, all those wise, Greek philosophers?"

My hostess just threw her head back and roared with laughter, as did the three other gals standing around me. I was stumped at what was so funny, until she said, "Samantha, Pluto is a dog in the Funnies. I think you mean Plato."

Slowly, I felt the blood creep up into my neck and face. Of course she couldn't know that Pluto was even more foreign to me than Plato. The Funnies were one of those no-nos I was never allowed to read. I don't know when I felt so embarrassed at my lack of education and worldliness, and Ray nowhere around with his ribald humor to rescue me, to poke fun at my ignorance in a way so I could laugh, too. Instead, I turned from the group of ladies hoping to disappear from the face of the earth and bumped right into this short, tough looking man in uniform. Crocker, was on his name tag, and a Lieutenant Colonel's gold leaf on his collar. I excused myself. He grabbed me around my shoulder, and said, "And where have *you* been all my life?"

I was anxious to put the embarrassing faux pas with the ladies behind me, so I may have sounded more friendly than I should have. That's the only thing that could have happened to give him such an idea. I was very nervous and not thinking too clearly when I proudly told him I was married to Lieutenant Malorry, who had just left on TDY.

"So you're on the loose, huh?" he said with a twinkle in his merry, wicked eye.

Right then, I knew I had made a mistake. It seemed no matter who I talked to, I was putting my foot in my mouth; it was the story of my life. Now I had to get out of this somehow. Standing head to head with him, I knew his being in uniform at a party was a dead giveaway that he was here on TDY – alone without his wife. Of course he really wasn't all that old, looking back, probably in his early 40's, but I thought, then, he had one foot in the grave. Not that it would have mattered, you see, if he'd have been younger. It's just that his being *old* made him all the more repulsive. Ray had already explained quite a bit to me about the Army, about how some junior officers traded favors from their young wives, for promotions. He didn't have to explain it too much; I'd already had quite a few offers in my ear on the dance floor, but I would laugh them off and act like it was surely a joke. Dismissing such booze-happy comments, I was confident in my husband's ability; I knew that whenever he got promoted it would be on his own merit, not mine. We'd even had discussions on that, so I was never afraid to look an old codger in the eye and let him know he was barking up the wrong tree. Lieutenant Colonel Crocker was waiting for my reply. My face felt like it was on fire, but I realized the ploy immediately, and said, "If you'll excuse me, I have to get home."

The kids were already in bed asleep; a friend down the hall had been looking in on them. I was sitting in the living room when I heard the hall door open.

Out in the hallway, this Crocker guy came waltzing in with a beer in his hand. "Fancy meeting you here," he said with a grin.

Being reared by a southern father, a drop of honey had always been my first line of defense. At work I had been known as the customers' complaint lady, I could always quiet a ruckus. Shushing him, I motioned him out of the echo-y hallway.

The minute Crocker saw the pool table, he grabbed a stick.

"Wait a minute," I said. "I don't think you were invited to play."

He ignored me, and began racking the balls.

Since our meeting at the party was so brief, I really didn't know him, but his high rank intimidated me. I just stood there, watching, trying to decide what to do.

Finally, he said, "All right, I'll leave after you play me one game."

"Is that a promise?" I asked, relieved that he was at least recognizing that he wasn't welcome.

"Promise," he said.

When it came my turn to shoot, he disappeared into the hall. I put my stick down and followed him – I was very protective of my kids. In the kitchen, he was helping himself to a beer. That really got my dander up, and if he woke up baby Sean, they'd *all* be up. I *had* to speak up, "I really think you better leave... *now*."

Irritated, he turned on his heel, took the beer, and left.

The whole night was so upsetting that I took a tranquillizer. It was a couple hours later when I woke up with this same, strange man in my bed.

Ray was looking at the expensive Bulova watch. I could see that he was having a hard time telling me. "Sam, the Inspector General just doesn't think you should press this issue. He says that he knows Crocker. He's a horse's behind and pulls strings all over the place, and by the time he got finished with your reputation, you wouldn't want to show your face anywhere, again. In fact, the IG said his own wife had experienced the same kind of thing when she was much younger, and he advises us just to drop it, okay?" he said, fingering the gold piece.

"You mean to tell me that I can't lock my doors; anyone who wants to can walk in here any old time, crawl into my bed, feel me up, and I can't do a blessed thing about it? I can't believe it! I just can't believe it! This *is* the *United States* Army, isn't it?" I asked.

Ray was defensive. "Hey, what can I do? This is a *man's* Army. You're lucky they let you and the kids even *be* here with me, that was made very clear – *Don't rock the boat, Lieutenant.* You know the old saying: *If the Army wanted you to have a wife, they'd issue you one?"* Ray laughed in his dry, sardonic way.

The gold watch lay in my drawer for weeks. Ray heard via the grapevine that Crocker wanted his watch back because it held "sentimental value" and "was irreplaceable." We laughed at such audacity. I guess I was luckier than most, my husband was still on my side.

T he housing list, set up by rank and bedroom requirements, was the subject of conversation amongst us families stuck in Building 650. Enlisted people had separate housing. Ray, being only a First Lieutenant left us at the bottom of the list. Many families who had come from another overseas assignment, Inter-Theater Transfers, were allowed to let their previous overseas' time accrue for seniority; we didn't have a chance at getting a house.

Despite the large *Private Quarters-Keep Out* sign at both entrances, the young MP's kept up their habit of walking through regularly "to make sure the Fire Exits weren't blocked," often catching me in grumbling disarray.

This was when we got to really know the Daniels, who now lived directly above us.

When Major Daniels first asked me what I wanted to drink, I answered, "Oh, just anything you have the most of."

"My God, how much are you planning to put away?" he asked in his teasing way.

Embarrassed, what I meant was, whatever was the least expensive, but instead, when I explained that I really didn't much care for *any* of it, that I usually drank Pink Squirrels or Brandy

Alexander's, much too fancy to make at home, he suggested a Gin Gimlet, a sour drink with gin and lime juice. I loved lemons, and the best label gin was only eighty-five cents a quart at the Post package store; I was safe on that score. Gimlets became my standby, but, of course, I would always try anything once.

After our introduction to tequila with the Daniels one night, Major D., an Infantry officer, taught Ray how to line up troops. Being in uniform for the first time in Ray's career was new and demanding. Having been in civilian clothes and exempt from such responsibilities as being Parade Leader, in his function as Troop Commander, he was surprised to read the small print at the end of his orders, "... *and other duties such as the Commander so desires.*"

Major D. had his work cut out for him.

"Atten-*shun!*" Ray yelled out the third floor window at the tree tops.

"Pretty damn good for a pansy," Major D. exclaimed, referring to the brass Intel insignia of a splattered pansy Ray wore on his uniform.

Ray held up his glass in salute to the obedient statuesque troops. He was nervous about having to give parade commands to the men of the company to which he was assigned. Major D. became Ray's tutor on that score, and many nights, before too much booze went down, we would hear them train in front of the huge wall-to-wall windows where the tall pines would be forever stand-ins for invisible soldiers.

This training was soon tested as Ray's Commander directed that he put the troops through their paces, many of whom played softball on the same team with Ray, and who had great respect for him as their very competitive, winning pitcher.

On the day of his initiation into this new role, Ray came home red-faced to tell me that when he had the whole unit on the parade field, he gave the command, *Forward March.* Of course, the whole field of troops started towards him in military precision. "When that whole parade field started coming at me, I drew a blank. You know, that special command, to get the troops to turn right and march off the field, that Major D. has been teaching me? Well, it totally escaped me. Unfortunately, that didn't stop the troops; they kept on coming straight at me. Afraid they would trample me, I stuck my arms out, and yelled, *Whoa, damn it, whoa!* Oh, boy, I'm never going to hear the end of *that,*" he said, shaking his head.

Ray was known for his Irish humor and quick wit, ready to razz anyone about anything, to whom, or about what, mattered little. Consequently, there were many just waiting for such an opportunity to return the favor. "Whoa, damn it, whoa," was an unbelievable chance to get even.

Sophie Daniels, who went by *Soph,* took me under her wing. She was only pint size, but her stature was enlarged in my eyes by her vast experience as an officer's wife. When I apologized for my ignorance, her response was, "You're a breath of fresh air, Sam. Don't worry, you'll learn quickly enough!" She and Major D., as he was known, had met at college, which, in itself, drew my respect. But Soph had some personal problems. Her face was scarred from a recent auto accident, and she would cry for hours as I listened, and listened – the more she drank, the more of her pain she would reveal. Convinced that at age thirty-five, just around the corner – her "doom's day" – Soph was intent upon finding a Japanese plastic surgeon to right her with the world. Then, if her husband continued to chase every skirt between here and tomorrow, she would still be young enough to find someone else. She said she loved him and their two adorable children, and claimed their sex life was superb, despite his being "hot to trot" with her best friend in their last assignment. After this girl had to have an illegal abortion, Soph was now intent on getting *him* a vasectomy. The Daniel's coming to Japan was no accident; he had requested the tour for these personal benefits.

The infidelity of her husband was a perplexing thing that Soph and I hashed over daily. I knew she wasn't imagining things; already I was having to watch my every move with him myself. When we played cards, Major D. kept his knee pressed against mine, would touch me somewhere under the table. Unbeknownst to anyone else — when I took a glass from him, a card from him, a plate from him — he managed to somehow *touch* me. This constant physical barrage became so disconcerting, it was difficult to concentrate on our Bridge game. Yet in conversation, he would belittle me openly, tease me to the point of embarrassment, until I felt like crying at his witty cruelties. Besides this, Ray's already sarcastic humor was beginning to turn on me for the first time in our seven years of marriage. Keeping the secret, under my ready smile, became a challenge, and the frustration made my quiet anger grow as this cheeky man-around-town pounded away at my inner reserve. Because Ray was obviously in awe of him, grateful for the personal attention and friendship, this new cat and mouse game created even more confusion personally, for me.

Each party, the guests seemed to get drunker and their behavior more daring. A dinner thrown by Colonel Benton to introduce his newest young girlfriend – while *the wife* was back in the states keeping the children in school – was no exception. *And to think we considered ourselves of special distinction to be on the invitation list!*

At first, I was dumfounded that this senior officer had the audacity to flaunt a young single girl amongst us, but his rank and position seemed to justify his doing anything he pleased — after all, he was the Post Commander. When, at a formal sit-down dinner, Soph laughingly told me of the Colonel's ramming his hand up her dress under the table cloth, and she was still laughing when she explained that his girlfriend on the other side of him had *her* hand under *his* napkin, and Soph was wondering just *what* the guy was going to try *next* – I knew we had crossed over the line. The terrible thing about it was, as time went on, these events began to feel less and less strange. In a moment of deep despair, I realized that Ray and I had slipped past the point of no return: Nothing seemed to shock us anymore, not even the stories the guys told about the "honky-tonk sweeties" they found off Post, in Tokyo. Both our husbands threatening to ditch us halfway through every party, and go out stag, only buried the anxiety deeper. After an especially drunken bash, they *did* go.

When Soph and I realized Major D's car was missing, as well as my car keys kept in my handbag, we searched our car with a flashlight. Not finding them, and knowing we were stuck at home with no way to chase down our straying husbands, we sat up until morning, drinking coffee and talking, while I listened to one angry story after another of her adulterous husband.

It was daylight, and the kids were up, when the guys got home. We had breakfast on the table with bloody Mary's for us adults. When my missing handbag, with all my ID cards, money, checkbook, make-up, and tranquillizers I now used for the awful hangovers, was mentioned, we called the Provost Marshall, downstairs, and asked how to report it. It was Major D. that started to recall that to keep us from following them the night before, they had hid the handbag. *But, where?* They couldn't remember, but the more vodka they put away, the more of the events of the previous night came to mind. Finding the handbag in a cabinet, high up near the ceiling that had been used for storage, it was clear neither Soph nor I was meant to find it without a ladder. In our rekindled inebriated state, the whole affair grew more humorous by the telling. "We had to get as drunk as we were when we hid the damn thing, in order to remember where we put it," Ray told the Provost Marshall when he reported finding the handbag.

In the hilarity of the moment, the anger I carried at Ray's unconscionable behavior the previous night got tucked away with the Korean party photos, and before that, the softball tournament Wac – the list was slowly growing. His many TDY trips to Vietnam and Okinawa (where the dancers *started* in the nude) and where his appetite for "slant eyes" could be revisited (He always said he didn't believe in playing an away-game at home!) only piled fuel on the angry fire smoldering within.

My religious upbringing that taught me as a wife I was to be subservient to my husband, was only an excuse my mind used to shroud my sleeping emotions. But in actuality, it really was a throw-back to our first Christmas party, only a year married: At the dinner table, with me sitting across from Ray, one of the gals he worked with, very drunk, had crawled onto his lap, hugging all over him, while I looked on – unbelieving. At home, I just blew my stack, screaming in rage at this girl's "disgusting behavior," which he seemed to enjoy, making it worse. Ray let me finish, and then calmly pointed to the shoes he had just removed, and said, "If I put them back on, I am walking out of this house. I lived with jealousy in my parents marriage my whole life, and I will *not* live with jealousy in *mine*." The actual incident had long been forgotten, but the threat remained. Having gone through a bitter divorce once, I was determined to never subject myself to such pain again.

M y eyes came awake in the dim, early morning light with someone shaking my shoulder. I looked up into the anguished face of Soph, obviously still half asleep herself. Ray was on TDY and the first thing I expected to hear was that his plane had gone down, but before I could get the words out, Soph said, "President Kennedy was just shot, Sam."

"Oh, my God, where?"

"In Texas," she said.

"Texas? That no-good Johnson! I bet it was him," I said before being fully awake. Suddenly, an overwhelming feeling of sadness came over me, and trying to choke back the embarrassment of my ready tears, I said, "You know he was the first president I was old enough to vote for?"

Living in DC had been so exciting; it was the first time I had read a newspaper in my life. Before that, in Michigan, during the November election, I'd stayed up the whole night, without Ray, watching the returns. The next day, the Inaugural festivities had me totally absorbed, so much so that I defended with vigor *The Porter Sentinel* to my angry sister-in-law, Ro, ranting about the "poor taste" of a newspaper that would spread across the front page, in living color, the President's party with Sammy Davis, Jr., "a Negro," planting a shocking kiss on the cheek of the, now, President's sister. Ro said, "How awful!" I had responded, "I think it's pretty Christian, myself?"

Remembering such moments, I felt like the Kennedy's were my own private family. *Jackie, she has such class. Is she all right? Where were the children?* The unanswered questions went on and on as we hovered near the radio straining to hear every word we could extract from our limited news casts. Our TV was mostly rerun shows that were dubbed in English over Japanese, so we missed the round-the-clock coverage the folks back home were getting. It was nightmarish, even so.

The Japanese were also extremely fond of our young American president. A young waiter at the Officer's Club, whose name was Sabu, had a haircut like JFK's so we had nicknamed him Kennedy. He just beamed at the proud association. When we walked into the club the next time, he quietly asked us to refrain from using that name now, to please call him Sabu. "You understand?" he said, bowing very politely.

There was no way to describe the estrangement we felt, being so far from home. I'm sure the tragedy was inconceivable to everyone, everywhere, but we felt alienated as stepchildren. The sadness lay especially heavy on my chest. Kennedy was just a president, after all, that the whole world mourned. My lifetime of grief was personal, buried and unfelt beneath a make-believe life, a contrived picture-perfect family, which now extended into a citizenship I couldn't quite grasp; within a sea of foreign faces surrounding us with strange voices that uttered indiscernible words; smells that insulted, offended; tastes unfamiliar; doors with no locks; walls with no warmth. *Solace, where to go?* How to abide the bullet that shook the world that November day. Seeing little John John in salute: It would be years before I understood its symbolism, of the traumatic loss of my mother to my own three-year-old world for whom I had not yet been allowed to grieve. *Now*, I cried, but the tears didn't seem to penetrate through to my soul, register relief. The helpless, angry feeling of loss, the sadness of grieving, all foreign to me, remained, obstructing the very fabric of my world. Not understanding with my three-year-old heart – not even a little bit – the sadness rose up as a rock in my gullet. I drank to push it down, I drank to keep from feeling the pain – not knowing *why*, I just drank.

T he Daniels finally got housing in the lovely officer's area way on the other side of Post. After her long awaited appointment for facial surgery in Tokyo, Soph was staying in a hotel there until the bandages could be removed. She called me daily, and while Ray was out of town one night, over the phone, we both, in Soph's colorful words, got "royally, stinking, boo-coo drunk." *Out of my mind, drunk…*

The roads were dark, and I doubt that I really knew where I was going, or why· I was searching… driven… I found the Daniels new quarters· We had not been invited over since they moved· Ray assumed, due to his junior rank, we had only been chosen as the recipients of their friendship earlier because of the close vicinity of our temporary quarters, and, no doubt, would not see them again socially, but Soph had continued to keep in touch, by phone· No matter…

Vaguely, I remember walking through their house· Most of the night was a total blank, but fuzzy flashbacks would haunt me for months… years… The huge wrought iron bed, lying there on my back while he pumped me… I remember distinctly sneering into his face, "You bastard· You son-of-bitch·"

He laughed at my awkward, good-girl attempt at profanity as he stood up and watched me struggle with my buttons… my fingers fumbling, my head spinning… the room fading and coming back·

Sitting on the edge of the bed, I said, "You ain't got it, Honey, not even close· What a joke, you are, all your talk·"

As I pulled myself together, I looked over at the end of the bed to see four little sets of knuckles grasping the bed rails, four little eyes peeking through them…

Running, running, I remember running out of the house into a black, empty void knowing I had passed into some kind of unforgiving hell.

The party after the party after the party usually ended up at our house. Ray and I didn't seem to ever want to face *the end*. He was looking in all the cabinets for another bottle. There were people roaming all over the house, drinking, playing pool. I was standing next to the wall. Slowly, I began to slide down it, onto the floor, into a heap. Ray came and grabbed me by the arm, dragged me into the bedroom, and threw me onto the bed. It was dark, but he left the door open. The sound of the laughter in the next room made me feel like puking... In the closet, from my purse, I got a Dramamine and two Miltowns. Just making it back to bed, I upchucked over the side of the bed. My head was spinning, but I was awake enough to see one of the young pediatricians that treated my kids – for all the staph infections they were getting from this god-awful dirty building the Army wouldn't clean up – coming down the hall, the married doctor. He came through the door, carrying a drink.

"What's the trouble; you sick?" he asked gently.

"Yeah, I justook two Miltowns," I said, having trouble articulating my speech, "and they camebackup."

"Where's the bottle?" he asked.

"In my handbag," I said, pointing to the closet.

He found it, and pulled out the pills. "Here take these," he said with all the authority behind his Medical Corps brass as he held out four tablets.

I said, "I already took two, but I upchucked'em already."

"Try again. Maybe, this time," and gave me his drink to wash them down.

My head was spinning like a whirlwind. I put one foot on the floor to stop it, then I started to cry. "Oh, God, help me, God. Please help, me. *Somebody* help me," I pleaded.

Suddenly, I saw my mother up above me in the clouds; I was sure she was my mother..."Mama... help me. Please help me, Mama... Why did you *leave* me?" I yelled out in anger.

Then I heard Ray's voice coming from the doorway. "Go to sleep, Sam. Your mother is *dead*," he said disgustedly. "Go to sleep."

I wilted into sobs as he walked out of the room. In the darkness I saw the doctor squatting down in the shadows with a drink in his hand, quietly watching. I closed my eyes, and fell into sweet, sweet oblivion.

We were kissing. The lips were warm and soft. The kind and gentle hands felt so good all over my body. I was responding with a welcoming passion I had not experienced in far too long. One of us lately, Ray or I, was always too drunk. The touch was from heaven: tender, caressing – of wanting, of caring. I felt like my whole body would open up to this feeling of warmth... of love... My right hand was sliding up the smooth skin of soft, warm flesh... up... up... Into the air, I stretched my arm... My hand reached for the hand that had been stroking me, to do it some more... when the bracelets slid under my fingertips.

The lips on mine were *a woman's!*

"Oh, God," I screamed. "Ray, there's a woman in my bed." To the top of my lungs, I screamed, "Ray, help me, there's a woman in my bed."

Ray appeared in the doorway again. "Sam, you're dreaming. There's *no one* in your bed, go back to sleep."

My body broke into shattering sobs, my chest crumpled up. Sleep... Sleep... My eyes would hardly stay open... could barely focus...

Stooping in the shadows and sipping his drink, out of the hallway light, was the outline of the doctor – still watching.

The puke was dried to my hair, my face stuck to the pillow, I thought my head would break open from the piercing sunlight coming through the window. I got up and went into the kitchen. Ray was drinking a cup of coffee. Riki was there, and I asked her to fix me a cup, with brandy. "Ray," I said, "there was a woman in my bed last night, did you know that? She was feeling me up, kissing me, and Doc..."

"Oh, don't talk nonsense. There was no woman in your bed, Sam. You were dreaming, really flipping out. You were talking to your dead mother, too. Did you know that?"

"Here, Ray... Did this little charm from a lady's bracelet come off of *a dream?*" I asked waving the little gold trinket, imprinted with Laos, (the country the U. S. was denying having been in) before his eyes.

His face fell like a punctured balloon. "Where did you get *that?*" he asked with unusual interest.

"In my bed, right next to my pillow."

Without another word, Ray continued to drink his coffee and stare into space.

The spiked coffee brought me back, in a fashion. It would hold me over until I could get a shower, and something in my stomach. Riki changed my sheets while I was in the bathroom. Only a few minutes later the phone next to my bed rang. I answered it. An anxious woman's voice asked, "Did you find a gold charm this morning?"

"Yes," I said. "It's right here, on my dresser."

"I'll be right there. My husband got that for me in Laos; it's very special; don't lose it."

"Who *is* this?" I asked out of curiosity.

"Doc's wife, you know, the pediatrician? We only met for a minute last night, before you passed out," she said.

Yeah, *while* I was passed out as I never saw her, but all I said was, "Okay. It's here if you want it," and I hung up.

Ray left before she got there. Still, he said he didn't believe it. He never believed anything I told him, not ever – just like Daddy.

That night there was another party, up on the other end of the third floor. I went up by myself for a while. The morning brandy, the lunch-time Bloody Mary's, the afternoon wine – by evening, I was in rare form. In the bathroom, I found a long bug with a bunch of legs on it, crawling. *Wouldn't that scare the peewadden out of somebody? I* thought, as I picked it up.

My hostess, a Major's wife, screamed. "That's a centipede, you fool, you wanna get me killed?"

"Oh, I'm sorry," I said, hugging her, rubbing her arm where it had sunk itself into her flesh.

"You're drunk, Sam... Go into the kitchen and get something to eat," she said, and pushed me away.

I was sitting alone, trying to eat a bread stick covered with dip, when Dr. George Burns (same as the comedian) came into the room. Doc Burns was my Duplicate Bridge partner, a young bachelor and one of the other pediatricians who treated my kids. All of the doctors knew me, my kids, our family. Besides the solid thick patch of acne-like sores I had developed over both cheeks, one of us had a staph infection coming or going somewhere on our bodies all the time: Sharon had sties in her eyes; both Kelly and Sean had boils on their bottoms; I had a boil embarrassingly start from an ingrown hair on my upper thigh, near my panty line. Even Riki got an infection in her foot from her ill-fitting shoe. Ray, whom everyone knew because of his softball championships, rubbed a strawberry on his elbow, pitching, and nearly got blood poisoning – he wouldn't soak like the rest of us! The doctors had reason to know us by name, and they were furious at the Army engineers for not painting our apartment to kill the staph. Doc Burns was the one who asked me to be his partner once, when Ray was out of town. After that, we started making it a regular team thing, even when Ray was in town. Ray had his own partner; they played to win. I wasn't very good in Duplicate, but Doc didn't care if we won. He just liked to play for the fun of it, to have something to do where drinking wasn't the main event. The minute he walked into the kitchen, I broke down in tears and told him of the previous night's startling event.

"Did you know about her?" I asked, begging for him to believe me. "Her husband gave me four more Miltowns and was sitting over there watching us, can you believe that?"

After listening for a long time to god-knows what I said while I sobbed my heart out, gently he put his arm around my shoulder, and walked me to the door. "I'm going to help you, Sam. But now I want you to go home, drink some milk, and go to bed. I'll be over to talk to you and Ray, tomorrow."

Doc Burns never did answer my query about the doctor's wife, but I remembered, when I sobered up, some of the gossip... and why they weren't invited to many parties.

In the living room, when I walked in, they had been talking for a few minutes. Ray was very subdued, and serious. He was telling Doc Burns how I had run down the middle of the street one night, outside our house, "so fast I thought I would never catch her and get her back inside. She said she was going *home* — wherever *that* is."

Dr. Burns was saying, "Your wife is very ill, Captain; she needs treatment. I'm putting her in the hospital right now." Turning to me, he said, "Sam, you'll need your toothbrush and slippers."

Mentally, it registered in my brain that even though they were both Captains, now that Ray had been promoted, Doc must have outranked him, the way he was handing out orders that were being meekly followed.

Speaking to Ray, Doc Burns said, "You can bring her in your car. I'll meet you at the hospital check-in desk," and slipped out the door.

The medic was feeling for my pulse. "Are you sure you're alive, Mrs. Malorry?" he joked. "It doesn't appear that way."

"I don't feel like it either," I said, but for the first time since I had landed in this place, I felt hope. At last, somebody was going to help me.

The social worker was staring right through me. "Don't tell me you don't *know* that when you flash those big, brown eyes of yours, you are giving men the come on."

How dare he say such things to me, I thought, but my anger was buried so deep, I hardly responded. He just didn't know what he was talking about, but it helped none to defend myself. *Why* did *the men keep coming on to me? Why* did *I go over there and lay down for that scoundrel, when I hated him so?* I couldn't begin to understand as yet that, with my bizarre behavior, I was *literally* saying: *Fuck you, you contemptible jerk!*

Three weeks later, I was released in time to get our clothes packed, and ready for our ocean voyage home. In the bottom of a drawer, I found the engraved gold watch that had been dropped out of the pocket of that rude night intruder, way back when. As I wrapped the expensive gold watch in newspaper, and put it in the bottom of the trash, I thought that Crocker was not the only one that had lost something irreplaceable that night.

Ray had special orders to have the kids and I air evacuated home, but traveling by ship was slower and easier to adjust to the "environmental change," the social worker and the doctor agreed. Since Atlanta was the only place that really felt like home since I married Ray, Atlanta was where we were headed, the five of us. There, the Army would provide psychiatric help in finding the *real me* buried under the sunshiny bright, good-girl exterior this social worker had just begun to penetrate.

Ray's choice to stay at Camp Yuhi without us was his to make. He was angry with me, and embarrassed. The same social worker began to see him regularly, digging into his past, Ray told me.

"So, Captain, are you saying you sat next to your mother at the dinner table for eight years, not giving up that seat even though two baby brothers came on the scene during that time, and took her other side?"

"That's right. When Matt came, Rich was the one got moved. I stayed."

"Leaving you safe and secure at her right hand?"

"Yeah. I guess you could put it that way."

"Until your baby sister came... *She* finally unseated you, *took your place!*"

Ray said he came up out of his chair, and almost coldcocked the guy.

That was his last session.

Soph wasted no time in her attempts to get even, by propositioning Ray tit for tat, to which he declined, he *said*. I would never really know the truth. Actually, I didn't care anymore, my own truth was terrible enough.

◆

CHAPTER TWO

"Savannah:" 1967

Love is like an umbrella. You can use it to protect, or to poke someone in the eye. Ray and I had become good at doing both to each other.

Always on a winning team, Ray has done his very best at every opportunity since he was born, it seems to me. All the times he didn't, I think it was his best, at that moment. However, in Baltimore, at the Army Intel Advanced Course for junior officers, he was being a cad. A man away from home without his wife, he was behaving like so many of the guys all around him did. He seemed to be looking for someone to love him for who he was and appreciate how hard he was trying. All I seem to remember doing at the time was to sputter around, cry, beg... But I really never knew what Ray was all about then. I was caught up in my own world of desiring to be perfect, but feeling fear, shame, and sadness. What I wanted was to be nurtured, to be loved for who *I* was. We were both caught up in our own little worlds of need that was invisible to the other. So Ray reached out to this girl.

She was young, innocent, and supposedly a virgin – something he said he never had and always wanted. He was older than the other guys, their superimposed leader. It looked as though he had a bummer wife, if he was gadding about, bringing this eighteen-year-old to the parties – and then I showed up. One day without calling, I just showed up in the car with the kids.

Ray was supposed to be there for a three-month school. He had been gone for one month already. I was trying to follow Kelly's doctor's advice, for him to have more male role models. Loran and Janice Spencer were the parents of David, Kelly's friend, who lived down the block from us. I had been spending a lot of time with them.

One night before Ray left, Loran had gone to Happy Hour with us at the Officer's Club. Loran was on the chubby side. He had a lower lip that protruded as though he was pouting, or chewing tobacco. We got out of the car, Loran's car. I remember that because it was parked on the street in front of our house, so it must have been Loran's car; ours would have been in the driveway — all three of us were drunk. Janice was at home with

David; Sharon was babysitting ours, inside. Maybe we had planned to go out to eat and ended up at Happy Hour. Somewhere, who knows where, somewhere to get drunk.

Ray looked so sharp, like always. He had a Hollywood haircut – flat on top and long on the sides. The pale yellow turtleneck shirt, really a mock turtleneck, brought out the blonde lights in his hair. He couldn't stand the neck too high up, said it made him feel like he was being choked. He wore a dark blazer over it. I was skinny then, all of 105 pounds. I had on a pearl white, two-piece dress. The skirt was cut tight and high, almost to my bikinis; my legs were tan so I didn't need hose. The top was sleeveless and overlapped the skirt's tight waistband. *God, I was skinny.* The dress was made of cotton, a knobby cloth that looked like needlepoint, a kind of cross-stitch woven into it. The simple round neck had white pearl beading, white on white; I always liked that combination. With this mini-skirt, I wore bone t-strap medium heels – you know, the higher the hemline, the lower the heel? My hair was teased, sprayed perfect, still like Jackie Kennedy's. It was 1966. (Domini and Bev had just visited us. Dom was such a swinger – from Porter, Michigan, one of Ray's old highschool gang that managed to evade prison. We'd taken them to Kitten's Corners, a night club in downtown Atlanta, where girls dressed in cat suits and were in cages doing gymnastics. The Twist was in; Ray and I could really do it like nobody else. Ray could Twist almost to the floor. When we'd dance, all eyes were on us. The floor would clear completely when Ray started into his routine. This particular night, he was really into it, and I got tired and backed off the floor with everyone watching him. He was so limber, on one foot and going to beat the band, when he finally looked up and saw everyone looking at him. The crowd roared and clapped. Ray was a real stage person; he loved an audience. He got turned on from their attention. And when I was with him, I felt his confidence, and shared his spotlight. We were the cat's pajamas, we were. What a pair, people said. That night at Kitten's Corners, Ray was in his glory. The girls in cages doing their thing had nothing on him, *he* was the star. Dom and Bev had fun too. They stayed with us a couple days; we showed them a really good time.)

It took a couple drinks for Ray to get wound up. At the time, I thought he was the magnet. But maybe I was the one that drew people with my natural looks of Cherokee and childlike innocence. I was often told it was magnified when I got a little booze in me, my inhibitions dropped from behind my good-girl mask; I loved everyone. There were no strangers or bad people, *only God's children*. Daddy had taught me to love everyone. Didn't Jesus love the whole world? *And I did*, no boundaries, never a reason to say *No*. I was open, wide open, to *everyone*. My arms were open to love, at least that's how I felt that night when Loran stayed behind and walked with me; Ray always walked a yard or two ahead.

Loran had his arms around me and was pulling me into his big, soft chest. He was crushing me, his mouth all over my face, his tongue reaching into my mouth. Ray was right in front of us. *What a jerk! Didn't Loran even care that my husband was two feet in front of us?* I started pushing him, pulling myself away, out of Loran's clutches just in time; Ray never saw it. If he did, he never let on because he was headed for the front door.

When Ray got his fill for the night, he was ready to call it quits. Enough is enough, he'd say, and head for the sack. But I was *never* ready to quit. A sipper, late starter, I always wanted to keep going, find someone to love me, look at me, hold me, *touch* me. I wanted to be a woman, *for a man to help me be a woman;* I didn't know how. But a man could make me into a woman, the right man could, and there was only one right man who was always ten steps ahead of me. I just couldn't keep up, in drinks, walking, dancing, eating, jokes, he was always way ahead of me. *I just couldn't keep up.*

Driving to Baltimore, the kids slept. The road was empty, and I drove Highway 95 all the way – ninety-five miles per hour on U. S. 95 North. I got into town and found Ray's apartment he had rented with his Army COLA money, he shared it with another guy, he said. When I'd call, usually I was drunk, crying, begging for him to love me. When I was sober, I was usually irritable, angry that he was always ten steps ahead of me; it is hard to explain.

When Ray saw me, he acted strange and stand-offish. He hugged me, or let me hug him, and headed for the car. Sean was so cute then. He was just three and a-half and a house of fire. Ray grabbed him and threw him into the air. Sharon threw her arms around her dad's neck; Suzie stood silent, waiting, like she always did, for him to notice her. Kelly was already up the stairs.

Ray had already used the guys rent money, he said, so we couldn't ask him to leave. It was an apartment building that was full of lieutenants. They were all sharing, partying; all in the school were waiting for 'Nam. Some had orders, some didn't. Ray had his assignment already, but this course came first. His being older and the only Captain gave him an edge, not to mention "smart, and full of pee and vinegar," as his grandma would say. At the Post swimming pool, I played bridge with the wives while Sean showed off for the whole world, just like his dad. Kelly was right with him, but Sean was Lieutenant Buckner's favorite. Sean called him Puck.

Buck was from the mountains in North Carolina. He wore dark rimmed glasses, a straw cowboy hat, and he was usually the one without a date. He was engaged to Jo, a nurse back home with "big tits," the one he was going to marry. Just because he "didn't have anyone else," he said, when he got drunk. Ray would settle down on the couch to watch a ball game and the lieutenants across the hall would start partying. The music was loud; I would wander over. Buck was the one I gravitated to. He had a homely-duckling kind of look, but he had a terrific personality that opened me up – and he thought I was something. He would tell me every minute he was with me, "You're really something," he'd say, and pull me to him in a dance step. We'd dance and dance, while the other guys were hanging out with their girls, on the couch, in the bedroom, but Buck and I never sat down. We were always dancing or standing up at the little corner bar. He'd push his cowboy hat back, and take his glasses off when he started getting a buzz on.

Let's go to a movie, he'd say, and we'd go to get Ray.

"Come on and go to the movie with us, old man."

Ray wouldn't budge. Instead, he'd pull money out from his pocket. "Buck, here, you take her; I'm watching this ball game."

One particular night, when Buck and I went to the movies, half way through the feature, Buck said, "This isn't right, your husband always giving me money to take you like this."

"Oh, it's okay, not a jealous bone in his body." *I just didn't know…*

It was too nice a night to go back in. The movie was a funny one, something to talk about. Buck and I walked across the street to the empty lots. The ground was dug up in spots for new houses. We sat down on a stump for a minute. The stars were out in full shine and the moon hovered over us so I could see Bucks face. He seemed to like me so much, and I liked him. He put his arms around me, and I let him. The booze was wearing off just enough to make me tired. I needed some arms, some loving… He was kissing me… God, was he into it; and I was ready. It had been so long, weeks... Back in June, when I first got there, Ray hadn't even wanted sex. I'd been there a whole week before he got around to even touching me; I just couldn't stand it any more. It was only two more weeks and I had to have the kids back in school, and then he would be leaving for a whole year. I had to have loving, holding, kissing, caring, someone wanting me. Buck had me by the buttocks... the other hand under my head. He had me down on the ground and was into me before I knew it. He was so warm, and he filled me up. I wrapped my legs around him and went at it like I'd been itching to since I was born.

"You're some kind of good," he said. "Some kind of good."

We walked for a little while more, hand in hand.

"God, I think I'm falling in love with you," he said.

"Oh, God, no, we can't... *I* can't."

"You don't really *love* him, do you?"

"Oh, yes, I really do, but he acts like he doesn't want me anymore; I can't figure it out. When I came up here, I thought he would be so happy, want me around. But he just lays on that couch watching ball games and ignores me completely. At parties he's off by himself, talking with everyone else."

"God, you're one hell of a woman; I can't understand him. But *I* want you."

"What about Jo? You're engaged to Jo."

"I know... I've *always* been engaged to Jo; she has these big tits."

"Well, as you can see, I *don't!*"

"I want you, Hon," he said coming close to me again as we walked. "I want you and he doesn't, can't you see that?"

The words broke my heart that someone else could see it too. I had hoped maybe it was only me, *my imagination* – like I told myself it was.

We parted at the front door. The house was dark and Ray was already in bed, asleep; I slid in beside him.

The next morning, I waited for Ray to be gone. He usually left for school by 7:30. In minutes, I had the kids rounded up and packed; I had to get out of there... fast.

We were in the car ready to leave. Buck came out of his apartment and saw us. He came over to us just as I had backed out of the parking space.

"Hey, what you doing, Babe? Where you going?"

"Home," I said. "Home..."

"But, why? *Why?* I thought you had two more weeks?"

"I got to get home... Tell Ray I left, will you? – if he even knows I'm gone – that I had to get home."

Buck was reaching into the car; he had me by the head, by one ear. I could tell he wanted to kiss me, but the kids were all watching, listening. Sharon was fourteen going on twenty-one. Sean was screaming, "Puck. Puck," reaching out with his arms.

"Hey, Tiger, you be good, you hear? And you too, big shot," to Kelly. He patted Suzie on the head, reached past me and pinched Sharon on the arm. "Y'all be good, y'hear? Take care of your mother; keep her straight."

His hand came back to my ear; I wanted to kiss him, too. The tears were stuck in my throat, that achy kind of stuck that feels as though they've been there forever. "You're some kind of good," he whispered in my ear and turned away from the car.

The trip back home was the slowest I'd ever driven. My heart was broken. *I had a husband that didn't love me. Guess he never really had; only married me because I got caught with Suzie, and, finally, the rest of the world could see it. Don't think about Buck... At home...*

Bunny Katzman, Mrs. Heizleman's brother, was so funny, the attorney in the family. Bunny always liked me, and even when his sister fired me for turning her in to the Labor Department, he still kept calling. He brought his wife, a "goy," to one of our parties, and tried to get me to go meet Jimmy Carter at one of his presidential campaign donut stops. Bunny said, "You want a divorce? Before your husband goes off to war? This makes no sense. Wait already. If you're lucky, maybe he won't come back."

Ray only had two days at home before he was scheduled to leave for 'Nam. Buck and I had been on the phone every night; he was begging me to wait for him, he wanted me, to marry me. He loved all four of my kids, too. "There's nothing wrong with any of them that a little fatherly attention wouldn't cure," he said. I believed, then, he was right. I told him what Bunny thought. I said, "I have to wait; it wouldn't be right sending Ray off under such terms."

We were sitting on the couch sipping on a drink. Ray didn't seem to want the booze, and I didn't either. I guess we had gotten enough to drink lately, but we always smoked together – sometimes a whole pack between us – just talking.

"Why did you leave so fast?" he asked.

It wasn't easy telling him about what happened with Buck, about his wanting to marry me, raise the kids, and my inquiring about a divorce.

Ray didn't look at me, just stared into space. After awhile, he said, "I went to see a Catholic priest."

"A *priest!* Why, a Baptist preacher going to see a priest?"

"I'm not a Baptist preacher anymore; don't even say that. But a Baptist would tell the whole world and I needed someone to talk to confidentially. You know, the Corps."

Yeah, I knew. The Intelligence Corps was always up there on his list. "And so? What did he say?" *Silly question, asking a priest about a divorce.*

"He told me to listen to my heart."

Ray took me into his arms then and kissed me gently, and with such caring, I started to sob. I had waited so long – being difficult, drinking too much, carrying on in anger. Booze always let it out.

We got up then and went into the bedroom. He laid me down on the bed and kissed me and kissed me, and then he said into my ear, his voice cracking, "Everybody has to have *somebody* to love them just for themselves." His body broke into shaking sobs as he hugged me all over, holding on to me like he never, ever had before.

My arms were never so open, so receptive, *so needy.* I hugged him and kissed him and opened my heart and body to him. I was *that somebody.* I had to be! If he wanted me to be, I *had* to be.

Buck called every night for a month after Ray left; his departure date was one month after Ray's. I was so confused. Buck didn't believe my husband really loved me. "He's just telling you all that because he's afraid of losing you," Buck said. "I'll be back through Atlanta, and I'm coming to get you, I promise. I want you to write me."

"I'll see," I said. "I'll see."
I was so confused.

Happy Hour was where I met Denise for drinks. She was alone too, separated alone. I didn't really trust her, but she was always there, waiting. She had a nice, sweet southern way that kept me off guard. Ray said her ex- had been a real prick; had bragged about how he screwed around with "anything with a crack," and wished he could "get a mouthful of Brenda Lee's pussy." It made me sick every time Sharon would play Brenda's records Ray had in his Baltimore apartment. Denise came from a highbrow family; her father was a college professor. She acted like she had class, and I envied her. When I talked to her, I spilled everything. She was always there, listening, egging me on to talk. I told Doc Hanks, "She's the kind who is better to have for a friend than an enemy," and he said right back, "That's a fallacy; there is no such person. Better to leave her alone; she'll never be a true friend." *How could I do that?* Denise was all I had – besides Sharon was acting fifty years old lately, the other three kids were one big blur in my mind, but always there in the background, having them to feed, clothe, keep clean, know their whereabouts, try to keep track of them until they were in bed at night so I could sometimes go to Happy Hour... One night, a guy followed me home. It was dark. Late. Sharon came downstairs. The minute I hit the bed, I came to. She was there when I said to him, "What are you doing in my bed, my husband's bed? Get out." Sharon shoved him out the door, and she was angry. It was dark and no one saw, no neighbors saw, the kids were asleep. Except Sharon. I told her, "I didn't do anything to egg him on, he just followed me. What could I do?" She got more angry.

God, what am I going to do? Sharon's mad at me; I have to stop doing this stuff. Denise isn't good for me; she sits and sips while I get snockered. She really isn't a friend. What's she up to, anyhow?

That morning, Dr. Hanks had seen me; I'd kept my promise to call him if I ever felt suicidal. "I'm going to put you into a group that happens to be in session right now. I'll be here, waiting, when you finish."

This was my first experience of this sort. I sat there, looking around from face to face as they looked back at me. The group was mixed in ages and gender. Being the newcomer, I figured it was up to me to say something, to break the silence. "Well, what happens next?" I said sort of giggle-y, embarrassed.

One of the young men said, "We are supposed to talk about something important to us, no holds barred."

"Let's talk about the Vietnam war," I said.

"No, no no-o," a young woman said, holding up her hand. "We are supposed to talk about something *close* to us. You know, something *personal*."

Looking her right in the eye, I said, "When your bed is empty, and your pillow is all you have to hug at night, I think that is about as *personal* as you can get."

The social worker sitting in with us stood up and immediately dismissed the group.

Dr. Hanks was smiling. "Well, I guess we finally found out what you are angry about, *this week!* Having to give up your husband to this war has got you very upset."

"But, how can *I* be angry, when *he* is the one over there risking his life?"

It was Saturday night at the monthly Geographical Widows party. I hated being with them, but it was the proper thing to do for a night out. I played bridge with them sometimes. Denise subbed in the group too. Instead, this night we ended up at the bar. "I hate that group," I said. "Did you hear that Bet's husband was shot down? And they finally found Mary's husband's body? Still no word on Roberta's, though. I just can't stand it any more."

That's how we started drinking and talking, about how awful it was to be with wives whose husbands definitely weren't coming back. And then *he* appeared out of nowhere, at my side.

Denise left, I guess.

Quietly, he sipped on his drink he brought with him. When he finally spoke, it was a soft voice, with the southern cadence I loved. His light, curly hair was dipping into his forehead, and when he turned his face to mine his eyes were pools of easy blue.

"Hi," he said. "Is this seat taken?"

"Hi," I said back. "No, it isn't. Well, yes it really is," I added with a slight apologetic note. "But he won't be back till September."

He was quiet, solid. There was something to him, not the usual flirt. Just nice. "He in 'Nam?" he asked, picking up my left hand, playing with my rings, *touching* me. *Oh, God...*

"Yeah," I said, "I'm meeting him in Hawaii next month; we're halfway there."

It was quiet for a minute, both of us just staring into space.

After some silence between us, he asked, "You like to drink?"

"Naw. That's why I order Grasshoppers; I like the glass," I said, lifting the stemmed goblet daintily to my lips.

"Hungry?" he finally asked.

"I guess I should eat; I'm not really hungry. Of course, I never *am* when I'm drinking, but I guess I should."

"Good. Let's go eat," he said, and took me by the elbow and walked me into the dining room.

"You just get back from 'Nam?"

"Yeah."

"When?"

"This week."

"God, I hope my husband gets back."

"Yeah, I hope so, too," he said. "Where do you live?"

"Right up this street, near the Post."

Half way into the meal, he asked, "Do you have your own car?"

"Yeah."

"Do you want to go to a party?"

"Where?"

"Across town. A friend of mine is having one."

"Oh, I would never find my way," I said.

"I'll drive your car, just get me to the expressway."

"Where's *your* car?"

"Don't have one; I'm just processing out. I live in Savannah."

My Ford Falcon had bucket seats. "Guess my husband was smart when he bought me this car before he left."

We laughed.

"Neat car," he said.

"Yeah, everything my husband gets is neat."

"Yeah, even his wife."

"I shouldn't be going with you."

"Why not? Do you think he isn't doing the same thing?"

"Is he?"

"I think so," he said, turning to look me in the eye. "I never saw anyone over there who didn't. It's a war, and a guy wants to, has to." He reached then for my shoulders and pulled me over, across the gear shift divider.

"I have a problem with sex," I blurted right out, I guess I had just enough booze in me. "I want to have orgasm, but I just can't seem to. It just won't let go, for some reason. This guy, Loran, told me I was frigid, one night when I was drunk, but I remember it. He said I couldn't if I wanted to, that I was just all talk. Do you think that's true?"

He squeezed my shoulder and reached his hand into my pixied hair. "It's not a big deal," he said. "Don't worry about it. I'm not asking for anything, I just like you."

It was such a good feeling. I didn't have to fight to protect myself, to explain myself anymore. He understood. *He just liked being with me.*

We got to this big house over in North Atlanta. Cars parked all over the place. We walked right in and went into the bedroom where everybody was talking, where all the coats, wraps were. The hostess, I guess, was in there telling the others to change into something more casual. There were all kinds of clothes on the bed in the next room. "Be comfortable," she said.

This was different, and I had just enough to drink to be agreeable. I had on my baby blue, sleeveless, crepe tent dress that just covered my bikinis. It had a French double ruffle on the bottom of it that made it stand out really cute. I found a pair of sloppy jeans and a shirt. He took his uniform off, put on jeans and a tie-dyed shirt. He was waiting for me at the door. We went across the lawn into the rec house, a big carpeted room painted pink. There was a piano, and a guitar stood against the wall. Everyone was sitting around on pillows, talking softly. No one was drinking or smoking. It was a subdued atmosphere, soft lights. I sat right down to the piano. *Smoke gets in your eyes...* the song I played. The piano didn't seem to go with this group, but they listened, and talked, and talked.

Savannah (I couldn't remember his name) just watched me. Talking really quiet, telling me I was a beautiful girl. He said, "You already know that, but, do you *really* know it?"

"You mean inside? Do I *know it inside?* Well, no, not really. People tell me that, but my husband has *never* told me."

"I'm sure he thinks it though," Savannah said. "He'd have to be blind."

He didn't put Ray down, he talked about him like he was just a guy at a war, and Savannah was a guy that was finished with a war, very matter-of-fact. He was quiet, calm, nothing like Ray. He was comfortable, I didn't have to talk. I could just sit there, and listen, watch. He held my hand, just held my hand and looked at me, steadily. It felt so good just to be seen. Someone played the guitar. Some of them sang, *If I had a hammer...* The sound and atmosphere was so relaxing, not having to prove anything to anyone, tell anyone my husband was over there, dying, maybe, and I was scared to death. I had these four kids I didn't know what to do with. Kelly was stealing, getting into trouble in school. Sean was climbing trees, I couldn't keep up with him. Suzie was too quiet, and Sharon was mad at me – I was sorry. But tonight I didn't have to think about all that, or of Ray – if he really loved me, or what I was going to do about Buck... Just sit and listen to the music, feel the warmth of a hand on mine...

It was time to go home, a long drive back, so he said he'd drive me. He was staying on Post. We were back in the bedroom to get our clothes on. I had just gotten on my dress, bare-legged in my t-strap shoes. I looked and felt like a flapper – like my mother must've looked back in 1939, the year she died. He had his shirt on and had just zipped up his uniform pants. He was reaching for me, kissing me on the forehead, on my cheeks... my neck... On my eyes his lips felt so warm... gentle... On my ears... His warm hand was on my thigh... between my thighs... slowly... up he was reaching... He felt for my... under the narrow panties... warm... His hand was so warm... easy... just his touch let it go... my insides let go... the whole inside of me let go and convulsed into a gigantic spasm. He slid me back onto the bed that was covered with wraps all piled up under me. He was on me, I was writhing, my whole insides were opening up, reaching... begging... grabbing with my legs, moving... Oh, God, he was warm... his hand... his body was full and warm and... *Oh, God...* everything let go, the whole world from inside of me let go... *Oh, God...* I was coming... I was coming... *Oh, God... Oh, God... Oh, God...* He was moving... slowly... warmly... quietly. It was so even, so beautiful, so sweet... He was holding me, and moving me, and I was feeling the most... most... There was no explaining it... Orgasm! Finally, it broke through the gates, the closed up gates for all these years since... the first time it broke through. This person was so gentle, so kind, so caring... warm... He just liked me, that's all. *He just liked me.* I was beautiful, *inside,* he said, inside of me was beautiful. I was a woman; I really *was* a woman...

All the way home, I cried, while he drove and held my hand. "I can't believe it," I kept saying. "How did you *do* that? I feel like the whole world just opened up inside of me. Oh, my God, how *did* you… ?" I kept asking.

He just held my hand and kept driving.

I really didn't have to say anything, and neither did he. *The damn had broke; I was a woman!*

He kept his warm hand on mine… He was warm, soft, gentle — on his way home to Savannah, from the war.

D enise just listened at the bar as I told her about Savannah. "I came, Denise, I finally *came*… After all these years; can you believe it?"

"Wonderful, Sam. Isn't sex great?"

I cried… sobbed… tears poured out of me. "Oh, God, I feel so guilty. What have I done? Oh, God. How will I ever face Ray again?"

She patted me on the arm and ordered us another drink.

The drink was sitting on the side of the tub, the water was warm. Sharon was still up. "A bath will be good for you," she said, and took away my glass. I wanted a cigarette. She got a sand ash tray that wouldn't slide. I said, "Just close the door behind you."

Under the water, I had forgotten to take my watch off – the one Ray had bought me on a trip to Japan, the year before. He had the band made special to fit my small wrist. I looked at it, and started to sob; I loved him so much. *What have I done? Oh, God. Oh, God…* I slid the watch down between my legs… *I should tear the bejesus out of me… I should rip my cunt to shreds… Oh, God…* Through the bubbly water, I shoved the silver metal into me, to rip, to kill, before I threw it across the room. And then I cried, sobbed: *Oh, God, I want to die… I don't deserve to live… Oh, God…*

T he Hawaiian air was warm and breezy. Ray and I were bare skinned, letting the breeze blow over us. We had managed to have three orgasms each that first morning. He was tan; it was hot in 'Nam. The sun was hot, the napalm was hot, the girls were hot — *but he didn't' tell that part; Savannah had.* That was how it was, so I knew.

Ray heard about all the Happy Hours and the couple times I had been followed home, about Sharon getting so angry. How I had been reaching, looking for something, someone… And about Savannah, how I'd reached orgasm so unexpectedly when I wasn't even thinking about it. That's when Ray told me about Baltimore, about the girl.

She was the band leader's daughter. The Brenda Lee records that we found, were hers. She was there in the apartment with Ray – until I got there. She'd run upstairs; the lieutenants knew, everyone knew. He had taken her to the class parties. They were all so shocked when I showed up. "You were so beautiful" Ray said. "The guys couldn't understand why, *with a wife like that – you're crazy man*, they said."

And I died, right then, I died inside. All that time, Buck knew. He *knew*. That's why he kept telling me, your old man doesn't deserve you. *He knew*. But he didn't tell me, nor did Ray that last night before he left for 'Nam, when he made me feel so sorry for him. After I told him about Buck, that's the least he could have done. Instead, he just told me he had made a decision after talking to the priest, to come home and ask me to love him for who he was. And I did, I did, I loved him so much. And now I could really love him, now that I was a *real woman*, now that I was whole. Therapy had finally worked, I had let go, after all the years of holding back.

"To the *parties*, you took her? With everyone that I met?"

"Everyone."

"The wives? Who I played bridge with, at the pool?"

"Yes, she was always with me, every time you called. One time we were in the middle of sex; you were drunk."

"Oh, I remember. You hung up on me, and I called Buck, crying. He never told me." *God, he never told me.* "How *could* you? Just like Major D. did to Soph. How could you humiliate me like that? After we talked about how rotten it was for Major D., for an officer, to do that to his wife?"

But I couldn't really complain. Look what I had done, I didn't deserve anything else, did I? It was only fair.

When I told my friend, a Colonel's wife, I was crying, "Why did he tell me? I never would have found out. Why?"

"To hurt you," she said. "To get even, that's all. It's a male ego thing. It's over and done with – now that he's even with you."

"Why didn't you *tell* me?" I was asking Molly over the phone. We met in Baltimore. "How could you play Bridge with me? All those hours we spent together, talking — about everything, our husbands – and never tell me he had a girl there?"

"It's just not something you tell, you know. We thought Ray was a big jerk after you got there; it just didn't figure. It hurt *him*, not you, don't you see that?"

When I started bawling, she hung up on me. How it hurt,

how it hurt. She was a Boston blue blood, and I was feeling every bit the slut Charity, my step-mother, had called me when I was so young and innocent, that hurtful misjudgment of me that pushed me into Huey's waiting arms so long ago and started me "on the road to ruin."

Whatever kept me putting one foot in front of the other, I wasn't sure, but I found a job and swallowed it. The unanswered letters from Buck stopped coming after I asked him why he didn't tell me? He said he wanted me to love him for himself, not out of spite. I told him that everyone thought Ray was a real cad, "and I'm not writing you back anymore, Buck," even though Buck said he loved me and wanted me to marry him for sure, now that I had "no reason to stay with Ray."

"My kids."

"*I'll* take care of your kids," Buck said.

Ray was home a month when the phone rang at midnight. It was Buck calling from the airport. He changed planes in Atlanta and wanted to see me. Out of a sound sleep, I told him, "There is no way I would leave Ray, I just couldn't. Right or wrong, I had three of his kids and he has adopted mine; I have given my commitment once and for all." Besides, I told myself, if I could live through all of this, I figured I could live through anything.

We were driving home from Happy Hour. It had started as "a required thing" by Ray's CO, a full Colonel, whose wife was an alcoholic, small and frail and pitied while her husband kept on ordering her drinks. In trying to please this new boss, we had gotten in the regular habit of going to the club on Friday nights. I was furious at such a demand. Defensive, Ray was determined to not "get my ass in a ringer," he said, when I complained. In the car, I was screaming at him, how mean he had been, more concerned about this jerk of a boss than me, "I hate you, how I hate you," I screamed, and opened the car door...

He grabbed me and screeched to a stop. "Have you really *flipped?*" he yelled and locked the door. He pulled me over next to him, and took off for the Post hospital, right then.

We were standing at the counter, Ray was checking me in, was telling the medic that I was drunk and had tried to jump out of the car, that he couldn't do anything with me.

The outside hospital door was standing open to the left of us, and I started toward it. The medic yelled at me, "Hey, Ma'am, come back..."

Slipping out of my shoes, I started down the stairs, out into the grass. Across the big green that ran the length of the hospital, I took off like a streak. God, did I run. *No way was I going to be put back into that damn hospital, there was no way!*

The medic caught me, but he was huffing and puffing, "Goddamn, lady, you a runner, or something?"

"No, just Cherokee," I said, laughing.

"What's the problem?" he asked as we walked back with his hand tightly on my arm, both out of breath.

"Oh, he wants to lock me up so he can do his own thing, I guess."

"Well, you don't sound like anything's wrong with you."

"There isn't, that sobering up won't cure. I just had too much to drink; I always get mad and stupid when I drink. I'm seeing the psychiatrist right now for it, he gave me some pills."

"Well, if I let you go home, will you promise to not jump out of the car, to take your pills and go to sleep?"

"All right, it's a deal, if you won't put this on the record."

"You got it," he said winking.

When the phone rang, I was in bed, almost out. Ray was still up, sitting in the other room, watching the news. Lately, he usually didn't drink as much when he saw me getting drunk. I could hear him talking softly, but he learned to whisper in a saw mill, so I could hear every word. It was Denise, who had been sitting with us all night. It was becoming plain Denise had her eye on my husband.

Ray was saying, "She promised she would go to sleep if I brought her home, she's out cold now... No, I'm all right... Sorry we left like that... Uh, mm... Yeah, she told me about him. One of these days she'll get her head straight, one of these days. You're sweet to call."

That was when I figured out that I didn't have to drink all those drinks stacked up bought by somebody's boss – or *a friend*.

Buck married Jo, we heard, and none of this was ever spoken of again. Ray and I appeared to be the happy couple, as long as I stayed sober, and I tried. The times I didn't grew less and less. "As you learn to verbalize your anger," Doc said, "the urge to act out will gradually disappear." Until then...

That following year, Ray got orders for Bangkok, just days after I had gall bladder surgery. Our family was to be ready to travel in six weeks. Recuperating, I was still yucky sick, but I thought that anything was better than staying behind, without him.

◆

CHAPTER THREE

The Major: 1968

In a small clandestine operation within the busy international city of Bangkok, two U.S. Army officers were engaged in the day-to-day transactions of running some very important business for the pentagon: Keeping track of the Russian KGB agents whenever and wherever they were spotted, in their cars, in restaurants, at the Sunday market – in short, an intelligence collection agency. Ham radios were conveniently, or inconveniently, placed in bedrooms for on-call duty twenty-four hours a day, cars were specially equipped to pick up whomever. On the second floor of the Demure Building, within walking distance of the Rama Hotel, were the headquarters' offices of the Far Eastern Activities of Mission Affairs, a military intelligence unit otherwise known as the FEAMA MI, HQ. Major Ray Malorry, the younger man and assistant to the unit commander, who now would rate all twenty-seven of the men in the office, was standing ill at ease. Not having been invited to sit, he awaited a response from his new boss.

Lieutenant Colonel Koche, the Company Commander, was unconsciously rubbing his chin while leaning back in his overstuffed leather chair staring blankly out the spacious window which surrounded him. Instead of the usual U.S. Army uniform donned by other military personnel stationed in the area, clearly displaying the name, rank, branch, and unit of same, the short-sleeved, white, open-collared dress shirts these men wore kept such information hidden from persons "not having the need to know." Koche, like Malorry, was a reserve officer who had been given a battlefield commission despite the man's lack of education. Malorry didn't hold this against him. Koche seemed defensive when he disclosed his having joined up at seventeen without finishing school. It appeared he was smart enough, though, to manage a sweet little job out of the limelight by keeping a very low profile, very low. *This place was unheard of, for god's sake.* The Intelligence Corps had its beginnings with men like themselves, now finagling to remain undercover because they ate up the intrigue, not to mention the aura of prestige that went with it. They believed they were the elite of the elite: hand picked, for the most part, because of their exceptional character and impeccable background, who had been taught to lie, steal, and break locks, to name only a few occupational skills acquired in the line of duty. Because the undercover world of espionage was beginning to shift, due, in part, to the bad press Vietnam was getting, and from the long-haired "peaceniks" parading their signs, an assignment like this was hard to come by. At this point in his career, Major Malorry considered himself fortunate to even get a command on his record, and in Branch, no less. The area running amok with the elite of the spook arena, working with the American Embassy and The Agency right under the noses of the KGB, only sweetened the pot. Since the financial strain of his four very active kids was ever increasing, the added COLA money loosened up some recreational dollars, as well as paid for three live-in servants. Training this native domestic help to keep an American style house without speaking a common language, was keeping his wife *plenty busy*, as their Chinese cook would say. But it helped the Thai economy, they were told.

Ray looked over the head of the man who had just twirled his chair around to look at the twisted gnarled traffic in the street below. The noise of squealing wheels and grinding breaks pulled their attention from the moment. "Damn," Koche said under his breath as he leaned forward to investigate the debacle. "That damned hotel traffic," he said, shaking his head. He was a thin, wiry man who didn't fill the huge padded chair. He sat back, settling into it, and finally turned around to face his new Operations Officer, and perhaps undeclared opponent. His face showed no emotion as he threw a page of figures back across the desk. "Major, you're mistaken. This money was for legitimate expenses. As the CO of this unit I have the authority to approve funds on a need-to basis, *as I see fit.*"

"Yes, Sir, I understand that. But the use of those funds must be documented in some fashion, that is all I'm telling you." The Major was still standing erect, his shoulders leaning inward. "Just for your information, Sir."

"That's fine. I'll mention this to Dirk when he gets…"

Just then the door opened abruptly. They were both facing it, surprised at the uninvited entrance of Mrs. Beverly Koche, an attractive dark-haired woman of a medium-to-plump build. The door slammed shut on its own volition announcing her presence.

Literally ignoring her husband, Beverly Koche stepped to within arms length of the Major. She locked her otherwise beautiful, penetrating and angry baby blues onto his. Standing in a broad stance with her hands poised on her hips, she looked boldly into his face. With a wry smile, she said, "Well, Major, shall I get you an apron?" Her voice was dripping with sarcastic sweetness. "I understand you're taking over my job?"

Ray Malorry was not one to treat any woman with deference, in fact, he was rather nonchalant about the niceties society sometimes bestowed upon the "weaker sex." More times than not he would forget to stand when a woman entered; he rarely, if ever, lit their cigarettes; his wife was often left in the dust just walking from the car to the house. Consequently, holding a door open was a gesture foreign to him. Conversely, among his male peers, he was never one to take a walk at the plate, or turn from a challenger. *The Win* drove his personality (he already had a ping-pong tournament going at lunch in the office) and taking on this female was no exception. Malorry, a former – underline *former* – Bob Jones University preacher-boy from way back had given up the pious religious crap when he joined the Army, but he had not thrown out the baby with the bath water. Thus far, he – a meticulous accountant with honesty and integrity, a matter of personal pride – had the upper hand with his new boss. A calculating gamesman, the younger officer turned to the senior now for some direction.

The older man had not moved a muscle or given any reaction to what he had just heard. It was his wife in the first place who had put the word out that the men would be rated on their efficiency reports according to the sociability of their wives. When the Major's wife, Samantha, heard it, she had come home fuming at the woman's archaic mentality, not to mention audacity. Since Malorry was the Rating Officer, and Lieutenant Colonel Koche only the Endorser, Malorry had immediately called all his married officers in and let them know, *unquestionably,* Efficiency Reports were their own making, *not* up to their wives. And, certainly, what the ladies did or didn't attend had no bearing on anything. Derived for their aid and solace, social functions' attendance was purely a matter of personal choice, *not to please anyone else.* Ray was now expecting this man to back him on Army code, to stand up to this... this brazen woman, but no-happen, GI. The man just sat, leaning on his elbows, looking up at the younger one, waiting with mouth ajar.

Major Malorry cleared his throat and took a deep breath. He had a piercing, almost fierce look that emanated from him, his broad jaws set in determination as he looked unflinchingly into the eyes of Mrs. Koche. His withheld anger made his own already large eyes appear to burst from their sockets, anger more at the man for allowing such unabashed daring than at the woman for being so ignorant as to think she could possibly be an honest-to-goodness threat. Pointing a finger dangerously close to her shoulder, he spoke through bared teeth. "Ma'am, the day I see the brass on your shoulder is the day I will take orders from you." Turning on his heel in true John Wayne style, the new Major swiftly and deliberately left the room.

The subject was never again broached between the two men, but rumors flew hot and heavy. The word out was, that the Major's wife, Samantha, from then on, was to be given the cold shoulder, publicly shunned. Ultimately, Samantha became a believer when she would arrive early to someone's home for an official Coffee, sit on the end of the couch, which would conspicuously remain empty as the ladies would arrive one by one, and sit elsewhere. On rare occasions, the wife of the senior in country, Colonel Bantos, might visit; her name was Evelyn. She, only, would sit next to Samantha, pat her on the leg, and smile. It seemed Evelyn knew what was happening; her kind attention seemed to make the tension in the air even more pronounced – it was to be a long two years.

She usually waited for him to make the first move, her generation's thing. Women were not supposed to be that forward, but it really was more her fear of rejection, so Sam made a habit of waiting. Sometimes she was disappointed and realized too late that he was just as afraid as she was... She remembered such moments when she stood before the Thai class, terrified, a lesson she had carried with her. Someone had told her how frightened the students were of failing. Their families had put a great deal of effort into having their children learn English so they could earn more money in their shops. At first, when she had taken on this challenge of teaching students preparing for college in the States, and she herself never having had the privilege, she wondered where she got the nerve, actually. *How could she attend college with four kids, not to mention the money, or being smart enough?* But it had always been her life long dream, wishing, and hoping.

Here in Bangkok, because of the immense heat, the Army had reimbursed them to hire three servants, one of the agreements the government of Thailand made to allow the U.S. to be there. Sam needed something to do. In the early morning, at

5:00 or 6:00 a.m., it was still cool enough to move about physically without passing out, so she bravely answered the ad, posted on the Officers Club bulletin board, to be a TESOL[2] teacher in the American University Association training program. (She would teach in the same building later used by Robin Williams to portray that position in his movie: *Good Morning Vietnam.*) Sam was chosen immediately from the many applicants. Her Midwestern sound, slowed by the *southern* – living four years in y'all country in Georgia – had made the perfect syntactical mix, according to the Cornell University professor who ran the TESOL program – besides the fact that she used good grammatical English. She had worked hard on her speech since she met up with Bonnie the year of her divorce. All those *You knows* had driven Bonnie crazy, making every moment of their conversations together so tedious that at some points Sam was ready to quit and give up on *becoming a lady.* But she had stuck it out and landed a real Bob Jones University boy – even though Sam didn't wear hose to drive-in movies as Bonnie expected, her feet up on the dash board in her sneakers had really blown Ray's mind. He appeared truly sorry, for quite a few months, that he had been *obliged* to marry her — until his Colonel had come to their house to see if he couldn't settle things between them.

Sam was riled up about the Army postponing a lie detector school for something as trivial as the softball tournament in South Carolina. Appalled that the big, monumental U.S. Army had behaved so childishly, her staunch German work ethic had reared its determined head. "I'll go see the Commanding General," Sam yelled at him.

Ray laughed in her face while pointing out that it was the "Commanding General who was softball crazy" and had personally rescinded Ray's orders to allow him to pitch in the championship.

Sam had blown her stack then. "Oh, my God, what do you mean? How can a grown man behave this way, much less someone in charge of so many people? And the money... Why, it's beyond human imagination."

"Welcome to the real world, Sam."

That night Ray mentioned at dinner that his CO, a Colonel, was coming over to visit them." What ever for?" she asked in alarm.

"To talk to you and explain about the softball tournament. So

---

[2] Teaching English to Speakers of Other Languages

you won't... so you'll understand."

The house was spotless, as usual, and her dishes all put away, kids in bed, when Col Traehan arrived. Sam took him into the kitchen, sat him down to the table, and asked if he would like a cup of tea?

He was delighted. "Yes," he said, "I'd love one."

She served him from her best cups and saucers, a leftover first-wedding gift. This was an opportunity seldom presented, but often dreamed about.

Ray sat with them a few minutes, and then one of the kids was crying so he eagerly disappeared upstairs.

These few minutes alone allowed Sam to voice her displeasure with the turn of events. Her distress at such shenanigans did not leave her mincing words, "Well it just seems to me that the business of preparing someone for something as important as a lie detector examiner should take precedence over *fun*," she said right out.

"Mrs. Malorry..."

"You can call me *Sam*."

"Yes, I can see how you would feel that way, Sam, and generally speaking, it does. But you must understand that sports in the military is one way the troops have to keep physically fit. The physical part of their training is extremely important. Do you agree with that?"

"Yes... Well, I never thought of that."

"And so... exercise, per se, is not exactly exciting. In fact, it is rather dull and boring to someone who has a sharp mind and ability... such as your husband. So the military has... tries to find ways to stimulate and challenge those physical bodies, in order for them to stay fit."

"Oh. Is *that* why they have all these tournaments: golf, soft ball, bowling leagues?"

"Precisely."

She poured him more tea.

"In your husband's case, our softball team has been lucky enough to have your husband as a leading pitcher, and we have beaten all the teams here. Now we have the chance to try and beat all the teams in the whole area, scheduled up at Ft. Jackson. And if we win that, we can play the other areas."

"Yes, yes, Ray has explained all that to me. But..." She was getting impatient.

"So, it has made the boys work hard, and stay fit."

"Oh," she said, "so they would make it to that conference. That's interesting; maybe the General is not so childish, huh?" she said with a silly grin. "Just a little ball happy. You know when Ray won the golf tournament last month, he gave Ray a set of golf clubs, his old set, and a picture presenting them. Of course, Ray was embarrassed because the clubs were the General's old second-hand ones. I guess the General thought because *he* had played with them, it made the clubs special somehow, even though they were beat up." She was trying to stifle her giggle. "But not Ray, he was really disappointed. His own set was new and much better looking... and that awful bag was so ratty. I told him he had the *honor, but not the glory.*" At this, she could not contain her laughter.

"But it got quite a few boys out there who might not have otherwise played. Do you see?"

"Sort of a sales thing, like *selling exercise*, is that what you're saying?"

"Precisely," said the Colonel in a relieved sort of voice. "Not to mention the sportsmanship that is learned from playing on a team," a concept that was truly lost on someone who grew up as an only child to a single parent.

The next day Ray came home from work just beaming. "Boy, you really impressed the Colonel. He said you were *a highly intelligent lady* and that I should be proud to have you for my wife."

"You mean you didn't think so before the Colonel told you that?" she asked in wonder.

He bowed his head, but the pride in his face could not be hid. There was no doubt, the Colonel made her young husband aware of a side of her he hadn't noticed before. All those little things that had disappointed him had built up – the bare feet, without hose inside her shoes; the tennis shoes on the dash board at drive-in movies — He hadn't made a bad choice after all; he could wear his wife on his arm again. She was intelligent; the Colonel had confirmed it.

◆

CHAPTER FOUR

The Big Heat: 1970

Keeping very busy had worked for me before. Teaching English very early in the morning before it got unbearably hot, three classes 6:00 a.m. to 9:00 a.m. daily, at AUA, was just the beginning. Six-week terms with twenty-five to thirty pupils each put me in touch with considerable number of students over the course of our stay. The first day, I remember how terrified I was standing up at the front of the class, worrying that I would offend a Buddhist by pointing or unconsciously sitting on the desk and inadvertently swinging my feet at them; so many things to remember. But when I looked out at all their faces, seeing how frightened they  were of me, and remembered hearing how their families were scrimping to send one of the younger ones to college in the States, and I was the one who had the power to help make that possible, I forgot my own fears.

Teaching was enjoyable as my job was to put sounds to the words they had learned through book study. Remembering all the many sounds for just one letter in the Oriental languages was an especially challenging task. Their favorite word game was what I called *Thinking English*. I say a word, call on a student, who then says the first English word that comes into their head. They absolutely loved it, and it was the highlight of the end of every class session. They got so good they would do it with one another. They were delightful students, particularly respectful and appreciative, who loved to bring gifts, or write letters such as this one:

Dear teacher,
We all students of the class fell deeply in your kindness, which is inculcating to be clever, since the beginning to the end of term.

During the time of education, it's beyond to understand the condition of knowledge, and seem to get lost in way, but you have brought in a right one, and give get off to a flying start, which would bring succeed to all of us.
We are congratulate and please receive our best wishes in this occasion. Thank you very much.
All of your students.

The remainder of my teaching day was spent mostly in our huge air-conditioned bedroom, where I set up a card table to put together all my lessons using pictures with English words and sentences under them. It was this training that enabled me later to help Sean learn his alphabet, through phonics and visual aids, when we were asked to remove him from kindergarten at Bangkok's American School.

Sean was unable to sit still even for stories, without the kindergarten teacher holding his hand and stroking it as she read, she told me sadly, as she really loved him. "He's such a sweet child; I just think he is too young right now and needs time to mature a little. December boys are always slower, it seems." The school sent him to the school psychologist, just retired from the penal system, for an exam, who pronounced Sean a "sociopathic personality" on the spot. "He was up on top of my file cabinets while I was getting a pencil out of my desk drawer; your son obviously has no respect for authority." Besides being quite angry at such a drastic assessment of this darling five-year-old child, my anxieties surrounding my children, and how to teach them to be the best in all the world, mounted. We found an English free-school run by an Asian Indian woman, who allowed Sean to learn at his own pace by letting him play, but learn when he wanted to, in the hopes he would be able to go back into regular school the following year, which he did.

During the afternoons, I took in individual students that needed extra help with their English. It was during one of these sessions that I had allowed Sean to go with Bobbie, a young lieutenant's wife, who lived around the block in an apartment complex which had a nice swimming pool. Sean was an excellent swimmer, he had learned to jump off the high dive at the last Post pool and had earned his swimming patch at age four. His dad had taken him out on the ocean waterskiing, already. Although I was not a swimmer, Ray was an excellent one, so I had little concern about Sean's water safety.

Sean was only gone a short time when he appeared at the front door with Bobbie holding firmly to his hand. The girl was visibly upset and appeared to have been crying. "You're not going to believe what Sean just did," she said.

"Oh, yes, I'd believe anything," I said, laughing.

Bobbie explained that she was reading at the side of the pool, when suddenly she heard, "Bobbie, look at me," he called. "Up here, up here."

When she finally spotted him, Sean was standing on a ledge of bricks that ran under the windows of her apartment, three stories up. She immediately ran over to the building and yelled up at him, "Sean, you come back down here this instant!"

"Okay," he said, "I'll just go down the other side."

"No, you don't. You come back down the same way you went up." Bobbie then explained that she had just taken him into her third floor apartment for a drink, and he had seen the pool from inside. Barefooted, he had climbed the corner bricks straight up.

Bobbie's demeanor stopped my laughter.

"It isn't funny, Sam. When I looked up and saw that kid three stories up, I nearly fainted."

"Oh, my God. Oh, my God." Grabbing Sean and hugging him, we were both crying and laughing at the same time. That's what they say about his hyper-kinesis, he's not afraid of anything. He loves to be high up; he used to be up a tree when I went to call him in for lunch, back in Atlanta. I would look up at him, and say, "By the time I get home, you better be there waiting for me. He would scamper down the tree, run home two doors down, and be sitting on the front step, waiting, giggling. You have to be on guard every minute, although he does mind very good when you tell him anything; you just have to be fast. What is he going to try next?" I wondered aloud.

"Whatever it is, it's not going to be with me," Bobbie said.

Besides my week-days teaching, on Sundays, I played the Hammond organ at the Protestant chapel. After completing the Red Cross Volunteer training, I worked at the hospital one day a week. At Christmas, I hosted a special Coffee for fifty ladies and invited the wife of Ray's Bob Jones' college buddy, who was the medical missionary doctor for a twenty-five-bed leper hospital up country, as a guest speaker. The huge tree was loaded down with gifts, new and used, brought for their children and those of their village. At another of the ladies' luncheons, hidden behind the stage curtain, I donated my limited talent by playing my entire repertoire of pop songs as background music.

Our home, in the evenings, was open to officers and enlisted personnel alike. Chan, our Chinese cook, would stand at the gate watching the road for Ray's car, and count the heads inside, so he would have the dinner table set for the correct number by the time the car came into the yard. With the help of our three servants, to whom I'd given personal training through diagrams rather than depend upon their English and my Thai, we were able to give sit-down dinner parties that were the envy of many. But still, at parties, Coffees, dropping in at Ray's office, it was as though I was invisible.

No, this tour could not end too soon for me despite all the happy moments with my English students; teaching my cook's wife, our sew girl, with the help of a calendar and pictures in my Medical Guide, to count the days of her menses in order to conceive a child after three years of marriage; breeding our little ten-pound shaggy-faced terrier (just one of six dogs that had free access in and out through the two-way screen doors) with a Chinese consulate's male dog in our house, we were allowed to observe and learn first hand nature's fascinating ways and watch three puppies come into the world. Our experiences went on and on

It was true; I was never accepted by the CO's wife or "her girls" no matter what I did. This behavior hurt me deeply. *Women! Dr. Hanks was right, I should leave them alone — they were my Achilles heel.* A rare exception was Evelyn Bantos, a woman senior in position by virtue of her husband's rank (outside of the Commanding General) to everyone in country.

The Bantos lived in one of the nice apartments in a high rise building that was fully air conditioned, unlike our large Chinese house which only had the bedrooms cooled, for sleeping. We chose the house over the apartments in the beginning because we were leery of all the drugs we'd heard ran rampant in the buildings. The Bantos girl, the same age as our Sharon, had gone to bed early one night and slipped out the window with the intent of going down the fire escape to meet a GI she had been forbidden to see. Her glasses had fallen off and, with her poor vision, she plunged twelve stories down, to her death. Because of Evelyn's kindness to me, I was intent on returning it somehow. I used this moment of opportunity.

We arrived at the Bantos apartment with a baked ham to pay our respects and give our condolences. We were welcomed with open arms. Col. Bantos took Ray into his study with a pot of coffee, a bottle of cognac, and shut the door.

Evelyn and I sat down in the living room where she had already fixed herself a high ball. I was a very light drinker these days. Always on my best behavior, I accepted a glass of white wine. Evelyn was middle aged, and a lovely person who I looked up to. I was still a young officer's wife who thought colonel's (and their wives) were next to God, so I sociably sipped on my wine and listened, while she began talking about her daughter.

Between sips, Evelyn was saying, "I had no idea she had anything like this on her mind. She had her hair up in curlers, ready for bed, and disappeared into her bedroom. How could I know she had fallen for this guy? Her father... my father used to tell me..." Then Evelyn began at the beginning, *her* beginnings back home in Missouri.

I continued to listen.

Evelyn talked about her father, *God rest his soul,* and how she loved him.

She talked of her father's love for her, for her husband, for her children, and for this beautiful daughter, just seventeen, struck down in the prime of her youth...

Still, I listened.

Working her way up to the present in a winding, free flowing tearful monologue, she argued the reasoning behind her decision that brought her family such a tragedy.

I cried with her, as I listened.

She talked, cried, reasoned, and sipped. More words, tears, and sipping...

Five hours later, Evelyn had talked herself sober, and she had finally resolved the issue of guilt. She had a good foundation of trust and mutual respect with her daughter, she believed. *Where had she, as a mother, gone wrong?* she kept asking, until she had answered her own questions through her father's words.

I sat in awe at the process of grief and how the soul had the innate desire to make peace with itself, and I was amazed at the ability of the human spirit to heal.

Colonel and Mrs. Bantos ushered us to the door with their arms around each other. There had been no one else, they said, no one who cared enough – to listen.

The tropical night air had cooled to a tolerable 100° degrees. Inside, the ice cubes began melting even before the drinks were poured. Glasses, snug in their coaster-socks, soppy with condensed moisture created a slick, watery film over the bar.

My elbow kept slipping off the edge into my lap, as I held the cigarette and it's spiraling smoke up in the air, away from my face while I talked. Halfway up my arm, the sharp edge of the blue Formica had already rubbed a mean-looking strawberry. "For god sakes, am I really such hot stuff, or what?" I said, giggling, propping myself back up on the bar.

"Sam, you're always hot; you know that. But tonight you're cooking with gas." One of the younger GI's, really waiting for seventeen-year-old Sharon to finish her homework and come downstairs, was hovering over my shoulder. "When you get to Pennsylvania, those War College hoity-toities will have to move over."

"Hey. I don't mind if they do," I squealed, raising my drink straight up into the air above me. The sound of clinking glasses muffled the approaching saam-lair in the soi. They all knew the tough two years that lay behind us. I was so noticeably ignored at all social functions for my outspoken opposition to Mrs. Koche's tactics that it seemed to become the joke of every unit party. Her rejection, and seeing the wives following her bidding out of fear of reprisal from her husband, was a daily bitter pill. For the hurt and lonely isolation, putting my energies into other things had been my savior. Proud of the array of accomplishments, and the end in sight of the unbelievable daily stress, I was full of high energy, feeling in rare form – and I knew I looked my best, because it was *that time*. Ray would sometimes comment, "Your eyes just sparkle when you're *in heat*." But he was too overwhelmed with his own excitement, besides being absorbed in his dice game, to notice me at the moment.

Like this, many times we had sat here, at this twelve-foot bar in the center of our enormous Chinese house with the round doorways, the slowly twirling ceiling fans easing little the intense heat of an ordinary Bangkok night. There usually were several guys sipping, yakking, and someone always getting drunk, to pass their time until they could get back to the good ol' U.S. of A. But tonight it was not one of those nights. It was *our* night: Major Ray Malorry's family who would be facing *Goodbye Charlie* blues and the jitters that always accompanies a new assignment. Despite the constant battle Ray had fought with Commander Koche – finally ending with the IG making a special inquiry, at Ray's request as Executive Officer, culminating with Koche's much warranted official reprimand and eventual forced retirement, we later heard – Ray's men and their wives, for the most part, within Ray's area of command, looked up to *The Major* with respectful affection, his Irish humor always abounding.

As would be expected, Ray's flamboyance was at its highest peak, telling his tale of receiving the creme de la creme staff assignment to the U.S. Army War College, in Carlisle, a vindication of sorts for the past two years of virtual hell. Tonight Ray was ecstatic, telling his tale to everyone that came through the door, and each time slanted to the particular listener. Ray's stories could liven up any group, anytime, anywhere, and I never tired of hearing them as they never, ever came out the same. But some stories took on a special life of their own, like this one, a new claim to fame in this man's Army. Ray would never be an ordinary reservist again; his time had finally come!

Besides the several GI's Ray had brought home to dinner, the ones who showed up for after-dinner drinks were mostly the younger ones in their early twenties, hoping mostly to get a peek at either of our teenage daughters. Round eyes, innocence, and free beer. What more could a young guy, far away from home, ask for? Jim was one of the few single officers. Already a Captain with no one to spend his money on, save our Sharon, we called him Diamond Jim.

Because he was a young, clean-cut twenty-five-year-old, we allowed Sharon to go out to dinner occasionally with him "for the experience," I suggested to Ray. She was just ahead of the drug culture that had come in during the decade of the '60's and still preferred beer, unlike her fourteen-year-old sister, Suzie, and most of Suzie's peers. We believed then, that beer with a Known was better than drugs with an Unknown, even if he was eight years her senior. Besides this, he was easy and fun to have around, just a good friend.

One night recently, Sharon had come rushing down the bedroom quarters' stairwell, bursting through the door with her fingers to her lips, "Sh-sh-sh," she whispered. "Jim is paying the saam-lair driver and *is he loaded*," she said, giggling, running over to the power switch by the door to cut off the huge fountain in the yard.

A hush came over the room, waiting for the buzzer at the gate to sound. Since our recent burglary, the gardener, who manned the gate, was suspect and let go. Chan, our Chinese cook, had temporarily taken over that job. Tonight he was sitting out in the guard shack keeping an eye out for Jim. Even though the house backed up to the emptiness of high-walled farm lands, in front of us was a huge Chinese mansion surrounded with lovely gardens and fountains bringing many visitors. Leaving the gate unlocked was not something that was knowingly done. When Sharon had tried to have a secret rendezvous with one of the Thai boys down the soi, in the vacant maid's room downstairs, Chan had intercepted him with a rigged-up bucket of water setting on top of the archway, over the door – the handle tied to a rope attached to the bucket. When the door opened, the boy came through it, and got doused. "Cooled off the young stud, the Chinese way," Ray said, chuckling, *after* he chewed Sharon out for messing around with a Foreign National. Chan was asked to rig up the bucket again tonight, for our Jim, as he was expected, after bowling, to be three-sheets-to-the-wind. At the sound of the buzzer, Ray looked up from his game, and yelled, "Come on in, Jim, it's open." There was a silly hush in the room.

In the stillness of a country May night, the sound of the hinges squealing could be heard, followed by Jim's voice screeching into the air at its highest pitch, "You gotta be shitting me, People! What the hell *is* this ?"

The sound of laughter broke out into the room as the herd stampeded out the front door, down the three wide arched marble steps.

"Holy Christ. What the hell you doin' to me, guys?" Jim was saying, wiping the water from his face, laughing. "Look at my bowling shirt. It's soaked, for Christ sake."

Ray had his arm around the young man's small shoulders. "Jesus, man, you look like you need a towel, or something."

Just then someone turned the fountain back on and Jim's eyes shot over toward the spaying water. His eyes got big, and at the same time he started to pull Ray toward it.

"Oh, no you don't, fellah," bellowed Ray. "Now we're even. *This* was for last time," he said, pounding Jim's wet chest. Blocking the path to the fountain, Jim was led carefully through the door, into the room with music emanating loudly from the stereo. *If you could see me now* sang Shirley MacLain.

Tonight, we were into some heavy conversation, Jim and I. "This new assignment has me terrified," I confided to him. "It's scary enough just going back to the States; we've missed so much these two years."

Jim reminded me then of some of those things. "The space walk was something else, huh? Even if it was on news' reels. The Thai's are not too big on news, like the Detroit riots. The burning of California's Watts sure didn't get big press, either."

"Yeah, most of those back from Home Leave seem to think that Bangkok is a safer place for our kids right now, can you believe that? If a grand's worth of heroin can be gotten from any taxi driver for *cheap money, M'da'am* of two bucks *here*, what can it be like back home?"

"You know, Sam, kids as young as your boys – Kelly, isn't he ten now? And little Sean, as young as he is – are getting caught every day with hard drugs."

How well I knew. Kelly had given us a royal scare when he had snuck into my handbag, while I had the house filled with five tables of ladies playing Bridge, took money out of my wallet, and left in a taxi. It took the entire bunch of Ray's GI's to find him at Pataya Beach, two hours away. Lucky for Kelly, and us, he had not met up with any harm, but our anxiety surrounding his questioning behavior – since he was born, in fact – was only heightened.

The more I thought about it, the more frightened I became. Like other parents, we had rarely spoken of it. Instead, we usually talked about the long hair. It was *in* back home, we were told, although we saw little of it as the Thai Police discouraged it by not allowing any Hair to deplane anywhere in the country. A quick shearing in the tiny cubicle of Pan Am's rest room was a common detour for well-off hippies searching for cheap drugs. The Army still frowned at Navy's beards, but the biggest shock was seeing men wearing jewelry. Ray had already succumbed to a gold chain around his neck. All these changes were disturbing enough, but to be confronted with three years ahead of us with nothing but full bulls and light colonels all bucking for their general's star, not to mention their starry-eyed wives – *especially* their wives, if they were anything like Beverly Koche — made my first induction as a lieutenant's wife way-back-when in Japan seem like patty-cake in comparison.

Ray had no idea of my trepidation as he had not given me a

minute of his time or attention privately as yet. Private was not his way. He was the type that always had to have a third party to play to. Whether it was one more or ten really didn't seem to matter as long as it was never just the two of us. I had learned to appreciate every little innuendo in his stories the same way he read every word of every letter I wrote back home — how we really communicated with each other. But sometimes I needed to have instant feedback, a kind word of understanding, reassurance. *Too much to ask?* I didn't think so, and sometimes not getting it, in special moments like this, for instance, left me a little agitated way down deep. And since showing anger was a big no-no in my growing up, the alcohol had a way of easing the pressure. Of course, I didn't recognize the feelings as anger, to do so would have meant I was OK. According to the latest fix-you pop-psychology craze, Transactional Analysis,[3] I was in need of serious "fixing."

Jim must have sensed this as he kept my glass filled and a typical can-you-top-this dialog going at our end of the bar. At the other end, Ray proceeded to get royally, stinking, boo-coo drunk. I knew this was going to be "one of those nights" when I looked over Jim's shoulder, just as the screen door closed behind Ray's last chess partner, to see Ray heading for the couch.

All four kids had been asleep for hours, even Sharon. She was an early riser – all that bouffant hair and eyeliner, she never stayed up late. After she'd gone upstairs, Jim and I managed to put away quite a few. As I talked and re-propped my sliding elbow on the sweaty, slippery bar, Jim would pull my elbow back up, mop the bar, and continue to tell me about some adventure in his first, or second, was it? tour in 'Nam — or about his aunt Sadie. God bless those aunt Sadies, bayonets and napalm were getting to be old-hat.

This, the hottest time of the year, ice melted before it could cool the drinks. The night air was some relief; it would get down in the 90's before morning, humidity the same. I'd sent Oobaan, our newest gardener, for a saam-lair, an open-air three-wheeled, bicycle taxi, and I got up to see Jim out, until it came.

Ray was snoring unconcernedly on the couch. I took one look at him, and then looked back at the lonely bar lined with empty glasses and smashed beer cans. The buzz of the overhead fans made the empty silence scream at me over the soft sound of

---

[3] Eric Berne, *Games People Play;* James & Jongeward, *Born to Win.*

Johnny Mathis, who had a way anyhow of tugging at the pent up emotions that had piled up. *Thirty-some years of denial and just enough booze.* I darted back behind the bar and grabbed the small handbag I kept there, for emergencies. It had baht in it, enough for a round trip, that's all I would need. It was Bangkok and I was a round-eye on the loose. *I'd show Ray he could sleep through hell; I'd get along without him!* As the screen door closed behind me, the record changer jammed and Humperdinck was singing, *Plea–se release me release me release me.* As I walked across the front yard to the gate, I laughed to myself, wondering how long it would take for someone to wake up. Yes, anyone wake up and *miss* me.

Jim saw the small clutch bag in my hand and his eyebrows shot up. His concern struck me funny. He should have *known* he was not my type, otherwise would Ray have gone to sleep? Sometimes guys were dumb; I giggled. "I just have to get out of the house tonight, go somewhere to cool off. Don't worry, I have enough money to get me back home. I just want a ride in some night air, just for a few minutes. This heat. Ray will never miss me."

Jim's apartment was only a five-baht ride. He was hesitant to get out and leave me. I assured him again that I was a big girl. "Mai pen rai. No sweat! Don't worry, GI," I said, smiling. He just looked at me, questioningly, but then he headed for his hooch as I motioned for the driver to turn around, to go back home.

As we passed the next soi, I thought about it being the street on which Mr. Donney lived, Ray's golf partner. He worked for Ray in an administrative slot who referred to his boss as The Major. Ray was a man's man, and having unaccompanied males around had been an ordinary thing; wives were a third dimension Ray had trouble dealing with, so he surrounded himself with the strays. Mr. Donney, a hilariously funny Irishman from Brooklyn, made no bones about his preference for Oriental women. He was attractive enough, behind his heavy horn-rimmed glasses, but I never really noticed men's looks. It was their manner and the way they spoke to me that turned me on, and Mr. Donney definitely did that. It was how he treated me with deference, always managing to say something to include me into the conversation. It left me feeling warm to my toes. He sometimes joined us for beer before he went out, but tonight he had been conspicuously missing. *Wonder if he's home yet from his night prowling?* I tapped the driver on the shoulder and motioned for him to turn right. I was too drunk to remember the Thai word. It was a sharp turn and I thought for a minute we would roll over into the khlong water, the open drainage ditch along the side of the road. It smelled unusually foul tonight. *Too bad all those beautiful pictures of this country couldn't begin to relay the strange mixture of the stench and flowers that this place produced.* "Here. Here," I said, as we pulled into a lighted area of apartments. I gave him twenty baht, a whole dollar was more than enough. I was too tired and impatient to wait for change.

The Indian guard was asleep against the wall of the apartment building. I scanned the parking lot for a vehicle with a FEAMA sticker that could be Mr. Donney's car, but my eyes were so blurry from the booze, I couldn't see. I knew which apartment was Donney's. Ray sometimes left messages, tee times for him under his door; the phone system was not very reliable.

Up one flight of outdoor cement steps, I climbed. At least there was a breeze through my Thai silk jumpsuit my sew girl had made for me, without a pattern. I was a slight size five, fighting to maintain my meager hundred pounds or into the hospital I'd go; Bangkok belly had taken its toll. Beer had been my prescription at every meal, doctors orders from a big strapping Austrian female M.D. at Fifth Field Army Hospital. My Milwaukee background prepared me for her simple remedy, and I did like beer. My stomach was churning just now as I reached for the door knocker.

No one answered, but the Indian guard woke up and came up the steps. "He not home, M'da'am; Mr. Donney gone," he said, standing there, waiting for me to speak, or leave.

I did neither. Instead, I turned, and went to the top of the stairs, and sat down. Suddenly, I was getting very ill. I reached into my bag for a Dramamine – that always did the trick. When my stomach was calmer, I would decide what to do. I leaned against the bannister and closed my eyes for a moment. The Indian shuffled past me, down the steps. He'd done his work for the night; he could go back to sleep. I wasn't really thinking about where I was, or what I was doing, just reaching out for something, someone...

An irritated Mr. Donney was shaking me awake. "What the hell are you doing here?" he asked with so much venom I got suddenly shy.

"I don't know, Donney. I thought it would be nice to talk to you for a while. Ray fell asleep He got really drunk tonight, you know our orders."

"Yeah, I know. I didn't think I could handle it all night, after hearing it all day. Come on," he said, with unexpected gentleness. He took my arm and pointed me in the direction of his door.

"I'm sorry, Donney. I'm really not quite with it. I just got very sick before and took a pill. Jim and I already put away a few at home."

"Yeah, I can tell, you and me both. You shouldn't be here, you know," he said opening the door, and turning on a rickety floor lamp.

"Can I use the bathroom?"

"Yeah, I wasn't expecting guests. You'll have to overlook a bachelor's mess."

At the end of my period, I realized I didn't have any Tampax, *but I had on black underwear.* The cramps had gotten worse ever since the IUD was put in, the past week had been one of my worst months; I was glad it was over. Now I was smack-dab into ovulation, but I had no intention of taking my clothes off. On the john, I was falling asleep anyhow; I just wanted to lie down…

The apartment was one room, with a table and chairs to one side. The bed was nicely made, and Donney was sitting on it, waiting. "What's the deal?" he asked me.

"I just needed to talk to someone, you know?" Then I started to cry.

He got up and put his arms around me and held me, just held me. *How long had it been since Ray had done that? Was that asking so much?* Then, I said it, "I'm afraid to go back home, to the States; maybe I could stay here?"

He was tall and lean and he had taken his glasses off and was looking down at me through his wavy hair. He had the bluest eyes. I never had really noticed them before. Ray always bragged about the blue eyes of the Irish. Donney just hugged me, and in his Brooklyn accent, he said, "I don't know about you, but I'm beat. And I gotta work in the mornin', rememba?"

Yes, I did. And then we kissed for the first time. He was so gentle and caring; I started to cry again. He put his hands through my messed up hair. My hairpiece came loose and fell off. We both giggled as I caught it before it hit the floor. It was a small bunch of curls the beauticians could pin in, to give me height. I felt for the flat top of my head. He just laughed, and ruffled it up. "I don't think we're very good at this. Maybe we should try pinochle," he said, and disappeared into the bathroom.

The bed looked so inviting that I lay down on it, on top of the covers – just for a minute. The air-conditioning felt cool, and I was too sleepy to think. The antihistamine had left my mouth more dry than usual, after booze. That's all I remember before falling asleep.

Later on, I was in the middle of a strange dream. In it, I was hooked up to this wagon, like a horse. I had the harness and straps all tied around me so that I could pull the wagon. There were five people in it, and it was very heavy. I knew I had to pull it, and I tried, but it was very difficult; it barely budged. I was desperately afraid I would not make it. At that moment, I came awake to find my body locked into the missionary position. I felt the strain of moving very slowly, very slowly, rocking, rocking. The effort was tiring as I tried very hard to keep up the rhythm, rocking slowly... It was wearing me out... Slipping back into the dream... trying to get the strength I needed to keep going, rocking, slowly straining, pulling...

At daylight, the sound of an electric shaver woke me with a start. My surroundings and lack of clothing brought me bolt upright, out of bed. *Oh, my God; how am I going to face Ray?* Donney came out of the bathroom, all dressed, just as Ray picked up the phone that was ringing on the other end. "Where are you?" Ray asked.

"You don't want to know, I'm all right. I'll be home in a few minutes. Is anyone up yet?"

"No. I slept on the couch. Didn't even know you were gone."

There was a penetrating silence on the line

Ray said, "I think the record player's broke."

Finally, I said, "I was hurt that you fell asleep."

"For God sakes, Sam, I was drunk!"

"So was I."

"So we're even, right?"

"I guess," I said, and hung up the phone.

Donney was just standing there, staring at me. Then he shook his head and turned away.

I wanted to explain, to tell him about the dream – that I didn't really remember him even though I knew he had. I started to reach for him, to have him face me; I should say something...

Instead, he turned to face me on his own and took me into his arms. "Don't worry about it," he said. "It's just one of those things, you'll make it all right. Going home is rough sometimes." Then he kissed me softly on my forehead.

In hopes that I could get back to my house before anyone else woke up, I rushed out the door.

A few days later, Sharon asked me where I went that other night? I said it was *my* business, no one else's.

She said, "Oh."
No one ever mentioned it again.

With everyone taking their turn at saying farewell, we partied for three straight weeks. It was strained to have Mr. Donney around. Sometimes I would catch him looking at me, but we never spoke privately again. He had been my husband's right-hand man and best friend – I was sad and ashamed – but in unexpected moments, I would feel the pleasure that only tenderness can bring.

◆

BOOK TWO

A Make-Believe Family

"The roles in dysfunctional family systems... are not chosen or flexible. They are necessitated by the covert or overt needs of the family as a system... to keep the family in balance. In dysfunctional families, the individual exists to keep the system in balance."

– John Bradshaw
The Family

"All families are in balance. The question is, however, what is the cost to each family member to maintain that balance."

– Virginia Satir
People Making

"The psychotic withdraws from his environment in favor of suffering or bliss within a world of his own fabrication... I am not saying that addicts are psychotic per se, but that their response to anxiety moves beyond an absolute escapism."

– Lerner & Tefferteller
The Addict In The Street

"You can drive the devil out of your garden, but you will find him again in the garden of your son."

- Heinrich Pestalozzi

CHAPTER FIVE

Ousted: 1973

Ray was on the phone in Pennsylvania asking if I was ready to start back home soon? He was babysitting the younger ones while I took a weekend drive to visit Sharon in her new apartment, in Fairfax, outside of D.C., a two to three-hour drive. It seemed strange for him to call like this, usually he was easy going about what I did, and he sounded so serious.

"Why? Don't you think I can drive this big car at night by myself?" I said to tease him.

"It's not that, Sam," he said quickly.

Even though I had driven all over the country with the kids while he was overseas fighting two wars, he never seemed to think I was really capable, as though he thought that a fairy godmother came and transported us when he wasn't around to shoulder the wheel. My preferring to drive at night, without the sun in my face, didn't seem to register. He hated night driving himself, so on cross-country trips, he and the kids slept and left me to enjoy maneuvering the road with the truckers – and this was such a short trip. He treated me like I was his charge, or something, as when crossing the street, he would take me by the hand and hold it up, into the air, and pull me as though I was a young child. Ray, I would squeal, *I'm* supposed to take *your* arm. Usually his protectiveness drew laughter from me, but sometimes, when I was intent on getting something finished, it got in the way. The sarcastic tone in my voice, which was rare for me, caught him. He began to explain, "It's just that we need to talk. It looks as if we're getting orders after all," he said rather dejectedly.

"Oh, no," I said, sharing his attitude. I was just finishing my first year of college, and Ray had gone back to school nights to eventually tackle his Masters. We had hoped to stay put at the Army War College so Ray could maybe retire there as a civilian in the same job, three years away. He'd revamped the whole secured library system, making his presence known with both the staff and faculty, and even the students; hard work and Happy Hours had paid off. By then I would have my Bachelors. We loved the area, the small town atmosphere of Carlisle, and it was so convenient to Sharon for a weekend jaunt. "Orders, to where?" I asked, getting a little nervous that he hadn't just spilled it out like he usually did. He was so full of mischief and kept me constantly on guard.

"Well, I'm not exactly sure yet, " he said with a flat tone so unlike him. "Aren't you finished with your paper yet?"

"Sharon's typing the bibliography right now. If you're that anxious, I can take her to dinner another time for helping me."

"Great," he said in relief. "Don't speed, or anything." We both laughed; telling me not to speed was like telling a dog not to bark.

Sharon had typed the report due for my *Child Growth and Development* class, a case study on a third grade boy that I had observed all semester. I had spent my whole life trying to improve my self-taught typing skills, and here Sharon typed an incredible 100 words per minute, with no errors. Even though she had excellent grades, college was not in her plans. When she had started her Office Practice major at Carlisle High, with the driving ambition of becoming a secretary in Washington, D.C., hoping to live with her girlfriend from Bangkok who was now there, I didn't really think she was that serious. But before she was even graduated, she had proven herself by landing a job in a Senator's office through a Colonel up on TDY, who we met at Happy Hour. The Colonel's wife was Office Manager for a Senator.

Before Sharon's interview, on the way down in the car, we asked her, "Who is the President?"

"Let's see," she said, "It couldn't be Kennedy; I know he's dead." She thought awhile and gave up. Our living within the cocoon of the military establishment, and overseas, had isolated her from more than we realized; she had no political sense whatsoever. Ray gave her a short course in government those two hours, which didn't help her relax any when she realized how little of those subjects she had absorbed in her young life.

That morning, while we waited in the car, she passed her testing with superior skills. She said her knees were literally knocking together. The Senator's administrative assistant was impressed with how visibly scared she was and how little it had affected her scores; she was hired on the spot. Already past her eighteenth birthday, we got her a used Ford Mustang for graduation and she was on her way the very next day to report to The Hill for entrance into her new grown-up life. Since then, she came home often, and we went down there to help her to set up her place. Leaving this area would make that harder to do. Thinking of her being completely on her own without us had me a little worried. Still so tied to us, to our opinions, she would call and ask me things at all hours of the day, or night, but I was just too happy to be there for her.

Driving home, north, through that beautiful farm country in Maryland, and then into Pennsylvania, my mind drifted back over our lives together. I started thinking about all the places we had moved to, and left. Now here we were again. *Please God, not another hardship tour!* All along, Ray had been reassuring me that he thought he might squeeze by just three more years until retirement, without one. These last three had been packed full of one new challenge after another. Although Ray had always told me that he would see to it I got to college some day, so I'd finish my high school correspondence course, I believed, but never had I dreamed it a real possibility. For one thing, I really thought I was too dumb. Passing the GED required and then the SAT, made me realize how little belief I'd always had in myself. That first day as a freshman, feeling so ignorant, lost, and out of place, I remember looking around the classroom for the cloakroom to hang my coat, since there were no lockers. At my age, the kids thought I was a professor. Although, when I was with Sharon, we were often believed to be sisters. Once when Sharon came to a War College party with us, she had her hair done up in her natural blonde twist; I had cut my graying brunette hair into a long frosted shag. In the ladies room, I heard one gal whisper to her friend, "Can you believe it? She looks more like the daughter."

Ray's being made the Staff Security Officer was a true plus for his career. He was still hoping to make lieutenant colonel before his twenty years were up. Not only was he able to exercise the tact he had fought hard to learn, after being reprimanded for the lack of it in his early days, he had a vibrant personality that drew people to him, or repelled them, depending upon which side of the law you were on, and sometimes what kind of person you revealed yourself to be at Happy Hour – a big social yardstick the Army, too often, used.

We both had more energy than sense. As down payment on our first house, we finished all the interior wood ourselves for *sweat-equity*, the builder called it. The kids got their friends to help us every night for free suppers, but when Post housing came available, we were fortunate to sell our house. Ray could walk to work from Quarters and I could have the car for school. Living on Post for the first time since our stint in Japan, ten years previously, the kids didn't need taxiing to all their sports' activities, or to the movies, and the dogs could run along the creek without a leash. Social parties went on at the club every week with a formal dinner dance monthly, with dress-uniform regalia and floor-length gowns. Drinking was definitely *in*, but my drink had become virgin screwdrivers, or my eyes wouldn't focus the next morning, to study.

Through the psychology course I had just finished, I began to see everyone in our family differently. Every course I took seemed to uncover a different aspect of my ignorance, showing me things in my upbringing that were missing, or badly distorted, which in turn affected my kids.

In second grade, Sean had trouble learning his alphabet, a serious memory-blank problem. One day he'd remember a K and the next day he wouldn't. Together he and I made a collage on cardboard of magazine pictures, matching sounds to the letters, similar to how I'd taught the Thais the year before to pronounce English words they could already read. This picture lesson was in front of Sean daily while he ate alphabet cereal, at breakfast. Soon after moving into the new house, he started wetting the bed. The pediatrician put him on Ritilin for being hyper-kinetic (a fancy word for hyperactive) and his bed was never wet again, unlike his brother Kelly, who, unfortunately for him, had never been given medication; Kelly was well into puberty before his bed stayed dry.

Sean's medication also made a tremendous change in his behavior. His teachers raved at the difference in his concentration, sometimes "too intense," it seemed, and why I had such keen interest in doing this case study. Since Sean was in the same grade in another school, I could see how other boys his age behaved *without* medication. The experience had been an eye opener. Being in the classroom on a regular basis so that the kids became accustomed to having me, forgetting about me, I was able to learn more from observation than from any text book.

Kelly, senior to Sean by three and a-half years, had average marks in Junior High, but his teacher would tell us continually how much more capable she believed him to be. His third grade teacher's opinion that he "lacked responsibility," which had sent him for his first psychiatric evaluation at Emory University, in Atlanta, where I had been seeing Dr. Hanks, I was not too surprised to hear, after several interviews and testings, "Your son is feeling overwhelmed by females."

After all, I told them, he lives with a mother and two older sisters. "My husband is in Vietnam for a year, before that he was away to a three-month school in Baltimore. Also, Kelly was only thirteen months old when his dad left for Korea for a year, so you see he *has* been with nothing but us females, except for his baby brother — but what can I do about *that*?"

The head doctor had responded with reassurance. "Until Kelly's father returns to the home, Kelly needs to be around some adult males on a regular basis, i.e., boy scouts, a father of a friend, something of that nature. And when his father comes home, the problem, no doubt, will right itself."

Uneasy about Kelly's behavior, I wanted to believe Ray's assessment that most of it was "just being a boy." As parents, we didn't really push for high grades for fear it would hurt more than help.

Kelly's little scrape with the MP's though, had heightened my fears. On the younger and smaller side in his age group, he was chosen to be a lookout while the older boys broke into a cold locker and stole beer. Trying to "put the fear of God into Kelly," the MP told us he had been unusually stern. We hoped he would find other kids to run with. After that, Kelly became friends with one of the boys whose father was in the present War College class, and just one of the many Happy Hour regulars we got to know.

Driving like this, sunset and twilight approaching, always reminded me of how much mastering the wheel was so much like life. I loved driving anyway. After a while behind the wheel, I began to feel as though the big machine was merely an extension of my body – feeling every bump, swerve. Then you think you see something down the road, a sharp curve that might seem scary. Your adrenaline starts to flow, your hands clutch tight to the wheel, but you keep on moving, closer... closer... And then you reach that ominous turn and find it so slight, your tension not needed – so much like facing orders to an unknown place, but anxiety was my middle name. It was hard to control where my family was concerned.

Take Suzie, smack dab in the middle of her teens, the quiet one that seemed to worry me the most. Ever since leaving Bangkok, she had seemed openly rebellious to us, and sort of depressed most of the time, bad dreams at night. She started walking in her sleep too, which really concerned me. With Sharon now on her second year out of the house, I was starting to really see Suzie for herself, instead of always in some fight with her sister. Her attitude seemed cynical for a fourteen-year-old, throwing suicide jokes around like it was funny. Finally, I insisted she go with me to the Post psychiatrist. But with me staying in the room, as she'd made me promise, there seemed to be no real connection made. At least she knew where to go if she needed that kind of help, the doctor told her. *Was she smoking more than cigarettes at the ball field after dark?* Until she came home high and red eyed, grinning at her dad when he told her not to come home like that again, we weren't sure. Being careful not to accuse our kids of anything without cause, we tried to be concerned, but not overbearing, parents – as my dad was with me. Ray still didn't think smoking pot was all that dangerous; few did as yet. I disagreed, especially in private. Often I would ignore things Ray did or said in order to maintain a united front. We'd argue in whispers in the bedroom, or when we got a chance away from the kids. All in all, as parents, no one tried harder, or could care more than we did; certainly, for sure, our kids had to *know* this.

It was almost dark when I drove into Carlisle Barracks housing area. The woodsy road on which we lived wound around the General's quarter's, commonly referred to as The Castle, a large white stone fortress hidden behind rolling lawn and shrubs. We had been invited there, as were all students and new staff and faculty, for a meticulously prepared and served full-course, formal dinner. The guest of honor on that night was a nationally known economist who was speaking at the college. Dinner completed, we were led into the library for after dinner drinks and conversation. A polite, stiffly somber evening was a reflection of this General's reputation. Conversation was nil as few were going to chance a slip of the tongue. Most of us were afraid of him; kids would sometimes stray up the walk on their trikes with anxious parents at their heels. Our kids were too old for those kinds of mishaps anymore, *thank God!*

As I pulled into the drive of the redwood A-frame, which backed up to a shallow tree-covered creek, two black shiny noses poked through the living room sheers that hung behind the couch. It was clear, silver-haired Gigi and blonde Zsa Zsa, our shaggy mops of Thai terriers, second generation bred from of our ten-pound Ti-sip in Bangkok, were keeping careful watch. As I entered the house, all was quiet save these two, now sitting on the kitchen tile at the door, right next to the edge of the carpet. Trained as puppies not to tread on the living room rug, they sat obediently, yipping and yapping, as though they had never, *ever* trespassed beyond their assigned boundaries.

Chuckling at them, I didn't hear Ray come up behind me. Turning on my heel, the look on his face took me by surprise; rarely did I see this man with a serious expression. His Irish humor was never more than a breath away. Hugging and kissing me, I stood tense. Ray always kissed goodbye; I was the one to kiss hello. Alarmed, I asked immediately, "What is it? What? Where is everyone?" I could hear my chest thumping in my ears.

"Come, sit down," he said and pulled me by the arm to the couch. "The kids are at the movie, and we only have a few minutes before they will be here. That's why I wanted you to come home early. Last night, about 7:30, Kelly was supposed to be at the movies and... Well, he got into trouble again." Ray's face was devoid of color. This storytelling of his, always building things up to such a pitch that by the time you got the punch line, you were on the edge of your seat...

"Ray, please, tell me first what Kelly did? You can fill in the details..."

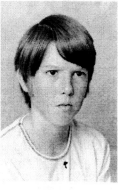

"Well, he got picked up by the MP's again. He robbed the house next door with the new kid he's been hanging around with, and this time, in the interrogating room, the General was behind the two-way mirror, listening and watching... We have one week to get Kelly off Post, and one month for me to find another assignment."

"What do you mean, robbed... When? Who? *A week?*" I shrieked. "The Army can't do that, can they. How?"

Ray then explained how a military post was really a small dictatorship within a larger one: in fact, the entire military establishment was one inside the government. The General was in charge of this one and "he could damn well do what he wants," Ray was saying. "When he saw Kelly being questioned, without showing any emotion... Apparently, Kelly just sat there staring... the other kid was carrying on with big tears. The MP's tried to persuade the old man that since Kelly had buried the money, not spent a cent of it like the other kid – who went right out and bought himself a TV – Kelly should receive some leniency. But because of my job, I have to be above reproach. I can't very well bust some Colonel for screwing around on his wife at some cheap motel and ruin his career chances, if I can't control my own kid. It's Kelly's second offense. The father of the other kid... *His* career's in the toilet. But he at least isn't being singled out; he'll just go quietly on his way like the other students."

Ray had been right, I might very well have wrecked the car driving home, if I had known. He was trying to explain, but my mind was flying, going in circles, the terror I felt inside had no words; I had failed miserably as a parent, and here was the proof Dr. Hanks was right: I *was* lacking a great deal from my own mother-void, all those missing puzzle pieces he said I may never find, *never find*, the long, long search for them just getting started in school, and now everything was coming apart. We were being publicly shunned, again. In disgrace. The two years in Bangkok had already taken its toll on us, but at least *there* it was not something *we* had done... But now, here, it *was* our fault. How could I go on, face everyone? *How could Ray?*

"Get this, Sam, you're not going to believe this, but all Kelly took were some cupcakes, spilt candle wax all over the house. The piggy bank full of change, around $300, they split between them."

"Next door? Our friends, this next door, in *this* house?" I was dumbfounded. We lived in one end of a duplex next to Colonel Benton, a faculty professor, a real brain. Len and Loraine had become a regular fixture at our house, for Happy Hour on Friday nights since the day we moved in. They would come over with drink in hand right after work, and invariably Len would pass out in our living room while Loraine would talk and drink, drink and talk. We finally had learned how to steer them to their house, next door, for food they were always inviting us to eat, and leave them while we maneuvered ourselves out the back door, without them. Because they were such great people otherwise, and he also out-ranked Ray, we tried not to make too much of it. Len was a boy scout leader, and would take his big RV on camp-outs *in order to dry out,* he said once. His son, Kelly's age, would brag about his big camping weekends. Kelly was apparently more envious than we thought. Afraid of what could happen, I gave Kelly all kinds of silly reasons why he couldn't join scouts: Ray wasn't a camping kind of dad, we'd say. Accidents could happen, costs too much. But beyond the alcoholic part with Len, it really was my fear of the sex business; I didn't trust *anyone* with my kids. *What happened to me was not going to happen to any one of them.* It was just easier to say no *always,* to continue to keep the *No overnights!* rule we'd always had. Neither did we use babysitters; Sharon and Suzie were the only ones I had ever trusted – our kids just understood that.

The choices we had in assignments were: Korea for a two-year accompanied tour, or Atlanta, our old stomping grounds. Ray, having been to Korea, knew much about it. A filthy country first of all, he said, worse than Japan was, and secondly, we heard it was the gateway for hard drugs coming out of the Orient. Keeping your kids away from it was one hell of a job. The drawback to Atlanta was, Ray would have reserve units out of town every weekend, but he'd be at home for two days a week to compensate for it. Our old friends, the Whites, who still lived on their farm in Alabama, driving distance from Atlanta, were the first ones we called. Asking for their help in taking Kelly for the remainder of the school year, about six weeks, until we got moved; they accepted. We had no idea where else to go with him. We were barely making ends meet financially, since we'd used all of our excess funds on college tuition, and both of us had finals to take yet, or lose all that time and money we'd spent on school. In the mean time, we had to deal with Kelly.

The Post psychiatrist was booked solid, and I was told it was a year's wait to get in. A week was just not enough time. We put Kelly on a plane, and prayed – how I prayed. For what, I didn't know. *For a miracle, to fix our son?* Something was drastically wrong with him, or the General wouldn't have reacted like that, would he? Ray wouldn't hear of our seeking help for our family through other channels, go over this General's head. That would really finish Ray career-wise, who was happy that he wasn't kicked out rather than just be relieved of his position.

Ten years back when I was in therapy with Dr. Hanks, he had told me, "You take care of the girls, Sam. Leave the boys up to their father; boys need a father's discipline."

"What happens when he doesn't do his job, and they get into trouble, then what?"

"That'll be his worry, not yours." *Easy for a doctor to say!*

We had condolences from the parents of the other boy who felt we were being unduly and harshly treated over this – a feeling often, openly expressed, but we could do nothing. Here, the General was God.

We arrived in Atlanta right in the thick of Watergate. At the guest house, the hearings on TV absorbed the attention of everyone. Sharon had left the senator's office and was working for *Citizens for Nixon*, a group that was fighting to hang onto the White House. I was frightened for her involvement when I saw so many getting dragged into the mess as witnesses. She was the star of our family, the one who kept us holding our heads up; we hadn't totally failed. *Where would she go from here?* She took a short job at Treasury, under Schultz for a while, until

Gerald Ford was sworn in. There, Sharon landed on her feet, heads up, supervising a dozen people in the White House. She was making us so proud; Ray never met a new face with whom he didn't share the success of our oldest daughter, our ego's lifeline.

We immediately got Kelly into counseling with a child psychologist, who, we found out too late, was a Skinnerian behaviorist with strict authoritarian leanings. His judgmental and condescending attitude, together with his method of giving merits as positive reinforcements for efforts made and ignoring behaviors which we were hoping to eliminate, seemed only to irritate rather than help. Feelings within our family only grew more tedious when Kelly ran away again, this time taking a bus to South Carolina. When the police called us, we had to go after him in the middle of the night. After a week's restriction, Kelly promised to do better. It was months later when Kelly again forced himself into our consciousness...

Ray was pouring his one vodka Gibson martini. I had put my foot down; only one drink. Of course his *one* was poured into a grog glass so big around that I needed both hands to pick it up without dropping it. We were on our way... again! Dan and Dot, from across the street, were going to dinner with us at Steak & Ale. We were well into the alcoholic din of dinner preparedness – a must when friends were involved.

Dan was a government employee and a sweet friendly southern boy who shared many of the same values as Ray – a corner lot with the nicest house and lawn on the block, a finished basement with a pool table and a bar, a pretty, active wife who ruled the roost and who threw parties almost as good as we did — and kids who didn't embarrass them, that is, who stayed out of major trouble by going to school and graduating proper, and then whatever... They had two girls almost ready to do that, when the oldest one would suddenly decide to get married with a big fancy wedding in the living room with just their family, a quick, hush-hush affair with a cameraman dictating the moments to share later with the child that had dared to already be conceived. 1974, pregnancy out of wedlock was still the unpardonable sin – and always would be to a Southern Belle.

Sharon, at twenty-one, still in the White House, had already made her first life blooper, marrying an alcoholic con she would soon divorce.

Suzie, now seventeen, was well into her teen-age madness, secretly managing two abortions following drug-horror "fruit salad parties, colored pills of god-knows-what downed with alcohol," one of her friends reported. *Would her brain survive the insanity struggle we were witnessing as she grew closer to facing life without Mom and Dad?*

Kelly we still accepted as our biggest challenge as parents. His running away, or worse, loomed over us continuously.

Sean, in puberty, had grown out of Ritilin, and was switched to the antidepressant, Imipramine "so he would eat more, sleep more, and grow more – and learn more, an aside." His success with his music quelled my anxious worries about his future. After breakfast and his meds every morning, he practiced the big Gulbransen organ and the baby grand for half an hour each. Now in the school orchestra, he was playing the horn Dan had taught him to blow with a few short lessons on his old beat-up coronet. Yes, Dan had fit into our family fine.

We are into laughter in a big way. Ray likes to keep everyone in stitches, with his Red Skeleton humor learned from his dad, and funnier with every drop he drinks, also like his dad. He is on his umpteenth joke: "…This guy decides on the third hell. No fire, no snakes, just standing in shit up to their belt buckles. But they all held coffee cups, sipping away, with an angel, no less, pouring refills. How bad can this be? *My* kind of place to spend eternity, the guy thinks. So he jumps right in and gets a nice shining cup filled with brimming hot coffee. He's just getting acquainted good, finishing his second refill, when the angel yells, *All right guys, down on your knees, coffee breaks over.*" I'm screaming with giggles at Ray's way of changing his stories in some small way so I never, ever get bored. You can tell by the version he tells what he thinks of his listeners. For instance, this time he says *shit* right out, so he doesn't think Dot so much of a lady as she likes to think of herself, I never can figure… I'm thinking this under the heaviness I'm feeling, the vodka getting to me. *It's time to eat soon; we better get going,* I'm thinking, when at the back door, we hear a loud knock…

Next, I'm out on the driveway. The squad-car is sitting in the dark street with its lights flashing, the uniformed cop telling my husband that someone saw his son just drive our Oldsmobile into the ditch, up the road. "You need to come and get it out."

Ray turns to me, still with the grog glass in his hand. "Where's Kelly? Isn't he downstairs watching TV?"

"Yeah, I thought so. Suzie's down there with them both."

Ray disappears into the house just as Dot squeezes my hand, telling me discreetly, in her genteel way, "I'll see you," and walks on down the drive. Dan puts his arm around my shoulder, and says, "Guess you got your hands full right now. We'll catch y'all later for dinner. Talk to you tomorrow, y'hear!" He gives me a hug as he follows his tiny blonde wife across the dark street into the rambling ranch-style that sits behind the blinking lights.

Inside the house, Kelly is standing in the middle of the family room, the cop's behind me, and Ray, with eyes bulging in anger, is speaking loudly to our firstborn son. "Where's the keys? Tell me, where're the keys? I left them on my dresser. Where *are* they?"

Kelly's brown eyes are larger than usual, a shrimpy for his age, still only my height, and looks up at his dad as though he really doesn't know what he is saying, as though *Kelly* is the one with the almost empty grog glass in his hand, not his dad.

Ray's voice is getting louder. I'm beside him, shaking Kelly, pleading, the anxiety bursting through the numb that has become my insulation. "Tell your dad where they are, Kelly," when finally the policeman steps around me, reaches for Kelly's shoulder, gently taking it into his mammoth hand. "It's all right, Son," he says, softly. "We need to have the keys in order to move it. Otherwise, it's going to cost your daddy a little money to move out. With the keys, we may not have to get a wrecker."

Kelly says very matter-of-factly to the cop, "They're on the roof; I threw them up on the roof," and is pointing upwards.

"For gods sake, *why?*" Ray yells. "What the hell did you do *that* for?"

"So you wouldn't know it was me, so you'd think it was stolen." Suddenly Kelly breaks down into tears.

Finally... There is some kind of reaction, some kind of visible emotion. *See, I knew he wasn't the sociopath that Army General insinuated he was.*

Minutes later, we are at the car stuck in the ditch, on a back country road bordered by thick woods on one side. Fortunately it is near some houses. The brights tipping up glare into the house windows where someone had seen a teenage boy run from the scene. The cops are wrestling with the car. Ray's loud voice is assuring them that he can get it out. He speaks with such authority no one ever seems to question him. Self-assurance, that take-charge air which first drew me to him, a knowledge about life, things, people. He always knows just what to do, how, when, where, who... Ray is in the car and there are people around me, speaking to me, consoling me about my son "growing up *eventually.*" I am having difficulty responding. I can't seem to find the words, think the words. These people are only strangers, but still, they must see that I am... They must be able to smell, hear... Oh, god, here is my kid in trouble with the cops, and I am not really *here*. What kind of mother *am* I? Ashamed and frightened, I can't even put two thoughts together out of the alcoholic blur.

Inside the police car, we follow my husband the few country blocks back to our house. I'm so ashamed. I try to keep quiet, but the words tumble out, fear, horror. "Is Kelly in trouble?" No, the cop assures me. "Teenagers take a whole lot of patience especially in this day and time. All these drugs... He'll be all right. The boy's got parents that care about him; you can see that." *Can he see that? Why can't I feel that? What are we turning into? Oh, god. Just what I was always afraid of.*

It was that night, in the dark, standing by the side of the road that I knew I would have to find a way to get our lives together, and completely sober again. Even though I had been trying, since forever, it just wasn't good enough. There were too many people like Dan and Dot, parties, and Ray had grog glasses everywhere. Problems came out of nowhere that I had no idea how to solve, feelings that were bursting to be felt, memories I had managed to forget were getting more vivid with my Journals. Anger that was exploding inside my head when I could hold it back no longer. *Just a few drinks are better than running,* unless I could get Ray to bed before *he* had too much. Having sex was my only outlet, sex with abandonment, a new kind of sex that I would never admit to having – much less enjoying – while sober. There was just too much to feel and not enough ways to get it all out without help of just a little emotional lubricant... a little wine, a little vodka...

At my next session with Dr. Hanks, I expressed disgust with myself, my fear at my not being able to *be* there fully at the moment I was needed, as a mother. I was out there somewhere in some half-stupor, looking through a dense fog, hearing muffled voices, really only half hearing. In the past, this doctor's kindness had sustained me, had taught me to begin trusting myself, to begin to hear myself, feel the knot in my stomach before it got to my head and blew it apart.

"Your anger builds up because you have conditioned yourself from babyhood to hold it, hide it, keep it in, until you *can't* any longer. Then you use alcohol to give you an excuse to let it out, something to blame it on. It's not *me*, it was the booze, you tell yourself. As you learn to express yourself in more appropriate ways when situations arise that upset you, you will find the need to use booze less and less as a cover for your behavior. The times you'll resort to it will be further and further apart, two months, three months, six, a year – until one day you will realize you no longer will need it at all."

"Yes, I think you're right. It used to be every Friday night – Happy Hour. Now it's once a month, usually right after payday!"

We laughed together; I realized that my previous pattern of difficult very sick monthly episodes had shifted from my periods, since my hysterectomy, to monthly drinking too much I was now blaming on availability of money, at payday. "Why do I have so much trouble dealing with whatever when it happens, why?"

"It seems you have a great deal of anger hidden deep inside, anger at men, at women, at just about everyone you ever deal with. That parent tape in your head still tells you, "Keep still." *Daddy's very words, accompanied usually with a big, fat pinch twisted to hurt!* "As you settle the score within, you'll be able to face the present moment for itself without the past spilling over. Ray is just a symbol of all those other pseudo dictators. It isn't that you are angry at *him* so much. A little," he said with a grin, "but not so much."

Quickly, my mind shot to my kids. "What about my kids? Until I get to that place you're talking about, how are they going to make it?"

"Just remind yourself of one thing – this is very important – as long as you live, remember: *You did the very best you could with what you had.*"

In order to finally get the two course credits Ray lacked for his bachelor's degree, with the final intention of obtaining his Masters before retirement just around the corner, he wrote for his credits from his alma mater, Bob Jones University, Greenville, South Carolina. His request was denied in a personal letter from Dr. Bob, "… because you are not living in the place God would have you."

Ray was very angry, not only at the audacity of the elders of the school to make such a judgment, because he had voluntarily left the ministry he had prepared for while there (and married me, a divorcee, after volunteering for the draft) but due to the federal investigation of BJU for discriminating against minorities, thereby cutting off government funding, the University of South Carolina withdrew their long time agreement to honor BJU's independence and non-accredited standing by providing State accreditation.

Ray went to the Dean of Mercer, Atlanta — a Baptist, but very liberal school – where he was not only accepted, but taken under wing by the Dean herself who taught a social psychology course. I was allowed to monitor.

The students sat around a large, oval table, with the Dean at one end, and Ray at the other. When the subject of B. F. Skinner was raised, Ray and the Dean went at it. She defended the famed psychologist and his behavior modification techniques.

Ray vehemently disagreed with being compared to rats in a maze. "He's left the human aspect out of his theories; we have a will, therefore choices," Ray contended, this a running argument.

The subject of drugs and alcohol addiction was given as a personal study and report. One night driving home from a particularly poignant class, as Ray turned into the last street that led to our neighborhood, he pulled the car over to the side of the road, and stopped. "I want to tell you something important. This class has shown me things I never gave any thought to before. I think you are right, maybe I do have a problem with booze, and I want you to know that I intend to make some changes in that direction."

It was a night I would remember. Ray had never come close to admitting he could be *wrong in anything*. It was one of the hardships of living with him; it seemed he was *always* right. How I had studied and searched for answers to our family's problems, and, although it would be thirteen years before he would actually fulfill this promise, it seemed, until this moment, I had been pulling the weight all by myself.

◆

CHAPTER SIX

Things... 1975-1976

The sign read, *Reserved - Probation Officer*. My heart seemed to fall into my stomach as I pulled into the slot next to it, marked: *Visitor*. Kelly, sixteen, was the first one of our kids to be arrested and locked up. A few minutes early for my appointment with the Fulton County Juvenile Court psychologist who was evaluating Kelly, I reread the questionnaire we had filled out following our first visit, and the notes of explanation I had added to support the legal petition Ray had filed.

Writing was my strong suit, Ray had little patience for it. Not that he wasn't good at it; he had been forced to learn from a boss who returned telephone notes, edited, but he was loaded down with his Masters' program at Georgia State – in criminal justice, no less– trying to prepare for employment upon his twenty-year retirement, come springtime. At first glance, several pages of typed information, including Kelly's school attendance and performance records, seemed to offer little insight. The *just a boy* explanations by his dad through the years, and even some of his teachers, revealed "little deviance from the norm" overall, but his temper tantrums – banging his forehead on the floor so that it was swollen for days; difficult toilet training, i.e., holding and smearing feces until age four; stealing and running-away behavior; bed-wetting until puberty – was indication enough, from my reading, that Kelly had a problem. Determined stubbornness, I personally called it, determined to *not* do anything he was asked to do. There was no question he was his father's son.

This was the fourth time Kelly had run away since he was ten. Since that evaluation in third grade, when his teacher had requested a mental health evaluation due to his apparent "lack of responsibility," revealing he was "overwhelmed by female authority figures" and needed more "male modeling." It was in this spirit, trying to leave the disciplining of the boys to their dad, that I left Ray in charge of Kelly and Sean's school enrollment for fall term. As a celebration of sorts for Suzie entering college, over labor day, I took Suzie and her girlfriend to Savannah Beach. If I wasn't around, Ray would then be forced to deal with all the little ins and outs of the new school year, to which he seemed otherwise oblivious. Getting Ray's help in anything required real determination. His Irish mother said it was only gotten by "knocking him down first to get his attention — *before* you asked!" Being thrown in Juvenile Hall seemed one heck of a way for Kelly to do that. My guilt at not being able to stop what I had foreseen coming for years, and fear for what lay ahead, was only hidden by my extreme anger, both at Kelly for being detained in this loathsome place, but much of it, rightfully or wrongfully, was aimed at his dad – and I still had trouble forgetting about Kelly causing us to be kicked out of the War College. Each one in the family had suffered in our own way from that terrible upheaval and public humiliation, and it wasn't clear to me who was at fault, or what Ray or I had done, or not done, to bring our family to such ends. Clearly, I was beginning to personally experience the "consequences" of which Dr. Hanks spoke when his recommendation, for a father to take responsibility in the disciplining of his sons, was ignored.

It was at the suggestion of Ray's civil law professor that he had found a juvenile attorney and filed an "Unruly Child Petition." To me, asking the State of Georgia to intercede on our behalf, even with a kid over whom we had little control, did not provide any real solution – not for Kelly anyhow. But since I wasn't there, and Ray's handling of his son was left up to him, he said he was doing it, *my way!* After I had complained for years of Ray's lack of involvement, I felt I had little recourse but to support his decision, at least he *made* one, and it would be hell to pay from then on if I didn't.

Inside the temporary detainment center, the air reeked of Pinesol. Allergic to the beautiful Georgia pines that covered our backyard, just the smell made me itch. The starkness of the gray walls and bare wood floors reminded me of grade school, a strange mixture, and for some reason reminded me suddenly how quiet Kelly seemed to be lately. Although it was puzzling, it was a pleasant change from the non-stop, very loud, intense talking of his earlier days. I complained to one of our neighbors once, a kindergarten teacher, who'd told me to, "Just listen to him!" "My god," I said, "that's all we *can* do!"

Dr. Shoenfeld met me immediately. He was tall and thin, and wore glasses. The studious type, I surmised, not a jock like Ray. I immediately pegged him as one of those pacifists who had marched against the Vietnam war, while my husband was dodging bullets.

The desk was large, cluttered, and it literally filled the tiny office. No frills here, but *good enough for government work.* The doctor directed me to one of the two chairs directly in front of him, a parent conference; Kelly wasn't to be here.

Nervously looking at the empty chair next to me, I said, "My husband had a class. He's out of town every weekend commanding his reserve units, you know, leaving weekdays open for school. He's already missed several on account of Kelly, and since he's on the GI bill, he can't miss any more."

Dr. Shoenfeld ignored my apology. "I've spent the better part of three days with your son," he said. "He's a very troubled boy."

"Yes," I said, "I agree. That's why I tried to be as honest as I could in this," I said, waving the typed pages in the air, copies of which he'd already received. "We just don't know what to do about him. This summer, the father of one of his friends invited him up to Tennessee, to stay and work on the farm. We relented, thinking it might help, get him away from this crowd down here. We just couldn't take his sneaking out any more nights. I don't know if it was the right thing to do. Ray doesn't..." *Guilty, I felt so guilty, as though, by letting Kelly go, I had given up on my kid. Somehow I had to make this doctor understand what we had been through.* "Going out that basement door after we were in bed, asleep, walking the streets all night leaving the door unlocked so that his sister has screaming nightmares, hanging out in the woods at that filthy abandoned shack full of beer cans, candy and food wrappers, pot paraphernalia... I took pictures... Here... Look... And it's right under the nose of the school, right in the next field... and the cops won't..."

Seemingly disinterested, the doctor ignored the pictures, and said, "Tell me about Sharon. She's the oldest, right?"

I nodded. "She was from my first marriage. But Ray adopted her very soon after we were married, she had just started school." My anxiety was beginning to burst through my steel-like veneer. *Why wouldn't he listen to me about Kelly? Asking me about Sharon, as though my whole motherhood was on trial.* I folded and unfolded the wadded up Kleenex I held in my lap. Finally, I smiled, and through trembling lips, I said, "She doesn't live at home anymore. Several years she's gone already. Why, what does Sharon have to do with anything?" By now I was on the edge of my seat, the Kleenex in a ball again.

"You hardly look old enough to have a sixteen-year-old, much less one twenty-two!"

My age is what always got us into this private stuff. I still cringed in shame having to answer questions about my past. With an exasperated sigh, I said, "I was fifteen the first time I got married, and sixteen when I had Sharon." *Would revealing this regrettable fact ever get any easier?*

He must have sensed my uneasiness, my irritation, his face lost its smile. "How did Kelly feel about his oldest sister?"

"Oh, we knew he hated her when he was little. He used to draw these pictures, you know kids. Kelly was good at it, too. Funny stuff; ugly monsters. He'd write "Sharon" all over them. We'd just laugh," I said chuckling, but inside the feelings of mounting fear I got when confronted with things for which I had no answers rose up to grab me in the throat, literally closing it.

The doctor leaned back in his chair, and stared at me through his bifocals, studying me. Apparently this guy had no humor.

Self-consciously, in a high-pitched, cracking voice, I said, "Don't all little boys hate their big sisters?"

Dr. Shoenfeld bent closer and spoke quietly, his serious tone a subtle rebuke. "In the only safe way he knew, Kelly was trying to tell you... things."

This doctor's assessment of Sharon, of someone he'd never even seen, put a knot in my stomach. I was looking him straight in the eye, trying to digest his words: psychopathic, sociopathic. *Then my mind raced back, remembering... the psychiatrist's ugly pronouncement, soon after I got pregnant with Sharon, of the mental condition of her birth-father, and his mother's angry reaction, unbelieving.*

Dr. Shoenfeld was saying, "Sharon wasn't a happy little girl at your remarriage, I take it."

Thinking about Sharon always did make me anxious. "Since she was born, I was conscientious about putting her first, even when I was divorced and dating, always."

His rapt attention to everything I recalled about Sharon made me realize there must be something more to it than I was admitting. I told him then, about her running away, back when she was eight.

"*We were in Oklahoma for a three-month Army school on the way to our new home in D·C·, where Sean would be born the following year — a third move in little over a year· We had driven across country, and were living out of suitcases in a tiny furnished apartment· I had just scolded Sharon for the umpteenth time for not brushing her green teeth, when out of the house she ran, carrying a brown grocery bag filled with her clothes· Ray happened to be at home, and took out after her in the car, only to find her sitting on the curb, outside the playground, waiting for school to start the next morning· When Ray caught up with her, he asked her how she was going to eat? Pick up all those pop bottles and buy candy and gum, she said· Back home, I sat her down by ourselves in the bedroom, and asked her what was bothering her? Through her tears, she told me, I do love Daddy, and Suzie, and Kelly, but I really liked it better when it was just me and you, Mommy· Her pediatrician told me to give her some special alone time, just us two, out to a movie, or somewhere without the other kids· He said she was reacting to Ray being home after his being gone to Korea for a year; she'd gotten used to having me to herself again· From then on she got my every spare minute· In fact, there were times when she got too much, my husband says· I tried hard to be what she needed, wanted – I tried so hard· I was worried she would run away again, back to Milwaukee to my first in-laws· I didn't realize just how afraid I was of this until she had graduated, and left home· It was like a great weight had been lifted·*"

Dr. Shoenfeld was listening intently, as though there was something else. Psychopath, such an ugly term. It tore away at me. I'd already read what little I could find on the subject, ever since that school psychologist in Bangkok had suggested Sean be held back a year, to mature. His observation indicated to him that Sean's personality sharply resembled hardened prisoners he'd met. He told me rather angrily, "If ever I've seen a perfect example of this personality type, it is this kid. He has no respect for authority, and he's fast. Why, he climbed all the way to the top of my file cabinets before I could get my pencil out of the drawer." Giving such a devastatingly cruel label to a five-year-old angered me, but by "a counselor just recently retired from the federal penal system, for god's sakes," as Ray characterized it, I wanted to shout, *Not my beautiful, sweet child. Hyperactive, yes!* I didn't believe such nonsense then, and I wasn't about to believe this person now. *Although Sharon's birth-father did spend three years in Greenbay Reformatory. No, she couldn't be like him; he hadn't lived with us since she was a baby, she hasn't even seen him since she was three.* I remembered then how determined I was to show the world that her genes had nothing to do with how she would turn out. My love and discipline would conquer all. She was smart, and beautiful, and making us so proud! Picturing her now as this evil, murderous villain with no conscience, "No, no, Dr. Shoenfeld, you must be mistaken. That's a *criminal* personality; that can't be true!" I was almost crying now from the confusion of anger and fear clutching at my insides. The image of Sharon in her big, beautiful office, calling me almost daily on her government WATS line..."Didn't Kelly tell you his big sister works in the White House, with a top-level security clearance? Why, Sharon's salary is almost *twice* her father's, and he's a Major in the Army."

The doctor's intake of air made an audible sound, his eyebrows wrinkled as he looked away momentarily, seemingly to gather his thoughts. As he turned back to me, he spoke in a tone of exasperation, "Mrs. Malorry, I don't think you quite understand how adept some psychopaths are at climbing the ladder of success. Look at Nixon."

"Nixon?" I blurted out. "Oh, I don't want to hear this, really." Now he had quit preaching and gone to meddling, as Daddy would say. Sharon had gotten us tickets to Nixon's second Inaugural Ball. "Nixon wasn't doing anything any other President hasn't done before, and will probably do again after all of this is forgotten. Besides, he's the one who finally got Vietnam stopped, isn't he? Why, in foreign policy wasn't he absolutely brilliant?"

"I never said anything about brilliant." Dr. Shoenfeld leaned over the desk that separated us, and said very quietly, "What you are dealing with is a person who has an agenda that supersedes all other agendas; their success will not be interfered with. And they will use anything, *anyone*, to accomplish their goal. And sometimes, when one child receives undivided attention from a single parent, they don't want to give it up, so their goal in life is to get it back – *or get even*, so to speak, through whatever means. This sets up a lifetime pattern of behavior. By the way, I'm curious, were there any incidents, falls when they were little, that were unexplained?"

"What do you mean?"

"Oh, you know, accidents?"

I thought a minute. "Kelly slid down the stairs once. He was nine or ten months old. The four of them took baths, well there was only three then — they took baths together. Sharon was at the top of the stairs holding Kelly in a towel. I was at the bottom looking up and talking to him, when Sharon suddenly lost hold somehow. I thought he must've been wet still. It really scared me at the time. Kelly slid all the way down those bare wooden steps, bouncing all the way. My stomach was in my throat, but Kelly just giggled, as if it was a game or something. His pediatrician said babies were so relaxed they seldom broke bones when they fell like that."

"Yes, well, I'd say he was fortunate, but that's exactly what I was talking about. Accidents: accidentally on purpose."

That New Year's Eve in Bangkok, when she sent her elbow into me, accidentally, she said, to get away from the drunken G.I. begging her to dance. So hard she shoved me, I went sailing, landing on my tail bone, cracking it, rupturing a disk in my neck; I came to in Ray's arms. Years of headaches neurologists have attributed to that fall. A fleeting thought as I was flying through the air, was, she had done it deliberately. How else could I have gone so far in the air off that stool — accidentally? Naw, that's sick. Why would she? Such great fun we've had. She calls me six times a day. Preparing dinner, I feel as though the phone is growing out of my ear.

Then this doctor proceeded to tell me *more things*...

*C*ertainly none of this could be true; Suzie, tell me it isn't so, I was thinking. "Ple-ease, Suzie! I need to talk to you," I said to the back of her head. The long, immaculately kept hair of my second daughter was bouncing as she scurried down the stairs below me to her hideaway, where she and Kelly had their own bedrooms. The winding stairwell to the finished apartment was dark, but I plunged down it, trying to catch her before she slammed her bathroom door in my face.

The finished basement, complete with built-in kitchen, full bath, and a sunny living room that opened out onto a lovely tree-shaded patio, providing unusual privacy and freedom — a music-loving teenagers' dream – had been turned into a mother-in-law's suite by the previous owner for an elderly mother; both had died in the house. White funeral mums growing in the backyard fed Kelly's paranoia; he was convinced ghosts abided within the beautifully paneled walls. Even though my laundry-room, in the extra kitchen, provided me with ample excuse to be down there, and the unfinished basement still left enough room for our pool table, which Ray and both boys used almost daily, the drawback to all this roominess was a windowless bedroom, for which Kelly begged: "So the camois [burglars] can't get in." (He never really got over them coming in through his bedroom window in Bangkok, exiting through the front door with many of our high-valued State-side wares, actually taking Ray's wallet he kept under his pillow while he slept, filled with Thai baht. We were told by the MP's that a knife had been held at Ray's throat during this take, in case he had awakened, so we had some sympathy for Kelly's fears. It had taken us all some time to get over this frightening event, which led to our obtaining six "camoi dogs" that had the run of the house from then on.) The fact that the sliding glass doors to this apartment Kelly and Suzie shared, had no outside lock, was always in the back of my mind; *but it would not be used as a regular exit,* I told my questioning inner parent. I rationalized that these kids were both too apprehensive to ever leave the door unsecured.

Upstairs, the basic three bedrooms left an extra leave-it-a-mess room next to Sean's, just for my ironing, sewing, and painting, while doubling as a guest room for Sharon. Cathedral ceilings, gas logged fireplace, a separate breakfast nook with an extended space ideal for Ray's antique desk, a huge built-in bar — complete with padlocks which we promptly removed, we trusted *our* kids – occupied it's own area adjoining the family room. All this on Ray's choice of a corner lot. Short on cash for a down payment, after our college tuition had drained us, VA's low minimum overcame the gnawing hesitation I'd felt initially at the basement's too-convenient outdoor exit. With one child already out of the nest, giving Suzie and Kelly more space would provide an extension of my own freedom begun in Pennsylvania, as a freshman at State College. We had been in the house two years already, Suzie's last year of highschool had shrunk to one semester since Pennsylvania schools had put her way ahead of Georgia in required credits. Kelly was a freshman in the same school. The unanticipated result of this living arrangement was that I would rarely see either of them except at breakfast, and an occasional supper.

Talking on the run like this was about all I could manage, especially with Suzie, now graduated, going to college and working at Burger King. But I was insistent, "Kelly told the doctor some things, about you kids. I just know they can't be true," I was saying into this new emptiness in our relationship that began the night she hadn't come home.

In the past, Suzie's good sense had often astounded me, and I was hoping she would have something profound to offer now regarding her brother's revelations to Dr. Shoenfeld. I had wanted to ease into it by explaining that Kelly, missing, again, for three days, had been found on the street, hours away in Nashville, standing on the top of a parked car "high on something." The Atlanta police now had him down at Juvenile Hall, and was holding him until the doctors all, respectively, finished their evaluations. The M.D. was satisfied that Kelly had, in fact, swallowed the entire bottle of asthma medicine the Army Post pediatrician had given him. I had been trying to get this psychological evaluation done at the Post psychiatric clinic for the past year, but the waiting list was long, and Kelly's behavior apparently didn't appear serious enough to warrant immediate attention. I could no longer run from my suspicions, that something was basically askew with Kelly since the War College incident had brought everything to a head. I knew everyone in our family had suffered from it, but this prison Doctor Shoenfeld had to be one of those behaviorists popular in the '60's, still trying to lay the world's ills on the doorsteps of us parents. Surely Suzie would confirm my belief that his outlandish conclusion, labeling her sister Sharon some kind of maniac, was nothing more than the wild imagination of a book-happy Ph. D.

Trying to jolt Suzie's recently declared disinterest in the family, I blurted out the terrible accusations. "This doctor said Kelly is the product of a psychopathic sister who is out to destroy our family, and that she, Sharon and you, Kelly said — since he was real little – you four kids have been messing around."

Suzie's back was still to me.

In a thin, raspy voice, I added, "... sexually."

Suzie stopped, and spun around to face me.

Looking into those clear blue eyes that would light up a darkened sky, the whole thing seemed so farfetched, disgusting.

"It's true, Mom," Suzie said flatly. "Kelly's telling the truth."

"But Suzie, this doctor said Sharon had forced Kelly to... to... to do awful things."

"It's called *oral sex*, Mom."

My fingers pressed against my lips, *these sex-liberated children.* "No! No!" I heard myself whisper, "Tell me it isn't so."

Instead, she said, "Kelly used to gag, sometimes he even threw up; he hated it."

Tears clouded my vision as I looked into those eyes so like my dead mother's, but I had to find out. "He said, you... you and Sean..." I just couldn't bring myself to say it. Sean was six years her junior, very young when all this presumably started.

She looked at me with a perverse grin, almost flaunting the confirmation. "Yes, Mom, I did, but Sean *loved* it!"

"No! No-o-o!" I cried, not wanting to believe. "You didn't! How could you? Sean was so *little*."

"Oh, he was big enough," she giggled insidiously.

Was this the same Suzie who decoupaged birds? Who did hours of needlepoint flowers for a special Mother's Day? The same kid who came home at thirteen, in Bangkok, furious with her Baptist missionary friend for having the audacity to suggest that Buddhists were going to hell? Always responsible, loving, thoughtful, a kid for whom you went to bed, saying, "Thank you, God." No specific time to be home was ever required, as was for her siblings, so none was ever given. This beautiful, considerate child had gone to work one night, and an entirely different one had come lazing in the next day around noon, grinning, totally unimpressed with our anxious worry. She gave no explanation other than, "I'm in love!" We were certain this must just be a passing teen thing, a plea for independence. Surely our seventeen-year-old-going-on-ninety would soon return to us.

Suzie was continuing, "But it didn't *mean* anything to me, Mom. If it wasn't Sean, it would've been a Coke bottle," she said now without a hint of embarrassment or, God-help-her, remorse.

"A *Coke* bottle? Oh, my god! Penetration? When? Where?"

"When Dad was in Vietnam, things were messed up. All that stuff with Sharon: her shoplifting; that night... Remember, you caught her smoking in bed, in the dark, and she threw her lit cigarette on her dresser – She was holding your wrists, you were screaming, watching it burn. When she finally let go, she got the butcher knife and ran into the backyard... That's when Mr.

Boatman, next door, got the knife... Don't you remember all the cigarette butts and dried up bloody Kotex you found in that little attic room next to our bedroom?"

Just the thought of it, gagged me.

What kind of a girl throws dirty sanitary napkins in the attic? I had asked a counselor. One with no self-esteem, she said. But, why? With all the attention I gave her since she was a baby? Suzie seemed surprisingly cooperative, almost glad to be questioned. "Then Dad came home. After that, in Bangkok is when Sean — I was in puberty, remember?"

How well I remembered. Suzie's constant red eyes, her sleepy, no-care attitude. Her best friend was sent to Europe for treatment for heroin addiction; I had been frantic. "You know how puberty is, Mom," Suzie said, with a smirk on her face, and iciness in her voice.

It was too easy to write off this arrogance as anger over a sister-spat, but ever since their summer vacation to Florida together, when Suzie reported that Sharon had "beat the crap" out of her one night. Apparently Suzie made the mistake of sharing her recent sexual missteps with her sister, in the car. Sharon got very angry, "You slut!," she yelled, stopped the car, pulled Suzie out, and let her have it right there along side the road. Since then, Suzie would go into an absolute rage at just the mention of Sharon's name. Now this! Shock, confusion, I felt as though I was sinking into a black hole. My stomach was all I was conscious of; I felt my hand clutching it, just as Ma Schultz, my first mother-in-law, had – every time she would blame *those awful boys* for the trouble her son... But these weren't *those awful boys*, these were *my* beautiful, intelligent daughters.

Begging, pleading for some kind of denial — so we could go back to that place where we had been, my anger at Ray momentarily forgotten, where things would be all right around the corner, where things were never as bad as they seemed – barely audible, I said, "How *could* you?"

Suzie had turned away, as though to dismiss me, when my words stopped her. She faced me then, and threw me an incredulous look. With her chin in the air, she said, "Uh, you mean, how could *you?*"

"Me-e-e?" I cried. "Me-e-e? What are you saying? I didn't *know*." By this time I was screaming, " I had *no idea!*"

In a flat monotone, Suzie's answer came trigger quick, "Why *didn't* you know?" The light in her blue eyes had turned to dark pools, her voice low, controlled, and filled with unbelievable rage.

"Why *didn't* you know, Mom?" Her staccato words were driven, dagger-sharp, "*Why* - DIDN'T - *my* - *mother* - *know?*"

Days later, the long letter which I wrote to Sharon, begging her to seek help from a good psychiatrist, was answered, but I never saw it. Ray intercepted the letter, read it, and destroyed it, saying, "It was too awful for you to read." *The big protector.*

How unfortunate it was for me to not have learned, first hand, of Sharon's anger towards me then. We could have dealt with it head-on and maybe by-passed so much of what lay ahead for our family. Instead, the whole thing was tucked away, out of consciousness, where it would fester for years, allowing Sharon's presumed hidden agenda to continue unchallenged.

How this terrible thing had happened inside my family, and right under my nose, so to speak, was too monstrous for me to acknowledge in itself. But to have been so completely oblivious to the results of the control that I had unwittingly granted Sharon, which she learned to wield with such subtlety, yet in bully-like fashion after having placed such trust in her, the *Why* of it all was just too incomprehensible. But it was the searing words from Suzie's mouth that struck at the heart of me creating the driving need to understand. The life-long repression, that had built a wall around me, had acted as a solid fortress, making me as-though-blind to what lay outside that protection – my family, sadly, its recipient.

Kelly, still in Juvenile Hall, was acting very listless, gaining weight, while awaiting the State's next move. I became impatient, and sought help myself from Dr. Hanks, who suggested we bring Kelly home and try him on lithium, the treatment very new to this country (which we were to learn was used primarily for manic depressive/bipolar illness). Dr. Hanks was anxious to try it with Kelly. In lieu of this option, as Ray absolutely refused to have Kelly back in the home just yet, a psychiatric hospital took Kelly for a thorough evaluation, ultimately diagnosing him with hebephrenic schizophrenia, i.e., "becoming schizophrenia." It was the "explosion of the world" dream he had while in Juvenile Hall, that pointed to this diagnosis, we were told, a common feature of the beginning of this illness. Kelly was then accepted by Devereux School, an expensive private residential treatment program, for the remainder of the year, which would accept our military health insurance at only $100 additional cost per month. There, Kelly was put on Thorazine, which pushed his weight up into full blown diabetes, genetics from my father's side.

By the time Kelly came home at Christmas for a visit, he had shot up six inches in height to over six feet tall. So fast was his growth, that he seemed unstable in his footing, but the strict diet care he received in Devereux satisfied us that he was being well supervised. He definitely wasn't sneaking out at night as he had been for the last year, while at home. This was Ray's main objective, a goal he had not been able to accomplish himself. The one time Ray caught Kelly coming in the basement door at 7:00 a.m., Ray met his son with his fists in his face. On the floor, Kelly was in shock, and tears flowed when Ray yelled at him to "get up and fight like a man."

Standing behind in unbelieving revulsion, it was more than I could take. No matter the Irish way of doing things, Kelly was still a child. It was then that I realized, my husband had never had the right kind of parenting himself either, the same as I hadn't. What a pair we were, as hard as we had tried, we had nothing of substance to fall back on in such dire circumstances. At least for one whole year, with some professional supervision, maybe Kelly had a chance. *Just, maybe!*

Now, with one major problem in our family seemingly under control, I was allowed to concentrate on Suzie and Sean, which seemed minor in comparison, at the time…

*H*ail & Farewell Party, the announcement read, an expected attendance for an Officer. It was the way the military had of welcoming newcomers to the unit, and at the same time saying goodby to those leaving for their next assignment. Sometimes, someone had been where you were going, and they could give you some pointers, but mostly you were left to wonder for weeks just what the future held for you. It was not too often, though, that retirement from a lifetime career was the reason for leaving, especially for someone so young. Life begins at forty, we're told, and at forty-three and thirty-nine we had barely begun to wake up. At least this is how I viewed ourselves as Ray and I faced our long future ahead of us. There were no retirees expected to be there who could tell us what was in store.

It was also Christmas time. We'd had our fill of holiday rounds; *everyone* seemed to throw a shindig then; the unit social calendar was not any different. This particular party was combining everything into one. The Ladies, as we wives were referred to, would have an excuse to get a new outfit, hairdo, and all the trimmings. I was fortunate as I already had a beautiful gown I had only worn once, which I had designed and sewn for the Inaugural Ball, in D.C. It was silver crushed velveteen, with a black and sparkly hand-crocheted Mandarin collar, which I also did, A-line to the floor with long fitted raglan sleeves. Cuffs matched the narrow collar and set off the softness of the material. Silver shoes and bag were still in the box on the shelf, waiting to be worn. I was excited to get dressed up as I knew how much Ray would want to dance; he always did when he was drinking. At his Retirement Party, I was sure he wouldn't be holding back, not with everyone buying him free drinks all night. My hair had grown out just enough from the permanent and silver frosting so that it pulled into a nice up-sweep of curls.

Despite the normally busy schedule we had, I was ready for this party well in advance. Ray was in school getting his Masters, I was finishing up the quarter at Clayton Junior College, Kelly was with us on Christmas vacation from Devereux, and Ray was sending out resumes ahead of his retirement date, in March, just around the corner, Suzie was in college full-time, but working part-time at a popular steak house, and spending more nights at home than in her own new little apartment. Sean seemed to have settled down and accepted his despised sixth-grade teacher, after he had sat in the principal's office the first two weeks of the term, rebelling, saying he was *not* going to that terrible teacher's class (He was right, she *was* a terrible teacher, I would learn much too late!). Now, taking Imipramine every morning at breakfast (instead of the six Ritilin he'd been on since third grade) Sean would

spend his regular half-hour at the organ or piano in serious practice before racing off to school, his favorite thing; he loved school. After the music director sent a note home: "Please get Sean a new horn," Sean was accepted in the school orchestra playing his new trumpet, and was one day hoping to get into high school band.

Things were generally in an uproar anyhow, nearing the holidays, but this year there was no let up. I had been smoking at least three packs of Winston Kings *before* I had my first one at a party. My weight had dropped back down to 105 pounds, where it was in Bangkok — there was no problem getting into that dress! But even so, I was laying off the salt, and eating very little. I would take one bite at meals, and then smoke the rest of the sit-down times with my family. When the phone rang, I ran for my cigarettes first, before answering.

"Mrs. Malorry? This is Mrs. Green. I work in your husband's office. There is something I think you should know."

"Oh, yeah?"

"I don't know whether you know the little blonde girl who works for him?"

"Nadine? Yes, I've met her."

"Well, she is carrying on something shameful with him, right out in front of everyone. It is the talk of the whole office, and I know if I were you, I would want to know."

I said, "Thank you... I think," and laughed in embarrassment. "This is the first time I've had someone call me and tell me such a thing. I'm not sure what to say."

"That's quite all right, dear, I understand," she said, and hung up.

When Ray came home that night, I asked him immediately who Mrs. Green was. He said, "Oh, she's an ol' biddy in the office, why?"

"Well, she called me just a little while ago, and told me you and Nadine were carrying on, I think she called it, right out in front of the whole office. Are you?"

Ray burst into laughter, got red in the face, and then proceeded to tell me it wasn't him, but his buddy, who was also married, "I'm just covering for him to throw people like Mrs. Green off. Don't pay any attention to her. She is just an office busybody with nothing better to do all day than sit around and gossip."

It was settled. I wouldn't let "some ol' biddy" spoil my good time at our last official function.

The night of the party, the mirror returned my confidence; I felt as though I looked better than I had in months. Many things were being talked about with Dr. Hanks, still our family psychiatrist. He was also seeing Suzie after she had been close to suicide months before, and, against Ray's wishes, I had brought her back home to live, temporarily. Dr. Hanks would spend time alone with Ray, and then with me. They were usually laughing when I'd walk in; I felt as though they were having their little boy-jokes at my expense. Probably just paranoia, no matter, but it was helping Suzie, and I was letting Sharon go, hang up the phone when she sat and giggled on her Watts line with nothing really to say, passing time until the latest man in her life, working down the hall, came to take her to Happy Hour. Trying to make dinner with the phone stuck to my ear, she really seemed to just want me to *Be there, Mother*, and so I was. Afraid to put a stop to it, until Dr. Hanks helped me to realize that I was "still being controlled by Sharon hundreds of miles away, via telephone." When I would hear her giggling conversation with her co-workers while I was trying to cook, I was learning to simply say, "I have to go now," and hang up. Saying *No* to anyone had always been a difficult thing for me to do, but to my children, it was major. My father *never* said *Yes*, it was always, "We'll see," making me determined to *not* be like him.

At the party, it wasn't really unusual for Ray to wander off and leave me standing alone, but it would only take a few sips of alcohol to take away my fright, to find someone to talk to or dance with. I hated women's functions, rarely went to them, as I had no clue how to interact. My discomfort level was so high, Dr. Hanks told me repeatedly, "Leave the women alone, they're trouble for you, and you don't need any more of that!" When Ray politely bought me a drink and sat down with several older ladies way in the back, away from the dance floor, I thought he had put on his best behavior for our last party, as he sat with me for a few minutes. Soon, he was off to talk to someone on the other side of the room. The band was really good and playing some of our favorite swing tunes. *Where is he?*

In the middle of the dance floor, having the time of his life, was Ray dancing up a storm with Nadine. She was very young, newly divorced, with a small child. I had sent her a canned ham at Christmas, *before I knew,* home baked cookies, and German chocolate cake. I talked with some of the ladies who were much older than I, but I felt totally out of place. Finally, to keep from breaking down into tears in front of them, I went into the ladies' room and stayed. Sitting on the commode, I smoked one cigaret after another trying to hold back the tears of anger, but mostly hurt. Although I was tempted to just get into the car and go on home, I had never done that, beneath my dignity. Besides, I didn't want to give him any excuse to go home with *her!* So I sat hidden away, until Ray opened the door, and yelled, "Is Sam in here?"

We left arm and arm, Ray laughing his belly laugh, telling his stories, otherwise ignoring my presence, until we went to give our Holiday wishes to the commander and his wife, our hosts, and Ray referred to me again as his "Rent-a-Wife."

Trying to minimize the obvious inebriated state Ray was in, I said, "Oh, don't pay any attention to Ray; Christmas and retirement together are a heap of good cheer!"

The Colonel knew us from our War College days, a student in that last class when Ray got relieved and transferred here, to Atlanta. They were the best of friends, closer than most CO's and their staff. He gave me a southern hug and gentleman's kiss. Laughingly, he said, "Poor Sam, Ray just embarrasses you all over the place, all the time, doesn't he? Well, don't let it get to you; we all know him, and we understand. You've got to be a saint," and hugged me again.

In the car, I let the silent tears roll down my cheeks. My last party, and I had spent it sitting with old ladies while my husband danced the night away with his little blonde secretary. Not one dance; *not even one!*

It was after two days of brewing over this in silence, when I finally got up enough gumption to address my anger and humiliation. Ray was sitting at his desk, studying. He ignored me at first, until I threw something at him and it landed on his desk, breaking the glass top — *that* got his attention. We were screaming at each other, my choking on my tears, his denying, until in desperation I rammed my fist through the narrow window beside the door.

Dr. Hanks was most upset at hearing about this. "Glass cuts, and your wrist is not protected in such an outburst. You better find another way to express your anger, *safely*, like pounding on a pillow."

Days later, Ray brought home a picture taken of Nadine getting promoted. She was standing between him and the Colonel. Ray had his arm around her, and it was apparent he was goosing her, from behind, and he was having a good laugh.

This picture of Nadine remained among the Army photos and newspaper clippings collected down through the years, until one day, after years of lithium, when the box was opened, the picture that was worth a thousand words – had mysteriously disappeared.

◆

CHAPTER SEVEN

Sean: 1981

He was in a fight against time. It was his coming of age which loomed over him, of being cut loose of his moorings. Behind every thought, woven into daydreams, he was reaching for a girder, for something... He swallowed the handful of Quaaludes with the last of the beer. The large shopping mall was growing quiet with one shop after another closing, the black iron gates being pulled to in front of their huge glass windows. In his crouched position,

behind the large potted shrubbery, Sean knew he would be spotted soon by the friendly guard who worked the night shift. Sean's part-time job, sweeping up at the high-fashion hair solon, put him in the old man's path many nights. By this time, the drugs from Sean's cool owner-boss usually had him already high. The six-pack of beer, out of the small frig in the back of the shop, he'd guzzled down without a breather to cover for his reefer-red eyes, should anyone care.

Going home had long ago become a drag anyhow, he thought, sneaking in through the garage, past the bedroom door his parents usually left standing open. A thing his mom did, he thought, just to let him know he was never really putting much over on her — *what she didn't know...*

The drugs fogged his brain as they kicked in – a hushed lullaby, the soft hum of home euphony to soothe his troubled soul. Heavy footsteps briskly approaching gave him a start, telling him it was time to split – go find his baby, his lady, *his woman.* Then her words cut through the din, mingling with the footsteps coming closer... *No, Sean, this is how it has to be,* she was saying *through her tears. My dad doesn't fool around... He has a shotgun, for the store. My not being a virgin was bad enough, but when I thought I might be pregnant, he went berserk. Besides, a good Catholic just doesn't do all that... that... kinky stuff. It's... it's... I just can't anymore... you and Jason. It's too far out for me; I've hurt my dad enough already. She was sobbing uncontrollably... Withdrawing into that beautiful carrot-colored head, behind those crystal clear blue eyes, she was pushing him away, closing herself off, turning her back to him. In the early dawn stillness, she slipped noiselessly through her front door. He reached for her, caught her sleeve, pulled her, pleaded. She turned to face him one last time, and tore his hand away as though he was a wild root sorely growing being ripped from her depth. I'll love you forever, she whispered, and eased the door closed... Her words were reverberating in his brain, the gentleness in her voice, the desperation, the finality gripping his gut tight as a tourniquet.*

He reached into his pocket for his last Marlboro squashing the empty box with the hand he maneuvered all over the keyboard: putting in the base, the rhythm, the background to whatever tune his brain sent through the other. As he brought the cigarette to his lips, it grew to the size of an elephant's trunk, and the fire from his lighter lit the end of its tail.

"I'll let you out this door, Son," the old man said. "Better not let that black-and-white spot you weaving or in the slammer you go." His laugh, tempered with fatherly concern, passed over the dark avenue of death and reached through the dulled senses.

Sean grinned, and gave him the salute he'd seen his father give hundreds of times, a sign of acknowledgment, of respect, and said nothing as he followed the uniform with chains hanging, keys rattling a tune of their own.

The heavy mall door closed behind him, and the stifling mug of the Florida heat hit him sending him reeling. He expected to be grabbed by that SOB cop waiting to send his sorry ass back to Juvie. But his black Irish luck held as he staggered through the parked cars, down the lighted boulevard, around the corner into the caul de sac of manicured lawns, across the grass of the darkened house, around the back to the bedroom only inches from the swimming pool in which his father had thrown him — *wasn't it just the other day?* – to the window he had slipped out of so many godforsaken nights. His fist going through the glass sent blood spurting everywhere, but he was numb to its sting. The lock on the sliding pane easily opened, and he slid one of his wide shoulders sideways through the space his slight body had easily managed before, tearing his shirt on the jagged edges.

His quilt-covered bed was as he had left it when his mom had given her last ultimatum. *This time you have gone too far, Son; you cannot continue to live here.* Her anger was overdone, to keep her from caving in. He knew this time he had scared the ever-living-bejesus out of her when he drunkenly crawled across the threshold, bleeding from his chest, arms, and shoulders... Taken to Emergency by the cops she called, ultimately being told his wounds were not from being mugged, but "self-inflicted," was just too much. He had used a beer can to scar up his body and thrown his wallet away – for nothing it turns out... Snatches of conversation between the suck-ass cop and his dad... *He's a little short in the brain department or he would've found a way to get scratches in the* middle *of his back,* a policeman's derisive laughter. *Well, you know, he's a Special Ed student,* said his father, hints of sadness. *He has trouble figuring out the small details sometimes,* compassion... *Yeah, that's too bad,* says the cop. *Why they end up as flunkies for some mean dude who can think for them.*

The assholes. They thought he was passed out drunk, but unfortunately his ears were stone cold sober.

On his dresser his junior picture, complete with his going-to-church sweater under his favorite navy and red windbreaker and his shitty-ass smile, still sat. On the wall hung the remnants from tenth grade photography. He loved that, and he wasn't too shabby at it either, seeing beyond the lens. "But it costs too much. Stick to your music; we've put a bunch of money into that, and you are good at it, Sonny," his mom would say, hugging him, rubbing his back, pulling her fingers through his thick curly mass reassuring his frightened soul.

Thinking about her just now made him angry...

He stumbled through the front marbled hallway, missing the white ceramic Saigon elephants his dad brought back from the war. He rounded the corner, habitually avoiding with his heavy boot-like shoes the light plush carpet in the living room where his beloved baby grand shown as a beacon in the shadows. In through the family room instead, where they lived: his mother and father, with his martini and her wine, listening to *Hooked on Classics,* or some such tape... His father directing the orchestra like Bernstein, telling time and again of sitting on a Miami beach next to the famed conductor, who was old and skinny in his swim trunks, swilling down straight booze in the midday sun. Just one of his dad's stories of investigative intrigue, this one during the

Cuban crisis. A polygraph assignment from JFK's brother, Bobby. Pride mingling with contempt for the liberal democrats playing to the pinko commies. Whatever that was all about went over Sean's head. He only heard the music, and felt the passion he so wished to emulate.

Beyond, the breakfast nook beside the kitchen was the perfect fit for the octagon table they'd gotten in Tucson. Oak Parque, one of his mother's treasures, and where he and his dad sat by the hour playing chess while she hovered: cooking, cleaning, humming... The drapes were drawn, hiding the cactus rock garden below the large picture window between them and the pool, shaded by the spreading Schefflera.

He hesitated, turning into the kitchen, a couple steps to the refrigerator... Looking for something to drink... *No milk... No juice...* His parents gone, the refrigerator was bare... Lost, agitated, fumbling for direction, feeling his anger, *fear,* again, well up to choke him, he headed back into his parent's bedroom.

The blinds were turned downward letting the street lamp from the busy boulevard, that abutted their yard beyond the high shrubs, shine into the room. Streaks of light fell across the huge four-poster bed: a Paul Bunyan, another of his mothers' cherished. He passed the mammoth dresser on which a mirrored hutch reflected himself, his auburn hair bushy from wind in its curl. On one of the decorator shelves bordering the tall mirror, the jewelry box lay he'd given at Christmas... When opened, it played... *Somewhere my love... there will be songs to sing...* He knew she loved that... from *Dr. Zshivago...* Remembering now, and how she had cried when the small child's mother died, *just as her's had...* On the Russian guitar-like instrument the dead mother left to the boy, he learned to play that haunting melody... Just as *she* learned to transfer such sadness onto the keyboard, *so now did Sean...* On the silk cover of the wooden box was a print of a famous impressionistic painting, of a little girl in a flower bonnet holding a puppy dog... When his mother saw it, she exclaimed, *It looks like you, Sonny...* and was smiling, until she saw the look on his face and caught herself, probably remembering his childhood wishing that he was a girl *so I can wear pretty clothes, Mommy...* He wanted to sew on her sewing machine, too, but she said, *No, only girls sew; boys play ball and build go-carts* — and so he did all that...

He passed quickly by the memories, the dressy red slipper he'd made for her in ceramics class, the wooden bookends in wood-shop, the snapshot of them, Ray and Sam, when he was a child: Dad, so hip looking in his blonde, flattop DA, his light turtle neck and dark jacket standing behind Mom, his sexy lady with her bouffant hair and pink minnie-skirt sitting cross-legged on a bar-stool snuggled safely in his arms, taken during that summer they moved to Bangkok. He was a bitty thing, a scant five-year-old just learned to swim and dive off the high dive. At the fancy hotel *he showed them*, the day they arrived in the sweltering tropical heat, while they were all arguing over what to wear to Dad's new boss's welcoming party... He found the mezzanine that jutted out above the pool... The Thai man dragging him dripping through the lobby "to Mummy." His mom in tears, frantically hugging him for dear life; his dad laughing.

Back in the small master bath, the thick carpeting muffled his footsteps. Flipping on the light, it blinded him for a moment. Inside the medicine cabinet his mother kept her pills: insomnia, headaches. Pain in recent years kept it filled: Restoril; Atarax; Vicodin; Fiorinal w/codeine. Valium — the bottle was almost full. She said once she was afraid to take it, afraid of becoming addicted... Into his mouth he poured the contents of the whole bottle of pills, and swallowed them with water direct from the faucet. He wiped his face, and staggered back through the bedroom. Passing the dresser, he spotted the keys to his mom's Honda, and a tube of her lipstick...

In the garage, he managed to get into the car. Backing out, the mailbox was in his rearview mirror... *Aw, shit...* he mumbled through the cloud quickly settling into his brain. Out on the main thoroughfare, the wheel had a mind of its own. It headed down, and around, through, and into the subdivision where Melissa lived. The night was bright; a full moon lit the whole street. He pulled up in front of her house and stopped, dead. He felt safe here for some reason, near her. Although drowsiness was overtaking him, the vision of that shotgun lingered in his mind's eye. He turned and locked his door, and reached over to the passenger side, locking that one. The effort took all his strength as he collapsed on the seat; he let his eyes close in restful sleep.

Tapping on the window... banging away... An angry male voice... very angrily... yelling his name...

Aroused. *Fuck you... Fuck you to hell,* he was saying inside his marshmallow head. *She's my honey, my lady, my WOMAN!*

Still the loud frantic banging... The male voice yelling, "You stupid bum, wake up or I'm calling the cops."

Fuck you, you SOB. She's mine...

There was a crashing of glass, and then quiet oblivion.

Back in his mother's kitchen, on the light marble counter top there was a tube of bright melon-red, Revlon lipstick laying open, extended, cap missing, next to words scrawled in a child's script:

I want my wommy!

Such was Sean's story.

It was as if the child came alive as she painted, the tiny face with the sad eyes peeking through the colonial style window. The grids were similar to the ones in her present house – one of the things that attracted her to it in the first place, so cozy looking, clean and white, small panes set within each frame. She wanted to have the child's nose pressed against the glass, looking out, as though saddened at having to stay inside. She had seen a picture like that once in a Campbell's soup ad. Working on the small 10 x 20 canvas from time to time, whenever she had some hours where she wouldn't be disturbed, was something she looked forward to in the back of her mind. The beach was one place she found where she could make a mess, and leave it until she was ready to pack it up for another day. Sometimes she would spend a week, or more, just painting. But it was rare that she got to it anymore, with her Real Estate business taking so much of her time, not to mention energy. As she painted and worked on the expression in the eyes, she was thinking of Sean, her youngest son, and wondered where in the world he had gone? It had been nearly two weeks... Even though, in her effort to shake him up, she had made him move out, his not calling just wasn't like him; she was frantic with worry. Not knowing the whereabouts of Kelly, for months sometimes, the last five years had been a regular nightmare — being hospitalized every other month for "psychosis," out of his head, or on drugs, or both. Who knew? Sean had threatened several times of late to go "live in that barn with my brother, or on the street, *wherever he is.*" That threat hanging over her head had been what kept her from putting her foot down before, *but just how much can a mother bear?*

For almost Sean's entire life, now more than seventeen years, she had spent watching out for him in the hopes that she could keep him from a life like Kelly's: seeing to his medication since third grade, taking him to the pediatrician on a regular three-month interval, keeping tabs on his weight. The meds for hyperactivity cut Sean's appetite, and had she allowed him to go unattended, he would have dwindled to nothing – he was so small to begin with, a meager five pounds at birth. She had worked hard at delivering him on Ray's thirtieth birthday, even though her due date was three weeks off. So ignorant, she was then, about the health of the fetus, as was everyone, it seemed, even the GYN doctor, who prescribed the Dexedrine for her tiredness, apparently had little knowledge of such dire consequences the unborn child could suffer. Her slight fifteen-pound weight gain was admirable, she had thought, not detrimental to the baby as would eventually be determined. Back then, in 1962, it was just the beginning of the drug scene, when it was rumored that even Jack and Jacqueline in the White House, just down the street from the hospital, were given mass doses of the drug by injection from their M.D. friends. Drug use was becoming commonplace: speed for tiredness, the end-all cure.

The oils on her canvass wanted to run together. In all the classes she took, this, a recurring problem; she was not really a trained artist. The lights in the eyes seemed to disappear, the look in them gathering gloom. *Funny how it looks like Sean, this funny little face, so sad...* Sam laid down her brush and changed the station on the radio from soft ballads to classical. The lyrics were what got to her, made her sad enough to cry sometimes. *Memories.* With classical, there were no words, just feelings allowed to flow unrestricted, *and unnamed.*

She had just freshened her brush in the hopes of getting a cleaner look, when the sharp knock at the door sent Ray rushing past her, to answer it. He could read the paper or work crossword puzzles for hours so that she hardly knew he was around — until he got hungry. Now he was speaking to someone, the landlady who had rented to them before the season was officially open. Even though it was too cold to be on the beach, they loved to be there in the quiet and walk in the moonlight, listen to the beat of the waves upon the sand. They needed a break after what Kelly, then Suzie, and now Sean, was putting them through, one thing after another. And she had thought Sharon a challenge, but eventually thinking her an angel by comparison. *But little could she consciously acknowledge; better let sleeping dogs lie...*

"Oh, sure, I'll be right there," Ray was saying. "I'll just tell my wife."

He was yelling over his shoulder as he went out the door, "There's a long distance call for me at Ms Nebs; I'll be right back."

The nerves in her stomach took a little leap. At the sound of the telephone, she was beginning to jump of late, why they had thought being up here at Savannah Beach, way up in Georgia, their yearly summer vacation hide-a-way while living in Atlanta, would provide them freedom from that intrusion for a while; she needed it. *Must be someone from work,* she thought, trying to shrug off the unsettling feeling.

She was ready to mix some lighter skin color, when Ray rushed back into the small cottage. "That was Jim, from across the street, telling me the police had come to his door looking for us. Seems Sean came over, broke into the house, and took your Honda."

"Oh, my god... I knew I shouldn't have left those keys, I meant to... The police? Why the police?"

"Sean is in the hospital... Apparently took a bunch of pills."

"But how did they find him... Where?"

"Melissa's dad found him in the Honda parked in front of their house, out cold. Car doors were locked, and when he couldn't get him awake, he called the cops. They busted the windshield... Good thing, or it might have been too late."

She grabbed her stomach, feeling ready to retch the delicious seafood they'd just eaten. "What do you mean, too late?" she asked, looking up into his seldom serious face. "What?"

"Guess he was drunk, of course, but they pumped his stomach and think he had a mess in his gut: Quaaludes; Valium; who knows what all?"

"Valium... Oh, my god," she said, feeling the cramp hit her stomach. "There was a bunch in my medicine cabinet."

"Yeah, no doubt. They'll know more in the morning. Think we should start back... I'm gonna fly, and let you take the car; I can handle the police better. You can call me on the way down; you always like to drive at night anyhow," he was saying, a questioning tone in his voice.

"Well, if you think so. I was just getting ready to call it quits for the night, trying to avoid a headache. Aspirin and coffee should do the trick, keep me awake, besides." Her voice sounded too calm, and lightly agreeable, while a volcano was ready to erupt from within.

"That's my girl; I knew you'd see it my way," he said disappearing into the bedroom to call a cab for the airport, and pack.

Ms Nebs was close to eighty and loved to brag on her agility and independence. She had a beautifully wrinkled face that showed years of endurance. Sam had taken several snapshots of her, a closeup, with the intention of painting her some day in the future. Flattered by it, the old lady was friendly, but knew how to keep her distance, giving her guests the space they sought in her cottages. She was standing at the door, now, saying, "I know you are so neat and clean, and always leave things ready for the next one, unlike most of the others. And I appreciate that, Dear... But leave all that now; you need to get on the road, home to your family."

"Thank you so much. You don't know how much we needed this get-a-way time to ourselves. These boys are going to be the death of me, yet."

"Yes'm, I know all about boys, I raised three of them myself. It takes a lot of tough stickin' to it, sometimes. And a little help from the good Lord don't hurt," she said with a smile.

Sam knew that was the way many Southerners spoke, and in some distant part of her, she felt comforted. Yet on the surface, she really resented such God-talk, making her shut down inside. But she was as polite as any Southerner, having been brought into this world in a Tennessee farmhouse. Her childhood, though, being spent for the most part up North, with the exception of those couple years her daddy went south for a job and an education. He'd taken her with him, finally, where she'd learned to say: *Yes, Ma'am,* and *No, Ma'am* as part of her upbringing, which she had, in turn, imparted to her own children, their returning so many times to live in Atlanta. The southern twang to her speech had lingered for many years, and was easily resurrected when in an earshot of a soft *Y'all.* In fact, it was so easy for the whole family, that when they'd landed Stateside after being out of country two years, the minute they set foot on U.S. soil the kids slid right back into the *Y'all* they'd left behind.

Maybe that is why leaving this place left her feeling sad; she really didn't know why, except this time she figured she did have a reason. Georgia was more like home than almost anywhere else. But Clearwater was now home, and it was a good ten-hour drive. She put her foot on the accelerator, and eased out of the sandy road that housed Ms Nebs' cottages. The night was clear, no rain in sight, and she had a full pack of cigarettes in her lap.

Heading across the long causeway that separated Tybee Island beaches from the beautiful city of Savannah, she recognized how interconnected this place was with her family. She remembered bringing Suzie here the summer she had graduated, and before she was to begin her first year of Junior College, the year that all hell broke loose in their house. She, Suzie and her best friend, DeeDee, played gin rummy by the hour for one-tenth of a cent a point. It was one long tournament, and she had come out the winner. No matter how they situated themselves, switching seats continuously, the girls couldn't get ahead of her. How many times they had started over, they said, to give themselves a fighting chance. Very surprising, she thought, for someone who had never had a deck of cards in her hands before she met Ray. Her daddy called them *The Devil's Bible*, and allowed her only Bible Lotto and Scrabble, no games that had any cards in them for fear she "might learn to handle them" and start her on the road to ruin. Sam had learned to play Gin Rummy from Ray on their honeymoon. She had to smile, thinking about Ray, then, how timid she had found him to be, nothing like the smart mouth that gave one the impression that he was afraid of nothing when they first met. Every day she was learning something new about him, things that would surprise her so unexpectedly, like his wanting to take a plane right out, spend all that money... He really *did* care about his kids, after all. Sometimes his seeming indifference left her aching inside for them, for their wanting so much of his attention, his approval. It was something she believed she shared with them, if truth be told.

Nearing St. Augustine, on the north Florida coast, Sam remembered the Holiday Inn right next to the expressway. She turned in at the well-lit sign and parked under the street lamp. It would be safe to get out here and use the rest room. *After all they were lifelong customers; who was to know?*

On her way out, she walked by the pay telephone and dug into her purse. No change; her collect call, Ray answered.

"Where are you?" His voice sounded far off and strange.

"I'm at the Holiday Inn in St. Augustine, remember?"

"Oh, yeah. Are you all right?"

"Yes, just tired, and worried. How is he? Did you go to the hospital?"

"Yeah. He has a good doctor, some Latin guy with a thick accent. Says Sean was a lucky boy that someone found him... He is staying right on top of the situation, so no need to worry... Just keep awake; you can sleep when you get home."

"Did you get to talk to Sean?"

His voice sounded hesitant, but only for a moment, "Oh, no. He was sleeping," Ray said. "I'll go in the morning. I just got back a minute ago. Flight was only a few minutes; took longer to get home from the airport, actually."

"Okay, Honey, get some rest. I'll see you when I get there. Not much traffic, and I'm wide awake. Take care, love ya."

"Love you, too."

When she walked into the kitchen, Ray put the newspaper down he was reading and stood up to greet her. "I didn't hear you come in. Did you see the mail box?"

"Yes. Did Sean do that?"

"Yeah. The car is a little messed up. The cops have it impounded... It's a miracle he's..."

"Have you talked to the doctor yet?"

Ray came from behind the table and walked over to her, standing close. He always kissed goodbye, no matter how upset or angry he might be at her, but she was the one to kiss hello. When he came to her now of his own volition, as he had that other time in Pennsylvania, she grew wary as he reached for her. "I have something to tell you." He was holding her by the shoulders and looking directly into her eyes. "Sean was in a very bad way when they brought him in, they were not sure he was going to make it. I would've stayed at the hospital..."

"Oh, my god, he's not... Ray, what do you mean? Is he okay?"

"Yes, the doctor said he never left Sean."

All of it hit her too fast, her head was spinning, from the driving, the caffeine, the worry... Thinking Sean was over the worst, and sleeping... As Ray had said on the phone..."What do you mean, you didn't *tell* me?" She almost screamed in shocked disbelief.

"I didn't want you to know, on the road, for fear you would wreck the car. Dr. Comas..."

"How could you not *tell* me? I'm his *mother*..." The tears were burning her eyes.

"Listen to me, Sam. Dr. Comas felt positive about his pulling through, and he agreed to stay at the hospital and monitor. If Sean made it till morning, he'd be out of danger. He told me to go home and get my rest. There was nothing I could do there; Sean was sleeping, and I wanted to get your call. I didn't want you to call the hospital for fear they would tell you."

If Sean made it till morning? If? Her body functions seemed suspended, her lungs collapsed, her stomach sucked into her backbone... The shock of hearing that her son had lain at death's door and she wasn't with him, or even knew of it, while his father *knew and didn't tell her*... She could feel the screams of outrage mixed with fear come from somewhere inside... *No... No... No... I have to go to him.* Here, Ray was doing it again, treating her as if she were a child needing protecting, as when he'd kept Sharon's searing letter from her. *How dare he?*

Then she heard him say, "Dr. Comas called at seven this morning to tell me we could see him as soon as you got here; Sean's awake."

"Oh, my God. Oh, my God." Anger was just below the surface, but she was pushing him away, pounding on his chest, "Why didn't you tell me that *in the first place?* Always building things up to some kind of gigantic crisis. You and your Irish storytelling." Relieved of the terrible fear that had gripped her, she grabbed her face, pulled at her hair as she let the outrage at his patronizing behavior begin at a slow boil. "How could you do this to me?" Her voice was suddenly too calm, too steady, "Why didn't you tell me last night?" Her voice was starting to get higher. "You had no right to keep such a thing from me; I am his *mother!* I had a right to know." Her voice was rising to a pitch…

Lamely reaching for her, he said, again, "I was afraid you would wreck the car."

By now she was screaming, "How dare you… How *dare* you… You had no right to keep such a thing from me… You have no right to decide what is *best* for me. He is my son and I had a right to know the truth… Don't you *ever* keep such a thing from me again." *Still playing the big protector, and Sam, the weak, and fragile one. How many times did they have to face this same kind of thing in their relationship? When would he realize that his wife was as strong as he, and probably stronger, should the truth be tested?* The anger suddenly went out of her as she broke down into convulsive sobs. Doubling over, she wrapped her arms around herself. So like a small child, she was crying now, receding into a whimper, "Don't you understand? I am his mother… *You had no right.*"

S uzie, who now lived with her new husband in Tampa, was already in the lobby waiting for them when they got to the hospital. Seeing her youngest daughter so unexpectedly gave Sam reassurance that maybe she had done something right, that a sister would care enough about her brother to take off work. "Dad called me last night, Mom," she said and walked in step with her to the elevator.

"Had you heard anything from Sean?"

"No. The last I saw him was a couple weeks ago, when we were over for cards."

"Just can't figure this."

"Did Dad tell you about the lipstick? On the counter? What Sean wrote?"

Ray interrupted, "Yeah. I meant to tell you. I washed it off already. He wrote all over the counter top. I didn't want you to have to clean when you got home; I knew you'd be tired."

There he goes again, protecting me. Suzie, a psychology major, said, "He wrote, *I want my w-o-m-m-y!* Isn't that interesting, Mom? The spelling?"

"Oh my," Sam said, grabbing herself, as the realization hit her in her gut, the terrible sadness her son had hidden beneath all the drugs, and acting out... *How could I have been so blind — the perfect storm?*

She was thinking aloud. "He called Melissa, his *woman.* She broke up with him, you know, the day after we made him leave... I guess it was just too much..." she said drifting off into that ocean of fear that seemed to await her, to swallow her... Fear of her father was nothing like this wrenching terror inside that reminded her she had never known how to mother any of them, but at least she had thought she had done *something right* with the last one. She was older, and finally made it through all those classes where she learned a little about them, *about herself, and all the things that were missing, so many things.*

They were in the small visiting room the mental health ward used for private visitations. Sean was sitting in a wheelchair, wrapped in a white canvass smock tied in back, with his arms swallowed deep inside. He had a far-off look in his eyes, a slight smile, and saliva was dripping from his mouth. There was no recognition whatsoever when she walked up to him and threw her arms around him, sobbing. "Sean. Sean. What have you done, Son? What have they got you in?"

Ray answered for him. "That's a straight jacket. The doctor said he was afraid he would try to run if he didn't use it, from Sean's past history. I told them about the hospital in Tucson, about his dismantling the alarms... Guess the doc didn't want to take any chances."

Sam dismissed the information, as she did most of Ray's overly dramatic pronouncements, trying not to let it anger her. She hugged her son, and shook him by the shoulders. "Sean, Honey, we are here now, you're going to be okay," she said, rubbing his back.

Still, there was no sound, staring through her with no sign of life in the eyes, just a mouth turned up into a vacant grin, a constant drool.

The tears would not stay back as Sam continued to speak softly into her son's ear, rub his shoulders, his back...

Suzie seemed to be visibly shaken, also.

Ray just stood aside, and watched, silently.

Sam clutched Sean's head to her breast, and, as she had when he was an infant to hasten his sleep, began putting her hands through his hair. Speaking softly to him, "Sean, Son. We love you; we are here now. We love you." She kept repeating the words, and never stopped the touching while she let the tears flow unhindered, her family standing motionless, without speaking, watching.

They were asked to stay only a short while, it not being regular visiting hours. The doctor had ordered more tests, but they were welcome to come back later in the day.

The evening visit was no different from the morning. Suzie was there when they arrived. She stood in quiet abeyance, watching, as Sam tried again to communicate with her youngest son, in vain.

The terrible possibility was not voiced aloud, the fear that Sean would be another Karen Ann Quinlin, the teenager who still lay –for five years already – in a New Jersey hospital bed, brain dead, a virtual vegetable, the parents not knowing for sure, as some conjectured in the press, if the alcohol consumed had been combined with other drugs. Sam had known about the use of drugs by her kids. It would be a fool to have ignored the fact, taking them to doctors, psychiatrists. All that trouble with Kelly, and his ultimately being institutionalized his sixteenth year with the schizophrenia diagnosis. Then Suzie turning into a screaming stranger after her high school graduation. All of this paled in comparison to seeing her baby in such a state now. She knew Sean had never been the brightest of students, with his severe learning disability that had been referred to as *minimal brain damage*, an ugly description that was shortened to MBD by the pediatricians who treated him. But despite his hyperactivity, he had eventually excelled in music, which used a different part of the brain. As a kid, he had a sparkle that his teachers and coaches recognized. One coach had said that Sean wasn't the best hitter on the team, or the best fielder, but his enthusiastic spirit made up for all he lacked in size and ability, thus he was usually one of the first chosen for a team. Hoping for that fighting spirit to somehow pull him through filled her thoughts.

It was the third day that Sean, during their daily visit, looked up into his mother's face, and smiled. *Acknowledgment*. Her son was back, the light in his eyes shown when he spoke, and his response grew more pronounced every day. Suzie made it a point to be there, also. A surprise, considering the contemptible, distancing attitude she seemed to portend toward all three of her siblings in the recent past. The second week of Sean's stay, Sharon even flew down from D.C. with Candi, her baby girl, for a few days, another surprise! Attempted suicide was a new thing in the Malorry family. But they had no idea how to reach Kelly, believed to be somewhere in the Atlanta area where he had gone to high school.

Visiting Sean daily was a given. They were informed that their visits were being used as "a reward," to keep Sean in line, or "punishment," by losing the privilege of seeing them. The threat held over his head by the staff seemed harsh to Sam, but she was told that there was nothing else that seemed to work. Never once did Ray complain, or not want to go. But keeping the appointment with Dr. Comas, as requested, that first week "to get a rounded history on Sean," was what opened Pandora's box.

S he was trying to explain again about the many problems in her family. "There is just so much to tell; I don't know where to begin," Sam said, glancing around the beautiful office decorated in artifacts she recognized as foreign, from her own cherished collection. It had been several weeks since Sean, under the Baker Act by the State of Florida, was put under the care of Dr. Comas; she and Ray really had no say in the matter. They had tried to make several appointments, but something kept interfering with the schedule. First, Sharon had driven down from D.C. with her toddler; then Kelly had unexpectedly shown up, and admitted himself into the county's area mental health hospital for his intermittent anti-psychotic treatment, leveling him out on lithium, what Dr. Hanks had suggested, way back when. Without Ray, Sam had managed several sessions concentrating on Sean's unending story – three large file folders crammed with reports, every three months since kindergarten. But the doctor seemed much more interested in *her*.

"Your paintings..." he began while she was forgetting to tell him about Sean's latest AA counselor who had pushed her into painting her feelings. *If only Ray... but he had blatantly refused to come along. When she had asked, Ray was fuming, his voice so loud and angry, his eyes bulging. There's no way I'm going to go to any damn psychiatrist, plain and simple. No, he said pounding on the table as he got up to leave. Close to tears, she had asked: But what am I going to tell Dr. Comas? Tell him anything you want; I'm just not going.* Dr. Comas was saying, "Let me see what you brought."

"Well, I am not very good, but I really love working with oils. When things get to be too much... Up at Savannah Beach... We went up there to forget about all the trouble with the boys, with Kelly, Sean, not knowing where either of them was... and this little girl I was painting seemed to turn into Sean. The eyes are so sad, dark, I couldn't get them to lighten up... Then the call came that you had him here. See, this child looking out above the snow-laden window sill? I guess why it is so horribly sad, I had started it after I'd seen the movie, *Dr. Zshivago*. The night of the mother's funeral struck a nerve... Zshivago was very young and alone, at his aunt's house... He looks out the window as *Laura's Theme* is played on the malinkka: *Somewhere my love*... The child sees a leaf or two flutter by his window in the wind and realizes winter is coming, and his mother is out there, alone in the snow. The painting looks like it could be in Russia, the coldness of it, don't you think?"

Dr. Comas studies the painting, and says, "This depicts sadness and despair. And look at this window, with the crossbars on it. Like a prison. Who *is* dis child?"

"I thought it was Sean at first, since I started it when he first left. But the child is so young – except when I painted the face, it seemed it was Sean's face bleeding through."

"Did anyone ever tell you that Sean looked like you?"

"Yes, we hear that a lot, but... it looks more like a three-year-old."

"How old were you ven your mother died?"

"Three," she said, startled at the connection.

"You have never dealt with the death of your mother," he said, very simply, but definitely. "You are living in a prison of your own making. See it here?" Shaking his head and pointing to the wooden trim around the windows, looking like jail bars. "Der is no hope here, only despair."

This doctor had just described to Samantha the feelings inside she had learned to live with for nearly half a century. From her looks and chipper personality, though, no one would have ever guessed it. *She had done well with her make-believe face, for so long...*

"You see, you have never *really* dealt with the death of your mother. That is what we will do here. Together, you and I."

"But, I had therapy with Dr. Hanks, extensively, some years ago. I thought I had done so well after that year with him. *It's just that lately...*"

"Perhaps... Now, look at dis other painting, of the tree. Trees are mirrors to the psyche... Dey tell us so much about who we are. Look at the shape of dis large limb. What does it look like to you, apart from the tree it is attached to?"

She was embarrassed suddenly, seeing the shape of a large penis seeming to emerge through the foliage, hanging suspended. Her face turned beet red when she said, *penis*.

"And do you see the trunk of the tree? What does that look like to you, dis here?" he asked, pointing to the slight curve in the bark. The rippled indentation resembled the backside of a woman's buttocks showing from behind the towering appendage.

Sam covered her mouth with her hand, "Oh, my god, what does it mean? I certainly never *intended* to draw such things... How awful."

"Yes, the subconscious will tell on us most vividly sometimes. It seems dat sex has played a huge part in your life, hm?"

"Well, a little. Men keep coming on to me; I just hate it. Every man I meet... Even my first psychiatrist at Walter Reed, where I was sent to get my tranquilizers renewed, tried to give me a key to his apartment, can you believe it? I wish it would stop, and sometimes..."

"I tink you may be telling deese men someting, dat sex is the only way you know how to relate to them, to have intimacy. Is dat possible?"

"Intimacy?"

"Yes. Do you have intimacy with your husband?"

"I *think* so... but not really... Sometimes... Oh, I don't know."

"So, we have much to work on together, don't you tink?"

"But what about Sean? And Kelly is in the hospital right now, also. Ray and I had to go to an orientation for parents of mentally ill, a support group. And Suzie... She is drinking so much, and is so hateful to everyone. Sharon is here too, now, thinking she is pregnant by her next door neighbor, no less. You know she is still married and living with her husband? And Ray, he was in a bad way last Christmas, when all the kids were home. He was in the middle of a big deal at work; he'd been working on some kind of new secured radio for the government, this hostage business in Iran... He finally went to Sean's last psychiatrist who put him on heavy antidepressants, for several months. He seems okay now, but he is so distant to me again, withdrawn. He's not here with me today because he hates hospitals and doctors, especially psychiatrists. There is so much going on I just can't tell which way to turn. I'm very confused."

"Until you settle the past, it is always popping up to confuse the present. It is like trying to build a house by putting the roof on first, without a solid foundation. Poof, in the first wind, it goes - - all your effort."

"I am so tired, too."

"Yes, you are working so very hard and going nowhere, but in time..."

Time? That is all it would take? After weeks turning into months of delving into painful memories, Dr. Comas explained to her that psychotherapy was like surgery on the psyche. It is as if you are walking around with your insides hanging out, bleeding, hurting... Twice a week she had entered into a kind of frustrating no man's land where she fought to keep control, but was losing in her battle, as control had been her defense against facing all those forgotten memories, things she had unwittingly repressed as a child "in order to save your sanity," he told her. It was in the middle of such an agonizing state of mind that she was asked to take Sean out of the care of Dr. Comas, and relocate him to a treatment hospital up in the Blue Ridge Mountains where some of the medical students, from a major southeastern university in North Carolina, did their psychiatric residency. In the middle of a very hot summer, it was her lot to drive him, as Ray could not get away.

Samantha was nearly exhausted from the nineteen-hour nonstop transport she had driven while Sean fitfully slept.

His spaced-out condition was due, in part, to the major anti-psychotic tranquilizers given by Dr. Comas, in Florida. It was on this long trip that she became acutely aware of the terrible truth of her child's helplessness and emotional dependency.

She was directed to the executive offices of Hilltop House, located above the lavishly restored stone mansion, for Sean's admittance, although Dr. Comas had said he was already accepted. As she sat back into the uncomfortably hard office chair that had held her weary body for well past her allotted hour, her tears oozed intermittently from her tired eyes as she sat in consultation. The little, round, white-haired lady had been a kind of caring confidante, writing few notes in the course of her social history taking as Samantha poured out almost a lifetime of pain and struggle. She tried to somehow impart a more total picture of herself and her treasured family, finally divulging the recent precarious marital separation between her and her frightfully withdrawn husband, though living still in the same house.

It was now the other woman's turn to speak. As she did, Samantha listened attentively, feeling the kindness in the older woman's voice as the words fell softly from her lips. No one in Samantha's entire life had ever spoken to her with such candor, and yet so gently. "I've come to term someone like you a bottomless pit," the woman said. "Since your beginnings, you have been the object of considerable abuse, and not ever knowing real love and caring for, you are to love as a hole in the sand is to water: One can keep pouring the water into the hole, but it gradually seeps away. In order to keep the hole filled with water, one must have water replenishing it continuously to keep the sand even moistened."

The woman then looked Samantha directly in the eye. Reaching for her hand, the woman said ever so quietly, "So are you with love, my dear! You must have a constant supply of love showering over you because there is nothing there to catch and contain it. No doubt, if real true love came and hit you in the face, you would not recognize it before it had already slipped away, through the *bottomless pit.*"

Samantha shamelessly let the tears flow as the pronouncement of her condition hung in the air. *When would the pain be finished?* She felt the words as daggers, be they ever so veiled, piercing her to the quick. Was it not enough that this woman had just delved into her very soul as she extracted the tedious history of her *special child*, the newest young teenager this exclusive mental hospital was admitting for residential treatment, and the third of her children to be labeled mentally and emotionally unstable? Was it not too much for this mother of four – who was already a grandmother, as well as a wife for twenty-five difficult years – to hear herself, Samantha Sue, being compared to a hole in the ground?

What a synopsis of her forty-four years on this earth having conscientiously and deliberately committed herself to the loving and serving of others, fervent in her desire to emulate the Jesus of her childhood training. *Could it be that she truly did not know this love herself?*

TREES
When the pain is so great another step I cannot take,
I think of the tree He bore.
When I think of the weight that a million have borne,
in like pain as I,
I know why He stumbled and fell from the weight of us all–
as they've come to tell.
An example is He? This Jesus of three? As He suffered for me
To teach me to go, all the way, all alone – to the finish,
or more?
How can I know if this man of yore really meant to be
My inner truth, my inner self, my sensitivity,
my borrowed strength, my shining light, in pain or in night?
I cannot tell.
'Tis much too awesome, this meaning true,
how my pain seeks its refuge in words such as these – and in trees!

–L. L. Morton, 1981

The words of the social worker had cut her to the quick. Now, on her long drive home alone, Samantha had time to ponder them. Feeling absolutely broken, she felt as if her very insides had been pulled from her and been left bleeding. *A bottomless pit?* Hearing this had the affect of her questioning all her therapy with Dr. Comas. If she had no hope of changing herself, not ever, how could she go on?

As she looked up at those beautiful mountains she was traveling through, Sam was reminded of hearing her father, when discouraged, repeat the Psalmist's words: *I will lift up mine eyes unto the hills, from which comes my strength.*[4] Keep looking *up*, her daddy would say.

She had always believed that nothing was impossible if one wanted something bad enough, and worked at it. Wasn't it Jesus who said, *If you have the faith of a tiny little mustard seed, you could move a mountain?*[5] She had to believe, she just *had* to, how else had she gotten this far? Although the stark declaration about

---

[4] The Bible, King James Version, Psalms 121:1
[5] The Bible, King James, Matthew 17:20, paraphrased

her had begun to weigh upon her, she was reminded of the words this new Latin doctor had spoken to her. Surely all the time she was spending with him would help her find *some* of her missing pieces — Dr. Hanks had referred to so often in her therapy – so she would be more than just a *hole in the ground.*

Then, from the car radio, she heard Barry Manilow singing, *I had it all… all the time…* [6]

In her twice-weekly therapy sessions, Sam was eager to understand. Hypnosis was covered in one of the classes she was presently taking at Eckerd College, enlightening her to its possibilities. "Dr. Hanks suggested trying it once," she said, "but I was too afraid to let go and let him take charge of my mind, as much as I trusted him."

"You don't really trust *anybody,* do you?" Dr. Comas said as he watched her so closely she felt he could see through her.

Her face would always get flushed as she would look away, toward the tall, rubber plant standing in the corner.

"But you vill," he'd say reassuringly in his broken English. "Ven you are ready; ven you are ready. You cannot rush deese tings. It is not what you learn up here," he'd tap his head, "but what you *experience* in here," and pound his chest. Then his face would break into that broad, square smile that would send her on her way somehow feeling hopeful. He was her new lifeline, and how relieved she was when he reminded her, again, "Together, vee vill do dis, together, yes?"

◆

_____

[6] *Words & Lyrics by Barry Manilow and Marty Panzer, 1978*

BOOK THREE

A Make-Believe Jesus

"My salad days, when I was green in judgement."
—William Shakespeare

"The archeologist's material resists his inquiry... [same as] the psychoanalyst faces the literal unconscious resistance... For just as civilization is a web of deceptions, the mental life of the individual is a highly sophisticated system of falsity...

Not even dreams are safe from the sly work of the censor who lives in us all, denying the undeniable, making palatable the unpalatable — especially to ourselves... What is obscure must be made clear... Digging down from layer to layer, he seeks the buried city."

– Edmund Englemon
Berggasse 19: Sigmund Freud's Home and Offices

"... a terrible kind of cruelty, no matter how well intended, in demanding the denial of self when there is no selfhood to deny."

— James W. Fowler
Stages of Faith

"What's in a name? That which we call a rose
by any other name would smell as sweet."

"Give sorrow words: the grief, that doesn't speak
whispers the o'erfraught heart, and bids it break."
— William Shakespeare

CHAPTER EIGHT

Samantha Sue

It was almost automatic now. When she walked through the door of his back office, the room where she most often felt like a small child again, she would relax and feel herself lose the present out there in that black void of nothingness — a triggered response. On the same couch, behind the same low coffee table, a tall glass of water would be poured waiting for the need to lubricate her throat and let her speak unrestricted.

I really was never quite sure if … except that I was bad! Yes, I was bad the day Mama died… I was being punished. I remember that little three-legged stool by the window, and looking up at the sky at the falling leaves. It was October, nearly winter. The trees were almost bare. Here and there a leaf would flutter to the ground…

"What are you tinking?" Dr. Comas said, leaning forward. "Where are you?"

"Looking for Mama," she said pulling her knees up to her chest… her eyes peering through him, into then…

I am little· My short pudgy legs twist 'round the buck-toothed legs of my little stool· Alone, I sit crouched, hugging my lap·

Enlarged snapshots line the top of the tall radio, smiling faces set in silver frames· There is one frown surrounded by Dutch boy hair, this one framed in wood· Me, by Daddy's Model-T, standing on Grandma's Sunday chair· In the corner fish bowl a gold, shiny streak slithers noiselessly through the water· All are out of reach of my tightly clasped fingers· An empty quietness soaks into my brain· Left behind· No licorice at the store· A sad feeling, again· Another new baby getting ready to come from inside Mama's funny, round tummy·

Is it *that* day I hear Mama in the kitchen? I want to get up but I remember what she's told me, "You stay here, now, and behave, till I say you can get up."

I sit back on my haunches and tuck the hand-me-down crocheted dress under my white-stockinged legs.

Is it from *then* comes the odor of bleach? It smells so good – wonder what it tastes like? The perfume of the laundry soap tickles my nose.

Then come the squeaking sounds of the door leading to the roof. Is she hanging out the clothes? The roof has no railings. "Stay off that roof," Daddy said.

A thread of hope. Maybe *Mama* will let me go out there, where you can see over top of the *whole* world. Sometime she might, I can tell, *if Daddy not see.*

Waiting. Waiting.

Me want... the licorice Aunt Jenny Lou always buys us; the ride in Uncle Wilbur's car. Even Cousin Marilee got to go, and she can't even walk yet, she's such a baby.

A baby... like Jesse Woodrow? "It was the nurse that give him pneumonia, leaving that window open when he already had whooping cough," Daddy said. *What is pneumonia? Could I get it?* Baby brother, who took away

Mama's milk, is gone·

Now *Mama's* quiet, sharp with me, combs my dark, stubborn hair over and over· It hurts when the comb pulls· I holler, and get slapped on the side of the head·

I pitch a fit, like just now, wanting to go along in the car·

The rubber band pulled so tight, hurts· Then the ribbon· I touch the right side of my head to feel it, where *Mama* has just tied it again· I pull at it a little, not enough this time for it to come loose, just so it won't hurt so bad·

The sounds from the kitchen have stopped· The funny quietness fills my ears; I can hear only the wind rattling the windows, and the tick-tock of the loud clock·

Where did Mama go?

Waiting·

A car door slams outdoors· I want to run to the window and climb up and look, but I sit still· In the yard below, Daddy must be in his overalls working on his car, bending over the dirty, sorry-sounding engine with the hood rolled back, and a Lucky Strike hanging from his lips· I can almost see him squinting through the haze of cigarette smoke curling into his nostrils; his hands, always cold, stuck into his pockets as he studies the sputtering engine·

A sudden pop-pop bang comes from the yard· I imagine the sparks flying every-which-way from the car and Daddy saying the bad, ugly words that make *Mama* wince, and bite her lip, and then hug me tight·

"Maa-maa, where are-rr you-oo-oo?" I sing to the tune in my head·

My eyelids begin to get heavy and want to close· I put my head in my lap· My arms hang down around my legs touching the smooth painted legs of the stool· My short fingers find the loops of the lacy, crocheted dress· They wiggle and twist, in and out the holes, pulling the pink into a bunch·

The sound of a streetcar echoes in the silence· The quietness hurts my ears·

I sit up and begin to holler, "Mama? Mama-a· Mama-aa·"

Again, I listen· A lonely leaf hits against the window· I

stiffen at the sound as I watch the wind carry it away. The quietness, the dragging, empty quietness.

In despair, I curl the toes of my high-top, white button shoes around the legs of my tiny stool. I bend over and hug my knees to my chest. Softly, I begin to weep.

Where is she?

The bright room full of windows becomes a shadow as I concentrate on listening for Mama, but I only hear the mocking of the wind, the sound of my own sobbing, and the tick-tock of the big, loud clock.

"Mama?"

My buttocks squeeze tight. Into my fist, I feel the wadded rope-like yarn of my favorite dress.

"Mama?"

My eye begins to itch, and I sit up and rub it red with my fist. A pain, knifelike over my eyebrow, makes me forget a lost tear trickling down my cheek.

"Mama," I whimper, one last effort.

An eon, or a moment? Shadow-like images dance in and out. Through the curtains, white wintery sky is all there is. A lonely bird flies through it. My eyelids keep wanting to close. I rock up and down. Up, and then down, fighting the sleepiness, straightening, pulling on my dress. My legs, ribbed in their white cotton stockings, dare to stretch out in front of me. Like a mushroom filling my brain, I am tempted; I strain to hear. A signal? A sign? My toes hug tight to the floor; I creep forward an inch; my stomach fills my mouth. "Mama?"

My ears pop inside with the effort to hear. Curious fluffy sounds come from back in the bedroom.

"Mama? Mama?"

Then I hear the soft sound of her voice calling my name. It is the sound of angel wings and snowflakes, of daffodils and black-eyed Susans, all, fluttering in the wind. "Samantha! Sammy Sue! Sugar, you can get up now. Come here; come here, Hon."

Downstairs, I stand small by Grandma. The black pay-telephone hangs just inside her living room, by the door leading into Grandpa's horseradish store. Grandma is hurrying, rummaging through her apron pockets. She finds a silver nickel and sighs a thanks to "sweet Jesus" as she reaches on tiptoe to drop it in the shiny slot·

I tug at her, but she's already stretching her neck to reach the protruding mouth piece· Speaking loudly into it, she says, "It's my daughter, please! Come right away... We don't know what happened·" Grandma's voice is high pitched, loud· "Please, *hurry!* She's in family-way and she's done fainted... No, no one was; she was alone·"

Alone? I yank hard on Grandma's apron· I am crying, "Gramma, Gramma, is the baby comin'?"

Grandma covers the mouth piece, and says in a harsh whisper, "Hush, Child, I cain't hear with you a-whinin'·" Then she turns back to talking· "Yes, I tell you she's fainted-dead-away... Her color? Not good... No, no blood that I can tell· Oh... Well, yes, we did find some water on the floor, next to the commode, but we don't know what it's from· The toilet seat's all bent and twisted... Yes, she must've fallen somehow; we just don't know· Please, *hurry·* The baby's due right soon, here, now·"

A rush of fear comes up from inside me, and I open my mouth wide, and scream, "Mama-aa·"

Over my mouth, Grandma's hand is quick· With the other, she grabs my shoulder· "Hush now," she says, shaking me silly· "I've got enough to worry about without you pitchin' a fit on me· You straighten up and be still, y'hear?"

I take a breath and swallow back the tear that is bursting through my resolve to *Hush·* A heavy weight closes in on me, like heavy giant doors to an ancient monastery shutting out the world·

Soft strains of organ music float over the tall room· The man up there in black is halfway to heaven, and Mama and the baby just beneath him· The high-backed bench is hard, and it hurts to sit· I squirm, and Daddy takes me on his lap, but that is hard, too· Everything hurts· Aunt Jenny Lou pulled my hair too tight; I keep pulling at the big, blue ribbon, bought special· The words of the man up there jumble with the events of the last days: Accident· *Pregnant; died·* Autopsy; inquest· Events I have no words for except *Hush, Child·* I hear: *Safe in the shelter of His arms; rest forever; no more harm; no more pain; forever·* They're closing the lid on Mama· The music starts again; Daddy takes me in his arms, and we go outside. He is crying, sobbing, but he still hugs me tightly to his chest. People say things to us, squeeze my arm, pat my back. All of them are crying, too. *Me be's bad. Punished... Had to sit...*

So many kin. "Cornfield relations," Grandma complained once. "Like to call themselves my kin, but stepchildren is all," she said. "That fat piece of a Myrtle... All that holy-roller-carrying-on, it's downright disgraceful, if you ask me."

The same fat Cousin Myrtle comes now and wraps herself around us. "The Lord help us, Child. God loves you; He'll take care of you. We pray for y'all every day."

"Thank you, Cousin Myrtle," Daddy says.

"Y'all come over to see us right soon, y'hear?" says gentle Cousin Tim.

For days, Daddy does not speak; he sits and stares out the window. At the dinner table, he stares at his food; he stares at me, too. Aunt Jenny Lou takes care of me, fixes my hair, washes my clothes, and makes me eat things I don't like. At night Daddy hugs me hard to go to sleep. Then is when I really miss Mama, her pale blue eyes that look like clear crystals glistening in the sun. Her smell, of warm milk and lilacs. Her laugh, at a prank she's pulled, sticking Daddy with a pin in his behind. Her squealing in delight at catching him with his pants down, and him playfully angry. Her impatience with my everlasting *questions.* Her anger at my stubbornness, at my strong will.

Aunt Jenny Lou tells Uncle Wilbur, "Getting Orin out for a ride might help. Maybe, over to the church? Might be the *Pastor* could get Orin to talking again, you reckon?"

Aunt Jenny Lou is wringing her hands, and fretting under her breath. She is still worried about the water on the floor. She says over and over, *I didn't leave that there, did I, for Dorie to slip on?* But no one knows. When the detectives come back again, she tells them, "Yes, oh, yes, we got on right good, living here together in one big house. You almost *have* to... 'cept for Dorie's moods." The words come out before she thinks; she covers her mouth as though to grab them back. Then she gets a cantankerous edge to her voice, "Well, she *was* moody; no sense telling stories about it. If she hadn't been near her time, I might never have gone in there to check on her. I might *still* be waiting *for her to answer me.*"

All this was weighing on Aunt Jenny Lou, besides taking care of me, and Daddy so funny quiet.

But when he comes home, he can't wait to tell the good news. "I've been to see the preacher," Daddy says, a touch of happiness in his face. "Now things got to be made right."

Down on his knees at Grandma's lap, Daddy is crying, "Please, before God, I beg you, forgive me of all I did to your daughter." The tears are running down his face. "Pastor Cunningham told me God would forgive us of anything, no matter what. And I've already asked the Lord to forgive me, but I need your forgiveness," Daddy begs, shaking Grandma's prayerful hands.

Grandma looks right on past him and thinks for a spell.

Daddy keeps shaking her hands, "Please hear me. Please let me have your forgiveness. I done so wrong by her, and I know it's God's way of punishing me for my sins." Daddy is bent over almost to the floor, sobbing. Into his handkerchief, he says, "If only I'd have come upstairs just twenty minutes sooner."

Grandma is thinking, staring... Finally, she looks into Daddy's pleading face. Very gently she puts her skinny hand on his shoulder, pats him, "Now, now, Orin," she says. "Dorie Mae is done gone, and we cain't live over even one minute of one day." Her voice gets shrill and high sounding. "And we didn't know either she was up there needing us. Twenty minutes might never have helped, just a doctor's guess."

Daddy listens intently.

Suddenly Grandma sits up straight, and leans close to Daddy. She speaks in a soft voice, husky with tears, "Leave that to God, Orin. Besides, Dorie Mae's left you with a mighty big responsibility here."

Aunt Jenny Lou has already fixed my favorite supper – wieners, but I decide to want an orange, instead.

Daddy slides his chair away from the table. "I'll be right back," he says as Maureen and Marilee stare wide-eyed.

Aunt Jenny Lou keeps her lips tightly shut until Daddy

has gone out· The wind from the harsh Milwaukee night blows through the slamming door, over my untouched food· "What a waste," she says with pursed lips, grabbing my plate· "You're getting downright spoiled, little lady· What you need is a board put to your behind·"

Maureen twists in her chair·

I can almost feel my bottom sting from the threat lingering in the air·

In awhile, Daddy comes home with a sack of oranges· "Had to go all over town to find some," he says wearily, dropping a large one into my lap·

"I don't want it now," I say, puckering up my lips, sneaking a look at Aunt Jenny Lou·

The sternness in her face draws out my tears, and I holler, "Aunt Jenny Lou's goin' to spank me·"

Daddy's face suddenly gets red, his bottom lip begins to twitch· "I don't want anyone else spanking her," he says as he gathers me into his arms· His eyes are blinking fast, blazing in anger, "You just tell me what she's done and I'll tend to her myself·"

Aunt Jenny Lou's piercing eyes speak for her sealed lips as she turns her back on us·

A sudden chill from the cold fruit clutched to my bosom shivers through me· It cuts through the heavy silence struck in the air as I nestle safely into the comfort of Daddy's arms, my daddy·

Aunt Jenny Lou and Daddy had a falling out over my "rearing," and particular she was about using that word, as animals get "raised·" Cousin Myrtle and Cousin Tim were good enough, then, to take us in, and to their holy roller church·

Holy Ghost Pentecostal was now Daddy's new church· For every service, the soft-spoken Cousin Tim was always standing at the front door, the head usher· Cousin Myrtle liked to tell how he married her when she was just thirteen, and bragged on how good he was to her, waiting for her to "get growed up before bringing her to his bed·" She seemed to like talking about hush-hush things: about growing together, you know... getting stuck, like dogs, and the doctor having to come and cut us "a-loose·" They were pretty embarrassing stories, trying to scare Junior and me *off of being nasty, our staying by ourselves downstairs every night. Everyone else slept upstairs. Junior's oldest sister, Laverne, was dying of tuberculosis; all the time she would cough and spit into a paper sack. Cousin Myrtle was afraid we would get the sickness, so we were not allowed upstairs, even for the bathroom. We had to use the slop jar out on the back porch, even when it was cold out, and at night. That was when Junior loved pestering me. He would come by my bed on the couch, just outside his bedroom, and pull his dooter out of his long-john underwear and shake it at me, just to scare me. Junior was four - a year older than I was.*

One day, Cousin Myrtle called me into the kitchen. "Come here, Sugar, do you want to see how the insides of a chicken gets took out? Junior, you too," she said.

She took us out in the yard, into the grass. What a site to behold, seeing her take the chicken by the neck, and twist it 'round and 'round, like it was a cowboy's rope, before she chopped off its head. While it's legs were still flailing away, she put the chicken under an upside-down cardboard box. "What's that for?" I asked.

"Until it stops thrashing around, it has life, and we don't want to get the blood all over. See, here, Hon, God gives life and it is hard to give up, so even animals fight to the very end."

Back in the kitchen, I watched as she pulled its insides out. She let me stick my hands inside it, just to feel how gushy it was. Pulling the white feathers out was fun, all the while listening to Cousin Myrtle talking about me and Junior being nasty, a big sin. While his mama's back was turned, Junior would stick out his tongue and make mean faces at me, letting me know I better not tell on him, so I didn't. When Laverne, already sick, got worse, we had to find us another place to live. A family from our new church took us in.

The new house was up three flights of cement steps, on the second floor. Ruby was the only child left at home and she scoffed at the term. She was eight. She had two grown sisters, both nurses. Her parents called Ruby "the special blessing."

Afternoon kindergarten accepted me because my

birthday was before the end of the year, just under the wire· Ruby had to walk me to school, hating every minute of it· She gave me strict instructions not to wave at her if I should ever see her with her friends· Otherwise, school was fun·

The new kids were assigned *buddies* to help them with their nap blankets, and to show them where the bathroom was· This one day, I had been begging my *buddy* to take me to the bathroom, but for some reason, she just looked at me and turned her face away·

The third time, with my knees together and holding my stomach, I was pleading·

The look in my buddy's eyes seemed to gleam with pleasure, the same kind of look Daddy got when he was chasing me with the vacuum cleaner, making me squeal, as if making me squirm amused him· The look, now, made me have cramps for sure·

My buddy had walked away from me again, so I neatly pulled down my breeches and squatted next to my blanket; I just couldn't wait another minute·

The kids were all holding their noses, saying, "Poo-poo, Samantha Sue," while the janitor was pouring sawdust all over the pile I had just made on the floor·

Tears wouldn't stay back· I tried to tell the teacher that my buddy wouldn't take me, but she was too upset with all the commotion in the room to hear me·

The principal and the teacher from the next room were there· The kids were all dancing around me, making faces· Then Ruby's older sister appeared in her nurse's uniform· "I've come to take you home, Samantha Sue," she said as she took my hand and walked me out the door·

Ruby's mother was waiting for us on the street corner· All three of us walked home together, me crying and pleading all the way, "Please, don't tell my daddy; please, don't tell my daddy·"

By the time we got home, I was almost hysterical from sobbing, fearing Daddy and what he would do to me for all the trouble I had caused· Finally, I laid down on the highest top step, as much from exhaustion than anything, having to be carried into the house, still begging tearfully for them to not tell Daddy·

At supper that evening, Ruby's mother said, "Samantha was sent home from school today, the flu I guess, Orin."

Just finishing my second hot dog, my most favorite food, was almost too much for me to believe, that Ruby's mother would really *lie* for me, but she had. Ooie, and God knew, too.

In the middle of the night, Daddy woke up with me retching hot dogs from one end of our big double bed to the other. After that, just the smell of hot dogs would make me sick.

We didn't stay at Ruby's house very long anyhow, not after Daddy did his hands and arms, singeing the hair on them the same as plucked chickens, for his being sweet on Charity.

Beth was the little blonde headed visitor to our Sunday school who came just often enough to get special welcomes from the teacher. Her hair always hung down her back in loose waves, accented by her white rabbit's fur hat and muff, articles of envy unmatched in our Sunday School set. It was because this Beth LeMay had just moved out of the Simms' boarding house into her very own home, with a housekeeper to look after her and her father, that we moved in.

That's how we came to be driving down that still, shaded street. The tops of the rows of trees met at the center, forming a cover over us as we drove. It was a strange, warm feeling, as though we had entered a new world, quiet and comfortable, protected from without. But Daddy was too intent upon the subject at hand to notice. "Listen here, Samantha Sue. About the Simms' boy," said Daddy as he caught the knob on the steering wheel, interrupting its spin. "You need to understand some things."

Up on my knees, I was facing him with my back to the door, my left arm hugging the seat. This traveling position had started out as a maneuver to see out over the dash board, but it turned out to be a defense against Daddy's quick stomp on the breaks, which once sent me flying into the windshield, shattering it. Remembering his unpredictable foot, the spider-shaped crack in the glass, and the lump on my head, I was half paying attention when his tone drew me in.

"You know Martin still lives at home," Daddy was saying, clearing his throat in his readiness to tackle the serious topic.

The elderly Simms I knew only on sight, in which pew they usually sat. The solid white, wavy hair of the burly old man always caught my eye. Daddy referred to him by his position as head deacon, but it was the *young* Simms who had Daddy's attention just now.

I remembered little of Martin, a slight shadow of a memory, of shenanigans in the church yard at Summer Bible School, a regular boy, if there was such a thing to Daddy whose suspicion of all young males seemed to grow with my age and, when mentioned, set the nerve in his lower lip to twitching. At the sight of it, my fist found the little hole in my middle and kneaded its way in and around the gnawing pain.

"And he'll be around from time to time, I imagine," Daddy continued, his voice rising in pitch. "So it's important that you understand how to act around men... even an older boy like Martin."

Looking out his window, Daddy spoke in a calmer voice. "A lot of Jews live around here; see all the expensive brick houses?"

I hadn't noticed exactly what kind they were, just that they were big, dark, and foreboding. I liked light-colored houses, and there were only a few of them, one or two sprinkled here and there.

"But never matter," continued Daddy, "Jews are God's chosen people, the Bible says. You know Jesus died for the Jew *first*."

Behind the massive brick I could just see men in beards and sandals all wrapped up in yards of shiny cloth called *garments* moving clandestinely in the cold shadows. But behind the painted wood I imagined people like us, Daddy and me, strolling freely, smiling, uninhibited by the less oppressive structure.

"We have to witness to the Jews, same as anyone else, even though they've rejected Him," said Daddy. "But it's *hard.*" His voice trailed off in his own thoughts as he pulled the car into the driveway of a small, white bungalow·

A big shiny Plymouth stood in front of us· I stretched my neck to see over it, into the back yard that was partially planted with a flourishing garden· Parked next to the back door was a boy's muddy two-wheeler· "Oh, boy, a bike," I squealed·

Daddy's face reverted back to his former seriousness, his anger difficult to hide when his eyes were blinking and his lip was pitching a regular fit, "Now listen here, I think the best thing for you to do is to stay clean away from Marty Simms," he said· "The best thing to do with any boys· And let me tell you, when any man tries so sit you on his lap, you refuse and get down as fast as you can, y'hear?"

"Yes, sir," I said with my practiced politeness·

"And above all, don't ever kiss anyone on the lips," he added for good measure·

His anger kept me from pursuing this new dictum· He must have sensed my confusion at the mysteriousness of his words· "Someday you'll understand why I'm telling you all this," he said·

Daddy surveyed the contents of the car and then hid his keys behind the sun visor· Even though the car was loaded down with everything we owned, it would be safe· We were now in the north end of town where the well-to-do folks lived, thanks to Beth's leaving only days before·

We were barely settled in our new surroundings, my sixth birthday and first grade just around the corner, when the LeMays came to visit· Daddy was a friendly person, and so was Beth's dad, Bob· A tall man whose shoulders filled the doorway, his voice was gentle, spilling over with laughter often at Daddy's seemingly serious words· Their lively conversation had settled into a quiet monotone behind the heavy door that swung into the living room· The Simms were gone for a run in the country with their mean dog, King, and Marty, leaving the back end of the house to Beth and me playing in the bedroom·

Daddy had bought a nice wooden cedar chest to keep all my toys in; it was crammed full· I loved kitchen gadgets, especially my new folding ironing board and toy iron· Beth pointed out immediately that her iron at home had a chord on it that "sucks up to the wall like a real plug·" But the latest in my long parade of things that simulated the grown-up life was a sink with a storage tank that let real water pour from its spigots· Beth chose the sink over the cordless iron, leaving me the leftovers until our fathers appeared at the door, suggesting a boring nap·

Beth had taken the other twin bed· Her shoes kicked off, her panties in a thin roll around her knees, she said, "Why don't you do it like this?" clasping her hands flat together and placing them between her legs·

I was watching, shaking my long, fat, Sunday-only curls in fear· "No, uh-uh; that's nasty," I said in a tone of fearful recrimination·

Through the wall, I listened for the sound of our fathers' voices· Reassured by its soft, monotonous drone, I put my fingers over my panties·

Beth opened her eyes and saw me· "It feels better this way," she said, exaggerating her moving·

"I like my finger-way better," I said, holding up my index finger, then sniffing it· I hated stinky things·

Suddenly Beth said, "I've got to go to the bathroom," and slipped her panties back up around her hips· "You can come with me," she said over her shoulder as she opened the bedroom door·

People said Beth was a spoiled child, since her mother had "run off·" I felt sorry for her, but mainly I was afraid of her, she was so willful· When Beth summoned me to do her bidding, I had a time refusing·

Sitting on the commode, my panties were hanging around my ankles, when Beth clicked the door lock shut· It must've been the silence in the air that hung on that sound, stretching it into tomorrow, as I watched Beth sink into the opposite corner of the white tiled room· She lay sprawled, with her head against the bathtub, her hands moving between her legs· Suddenly she jumped up and pulled me down on the floor in her place· "Here, let me show you," she whispered, pulling my panties completely off and throwing them aside·

My head was propped up on the hard tub when my bare buttocks hit the tile floor· "It's cold," I said, irritated, attempting to get up·

"No, it isn't," she whispered, determined, pushing me down· Then she backed away and pulled my legs apart· Down on her knees, she had me apart with her head between my legs before I had any idea what she was doing· Suddenly I felt the warmth of her tongue moving up and down, up and down on my most private part· I was absolutely astonished· This couldn't be· Get away· Stop, you terrible girl· But the words never came, the feeling so good and warm, I lay paralyzed, lost in a world of nothing-land, caught by a thread tied to my soul, while my need to pee ran over its banks, into her face· This horror so vivid, the boundary so fixed, even billows of warmth, of heaven set free could not escape its decree·

Beth waited, back in her place in the corner, while I sat on the commode· "Now, you can do it to me," she said softly, pointing· She was holding her legs open for me to see· It was an awful sight, all red and wrinkly· "Come on; come on," she kept saying·

As I drew close, the smell startled me· I must have made a face because she giggled·

"Come on," she said and pulled my head down· "Stick your tongue out like I did to you·"

So I did, even though I thought I would die right there, I was so shocked, revolted, and ashamed·

The squeak of the swinging door made us both jump up and grab our panties· I was frightened, and the cold water on my hands – trying to wash away our sin – only sent chills to my toes·

And Daddy was so worried about boys

I t was 1955, the second summer after my divorce. The cool east wind, blowing in off Lake Michigan, was lifting my skirt. My hair was a fright, blowing every which way as I anxiously clutched the APARTMENTS FOR RENT page torn from *The Milwaukee Journal*. Patience was one virtue I lacked as I waited for someone to answer the door. I held my skirt down and tried to correct my posture by standing erect, pulling my shoulders back. If they would just talk to me, hear me out. Usually they just slammed the door in my face. This time I really wanted to make a good impression. My lips felt dry, so I licked them, biting them to make them pink, anything that might help. I was tucking my silky blouse back into my skirt again when the door began to open, slowly. I should say something, I thought, and cleared my throat as I looked into the big blue eyes of the woman who was peeking out at me. I opened my mouth to speak, but my voice caught like it usually did when I was scared. My throat would just close up. The faces of Daddy and Charity flashed before me, and I remembered why I was there and swallowed hard. I cleared my throat again and told myself to speak directly and try to exude (my new word for the day) confidence. The woman was looking at me, waiting for me to speak. "I'm here about the apartment," I said.

"Oh, you want my mother-in-law," she said, "downstairs. But she'll never rent to a single girl... not one so young." The huge rumpled-looking Italian woman had a lazy, careless way about her, her voice low and husky. "My husband's sleeping," she whispered in explanation, without a hint of a smile. "He works nights, but his mother owns the house anyway."

"Would you mind telling me her name?" I asked. My voice came out soft and unusually timid.

"Bahliacho," is what it sounded like. "The same as mine," she added.

There was annoyance in the woman's voice, a touch of mockery that made me remember the Statdz twins and the fun they used to poke at me after I'd go and believe some silly lie they told. It was the sound that made me still hurt with memories of the long sanctified dresses I had to wear and my godly uncut hair Daddy plaited so tightly. A "woman's glory," he'd say. And the hurt from not being allowed to participate in all those school activities, the fun things like dancing or seeing movies, the feeling of shame. My teachers had really done their best to soften the pain of Daddy's narrow beliefs. But it was hard to quiet the sound still of all who laughed at me, the sound of scorn stuck forever in my brain.

All of this left me with the feeling of being on the outside, watching, never a part of anything. It was easy to understand how I had thought I saw a way out. To be married, to be a part of a family, to have one of my own. But it hadn't taken long to realize that the way out had been a joke. Marrying was like jumping from the needle into the haystack, leaving me the youngest divorcee north of the Mason Dixon line — an adult woman of the world, a status, though, worth every bit of the pain.

If I would only *look* like it. In spite of all of it, my whole sordid past, I could not seem to get over looking so young. I *felt* very mature and knowing, but all that sheltering in my youth from the sinful world around me — "in the world, but not of it" preached

Daddy, no friends, no boys, no movies, no laughter, no fun – must have left me extremely naive and vulnerable. Of course, I couldn't know this then, but this attitude of innocence was only perpetuated by my sincere belief in human nature, that the good, somewhere inside of all of us, would prevail.

How I managed to cultivate such a way of thinking when all I heard day in and day out was: "All have sinned and come short of the glory of God"[7] or "The heart is deceitful above all things and desperately wicked..."[8] was a mystery to me. Maybe it was the only viable way for me to rebel. Daddy could control my life to a great extent, but he could not force his beliefs into my head — although it might have appeared that he had for some years. My basic belief, that man is good and not inherently sinful, contradicted all of his Bible teachings. Maybe that was why I had a tendency to deny the bad in people, because I had heard how bad they were since I was little and refused to believe any of it. When it took me so long to see through Huey, my problem, I thought, was in finding his good; it was there, if I would just look for it. It was this blind faith in people, coupled with my strong will to get what I wanted, that pushed me past the slurs and innuendos I met up with almost daily. A snide smile here and sarcastic question there, all seeming to infer I was dumb.

Maybe because I had come up against it so many times lately looking for an apartment, I was all the more determined to prove everyone wrong — at least about getting along on a shoestring. And this fifty-dollar a month apartment, even though a third floor attic flat, fit into my shoestring budget. So when the woman said her name I could picture it in my mind, remembering how Italian was like the Spanish I took in school with some letters silent. I knew how complimented people felt when you could spell their unusual names, so I ventured past the message in her tone with a daring guess, "Is your name spelled B.a.g.l.i.a.c.c.i.o.?"

The door opened a little more and the woman's voice pleasantly changed, expressing interest. "How did you know how to spell it?"

"Oh, I have some Italian friends, and I guessed," I said, feeling my old confidence returning, knowing it must be *exuding* all over the place. Then, just so she wouldn't get the wrong idea, I leaned in close to the screen and spoke softer, more intimately, "I'm only eighteen, but I have a child. And I feel a strong

---

[7] Romans 3:23, New Testament, Bible
[8] Jeremiah 17:9, Old Testament, Bible

responsibility for her; I try to be a good example."

The woman had very round, luminous blue eyes that peered through layers of dark ringlets flopping about her forehead.

Something I said or did must have worked, *or maybe it was God,* because she opened the door wider. Her mammoth size, embellished by a hugely flowered yellow duster, made her appear well over thirty, even though she probably was not much older than I. Excess weight has a way of doing that; it made her look matronly, and let me feel I could trust her, tell her anything – and she was Italian. The ones I had known had always been good to me, so that when she showed surprise, asking, "Oh, yeah? How old is your kid?" I had no reservations whatsoever about telling her all about us.

"Sharon is just two-and-a-half. But my stepmother has agreed to keep her during the week. I work at a bank, days, and a custard stand, nights. So Sharon won't be here except on the weekends for awhile yet. And we would be very quiet. I don't drink or anything. I'm still working nights to pay off my furniture."

"Why don't you come in?" she invited, pushing the screen door open.

As I crossed over the threshold into her house, I felt that, at last, I was about to enter a world of unhampered freedom. Home. Mine. *Finally.* A place I'd dreamed of since the day Mama died and we'd had to move from one place to another. When Daddy married, I had thought, *that* was going to be my first home, but it wasn't; it was Charity's. Then when I married Huey, I thought, now *this* is it, but it turned out to be his mother's house. Even after we moved away from her, clear across town, I still had no real say in anything. Huey told me how to dress, what to cook, and what I could spend money on. He even tried to tell me how to fix my hair, just like Daddy had all my life. I couldn't believe it. So now, at last, I was really free, on my own, to do as I chose, and the excitement of it thumped in my chest.

In moments like these, I had to concentrate very hard on listening, for words — sometimes even full sentences – would fly by me amid the frenzy of my jumbled emotions. "My name is Mary," I heard. "And this is Anna Maria. What did you say your name was?"

Then I saw her little girl, the same age as Sharon, whose hair fell in dark ringlets also and whose large brown eyes looked back at me shyly as she clung to her mother's skirt. A playmate for Sharon was more than I had asked for even in my prayers. I wanted to jump up and down and shout and scream like I had done in *Holy Ghost Pentecostal* as a child. But I had since learned to maintain an impregnable front: cool and confident and responsible. So instead, I answered in a carefully controlled manner, "My name is Samantha Sue Schultz. But I like to be called Sam." Then I reached out to touch the child's curls. "Anna, " I said, "what beautiful hair…"

Curly's Custard Stand was the only drive-in restaurant on Milwaukee's north side. People came from miles around to sit in their cars and look at the teenaged carhops in their white shorts and red scoop-necked sweaters while they ate their homemade barbecue or scrumptious ham sandwiches and slurped on their thick custard malts.

I figured Curly's was a good place to work for a second job. After being at the bank all day, I enjoyed its lively atmosphere, and Curly let the girls eat for free. He put me behind the steam table during rushes. He said it was because I could handle ten orders at a time, but I could tell he wanted me close by when he would linger, just a moment too long, so our hips could rub, moving in and out of the close quarters. My pay was fifty-cents an hour, half the minimum wage and fifteen-cents less than the girls outside got. "And they get tips besides," I would remind him.

"But you get more hours," he'd respond in his feisty flirt-y way. That he wanted me near him was clear, subtly woven into his every movement: touching my shoulder, my back, my arm, picking a hair off my chest, scheduling me to close up with him alone "because you do such a good job shining the aluminum," then offering me a ride home by way of the Lake Front for a little "harmless" necking.

Even though he was married with kids, Curly seemed to think, as often happened, that "divorcee" meant easy sex. He'd volunteered his services, "whenever you're in need," he flat out said. The attitude was not unfamiliar to me. I had found my unusual candor in coming right out and talking about sex to be of benefit, too. It seemed to act as a shield of sorts so that touching, copping a feel, was rarely a problem for me, until Curly.

Daddy was the one who really taught me to flirt, after Mama died. It had become my only way of survival. To be coy and beg sweetly, always maneuvering his stolid fortress of a will just a degree at a time. For that was all one could expect with God and Jesus and the Devil all on his side — tiny concessions. It taught me patience and perseverance in dealing with men, the worry that had come to preoccupy my every minute of every day.

The screeching of wheels in the parking lot brought my attention back to the steam table. Through the window I saw a flash of red. It sent a tingle through my inner thighs, making me feel nauseated and breathless at the same time. I moved closer to the counter, bursting with the news of my apartment, as the tall and lanky Doc Bernhardt got out of his new red convertible. He wore his white high-collared uniform as casually as a pair of jeans, sauntering up to the window, hands in pockets. A shock of his dark, otherwise manicured hair blew loosely in the wind.

"Wow. What a sharp car. Business must be good, huh?" I said in warm approval.

Doc rested his elbows on the counter, leaning forward, his head all the way inside the window so that his face was inches from me. I was wishing he wouldn't get so close, he might hear my heart pounding as I looked into his sinfully handsome face. Dark coloring like his, like my own, had never caught my eye before. I had always been drawn to blonds with blue eyes like Hubert and then Ray Malorry, who, Mr. Simms insisted, had stolen my heart. But I considered Ray a useless cause even after I heard news that his wedding was off. Preachers just didn't marry divorcees, so I was trying to forget him. But there was something about this chiropractor that turned my insides upside down – and he already had a wife.

Doc was looking up at me, his eyes twinkling as he spoke. "You like it? How about a spin?"

"Sure. Anytime I'm not working. Whenever that is," I said rather lightly.

"How about a ride home? What time do you get off?"

The kinky-haired Curly hovered like a jealous husband. His rapt attention left me no way out now. I couldn't lie. *Why had I been so quick to agree?* I heard myself saying to Doc, "Sure. Why not. I get off at eight tonight."

I was asking for trouble, I knew, by the iciness of my fingertips and the beating of my heart, not to mention the pain in my stomach, as though I had already done what I'd kept myself from doing all this time.

Doc had pulled up at the back door of the custard stand as I was changing from my uniform into the dark jacketed sun dress I had worn to work. The short bolero provided just enough covering for the chilly night air. I looked at myself in the mirror, tempted to leave off the jacket. Still so conscious of my small bust, I habitually covered myself: jackets, sweaters, shawls. As a Christian girl, I felt covered was more chaste. Purity was a hard thing to convey as a divorcee, as careful and particular as I had tried to be. But the new air-filled bra that Mr. Simms had ordered clandestinely in the mail while I was living there (having it sent to the next door neighbor's – away from his wife's discerning eye) had given me considerable new confidence in my figure, so that purity had not been uppermost in my mind of late. It had something to do with the twenty pounds I had gained eating Curly's custard, filling out my bony frame, my age. It wasn't boys any longer I was beginning to attract and fantasize about, but men like Curly — and Doc, who was waiting.

Hurriedly, for assurance, I pulled my breasts in and upward, testing the plastic pockets filled with air. There was only a small decrease in size on the left side, a slight air leak that could be remedied by blowing into the plastic straw I carried in my purse for just such emergencies. *What a time for a girl's cleavage to disappear!* It was scary enough being with such a good looking guy who was so suave, so sophisticated, and so *married*: a taboo I had stuck to every time Curly brought up my "need." Now, in addition, I would have to worry about whether my bra would deflate. It was a stupid kind of bra, I knew, but I was so naive about such womanly things. I would never have dared to order such a thing for myself, no matter how embarrassed I was about my figure. But Mr. Simms had made it sound so right, so *necessary* to my well being, to look good in today's fashions, he'd said. So I'd taken the package, red faced, having hoped all along for just such a miracle. The uneasy feeling persisted at receiving this kind of intimately personal attention from him. But how could I say *No* to a man who had cared for me with such generous affection when Daddy had been gone and throughout my entire life, even though his interest in me seemed to have taken a turn somewhere along the way. When I'd think this way, I'd chide myself: not Mr. Simms – a deacon in the church and old enough to be my grandfather. *No, surely I'm imagining things.* But the collapse of my secret miracles I wasn't imagining. Soon I'd have to find another way to supplement my small bosoms, I thought, as I hugged the jacket close to me, stuffing the plastic straw tube to the bottom of my purse.

The steps creaked no matter how quiet we tried to be. *What would I do if a door opened and I was caught with a man – after being so explicit in my declaration of propriety? Trying to win trust with Mary. And Doc: What would I do if he tried something?* There were no lamps yet in the place, so we tiptoed carefully by the kitchen light flooding the house. I took him through the four large rooms, proudly showing him the secondhand dining room set I had purchased and paid for already. As I talked, I automatically kicked off my shoes, slipped off the pinching earrings and laid them on the table.

The dim light from the other room fell across our faces. I looked up at him, realizing he was looking intently at my ears, which were very visible beneath my short hair. There had been no physical contact between us yet, only kidding around. So when he suddenly grabbed me, covering my ears with passionate, breathy kisses, I was taken completely by surprise.

"Oh my god," he whispered, "you have the sexiest ears. You know I have a fetish for ears? I can't stand to look at bare earlobes."

Laughing right out loud, I tried ever so gently to resist his caresses, but he continued covering my face, my neck, and then my ears again with his warm moist lips. It was most embarrassing, trying to behave circumspectly after leading him on with every mischievous word and flash of eye.

Trying to let him think I was *with it* rather than let him know how dumb I really was — to be labeled a teaser would be even worse – I soon found myself flat on my dining room floor. Doc's passion rose to a crescendo as he maneuvered my body – completely clothed, my still-inflated miracles undiscovered, bypassing my panties and sucking all the while on the flesh of my ears, first one and then the other – up and down on the hard wood floor. It was obvious he had no concern for my new friend Mary, downstairs, who thought I was *not this kind of girl.*

Quickly, Doc was finished with me, hardly aware of my presence. He quietly pulled up his trousers that had somehow worked their way around his knees, saying nothing as he walked to the door. He patted my arm as he left me.

It was clear, I had *done* it. Though it may have appeared that I had given in, I felt violated. Raped, with no will in the matter. I felt so dirty, like a shiny spittoon that had just received its first wad of spittle. I had stayed a *good girl* even when I had wanted to *give in* with Ray, then Tony and Sully. Even with Curly, I could have. I wondered, now, what I had seen in this man as I watched his dark head disappear down the winding stairwell of my brand new home. *Was this the independent living I had waited for?*

Mary, now my baby-sitter, was very curious about me. I would answer her questions, but I learned to volunteer nothing. My early marriage was the big mystery, even though I was quick to tell her I was married a year when Sharon was born. It was plain Mary did not accept my usual explanation that I had married at fifteen because I hated my stepmother. This answer only drove her on to know all about me, pumping me after the wine she drank made her even more daring.

She would invite me to have pizza with her after the kids were asleep, a time to share things about herself, about her husband, Mario. It was just such a night when she was feeling unusually mellow, that she admitted peering from behind her curtained window to catch a glimpse of "that tall, dark and handsome man," in hopes, I was sure, of my telling her everything. I was still very reluctant to share any confidences, the memory of Charity, how she had betrayed my secrets, still too fresh in my mind. So I told her only that Doc was a friend from work who had given me a ride home. His picture was in the paper regularly for this or that benevolent act. What a publicity hound. Good business, he'd said, when I'd brought it up. But this really didn't interest Mary, a devout Catholic, as much as did his marital status. The *other woman* seemed to be the object of her imaginations. I refused to become one, in her mind or my own, as I continued to insist ours was just an *innocent friendship*.

"Oh yeah, " she'd say, chuckling, as my face would grow hot just at the mention of his name. I wanted to forget about him. Giving up my night job at the custard stand had been a relief, not having to see him, or Curly, anymore.

Though I dreaded her questions, Mary's interest in me both pleased me and made me uncomfortable. Not having to work a night job left me more time to socialize with her. She told me often that my "lack of male companionship was *unnatural* for one so young and beautiful," and she was trying continuously to find some *naturalness* in me. Finally, one very long night, her unending questioning forced me to remember things I was trying hard to forget.

It was a nice August day, the kind every bride hopes for: warm and sunny with just enough breeze off Lake Michigan to keep you cool and not enough to muss your hair, when Daddy said God was smiling on him and Charity. But he already knew that, from her finally saying yes.

It was the summer of '48, and already Daddy had waited and prayed seven long years for this day, I can vouch for that. He got down on his knees by the bed most every night. When I rolled over, I'd see him bent over his open Bible. By that time I was sleeping with my eyes open. That's why light in the room woke me so easily –moonlight, or street lights, or car lights shining in the window – and his crying. But he never gave up on Charity. I couldn't get him to even look at anyone else, but I tried.

First it was Edna at the Bible school in Georgia. I loved Edna. She would have been the perfect mother. So much fun. Always cheerful, like the sunshine in her hair. Edna made leaving all my friends in Milwaukee for those two years a bit easier. But she was on her way to India with that uppity missionary lady, Sister Mueller. She said her name "Miller," but southerners call things like they look so it always came out "Mule-r." It made her angry, but it fit her. She was white-headed, with terribly large bosoms. Right away she made a big fuss over Edna sharing her bed. Edna cried for weeks before finally giving in. Fighting God's will, Sister Mueller had said, making a scissor-like motion with her two fingers. I never could understand what that meant.

"Why do you make your fingers like a scissors?" I dared to ask her one day, at the big dinner table in front of everyone (except Edna was in her room "fasting and praying"). I was only eight then and Daddy always tried his best to answer my questions. But Sister Mueller seemed to think, by the tone of her voice, that I had no business asking.

"What does a scissors do?" she asked, kind of hateful sounding, mean.

"Cut," I said. "But I still don't understand."

Her voice went all over me, when she said, "Edna knows what it means, and *that's* all that counts."

Whatever it meant, it made Edna hush the instant Sister Mueller did her fingers.

The day Edna moved her clothes, I walked in on the commotion. Edna and the sober-faced Agnes didn't know I was there. Agnes was saying, "You don't *have* to move, either. Why, she has you plumb hypnotized, I do believe." But Edna paid her no mind. She just kept wiping her eyes, blowing her nose, and moving her stuff across the hall into the room with the double bed.

Agnes was my next choice, since Edna was clearly out. Agnes taught me to sew my first broomstick skirt. That's how I'd happened to walk in on them; I used her sewing machine.

Dark eyed and black-headed, Agnes looked a lot like me. Kind of sallow looking though, and bony. No doubt that was from the sick spells. She'd fall out flat and stiff, like marble, any old time. We'd all stand around and just watch her like she was dead.

But she wasn't. Everyone in the church prayed for her, but it didn't do any good. The doctor gave her pills, but she believed it was not having faith in God to take them. So she just fell out flat wherever it hit her: on the bench in the camp meeting, at the cannery where we went to take the peaches the Bible school students were allowed to pick free. She went down right there on the cement floor. It kind of scared me, but she seemed more embarrassed than sick when she woke up. Don't get me wrong, that's not why Daddy didn't take to her. He was nice to both Edna and Agnes, really. They were in his class at the Bible school in Magnolia.

It took Daddy three years to graduate, but he loved Georgia. It was a lot like Tennessee, where we'd come from to start: hot, and a whole lot of red mud. I never remembered Tennessee; I was only a baby when we left there. The first year of Daddy's school in Magnolia, he'd left me in Milwaukee with Mr. and Mrs. Simms. I had my first bad side-ache then, in the second grade, and saw the one and only doctor in my whole life. Daddy didn't believe in man's cures. He would have just "anointed me with oil," had he been there, and maybe spoken in tongues a little. The only time praying helped was the time I had that high fever before the measles. Pastor Dunham prayed, and my fever went down. I was broken out by morning, and Daddy said *God did it.*

I was forever being prayed over for being sick. From the time I started school, the nurse kept sending me home with tonsils full of white chunks and fever, with a note to see the doctor, but I never went. Instead, Daddy'd get down on his knees right then, with the note in his hand, and pray.

The Simmses didn't stop to pray. Right from school, they took me to this old man doctor. Even though he was nice, he was still *a man* and I was afraid for him to touch my tummy. He said there was nothing wrong, that I was just missing my daddy. But I didn't really believe it, I hated Daddy's praying so and was too frightened to tell. "Lonesome hurts really bad in the tummy, sometimes," he said.

"As soon as Daddy has enough money, he's coming back *after* me," I told him right off. The first time in my life that I thought about money being important. But since most things were wrong and sin, I couldn't want much. And Daddy *did* come back, just like he said. That's why I trusted him so; he always kept his word. Same as when he told me if anything happened to my new bike, I'd never get another one, even when it was stolen. No matter how much I begged, Daddy kept his word.

The whole idea of Bible school, to begin with, was Charity's doing. She had gone off to Bible school in Florida, so he figured he'd better get educated too, if she was to have him. Third grade schooling wasn't enough any more. He found this place in Magnolia, Georgia, out a ways from Atlanta, where he could work for his room and board and school as handyman.

Sister Heath ran the place her husband had left her: a lot of land, with magnolia and fig trees growing all over it, houses filled with family renters, cottages full of students, and a big Oldsmobile that Daddy drove. Sister Heath taught the homiletics class, about how to preach. What's more, she even preached on Sunday mornings, in the chapel. Up north they never had heard of such a thing, of a woman preacher. Well, they weren't missing much. She put me to sleep most always, never lifting her voice to yell and shout like the other preachers. You'd think she could've hit the pulpit once in awhile. Everyone thought she preached more like a Presbyterian than Pentecostal; no one ever dared say it though. But I liked Sister Heath, she always had time for me. She even came up to Milwaukee to visit, that year before the wedding. She woke me up out of a sound sleep very early one morning.

I was barely eleven years old and I already towered way above her — that's how I knew I had grown. I was foggy with waking up but I heard her say, "Just had to see you, even if it's only for a minute."

She hugged me then for the first time ever and laughed at the fat curlers all over my head pressing into her cheek. She never needed curlers with her long white wavy hair. She put it in a pug. I made up my mind that someday, I would wear my hair that way. I caught her one time with it down. She'd had the flu and I hid behind Lizzy, the Nigra maid, when she took in the food tray. Sister Heath's room was a regular mystery, her desk so full of things and her always busy at it. So I peeked every chance I got. I liked Sister Heath. She taught me that a woman can run anything she has a mind to – quietly. Sometimes I wished *I* could be more quiet – when I thought about it.

Charity was quiet, too, but in a different way. Sister Heath was a proud quiet, like she didn't have to defend herself to anyone, she just was. Charity seemed almost haughty in her silence, as if she was waiting to pass judgment. On her wedding day, for instance, Charity and her maid of honor, Myrna, clean forgot I was there. Being a junior bridesmaid makes you kind of invisible. We were all in the minister's study waiting for the right music to start up.

That was the first time I saw Charity with my own eyes, how she really was. I already knew about her sticking her nose up at the hair on Daddy's arms. "Icky" was the exact word she used the first time he tried holding hands with her, back when he first met her. She was only eighteen, then, and just graduated from high school, and Daddy was nearly thirty. It was at Ruby's mother's house. How I found out was from the awful smell coming from the kitchen. There was Daddy, with his sleeves rolled up, moving his hands and arms over the gas stove, flames a-leaping.

"Shu. What in the *world*; what stinks so bad, Daddy?" I held my fingers to my nose.

He laughed hard and said he'd done a mighty lot of chickens that way, and figured it might work on him. It did, too. Right before my eyes, the heavy black curly hairs turned to fine white fuzz, and rubbed right off then, but what an odor.

"Reckon it might turn that Charity's head?" he asked. His face grew red when I held my nose, snickering.

That was the first I had heard of Charity. I knew by Daddy's shyness how much he liked her. He was always so sure of himself around anybody, even strangers. It made me dislike her right off. But I never let on; I just made-believe I liked her – and smiled.

That's what I was doing in the minister's study, smiling. Charity had on flat shoes under her wedding dress; it was plain she hated wearing them, but she looked taller than Daddy even then. And she'd never slouch; her figure was her pride. Full bosomed, she carried herself above most women, looking down her slender German nose at them.

It was a borrowed wedding dress, from Charity's other girlfriend who couldn't be in the wedding because of her being big in the family-way. Mrs. Baumn and Myrna had just gotten Charity into the creamy-white lacy dress. It was a mighty tight fit. Charity's tummy seems to have bloated at a bad time. They brought a mirror for skinny Myrna to hold, and when Charity saw herself, she got really disgusted. First, she tried to flatten out her stomach, standing this way and that. She clicked her tongue over and over. The tone in her voice, so sharp and cutting, made my insides catch. The bad feelings of dislike, I'd kept deep down inside me from the very beginning, had company, but I still smiled. Then a sadness came over me from somewhere, and I felt a little like crying.

Charity took it out on the dress. "I wouldn't have chosen such a full style myself... not all these gathers here," patting her full stomach, her face looking like she had just gotten a whole mouth full of persimmon, "but, beggars can't be choosy." She spat the short cut-off words at her mother, giving her a sideways glance as if to say, *It's all your fault, Ma.*

Mrs. Baumn stiffened up straight; her kindness was like her shield. "Dear, I'm so sorry." (You could tell she really was.) "I had always planned on sewing your dress, you know that, but these cataracts... I'm afraid..." smiling at Myrna, then looking down at her hands, "...blood spots from pricked fingers..." Mrs. Baumn dwindled off then since no one seemed to be listening. It was clear she was hoping Myrna, at least, would maybe understand. But Myrna kept still, completely hidden behind the mirror.

Just then the usher came for Mrs. Baumn. With a tear hugging her cheek, she turned and smiled. "You do look lovely, Dear," she said. When the door closed behind her, I wanted to cry. Oh, what I'd have given for a mother like her. *How could a daughter be so mean?*

Charity kept clicking her tongue in disgust and smoothing down her dress. Myrna had put the mirror down and was undoing the flowers. They were bright red roses, at least a dozen of them. "Oh, they have such a good smell," I said, trying to lighten the air.

Charity turned to me: "Don't you know that flowers have fragrance? *Garbage* has smell."

I smiled.

Mr. Baumn opened the door. The moment Charity saw him, her whole being changed. He was smiling as he reached for her hand, "My dear, what a sight you are to behold. A vision of loveliness. Surely God has his candles lit for you." He was a gentle man, soft-spoken, and love was his flag. His mission: to bring God's love to the unconverted. His special calling: to "enlighten" daily the nuns and priests of the Catholic church, though some called it *gallivanting.*

Myrna handed Charity the roses. *My* flowers were in a nosegay and barely smelled. The music sounded; I had to go first.

"Do I look all right?" I asked, as I stepped past the mirror.

"Yes, you look nice, Samantha Sue," someone murmured.

I was trembling. Then I stepped through the door and saw Daddy, standing at the corner of the altar with his best man, my Uncle Clarence, Mama's closest brother. The butterflies started churning in my stomach, and I felt my face get hot with the sound of bodies turning in their seats, to look. Daddy smiled at me over the heads of all those people. I clutched my flowers and stepped onto the white sheet laid up the aisle. Walk slow... walk slow... I kept telling myself. Then I heard Charity's voice in my head, "Walk slowly. It's *slowly*, not slow," and I felt I was nearly running in my nervousness, but I kept smiling. I made it up to the front of the church without stumbling.

It hadn't been so bad when I was in Ellen Dunham's wedding. Even though I was little and scared then, I was proud to have been chosen for the pastor's daughter's wedding out of such a large congregation. It turned out to be a very big affair. There were two of us flower girls. Karen, the groom's sister, had kept me in tow. We looked like twins, they said, and little miniatures of the bride in our dark sausage-like rag curls. With Karen beside me, I knew, just by the feel of her, if I was going too fast. But being on my own, this way, was a different story. Not having anyone to stand up with, like everyone else, had left me plumb humiliated. But Daddy said, "No boy," and that was that; he was so dead set against boys.

There I stood, down in the front of the church, with Myrna next to me, facing everybody. Myrna looked nice with her brownish no-color hair all done up, and in her new pink dress she'd paid for herself. Charity had cut down an old pink one of her own for me. No one could tell, though; she sewed right good. Daddy and Uncle Clarence had on blue serge suits. Daddy wore one most of the time to church, anyway, and his still fit from his Bible school graduation.

The church was full, too, which surprised me, seeing a lot of them had to come all the way across town to Charity's church. She used to go to our church, where Daddy met her, but she got highfalutin away at school and switched to a quiet fundamental kind where they didn't shout, or speak in tongues when they prayed. Daddy called them *lukewarm modernists*, but said, to start off, he'd "have to compromise some, and go there with her."

We were waiting for the organ to sound that special cue for Charity. When it did, the whole church turned at once to look. But no Charity. People were standing up trying to see. The organist played the whole song through. I knew enough not to look directly at Myrna, but we were standing a little sideways so I could see her out of the corner of my eye. She was as still as could be. So I just stared at the back of the church and kept smiling. (People were always saying what a nice smile both Daddy and I had.) I knew Charity was always making Daddy late for things. But someone told me it was the thing to do, to make a man wait for you a little; keep him on his toes by not letting him think you're too anxious.

The organist sounded the music, again, from the bridal march.

Still, no Charity.

This time the organist played only a few bars and jumped to the ending. I knew what the organist was doing. Since I'd been playing the piano for the whole school to march into the auditorium since fourth grade and sometimes the end of the line came in the middle of the song, I used to do the same thing. But the song getting to the end for the third time made me uneasy. I'd heard about brides getting cold feet at the last minute. And Charity wasn't in such a dandy hot mood. But her pa seemed to cheer her; his being there had eased me considerably. The wait was beginning to stir up the same feelings in my stomach I got when I'd first heard about Charity refusing Daddy. It wasn't anger as Daddy wouldn't have that. He tore me up if I even acted like I might get mad at something. No, it was more a sick feeling, in the pit of my stomach, like... like there was a hole in the bottom of the world and I was falling through it.

Don't get me wrong. I loved my daddy. It was always just the two of us. We'd lived with anyone from the church that had a spare room for us ever since Mama died, when we'd left Aunt Jenny Lou and Grandma Evermardt's place. Daddy and me, we even slept together till I was pretty big. He would tuck his knees in behind mine to keep me warm. We were a choo-choo, till he stopped, saying I was too big. Then later on, my chair-bed got so hot, Daddy'd let me crawl up in his bed most of the time anyhow. That's what I'd done that night...

I woke up with him on his knees, crying. He said he'd done a terrible thing in the night, to his little girl.

"What do you mean, Daddy? I was asleep."

He acted like he didn't believe it. "Your eyes were wide open." He swore it. Then's when I knew I opened my eyes in my sleep, but I couldn't convince him.

He said he had to tell me, anyhow, to clean out his conscience with God. "Well, God has already forgiven me. And it's not anything like your Uncle Nathan in Tennessee did, to *his* girl." Daddy's lip was twitching, then, like it did when he got upset, and his eyes were blinking. "He got her in family-way, you know."

Shocked out of words, I just listened. All I could think about was his breaking my cherry and ruining me for my wedding night, like I'd heard a lot about in my new sixth grade class. "My *cherry*, Daddy," was what I said, and grabbed myself. I started to cry then. It was a Sunday, and we were missing church for the first time, ever.

"Hush, Samantha Sue, someone will hear. I didn't do *no such thing* to you. I just touched you with *my hand* was all – but I shouldn't have done *that.*"

You see, Daddy was such a good Christian, this just wasn't happening. Why, we prayed so much I know we must've wore God out listening. Every night and most of Sundays, reading the Bible, and praying against the lust of the flesh, or visiting the sick. But it *was* happening because Daddy kept on talking about it.

"Yes, Uncle Nathan messed around with his youngest girl and give her two younguns. His wife, Claire, she was sickly and... but he wasn't no *Christian*... still, I just want you to know I wouldn't never do anything like that to you. You *know* that, don't you?"

With my head down and looking at the floor, I gave a little nod.

"Well, *sure* you know that... although I ain't saying what I did wasn't wrong. But I just touched you was all." Then, still on his knees, he leaned over the bed, put his head in his hands, and just sobbed.

After he cried a good long time, he said, "It was the Devil got hold of me... while I was praying, just like our Lord in the garden." Then he commenced to beg me to forgive him.

Now, how could I forgive him for something I didn't know he'd done? But he was crying so, I did forgive him. It wasn't till later on, when some of them started whispering about such things back in the church ladies' room, about it not *fittin'* men should live unmarried – *without a woman,* and looked right at me – that I started understanding what he'd done. Inside, something was gone between us after that, and I started wishing, in spite of my sorry feelings for

Charity, that she'd give in·

The bridal march sounded again. There stood Charity on her father's arm at the head of the aisle. The organ gave an extra loud signal so everyone knew this was really it; they'd been fooled before. Charity stopped for a brief instant, like she had to catch her breath while the sound of the wedding march declared her moment. *It must make a bride feel like she's queen of the world for that one single speck of time.* Charity was smiling, looking straight at Daddy. Her flowers were jiggling some, but she held her head high, with her father towering above her. She walked slow... *slowly*... and Myrna and I turned our bodies, gradually, as Charity left her father standing at the corner pew, and walked on past us.

Daddy held out his arm and Charity took it. Then, I breathed what felt like air coming all the way from my toes.

The standing was the hard part, waiting for the song, *Thanks Be To God*, Daddy's request, while the bride and groom knelt. Daddy liked to think Charity was God's special gift, her name even God's way to say *love*.

It's not that I was jealous, but when the minister said, "Do you, Orin Otis Tuckermoore, take this woman..." How those words tore into me. Unexpected. Some folks would have said *surely* I was jealous. But there's more to it than that. I think it had something to do with my mama.

When she died – from the fall, they guessed, by the bent toilet seat and the bruise on her back; the police said it was accidental· But no one knows for sure how? Since I was thought to be the only one with her at the time, and because I wasn't quite three yet, they figured I was too little to relate anything· That must be the reason, no one talking to me about it, that things got so all locked up in my head later on, and maybe why I was so terrified of Daddy· He would go on about it: "If God ever sees fit to give me another woman, I'll know how to treat her·" He'd cry easily, too, and say, "I had this demon whiskey in me," and tell me how badly he'd treated Mama· Aunt Jenny Lou said he was bad – sometimes in bed in the next room, she'd hear his ornery meanness· Maybe that's why Mama was quiet so much·

Then, Jesse Woodrow, my little brother, wasn't right,

when he was born· Mama didn't truly believe it, though, until he died·

At the wedding, Aunt Jenny Lou, dark and curly headed, with clear blue eyes looking just like Mama, married to Wilbur Lee, the youngest and lankiest of Daddy's seven brothers, was there· The rest of them were all back in Tennessee, though, with his sisters and his pap· Except Beulah, his youngest sister· She was here in Milwaukee, but we didn't visit her often or stay too long· She smoked and cussed and Daddy didn't like me to be around her very much· But I was crazy about her, especially when she played the guitar and sang· She was so funny, talking about how every blade of grass had eyes and was looking at her· She painted pretty pictures, too· She said the farmyard she painted, when the puppies started to dance, she had to quit· Once she painted a big huge mermaid with bare breasts all over her bathroom wall· Daddy got so mad he wouldn't even let me go in there to use the commode until she finally painted some long, wavy hair over *the nakedness·*

Daddy looked very nice for the wedding· He'd finally gotten his stubborn hair to go back smooth, and his cowlick to lay down· His nervousness wasn't noticeable either· Sometimes his lip would jump and his eyes would blink fast and his voice might get a little high; but it was usually from being mad at me· Anyhow, his nervousness is what kept him out of the Army· I remember the day he went to get his physical for the draft· He had to go all the way into Atlanta·

In Magnolia, we had us a set of rooms in behind the chapel; but we took all our meals with Sister Heath and the students, in the school dining room· When Daddy had chores to do, I tagged on behind, watching, with him explaining things to me· But mostly I tried to find ways to be somewhere else· I'd visit the girls, Edna and Agnes· Or later on, after Cousin Essie came, I spent a lot of time at her cottage· Daddy might give in to that because she was "kin·"· Of course, I had school, too· The day the Army called, though, I was over at Sister Weelock's, Sister Heath's sewing lady, watching her sew curtains; I hardly knew he was gone· I remember it was near the time President Roosevelt died, at Warm Springs·

Daddy left early in the morning. When he finally came home, well, he was about as happy as a swallow in a redbird's nest. "Don't tell *me* the Lord don't answer prayer," he said.

Now, I knew lately Daddy had been fasting and praying more than he usually did, but I never asked him why, for fear he might tell me, and I avoided sermons like the hickory. Daddy couldn't keep this in though; he had to brag on the Lord. So I was in for a spell of listening.

Daddy said, "That doctor checked me over and it looked like I passed the physical right away. Then I told him about you, Samantha Sue, and your not having any one to tend to you, but me. I had to wait while he read over my papers again, real careful, and then he told me to hold out my hands, straight ahead. *Hold 'em still,* he kept saying. See, my hands were shaking, almost like I had palsy." Daddy held up his hands then to show me. But now they were as still as a board. "Don't know what got into me over there," he continued. "Next thing I knew, that doctor had wrote down on my paper, *Rejected due to nervousness.* Praise the Lord." For days, Daddy went around whistling. Until I was older, it hadn't really sunk into my brain that he might've had to leave me and go off to war. It was scary to think about, even then.

After what happened between us, that last year before he married, I got used to being away from Daddy. We moved to the Polish Mrs. Rupotski's who was nearly blind and wore thick glasses. Her questions about Daddy made her ever diligent in keeping an eye on me. Then we moved to the Ridell's where we had bedrooms clean away from each other. In fact, I hardly saw Daddy after that. He had his own kitchen fixed up in the basement, and I ate with my new family.

Jodi Ridell was younger than I was, born in her mother's change. Mrs. Ridell, a short and round, and kind of silly lady, never did forgive her husband for Jodi being born. He was a smart and good-looking man who repaired furnaces. She'd yell and holler at him, and get really red in the face, throwing pots and pans. "Men are out for only one thing," she'd scream, "and I'll show *you.*" She said she'd never sleep in *his* bed again· Instead, the three of us: Mrs· Ridell, Jodi and I, all slept upstairs in an attic room in twin beds, Jodi with her mother since she was born·

The Ridell's grown children complained about how spoiled Jodi was· She *was* a little trying at times· Even so, it was the first time for me that I didn't have to answer to Daddy every minute· Oh, Daddy might call me into his room for devotions, but I'd manage to leave the door open, to shorten the time· Jodi would come and stand at the door and stare with her bright blue eyes· Daddy would get upset, the Ridell's keeping us apart· He told me over and over, he was fixing to do something about it· Till one Sunday, he took me with him to visit Charity Baumn·

You have to understand about the Baumns· They didn't have a whole lot· Mr· Baumn was too sickly to work very much· Daddy told me that before we went, so I wouldn't say anything rude· Their house was a little unpainted shack way in the back of a bigger house, and the walk was covered with thistle bushes that scratched, and caught on our clothes· The owner was a Nigra man who lived in the front house· The Baumn's house was condemned, Daddy said· But as long as a person didn't move, the city let you stay on· Mr· Baumn couldn't afford any place else, so they stayed·

Mrs· Baumn let us into a large room with an old worn out linoleum on the floor· Spanking clean· I took it this was the living room since it had an easy chair and a lamp in it· Next to the wall was a cot, which turned out to be Charity's bed, but you could tell it was used for a couch sometimes· A dresser and bookshelf were on the other wall· Mrs· Baumn took our coats and invited us into the nice warm kitchen, where Mr· Baumn was sitting at his big desk, with his reading glasses on his nose· He looked up and smiled very friendly, and then Charity came in from the back bedroom· A curtain hung over the door, but I spied a sewing machine through it·

"Do you sew?" I asked Charity, smiling up a storm· That was my one true love, sewing·

"Only when I have to," she answered very politely, looking at her mother· "My mother does most of it, or used to before her eyes failed·"

Then Mrs· Baumn chimed right in, volunteering to show

me all of her needle work she'd done, pillow cases she'd
embroidered, trimmed with tatted and crocheted lace she'd
learned to do in the Old Country, Germany to her, hours
and hours of fancy proud things· While we were talking,
Daddy and Charity slipped off into the other room·

The three of us talked, then, on and on, being polite,
Mrs· Baumn telling me what an upstanding family she'd
come from, where needlework was a *pastime* – not a way to
dress yourself· She looked at Mr· Baumn sideways· He picked
up the look and started in about his calling from God, and
the Catholics, how *in darkness* they all were·

I'd been sitting a good bit by now· Daddy had told me
about the odd toilet before I came, so I waited as long as I
could, but I finally had to be excused· Mrs· Baumn was very
understanding, lifting up the trap door in her pantry floor·
The steps led down into the dark, to a cold, hard dirt floor·
Next to the wall was a dim light over a commode fitted
into a regular wooden, outhouse toilet· It just set there, up
on a high step, with no door, or walls around it· But it had
a real toilet seat on top of it, and a pull-chain flusher· The
hole in the commode was so dark, it scared me to sit on it,
worse than the outhouse in Tennessee at my Grandmaw
Tuckermoore's farm· I almost froze when I took down my
ugly, bloomer snowpants· I hated wearing them, but Daddy
insisted·

Back upstairs, Mr· Baumn handed me a big cup of
steaming hot cocoa· He saw that I was shivering, standing
next to the potbellied stove·

"Here is some warmth for your tummy," he said· He
talked kind of throaty like a frog· "God always provides us
with some measure of recompense for our labor·" His eyes
danced and you could tell he loved being funny· He was
always making jokes about God, somehow· I wasn't used to
that· Daddy said laughing at things made light of them·
"Spiritual things are too important to fool with; God is not
mocked·"

The afternoon had wore on, and it was getting time
for Young People's Meeting at church· I never missed· I
practiced the piano ahead of time, and maybe played for
service, depending on who else did or didn't show up·
Sometimes I got lucky· Daddy was proud of that, and was

beginning to let me go on the bus by myself, as long as it was daylight out· He'd come later on for regular church· Daddy didn't like me to miss, either, as we didn't have a piano at home yet· (He didn't know Huey Schultz, a friend of Jamie's – *my true love*, sometimes showed up early with his saxophone and played along with me·) Intent on not being late, I got all bundled up: boots, hat, coat, and mittens· Then Daddy told me to "Sit there awhile·" The day had tired me out so I leaned back in the chair·

Charity was sitting on the cot, and Daddy was standing up in front of her, fixing to tell her goodbye· It was plain he didn't know what to say next· I closed my eyes, letting him think I wasn't listening·

Charity said, "Don't you think Samantha's too bundled up for this hot house?"

"Naw· She'll be okay for a minute· She's asleep, anyway·"

Putting on an asleep-face, I was keeping my eyes still, letting my face hang down, my mouth falling open·

"Reckon... Reckon..." Daddy started to say something, but all he could get out was, "Reckon· Reckon..."

It got quiet again· I strained to hear but not a sound was coming from that corner· Then I hear Daddy trying to make polite talk· It looked as if he was giving up what he'd come to say·

"What's that there on your dresser? A pretty crocheted, book mark? A cross·" He admired that awhile, a graduation present·

Then next I hear that he's thumbing through her Bible· "Right expensive Bible... with all these pictures·"

Charity was quiet all the while· I wondered if she was frowning, or smiling, giving him the eye· But I couldn't see, and I didn't dare peek·

Next, Daddy's admiring the picture on the wall· I'd seen it: a sheepherder tending sheep in the mountains, like David in the Bible· Daddy cleared his throat, then, two times, trying to meander through, like he was just filling up time· "Look it, there, at that nice picture, of them mountains· Why, let's see... It looks like it's... it's a... a... why, it's a herpsheeter·"

I giggled right out loud·

That started Daddy giggling so much that he could barely get the words out· "I mean... sheepherder·" He was still laughing when he turned to me, and said, "Playin' possum, you were·"

By then, Charity was laughing, too, and Daddy's face so red· His getting tongue tied, though, must've been what did it with Charity, making her laugh; because she let him come back a lot after that·

I now pronounce you husband and wife," the minister boomed his last words. Myrna took the roses so Daddy could pull back Charity's veil. They looked at each other with solemn eyes, and shyly Daddy reached over and kissed Charity right smack in the mouth, his ears turning a bright pink.

It was the first time I'd seen them kiss. Even though I knew it was supposed to happen, it was unexpected, the way I felt. I remembered, then, when I was little, how Daddy had told me to never let anyone – *not anyone* – kiss me on the lips like that, not even Mr. or Mrs. Simms – *only him.* So seeing them kiss like this, right out in the open, made me feel sort of funny – as though I had accidentally walked in on someone in the bathroom.

Even though I was proud to be in the wedding, getting dressed up fancy, I thought the day would never end. Charity had finally talked Daddy into letting her cut my long braids and give me a permanent. With my new white patent leather pumps, and nylon stockings, too, I looked more grown up than ever, but I still felt on the outside of things.

The wedding dinner was in the back room of a restaurant, not at the big hotel downtown like Ellen Dunham had with the whole church there. Charity just invited the wedding party, the Baumns, and the minister. It was a bit ticklish, with Uncle Clarence married and Myrna engaged, but Daddy won out not having to pay for those two extra dinners. Daddy said, "Clarence's wife understands not being invited, and I don't care none about Myrna's boyfriend." Charity thought he should pay for them, but Daddy would not budge when it came to money.

Charity had worked awhile as a legal secretary and saved her money to have real pictures in a studio, up Wisconsin Avenue.

The reception that night, upstairs of the church, was what dragged on, with Charity and Daddy opening their wedding presents, ooh-ing and ah-ing over all of them, and there were so many. Even people who couldn't come sent presents. Charity wasn't much for show, you could tell. She said she'd much rather open them at home, like most other people did, but our church always did it that way. We didn't have any dancing or drinking, you know, so they had to do *something*. Daddy was thrilled, though, with everything going on, except the wedding cake. He pretty nearly choked on that, everyone watching and their feeding each other for someone's flash camera.

My insides was hankering for excitement, had been ever since I could remember. The Stadtz twin girls hadn't come, or any of their family, just their old fogy parents. My only friend that Daddy allowed over, Beth LeMay, didn't come either — not that it mattered since she wasn't much of a friend. She was a spoiled brat and thought she was better than I was, with her long, honey hair that she wore down so she could comb it over and over. Besides getting to go to ball games, she could swim in a real bathing suit. Beth could wear shorts and playsuits and blue jeans, too. She and her daddy visited different churches, and he worked at the brewery. Daddy didn't look too kindly on either one. He said a body should settle down and become a member of the flock and pay your tithes there. Even though the brewery paid good, Daddy thought it wasn't any place for a Christian to work – oiling the Devil's bandwagon. But being both with little girls like Beth and me to look after, they stayed friends.

From the start, I was awful uneasy around Beth, ever since that time when we were little. I hated her really, and I dreaded having to play with her. But I never dared let on to Daddy. Even though we never did do it any more, I just dreaded having to play with her. Trying to keep her mind away from it, I had to tiptoe around. She *loved* doing it, she said, even by herself. It made me want to throw up thinking about it, just like then, it tasted so awful. I never let on to her how good it felt, though. All my life I worried she'd tell. "Queer, sure as shootin." is what people would say. And Daddy just about catching us, his lip twitching so when he walked in, I figured surely he knew. Then Beth's dad came. Trailing right behind, head and shoulders way up there, and said for us to get ready: he was going to get us that big rainbow cone with all the colors. That's when I got sick, after the ice-cream. Daddy must've forgotten then, with me vomiting all over. It seems every time I was around Beth I felt the same sick-at-my-stomach, so I was glad she hadn't shown up at the wedding. Bob, her daddy, was there and brought his new girlfriend.

Maureen and Marilee had stayed home with their three baby brothers, all a year apart. I loved changing their diapers. Daddy didn't like me lifting big heavy babies, like she and Marilee did. But Maureen would sneak and let me every chance we could get. Their having baby brothers, when my brother and sister had died, made me so full of envy. I knew I sinned, always wishing so hard they'd be mine. "Thou shalt not envy" was one of the ten commandments. But I learned how to put a pin into my finger, instead of the baby, very quickly, anyhow. Leaving there, when Mama died, that big house full of younguns — Grandma's three girls besides – left me mighty lonesome.

Boys, though, were what was exciting. Any age. I wasn't allowed to speak to one, ever. If I saw one from my class on the street I had to turn away, fast, before they could speak to me, or I'd have to explain. Over at the Stadtz house, there seemed to be boys, of some kind, always.

The Stadtz twins were fifteen, and in the middle of a big huge family, so their folks never paid them any mind: so many kids hanging around. I'd started going over there on the bus Sunday afternoons, after Daddy began visiting Charity. Since the Stadtz's were church folks, Daddy never bothered checking on me. He didn't know the twins had an attic bedroom that could only be gotten to through a hole in the kitchen ceiling, up a ladder their folks were too old to climb. Their bedroom window had a big huge tree outside of it, making it pretty convenient for the boys. I had not been asked up there yet. The day I was, I knew I'd *be* somebody, like Donna and Doris Stadtz – identical in their dirty dishwater hair, cut off way short like a boy, worldly — the most popular girls in the church.

They were a little mean to me though, laughing at me all the time, but I had no one else to tell me things. And after I heard that sometimes Jamie Krause rode over on his motorcycle, I couldn't be there enough. I'd started liking Jamie before I went to Magnolia. All that while I couldn't wait to get back to Milwaukee to see him. (Paul Newman, in the movies I saw when I grew up, looked just like Jamie.) He'd grown considerably, but he was still shy. I'd catch him looking at me sometimes with those clear blue eyes, especially lately, since I got my hair cut. If Daddy wasn't so strict, and I wasn't so young, I knew Jamie would have liked me. He played trombone in the church orchestra, and I managed usually to sit on the second row so I could see him good. I was always hoping he'd show up with Huey some Sunday night. So you see I *had* to be friends with the twins.

Donna and Doris loved telling dirty jokes. One Sunday afternoon they read out a list of questions, simple ones, like, "How many times a week do you brush your teeth?" Then after you wrote out your answers, they turned the paper over and read a different set of questions, and you had to read out your set of answers. It turned out I was supposed to *do it* fourteen times a week. I laughed along with them, but they started poking fun at me telling me I didn't even know what I was laughing at, being as I was "just a child without no hair down there."

"Uh huh," I argued, "I have so got *lotta* hair there."

"You dummy," one of them said. "Don't you know you're supposed to *shave* down there, same as your arms and legs, and armpits?"

Now *that* was news to me. And since I never had disobeyed my daddy and shaved anywhere, I was feeling pretty embarrassed at my ignorance. So I hurried home and snuck into Mr. Ridell's bathroom and got his razor. I wouldn't have dared take Daddy's, but Mr. Ridell was so nice. He was the one who taught me to always say *Good morning*; no one else in the house bothered to speak. So I took a chance with his razor.

I couldn't wait to tell the girls in church what I'd done. That night, I caught them in the ladies' room and they both covered their mouth and giggled. I knew right then something was wrong. They were surely laughing at me, again, and I had no idea what for — but I soon found out.

All summer, waiting for my sick time, I'd been wearing a sanitary belt and pad (like they told me) for the thick, black pasty stuff that kept showing. They said I was about to *start* any minute now, and if I wasn't wearing something, I'd be mighty embarrassed. They told me serious as church, so of course, I did like they said.

Oh, it was an awful summer. It was the first time in my life I was glad I wasn't allowed to wear a swimming suit, or shorts, or slacks like everyone else. Then when the itchy hair started growing back in; well, you can't believe how uncomfortable it was, not to mention how awful it looked, my lankiness accentuating the protruding pelvic bone that already showed in my skinny skirts. I finally did get the message, though, and stopped wearing the pad. It looked like they'd been funning me all along. Still, I couldn't understand why; that's what really hurt.

Upstairs at the wedding reception, there was still a whole lot of wedding presents to open, and I asked Daddy to be excused. The bathroom was down in the back of the church. The lights over the piano and organ were lit, up front, so I hightailed it up there. Some kids were running around playing tag in between the seats. Horace Dolan (the kids called him Rolly-polly, only I wouldn't *never*) was slid down in one, sneaking a comic book. It was a sin to read comics, you know, and when the shoe clerks gave them out I had to refuse them and say, "No thank you; I read the Bible." I don't know how Horace got around his daddy, Mr. Dolan, being the Sunday School Superintendent. I would sure never take a chance like that to sneak a read *anywhere,* especially not in church. Daddy was right, boys *were* shameful sometimes.

Horace liked me, though, everyone said, since we were little. He acted like it, too. At summer Bible school he'd chase me, stick his tongue out at me, and pull my hair. But he was my own age and not very interesting. Since he was here, though, and he played trumpet in the orchestra, I felt better playing the organ, like it was *for* somebody. I'd watched the organist very closely the night before at rehearsal.

The sound of that organ was better than any piano ever. I knew I would have one someday, right in my living room – just like Arlene Krause, our church pianist. She was Jamie's sister-in-law. She'd invited Daddy and me over to her house once so I could play her Hammond. I'd really fixed it up as an excuse, though, for Daddy to get acquainted with her sister, June, who lived with Arlene. They both had the lightest hair you ever did see. Pure towheaded. Some said it was *too* light to be natural, but I asked right out if they bleached it. They both laughed, and June said, "No, it's pure German."

June was Daddy's age, real short and extra big busted. She sang like an opera singer for church specials. The boys always made fun of her voice and her bust. They'd stick their fists inside their shirts and push them way far out and sing high soprano, real shaky silly, the latest popular song on the radio, *June is busting out all o-o-ver.*[9] I'd try to keep a sober face, but I was so embarrassed because I liked June. She was nice and fun, besides her being sort of related to Jamie. She'd giggle with me in church right during the preaching – when Daddy'd let me sit with her. She liked Daddy, too, I could tell, but it never did her any good.

Horace Dolan kept looking at his comic book, acting like I wasn't even there at the organ. But I knew he was listening. He had on this silly deaf face and never did turn another page after I sat down. I was playing by ear, feeling for the right notes. I never looked at the keys, or I'd mess up. Pretty soon all the kids were gathered around, watching, asking me to play different songs: *In The Garden* and *The Old Rugged Cross*.

Then Daddy came down the stairs and all the way up to the front. He got hold of me by the arm. Daddy took one look at Horace almost catching him with his comic book, and the nerve in Daddy's lip started jumping. In my ear, he said, "Get yourself back up them stairs and stay put." Leading me back up the aisle, just as we were next to Horace, Daddy took a hunk of skin and twisted it, like he did to me when I was little and got rambunctious in church service. "I'll tend to you later." he whispered.

Horace didn't hear or see anything, but I felt it. I knew I'd have a bruise, it hurt so; inside it hurt too, especially since I had no idea what I had done.

Going up into the reception room, I felt the tears welling up behind my eyes, and my throat ached from holding them back. But I put on my smile-face. That was the best way of helping Daddy to forget to punish me later. I hated lickings; they hurt and left such embarrassing marks all over me that I'd have to wear long sleeved sweaters, even in summer.

We were on our way, in a taxi, to what Charity called The Honeymoon Cottage. It was a house in the ritzy suburb of Wauwatosa, whose family was going on vacation and needed someone to stay in it. Two weeks was just the amount of time we needed until the basement flat Daddy rented, on Cherry Lane, would be ready for us to move into. I'd begged Daddy to let me stay on at Jodi's till then, but, as usual, he said *No*. We had our suitcases packed for a nice stay, and since I didn't know what to expect, it felt just like it usually did when we moved: Daddy

---

[9]From *Carousal*, the Rodgers & Hammerstein Broadway Musical, 1945

would find us someplace, pack the car, and *then* tell me about it; he said I asked too many questions otherwise.

Charity's wedding dress took up half the back seat, so I had to sit in the front. It was a beautiful warm night, and the stars in the sky reminded me of when I was little. Sometimes I'd fall asleep in the car looking at them, but Daddy didn't mind. He'd carry me in and put me to bed, and I'd wake up never remembering how I'd gotten there. Daddy had my complete trust then. He was my whole world and there was nothing he couldn't do or fix. He always knew I had a spot for a hamburger or ice cream. His lunch box never came home empty, always a Baby Ruth, or some candy bar in it I liked. It never failed. I'd be there right when he got home, too. He'd get mad if I wasn't, so I always was. No matter what I was doing, or where I was playing, I'd stop and run home to hug his neck and give him a hello-kiss — until we moved to Ridell's.

Since we came back from Magnolia, Daddy had tried different jobs. But when he decided to get married, he told me he was going to stay at the motor factory. He tried working at the slaughter house doing the stabbing of the animals, since he was a farm boy and knew how just right. He did do all right, till he got to the sheep. "The other animals kicked up a fuss, but the sheep, they only stood still," Daddy said. All he could think about was Jesus and how in the Bible it said he stood silent before his accusers – like the sheep. Two weeks was all Daddy lasted there. Then he got a night job at a meat packing plant. But he couldn't sleep days. It was too light and he got sick headaches. That didn't last either.

Money was something Daddy never discussed. I never dared ask what he paid for anything. It was "rude and nobody's business," and I certainly never knew what he earned. But I did know one thing, Daddy didn't part with his money easily, then, only for his belly. I think it was because he was so poor as a boy, not having meat very much — beans mostly – sometimes only getting a single orange for a Christmas present. "Don't go much for such fussing, anyhow," he'd say, and that "Christmas was made up by man, not God." So I never got many presents either. I usually watched the family I was living with trim the tree and put out all their gifts. Oh, I got one or two, for sure. But I was always on the outside, it seemed — like in the taxi, the two of them in the back seat, together.

It was strange having someone else there. Charity was so quiet, she made Daddy, who was for sure quiet, sound like a real talker. The hum of the motor and the sound of them breathing let me fall off to sleep. The last thing I remember was crossing over the viaduct, towards Wauwatosa.

The lights in the cab woke me with Daddy paying the fare. Charity was unlocking the house door and told me to not let the cat out till morning. My eyes were so sleepy, I hardly opened them to look at anything, even the covered canary. Charity pointed me to where I was to sleep, a narrow day bed in the den. The people didn't want me in their kid's rooms, afraid I'd snoop, but they didn't know me. I never touched anything anymore that wasn't mine, not since Mrs. Rupotski made us move for my changing her clock forward, teasing her grown daughter who was always late for her date. My dress came off easily, and I slid into bed in my slip. I was too tired to even open my suitcase; Charity didn't complain.

The big fuzzy cat crawled up on my feet, like animals usually did to me. I was thinking about Daddy and Charity in the bedroom and what they were supposed to be doing. I lay there listening real hard for something, I didn't know for what – but not knowing made me listen all the more. I remembered, then, the day I first heard about *that*. It was from Theresa Booker, in my fifth grade class, who lived across the street at the big house with all the younguns – one of Mrs. Heath's houses.

Bookers had a tire swing hung from their sycamore tree that drew kids from all over· Boys too· That's why Daddy stopped letting me go over there, but I walked back and forth to school with Theresa anyhow· She had to wear pigtails, just like I did, and hated them, too· It was my last year in Georgia· I'd just turned nine· How that came up was by my telling Theresa about the Hadley's baby girl dying·

Mr· and Mrs· Hadley lived upstairs of the chapel· Mr· Hadley was a roofer and gave Daddy extra jobs now and then to buy my shoes and things· They weren't Christians, not born again anyhow· Nominal Christians, was what Daddy called them, in name only; they smoked nasty cigarettes· Mrs· Hadley was nursing the baby, but Daddy said her milk was like sucking a sugar-tit: a piece of rag, twisted, with sugar inside, not any good· So the Hadley's got some goat's milk, but it didn't help, and after a few days, the baby died· I'd begged Daddy to let me go up and see the baby; I loved babies· But he kept saying it wasn't right to go in on them like that· But for some funny reason that Daddy didn't explain then, after the baby was dead, he asked me if I still wanted to see it. Of course, I was scared to see a *dead* baby, but I went anyhow.

Mrs. Hadley, skinny and frail, in only a bathrobe (I didn't see anyone undressed much) was sitting on the floor next to the cradle, just looking. I slipped over by her and looked too. The baby's eyes were half open, and I wondered why nobody had put pennies on them yet. Daddy always told me that's what they did to dead people (or maybe he said it just to keep me from putting money into my mouth). It was so dark in the room I couldn't see very good. The baby felt too still and not warm. From the way Mrs. Hadley stared, I could tell she wasn't believing her baby was really dead. She had that hanging-on look, like I'd remembered feeling for years about Mama. And I remembered what everyone always said to me, "Your mama's with Jesus." So I whispered that to Mrs. Hadley.

"She's already with Jesus, ain't she? All babies go to Jesus, you know, *no matter what.*"

Mrs. Hadley looked hard at me, and then she started crying. Daddy called me out, right then, to leave. That night, the ambulance finally did come for the baby. Later on, I heard Daddy tell someone: "Sometimes children can say things just right." I didn't really know what I'd said, but I was telling Theresa all about it the next day.

"You know Mr. Hadley, the roofer... upstairs from us? Well, his brand new baby just home from the hospital... it got sick and it died... and Miz Hadley wouldn't let nobody come and get it and take it to the funeral or *anything.* So my daddy, he took me up there. Thought it might help some, I guess. It still had its eyes open a little, like it could see. Boy! It was *funny* lookin'."

"Well... did you *touch* it?" Theresa asked, really interested now.

"Sure did. I touched it, all right, but just for a minute. Miz Hadley didn't want me to, I could tell." Then I told Theresa, "I cain't wait till I have a baby some day."

Then's when Theresa let me have it. "Well... you *know* how babies get borned, don't you?"

"Sure I do," I said, poking myself in my tummy.

"Yeh-yah," Theresa had a real southern drawl, "but

it's how it gets there. Do you know that?"

Now, that was easy enough. I said, "'Course. God puts the seed there, and it just grows."

Theresa laughed so hard she bent over, "See there, I knew you didn't know. It gets there in wa-ter, from where you go to the bathroom. The daddy squirts it up there."

Well, I didn't believe any such thing. "From water?" I repeated it, to make sure I'd heard right.

"Uh huh... from water," she said again, real certain.

"I don't believe no such of a thing," I told her for the second time.

"Oh, yes. I know it's true, 'cause my Cousin Amy told me. And she's bi-ig; she's in high school."

"Well," I told Theresa, "I'm going to ask my Cousin Essie. She'll tell me the truth, not some fool story."

Then Theresa let me have the big part. "And it comes out at the same place it gets in."

"No... Uh uh-h, it don't," I insisted. This I knew for sure. "It comes out through your belly button. The same place God puts the seed in. Whilst you was asleep."

But Theresa said, "Them is just stories they tell little kids. Like Mother Goose, and all that."

I couldn't get over to Cousin Essie's cottage, behind the chapel, fast enough.

Cousin Essie was the daughter of Cousin Myrtle, one of our "cornfield relations," Grandma called them, back home in Milwaukee, the one who took us away from Grandma Evermardt's quiet Missionary Alliance church. Cousin Myrtle was a bit fat. The metal divider between two seats, in the second row of church, had to come out for her body to fit. Even though Grandma didn't claim any of them as kin, Daddy made me address Essie as Cousin.

When I told Cousin Essie what Theresa had just told me, well, let me tell you, Cousin Essie's eyes got big as saucers. When I asked her to tell me the truth, she made me sit down on the side of her bed and commenced to tell me all about her and Cousin Jed, her husband.

Cousin Essie was pretty tall and skinny and had real long dark hair she plaited and put up over the top of her head, straight up there, high, like a queen's crown. She had pretty blue eyes. Even though her teeth stuck out in the

front, could she ever sing, and yodel too, as good as any
cowboy·

Jed was even taller than Essie; when they sang, he
strummed the guitar· He was too shy to try to sing·
They'd do a duet together for night church, her singing and
Jed strumming· One thing funny about Jed, he had the
biggest Adam's apple you ever did see· And he was so shy
that if you looked at him straight on, he'd turn pink in the
face· He'd swallow, a big gulp, and then you'd see what
looked like a golf ball sliding down his throat·

Essie and Jed were so proud of each other, not having
any kids to fuss over, it was fun to watch them together·
But I especially loved listening to them· Essie had a beat to
her singing and wasn't shy a bit with her voice· She belted
it right out as good as any Ol' Opera woman I've heard
since, so I put a lot of store by her·

Now mind you, I never once doubted her; I was just
too overcome· Cousin Essie even got out the tube of jelly
they used, "Cause I'm so small," she said· "But there's no
cause to think you'll ever have to use anything like this,
Samantha Sue· Some people are just built that way· Doctor
says I might never be able to have children·" Her eyes
looked far away· "I'm so glad you come to me· You're
daddy might not be so comfortable in talking about such
things·"

"My *daddy?*" I asked, shocked stupid· "Does my daddy
know about this stuff?"

Essie laughed, then, and asked me how I thought I got
born? Oh my, I thought I was going to fall out right there·
But Essie kept talking on and on, just like her mama used
to· Cousin Myrtle loved talking about hush-hush things
better than anything·

Junior was a mean little runt then, but he grew up
taller than his big sister, Essie· I'd just about forgotten all
of that, and the bad ugly feelings Junior always gave me,
till Cousin Essie's talk·

For a week after that, I lost all my taste for food·
Daddy thought I had the flu, because when I ate, it'd come
right back up· Maybe so· All I know, the whole world looked
different from then on· I stopped liking Cousin Essie, and
her mama· I thought Grandma Evermardt was right: "white

trash and no kin of mine·" Not to mention how embarrassed I was to even look in Jed's direction· I was sure he'd of just died had he known his wife had told me all of that stuff· But looking at where my baby was going to come out, though, was what I just couldn't believe·

And Daddy – he and Mama. *She was pregnant and Daddy did it.* And now, he and Charity in the bedroom. It was just too much to think about anymore, and I fell asleep.

In my dream, a boy fairy, looking a lot like Huey Schultz, with blonde curly hair and clear blue eyes, with wings that flapped, had a big fat hose like a fire engine's hooked to him between his legs. He was squirting me up close in my lap, and I was soaking wet. I must've rolled over, and the street light woke me. The dream was so real, it left me feeling funny since me and Huey were still not speaking when we played our music together on Sunday evenings.

The water in the dream made me feel like I needed to use the bathroom. In the dark, I found my way. The light hurt my eyes so I would keep them shut. Sitting there on the commode, I was falling back asleep like I always did when I went in the night. My new white wedding slip was bunched up in my hands and it felt damp. When I looked, the slip was all full of red blood. Soaked. Blood was all over my legs, panties soaked clear through besides. I just sat there, feeling bewildered. *What in the world is happening to me? I must have a rupture inside of me causing me to bleed like this — like the rupture inside of Mama, they said, that made her die.* Finally, I got myself together and knocked on the bedroom door.

It was Charity, I asked for. But she was so sound asleep, it was hard getting her awake. "I need some help, quick," I hollered through their closed door. She came out then, rubbing her eyes. When she took one look at me, she said in her sleepy voice, "Oh. It looks like you've gotten your sick time, I mean your *menstrual* period."

"My period?" I shrieked. "You mean, the *curse*?"

"Your menstrual period," she said again. "If you think of it in a negative way, it will be a negative thing, when it really is just a natural thing that happens to a woman every month."

Charity fixed me up a makeshift pad till we could get to the store the next day. That night I sunk into a sleep so sound – as though I hadn't slept in a year. For the next few days, I slept, and changed my pad every hour I was awake. Charity complained I was wasting money, especially since I was having to use store-bought pads until she said her "ma could make us some free from old rags and mattress stuffing she'd saved." But I had to keep looking to make sure I really was a woman. The whole two weeks all I thought about was finally being able to tell Donna and Doris.

At the Baumn's house, it wasn't exactly a good night's sleep, the three of us all in a bed: Daddy, Charity and me, but it was a place to lay our head. Daddy said it'd do for one night. The next day, the most important day of my life up till then, kept me excited. I was going into my very own house, and us a family, what I'd always dreamed about since Mama died.

Mrs. Baumn let us have her bed squashed back up in the corner of their tiny bedroom. She took Charity's old cot, and Mr. Baumn must've taken the floor. I didn't really go in there. I was too tired from the long day at the Science Museum in Chicago. First dropping off our suitcases and then catching the North Shore at the train station, downtown.

After I'd confided in Charity and told her all about Cousin Essie and her mama, and about the Stadtz twins, she figured it was only right I should see the clear plastic manikin with a baby in its tummy. Even though it was only plastic, it still was a little embarrassing to look at, way up on that shelf in the middle of the place. Then Charity had to explain *everything,* out loud, about all the fetuses in embalming fluid kept just like they were when they were miscarried. People turned around to listen, like on a tour. It was so unusual to be talking about at all – much less in public. I *was* interested, but wished I could hide, Daddy and Charity holding hands besides.

The trip came about with me telling her so much. With her interest in everything I had to say those first days together, I told her just about my whole life – except the really *bad* things. The Stadtz twins were already off my visiting list since I'd told her about them. But since Jamie'd *had* to get married, and then to a girl he hardly knew, I'd lost my real reason to be over there anyway. I didn't want them to see my hurt at what Jamie'd done. I was afraid I couldn't hide it if they talked about it, and you knew they would. So it didn't bother me too awful much that the twins were put into the *white trash* category, along with Cousin Essie and her mama. I was beginning to see just a little why no one told their mothers *everything,* but I was beginning to like thinking of Charity as my friend; she hadn't passed over that line as yet into being mother – the enemy. To me, I didn't see how she ever could. Mothers were that something special: the good fairy and the perfect female goddess, all rolled into one. Her opinion grew more important to me everyday.

All in all the honeymoon went by fast with all the new things cropping up. One day at the Washington Park lagoon they let me take my own rowboat. Daddy never took his eyes off of me. You'd think since I looked so much older than eleven going on twelve (some even said I looked fifteen already), that he'd trust me more, not less. Since Ridell's, he was more strict than ever about knowing where I was every minute.

Going to *Highland Fundamental* Sunday nights, Charity's church, as Daddy'd promised, made it even worse. The young people's meeting there was filled with teenaged boys who made my heart beat so fast I couldn't hear the preaching. The boys (Charity called them "fellahs") sang and talked right up about God and being a witness at school, in the *Youth For Christ* club called *Hi-C*. They were different than at *Holy Ghost*. I told Charity in secret that I was excited to find out about such boys. Different than Jamie and Huey who just came to our church because they had to.

Lately, Huey, who was a year younger than Jamie, and much lighter haired and shorter, had started watching me with those same clear blue eyes that I had fallen for in Jamie. Huey's coming early to young peoples' nearly every Sunday night, playing his saxophone along with me, had put my insides into a turmoil of late — even though we never spoke a word, we just played together. With his eyes closed, he'd follow on his horn whatever I'd start: *Do Lord,* or *Peace in the Valley,* songs like that I knew by ear. He liked that. But I saw how he smoked cigarettes, outside. Donna and Doris said that he and Jamie drank beer, too, coming drunk to their house a lot of times. You knew just by seeing them they were a whole different sort than at *Highland.* But right away Daddy let me know he didn't like it *any*, my going up there to *Highland,* to "the modernists." But he was stuck for the time being, his being such a newlywed, to come right out and say *No* already. But one of these days, I knew it was coming. Meantime, I couldn't really miss having a good time Sunday nights. One way or other, I was finally around some *boys* without Daddy knowing about it.

The last night of the honeymoon, sleeping together edgeways in the bed, was mighty peculiar. First place, Daddy had on new pajamas. "Never had on a pair in my life before," he said. He always slept in his skinny underwear, but I never, in all my life, saw him undress. This he was particular about. He dressed out of my sight somehow, mostly in the closet, then he'd come out in the dark and get right into bed. Seeing him in pajamas got me tickled. We were giggling, getting our legs all stretched and dangling over the side, Daddy and me on each end, Charity in the middle. It reminded me of Grandmaw Tuckermoore's funeral. I had to tell Charity all about it. While Daddy fell asleep, she listened pretty interested.

It was during school, first grade. I remember coming home for lunch, turning the corner, and seeing Daddy's car sitting in the driveway. My heart literally froze wondering what I had done, it must be the end of the world. When I found my new Easter bonnet — with navy grosgrain ribbon that hung down my back - laid on the bed next to a suitcase half filled with my clothes, with great relief, I went squealing into the bathroom where Daddy was washing up. When he turned to me, I saw the sadness in his red eyes, as if he'd been crying. Daddy still cried a lot then. "Grandmaw Tuckermoore just died," he said, very quietly, "and we're going to the funeral."

I tried to keep my excitement still, while I got into the tub of hot water Mrs. Simms had heated special in the middle of the week. We didn't have an automatic hot water heater, so Saturday was the only day the heater was regularly turned on.

"Aunt Maudie and Uncle Reevis don't have a bathroom. Remember? Just the well, so scrub yourself good," Daddy told me. But he did it again, anyhow. As usual, he nearly rubbed my neck and ears raw, trying to get the dark off from the sun. He never did believe it wasn't dirt.

The Greyhound bus was slower than the train, but it was all Daddy could afford. The cigar smoke curled into my nose, no matter how I sat or twisted. By the time I got to Tennessee, I was green sick.

The bus pulled up in front of the US Post Office, a small brick building, the only one in Hickory Hollow. They called it Holler. Cousin Agatha, fifteen and the oldest of nine, came along and met us there on her daddy's tractor. "This is the only riding piece we have," Uncle Reevis told us.

Agatha was a chubby girl, with one long braid down her

back· She took charge of me, swinging me on the tire hanging from the huge tree· She loved to sing, and while we swung on the porch swing, she sang out long and funny stories· One I really liked:

> On top of old smokey, all covered with snow
> I lost my true lover for courting too slow.
> For courting's a pleasure, but parting is grief
> And a false hearted lover is worse than a thief.
> A thief will just rob you and take what you have,
> but a false-hearted lover will lead to your grave.
> The grave will decay you and turn you to dust.
> Not a boy in a hundred a poor girl can trust.
> They'll hug you and kiss you and tell you more lies,
> than the ties on a railroad, or stars in the sky.
> So come ye young maidens and listen to me
> Ne'er place your affection in a green willow tree.
> For the leaves they will wither, the roots they will die.
> And you'll be forsaken and never know why.

Lucky for me Daddy wasn't around to overhear and put a stop to all the "devil's made-up lies·" Agatha took me to the outhouse so I'd know where it was, and showed me how to get a drink from the well with the bucket and dipper· Going around the barnyard and seeing the animals was interesting, especially the pigs, how they grunted in all that thick soupy mud clear up to their bellies· I tried milking a cow, but her funny *faucets* wouldn't work for me; I couldn't get a drop to come out, unlike Agatha, who got it to come out in a steady stream, right into my mouth· I had my first taste of clabber milk, like buttermilk – that's just plain sour milk filled with chunks of clabber – with day-old corn bread broke up into it· But mostly, Aunt Maudie's biscuits were the thing I liked the best, how she mixed them with her fingers, that, and her homemade pork sausage fried brown, with my eggs·

That night, us little ones slept four or five to a big iron-railed bed in the living room with our feet dangling· We giggled and twisted and sang, till the grownups hushed up all our nonsense· We hardly knew we were at a funeral – until the next day·

When Grandmaw was brought in, they put her into the living room, in front of the windows, with the coffin lid left open· By afternoon, all the Tuckermoore kin had come around, some sitting in rocking chairs, some on the side of the bed, there were so many· Eleven children in all, still living· One by one they commented on how *good* she looked·

"Not no grey hairs to speak of·"

"And still kept it curled·"

"They done a good job fixin' it·"

"Fat in the neck," said another, now that they knew about the goiter·

It was a hot, lazy afternoon with the sun shining through the white curtains right into our faces· I'd crawled up in the wicker rocker next to Daddy, listening, everyone jawing and staring into their memories·

I remembered little of Grandmaw, except her rocking and spitting from her chew· She was terribly good with her aim· She kept a can down in the floor under a carved out knothole· She'd rock forward and reach for the knot, pull up the can, spit while she rocked backwards, and then rock forward, putting the can back into the hole, never missing a beat to her rhythm or a word to her talking· That's all I remembered about her· She cussed a whole lot because she was mostly Cherokee, Aunt Jenny Lou said, and I happened to get some of it, with my straight black hair, dark skin, and high cheek bones· Daddy was a little ashamed of this though, and tried to make light of it· Instead, he'd brag about his mama being blue-eyed· "Wasn't enough Indian to worry about," he'd say, but I was proud and told everyone· I liked feeling part of *something·*

Mamaw dying in her sleep so suddenly had them all in turmoil· Snatches of conversation lulled me into a sleepy spell; I just couldn't keep my eyes open·

"...fat tumor size of a grapefruit·"

"...only fifty-five years old·"

"So young to be taken; cut off her air in her sleep·"

"Reckon she knew it was a-comin'?"

"If I'd've just known, she could've saw a doctor·" said Grandpap, through his waxed handlebar mustache and his smoking corncob pipe, "but she never said nary a word about it·"

"My, how she loved her chew· Clean about it though," someone else said·

Then I heard Daddy's voice, cracking from the sadness, saying, "She was a *good* woman· Gone to be with Jesus, I know·" He'd wipe his nose, and to fill up the silence, he'd say, "Bless the Lord·" After awhile, the soft talking all ran together with the sweet scent of perfume, letting me fall back into somewhere like it – deep in my memory, a memory I could not really see, only feel· Soon, I was sound asleep·

It was the quietness then, all around me, that shocked me awake· The Tennessee sun was going down through the far window· I looked around at all the empty chairs, and there was Grandmaw, big as life (only dead), still laid out in front of me with her hands folded over her, her lacy cuffs catching the stream of evening sunlight coming through the window· Startled, I jumped up out of the chair and ran to the door· It was shut tight, and I couldn't get it open· I pounded and screamed till Daddy heard me, and came running· Frantic, I was almost crazy with fright· Pulling at the door, the closest to cussing I ever heard him; the door was locked by my little cousins to be mean· They were scampering about, giggling, with Daddy pulling at the door in high temper· "If someone don't find me that key, here, right quick, I'll tear me this door down·"

The giggling stopped then· Agatha had to be out to the hog pen, or she would have had them all turned upside down for the key· The fear of Grandmaw lying there, and me alone, when Daddy slid the key into the lock and got me out, had my heart in my mouth· Daddy took me then to the front porch swing· Usually when I got scared senseless of bees or dogs, he got all over me for crying· Not this time, though, as he held me in his lap and took to swinging me, while I sobbed into his shirt·

"Well, here now, no need to be so scared· Just a piece of clay in there in that box; nothing at all that can hurt you· The spirit's gone to be with Jesus· Still – your cousins had no business locking you up that way· Them *boys*, tsk tsk·" How Daddy seemed to hate boys· "We're just guests in this house, though, so we can't complain any," he said, and kept swinging me· "We'll be leaving here tomorrow, anyway·"

His petting me, then, was so unusual, I never will

forget how surprised I was. It stuck out in my mind always, every time he'd whoop me with a hickory or his leather belt, leaving welts and bruises all over my backside, and sometimes my arms got in the way. (He was careful to never touch my face, though.) It was those warm feelings from the porch that day I took along with me that helped me to remember, Daddy did love me for sure, even when I was scared to death of him and hurting clean to my heart.

A couple days after we got back to the Simms house, in Milwaukee, I noticed all our bedding out on the back lawn, with Mr. Simms taking a blow torch to the metal coil springs. Mrs. Simms was tight lipped and kept on hanging out all the bedding and clothes she'd washed, even though it wasn't all dirty. I couldn't get anybody to tell me anything. When I'd ask questions Mr. Simms didn't want to answer, the one I depended upon the most, he'd say, "If anybody asks you, tell them you don't know."

Sheepishly, Daddy finally did tell me. "It seems we brought back some unwanted visitors in our suitcases from Aunt Maudie's house, from the blood on the bed sheets. Bed bugs is what they call them up here," Daddy said. "But we call them chinches back home. They live in the fields and can get into your bed and lay eggs. That's why Mr. Simms blowtorched the springs. Ha-ar-rd to get rid of. Tiny blood spots on the sheets tell you they're biting you. They suck your blood, you know. That's why you don't stay in no sleazy flop houses overnight. Guess Aunt Maudie wasn't very particular." I knew from the look on Daddy's face he was mighty embarrassed when he said, "Shu, that's what happens when people ain't clean; they collect varmints."

It was then, I think, in the back of my mind that I decided I was a Yankee — but I didn't tell Charity this part, about the bedbugs. She already thought badly enough about Cousin Essie and her mama being our kin. Anyhow, Charity was too quiet, I had talked so long. By the time I got the story out, the sound of her and Daddy's steady breathing let me know she was sleeping sound. No telling how much, or little, she heard.

Later on that night, the overhead lights came on, blazing brightly, and I awoke from a sound sleep. Daddy was out of bed, just coming back up from using the commode in the basement, and he had on different pajama bottoms. Charity was blinking, half awake and over on the end, in my place, and I was in the middle, next to Daddy. I asked her, "How in the world did I get *over here*?"

In her sleepy voice, she answered, "Because you kick and wiggle too much," and went right back to sleep.

Daddy was upset, I could tell. But I was too sleepy to figure it all out, so I fell back asleep, too.

The next day, Charity and her mother had run to the store for a couple things to take to our new house. Mr. Baumn was out doing his *gallivanting*, and Daddy got me aside, finally alone. His lip was twitching and his eyes blinking like I hadn't seen in a long time.

"What in the world is wrong, Daddy." I asked, scared to death of his ire when it got up, and no one around to put him off.

"I declare, Samantha Sue, you caused me so much *embarrassment* last night."

"Me? What did I do?"

"Why, you know what you *done,*" Daddy said, mad now for sure. "You *handled* me, for goodness sake. *Must* have, because I had a terrible accident. Had to get up and change. The Baumns knew I got up, too. Tsk tsk. How *humiliating.*"

Handled, did he say? Did he mean *touch* him? My head began thumping just thinking about it. I couldn't imagine myself touching anyone – not Junior, or even my baby cousins. When I diapered them, I was particularly careful *not* to touch their dooter, still frightened from Cousin Myrtle's warnings about touching, although I did a whole lot of serious looking whenever I could. So I knew Daddy made a mistake, but I was never allowed to question Daddy's word, even if I *knew* differently, or he'd think I was arguing and whoop me right there. This time I *knew* he had to be wrong, "But I was sleeping sound when the light came on and woke me up.," I said.

"Listen here, don't tell *me*. I had to go *change.*"

It was the accusing meanness in his voice that struck down deep inside of me, especially since I didn't understand what he was really talking about. Cousin Essie had left out the *water* part (Theresa's words), about nature's curious ways.

"Please, Daddy," I begged, in fearful tears. "Don't you know me well enough, to know I wouldn't *ever* do such a thing to you, or *anybody?*"

"All I know," he said then, with his eyes blinking fast in rage, "I woke up with you next to me, so you *must've* done it. That's all I know."

As much as I wanted to say: *But Charity put me over there, and maybe she did something* — just what, I couldn't for the life of me figure out. Never had I seen him so furious, maybe because he couldn't strap me with Charity and her mother due back any second. Somehow I knew Charity had let this happen, but I just couldn't let myself be put out with my new mother and spoil everything – as long as I'd waited. Instead, I shoved the anger and hurt away, back inside, with all the rest from my whole life. All those feelings had piled up, but I think it was that day that things started going really haywire in my head.

Oh, I never felt too good inside, *ever*. First Junior, then Beth. Then it was Marty Simms before he left for the Navy. I was so crazy about him, too. I'd giggle, hiding the ugly feelings he gave me, but loving his attention, feeling like a proud five-year-old to have such a *big* brother, even though Daddy had told me plainly, the very day we moved in, to be careful not to let *any* boy or man fool with me. But Marty *made* me disobey, and it worried me a whole lot.

That, and the way Daddy himself seemed to like to see me squirm whenever he'd wash me when I was little. He would pull the towel through my legs to dry me, and I'd giggle, trying to hide how ugly the towel touching me there made me feel. Daddy's face would color some, and he'd giggle himself. It got so I dreaded his coming into the bathroom for my baths. Until one day, in Georgia, I was about nine when Daddy got a little extra carried away with the towel and gave it a hard jerk. It caught me just right and smarted as it came through my legs. I jumped and grabbed myself, squealing, "Ouch, Daddy, that *hurts*," I said, as I fought the smarting tears that came to my eyes.

Daddy stopped giggling, and as he stomped out of the bathroom, he threw the towel at me. "Here, dry your own self. You're too big a girl for me to be coming in here like this, anyway," he said in his mean voice, and slammed the door.

Then, and for the first time that I can remember, the tears poured down my cheeks, like there was a barrel full inside of me. I just couldn't hold them back that day. Holding myself and hugging my bare naked chest, I hated my being a girl. That must have been when I started slouching so badly, trying to hide my body from the world. Because of my being a girl, Daddy wouldn't cuddle with me or even hug me very much after that.

All of these ugly memories, together with Ridell's penned up friendly pup, when, as a ten-year-old, I'd squat down to feed him through the bars and not push away his warm persistent nose, put me to shame. Having feelings in those parts, same as with Beth, convinced me I was the worst awful sinner in the world.

Charity's opinion towards *white trash* kept me from ever talking about any of it, afraid she'd think me trash, too, and blame *me* for it all. Daddy was good at that, turning the tables on me for any tangles I got into at school. Now this. *Was I really to blame, and in my sleep, no less?* I just didn't know who I was or what I was turning out to be. What I did know, I wanted to shake loose of my life and find me another one. And someday, *somehow*, I would.

There, at the Baumns' house, the last day of the honeymoon, things in my life took a whole different turn. From then on, I began showing my intense, angry feelings for Daddy that I'd kept hidden for so very long. Now that I had a mother, I could.

◆

CHAPTER NINE

Huey: 1950-1952

As I turned into the alley that cut across to Cherry Lane, the other alley we lived on, I had a feeling of dread. Of course it was a common feeling — dreading to go home – a feeling I had thought would ease up some when Daddy and Charity got married. But then I put too much store in motherhood, I guess, a misconception my new friend, Muriel Plummer, had tried continually to undo. Coming back at me after a particularly dogmatic statement I'd made quoting *my mother* — a term I had begun using since my little sister, Marcy, was born – Muriel, a year older than I and ahead of me in high school, would say, "Your *mo-ther* doesn't know *every* damn thing."

Muriel's language was what shocked me the most, since I was not allowed to use any slang whatsoever, not even darn, or golly, or gee whiz. But, in a way, Muriel's way of speaking pleased me, thinking how surprised Daddy would be to know his Christian landlord's granddaughter, members of the *German Pentecostal* around the corner — the one new friend, besides Beth, that he approved of – was so adept at keeping hid all her many sins. The two-faced fanaticism (Charity's words) prevalent in our religious circle had already begun to gall me. Every time I turned around, I'd hear something awful about a respected Christian. The minister that had married Daddy and Mama at Grandma Evermardt's *Missionary Alliance* church, Reverend Cunningham, nearly an old man, was caught molesting a teenaged boy in his study and fired. Then Missionary Mueller, who had come to Georgia and taken Edna off to the mission field, we heard, had been kicked out of the *Wyoming Hills Bible School* prior to that for showing her bare breast to a young female student in a seductive way. Daddy's hypocrisy was just as disgusting to me. Charity's outward perfection and high standards she had set for herself, although a good example for me, seemed lost all too often in her harsh, critical words that would cut me in two. So underneath, Muriel had an edge I was hesitant to admit to, when she would dig my *mother* at every opportunity.

Muriel, although attending the same kind of church as I, did all the things we were not supposed to do: She went to movies, danced in the gym during school lunch hours, drank when she could, and smoked regularly. She convinced me to take a puff one day in the bowling alley bathroom. After choking, more on my fear of getting caught than anything (Daddy had a super human smeller), I swore to *never* take up that awful tasting stuff. Being inside a bowling alley was, in itself, a daring thing, but Muriel would manage to think up numerous approved outings for us to cover all our escapades.

Saturdays we went shopping after my housework was finished. Muriel was an adored only child and her mother required little of her. Mrs. Plummer took to me from the beginning, encouraging me in cooking as I watched her delicate struggle with the strudel dough that would cover her kitchen table. She was impressed with my sewing ability and even gave me her old treadle Singer. I liked her, too, and when I went to the Plummers' house it was hard for Muriel to get a word in between us. Muriel never had to take any static from her mom about our friendship.

On Sundays, Muriel and I would take bus rides all over, sometimes ending up at Washington Park lagoon for a rowboat ride. Mainly we were looking for boys. If Muriel found one, we'd go to his house and I'd sit on the porch by myself and wait, day dreaming about being with Huey. He had been writing me notes at church for over a year. Tonight I had walked out of the house following that terrible whipping.

Tomorrow was the Brewers' season opening, and school would let us out for the game if we had a note from home. Milwaukee was baseball crazy, and even though the Brewers were just an amateur team then, it was the only one we had. Muriel, like her dad, loved baseball and knew every vital statistic about every player. Her dad had volunteered to take a car load of girls to the game, and since they were also Pentecostal, I felt certain this time Daddy would let me go.

But some things never change, and Daddy's opposition to *worldly doings* was as strong as the belt he laid across my front as I spouted out my anger at his unfairness, making me sit in study hall with maybe two or three other kids who were, like I was, too scared to skip. The sting of Daddy's belt made me jump up, letting the books fall to the floor as the wide leather belt came across my barely budding *flat* chest, as Charity so cruelly described it. I ran from the room with Daddy coming after me, fury blinking in his eyes, "What do you *mean* talking to me that way?" he spewed at me with his arms raising blow after blow across my back. My tears finally stopped him as I held myself in stinging pain, fearing my breasts were stunted for life now for sure.

In anger, I grabbed my purse and jacket and fled from the house, down the alley — a daring first for me – with Daddy running behind.

"Just where do you think you are going, young lady?" he yelled, a few feet from the front door. I had run a good ways and was prepared to run further if he had continued.

In defiance and pure hatred, I turned around to him and said, "I'm going to the police station and show them my bruises, ones I've still got from *last* week."

Muriel would have been proud of me. The anger had boiled over so many times of late, usually in a three-way tangle between Daddy and Charity, with me taking Charity's side no matter *what* the disagreement was. Her going back to work since Marcy was born left him wide open for disgruntlement continuously. He didn't want no mother-in-law tending *his* kids, he said, and I dearly loved my new Grandma Baumn. She had become my other friend, besides Muriel, making me even more determined in my opposition. When Daddy turned around and went back into the house, I knew I'd won. But it did not quell the storm inside, so I walked.

And I walked, and I walked, all the while my nose running, my eyes so blurred from the tears, I hardly paid attention which way I was headed. When I looked up and saw the White Tower Hamburgers' sign on 35th and Burleigh, nearly three miles from our house, I realized I'd been unconsciously going home — to the Simmses – to the only place I knew of where I was somebody who counted. I knew Mr. Simms would come and get me if he wasn't working, his hours so varied I never knew. I went to the pay telephone to call him. On the spur of the moment I thought of Huey and all the notes he'd sent to me at church, through his nineteen-year-old sister, Bernice. She passed them to me under the toilet stalls in the ladies' room so nobody would see and blab, especially Karen, who told her righteous mother everything, who would then say – *the Lord led her* to tell your parents. I was only thirteen, a sight away from twenty-one when Daddy'd said I could finally date. I didn't dare ask him to change it; he'd just say no and watch me more closely.

Huey, three years older than I, had begged me in his notes to call *him*, since we didn't have a phone, but I never had. Charity told me, continuously, how bad mannered it was for a girl to chase a boy; it showed her to be without any self-respect. But now the idea seemed rather appropriate in my anger.

Thirty minutes later I was sitting in Huey's jalopy under some bridge out at the edge of town, with two other couples in the back seat: boys drinking beer and the girls drinking "Dago-red." I refused the wine, of course, and stared out the window, scared of what lay ahead but determined it could not compare to what lay behind.

It was dusk, and the April breeze was blowing the tall weeds in the field. By summer, it would be covered with black-eyed-Susans — what a lot of people called me. I looked up at the bridge that shielded us from the cops' view, and as I glanced at the field again, I realized where I was. "Is that Highway 100 up there?" I asked.

Murmurs in the car agreed.

Huey asked, "Why? Something wrong?"

He must've seen the startled look on my face when one of the girls in the back seat continued, "Yeah, this used to be a cemetery, Rest Haven, I think. But nobody uses it anymore; it's all grown up."

"Yeah, I know," I answered quietly. "My mother and baby sister and brother are all buried – right over there."

Huey started the engine as quietly as he could with his dual pipes sputtering in the night. They dropped their cans and bottles out the windows as we eased out of the field and onto the highway, back to my neighborhood.

We drove past Muriel's church where I asked to be let out. They had a teenage evangelist there all week and Muriel and her other girlfriends from *Hi-C* club had not missed a night. I was supposed to be going, too.

Huey stopped at the curb outside of the church and turned his motor off. He pulled me over to him, even closer than he had before. I was trembling, everyone watching us from the back, and I worried someone from church might come by and see us, even though it was about time for preaching to begin inside. Soon I heard the quiet sound of necking: murmurs, and hands and arms slipping and sliding, an occasional whispered protest from one of the girls, and I knew they were not interested in me. Huey put his left hand between my shaking knees as I pressed them shut. His other one was around my shoulder, rubbing my bare arm up and down. I had not been physically touched by anyone in so many years, other than a little pat by Grandma Baumn sometimes (Charity hated hugging from me, and Daddy seemed afraid to anymore) that Huey's gentleness made me yearn desperately for it. He brought his left hand up to my waistline then, polite and proper; I sighed in relief.

When he asked, "Can I kiss you?" (a sign of a well bred gentleman, to ask, according to Charity) I melted into his arms, into oblivion. His kisses were like honey and hot chocolate amidst the lingering odor of beer and cigarettes and Juicy Fruit gum. The warmth of his body crushing mine made me know this was what I had yearned for my whole life – to be loved and held, as well as respected. I could've stayed there forever. Now I knew what Muriel was talking about. It *was* heaven, but I knew I had to stop. I did not want to go *all the way* like she did. Charity's purity was a star I'd hitched my wagon to in my head. So I tore myself away from him – that haven of rest, like the one the song in church talked about that Huey and I practiced so often together before Sunday night Young People's. The song started running through my head as I walked towards the church.

> [10]My soul in sad exile was out on life's sea
> So burdened with sin and despair
> Then came a sweet voice, saying,
> Make me your choice
> And I entered the haven of rest.

The soft mellow sound of Huey's sax filled my head, along with the rest of the words:

> I've anchored my soul
> In the haven of rest
> I'll sail the wild seas no more...

With Huey's promise to pick me up from school soon, I floated through the door of the church and slid into the last pew filled with Muriel and her other girlfriends.

The young good looking sixteen-year-old from Texas was playing his guitar and singing *Peace In The Valley*. My heart was thumping so hard, I was sure he could even hear it way up on the platform. I had to tell Muriel all about Huey, so I wrote sketchy notes, but her attention was on Brother Buddy Doogan.

We sat through his fiery sermon, and his eyes kept coming to mine, keeping my nerves very taunt after such an explosive evening. I knew my face was in a flush, and was afraid my hair was a mess. With Brother Buddy's attention continually resting

---

[10] Lyrics to the hymn, *Haven of Rest* were written in 1889 by H. L. Gilmour and music by Geo D. Moore.

upon me rather noticeably, I felt elbows poking me, and Muriel passed a note, "He's eyeing *you!*" I couldn't even peek in my mirror to find out what in the world he was seeing. I didn't think I was special looking, so I must have looked a sight, I thought, sneakily wetting my finger and straightening my Vaselined eyebrows. I bit my lips to make them pink, the extent of my makeup, other than the plain loose face powder Charity approved of for the shine on my oily skin.

Brother Buddy's final exhortation to bring us all under conviction so we'd come forward was, "God said, *All* have sinned and come short of the glory of God." But none of us went forward until after the benediction. Then we bombarded him, one of the girls finagling a ride home for all of us.

Muriel's mother smiled and told us to be good.

Under her breath, Muriel answered, "We will, and if we can't be good, we'll be careful." And someone else added, "And if we can't be careful, we'll name it after you." We were all laughing as we piled into Brother Buddy's nice car he'd driven all over the country. We couldn't get enough questions out, wondering how he got out of school? And where he learned to play the guitar?

Sitting on a lap in the back seat, I could see his eyes in the mirror. He addressed one question to me, everyone silent and poking me and each other. "Where are you from?" he asked, the dreaded subject.

So many knew I was born in Tennessee, I couldn't lie, so I told him, but assured him I only lived there a short time before moving to Milwaukee.

"I *thought* you were a southern girl. How about that, a southern girl raised in the north." It was the first time anyone seemed delighted to hear I had southern beginnings.

At the corner near my house, I told him to stop. He asked me if I was coming back to church, which pleased me even though I was the first one to get out of the car. But I didn't give him a chance to say more, for fear he would ask which house I lived in.

There was so much happiness in me, I could hardly contain myself. I must have been grinning from ear to ear until I turned into the alley. Then the fear and dread fell upon me like a torrent of icy rain when I thought about Huey and his tender touching and kissing – and Daddy waiting for me at home.

There was a light on in the living room, over the chair I had been sitting in before I left, the only easy chair in there, given to us by Grandma Baumn. We'd gotten an upright piano, too, that took up most of the tiny room, besides the bookcase Charity prized from her childhood and the big old floor-style radio someone else had given us that kept me company when I baby-sat Marcy. Daddy would have had a fit if he knew I played the sinful radio, listening to the comedy of *Baby Snooks* and *Henry Aldrich* and to the dreamy music of Nat King Cole.

Daddy was on his knees by the chair when I went in. "I'm here, Daddy," I said, holding my breath.

He turned to me, then, tears bursting through his quietness. "I thought you were never going to come back," he said. "I've been praying for God to forgive me for striking you in anger... and now I need *your* forgiveness."

Somehow the anger I had felt towards him melted away at his tears and his softness, like it usually did. And, as always, I hugged him and told him, "I forgive you, Daddy."

I waited a minute, and he said nothing, just let the tears fall down his cheeks.

"I went for a long, long walk and ended up at Muriel's church," I said. It was close by, so I didn't have to lie about who'd brought me home. Telling half-truths, leaving things out, had become my way of easing my guilt and still stretching the rigid limits Daddy had put upon me. Tonight, though, had been the first really daring thing I had done.

As I undressed and combed my long hair into its pageboy setting, I told myself I had stayed a *good girl* – and let Huey know it.

I closed my eyes as I rested my head carefully onto the pillow, so as not to mess up my hair. It would be pressed, smooth as a curler setting, by morning, turning at least once in the night to press the other side as well. I don't know when I stopped all that wiggling in my sleep; now, instead, I slept still, like a doll, just like I finally had learned to sit in church.

Thinking about the whole night, and the subdued tone in Daddy's voice when he saw I had come home – after going to church, no less – I somehow knew I'd seen my last whipping. The butterflies in my middle churned away as I felt sleep overtake me, remembering the feel of Huey's arms about me. I was there, in the field, full of high, tall flowers waving in the breeze. I heard a voice — just like the one I'd heard often opening the *Henry Aldrich* show, calling, "Hen-ry. Oh, Henry *Ald*-rich!" Only this time, the voice was calling, "Sa-*man*-tha... Oh, Sa-man-tha *Sue*-oo..."

Then I felt myself running, slowly and effortlessly through the fields, with the wind blowing gently through my long, smoothly curved hair and the black spotted yellow flowers almost reaching my face, the soft, feathery feel of the tall, wispy grasses caressing my bare skin. And as Henry Aldrich always answered his mother, I called back – like an echo in the wind, *"Com - ming... Moth - ther!"*

I t was almost free, the studio photograph: an indelible memory of my last day of innocence. I begged Daddy persistently to let me get my picture taken and he finally agreed, if I'd pay the dollar out of my own money for the Easter special. Since he'd come to me often to borrow, he knew that I almost always had money – from my fifty-cents allowance and baby-sitting – hidden away.

The studio was on a bus line, as everything in Milwaukee was. I held my breath hoping I'd get to go by myself, or at least with Muriel, and maybe sneak a few minutes with Huey to neck in his car. Huey had been after me of late, when I'd tell him I loved him, to prove it – a slight damper on my enthusiasm. But, in the end, the affection waiting in his arms always drew me. Even without ulterior motives, to be accompanied by her entire family *anywhere,* especially on the bus, was humiliating for any fourteen-year-old. But for some reason, Charity insisted she, Daddy, and Marcy were going along. This was not unusual. I felt Charity was trusting me less and less since the episode at school, back in eighth grade, when Mr. Garbe had asked me to stay after to help him. Daddy took off from work, and both he and Charity showed up at the principle's office, protesting such "irregular behavior."

Mr. Garbe, one of my first male teachers, was a very kind person. He was married, with several small children, and he said the way he hired baby-sitters was getting to know them after school. The girl he was using was graduating, and he'd taken a shine to me. Charity misunderstood my obvious crush on him after I was promoted a half grade ahead to his home-room. It was my "intelligence and maturity" that brought me to his attention, he said. Charity was highly skeptical of this, although I wondered what she thought it was since she told me at least once a day how *skinny* I was, how *straight* my legs were, and how simply *flat as a pancake* my chest was, which really hurt. (*Her* measurements, she bragged, and I repeated proudly since I'd heard they were the same as Marilyn Monroe's, were 36-26-36.) Apparently she thought I must be *throwing* myself at him, so I stopped confiding in her after that, telling her as little as possible.

Charity's snide remarks about my being boy crazy didn't

help either, since that was the only subject I really wanted her advice about. She offered advice about everything. Already, she had changed my eating habits, making me taste *everything,* even things I hated, like cabbage. She influenced my way of dressing, pointing out my bad taste in color and design combinations. No plaids with checks. The style for a skirt in school was very tight and long, to the ankle, but Charity and Daddy frowned on that. Since I sewed, I could make it long, but I would roll it up under my sweater in the house, and let it down when I got around the corner.

Charity's fancy tastes were a striking contrast to her poor beginnings. She preferred one pair of expensive shoes to ten cheaper ones. Sometimes I was forced to wait for a good while for something new, unlike what I was used to; Daddy had always spent most of what little money he had on me. Too, we had managed to live in the best of homes and neighborhoods. It was the well off folks, whose children were grown and gone, who were able and willing to take us in. The subject of *white trash* was a subject Daddy brought up often, especially when visiting the sick and disadvantaged many Sunday afternoons. To him, *white trash* was people who didn't care about themselves enough to keep clean. "Soap is cheap," he'd say, "and there's no excuse for anybody to be dirty, no matter how poor they might be."

Daddy was very careful about who we lived with. Besides his insistence that he be the only one to correct me, leaving a wide open space between me and the lady of the house, Daddy's refusal to let me participate in any of the household chores that busied most children growing up not only added to my feeling of isolation, but this aloneness was to become an accepted way of thinking and feeling about myself. To some, these restrictions made me appear, in adulthood, as a spoiled and kept child: which, in fact, in a way, I might have been. Charity often said how *lucky* I was to see how so many people lived. Maybe *that* was what irritated her about me.

Something kept Charity riled continuously. I guess it started the very first day we moved into Cherry Lane. She and Daddy had gone off shopping and left me at home alone. Of course, it thrilled me to be in my first, very own house. I couldn't wait to get the boxes of wedding gifts unpacked that Charity had shoved into the large pantry, but not until I had unpacked my own clothes, or rearranged them, as the boxes stacked in an A-formation became my dresser. In my head, I was already planning to replace them with orange crates, and sew frilly curtains to cover their front.

Eventually, Muriel would give me rolls of birch bark to cover them.

After my things were taken care of, I scrubbed the large kitchen floor on my hands and knees, like Mrs. Simms always had, and like Mrs. Dunham had taught me while I was helping her out after Pastor Dunham took sick.

All in all, that first day was one of my happiest ever. The first thing I did was to take off my shoes. Going barefooted was strictly forbidden. Daddy remembered all too well the days of the depression when many were without shoes, and he swore, often, that his family would never go without them again. Bare feet in farm country in those days were a sign of poverty, and I never, in all my life, had been alone in any house before where I could sneak and do it. How my toes loved the feel of freedom and my feet the smoothness of a clean floor.

Charity had bought pretty strawberry edged paper with which I eagerly lined every pantry shelf. Setting out the complete set of hand painted apple dishes just so, I used all the creativity I had longed for in all those other homes. But my efforts and talents were not appreciated by my new stepmother.

Charity stormed through the house, first literally sobbing at my "audacity" (she used such big words) to open her personal cards and wedding gifts. She had neglected to tell me about the *Thank You* cards she intended writing. "Now, how am I going to remember who gave me what?" she cried in disgust.

That seemed so simple to me. "Just write, *Thank You for the wedding gift.*"

She screamed at that, telling me the proper thing to do to show *real* appreciation was to name the item given. Then she sort of caved into her middle, and broke into sobs. "How am I *ever* going to teach you?" she said as if it was a useless cause.

Boy, what all I had to learn, and believe me, she made sure I did – hearing things over and over again.

When I begged tearfully for forgiveness by throwing my arms around her neck, she flung me hatefully away. In the same tone she often used with her mother, she said, "I don't go for quick kiss-and-make-up deals."

This hurt bad enough, but when she went around in a pout for a week, not speaking, I determined in my mind I would be very careful before I got her goat again. This was not so easy, since most everything I did or said got her goat, even the way I said things — *especially* the way I said things.

When I'd say "maynaise" with only two syllables, Charity would have a fit and hold her ears. "The word has *three* syllables," she'd say and spell it for me. Fortunately I disliked *may-on-naise,* so I didn't have to say it often. Daddy and I always had a problem with language, coming from the south, and then hearing all the first generation Europeans all around us just confused the dickens out of me. No wonder I nearly failed English in first grade.

That year, I had gotten marked F (for Fair) in Language, and I was extremely frightened to have Daddy see my report card. Thinking the teacher had somehow mixed me up with someone else who used bad and sinful language, and feeling certain Daddy would never believe the truth, I changed my grade by adding a bottom line (and an ink smear) to the F, making it into an E (for Excellent). Daddy signed the report without a word about the smear, but then I couldn't get it off, or the line I'd added. I tried Mr. Simms's eradicator but the mess just got bigger. In the shoe box it went, way in the back of our closet. For a whole week I held my breath whenever Daddy dressed in there. Finally, the teacher's notes of inquiry got past me and into Mr. Simms's hands, and it was he, after gently prying the secret out of me, who explained that *Language* was the subject of speaking, and my use of *them things,* and *hisself, heared,* and *sleeped* (among others) had gotten me the F. He took Daddy aside, who turned into a lamb right before my eyes after their talk and didn't give me a licking. That was when I knew Mr. Simms could do *anything.* And now Charity was not far behind him in my estimation.

The biggest and most important change that Charity caused inside of me was rearranging my beliefs and attitudes towards the scriptures. For the first time in my life, I questioned the way I had been taught. Of course, I had always been ashamed of our being Pentecostal and would cringe when the kids called me *Holy Roller,* telling strangers at the park, sometimes, that I was Baptist. It sounded like such a common, ordinary religion. But Charity and Daddy's talks, that always ended up in a heated argument about Acts 2:4, where it tells about getting the baptism of the Holy Ghost with fire and speaking in tongues — the basis of their differences – shed a great deal of light on the subject.

Charity didn't take this scripture literally, she said, but believed the Holy Ghost came into your heart as part of being *saved,* not a special blessing. Receiving God meant you got the rest of the trinity along with Him — Jesus, God, and the Holy Ghost too. The *tongues* part was just a big misunderstanding. The main idea she was getting at was all that shouting and taking on so that we did in the Pentecostal church, and why people called us *Holy Rollers*, was just a bunch of showy emotionalism, not anything to do with the spirit of God. I knew exactly what she meant, as I remembered, still with utmost shame, my "getting the baptism" when I was only six years old. We were living with the Simmses.

It was on a Sunday night, after I'd spent the afternoon playing with Beth. She was such a trial, never wanting to play house, only primp in front of the mirror with lipstick she'd hid. Mainly, though, what she wanted was for us to go into the bathroom and *be nasty*. Trying to keep her mind away from it, when she was selfish and spiteful, like she usually was, I'd give in to her. That day, I'd finally gotten her to play house by letting her wear Mrs. Simms's old, flowered straw bonnet. I really wanted the hat for myself, but instead I put on Mrs. Simms's old, brown rayon stockings that I rolled over the round garters she'd given me. The garters themselves were so big I had to tie knots in them to keep them on my knees and the stockings so long I had a mighty big roll between my kneecaps. Later on that night, come time for church, I was reluctant to give up my making-believe I was grown up — my constant daydream – so I put my white cotton Sunday stockings over them, pulling them all into a big fat roll over the knotted garters. My long *sanctified* dress came in handy to cover up the bulges.

After preaching that night, I went forward – the singing of *Just As I Am* always did make me feel so sinful. Of course, I believed I was already born again, "saved when I was three," I told everybody even though I really didn't remember a thing about it. But Pastor Dunham had preached me right under conviction, about "thinking" sin — as bad as doing it. All afternoon I was "thinking" about sinning, every time Beth got tired of the game we were playing. So I was "strongly under conviction" and went forward to the altar. If I could just get the baptism I'd not sin so easily, I thought.

Going forward in our church meant a lot. Everyone in the whole church is looking, and the minute you raise your hands to pray, they all come up behind you and cry out loud to the Lord with their arms in the air, saying, "Bless her, Lord. Make her heart right, Lord. Fill her, Lord."

Daddy had his special place at the corner of the altar, where he always knelt. So I picked a spot where he couldn't see me very well, where the altar bent inward. I *went forward* every now and then so Daddy wouldn't take so long in Bible reading, preaching at me, but I never stayed more than a minute, before I headed for the ladies' room.

What I didn't expect at the altar that night was Mrs. Simms coming right up next to me, kneeling and praying very softly in a sing-song voice, "Have thy way, Lord. Have thy way, Lord." She wasn't one of the loud ones, maybe because she was nearly deaf.

By this time, I was pretty miserable, feeling sad from the preaching and the music and all tore up inside from being with Beth all afternoon. So I raised my arms up high and started in crying for God to help me. I *did* need help, and this was the only way I knew to ask for it. I pleaded, with tears running down my cheeks, "Help me, Jesus. Please, help me, Jesus."

After awhile, the feeling of all the loud praying got to me and I was rocking hard, back and forth on my knees. Then someone laid me down on the carpeted floor, still with my eyes tightly shut. *Struck under the power*, at last, I could hear Mrs. Simms as she put a coat over my legs. This was a real new experience for me, except I'd seen it happen all the time after Sunday night preaching. So without really thinking about it, as any six-year-old would, I did what I'd seen. I started kicking my legs and shaking my arms and yelling, "Glory. Glory. Hallelujah, Jesus. Glory."

The coats — by this time there were several covering me – kept getting strewn about. I heard Mrs. Simms right next to me still praying quietly and pulling the coats back on top of me. After about the third time this happened, I suddenly felt the cold air hit my bare thighs – reminding me of the wad of stockings I'd forgotten I still had on. My heart almost stopped, but I never let on. My tears started coming in earnest then, after I peeked and got a good look at Mrs. Simms. She was funny anyhow, always primping to get her hair to cover the hearing aid cord she wore, hiding the batteries inside her bosom. Loud noises would make her jump and yell, "Mercy," as she'd grab her chest to cut the sound. Seeing her one hand reaching for the controls of her hearing aid tucked between her breasts (I was carrying on so loud), and the other hand firmly holding the coats so I could not kick them off again, still praying, "Have thy way, Lord. Have they way," made me so tickled I had to fight the giggles. Instead, I yelled all the louder, aiding *the spirit* to come a little quicker. Soon, I began hearing myself say something like, "Shun de da da... Shun de da da..." (what Daddy always said) and other mumbo jumbos that I could get to roll off my tongue.

Then all was quiet, and I heard a voice here and there thanking God for my filling.

Karen's mother began her interpretation. She was always interpreting right out in the middle of church service, sometimes her own tongues or someone else's. She was a tall skinny lady and always wore a dark felt hat shaped like an upside down boat, even at night church. The hat was filled with feathers and covered with a veil. Her favorite dress was a black and white spotted affair with a big white collar. The big hairy mole on her chin wiggled when she spoke. She'd stand up with her eyes closed and hold out her arm, as though she was Moses parting the Red Sea; Pastor Dunham would stop the service. We'd all bow our heads while she "exhorted us" very quietly in the spirit. Now she was doing it over me. I lay still with my eyes tightly shut while she gave the interpretation, of my *speaking in tongues*, in her shaky, whiny voice. "I am in your midst, sayeth the Lord. Listen, and I will speak. The Lord be exalted. Another soul sanctified and set apart for my work." My tongues were short. Usually the interpretation was very long and had something about "abomination" in it.

When I opened my eyes that night from the floor of the altar Daddy was beaming at me, never noticing my stockings. Mrs. Simms, thankfully, never mentioned them either. Mr. Simms ignored the whole event, never mentioning it once to me. And I noticed *he* never went to the altar. So Charity's view, which she so hotly debated with Daddy at the mere mention of it, helped me to admit, to myself anyhow, just how ugly I really had felt about the baptism of the Holy Ghost all these years. But if I knew what was good for me, I'd keep my mouth shut to either of them about it. Daddy would say I had blasphemed the spirit; Charity would say I was a fake and a liar, testifying all those years, even at street meetings, a subject I stayed away from. In fact, there were few subjects I could bring up without bringing Charity's wrath down on my head.

My hair seemed to be the latest thing for her to pick on. The morning of my picture studio appointment, I carefully fixed my face in my usual way, combing my hair into false bangs. Daddy would not let me cut bangs, and bangs — that Mamie Eisenhower wore – were the thing. So I pulled back the long hair on top, pinned it, and let the ends fall forward in a nice wave that fell just above my eyebrows, looking very much "in." My hair was longer than it had ever been, falling half-way down my back and curling up in a round, smooth roll all around, also the latest teenage look.

"Get that hair out of your face," Charity screeched. "Why do you want to look like every other Tom, Dick and Harry? Fix your hair off your face so you can see."

She pulled at it, messing it all up. So I started over, trying to make it higher on my forehead to please her.

By this time, I was fuming inside at Charity. And when I couldn't contain it any longer, the tears spurted out, messing up my face. I redid my face powder, ending with a touch of Vaseline on my black eyebrows and eyelashes to clean and darken them.

Hoping we could leave, the next time I came out of my room, Charity yelled, "What have you got on your eyes?"

"It's only Vaseline," I insisted.

"I don't believe it," she said, wiping her finger across my eyebrow and looking at it, almost disappointed not to find any black mascara.

"Wipe that mess off your face," she said then. "Do you want to look like some cheap floozy?"

For the last time, I disappeared into my bedroom, determined not to cry again or I'd be late for my appointment.

The photographer was waiting when we got there for me to put the black velvet drape over my bare shoulders, like all the girls at school showed in their pictures. Huey wanted one for his wallet. But at the sight of the drape Daddy's lip started twitching, so Charity said, "There's no need to change clothes. Your suit looks just fine — if you'd open the lapels like you're supposed to. Why do you pin it closed like that? It looks so stupid," she snapped.

"Because this is the style," I said, "to wear a suit with no blouse under it." I just *had* to be in style, I had spent too many years looking different than *everybody*.

"Style. Pile. What next?" she said and shoved me into the dressing room. "Comb your hair over," she ordered again, knowing full well I had already combed it twice at home, but I'd been pulling at it.

The photographer was impatient, listening to the embarrassing dialogue between us. Daddy kept still, tending to little Marcy. I unpinned my hair again and combed it to Charity's satisfaction.

"There. Now we can see your face. Who wants a picture of all that hair?"

Finally, the picture was taken, a

moment I wanted to forget now locked in time, and I hurried to get us all out of the studio. I was burning with anger and shame. All the way home I sat as far from them on the bus as I could and tried to leave Charity alone.

When I got home, I disappeared into my small, dark bedroom, trying to get some kind of solace for my wounds. My quietness, though a rarity, always killed Charity. She finally tore into my room, jerking aside the curtain (the only means of privacy I had from the kitchen and Marcy's crib outside my door) with the pretense of using the closet, the only one in the house — a rod hung at the end of my tiny room with a curtain strung across, in front of it.

"What are you doing now?" Charity asked, with a sharp edge to her voice, seeing I had combed my hair over, my way, and changed my clothes into the "worldly and unladylike" blue jeans Daddy'd finally agreed to let me wear around the house. I had put on a new blouse I'd bought on sale with Muriel. It was a white cap-sleeved rayon with a mandarin collar and large circles of pink, purple and black printed all over it. A popular item. But when I bought it, I neglected to try it on and realized when I got home that a black circle covered each breast perfectly.

"What did you buy now?"

"Just a blouse," looking down and slouching my shoulders forward, hoping she wouldn't notice.

"Just look at that," her laughter filled the room. "How silly, and as flat as you are, to bring such attention to yourself," painting with her finger around each encircled breast.

"I'll wear a sweater," I said, crossing my arms defensively over my chest. "It was cheap."

"It looks it," she spat at me then, bringing me to tears again as she just stood there, hanging and rearranging her clothes on the hangers looking dreadfully mean-faced, as though she was trying to think up something else spiteful to say.

Finally, I said it; I just couldn't help it. The look in her eyes cut me to my insides. "I *hate* you. I *hate* you. I *hate* you," I screamed, crying uncontrollably, sobs coming in spasms, almost choking me.

"We'll, I'll be so glad when you get old enough to get out of my house *and my life*," she spit back at me and trooped out of the room.

Following her, my heart galloping so I thought my temples would burst, I said, "Well, it won't be long now. Just as soon as I graduate." I never felt such anger. Letting it out was not like me, and things came out all tongue-tied and strange sounding. The top of my head felt like it would pop right off. "What do you think I'm taking all those extra credits for? Chorus? And choir? Playing piano for them instead of having study hall, making me have to bring homework home?" By this time, I was really screaming. "I'm trying to have enough credits to graduate when I'm sixteen. I want to get out of *here*, too; just two more years." I yelled, following her back into the pantry.

"Can't be soon enough to suit me, you *ungrateful little slut,"* she spewed at me, shoving me aside as she walked past me, like I was scum of the lowest caliber, just how I was feeling inside.

Those words, *ungrateful little slut,* is what did it, when I'd kept Huey away for the past year, in the face of his constant pleading. *How could she call me a slut?* I really hated sneaking around with Muriel. But Daddy didn't allow me anything enjoyable to do and had already denied my playing on the basketball team after school. Then Charity had put an end to my cello lessons on Saturday mornings, which "interfered with house cleaning." I didn't know which one I was more angry with. Ice skating in the long Milwaukee winters was not even allowed, when I'd beg to do one thing that was free and out in the open where he could check up on me. Daddy'd say I had enough to do – but none of it fun. Actually, I'd done well, holding it all in thus far, I thought. But those words, *ungrateful little slut,* did it.

Inside of me, something just snapped. As I drew a deep breath, a calm came over me from somewhere. Slowly and deliberately I walked back into my bedroom and started changing my clothes into a skirt I could wear outside of the house. Walking through the kitchen, I felt myself being propelled out the door, with Charity asking at my back, "Just where do you think you're going now?"

"To the drug store," I said, over my shoulder in a monotone unlike me. "I'm out of hair-set, and I'm baby-sitting tonight for Haley's from church. Remember? I already told you."

With Charity staring after me, I left. All the way to the corner the anger of her words flew around inside of me. The more I rehearsed them in my head — the feelings from my entire past closing in on me – the more despicable I felt. I was not loved by *anyone. No one.* I was rotten and *ungrateful.* There is no one. *No one who cares. I'm a slut. I'm a slut. I'm a slut.* And then I found myself inside the phone booth dialing Huey's number.

In a thin voice that didn't even sound like me, I heard myself say, "You know what you're always saying to me... to do... lately?

To *prove* it?"

"Yeah?"

"Come over tonight where I'm baby-sitting and I will."

I t was after 9:00 p.m. and still no Huey. I had told him 7:30 to give the Haley's plenty of time to be gone, and me time to be sure little nine-month-old Bobby was asleep. I was nervous enough without him being awake. The dishes were all done up, the front porch light on, as I'd promised, and soft strains of Nat King Cole were coming over the radio. Since I always stayed the night with the Haley's and rode to Sunday School with them the next morning, I had worn my church clothes — my only store bought outfit – the suit I'd had on for the picture taking that morning. It was a soft gray wool flannel with trim squared shoulders with a peplum jacket. The skirt was long and very narrow, with a slit up the back seam. I had the lapels pinned together, to look like it was the popular button-up Peter Pan style, with a strand of pearls under the collar. I was getting a little warm, as busy as I'd been, but I had only brought pajamas along. I'd combed my hair a dozen times and brushed my teeth twice. One of the lamps over the end of the couch was lit. I had just put a stick of Spearmint gum into my mouth when the doorbell rang. I ran down the steps to the door.

"I thought you weren't coming?" I said as Huey stepped into the echoing stairway, leading up into the Haley's upper flat.

"I had to take three buses and one streetcar. My car's broke down," he said, sniffing. "It took me two hours."

The odor of tobacco was all over him. I immediately began to worry that he might try to smoke. His coming on the bus was quite a surprise. I didn't expect Huey, or any guy of seventeen, to go anywhere on the bus. I was secretly pleased. He let me walk up ahead of him, slipping off his jacket the second he got through the door. He dropped it on a chair and grabbed me around the waist, holding me tight up against his wide, flat chest and kissed me. His short and stocky size surprised me, as we had always been sitting down in the car. Even though we measured the same in height, I felt like I towered way above him. He had never French kissed me before either (another no-no of Charity's), so his tongue inside my mouth was unexpected. He laughed at my embarrassment from the kiss. My face must have turned pink, it felt so hot to my icy cold hands. Huey took hold of one, led me gently to the couch, and pulled me down next to him. His arm was around me as I looked at him out of the corner of my eye, waiting.

"Well... ?" he finally said, turning to face me with his thin lips curving into a smile.

I shrugged my shoulders and raised my eyebrows in answer. It was the first time in my life I had no words. I think my throat had completely frozen, with the gum separating in little pieces in the back of my mouth. Finally, I got out the words, "Now what do I do?"

His black curly eyelashes squinted closed when he chuckled and said, "Well, lay down."

"But," I stammered, "on my stomach or on my back?"

Laughing right out loud this time, still with his arm around me, he looked at me and thought for a minute. I knew my knees were actually knocking together. "Turn off the light," he ordered, without further explanation.

So I did, while he untied his wing tip shoes, and loosened the buttons on his long-sleeved, blue shirt. He was good looking, even though he had a regular German "schnoz" as Muriel called hers. His wide, straight, black eyebrows, contrasting his light blonde and very curly hair (combed back into a long duck's tail) were prominent characteristics of German families. He pulled me down onto his lap, slipping his shoes off one by one (I was in my stocking feet), and whispered into my ear. "Lay down," he said, while he gently eased me down onto the couch.

No one had ever explained this part to me, not even my white trash Cousin Essie. But from the animals I had seen I figured I should be on my stomach. I lay there thinking about whether I was supposed to take off any of my clothes, and *when?* Whether to turn over, and *when?* Huey was lying next to me on the edge of the couch, his left hand pulling up my skirt, before I had time to wonder *anything* too long. He got his hand all the way up to my panty girdle and let out a "tsk" in disgust. "Oh, for Christ's sake, you have a girdle on," he said, feeling for the detachable panty snaps. The small piece of cloth came completely off in a matter of seconds.

"All *right*," he purred in approval.

While he was kissing me, he began rolling over on top of me, separating my legs. He unzipped his fashionably pegged, blue gabardine trousers. "Put your legs around me," he instructed.

I did, feeling something small and warm being pushed up into me. It burned, with a slight sting.

I swallowed my gum.

He moved his body up and down two or three times, and then got up. "I think you might bleed," he said.

The couch was a solid pale gray and I panicked, worrying how I would *ever* get any blood off of it. I jumped up, grabbing the panty crotch that had slipped under my head. I ran across the carpet, thankful of its many dark colors, as I squeezed my knees together, feeling something warm ooze from me and drip down my legs as I ran.

Huey was sitting on the couch with the light back on; he'd already put on his jacket. The Andrew sisters were singing *Sentimental Journey* on the radio. Quickly, I checked the couch for stains and sighed quietly in relief. Huey was putting a stick of Juicy Fruit gum into his mouth and was holding one out to me, unwrapped. I took it, as I sat down next to him. He took my hand, and we both sat and stared straight ahead. And chewed. It seemed like the silence went on for an eternity.

Finally, Huey looked at his watch. "Guess I'll hit the road," he said. "It's a long ride home."

I walked him to the door with my arm in his. He turned; we kissed lightly and quickly and tiptoed down the steps together. As I locked the door behind him, my stomach did a flip-flop, realizing that what I'd waited so long for was over. I went back through the house towards the bedroom to check Bobby and glanced at the clock on the way. It was not quite 9:30. Huey had not even stayed a whole half-hour.

Sleeping was a nightmare, tossing and turning, waiting for the Haley's to finally come in towards morning. My mind never stopped roving from one thing to the next. I wondered what all the talk was about. Sex. It was so quick and uninteresting. Except for the sharing of the personal part of my body, which was annoyingly tender, I wondered what all the hullabaloo was about. All the funny words I'd heard to describe things, like *prick*. It *did* feel like something had pricked me. And I *did* get *laid* down. But I couldn't understand what the "f" word came from. If I had not felt so guilty, I might have giggled. Deceiving the Haley's concerned me greatly. I always worried about other people's opinions. *Jesus first: Others next; Yourself last* was a plaque on my bedroom wall at home. The Haley's were so nice and hired me often for baby-sitting. She liked my helping out with everything in the kitchen. She was friends with Huey's oldest sister, Genevieve (everyone called her Gen). I worried Huey might brag about this to Bernice, they were so close, and she might tell Gen. What would any of them think if they knew I was *that kind of girl*. And then, to top it all off, after all the anticipation was spent, the whole thing seemed rather dull — a foolish and embarrassing dream.

T he full impact of the bizarre happening of the night before had hit me with the sting of the first morning urine. And the panty girdle that I had to wear to hold up my stockings hurt as I walked with Karen and Janet up onto the platform, to sing in morning service.

We had our heads close together in order to harmonize. The song book lay open before us on the pulpit that overlooked the center aisle. Gray and green checkered cost-cutting linoleum lined the floor before us. We stood directly opposite the main entrance. The amber-glassed double doors leading into the church gave a golden hue to the large room. Palm Sunday. Everyone seemed to be there; there were few empty seats. The organist gave us our tones as she finished the introduction. I was singing the low alto, the part I had sung in all-city chorus. I read music well; Charity had harmonized a lot with me. That's how I'd learned to play piano chords and accompaniment, hearing all the parts. Karen, Janet and I started singing:

> [11]*It was alone*
> *The Savior prayed*
> *In dark Gethsemane...*

I glanced up at the congregation. The door of the huge church opened and the sunlight poured in as Huey stepped through it and walked a few feet to the last row. He took his regular seat, on the end by the center aisle. He was stretching his neck to see. I looked back down at the song book. My voice gave a crackling sound, somewhat off key. The girls kept singing, as though it wasn't happening. My stomach began to quiver, my throat closed; no sound was coming out. I couldn't look up. And suddenly, from the pit of my stomach, almost like a fountain of water, came a pulsating giggle. I tried to swallow it, but the dryness choked me. I covered my mouth with my finger tips and held my lips. Even if I hummed, I'd giggle. The girls kept singing. At the end of the first verse, Karen closed the book; we were supposed to sing three verses.

As we reached the hidden passageway leading around into the back of the church, I burst into tears.

Karen and Janet both just looked at me.

"I'm so sorry for messing up," I said through my tears. "Something happened to my voice."

---

[11] *Alone* was written by Ben H. Price.

They still just looked at me like they didn't know what to say. We had sung together many times before.

"I don't know why I started laughing. I was so scared you'd think I would have cried," I said still crying, then laughing, then crying again.

They kept looking at me very puzzled. Karen was the one to speak. She was nervous talking to me, I could tell, but she was always sympathetic when I could sneak in a conversation with her. "It's okay," she said, patting me on the arm before quickly slipping into the service to sit with her mother, Janet smiling and following on behind.

The ladies' room, usually filled with young mothers and their crying babies, or with old ladies resting in the rocker or lying on the couch, or with gossiping teenagers, was strangely empty. Thankfully, no one could see me sobbing, too ashamed to show my face through the whole service. *I wished I was dead.* Now Karen would surely never be able to come over to my house. Her mother hated me. I was not *well supervised* and a *bad influence* on Karen since her brother had married the minister's daughter. I had liked Karen always, since we were the flower girls together. I thought she felt the same about me, but her mother had certain ideas about what *Christian girls* should and should not do. My hanging around the Stadtz twins had fixed it for me.

Oh, how I yearned for friendship, but it seemed to skirt me everywhere I went, except for Muriel and, of course, Beth, who I hated more than ever. The older she got the more interested in sex she got, whispering, when no one was paying attention, to come into her bedroom on our family visits, but I never went. I was convinced she was *that way* so I avoided her. We hardly ever saw any of Mama's Evermardt kin any more since Daddy married. He was still very stand-offish about people I liked. So Huey and Muriel had become my only real friends. Huey seemed to be anxious to see me every time I'd call; even his mother sounded excited when she'd recognize my voice. She was as nice to me as Bernice. His older married brother, Rodney, sat behind me in choir and would pull my hair and tease the daylights out of me until I blushed. Gen's husband, Arnold, was the choir director, and he treated me nice too. Mr. Schultz, Huey's father, never spoke much. His English was not so good. He just played his big tuba in the orchestra. The Schultz family had all the money in the church, Mr. Simms said, and no one dared step on their toes. He would complain about them after a big fight in the board meeting. He was the only one that had as much to say as they did. Besides money, he drew great respect, his being the father of two missionaries. Feeling a part of the Simms' family had always made me feel good, but what would *any* of them think about me now if they knew?

Charity came looking for me. I could only blurt out the disgrace of my giggling before the entire congregation.

"You simply had stage fright, Samantha Sue," she said matter-of-factly, as though it wasn't so important. "A bigger crowd than you're used to. And when a person is very frightened, they either cry – or laugh like you did."

How easy she made everything sound sometimes. *Oh, why couldn't she have been this nice to me yesterday?* I thought, as I rose to follow her out. But it only took one step for the stinging to remind me that it was too late for her kindness; too late for anything. Like the woman at the well the preachers loved talking about, I was now *ruined* for life.

O fficer Schmidt, the young police woman, was sitting on the edge of her desk. "Let me get this straight," she said, swinging her pencil back and forth, then sticking it into her full head of red, curly hair, "You're only fourteen, and you're here *voluntarily*. You do know what that means, don't you? No one's threatening you?"

"Yes, that's right," I said. "I told my dad about Huey on my own... after church last night. I felt so awful, and Rudolph, this friend of ours — he used to go out with Huey's sister, Bernice, and knew all about Huey and how he does with girls – saw me crying in church and..."

Officer Schmidt broke in, "Are you pregnant?"

"No. I told you..."

"How do you know?"

"Because. I have my period. Right now. That's why I decided to tell."

"You mean to tell me you've been shacking up with your boyfriend for over six months and you finally decide to tell your old man *voluntarily*? Hard to believe. Why?"

Her cold unbelieving manner was beginning to irritate me. "Because..." I burst into tears. "I told you. Huey drinks."

"Didn't he *always* drink?"

"Yes... but... he's been drinking so *much* lately. See, he used to kiss me and neck a lot with me. I liked that. But since I gave in..."

"Why did you give in?"

"I told you, I hate my stepmother. We had this fight. And Huey kept asking me to... to... saying he loved me."

Again, I began telling the whole story. Officer Schmidt had finally sat down in her chair and was saying, "Incredible! Unbelievable! You live here? In *this* city? And go to public school? And you have never been inside a movie theater in your life?"

"That's right."

"You were never allowed to say *Hi* to a boy? What if you did?"

"Oh, I'd get it."

I told her, then, about the whippings. And about the last one, when I first called Huey.

About an hour into the interview, with Charity and Daddy sitting downstairs in the Safety Building, Officer Krantlevich, another police woman, came in. Officer Schmidt turned to her, "She's all yours."

Officer Krantlevich didn't even sit down. "Okay kid," she said, standing right over me, looking through her straight dark bangs. "So you got caught shacking by the old man, and you're here to cover your ass, that right?"

"No-o," I said, crying again. "My dad and stepmother brought me here. They swore out this warrant for Huey's arrest because *I* told. Myself. About Huey. I'm sick to death of his being drunk, and not being able to... you know... come, and he's getting so fat. And *heavy!* Oy. Last week I thought I'd smother under him, when he fell asleep, and I couldn't get him off me. And when I finally did, he cussed and swore at me all the way out the door. He almost woke up my baby sister, threatening to tell my dad and the whole world all about it. *I'll tell everyone what a whore you are*, he was yelling real loud. So I decided at church last night, after talking to Rudolph, to tell on myself. Rudolph said because my dad was a Christian he'd take it right – if he heard it from me. That Huey was a scoundrel and had done that to at least two other girls that he knew about, and did I want to keep living under such fear? He said my dad wouldn't whip me. He promised, on his word. So I decided to go right home and tell, before I got scared again, before Huey had a chance to blab."

"What did your dad say?"

"I'll kill him. I'll kill him," he said at first. But changed his mind. He said he was just mad. Then he asked me why I didn't *tell* him I wanted to date so bad? Isn't that a laugh? When he'd told me since I was little to not be thinking about any kind of date till I was at least twenty-one."

"She's never been inside a movie theater," Officer Schmidt interrupted. "Church is all."

Officer Krantlevich's eyebrows shot up. She sat down and her tone got softer. They both began asking questions of me then, left and right. Shaking their heads, repeating "voluntary" over and over.

"Do you understand you will have to testify, in court, against this guy?"

"I do?"

"Yes. Are you willing to do that?"

"I guess. Is it public? Can anyone be there?"

They were both nodding their heads.

The thought of it almost choked me, but I repeated, "I have to. I don't think I have a choice, do I? My dad is sitting downstairs, waiting for me."

"Well, let's get a physical on you first and make sure you're not PG."

"But I told you..."

"I know, Toots, what you *told* me. But it's for the record. Only take a second. The doc's gotta sign the paper."

Officer Schmidt sat down next to me as I scooted up onto the table. She grasped my hand as I lay my head down, and the doctor put my feet into the stirrups sticking up. He still had on his felt hat shoved back to his hairline, and a dark, wool scarf hung around his neck over a plaid flannel shirt. I noticed he did wear a tie. He spoke through his teeth clenched over a fat, stubbed-out cigar, "Slide yourself back down here, towards me."

As I did, he separated my knees that were locked rigidly together.

"Ever had a physical before?"

"No. Never. My dad would usually pray for me, except once, when I had a side ache, the people who took care of me took me..."

"I mean a pelvic? Ever put your feet up like this before?"

"No," I said, "and I've got my period today; I'm wearing a Tampax."

"That's all right. I've seen a lot of Tampax in my day," he said as he pulled it out.

The cold instrument slid into me, and I gripped Officer Schmidt's hand. She squeezed mine back, "Hang on kid. It'll be over soon."

It was.

"I'm so sorry about this," she said, kindly, as we headed

back towards her office.

The two uniformed women were talking in the corner of the room, with a male cop in street clothes (a detective they said) eyeing me and nodding at me, while other cops in uniform stopped at the door and looked in at me. The three of them came back over to me, explaining, again, about *voluntary*, that I didn't *have* to do this.

"Yes, I do; if my dad says I do, *I do*."

They all three shook their heads in disbelief.

"Because you're only fourteen, a minor," the detective said, "the court is appointing you a *guardian ad litem*. You will be assigned a probation officer at that time."

Hearing this, my eyes and mouth flew open.

"No. Don't misunderstand," he said, calming me. "You are not being put on probation. You just have to appear to be assigned. They will explain it to you then. Will you be here?"

"Yes. I'll be here. What's going to happen to Huey?"

"He'll be brought in and questioned and charged with CK & A. That's *Carnal Knowledge and Abuse*. *Rape* won't hold because you were willing."

"Yes. My dad said he wanted Huey put away, so he couldn't ruin some other girl's life."

"I know. But you have to *testify* first, and then it's up to the judge. Meantime... Think it over. The *voluntary* part I explained to you; you can change your mind."

Downstairs, Daddy and Charity were waiting for me, five hours in all. Charity was sullen and wouldn't look at me. She was still upset with me because I wouldn't let her into my bedroom when I was telling Daddy about it. I had been ready to tear into her with my bare hands, till Daddy stopped me, and told her, "Leave us alone." I was sure this whole court thing was her idea, just like Mr. Garbe at school. But I was glad it was all out in the open. "The whole world will know now for sure," I said to them. "The Schultzes will tell everyone."

Daddy said, in a quiet voice, "I don't think they'll be so proud to tell things on their own son."

Daddy couldn't take off from work so Charity had to go with me to juvenile court. I was taken into a room alone, with several probation officers all sitting around a big table. I was asked many questions over and over. One in particular. "Do you have any other living relatives?"

"Yes, my Grandma Evermardt. My own mother, who's dead. Her mother." I didn't even think of Aunt Jenny Lou or Aunt Beulah.

"Do you want to go live with her?"

"Oh, I'd really love that, but I think it'd hurt my father too much. I couldn't do that to him, I just couldn't."

Everyone there made it clear to me, it was *my* choice, but it really wasn't because I didn't think Grandma Evermardt could take me. Since her TB, after Grandpa died, she wasn't well enough to even look after her own. For the five years she was in the sanitarium, they just about raised themselves. But the idea was secretly gratifying.

On the walk to the bus stop, Charity wanted to know everything that went on.

"Oh, they asked me if I wanted to live with Grandma Evermardt."

Startled, she stopped in her tracks, "What did you tell them?"

"I said, *No.* That I was afraid it would hurt Daddy too much." My tears wouldn't stay back then.

Relieved at my answer, Charity said, with a touch of kindness in her voice, "Oh, I'm so glad you made that choice. It would have killed your father."

We walked and talked together, then, my explaining to her about the guardian thing being just a technicality.

Charity was warming up to me for the first time since it all came out and asked, "What other questions did they ask you?"

"Oh, they wanted to know how many times it'd happened, and I told them."

"Only twice, right?"

"No. Goodness. At least a dozen, or more." I said. "I couldn't count them all."

Charity seemed absolutely stunned at this news. "I thought it was twice, and the first time he *forced* you?"

"No. You didn't hear right in the other room. I told Daddy just how it all happened."

"Where, pray tell, did you do all of this? In his car?"

"Mostly."

Right then, I was afraid to tell them about baby-sitting at Haley's, afraid they wouldn't let me do it anymore, and I needed the money. They didn't pay me much for taking care of Marcy. I added, "But sometimes we'd go to the little empty park full of trees, by his house where he'd lay me down on the bench. I hated it, always afraid someone would come back in there. It got so he only wanted to see me long enough to get it over with. He only came to the house once, that last time. No one saw, I don't think. He turned his lights and motor off, like I told him to."

"That nosey old Mrs. Plummer, I'll bet *she* saw. She doesn't miss a thing, with her pitter-pattering always to the window at the least little sound in the alley. Tsk tsk. How awful."

"I listened for her and I never heard anything," I said, trying to ease Charity's mind. She was so worried about other people and gossip.

As Charity thought about all of this, you could just see her face settle, slowly, into her quiet cool front — the one I hated, but it seemed to be the only one I saw much of anymore. She spoke little to me after that and seldom with any kindness. *I really was a slut*. Now, Charity finally had proof of it on paper.

I t was 11:25 pm, five minutes early, and I was home from my first real date. Quietly, I slipped through the kitchen door into the dark house. It had been tedious being Donny Morrison's date. I'd told his little sister, Margie, the closest thing to a best friend at *Highland Fundamental*, that I was now allowed to date. When Donny, nineteen, and president of Young People's there, showed up at my door after school and asked me to the toboggan party, I was not only shocked but so scared that I hardly ate all week. I had to pinch myself all night to make sure that, after the nightmarish events of recent weeks, I was really on the top of that toboggan run, wearing the wool slacks Charity convinced Daddy I must wear, or freeze. It was going to be a long winter, already this much snow and it still October.

Donny had just broken up with Sheri Peeks from *Gethsemane Baptist*, with whom he'd had a PG scare (some even said she'd had an illegal abortion and was so angry that she broke up with him). Of course, I had a strong belief that Donny was a nice Christian guy and nice Christian guys didn't do things like that. But hearing this did make me nervous, worrying he might try something – especially if he'd heard about me, even though Huey's and Donny's acquaintances were totally foreign to each other.

The talk was that Donny, madly in love with Sheri, was just trying to make her jealous. *But why me?* He had always been sweet to me when we waited for the same bus, going home from church, but with so many other girls out after him? It never occurred to me I might be pretty or likable in any way. In fact, I always wondered why I was asked to be in so many weddings. People were just being nice, I was sure. Daddy didn't believe in compliments. Nobody did then. They only puffed up your head, it was thought. But even though at first it seemed to irritate Charity,

I did sense Daddy's being rather proud of the way I had taken to housekeeping and tending to Marcy. Even so, I was sure Donny's invitation was some kind of joke and waited all night for him to try something. But he just acted natural and held my hand walking up the hill. His arms were around me in the toboggan, too.

Back at the church we had eats, followed by some singing and devotions, which Donny got up and led. He was good looking, with his brown, very wavy hair. I felt proud to be his date. *If he only knew,* I kept thinking, as he drove me home. As cold out as it was, I suggested he not get out of the car to walk me to the door. He didn't object. I wanted to ask about Sheri, but was afraid of prolonging the good night. I literally ran into the house. Home! I couldn't believe I was actually glad to be there. Dating was more scary than I'd ever imagined.

As I closed the kitchen door behind me, I let out a thankful sigh, knowing it was important to show Daddy I could be trusted. I took a quiet step across the floor and heard Daddy's voice through the darkness call me, from his bedroom.

"Come in here, Samantha Sue. I want to talk to you."

"What is it?" I whispered, shoving my hands into my jacket pockets as I stepped past Marcy's crib in the dark.

"Listen here," he began, "I've been laying here thinking, about you... and I just don't see how in the world I can let you go out with any more boys. I just can't."

Charity was silent.

For some reason, it really didn't seem like a surprise. Daddy was always changing his mind about things. He couldn't stick with anything to save himself, it seemed, except to keep saying *No* to everything. So I was used to begging.

"Why? For goodness sake. I'm home on time, and Donny... he's such a nice fellah. He didn't even try to kiss me."

"Well, I'm glad to hear *that*. But if he had, well, once you've given in, it's mighty hard to say *No*. And..."

"Daddy, what do you mean?" I almost shouted. "There's no way I'm going to give in to *anyone* again. Not after what I've been through. No way."

"But... a girl gets to likin' it after awhile, you know," he said, with a slight coquettish edge to his voice.

"*Like* it? I hated it. Every time. *Always*. There's no way you have to ever worry about *that*."

"We'll, I will," he said flatly. "So you can forget dating. I just can't go through the worry here, like this, all night."

It had been a dream. I knew it. It was too good to be true.

Tonight really didn't happen. But I didn't give up easily. "Now, what am I going to say? When someone asks me out? I've told *everyone*," I wailed. "And everyone saw me with Donny. *Everyone*."

"Just tell them, *No*," he said, like it was an ordinary answer to an ordinary question. My spirits fell like lead, and the anger at Daddy closed in on me like prison gates, almost smothering any hope of the future. There seemed to be no way out.

I t was barely five weeks since that horrible day at the Safety Building, when Daddy charged Huey with C. K. & A., and only the first week of November. The early snow had frozen the city into rigid narrow roads, and the overcast skies seemed to reflect the spirit of doom that hung over our house. I was ashamed to go to either church, arriving as late as possible and staying out of the ladies' room for fear I'd see someone and have to explain. In school, I was only there in body; my grades were slipping — except in Biology. Mr. Robbins, a big good-looking ex-Marine, seated me in the first row and kept me involved every minute of every class. In there, I was too embarrassed not to study.

At home, Daddy had started his fasting and praying. I'd find him in the living room most of the time, on his knees. One day in particular, he called me in. "Samantha Sue, I've decided what I'm going to do about you and this court thing. I've been talking to our new pastor, Brother Daugherty. And he says Sister Dunham is now out west somewhere — California, I think – since Brother Dunham passed on. And he thinks she'd no doubt love to have you come out there and live with her. She always liked you, didn't she?"

"I think so," I said, trying to hide my excitement, perturbed over Reverend Daugherty knowing about everything. "But did you have to tell *him* about it." I asked, reproachfully.

"Don't you no never mind about that. He's the shepherd of the flock. That's what he's supposed to do, advise us."

"But he'll tell *everyone*," I cried, remembering all the stories we heard coming from the pulpit that we knew originated in someone's family sometime, somewhere, but just disguised enough to keep anyone from being able to complain about it. But since he already knew, I latched onto the hope that maybe he could arrange something with Mrs. Dunham.

It was during her husband's terminal bout with cancer that Daddy let me work for Mrs. Dunham. They had rented one of Mr. Ridell's houses after they were forced to sell the parsonage to pay for doctor bills. She was devastated at losing her lifetime home where she had raised Ellen and Billy.

Mrs. Dunham was proud and beautiful, dark complexioned like her whole family. In my mind I could see her round, happy face set off by a large, black picture hat and a V-necked black dress. Pastor Dunham believed a minister's wife should only wear black, but his wife's necklines, revealing her full bosoms, became the talk of the ladies' room. Mr. Simms would laugh when I'd tell him what I'd heard.

"Jealousy," he'd say, with a twinkle in his eye. But she was above the gossip, I knew. I helped her clean her house, washing her delicate knick-knacks and stem-ware. She showed me how to clean hardwood floors on my hands and knees. Daddy thought working for her was like working for God and never complained. She paid me a little, too. My admiration for her was equal to Mr. Simms. High. And the thought of living with her was just the most exciting thing that could happen to me.

"I'll pray about it," Daddy was saying, as I floated on my way.

California, huh? To be near Billy, no doubt, now that he was preaching too. Ellen had moved also. *Wonder if Mrs. Dunham wears red, now that Pastor Dunham's gone?* He always said it portrayed the wicked Jezebel's heart and the reason he disapproved of lipstick and fingernail polish. He had definite ideas, and when he preached, he'd pound the pulpit and would often look me right in the eye. There was little he said I didn't understand. "If it's fun..." he'd yell, "ru-u-u-n from it... because it's no doubt sin-n-n," and he'd bend his head over the pulpit and shake his jaws as he said "sin-n-n."

My first recollection of Pastor Dunham was when we first started attending *Holy Ghost Pentecostal*. It was just a few months after Mama died; I had just turned three, and Daddy wanted to enjoy the night services without keeping me up. So he rigged up a cot in Pastor Dunham's study, a little room next to the platform, near where Daddy normally sat on the second row. He put me to bed soon after the service started, especially if I'd had a big day.

The tiny room was pitch dark, and I'd stare at the light coming under the door and listen to the singing until I fell asleep. I'd wake up sometimes to see a silhouette in the dark: Pastor Dunham on one knee, his hair in a pompadour, never mussed, praying just before his sermon. During the offering, the orchestra would play and he'd duck in for a minute. Sometimes his prayers got a little loud when he talked to Satan. "I rebuke thee, Satan," he'd say, and sometimes he'd cry or speak in tongues. "Bless me, Lord. Speak through me, Lord." It seemed he was wrestling with the angels he preached about. My favorite sermon was about Jacob hanging on to the angel. Climbing the ladder back to heaven, Jacob was saying, "I'll not let you go till you bless me... I'll not let you go till you bless me." I thought about that often during the three years Pastor Dunham fought death, till his thick hair finally turned into what, they said, looked like a bale of hay. His funeral was preached by Billy, an exciting funeral sermon.

But then, Billy's sermons were always exciting. He played trumpet very jazzily, some folks complained, but most people liked it. He'd play first, then throw his horn high into the air and catch it, with us all holding our breath. All the while he'd be singing:

> [12]*Hand me down my silver trumpet, Gabriel.*
> *Hand it down; throw it down;*
> *Any way, just get it down.*
> *Hand me down my silver trumpet, Lord.*

The funeral sermon was just as exciting. Looking and sounding just like his father, it seemed Billy considered it a victory that his dad was finally free of the awful curse of pain and sickness. And the verse he used was in Revelations somewhere,

"... and I shall put the moon under her feet... and Brothers and Sisters, let me tell you here this morning, that God has put the moon under *his* feet. Praise the Lord."

The whole place broke out in shouts of excitement. I thought it was going to turn into a regular summer camp meeting with everyone rolling in the saw dust. It was a funeral I will never forget. But it was sad, nevertheless, for me.

Because I was in so many weddings, and worked

---

[12] *Silver Trumpet*, Lyrics by unknown.

for the Dunhams, I guess I got to see a side of them most people never saw. At one wedding rehearsal dinner when I was a junior bridesmaid, the tables were set in a square design. Mrs. Dunham was sitting with the ladies, across from him, looking as beautiful as she always did, when Pastor Dunham stood up and grabbed a camera and took a flash picture of her, surprising her. Then he pulled out the hot flashbulb and pitched it over at her, landing it squarely in the crest of her bare cleavage. She squealed, "Mercy," but picked it off and tossed it right back at him. Everyone howled with laughter. I was so shocked, I blushed. But I loved them both all the more after that. After Daddy's talk, I went around for several days in complete ecstasy, thinking about maybe becoming part of the Dunham household.

When Daddy called me back into the living room, I was holding my breath. His words couldn't have been more disappointing, "I've been praying about this thing and Sister Dunham. No need to bother her, I think. Instead..."

I hardly heard a word after that as my spirits plunged. Daddy seemed good at building up my hopes, only to let them fall.

But Daddy was talking on, "I'm thinking about sending you to that school in Texas, the one Brother Buddy Doogan was from. You liked him, you said."

"Yeah, I did. But I didn't know girls went there."

"And you live in strict surroundings, careful about you, I understand. With chaperons."

After a few days went by, while I crossed my fingers and asked God, if there was such a being, to help me get out of this mess somehow and away from here, Daddy finally called me in again, "Look here, Samantha Sue. I've been praying a lot, and seems the Lord is telling me that there's no need to run from this thing. I think you can just go to school here, like you've been doing, and mind your business and keep your nose clean, and we'll come through all right. Huey hasn't bothered you, has he?"

"No, sir. Not at all. None of the Schultzes even speak to me anymore."

"Well, that's all right. You don't need to talk to the likes of them anyway."

"Why can't I date then?"

"Now, we've been all over that. The answer is *No*."

Daddy continued with his meager eating. His praying and reading the Bible in the living room never let up. Devotions were almost unbearable with all the preaching, and Charity staring at the floor. I never did enjoy staying home from school; even if I was feeling sick every month, I would go and upchuck in the nurse's office, rather than stay home. It had gotten so that I would use any excuse I could find to go to Muriel's, even during the week. Her neighbors had gotten a TV and sometimes I could sneak in a *Milton Berle Show*, although Muriel and her dad preferred *The Fights*. I think I lived a lifetime in less than a month, until Daddy brought it to an end.

"I've been doing a lot of soul searching here and studying the scriptures. In fact, our new Pastor Daugherty brought it to my attention that, according to the Bible, you and Huey are already married in God's sight. Did you know that?"

I couldn't believe my ears. This person that Daddy called a "good-for-nothing drunk," one he hated enough to have put behind bars, was now my husband? I just didn't know what to think anymore.

"Daddy," I said angrily. "That is in the *Old* Testament. Don't you remember, at Bible school, studying all that and explaining it to me? About the *Old* Law? That Jesus was supposed to have done away with it?"

"Well, true," he said, snickering just a little at my prompt correction of the new pastor.

A few days later, Daddy brought up the subject again. "I spoke to Mr. Simms about that very thing we talked about, and he agrees with you, Samantha Sue. You are right. That was how it *used* to be in the Old Testament. But it is something to think about, before you go and do a thing like that with some boy. How God *used* to think."

And I did give it a lot of thought, day and night, prompting me to finally call Huey.

His mother seemed pleased to hear from me. She said Huey was working hard and not drinking. It was a surprise to find that he had gotten a good job driving a truck. I knew he was going to church, I saw him there often, but avoided his eyes. Then Huey got on the phone and said he was saved now and was never going to drink again. "You know I love you. And if you'll just take me back, we won't have to sneak, now that your parents know."

This made me think, just maybe...

A couple days later, I got Huey on the phone again and just asked him right out if he wanted to get married and stop all this nonsense. "No telling what Daddy will come up with next for me to do. And I'm tired of living according to Daddy's whims and Charity's moods," I told Huey. When I told him about what the Reverend Daugherty had said, about us already being married in

God's sight, Huey did not object. In fact, he acted like he was anxious to see me.

Daddy was on his knees, praying, at his usual place. "Daddy," I said with steadiness, almost to the point of sounding stern, "I've decided to get married."

He raised his head out of his hands, and I could see he'd been crying again. "Married? To who?"

"Huey," I snapped. Before he could speak, I held out my hand to quiet him. "Don't say anything, Daddy, until I finish. We've talked it over, and he says he's saved now and has quit drinking. And he has a good job. I haven't seen him yet; I wanted to talk to you first. But I've made up my mind. If you don't sign for me, we'll run away."

"Well... if you're so *determined*," he answered without any real conviction in his voice.

"I am," I continued. My mind was so set on having to beg, and determined I wouldn't, I hardly paid attention. But I was relieved he wasn't putting up any fuss. Then I thought about school and Mr. Robbins and how much I loved Biology, and I wavered. "I did really want to finish school, first. But..."

When Daddy saw my hesitation, he quickly said, "A woman don't need no schoolin', all she needs is to know how to cook and clean and tend to younguns – and you know all that," he said with his face growing flushed.

The astonishment at his ideas about schooling stopped me cold and almost threw me off the track. Since he only went through the third grade, you'd think he'd want more for me. But then I remembered the past weeks and what misery I had been living in. Before I argued with him, I decided I'd better compromise in a hurry. "I do want to finish this semester in school. I think the end of January, between semesters – that's two months – would be a good time. That way, I'll have finished the tenth grade."

"Well, if you're that set on it, guess there's nothing left for me to do but sign."

The victory was somehow too easy, I kept thinking. Something didn't feel quite right about the whole thing, but I was too upset and confused to understand any of it. I just wanted out from under Daddy's rule, and this was the only way I knew to do it.

Charity was rushing to finish dinner. "I just hope *that Muriel* doesn't show up now," she said in her disgusted tone. "That's all we need."

"I told her the Schultzes were coming... to wait till later," I answered quickly, knowing Muriel's arrival, often halfway through supper, irritated the schnitzel out of Charity, who was so conscious of what people might say about her housekeeping. Muriel's quiet presence seemed to remind Charity of our landlady, Muriel's grandmother, above. We could hear her pitter-pattered vigilance, running to the window at every noise in the alley, and she complained about how much water we used, too. But we had to keep an amiable relationship if we were not to get thrown out on the street, since Daddy was unable to afford anything else. Coming over so early was Muriel's way of ensuring I could get out of the house quickly, I believed, although her own mother had dinner on the table the minute her dad walked in from work, and they finished very early. Charity was not that organized and often had the kitchen table full of stacked laundry, that Grandma Baumn had helped to fold, while I did up the breakfast and lunch dishes. Today had been an unusually sunny day, and the sheets had gotten dry outdoors. But the rest of the weekly wash hung in the small area of the dark, unfinished basement above the two ringer washers and stored portable washtubs just outside the kitchen door. The wash covered the entrance into our small, unheated sinkless toilet room (which I hated, and prayed no visitors would need) with its cold, icy cement floor. One of those very busy days, Daddy was even helping clear the table quickly, cleanliness being one of his priorities.

"Boy, they didn't waste any time getting over here, did they?" Daddy said as the doorbell sounded. Daddy answered it as Charity and I disappeared into our bedrooms to freshen up.

As I walked into the living room, Daddy was saying, "... is a good worker. You don't ever have to worry about that. She's not afraid of work. She's smart too, you know. Gets good grades in school. And sews her own clothes and her sister's too."

It reminded me of an auction for Negro slaves I'd read about in history. But I dismissed it. Daddy was just proud of me. It was clear, anyhow, he'd met his match.

Mrs. Schultz had a striking beauty that I never really noticed before, with her coal black eyebrows and dark flashing eyes and solid white wavy hair. She was very tiny and kept her black, curly lamb coat on. She spoke with a slight Old Country accent, sometimes mixing up her v's and w's and her r's sounding like w's.

"So. We are here as the kids requested," she said and smiled at me very warmly as Charity and I sat down. "I know they are in a hurry to get married. And there is no reason to wait, I think. What kind of a wedding did you have in mind?" She looked right at Daddy and smiled; her little round husband smiled.

Daddy cleared his throat, while Charity's uneasiness increased, her dislike for the Schultzes and their money almost visible in the stubbornness of her crossed arms.

Before Daddy or Charity could answer, I spoke up – it *was* my wedding. "I would like a church wedding," I said, looking at Huey for the first time. In spite of his embarrassment, his face lit up as he looked down at the floor.

Charity dropped her arms and spoke in her quiet, icy voice directly to me. "I think that under the circumstances, it would be a mockery to have a church wedding."

My whole body sagged as though she'd shot me with an arrow.

Daddy spoke up in a slow soothing way, "Well, I think it would be appropriate for the Pastor to *marry* them. Maybe he will tell us, can suggest something." Daddy grinned then, taking the edge off of Charity's remark.

Mrs. Schultz took advantage of his friendliness. "Would you be willing, then, to take care of the expense of a small family wedding? We could have the reception in our basement. We have the apartment building, you know, and the room in the basement is quite large. Several of the kids have had their's there... and baby showers."

Charity's flat disapproval flared-up in her tone, "A reception? We had not even anticipated..."

"But surely," Mrs. Schultz looked right at Daddy, "for your first daughter's wedding, you would like to give her a send off she vill wemember."

Charity colored but said nothing.

Daddy was always generous when his generosity was challenged. "Just a *small* reception then, for the family, in your basement," he said.

"That brings up another thing," Mrs. Schultz said, not waiting an instant for Daddy to recover, "Samantha will need something to wear for her special day."

"Oh, of course," said Daddy, "We'll be happy to buy her an outfit. Not a *long* dress though."

"No. I was thinking more of a nice tailored suit. Something she could wear for years to come. Bernice is a good shopper; she'd love to take her."

"All right," said Daddy. I could see him adding this all up in his head. "You know we are not well off financially; you understand that. We give Samantha Sue the best we can afford, but she will have to be content with something simple. Not too expensive."

"Certainly. Have you thought about the date yet?" Mrs. Schultz looked right at me.

"Yes. The end of January. During mid-term break."

"Good. It is settled then." Looking at Daddy again, she added. "Ve vill have to go to the court house, I believe, to sign for them both. Huey too. He's only eighteen. Here in Wisconsin it's twenty-one for boys. Going together vould make it easier. But that must wait, of course, until Samantha turns fifteen." She looked at me, questioningly.

"I'll be fifteen next week, the day after Thanksgiving," I said.

It was done — if I could just make it at home for nine more weeks.

Muriel started out by reminding me about all the times Huey had been drunk.

"Oh, he's quit drinking. His mom told me so, too," I said.

"And what kind of a job does he have? Driving a truck for that construction company; how long has he been there? Better yet, how long will he stay?"

"But, Muriel, I've been so miserable at home. *You* know that better than anyone, how awful my parents are, and even *they* are agreeing."

"Sure your father is agreeing, so he doesn't have to put out any more money on you. He's as happy as a lark. What about Charity? She's glad to be rid of you, too," Muriel said angrily. Then, abruptly, she started laughing, "But who's going to do her lousy dishes?"

The words struck me like a dart; my head was reeling. This was the last kind of reaction I expected from my best friend. "I thought you'd be tickled to death for me," I said, close to tears.

She ignored my argument, but instead, she said, "And the Schultzes. Why are they so con-sarned happy about you getting married?"

"I guess… Because they *like* me?" I answered timidly with a question.

"Humph. Bullshit. When is the court hearing?"

"Not until January. Well… Not at all, if we get married."

Muriel's look, then, said it all, hearing the answer to her question come out of my own mouth. Now I was all the more determined to see it through. I shut my mind to her doubts and dreamed every minute about the happiness Huey and I would have together, without Daddy or Charity to think about ever again.

On my fifteenth birthday, I applied for a part-time job at Woolworths. The manager hired me on the spot, saying, "Any girl who would look for a job on her birthday must want one." In Milwaukee the law was, you had to carry an average grade of eighty-five or better on your report card and could only work twenty hours per week, never past six o'clock. The forty-five cents per hour I was paid would come in handy, as well as get me out of the house. That night Huey picked me up for church and presented me with a small diamond engagement ring he had gotten on credit, for a ten-dollar-a-month payment (something neither of our parents approved of; buying on credit was the new thing and still considered very irresponsible). We sat together in church for the first time.

At school, kids came up and talked to me — kids I was surprised to find knew I existed. One girl told me, "Gee, you're nice. Not near as stuck-up as you look, being so pretty and never speaking to anyone." *That* was a shock. I was scared to death to speak to anyone, afraid they'd become friendly and find out I couldn't do anything. It was easier to stay to myself. The attention I was getting over the ring served to ease my insides somewhat. After I'd explain that I wasn't pregnant, I'd add, "My family always married young."

"Where is your family from?" they'd ask.

And when I'd tell them, Tennessee, they'd just say, "Oh."

But Mr. Robbins, in Biology, was not so easily put off. He came right out and asked me, after class one day, if I was pregnant.

I had only divulged this to girls, thus far. But I told him, *No*, and blushed. "Can't a girl get married if she wants to without being pregnant?" I added, with a teasing tone in my voice, "I *do* love him, you know."

Mr. Robbins had always responded with warmth and humor in the past, but this time he was dead serious. "You realize you are both too young; you both have a lot of growing and changing to do yet. When you grow, you change. And people rarely change *towards* each other. That's a fact. You usually grow in different directions. Few marriages last that begin this young. Believe me, I think you are making a drastic mistake."

"But my aunt and cousin were married that young, and

they're still married. Almost twenty years."

"That's unusual, believe me. You need to finish school. With your bright mind, you have so much open to you, if you get your education."

All I could think about was what Daddy had said about girls not needing an education, but I wouldn't repeat that. I knew Daddy was wrong, and that was not the way to think. Mr. Robbins' interest in me, pleased me. He was such a good teacher, no one could help learning in his class.

"Thank you for talking to me," I said to him on the verge of tears but still determined. "I intend to go back to school, but first I want to get a home."

Even though I ran out of his room, terribly upset, it was important for him to understand. He had been sympathetic when I had told him of Charity's new pregnancy, her morning sickness, and all the added work at home, having to quit cello. But this was something far different. Not Mr. Robbins, or anyone else, could possibly understand.

The wedding shower, thrown by Muriel and her friends — some I ate lunch with – was a surprise, and so many there. It was at Charlotte's house, a girl who had said little to me before I got the ring. She was very popular, played the flute in the school's marching band, and went to a different Pentecostal church. Her older brother, Benny, was very good looking, so she did not want for friends.

The girls all sat around me on the couch, asking one question after the other. Muriel had told them about Huey, I could tell. Muriel and her friends didn't think anything about virginity, or losing it, like I did. It was the drinking that worried them, though. His being "saved" was my only defense. As for my age, I continued to insist that I was *not* too young. Just like Nat King Cole's latest hit song, *Too Young*. The elegant wrappings on the personal gifts made me feel all the more undeserving. Silky under things, like I had never worn before, were just for me, not for my new home. This surprised me, too.

We were having cake and punch when the doorbell rang. Benny answered it. The door opened right into the living room where we were sitting so we could all hear. It was Huey, and he was obviously very drunk. "What the hell you doing with my bride?" he yelled belligerently into the frosty storm door Benny held open. "You fuckin' bastard, come out here and let me get my hands…"

Just then one of Huey's friends came up behind him. "Sorry about that, Buddy," he said. Huey had just plowed his car into the snow bank in front of the house. It was snowing hard out, besides, and his friend was drunk also, but more amiable than Huey. Hiccupping, his friend continued, "We just came from a bachelor party; I'll take care of him."

As the doors closed, all eyes were upon me. Right there I could've died, after just telling everyone Huey had accepted Christ and had "changed."

Charlotte came over and sat down next to me, putting her arm around my shoulders. The tears wouldn't stay back then. "Samantha, did you notice we gave you a *personal* shower, instead of the other kind?" she asked gently.

Shaking my head, I held my mouth with my handkerchief to hide the sobs.

"Well, we did that on purpose, just in case you change your mind. So you wouldn't have to give anything back."

The girls all murmured in agreement.

Their looks of sympathy turned my stomach and made me all the more determined to rise above that despicable feeling of being pitied. But there seemed no way to make anyone understand, I could see that. Shame hung over my head, and I knew of no other way to remedy it than to get married. They all knew; I was certain of it. And if they didn't, they and the whole world would, for sure, after the court hearing. At least, married, I would no longer *have* to be a virgin. Huey *would* quit drinking again, I was convinced of it, just as soon as we are married.

C harity was standing at my bedroom door with a pale blue, rayon, taffeta-like nightgown hanging over her arm. "Here," she said. "This is all we could afford after all the things Bernice strapped us with."

The rose, sharkskin, double-breasted suit, the kind of style Bernice insisted would last a lifetime, was the nicest thing I had ever owned. She found me a crepe blouse, double-pleated, to go under it, and I found a white felt, cloche hat that allowed just enough of my short, dark curls to frame my face. I'd gotten Daddy at an agreeable moment, and he had put a big bowl over my head and cut off my long hair. Short hair was coming into style, so I felt ready for my wedding day, even though the memory of the photograph flashed through my mind as I tried on the hat.

Bernice had taken me shopping on two separate Saturdays, and I was crazy about her. "Stick it to your old man," she'd say, looking at price tags. "It's the last thing he's going to pay for, so have a fling." She insisted I was being conservative, actually. A wedding dress would have cost a bundle. The French curved heels, in navy leather, were hard to find, my feet so small and narrow. They were expensive. But she knew just what would look good and keep me short. When she suggested looking for a "negligee," I refused, explaining that Charity had already told me she and Daddy would buy that, along with the pearls and earrings, for a wedding gift. I had expected to receive it at Christmas, but instead, the surprise under the tree had been the white figure skates.

The sight of the ice skates instantly saddened me to tears. *Why had they waited so long?* It was almost a slap in the face. Irony, Charity might have said, if she had been in my place. But Daddy thought the skates had really pleased me. Instead, they seemed to sum up everything, gift wrapped and tied in a bow.

The cheap, harsh-feeling nightgown from Woolworths, didn't really surprise me, and any color besides white – a reminder of my lost virginity, Charity's way.

Looking at myself in the mirror — at the two wide panels of hard, itchy lace, with one tiny pleat tacked under each breast, and how they hugged and flattened me – I burst into tears. Charity heard me and came rushing back into the room. I said to her, "Couldn't you have found something soft and full over the bust line to hide how skinny I am and not make me look so awful?" I was crying, hugging myself so she couldn't see me.

"Ach," she said with her guttural German, "What do you expect, miracles? You're flat as a pancake," flipping her fingers at my skinny body, "and straight as a stick, to boot."

Best wishes, I said to myself as she flew out of my room, more determined than ever to go through with this wedding in spite of everything. Huey was still drinking and now was asking for the little money I earned at Woolworths besides. Bernice was smart enough to suggest I not give him any sex until our wedding night. Just one more week, I thought at Charity's back, *and you will never, ever hurt me again.*

Our parents watched as Reverend Daugherty married us in his living room, with Bernice and her husband, Eric, as our witnesses. We had pictures taken in a studio and dinner with Bernice and Eric at a nice restaurant. Huey slipped out to the bar while we were eating and returned only minutes later, reeking of booze. The whole day became a blur in my memory after that.

It was as though I was caught rushing over a mighty waterfall. Things were getting worse, and I felt disaster ahead.

The reception that night, in the Schultzes' basement, was attended by both our families. At least a dozen Evermardts came. Huey had almost as many aunts, uncles, and cousins as I did. There were so many that my head was spinning as I fought to keep the smile upon my face, to keep from revealing the hurting inside. I didn't want anyone to hear Huey's threats all night to leave the party and go *finish getting plastered.*

As we left the basement, heading for Huey's parents' bedroom they'd given up for us, Rod, Huey's oldest brother, grabbed me, claiming the last kiss from the bride. He whispered in my ear, "You better make it nine months and a week, kid. Otherwise – no one will ever believe it!"

◆

CHAPTER TEN

THE MARRIAGE: 1952-1954

Another alarm clock was ringing somewhere in the room, again. Huey was cussing out every member of his family as he struggled in the dark to find the third clock, each set to go off an hour apart: the price one paid for not going away on a honeymoon. Huey was the baby of five kids and all of them married and living in apartments in the building. We wondered what to expect next. "Damn it. Let them ring," he said, crawling back under the feather quilt his aunt from Germany had made us. Laughter. How I longed for it. I prayed desperately that it was a sign of good things to come, but Huey wasn't laughing.

After being married a week, Huey had already started on his second job — at a gas station, where he met Norman.

The day he got fired from the station was the first time he brought Norman home. It wasn't only the black leather jacket Norman wore that made him look like a gang member, but his hair was greased back and his sideburns were long and shaggy. Like Huey, he was only eighteen, but also like Huey, he looked over twenty-one, drinking age. Whenever he was around, his eyes would wander brazenly over my body, head to toe, giving me the creeps.

But neither one of them was around long. As soon as Huey could get his mother to slip him a couple of dollars, with, "Don't tell Pa," whispered in his ear, he was gone "to get gas."

"I'll be right back," he'd say and take off, only to return home later and later, drunker and drunker.

While cleaning house, doing laundry, I would hear from Ma Schultz a new story every day about "Huey's trouble with the cops." His record had been so bad the year before that he had been sent to the Bible school in Texas (the one where Daddy was planning to send me) just to get him out of the state, away from prosecution. Huey finally quit school for good. His last arrest was for throwing a lit cigarette, "just for fun," through a car window, into the lap of an old man who was driving his classic Model-T on the road along side of him. Huey was already on probation for driving over a girlfriend's lawn, when she'd broken up with him, spinning his wheels and tearing up the sod.

"It's those boys he runs with," Ma Schultz would say, holding her stomach over her ulcer. "Huey is such a *good* boy. It's just *those awful friends* who influence him. Now that he's married, I know he'll settle down. Just watch and see."

Ma Schultz really believed he would change, and I was easily infected with her optimism. Hope was all I had left — until, on one of Norman's daily appearances, Huey begged for me to *Prove you love me; have sex with Norman.*"

It was almost dark when Huey and Norman got out of the car. Ma Schultz saw them first and grabbed me. We ran down the hall to the apartment of her sister-in-law who was fresh from Germany and spoke no English. Ma shoved me inside the tiny kitchen, whispered something in German, and ran back to her own apartment. Just as the tall German woman slid the chain into the lock, the boys walked past, out in the hall. Afraid to breathe, I was sure they could have heard my heart beating had they not been so noisy.

First, Huey went to his mother's apartment, then came out, cussing loudly. "Where is that mother-fuckin' cock-sucker, anyhow? She's gotta be around here somewhere. Don't worry, Norman. I'll find her for you." Their footsteps came closer and stopped; Bernice's door was just across the hall.

Bernice's high falsetto voice pierced the air. "No, Huey. I haven't seen her. Have you asked Ma?"

"Yeah. She said she hasn't seen her. Where in the goddamn is the bitch?" he was saying, as he left his sister's door.

In her chiding, cute way, Bernice admonished him, "Huey, is *that* the way to talk about your wife? Shame on you."

My ear was pressed to the door; the knock on the other side of it startled me. Huey's aunt, twice my size, reached her large hand over to me and patted my shoulder. She put her fingers to her lips in a "sh" and waited for the second knock. She pulled the door ajar, barely a crack, and looked through the chain. "Ya-ah?" she answered.

"Have you seen my wife? You know, Samantha?"

The woman just shook her head and shrugged her towering shoulders, like she usually did when she didn't understand, and rattled off something in German.

Huey sauntered off towards the upstairs, complaining about the "foreign bitch."

One by one I heard him knock on doors, looking for me, first to his sister, Gen's, and then to his brother, Rod's. Finally, Huey was coming back down the stairs and past our door again.

His aunt and I stood there, not speaking. She smiled as we listened, the terror I felt within undoubtedly written on my face as we heard Huey say, "Wait till I get my hands on that cock-suckin' witch, I'll beat the shit outta her." Their laughter filled the hallway as they walked on by, until the heavy outside door closed behind them.

In a few minutes, Ma Schultz came and got me. She was very upset and told me to stay home with her the rest of the evening instead of watching my usual television somewhere in the building. I felt I had narrowly escaped the dungeon or worse. Ma Schultz was my ally now, and I was sure it was her doing that Norman never returned. Nevertheless, the attempt had been made, and the thought of Norman after me haunted me, leaving no doubt now of Huey's *sexual perversion*.

Bernice and Ma Schultz were taking turns reading me the riot act – a customary occurrence about one thing or another. "Where did you go? How much money did you spend? On what?" I just sat there on the piano bench, red in the face, with Huey, still with his saxophone strap around his neck, saying, "Yeah, answer my mother!"

On the verge of tears, I knew Ma was right: I *did* sleep late most days; I just couldn't seem to wake up. And I *had* wasted money on yarn to crochet doilies, while the sun was burning up the clothes line, stretching it all out of shape so the sheets would drag in the dirt. Not to mention that I had not been around to help when the dry clothes had been taken down, off the line. And living here free, no less.

Gen and Rod, who lived in their own adjoining apartments upstairs, hearing the commotion, had slipped into the kitchen. Gen listened for awhile. Then she came into the room and spoke to her mother. "Ma. Listen to me. Look at this young girl. Think how *old* she is. Look at her. She is only *fifteen years old*. A baby! What was Bernice doing at fifteen? Huh, Ma? She wasn't even doing her laundry. No. She wasn't even ironing her own clothes yet. I remember how mad I used to get at you for doing it for her, and you're yelling at this kid? I think she is doing pretty darn good, myself." Gen turned around and walked out, with Rod following behind, leaving everyone in the room silently looking after them.

I never left the clothes line out in the sun again and made an appointment for my very first physical examination.

Ma Schultz decided maybe Huey would stay home more if we had some privacy. In the large basement, she fixed up a room at the end of it by hanging up a curtain and lent us the use of her old bedroom set. I'm sure she was tired of sleeping in the living room, too. We still ate with them, and she had started letting me cook a little. Mealtimes were really just a continuation of the day-long intimate conversation between us, as Pa Schultz said nothing, and Huey ate with his eyes glued to a comic book tucked under his plate.

But the new arrangement didn't change things, as Huey continued to go out night after night with one lame excuse after the other, always promising to be "right back." By the time he returned, he was usually very drunk. But Sundays, he never went out, it was "our day." Together, we went to church, and he would take me out to eat at some little inexpensive place afterwards. On that day, Huey was, what I then considered to be, a peach of a husband. He would stay with me all day and treat me special, with loving affection. I was convinced that if he would just quit drinking, we would be *happy* like this all the time.

Sometimes on Sunday nights, the whole family would have pot luck in the basement. It was fun, with close to a dozen grandkids all together, the little ones wheeling their bikes around. I'd play Parcheesi or Sorry with the bigger ones. I lived from one week to the next. Then one Sunday afternoon, one of Huey's friends called him, and he left. Just as I was finished dressing, to go with his folks to evening church service, he came home smelling like a brewery.

When Huey was drunk, he wanted one thing. Sex. And since that night at my house, when he fell asleep and pinned me to the bed, I had made up my mind that he was not getting it – not when he was drinking. It would become a contest of wills. This time, he grabbed my beautiful wedding blouse by the neckline, and ripped it right off of me. I was furious. "If you think you are scaring me, you've got another think coming," I yelled, holding up the torn blouse. As he reached for my wedding suit skirt, I got away from him. This really made him angry, and he started pulling all of our clothes out of the dresser.

Determined not to give in, I just stood and watched, not believing.

Like a mad bull, Huey began ramming his head up against the cement-block wall.

Still, I watched and wondered just what he was going to do next. His going out on Sunday was the last straw. I was going to *show* him.

When I threatened to call his mother, he grabbed one of his pajama bottoms and tied it around his neck, pulling it so tight that his face turned purple. Down onto the cement floor, he fell into a heap.

By now I was in tears, and suddenly feeling sympathetic. "Huey. Huey," I cried, and ran over to him. "What are you trying to do to yourself?"

He opened his eyes and rolled over and grabbed me around the legs, shoving me onto the bed. "Please. Please," he begged, bawling real tears. "Don't go and leave me here alone. I promise I won't do anything else," he pleaded, kissing me on the knees. Then, over my clothes, he put his mouth. "I love your cunt," he said and bit me through my clothes.

The sight of him, helpless, defenseless like a child, did something to me. I wanted to comfort him and kiss away his tears, so I brought his face up to mine and kissed him. His words of love and devotion were what I wanted to hear. As he helped me off with the rest of my clothes, my desire to love and protect him was all I could think about. Surely he really did love me and need me. Maybe his mother was right – he would change. Then we had sex after he said he'd "pull it out" in time. Married three months and still not pregnant. I was confident it would be okay.

The next day, Huey was sent home by the nurse at work with a headache, a slight concussion from the blow on the head he had received from the "car wreck," he told her, showing her the large bump from the basement wall. His sisters and brothers laughed when they heard about it. His mother said, "Oh, no, my god," holding her stomach. His dad said nothing, as always.

This crazy behavior, added to Huey's juvenile police record, which was completely unknown to me before we married, would now give me grounds for the annulment Reverend Daugherty had suggested one day, when I ran into him unexpectedly. "How's married life?" he had asked. The tears poured out of me as I told him how bad things had gotten to be. The Pastor's understanding advice that day never left the back of my mind.

"Sorry, dear," said the clerk in the District Attorney's office. "If you had run away, then you could get an annulment. But since your father signed for you, your only recourse is divorce."

I felt nauseated, and when I walked into the dark chambers of the stuffy old court house, where we had gotten our licenses, I had gotten dizzy. It was something about the odor in the place. My doctor's appointment was in a few days. Maybe Ma was right, something *was* wrong with me that I slept so much. The subject of this visit, though, and sneaking out without Ma or Bernice knowing about it, didn't help how I felt.

Ma Schultz was waiting, holding the back door open for me. The scowl on her face left no doubt that she was angry; her dark eyes were staring daggers right through me. With her hands on her hips, she asked, "Do you realize what day this is?"

"Well, yes. It's Friday."

"Yes, it's Friday, all right. This is cleaning day. Just *where* have you been?"

I knew she would be upset that I had not confided in her, but I was surprised at just how much, since I usually told her everything. Flushed, and a little shaky in my voice, I said, "I went shopping."

"Shopping? Not up at *our* store, you didn't; Bernice went up there looking for you. Where did you go?"

"Ma. What's this all about? Huh? What are you so upset about? My place is clean. I don't have that much to do, you know."

"Well, you could have helped me do mine then, since you two are not paying any rent. This is a big building to keep up. You know I do it all myself."

"I'm sorry; I won't go out on cleaning day again," I said, upset then, that I had to account for every minute.

When she heard the silent anger in my voice, she let me pass, and her demeanor grew soft again. She was my best friend, and I think she believed I was the only hope for her son. We had an unspoken bond between us, and I was beginning to understand my power with her. My new intentions would have to be a secret.

C harity was folding diapers and didn't seem too enthusiastic to see me. Her new baby, Philip, was two months old. I had only been over to visit her and Daddy once, when Philip was born. He lay asleep in Marcy's crib in the kitchen, and Marcy was down for a nap in my old room; we talked in whispers. It struck me, then, how convenient it must have been for me to move out – just in time for the baby. *Where would they have put him had I not left when I did?* I never gave it any serious thought before, just that they seemed anxious to be rid of me.

Philip's head full of ringlets perspired as he slept. Seeing him, I couldn't hold it in any longer. "Guess what? I just came from your doctor's office, and she told me today that the test came back positive. I'm pregnant! I'm so excited. I had to tell you first, for some reason."

Charity never looked up from the clothes she was folding when she said, "Ach. For your child to be born dead, would be a blessing from God."

Shocked at her words, I asked, "Why do you say that?"

"What does the child have? To welcome it into this world?" she said, staring into space. Then, as though there was no doubt whatsoever in her judgment, she answered her own question. "Better that it should be born dead."

Her words were like arrows piercing my heart, but I swallowed back the tempest inside of me, not answering her. Instead, I jumped up and offered to do the dishes I saw piled up in the sink.

The dishes had food dried so hard on them, I had trouble getting them clean. I was almost finished when Charity came over and reached under the sink for another huge dishpan full; I think every dish in the house was dirty. As I washed and scrubbed, I promised myself I would never keep house this carelessly. Her continual complaining of how much work babies were didn't seem to be an excuse. Babies or no babies, Ma Schultz was teaching me to never leave a dirty dish in the sink.

On the long bus ride home, Charity's words kept running through my head until I couldn't keep the tears back; she had been so cruel. But she had *always* been cruel. *Why had I gone there?* It just seemed important to tell Charity first that I was going to be a mother. I even used her doctor. The high spirits that had sent me to her, now plunged me into despair. But by the time I got home, my fighting spirit, that I liked to believe was from my Cherokee roots, rose up from somewhere inside of me. I decided that day to leave Charity alone. If I were dying, she'd be the last one I'd tell from now on; *I'll show her.* I'd show the whole world just what a good mother I could be. And Huey, I just knew this would be the trick that would straighten him out. "Becoming a father will do it," his mother would say, with such hope.

My own baby – it was my dream coming true. The dream I had carried all of my life, of my baby sister who never was born, buried with Mama. The dream of the three of us and how happy we all would've been together, if they had only lived. But now, I had another chance to be happy – at last. I would never be alone again.

The news of my pregnancy spread quickly through the building.

Ma Schultz was thrilled, as was Huey. He even started staying home more and talking seriously about getting our own apartment. It was a miracle.

We grew restless waiting for an apartment to become available in the building, so we found a nice little furnished place nearby. As part of our weekly rent, I baby-sat all day, every day, for the landlady's five-year-old son, Jimmy. It was through this job that I saw my first show. I got money for carfare downtown and lunch and enough to take Jimmy to a movie.

Pinky was the name of the film, about racism, with Jeanne Crain, Ethel Waters, and Ethel Barrymore. It was as if I was seeing my own life on the screen. Jeanne Crain, after living in Boston, and passing for White, goes back to the South and to her Black grandmother despite the mistreatment her race receives there. I could feel her shame and knew the wish she lived with — to be like everyone else. The feelings I had when the older woman died in her bed, were almost too much for me to bear. All the way home on the bus, I just sobbed, not knowing it was the similarity of the deeply hidden memory of my own mother's last moments that had come to the surface, almost choking me, while Jimmy kept patting my arm and telling me it was only a movie; "the lady *didn't really die*; it was just for the story," he said. Daddy considered movies *worldly, sinful, and of the Devil*. We heard in church that if Jesus came in the rapture, while we were inside the theater, we would surely be left behind. This threat was a fear I lived with my entire childhood. Now in the Schultz family, it helped that they didn't think the same way. From that one film, I could see how much I had missed without that side to my life. No wonder I was dumb about things, things most people took for granted. Now, though, Gen and Rod both had TV's, so I got to watch the *I Love Lucy* show every week. Lucille Ball being pregnant for the whole world to see, right along with me, was very special. Things in my world were changing before my very eyes.

That first week of my working, Huey and I fought daily. Anyone that got my attentions made Huey insanely jealous, even little Jimmy. Because my morning sickness was getting the best of me anyway, I let Huey have his way and gave up babysitting, which sent us back to his mom's.

The next small apartment that came available in the building was ours. It was surprising how fast it got furnished. Chairs, tables, rugs, all kinds of things were offered from everywhere. It was all hand-me-downs, of course, except a bright red couch Ma bought new, especially for us. Helping us to fix it up, she was as excited as we were.

Keeping Huey working and bringing in a paycheck, was the biggest problem. One of his brothers had finally gotten him in one of the plants he did business with. Everyone in the building seemed to want to see us make it, especially Ma Schultz. She had a key to our apartment, and I would find a stick of butter or a dish of fruit or some sausage setting inside my kitchen door almost every morning.

She would let me do my wash with her and taught me how to do laundry very properly – no underwear in the same water as dish towels! We put everything through two rinses and had to rub each piece on the washboard in the rinse water to make sure the soap was out. What a particular housekeeper she was! Her clothes line gleamed, with everything hung up to match: linens together, shirts, then underwear. She vacuumed every single day and washed her living room carpets with ammonia water every week, "so the grandkids don't get their knees dirty." On Friday, cleaning day, the whole house got a thorough going over. This is when I really got acquainted with Bernice. She lived at my end of the building, and it was easy to run down the back steps and knock at her door to visit. She was expecting her first baby also, three months ahead of me, and I had a lot of questions.

Bernice was the first one to talk to me about sex, asking me one day if I knew what an orgasm was. Trying to give her some kind of an answer without embarrassing myself, she saw my hesitation and laughed, telling me it was nothing at all to be ashamed of. "Women can enjoy sex, too. Try and let yourself relax and do it; Huey might like for you to." Even though they were close as sister and brother, I couldn't bring myself to talk about this with Huey.

Sex had been sort of hit and miss with us to begin with. Huey was a cuddler and would not go to sleep unless I was holding him, somehow. It was when he'd begin to touch me that I would get rigid, and feel awful. Even though I loved having him close to me during sex, how he'd hold me so tightly and tell me how much he loved me, when he might have forgotten to tell me in awhile, I just wanted to get the sex part over with. It always made me feel wretched, as with Beth as a child, feelings that I fought continuously... until I got pregnant. Something happened to me then...

Waking from an afternoon nap with the sun streaming into my bed, the swelling of those parts was something new, my breasts, too, as they grew more sensitive. In the bathroom, I'd find myself touching them, and more... At first, I told myself it was what I was supposed to do when I was pregnant. *Why else would I feel this way?* I'd remind myself of what Grandma Baumn used to say, "If you are hungry for something, it's what your body is missing, and needing." It wasn't until much later that I found out about the extra hormones in pregnancy, how they can wake up those feelings right smartly. But at the time, I didn't know, and I certainly couldn't talk to Huey about it. When he got drunk he would yell it to the housetops, as he already had done with my secrets about Daddy, using shameful words for the world to hear.

In my dreams, I spent many nights physically tangling with someone, usually Bernice.

Huey, too, was getting more obsessed with sex every day. Whether it was the swelling of my body, or he could sense my sexual parts waking up, which, up until then, were totally asleep, I don't know. Or maybe it was his own age, just turning nineteen, as sex was all he talked about. All I could think of was Charity's admonishing and quoting the Bible, about "children, suffering for the sins of their parents." *That sin*, no doubt, was *in the marriage bed,* she believed. The fear of my baby having something wrong with it, like my brother Jesse, a waterhead, frightened me beyond words.

Between my own body calling me to sin and my husband begging me too, I was in a constant frenzy to keep busy. I began to sew frantically for my new baby, starting with a whole new wardrobe for my six dolls that covered my bed.

Gen, a good seamstress, also, lent me her patterns, and help. All of the kids in the building had dolls for her to dress. Every cent I could pinch out of the budget went for material. The more Huey talked of sex, the busier I got, and the more he began going out again – when he'd almost stopped drinking.

Huey said he met a new friend to play with him in bars. It didn't take him long to learn that if he would take me shopping for new material, he could get out after dinner almost without a fight. I'd sew all night until I dropped into bed. There I'd stare out the window overlooking the street and wait for him to drive around that corner.

That summer, the first time in my life when I could wear shorts, halters, swimming suits, slacks, anything I chose, was the greatest. It was as if I had been let out of a cage, and Bernice and Ma Schultz were the fairy godmothers who had rescued me. Bernice gave me some of her old clothes, expensive things she was tired of. Rod's wife had given me a halter that tied, so I could adjust it as I grew in my pregnancy.

One day, I was outdoors playing with the kids on their little trikes, bent over pushing one, when Huey came home from work. Like Daddy, Huey wanted me right there too, when he came in, so he didn't have to look for me. I was bent over the little trike, in my new halter, when he grabbed me very tightly by the arm. "Get yourself upstairs and put on some decent clothes," he said, angrily.

"What's wrong with these?" I asked in astonishment.

"Look at you when you bend down; you can see your tits. It's bad enough they are so little; you don't have to advertise it by showing them to everyone."

All the way up the stairs, he hung onto my arm very tightly, a habit he had, bringing comments from the whole family about my bruises.

When we got into the apartment, Huey started in, "What were you out there showing off for anyhow?" he said, "All those workmen building next door, huh? Trying to give them a little teaser, huh?" He grabbed me again and brought his other hand up past my face, letting me feel the breeze of his swing.

Angrily, I ran out of the building and started walking. He followed me in his car, finally begging me to forgive him and get in. I never understood, till much later, how my growing and changing was affecting him. I believed that because I had said *I do,* I was already grown up. Little did I know how much of a child I was yet, and still in the growing process myself.

Incidents like this began to happen frequently, Huey getting angrier and angrier with me. If he started ranting and raving, the minute his mother would hear him, she would hide all the sharp butcher knives under her kitchen range.

It was in the midst of one of these fights, when he had really frightened me with his usual intimidations, that I took off early one morning, to visit my Grandma Evermardt.

It was at my wedding reception when I had last seen my grandmother, and then only for a minute, and nearly a year before that. I was eager to get to know her as a *free adult*. She lived way on the south side of town. It was a long ride to her house, and my pregnancy made me tired. After we ate her Southern fried chicken she showed me how to fix, we crawled into bed together very early. It was so much fun. She must've been close to sixty by then. Grandpa Evermardt, quite a bit older than she was, had died when I was a kid living in Georgia, and we missed his funeral. His early death put her into a TB sanitarium for five years, and her last three girls literally raised themselves. Grandma said she was *tired of younguns*, after raising sixteen. "But I still have a powerful lot of them coming around."

As we lay there in her bed, I started telling Grandma all about Huey, about all the trouble Daddy had put me through at the Safety Building, about being asked if I wanted to live with her. She hugged me then and told me how sorry she was to hear that I had not called her, "I would've taken you somehow."

She understood how I felt, though, loving my daddy.

"From the time you were a little bitty thing, your daddy never put any store by anyone's judgment where you were concerned. We couldn't, any of us, lay a hand to you. And that is where all the trouble came in with Jenny Lou, after your mama died. Jenny Lou was used to treating you like her own and to have to stop, well, she couldn't keep taking care of you under your daddy's rules, not letting anyone else but him tend to you. And you know your aunt. She is high tempered, and she and your daddy just got into it, one big tangle. Wilbur put a stop to it. Then your daddy sort of went crazy on religion, but we were so glad he wasn't drinking and carrying on anymore, for your sake, that we never tried to interfere."

The sadness in Grandma's voice, told me she really did care for me a whole lot. It was what I needed to hear from her more than anything in the world, being pregnant and carrying my own little baby.

I told her, then, how mean and awful Huey could be, but how sweet and gentle he was that nobody else ever saw.

"Sometimes, I love him so much, Gramma," I said, halfway to tears. "I just don't understand why he is so jealous of me. Being pregnant, no less."

"Well, someday, maybe all of this unhappiness you are having will be over, and you'll look back on it all and smile. Let's hope so. Life has a way of easing things, over time, you know."

"Oh, Gramma, I'm so glad I came over to see you. I haven't laughed in such a long time. Maybe you're right. Maybe someday, I'll be able to look back and smile, too, at all of this. But none of it seems very funny now."

Snuggling up close, we finally fell asleep. It was a time I will cherish always in my memory. A very special night. She had always been busy with her big brood, and Daddy had made it difficult for them to show me much attention, refusing most every invitation they ever extended to me. There were times in anger I had wished for her and Aunt Jenny Lou to interfere for me. But I understood, now, why they hadn't. They didn't know I needed them to, and I could never have told them.

As I left my grandmother's house that day to go back to Huey, I took her love with me. It would make up for Mama not being there to be "Gramma" to my new baby, just a little bit. And a little bit was a whole lot more than the nothing I had felt for most of my life.

Before I was too far along in my pregnancy, Ma Schultz convinced me to change to Dr. Oberman, who had delivered both Bernice and Huey. Like Mr. Simms and Ma Schultz, Dr. Oberman had snow-white hair and treated me with gentleness, as though I was something that would break. He was terribly upset that I was so young, and he made no bones about it, riding with me himself on the elevator to the delivery room after a trillion young interns had rammed their index fingers up my rectum — a teaching hospital. Interns being there created so much anxiety for me. On top of the discomfort and embarrassment, I was afraid Huey would see one of them and pitch a fit. Huey was prone to jealous rages, and his drinking had gotten even worse over the holidays. In the elevator, Dr. Oberman patted me, assuring me I would not feel any pain.

The last thing I remembered, after the nurse put my feet into the stockings and into the cold metal stirrups, was Dr. Oberman, thinking I was already passed out, saying, "She is just a child. A pity. A downright dirty shame."

But I'm sixteen now, doesn't he know I just had a birthday? When I awoke, the nurse was holding my beautiful baby girl. I named her after a girlfriend in school who was friendly and pretty. Although I had heard loud groaning, and screams from others from time to time, I felt nothing until I stood up. Then my stitches hurt. But when I held Sharon in my arms, all the pain in the world would have been worth it. She was beautiful, chubby, with a head full of black hair. It was like no other feeling in the world, and I wanted to hold her forever, close, just like then. This must've been why I had been allowed to live, when most of my family had died, I thought. Surely now, Huey would have real reason to stay home and never drink again.

My breasts were full of milk. I had to be bound and took drying-up pills. Nursing was not too popular, then, although secretly I wanted to do it more than anything in the world. But Huey wouldn't even consider it. He thought it was vulgar and flat out told me, "Hell, no, you're not." So I never even gave it a second thought. But the milk continued to pour out of me for days after it should have stopped. My body was crying out to feed my baby.

The night I went home from the hospital, Huey stayed home until eight o'clock. A record. He usually was gone by six. He said he had car trouble or some such silly excuse. I cried myself to sleep that night. There was no way I was going to live this way for very long. I knew it would take time and planning, but things had to change.

Maybe he sensed a change in my attitude because he began taking me and Sharon places. He took us to an apartment where a girlfriend of his buddy lived. Her name was Wanda Reese. When we got there, she looked at me as if I were a freak or something. I couldn't put my finger on it. I asked Huey when we left if I was still too fat to go out; it was only a week. Maybe that was what she was looking at, or maybe she didn't like babies. But she held Sharon and made a lot over her, asked me all kinds of questions about Huey, how long we had been married, as if she thought we had to get married and was surprised when we hadn't. She confided to me that she and Huey's buddy were *not going steady*, as Huey had told me in the car. We never went back there.

The next week, Huey took me to a poker party. The girls all drank wine, and the guys drank beer. I loved watching them, as I never had seen a game of cards played in my life. Daddy called cards *the Devil's Bible*. While Sharon slept on the bed, I got very interested and chatted with everyone. Friendliness was never a problem with me. As I was getting into the car to go home, Huey, who was pretty drunk, kicked the door of the car in, yelling at me for flirting with all his friends. "If you'd shut your fat face – smile, smile, smile, that's all you do, for Christ's sake. Shut it up, already."

The kids upstairs from the party heard us and came out. I was holding Sharon, standing in the blowing and swirling snow, with tears pouring off my face, falling all over her. It was so embarrassing. One of the girls whispered into my ear to "Dump that jerk." In my head, I said, *One of these days, I'm going to, you mean old thing.*

It was after Sharon was two weeks old and doing well on her formula that Gen had come over to watch me bathe her. Gen said she was planning to give me some tips, but that I was so very "agile" I didn't need any; she wondered where I had learned it?

"I don't know. It just sort of comes naturally to me," I said.

That night, Huey didn't come home for supper as he usually did, before he went out. Nights like that Ma got upset and began hiding the knives before he got home. When the birth of Sharon had not seemed to make a dent in his drinking, she started saying, "If it had been a *boy*, then it would have been different."

Since I had stitches, and the doctor gave explicit instructions to refrain from sex until after my six weeks checkup, I never expected Huey to come home and demand it. I had just fed Sharon when he came roaring into the apartment. One thing led to another, and when I didn't budge, he grabbed Sharon out of my arms. "What are you doing?" I screamed.

"It's my kid; I'm taking her for a walk," he said, and went out the door. I grabbed my robe and followed him down the hall. By this time, his yelling had everyone standing in the halls. We got next to Gen's front door, just in front of the banister that had an opening between the railings. Huey was holding Sharon, without a blanket in the cold hall, in one hand over the opening, screaming to the top of his lungs, "You goddamn bitch, you don't give me what I want, I'm going to drop this fuckin' kid, right now."

God, how I prayed, through my tears. Everyone in the halls were scared to death. Ma was standing below, in case he really did it, I guess. Bernice, who's own baby was just three months old, was standing behind me, shaking and crying, talking to him, trying to get him to give us the baby. Then Gen stepped out into the hall. She was a tall woman and had a stern look on her face, kind, but no nonsense. She looked calmly at her little brother and spoke to him like to a small child. "Huey, be a good boy, now, and give me the baby. I won't hurt you. No one will. Just give me the baby."

By this time, I was frantic. I couldn't take my eyes off my baby. Sharon was looking at the lights over her head and listening to all the sounds in the room, her little legs moving up and down in her nightgown. I loved her so much, and he knew it. He was jealous of her. I could see that then, and I knew, no matter what happened from then on, I would never, ever, trust him with my baby again.

Huey was still angry, and then Sharon began to cry. Gen walked over to them, very slowly, and reached both of her hands out and took Sharon from him. Gen put Sharon into my arms, and I broke down in giant sobs. That night, I swore, church or no church, Christian or no Christian, I was biding my time to get out of this marriage. My one fear was that I would get pregnant before

I could accomplish it.

It was late spring, and I had sewed a new orange dress, a square necked linen sheath. My weight was slowly coming down, so it fit very nicely.

We were having Sunday supper in the basement, with the whole family. Sharon was in her carriage, and I was sitting next to Huey at the long picnic table. Suddenly, I felt something wet and cold hit me and fall between my breasts. I grabbed it, squealing, as I pulled out an olive pit. I looked up and Rod was grinning at me, the same way he had always teased me in choir, long before I knew Huey. He just liked to tease me. I rolled my eyes at him, shaming him, and noticed Huey watching me pull the pit from my cleavage. Huey leaned over and put his arm around me.

Huey was anxious to leave, for some reason, and he kept his arm around me all the way up the stairs as I carried Sharon. Leaning close to me, he said, "You're getting to look pretty sexy lately; did you know that?"

"No. What do you mean, sexy?"

"Well, that dress, it fits like a glove. And your hips are bigger than they used to be. And your tits, they ain't so bad either, lately. And I noticed my brother looking at you."

"But, Huey, I didn't..."

At that moment, he put his arms around me and his mouth on mine, right there in the hallway outside our apartment door, and kissed me like he hadn't done in months, since before my pregnancy. Oh, how I fought him. Inside, I kept telling myself, *I can't fall for this stuff he's handing out. I can't get pregnant. I have to get away...*

He had me half undressed, though, while I was putting Sharon to bed. He began kissing me, again, all over me. He touched me and made places I didn't know I had – didn't want to have – feel good, and then he put his mouth all over me, and the feelings I had left behind in childhood came back to me as he turned around on me and put his tongue to me. When he put himself into my mouth, then, almost crying, telling me how much he loved me and my letting him do this, was when I realized what I was doing. I began to gag, and cry, and spit, and begged, "Please stop. *Stop.* You know this is a sin. Please don't do this anymore."

But in his passion he was oblivious to my cries and kept using his tongue all over me. Then he must have heard me, or felt me twisting out from under him, and he stopped and turned around, and kissed me and kissed me, and told me he was sorry he had done that to me.

He made me promise, then, "Please, don't ever tell *anyone, ever* that I done that to you. Oh, baby, I'm so sorry. I wouldn't hurt you for the world."

I fell asleep in his arms, believing that maybe, *maybe,* he really did love me. I was so confused.

But when he got drunk the next time, he wanted to do it again. And again. And again. And I knew I had to leave him, soon.

It was the second day of my menstrual cycle, when I was sure I wasn't pregnant, that I decided to call the ad in the paper which read:

> *Housework, live-in, young mother with child OK.*
> *Call 555-1000*

The ad had been in the paper quite often, and I was glad to see it again. I called from the drug store when I took Sharon for her walk. The lady that answered the phone had a soft voice. When I explained my plight to her, the woman, who said to call her Ruby, offered to call a taxi for me that night at eight o'clock and would pay for it when we got to her house.

This was surely God's answer to my prayers. I had been separating my clothes and had two small cardboard boxes stored just for this moment. Huey had quit his good job and wasn't even looking for one. His mother slipped us food daily, but I had no money. Packing was difficult, as few clothes would fit into the boxes.

The boxes were hidden in the closet, and Sharon, now six months old, was sitting in her stroller at my feet. She loved to stand up in it and pound her toys in the tray. I sat back in my rocker, crocheting, keeping my hands busy, waiting for eight o'clock to arrive. At seven-thirty, Huey unexpectedly came back home. If he even suspected I was leaving, no telling what he might do, to me or the taxi driver. So I was literally shaking until he left. I know he wondered something, since I didn't beg him to stay home, like I usually did.

My next worry was running into one of my in-laws in the hall. Even if I did get out into the taxi, I knew someone would follow me if they saw me leave. I kept my fingers crossed. It was almost dark and the doorbell rang. I ran to the downstairs outer door and opened it quietly so I wouldn't alert anyone with the loud buzzer that opened it. I put my fingers over my lips, and the driver nodded in understanding. He came upstairs and carried the boxes and the stroller out for me. I ran right behind him with Sharon in my arms, afraid I would trip and blow the whole thing.

We got into the cab, and I heaved a sigh as he closed the door and took off. No one had seen me that I could tell; the front door was rarely used. I was safely getting away to a new life, on my own at last. I hugged Sharon all the way, thinking how nice Ruby sounded.

Ruby was a tall, reddish blonde woman in her late thirties. She was on the verge of being overweight, and wore her hair down and pulled back, with a pompadour on top, like the style in the thirties. She wore tight revealing clothes, even around the house. Although she was kind and always spoke with a gentleness in her voice, I had a strange feeling about her. Something didn't quite jive. In the first place, her husband, Latham, worked as a printer for a magazine downtown. He couldn't have made all that much money. She didn't work at all, and the house was on the small size, not much bigger than the one my folks lived in, near them, in fact, in that part of town, and far from ritzy. Not where you'd expect to see hired housekeepers. Ruby's explanation was, "I just hate housework, so Latham pampers me this way."

The house had a finished basement. Sharon and I had a very small cubicle of a room, with a warped door that didn't quite close. It was held shut with a swing latch, easily gotten open from the outside, with any kind of flat instrument. Next to it was a very large room, with a double bed and crib in it. When I inquired about it, I was told it had been used by "Annie, the former housekeeper." She had found another job, and that's why I was hired. I would eventually get her room, in a matter of weeks, or days.

Several days went by before I saw either Latham or Annie. My curiosity had been aroused, so all my antennae were up.

The only housework that I was expected to do was light dusting and vacuuming, and fixing supper. For this, I received room and board for Sharon and myself, plus $5.00 per week.

Ruby hated to cook, she insisted. However, whenever I would start to prepare something, she would stand over me and "help" me, suggesting this or that, until the dinner turned out to be pretty much hers. I felt as though I was just acting the part. Ruby loved Sharon, though, and raved about her constantly: How smart she was; how blonde she was. She was forever pointing out the difference in our coloring. "Sharon looks like a Schultz," I repeated over and over.

On the evening of the third day I went upstairs, and found

the living room on the dark side, with music playing softly. Latham was sitting in his rocker, a TV lamp softly lit behind him. He was smoking his pipe, and an incense burner was giving off a very sweet scent.

Latham, tall and skinny, I was surprised to find, was a most unattractive brown man, with one roaming eye. His look just gave me the creeps. But amid my fears, I kept reminding myself how nice and attractive Ruby was.

The way I found him that first night was the way Latham would usually spend his evenings. After the dinner I had prepared for them, he'd settle back into his overstuffed easy chair in almost total darkness with his pipe and incense burner, wearing a small stocking cap. The cap really made me feel uneasy when I saw it, as I'd heard so many stories about white girls who married Negroes, about the dope they smoked and their strange ways. Negroes were a foreign subject to me, then, except to fear them. I was not too comfortable around men, anyhow, from my early training, with Daddy teaching me to not trust any of them. Now, the fear had come alive, compounded by the stocking cap and roaming eye.

After dinner, I would take Sharon for a walk in her stroller for a couple of hours. We went all over, just so I'd be out of the house and away from Latham. At dark, we'd go to bed early, unless Latham went out, in which case I would keep Ruby company. She never turned on TV. After I'd go to bed I would hear a slow methodical shuffle, in the other part of the empty basement, a big recreation room covered with squeaky linoleum. As the shadowy figure would pass slowly by the crack in my door, the swing latch in place, I would lie petrified in my bed, catching glimpses of the light stocking cap in the darkness. I knew then it was Latham's steps that would come to a stop outside my door, momentarily, and then continue on, fading into the other part of the basement. Annie never came home till late at night, and I only saw her a couple times before she left.

It was fortunate I met Annie before she had gotten her things completely moved out of her bedroom. She was packing on a Saturday morning when I knocked quietly, hoping Ruby or Latham could not hear me. Annie spoke softly, also. I asked her, "Why are you leaving?"

She rolled her eyes up into her head, and said, "Oy, there's too much to tell you. Just listen, don't *trust* them," emphasizing the words, pointing upstairs.

Now I was really interested, "Why," I asked, "What's going

on here?"

"First thing they did, was plant a pair of Latham's drawers under my bed, so Ruby could find them, and accuse me of having an affair with Latham," she whispered, talking so fast I could hardly keep up with her. "You know, blackmail? They've never liked me having *any* friends over, not too mention family! Of course, that was easy, my parents are dead, and my in-laws are trying like hell to take my kid, would use anything that would stand up in court. At first, I thought my in-laws had hired them, but found out..."

Just then, we both looked up to see Ruby through the doorway, standing on the steps. Fortunately, Annie spoke so quietly, we doubted she heard anything, but as Annie stood with her back to Ruby, rolling her eyes upwards towards Ruby, she mouthed words of warning, "Don't trust them; watch out for your baby."

Ruby knew all about the bad feelings I had towards my parents, and that I was afraid of my husband finding me. I refused to answer the phone, for fear one of the Schultzes might find the ad in the paper. For some reason I had never mentioned the Evermardts, and Ruby never knew that I had called my grandmother the day after I got there, and told her where I was. So Ruby figured I had no other people in the area. She said she loved having me, and "the pitter-patter of little feet around." She even suggested adopting me. "Oh, I couldn't go that far against my father, no matter what," I'd always say. She picked up this conversation, often. She tried to make me think she really cared about me. I almost believed her, until I talked to Annie, whose warning really scared me. It put me on the alert every minute of the day.

One evening, after dark, there came a brisk knock at the door. Latham quickly answered it, cracking the door only slightly to talk. In rage, he yelled, "It's lousy cops! What do you mean calling cops to my house? There's a Missing Persons out on you. Go outside. They ain't no way no lousy cops comin' into my house."

I went outside, to the squad car, wondering how such a report got filed?

"Your mother put this report out on you," the younger policeman said.

"My *mother?*" I shrieked.

"Isn't Mrs. Schultz your mother?"

"No, she's my mother-in-law. I am married to her son, and

I'm leaving him. It's none of her business where I am."

Surprised, and apologetic for such "misinformation and intrusion," the cops said: "She thought you had jumped off a bridge, or something; she was worried about you."

Laughing, I answered, "It would hardly be likely that I would jump off a bridge with a baby, a stroller, and all the clothes that I own, now, would it?"

"A baby? Oh, ma'am, we are truly sorry."

"You can call my grandmother Evermardt if you want to verify anything."

"Ma'am, we know. We already talked to her. We just had to verify her story. She didn't tell us about the baby, though."

When I walked back into the house, Latham hit me with a barrage of obscenities. I thought his reaction to the police a little bit overdone. There was some reason why he didn't want the police in his house. Maybe that really was dope he was smoking in that pipe, underneath the smell of the incense he burned.

On Sundays, Latham would take us all for a ride in his white Cadillac convertible, with the top down. Ruby rode in the front with him, and Sharon and I in the back. He would drive slowly for miles along the Lake Front, as though we were all on parade. But I figured, he must just like to ride around in cars a lot. I wasn't too worried about being seen by Huey, either. No one would be looking for Sharon and me in the back seat of Latham's car.

The first payday, Ruby only gave me a part of the money she owed me, and said she'd give the rest to me later. It really made me angry and I wasn't thinking too clearly. When I went for a walk with Sharon, I decided to call Huey. He answered the phone, and seemed happy to hear from me, telling me he had moved back with his mother, and had another job – this time at the factory with his dad. I told him where I was living, and that he could come and go for a walk with Sharon and me after dinner the next night. "Meet me on the corner," I said. I didn't want Ruby to know I was meeting him.

Huey and I met for several nights before I gave him the phone number. Ruby had a fit, so I didn't talk much around her. One of the things Huey and I talked a lot about was his mother. Although I thought a lot of her, I felt she was helping him drink by giving him money. He agreed, and asked me if I would come back with him if he would move clear across town, to the south side, away from his family where he might learn to stand on his own two feet?

Whichever way I turned seemed to hold catastrophe, but

here, my child's life seemed to be in jeopardy; I was convinced Latham was going to steal Sharon some night when I was sleeping. At least I knew what to expect with Huey; making one more attempt with him seemed the least dangerous. Besides, I still had a pulling towards him that I couldn't deny. We agreed he would pick me up the following Saturday morning. I called Daddy and asked him to sign for us to buy some furniture, so we could really be free of Ma Schultz. He agreed to cover it, up to five-hundred dollars.

Although I only told Ruby that I was merely thinking about leaving, she was extremely upset, and asked me to reconsider. "Huey is surely running around on you." But my fear of Latham was greater. Because Ruby was a woman, I still trusted her.

Quietly, the night before I left, I pulled out the boxes from under the bed and laid all my clothes into them. In the kitchen, I had a big thick cookbook from school that I loved. Ruby had raved over it. It included every kind of meat, how to buy it, cook it, and serve it. That night, I didn't sleep a wink, afraid I would oversleep and miss Huey. I got Sharon up and dressed to have breakfast. Latham was gone already. I heaved a sigh of relief and fed her while I nibbled at a piece of toast.

"Why aren't you eating?" Ruby asked, suspiciously.

"I'm just not hungry this morning," I said, casually. "I think I'll take Sharon for a little walk; it's so nice and warm this morning. You told me I could relax on Saturdays, didn't you?" I asked, looking back at Ruby as I carried Sharon with me down the stairs.

"Yes, of course," she said, unhappily.

Just as I walked by the downstairs entrance, Huey drove into the drive. I opened the door and ran out, giving Sharon to him. I ran back into the basement and got the stroller, and one box. Huey grabbed the arm of the stroller, and the box toppled off onto the floor. Ruby heard it and came running down the back steps. I turned to her and smiled, and said, "Huey came while I was walking, and we decided to go back together today. He found a nice apartment last night." Then I added quickly, "You can keep the money you owe me."

Her face grew flushed and angry. I ran back into the basement to get the other box. As I came up the steps to go into the kitchen, she stuck her arm out to block me. "Forget it. What is left upstairs is mine," she said.

"Very well," I answered politely, and picked up the box. Huey had the other one under his arm as he pushed the stroller, with Sharon in it, down the driveway. What a lot of maneuvering.

When I got into the car, I looked back at Ruby standing at the door, scowling, her mother love, gone.

Huey had found us a nice upper three room apartment, a back house, but on a streetcar line. It was on the near southeast side, towards the lake. Our new furniture was delivered that afternoon and Huey was as kind and sweet to me as ever, promising to keep working, and not to drink. We made simple love that night protecting ourselves from any future pregnancies, just in case this didn't work out. I hardly believed in anything anymore. But at least I was free of that creepy Latham.

Just how creepy, I was to find out many months later, when I ran into Annie on the bus and heard about Ruby and Latham being arrested on a morals charge. Annie had a friend in the detective division who told her they had cracked one of the biggest white slavery rings in the US, centralized in Michigan. Latham was the Milwaukee contact. Latham's scheme, through his standing ad in the paper, was to attract down-and-outers, such as Annie and me, who had no one, who wanted out of a situation. A child only added to the blackmail possibilities, having in-laws to hold over their head and then the babies were sold for adoption. So the ride around town in the open convertible was his way of *displaying his wares*. No doubt the police showing up to check on the Missing Persons report Ma Schultz gave, and my calling Grandma Evermardt, put the verification of my whereabouts on the police blotter – a real kink in Latham's plan and why he got so angry. Annie and I both felt it a miracle to have escaped from disappearing off the face of the earth. If I hadn't caught her before she left, and if she hadn't had a friend on the police force, no telling where each of us, or our children, might've ended up.

We'd only been in our new apartment a few weeks when Huey found that the bar just up the street would serve him. He came home night after night drunk, demanding sex. I had managed to quiet him usually, so we wouldn't get thrown out. At his parents' house, he could yell all he wanted. No one ever called the police there. But here, it was different.

One night, late in October, he was especially drunk. He had come home several times (to make sure I was there, I think), and we had argued. When I was angry, I managed to vent my feelings in ironing, so I had the board up in the living room. Sharon was playing on the floor. She was nine months old and getting around all over the place, pulling herself up on the coffee table. I taught her to put her tiny fingers on the edge of the wood, around the glass, so she wouldn't break it, pounding on it, and so I wouldn't have to clean her finger marks. It only took a few light taps on the fingers for her to learn to keep off of the glass. She was a darling baby. Everyone raved about her, how easy she was to take care of. She never fussed much or cried unless she was hungry or wet. When she was tired, she'd just lay her head down and suck her thumb.

After the third time Huey had come home this night, I had put Sharon to bed. Her crib was in the extra large kitchen, opposite the living room door. I sang to her as I ironed, and she was almost asleep when Huey came bursting into the house again. "C'mon, bitch, gimme a little," he said, knowing I would not even talk to him this time. "C'mon little Miss Bitch, open up to Daddy."

I still ignored him.

To get my attention, he went into the kitchen and pulled out the big heavy butcher knife. A farmer still at heart, Daddy thought meat needed to have a sharp knife to cut it and had made it in his shop. It had a solid steel-filled handle, extremely heavy. The steel blade was exceptionally sharp. Huey stood in front of me at the ironing board, holding the knife up in front of my face, grinning.

When I saw the knife up over my head, without thinking, I raised my iron up in the air to block the knife waiting to come down, I thought, on me. My iron struck the underside of the fleshy part of Huey's arm sending metal and plastic everywhere. I had forethought enough to pull the electrical plug when I saw the bare wires showing in what was left of the iron. Down on the floor picking up all the pieces, I cringed as Huey laid the knife on the ironing board. "You really thought I was going to *use* it, didn't you?" he said, silly like, and I remembered, then, Ma Schultz hiding the knives.

Screaming, threatening to call the cops to see this, I looked up to see Sharon standing in her crib, watching everything. I was horrified. *What have we done to that poor little thing with all of our fighting?* Always about the same thing, it seemed. I knew it was not good for her, and this time Huey had come close to using a real weapon. At least, he had made me believe he was going to. And Sharon saw it, as little as she was.

Huey laid down on the floor in front of the door and fell asleep. I couldn't budge him an inch. I was afraid to wake him to go out to call the police, as we didn't have a phone.

The next morning, after Huey went to work, I took Sharon

with me to the District Attorney's office. I swore out a warrant for Huey's arrest for Assault and Battery and was referred to Attorney Goldman, who told me to stay at home and wait. When the paddy wagon, a wire-grilled truck that was used to pick up drunks and prostitutes, came, I should keep quiet. The next day he would represent me in court and request the judge to issue Court-appointed Separate Maintenance for us, which would declare this a divorce case. Scared to death, I went home and cleaned up the awful mess in my house.

That night Huey came home from work meek as a lamb with a chocolate malt in one hand and a candy bar in the other. He'd gotten his arm stitched and bandaged at work. The wound was a nasty, gill-like slice right into the muscle of his forearm, evidence that his fist had been up in the air.

When the knock came at the door, Huey was down on his knees with his head in my lap, crying, begging me to forgive him. I was too terrified to move. Huey went to the door. Two big burly cops in uniform stood in the hall. Next to them, Huey looked like a little shrimp. They showed him the papers and waited while I got his jacket. As Huey went through the door, he turned and started cursing at me. "You goddamn cunt. You cock-suckin' bitch," he yelled and spit at me.

As the door closed after him I breathed a prayer of thanks that the police had come when they did. I was already beginning to feel sorry for him, tempted even to tell him about the cops so he could leave. Whenever he became penitent, there was no getting around it I was a softie where Huey was concerned. *How am I ever going to get through this thing?* I lay down on the couch and sobbed my eyes out – which of us I felt sorrier for, I didn't know.

To support my child and myself, I needed a way to live in this world without being susceptible to people like Ruby. My only hope was my faith in God and a prayer in my heart.

Two weeks after our court date, Huey came over after driving by the house in the middle of the night and gunning his motor to frighten me. Once his buddy pounded on my door, but when I complained to my attorney, this harassing stopped and Huey was given permission to get some of his things. Just for spite, I grabbed the feather quilt, but he took off laughing with his friends.

Even though I had not been to church in quite a while, word got to Daddy of my whereabouts. One afternoon, he and Charity came over to visit. *Why had they come?* Mr. Simms said once, "If you're looking for a reason behind something, look for the dollar sign." Daddy must've been afraid of getting stuck for the furniture he'd co-signed for because neither one of them seemed very sympathetic to my situation. Charity just sat there, staring, silent. Daddy was saying, "Your place is with your husband, Samantha Sue; I don't care what he's done. That's the way I believe; it's God's word. You made your bed, you lay in it." The nerve in his lower lip began to twitch in anger something fierce.

"Even after he's threatened my life, with the very knife you made me, Daddy?"

"Even after he's threatened you," Daddy said. "God will take care of you and protect you, if you trust in Him. You have to learn to *trust*, Samantha."

After they left, I lay down on the couch while Sharon still napped, trying to figure things out. Daddy had to know I had little money, but he didn't inquire about it or offer any. Even after I told him my rent was only paid for two more weeks and that there was just enough oil in the stove till then, Daddy turned a deaf ear. Too exhausted to cry, too hurt to think about it, I fell asleep asking God for help. I truly believed that somehow a way would be found for Sharon and me.

Days later, Mr. and Mrs. Simms came to visit. I had not seen them since before I got married. I knew how Mr. Simms felt about the Schultz family, so I was surprised to see them. Mrs. Simms hugged me lovingly. Although, as a child, I never remembered her as affectionate, she let me know, that day, that she cared about me. After I had poured out my heart to them, and told them all the awful things I had been through with Huey, Mr. Simms held his finger to his lips and said, "Shh. Listen, Sweetheart. Let me explain. You must understand I cannot interfere in a divorce situation because of the feelings of many in our church. But certainly, if my little honey girl was to come and knock on my door, asking for a home for herself and her little one, I could not, in all Christian conscience, turn her away. Do you get my meaning?"

I hugged them both. Through my happy tears, I said, "Thank you for coming. God really must be looking out for me."

A week later at the Simms, I had my old room back; the same one Daddy and I had shared years before. Sharon and I now slept side by side.

Within days, I went to work as a messenger for a big bank downtown. Mr. Doyle, who hired me for $130 per month, was so nice to me that I introduced myself as Sam. Maybe leaving the hurting and sad Samantha Sue behind would make a difference. "Sam" had a strong and healthy, worldly, yes — even masculine -- ring to it. I knew I needed to be all those things to take care of myself and my child, despite my thinking still not so clear as yet. Mr. Doyle was now my *at-work* father.

Mrs. Simms took over the care of Sharon leaving little money left after I paid her, and the $5 a month to clear Daddy's name of the furniture debt. Being welcomed back into the family, even by Marty and his wife, Leona, was scary, at first, hoping Marty was not thinking about baby-sitting me and the sexual games he'd played. Trying to forget it had happened, Leona was so nice to me, I almost did. Attending *Highland Fundamental*, singing in the choir and sometimes substituting for the organist on Sunday mornings -- on the same organ I had played the night of Charity's wedding -- helped. Daddy's marital agreement — to go there part time on Sunday nights -- had finally been forgotten. I still went to *Holy Ghost* with the Simms's sometimes, in spite of how I felt about being called a *Holy Roller*. I wasn't sure just what drew me back there.

Although I had filed for divorce, I still was not convinced I should continue. Huey's family was contesting it. Gen had told me once how badly she wanted another child and she was afraid she couldn't have one. If she ever found out I was not taking care of Sharon, she would spend whatever it took to get Sharon away from me. Her words were never out of mind.

One day Wanda Reece called me. I couldn't place her until she said, "Huey brought you to my apartment right after you had your baby. Upstairs?"

"His buddy's girl?"

"Well, I never was his buddy's girl. I was going with Huey for almost nine months when he showed up that night with a wife and a baby. Can you imagine how shocked I was?"

"My goodness. I remember thinking you acted a little funny, So that's why he was so anxious to get out of the house early every night."

"Believe me, I had no idea he was married. I felt so sorry for you; he was such a bum, and you were so nice, with such a sweet baby. Listen, I just heard you two were separated, and he was giving you a hard time. If you need a witness, just give your lawyer my name and number. He really hurt me. So anything I can do for you just let me know."

When the phone would ring in the middle of the night, and I'd be awakened to jukebox music and heavy breathing, Mr. Simms would say, "We'll get through this thing; we can last as long as he can."

When gossip about me began at *Holy Ghost Pentecostal* -- perpetuated by the Schultz's, I was convinced -- Mr. Simms would put his arms around me and say, "Nobody is going to hurt my little sweetheart, again. No sir-ee."

Still, I would sob myself to sleep, wishing for Huey to take me in his arms, kiss away my tears, and tell me he wouldn't hurt me again. But then I would hear about something else that he had done -- until one Sunday afternoon, my eyes were opened.

Catching up on lost sleep, I had taken a nap. Sharon, a darling child, already talking and singing *Jesus Loves Me*, was still snoozing away. I went out on the front porch to get some fresh air and warm spring sunshine. It had been six months since Huey and I had split up. Daily struggling with my inner feelings, wanting to do what was right, I was tired of the suffering I believed was the result of *my sin*. Reverend Ward, the highly respected radio preacher, happened to be a guest at *Holy Ghosts'* new building dedication. Talking with him, Reverend Ward had explained that because our church was in the "salvation" business and not in the "court" business, it didn't have the wherewithal to judge individual marital cases, as the Catholics did. So we depended on what Jesus told us in Matthew 19, that each person, with the help of God, had to judge his own situation.

There were times when I was ready to go back to Huey again. There were many people in both churches I attended who agreed with Daddy's opinion that I should. But Mr. Simms did not agree. "That so-and-so is nothing but a no-good scoundrel," he'd say. All these very thoughts were running through my mind as I sat in the sun, letting the warm spring breeze blow through my hair, when up the street I saw Huey coming in his old jalopy -- there was no mistaking it, the loud muffler with *duel pipes and mud flaps*. When he got in front of the house, he gunned the motor. He was cuddling with a girl; now I knew.

It was as if I was supposed to be out there on that porch, so I could let go of my foolish dream and go on with my life. I had been sound asleep only minutes before. Oh, how it hurt, though. I had known it in my head all along, but I hadn't really accepted it until that moment.

The clerk read off our names, Samantha Sue and Hubert Schultz, and motioned for us to come into the small room adjoining the main courtroom. We all sat around a table with the judge sitting behind it; he was looking through our petitions. Our lawyers sat side by side, and Huey and I were on opposite ends. The judge looked at Huey first and asked him, "Do you have anything to say about what is written in this paper," and held up a copy of the six pages Mr. Goldman had written, requesting our marriage be dissolved on grounds of "mental cruelty."

Huey shook his head, denying nothing. (He had dropped the contest of the divorce after his last shenanigan had been published in *The Milwaukee Journal,* about his stealing fur coats out of a downtown nightclub with a girlfriend. It said the cops arrested them just as they threw the coats into the Milwaukee river.) Huey said he would like to have the chance to try again.

The judge turned to me to get my response, and I began to cry. "I just don't see how that would be possible," I said, trying to stop my tears.

After he requested Huey and his lawyer leave the room, the judge turned to me and asked, "How was your sex life?"

Mr. Goldman told me to answer as simply and honestly as I knew how. I began telling the judge about how Huey wouldn't leave me alone when he was drinking, and how he insisted, time after time, on *doing it* in a perverted...

The judge's hand went up to stop me, "Did he ever force you to have oral sex with him?"

"Yes, that's what I was talking about, the *perverted* part. Yes, I guess that's what you call it. I couldn't..."

The judge held up his hand again and turned to my lawyer, "There is no need to pursue this further; bring the boy back in."

I spoke up then, quickly, before Huey came in. "Judge, I am very concerned about my child. I don't trust him with her, what he might do with her as she gets older. How can I protect her?"

"Leave that to me," he said.

According to the divorce decree, Huey was not allowed to visit Sharon without an adult of my choosing present, and was required to pay child support of fifty-dollars per month. The support money was to be paid to the clerk of court's office, as a matter of "undisputable record."

Seventeen years old and, at last, I was a free woman.

Finally I could date, after all those months. The time had dragged by slowly, waiting for my divorce. My lawyer had given me explicit instructions on how to avoid any possibly compromising situations, carefully trying to keep from giving the

Schultzes the least possible excuse to take Sharon from me. So the month following my divorce, I was long overdue for my first real vacation, a week at *Youth For Christ's* summer conference at Winona Lake, Indiana.

Bonnie, a new friend from *Highland Fundamental*, who also worked in the bank building where I now worked, invited me to go with her on the Greyhound bus. She talked a lot about Bob Jones University in South Carolina, which she had already attended for one year. She was saving to go back and finish. A tall, very well-built gal, Bonnie was a few years my senior, and I looked up to her in every way. She was teaching me so much, about how to dress simply and still look elegant; how to shop for *better* clothes on sale; how to talk without saying "you know" in every sentence; how to be a lady. She would have never approved of Muriel's ways. It was because of Bonnie that I finally got over Huey, though it came the long way around.

Winona Lake was hot and muggy. After we changed clothes, the first place to which Bonnie took me was the Bob Jones booth, a lounge with college yearbooks and school catalogues on display. We had just started looking through the reading material when in walked two of the best looking guys I had ever seen. One, especially. He sat at the desk facing us and began thumbing through a *Youth For Christ* magazine. The other one, a red-headed guy, sat over on the side in a big easy chair, right near Bonnie. She held up her magazine to hide her pointing finger and raised eyebrows. She was soft on freckles, and this one had a face full of them. But his friend had caught my eye with his sparkling clean look and his fashionable clothes. He had on a pink shirt, the latest thing. He wore the collar open without a tie. I loved his powder blue trousers, too, that matched the blue of his eyes. As he leaned forward, elbows on the desk intent upon his reading, his very light blond, curly hair tumbled into his face. I think it was that instant I fell in love. "What a doll," I whispered to Bonnie. I felt as if my heart had taken wings and would fly away.

That afternoon, she insisted we wander about the grounds separately. Bonnie's theory was that guys usually hung around in pairs, and if you were alone, you had a better chance of attracting one of them than if there were two of you. Trying to match four ways "lowered the odds," she said.

The afternoon loomed ahead of me; being alone was frightening. But I decided I'd spent a lot of money to get here, besides having to pay the Simmses to keep Sharon day and night for a week, so I was going to get the most from it. I couldn't help what kind of funny ideas Bonnie had. I figured she thought I'd hold her back because of something about me that wasn't up to snuff yet, she was making so much of me over, but I was just glad she'd invited me. It was her vacation, too. So I shrugged off the disappointment and dressed in my new black swimsuit.

In the mirror, I didn't look too bad. The boned top set off by thin white piping lay nicely over the curves of my chest, giving just a slight hint of cleavage. It was my one saving grace in the breast department. I didn't have much, but what I had showed nicely. The suit was the new bloomer-bottomed style one-piece, pleats opening up full around the hips, tucked into wide panty legs. The style covered all my stretch marks from having Sharon. The pleats had white set inside them so that when I walked they flashed. Confident that I looked as good as I could, I slung a towel over my shoulder and took off for the water, looking neither right nor left as Daddy had taught me to do when alone. "Never look a stranger in the eye," he always said.

Since it was the first day of the conference, not too many had found the beach yet; this was fine with me, as my "bare naked swimming suit" as Daddy called it, left me feeling self-conscious. I wasn't much of a swimmer, so I stayed in only long enough to get wet. When I stepped out of the water, I was embarrassed to find that the bottom of my suit had filled up like a balloon. I couldn't help but giggle at how I must've looked as I stood there, and under my breath, I said, "Bombs away, boys!" (the battle cry of the second world war I'd remembered as a child) as I tugged at the wide panty legs, discreetly letting the trapped water escape with a big splash onto the sand.

The day dragged lazily and quietly by. Late that afternoon I dressed carefully for evening service in a yellow cotton print. It had a black, rolled collar, scooped in the front and pointing to a V in the back, with a row of large black, shiny buttons dotting my backside, clear to the hem of the full gathered skirt. I put on white sandals over bare feet, against Bonnie's advice. Bob Jones girls *never* go barelegged, she'd said. When she didn't come back, I left for the cafeteria for supper, alone.

It was almost time for the evening service, so I walked slowly, hoping Bonnie would show up so I wouldn't have to sit alone in church, too. As I neared the chapel steps, I looked up to see Bonnie motioning furiously for me to hurry. I ran up the stairs before I realized it was the freckled faced guy who held the door open for us. Bonnie pointed to Red, who introduced himself. Then I turned and looked up into the chipped-tooth smile of his friend who, that morning, had set my heart on fire.

It sounded as though he said his name was Raymond Lorry. I asked him to repeat it three times. In exasperation, with a sarcastic edge to his voice, he said, "Just call me, Ray."

"I will," I said, with the same hint of sarcasm. Extending my hand then, I said, "I'm happy to meet you. I'm Samantha Sue Schultz."

He completely ignored my hand and asked me three times to repeat my name. Finally, as exasperated as he had been, I said, "Just call me, Sam"

"I will," he said. We both started laughing then at the same time, as he followed me inside.

The four of us sat together near the rear of the large open-air auditorium on one of the unpainted wood-slatted benches. The large mushroom-like buttons on my dress made me wiggle and squirm, like a small child, as I tried carefully to fit them between the slats. Finally, trying to shift the weight off of the buttons, I crossed my legs and rested one foot up on the empty bench in front of me. Bonnie yanked at my dress like a mother, indicating for me to put my foot down. I knew I had really embarrassed her.

Frank Boggs sang *Yes, God Is Real*. He could sing even lower in range than George Beverly Shea. (I took one of his records home for Mr. Simms.) The sermon was short, thankfully.

During the benediction, I had my head bowed and my eyes closed. When I opened them, Ray had just disappeared, without a word. It annoyed me, but I said nothing as we followed Red outside. Not sure what to expect next, I scanned the area looking for Ray and found him across the street, standing in front of a newsstand with his nose in a magazine. How rude, I thought, growing really angry then. We didn't have a true date, and maybe he had not planned on sitting with me, but still, he could have been more polite about ditching me. But I was not in the habit of expressing my feelings, so I kept up with the conversation as Ray joined us. Cheerfully, as though he had never left, he suggested we go to the drive-in for a chili-dog.

It was Red's car, so Ray and I were in the back seat. Because I was afraid that anything I'd say would come out ugly, I kept still. Ray's contagious personality took over the group, but I was determined not to give in to his clowning around. Surely he must've known that I was angry, and why.

We got our chili-dogs, but it seemed like the quieter I was, the more clownish Ray became. Red had turned on the radio to some hillbilly music. Ray said, like a disk jockey, "Now, Ladies and Gentlemen, you are about to hear the latest group to blow in, east of the Mississippi. It's Henry Hotsnot and his ten Nose Pickers playing, *I'll Get You Yet, You Booger.* Pick it out, Henry." He yelled it loud enough for everyone parked in the entire lot to hear.

A roar of laughter went up from all over, and I couldn't keep my pout going another minute. The giggles just exploded out of me, "Oh, you're terrible. I can't believe you," I finally said.

Until this moment, it seemed as though Ray was not really aware of my presence. He appeared to love an audience, the bigger the better. But the minute I started giggling, he turned to me and let out a loud belly laugh, getting everyone's attention. After the last announcement even those in the other cars were listening, as he said just as loudly, "Listen to this, folks; just listen to this girl laugh. She actually has a voice. She has a tongue. She can talk. But there's a hitch, folks. The secret is, you have to keep her stomach full."

I was almost choking from giggling so hard.

Then he turned to me and said, "Have I got *your* number."

My face must have turned purple from embarrassment, and suppressed anger, too, all of it together, realizing he was not going to admit to being rude earlier. Right then I knew this guy was really different, unpredictable, but hilarious with his sharp wit – "deadly with his tongue," some of his friends said. But for the first time in my life, I laughed at myself. And I loved it.

That was how we met Ray and Red. We spent the next five days with them, playing shuffleboard, miniature golf, and going swimming. When I'd come out of the water in my black bloomer suit, letting the water it collected hit the ground with a splash, Ray would go into his announcer's routine, "Ladies and gentlemen, we'd like to present you with The Black Bomber," I would turn crimson. I had no idea he'd been watching me on the beach that first day. He and Red didn't leave us alone much after that. For dinner we'd eat at the drive-in and always go to church at night. See, Ray was a Baptist preacher. He had just graduated from Bob Jones, and I found out the truth about him from Red, finally... that Ray was on his way home to get married to a girl he had been going with for some time.

Bonnie had stayed home from service that night for some reason she really didn't explain, but insisted I go without her. When I got there, I sat with the group from Bob Jones we'd made friends with. Strangely, Ray did not show up either. But Red was there. He sat on the other end of the bench. They all treated me like one of them. It was such a good feeling after all those years of feeling alone.

Going home by myself, across the big field towards our cabin, I got halfway there when I heard someone calling, "Sam. Sam." I turned around just as Red got into step with me, "Mind if I join you?" he asked.

"No. Not at all," I said.

As we sat on the porch swing, I finally got around to asking where Ray was.

"Did you notice the girl's class ring on Ray's pinkie finger?"

"Yes," I said. "But I didn't know it meant anything."

"Ray's on his way home to get married. His wedding is in three weeks. Ray didn't quite know how to tell you." Red said rather quietly.

I was crushed. I had begun to like Ray very much. But I didn't let on to Red. I just smiled, feeling thankful that at least I had taken Bonnie's advice and not let Ray kiss me, even if she had not heeded it herself. She and Red had necked up a storm in the front seat every night. She had also told me not to tell anyone about my past until I had to. But hearing about Ray, it seemed like an appropriate time. So, I told Red, "It's all right. I'm divorced, and I have a little girl. Preachers don't get involved with divorcees anyhow."

Then Red asked me all about Sharon and explained to me that, unlike Ray, he was not going into the ministry and was not bound by such convention. He was going into his father's jewelry business, but I really didn't hear what he may have been trying to tell me. My mind was on Ray, not Red, and I thought my heart would break.

It was a summer romance, I kept telling myself, as Bonnie later quizzed me intently about Red's every word. She said, "Red chased you? Running? Why, no guy ever does that unless he really *likes* a girl."

"Oh, Bonnie, that's your imagination. He was just doing Ray a favor, breaking the news to me."

"I'd say it was a case of *Speak for yourself, John*," she said, looking hurt that Red hadn't even asked about her.

The next day would be our last. I wasn't sure what to expect, but the guys showed up at breakfast just like they had all week, and we spent the whole day together. That night, Red and Bonnie got out of the car, went and sat on the front porch, leaving Ray and me behind. Ray had tried all night to kiss me, once putting the stick of gum he'd offered me between his own teeth. "Come and get it," he said, reminding me in his cute funny way that I owed him some kisses from all the shuffleboard games I had bet and lost. But I held my ground, determined not to give in. Neither one of us mentioned the conversation of the evening before between Red and I. Then we stood under the stars listening to the crickets. When he leaned real close and tried one more time to put his arms around me, I put my hands up in defense and pushed him away, smiling. "This has been a great week for me," I said, "I really had a good time with you." As he reached for me that last time, I slipped past him into the house. I couldn't have held him away another minute, but I was *not* going to let him have his way with me and then go off and marry another girl. It didn't register until much later that he was not wearing the little ring that last night.

When Bonnie came in, I was sobbing my heart out. "Oh, what a guy. Why did I ruin my life with Huey. Now I'll never be able to get a nice guy like Ray," I sobbed, as Bonnie patted my head, handing me Kleenex. I was feeling pulled in every direction, part of me so wanting to kiss him, part of me angry, part of me loving and caring, part of me saying, "No way, buddy. You're not going to have your last fling at my expense." It was Bonnie who put some sense into my feelings. She said I was vulnerable because of not dating before, so my feelings were exceptionally sensitive even though Ray was just a summer romance, like Red was to her. "Take it for what it's worth. Fun. A good wholesome time. And you didn't do anything wrong."

The closer to home I got, the better I felt that I had met Ray, even though he was getting married. I was very proud of myself for not letting him kiss me, too. Before I met him, I really had no idea what having fun was like — laughing, not taking everything so seriously. Although Ray and I had our sober conversations, agreeing about theology and spiritual things, nothing had ever stayed too serious too long. Laughing made the whole world look different. And I found out I had a lot of humor inside of me. The Evermardts were a gregarious, beer-drinking crowd. That was why Daddy kept me away from them. Meeting Ray had opened up a part of me I had not known existed — a happy fun-loving part. My life had been filled with so much hurt and pain that it was like finding a whole new me. My attitude towards myself and men took a turn right then.

Mr. Simms was thrilled to hear about Ray. He told me the same kinds of things I was thinking. Ray was my star, so to speak, to hitch my wagon to – "a prince of a young man."

The first of July, I moved into a large two-story flat with Daddy and Charity so we could provide a place for Grandma and Grandpa Baumn, both of them ill. Grandma Baumn hardly knew where she was half the time. I loved her so much I'd have done anything for her. We all agreed to try to get along for one year, no matter how hard it might be for us, until other arrangements could be made. Charity said, "We should put on a united front to the world." She was still not quite over losing her last child, born dead. She blamed me for having kept her upset. I never reminded her of her wishing that for my baby, not even when she would scream these accusations at me. But the adoration she had for her father was greater than her discontent. I had learned to live with my feelings about her, since she had no real say over anything I did anymore. I paid her well for baby-sitting, figuring Sharon had some playmates with Marcy and Philip. Daddy would manage to get Charity and me to stop screaming when we'd start. He had to sign a year's lease on the house, and they couldn't afford it by themselves. Whatever the reason, Daddy seemed to be much more friendly to me. I was surprised at how much smarter he was about a lot of things than I had remembered. Being able to talk to him as an adult was a new experience.

For the fourth of July, Huey had asked to take Sharon on a picnic. He hadn't seen her in several weeks. He had been broke and hadn't paid his child support, so hadn't even asked to see her. He had been complying with the court's request all along, visiting only at the house with Mrs. Simms or me in the room. He never stayed more than a few minutes. Mr. Simms said he only came to "feast his eyes," anyway.

I asked Huey where he planned to go on this picnic?

He said, "The Lake Front. We can listen to the concert on a blanket and maybe stay for the fireworks. Why don't you come along, so there won't be any problem with Sharon?"

I thought about it, knowing I wouldn't have even been considering it if I had still been living with the Simmses. But there was something subtle that had happened to me inside when I had moved back with my parents. It was a feeling of not being good enough, again. It was hard to explain or understand that feeling or why I said yes, then, to Huey.

The three of us enjoyed the warm day on the blanket. I did most of the talking. He did tell me he was playing his sax at night in bars, but he wasn't getting much for it besides drinks. He loved rock-n'-roll and kept switching the stations on his little portable radio trying to catch some of it. Sharon would bend up and down to the music. When I had to change her, he told me to go to the car. When I asked "Why?" he said, "Because... somebody might *see* her." His dirty mind really sickened me. Huey knew I had been out of town and so I told him a little about Winona Lake and meeting some nice people. I talked about my job and my plans to get my own apartment after the year with my folks was up. He listened, but as usual had little to say. I didn't like that part of being with him, having to do all the talking. It reminded me of when we were married and he had always kept his nose in a comic book at mealtimes. It occurred to me then, thinking back on it, that the comic book kept him from having to talk because maybe he didn't know how or was afraid he'd say things he was sorry for. Until I met Ray, I thought that all guys were quiet, only gals talked. Meeting Ray made me see Huey in an altogether different light. I had to ignore little things I was noticing about him now and tried to forget them while we devoured the delicious lunch his mother had packed for us. She was still hoping we'd get back together, I could see. Huey did play with Sharon a little, buying her a balloon in between trying to work his way on top of me to kiss me. I fought him all day long, but the continual teasing eventually got me aroused.

We left before the fireworks started because Sharon was so tired. As we drove home, she fell asleep in the back seat. It was pitch dark by the time we got to my front door. When Huey parked the car, he slipped over to me, as he had done in the old days when we were just kids – and I finally let him kiss me. He was so sweet and affectionate, and I could see that I had not gotten him out of my system yet. Before I knew it, he had me down on the seat and was maneuvering himself into me, and I let him. I don't know why. I just didn't have the will to stop him.

And then he was finished, sat up, zipped his trousers, combed his hair, and said, "Do you want to carry Sharon, or should I?"

Suddenly, it hit me all at once, in the pit of my stomach. Shame washed over me. Huey had been using me all this time. Muriel had been the first one to tell me; Mr. Simms had told me; the judge all but told me; Wanda Reece had told me; Bonnie had told me. And I knew it inside my own head. But it had never really sunk in, to my feelings, before. I had been so hung up on him that I had not even seen what was happening.

We walked to the door together and I looked at Huey as if I were seeing him for the very first time. I saw that he did not appear to be especially bright, a fact he had hidden behind a quietness that I took for intelligence. I remembered how shocked I was when he asked me if Chicago and Illinois weren't two cities. There we were, only ninety miles north. Music on Chicago's WGN was all he listened to on the radio besides. But then, maybe the music, that uses a different part of the brain, is all he heard.

And music Huey knew. It was the soft mellow sound of his saxophone that drew me to him in the first place, mixed up with the special feelings and excitement of our Pentecostal church. Its music played in my head through his horn, a beautiful magnetism that had held me and stirred me deep in my soul. Somewhere in there, I was sure, in all the feelings the church invoked in me, was a clue to the way I felt about sex and my own womanhood. All the preaching about the "lust of the flesh" being sin I understood as sex: the woman at the well, an adulterer, sinful — but loved by Jesus. Just like Daddy's terrible, painful whipping always came before his hugs and expressions of love, I had to be bad in order to get love. I was beginning to see, too, that my constant yearning to be held, by Huey or anyone else, had its roots in losing Mama. Our church had taken her place, making up for the security of the large Evermardt family all around me, why I kept feeling drawn to go back there in spite of the shame. Huey and his family were just another part of those feelings. No wonder getting him and that church out of my system had been so difficult. They both made me feel rotten, dirty, but their arms were always open for me. *Did shame go with love?* That week with Ray had made me see a whole different side of myself. Men, too. It was a revelation just to know there were guys who could talk, and laugh, and be with you without sex.

Maybe Huey didn't know anything else. I couldn't judge him too harshly. But one important thing I realized that day was that Huey really didn't love me or his child. It looked like he only loved sex. The rest of me he had picked apart — just as Charity had done – cursing me during his drunken rages. The ugly words I managed to forget, but the feelings they left, were only a repeat of what was already inside of me, feelings the church had instilled in me since babyhood. I had just never been able to see it before.

As I lay down to sleep that night, torn between the shame of remorse and the awe of wakening, I thought about the day. The fourth of July. Fireworks still thundered in the night skies all around me, celebrating independence. It was a good sound, a happy sound, the sound of freedom. Even though they celebrated freedom from another master — in another time, another place –

their thunder resounded within my spirit, within my soul. Someday, in another time, from another place, I knew I would be able to look back on this day, as Grandma Evermardt said, and smile. This special moment of freedom would allow that first small seed of self-love, so recently planted within me by that "prince of a young man," to take root, to flourish, and to grow.

Isn't life unbelievable how it keeps teaching me things? Wondering what was around the bend or over the next mountain, gave me a warm glow as I wandered off to sleep, loving this newest part of myself I'd just found, knowing that I would make it somehow.

Then I heard that last burst of fireworks going off all over town, a cascade of thunder that sounded like applause· I was taking a bow, a curtsy in my dream, and the applause continued· Ray was clapping his ring-free hands, laughing, laughing· Next we were on our bicycles riding off towards the horizon — Ray and I side by side· The applause rose, pushing us onward· Up the steep difficult hills we peddled together into the beautiful valley beyond· As we went over the last big hill, we passed a large marquee by the side of the road· It was lit up and in big letters it read:

WELCOME TO
The Black Bomber
and
HENRY HOTSNOT and his TEN NOSE PICKERS

◆

CHAPTER ELEVEN

The Divorceé: 1955-56

Being in my own apartment had allowed me some freedom, especially Saturdays. But the shrill sound of the distant telephone jarred my early morning sleep. Peering out of one eye at the ticking clock, I thought: *Not this early, my only day to sleep in.*

Dragging myself out of bed and walking on tiptoes past the crib, I noticed Sharon's little thumb was resting in her open mouth, her eyes tight in sleep. Up on her knees, she would rock herself back to sleep like this several times before begging to get up. She was so easy — a perfect child. I felt pride and satisfaction as I glanced at her silky hair that was usually pulled up in a ponytail. It was at just such moments when I would silently breathe a prayer of thanks for someone to finally touch, and hold, and love, and sew for besides my dolls. The jangling of the phone in the kitchen might wake her, I worried, as I rushed in to grab it. "Hello," I said groggily, wrapping the worn-out blue chenille robe about me.

"Hello Sweetheart," Mr. Simms said, on the other end. I knew by the friendliness in his voice he was still at work. "My relief got here extra early. You hungry?"

"When I get awake, I'm sure I will be."

"Chocolate crullers?" he asked, with a titillating tone, as though to arouse my spirits.

"Umm-hmmm," I said, trying to act enthusiastic.

After I hung up the phone, I walked into the bathroom and looked into the mirror. My hair could use a little trim, I thought, as I pushed my hands through it, yawning. I wondered what I was going to do about Mr. Simms. First the gifts: that horrible bra, the expensive navy wool A-line dress I'd told him about in Gimbals' window, the full length body girdle to wear under it — an expensive item I could never have afforded – and then the secondhand ringer-washer that was delivered without warning. "From your *godfather?*" Mary had guessed. Recently, too, he'd started stopping by on his way to work the night shift, seldom arriving empty handed — always calling, of course, to be sure that the way was clear. He didn't seem to really want anyone to know of his visits, not Mary, nor even Sharon, and it was becoming very uncomfortable. I had begun to get the uneasy feeling that we were carrying on an affair. *But how?* He never touched me. Oh, he hugged me often, just as he always had since I was five years old. But there was never a moment of indiscretion that I could detect. *So what could I say to him?* Nevertheless, the warning signals were up all over inside my head. But how could I stop it, whatever *it* was, that was going on? My confidante, he lingered on my every word, wanting to know of every silly thing that happened to me. *Maybe he was just getting old*, I told myself. I just didn't know, and I felt so alone.

When I looked back over my life, I remembered all the times Mr. Simms had come to my rescue and how, even now, he stood by me no matter that I had managed to turn my life into a confounded mess. Seeing through all the mistakes, he seemed to be able to see the part of me that was trying so hard. Sometimes when I would make a feeble attempt to object to his attentions, he would hug me and tell me he had a right, with his children grown, to buy his "baby girl" anything he pleased. Daddy had never been too much for gifts, other than candy bars. So invariably I would take the *tokens of love*, Mr. Simms called them. I was afraid not to. *What would I do if I was in dire need?* If I ostracized myself from him, who, *then*, would I turn to? I wasn't sure how it had all started, the quiet sneaky stuff.

When he began talking to me behind his wife's back, just as he and his children had done for years — knowing her hearing aid, no matter how she fumbled to adjust the controls hidden in her bosom, could not pick up his winks and mouthed words – I had a feeling then that things were not right. There was never anything that could not have been said right out in the open. Silly things, that would test my ability to keep a straight face. Often I wanted to giggle. *Secrecy.* That was what he seemed to want, to shut out his wife, to have his children, and now me, to himself. *Prized possessions? A feeling of power?* And what could I do? Who would I have turned to that day had he not visited me on the heels of Daddy's indifference, offering his home to me, pushing me to go to work? I was lucky to have found the messenger's job at the bank at only $130 a month! I could never have lived on that on my own, with a baby, at sixteen. I had learned to put up with his slyness and agree to his secretive whims out of sheer desperation. But now that I *was* on my own, making a little more money at my new job at the hospital, I would have to find a way to ease out of this bind I was in. His quiet tapping on the door was just another reminder of my unresolved plight.

Mr. Simms stuck his head in first to be sure I was alone. His hair had always been solid white, and wavy. It felt like corn silk, just like Sharon's. I remembered combing it when I was little — for hours, it seemed – while he lay back in his chair, eventually, inevitably, snoring. I would stop combing and creep away so as not to wake him wanting more.

He seemed larger in stature than he was because of his booming voice and the power he wielded. He was a college graduate — Iowa farmer turned engineer – and still on the church board at *Holy Ghost Pentecostal*. No matter who you were, you looked up to him and hoped he was on your side. I would be forever grateful for his going to bat for me against the Schultzes. When I'd recall fearful episodes in my marriage, Mr. Simms would shake his bowed head with mumblings of "Why" or "How" adults could allow such shenanigans to take place. "That bum is not worthy to tie my baby's shoelaces," he'd say, his eyes wet with tears, hugging me so tight to his chest sometimes I could hardly breathe. Then I would thank him, again, for coming to my rescue that day on the heels of my parent's rejection, their finding yet another *Christian principle* to shroud their callous *Whosoevers*. It was not surprising that the very sound of Mr. Simms's voice struck a responsive chord. It was warmth. It was safety. It was home. It was love – all I knew of it. So when he stuck his head inside the door and whispered, "Is the little one up?" I forgot my resolve and quietly closed Sharon's door before I poured him a cup of my boiled coffee.

The coffee was almost white with cream as he poured it, steaming, into the saucer to cool it. As I'd seen him do since I was a child, he balanced the saucer precariously on his fingertips, brimming full, and sipped from it, looking over his glasses as he spoke. "So-o. How's my girl? Any new beaus?"

"No," I said, as I nibbled on the sugar-glazed cruller. "I've just about given up. Except for being platonic. You know Dick Sully and Tony Panozzi? They still come around and bring me pizza in the middle of the night after they take their dates home. Aren't you having any donuts?" I asked him.

He shook his head as he continued to sip his coffee with a vengeance.

"They took me to Marquette's basketball game the other night. I don't know why Sully and Tony like to take me places. They took me out to eat after, too. I've told them each I only liked them as friends. You know... after Tony kissed me that night and got all flustered. Sully never did that. All the nights I've sat in his car just talking, all he ever did was put his arm around me when I was cold. So I had to stop Tony. To choose one over the other would split up a good friendship; I like them both too much for that."

Mr. Simms was listening intently to me, as he usually did, never interrupting me, just listening, so I kept talking.

"I'm not going to be like Billie Ann Murphy. She goes to whichever church the guy goes to – the one she's after. Everyone says we could pass for twins. She's gone steady with almost everyone in town and then dropped them flat. I guess they think I'm like her because of our looks, but I'm *not* like her in the least. Besides, it's nice, just being friends – not having to fight guys off. I just hate that. I'd rather stay home with Sharon and watch Perry Como on my new TV. Tony and Sully don't seem to care."

When I talked to Mr Simms, I had a hard time keeping to the subject sometimes, especially when the bad and ugly feelings would sweep over me. So I'd quickly switch to something else. "Tony says I'm a brunette Doris Day; do you know who she is?"

"Isn't she that blonde singer?"

"Yes, but he says she's in movies, too. He calls her a classy dame. He says I've got class, like her. That I have an invisible wall built around me, too, like she does, like I'm saying to everyone, *Come only so close... the untouchable beauty*. But that's Tony. Guess his crush on me has warped his judgment," I said, blushing. "Tony's Catholic, you know. He goes to a lot of movies. I've only been to a couple, when I baby-sat and had to take the kids."

Thinking about the way Sully and Tony treated me was confusing to me. I was really thinking out loud, "Either together or apart, Tony and Sully treat me like I'm another guy really," I said, trying to figure it out. Mary thinks our relationship is not *natural*, no matter that Tony is Italian. *Pooh with all your church*, she says. Underneath, I wasn't sure myself if I really liked it, being platonic, even though I said I did. "Don't quite know what to make of it, their coming around like they do," I told Mr. Simms.

"Well that's simple enough to figure out," he said, his huge hand swallowing the cup he carefully set into the emptied saucer. "You're a beauty, and smart young men can see beyond the *divorced*," he said, mouthing the word as if it was unmentionable.

Squirming in my seat, I answered him, "Ha. That's a laugh," I said, almost too quickly. "Tell it to the trumpet trio that just dropped me. You know I've been playing the piano for them. Horace Dolan, from *Holy Ghost*, plays in it. He told me that the mother of one of the other boys put her foot down and refused to let him continue if I kept playing. She said I was an *immoral influence* on her baby boy."

The anger in my voice was the only thing that kept me from crying, thinking about it. As careful as I had tried to be about my reputation. *Oh, how I hate women.* I had to fight the tears because I'd always cry when I got that angry. "They could've at least told me before I saw it in the *Youth For Christ* bulletin that I was replaced. I was lucky to catch Horace on the way in to the YFC rally. He was embarrassed to have to tell me. He used to like me when we were kids — remember when he was so chubby? — so I thought at least *he'd* look out for me, but he didn't. Right there in the auditorium, I started crying. I'd gone to hear that new young preacher that's getting so popular, Billy Graham, the place was packed."

Just thinking about that good looking preacher made me cheer up. "You know last summer? With Bonnie? When I met Ray Malorry? His friends from Bob Jones all seemed to think Ray looked and preached like Billy. Did you know Billy Graham went to Bob Jones University for a while? But he got kicked out, I heard. Someone said he was on the wild side, was too flashy. Don't know how true it is. They do favor each other somewhat, though, certainly has a commanding way about him — forceful, like Ray. Everyone listens, too, when Ray talks. Can't wait to hear him preach," I said, feeling the blood rush to my face like it did when I was embarrassed. Mr. Simms smiled as I put my hands to my cheeks and forehead, trying to cool myself off.

"You still writing Ray?" he asked finally.

"Once in awhile. I got him a week's meeting at *Fellowship Baptist*, Sully's church, for the end of September. He answers my letters right away, one skinny little page, about his meetings. How many souls..."

When Mr. Simms eyebrows shot up, I knew he was thinking things that just weren't true so I put him straight right then and there. "You can forget what you're thinking; Ray has not shown any interest in me since he found out I was divorced. Our writing is just business."

Just then Sharon's baby voice way back in the bedroom interrupted me. "Mommy... Mommy... Can I get up now?"

"In a minute, Honey. Mommy's coming," I called, as I scooted my chair back to get up. There was no real hurry as Sharon would wait for as long as I took.

Mr. Simms stood up immediately though. On his way to the

door, he reached for me, taking me by the arms, and shook me gently. Then he pulled my face up to look him in the eye. Whispering, he said, "One of these days... a prince of a young man is going to come along and recognize what a jewel my honey girl is."

He drew me close, but unconvinced, I held myself aloof, away from his usually comforting embrace.

He didn't force himself on me. Instead, he leaned down and kissed me quickly and ever so lightly on the lips.

Suddenly I was conscious of being undressed, and pulled the belted robe even tighter. With my other hand, I reached for the wide rolled lapels, the knuckles of my hand turning white as I pulled the skimpy cloth over my protruding collar bone: I could not seem to hide my nakedness.

Mr. Simms slipped past me through the door before he turned and handed me a small velvet box. *White Shoulders* cologne. "Maybe this will cheer you up," he said and mouthed, *I love you.*

My mouth flew open to protest, but he put his finger to his lips and said, "Sh-h." Then he was gone.

The stairs creaked at his leaving. I heaved a sigh of thanks that the majority of the Bagliaccio household worked late into the night at their successful bar and restaurant and would still be asleep. So far, nobody had mentioned the unusual hour of Mr. Simms' visits — only Tony and Sully's, and I had nothing to hide with them. *It's just a matter of time before Mary will say something.*

As I turned toward the bedroom, fingering the small velvet box in my pocket, I was remembering the day we first moved to the Simms' house and Daddy's talk about not sitting on men's laps and not letting *anyone* kiss me on the lips but him, ever. *Not even Mr. or Mrs. Simms.* Unconsciously, I wiped my lips with the back of my hand, wondering if *that* was why I'd felt so strange, so naked.

Sharon was standing up in her bed waiting for me. I reached for her outstretched arms. She was getting so heavy, I strained at picking her up, an armful. Solid and stockily built, *like Hubert*, Charity would often remark. Despite those hints of ridicule, I loved Sharon and held her closely at every opportunity. The underlying sadness deep within me was touched by her warmth and reassurance. Often, as now, I would hide my silent bottled up tears in her cottony hair.

Although I longed always to find someone to love me and

take care of me, it was Sharon, my motherhood, that I put before anything else. It was times like these with Sharon that I had looked forward to, having her finally all to myself in the evenings and weekends, even though being with her sometimes created anxiety for me.

People said I took exceptional care of Sharon, but there were times when I believed that I didn't feel the way a mother is supposed to feel — a part of me was missing: gone, had gotten lost somewhere. Sometimes I would find myself not sure of just how to behave with her. For the life of me, I couldn't remember much of anything about Mama, of any kind of loving exchanges between us. Memories that I knew were hidden under years of silencing myself, bits and pieces that would flash unexpectedly through my mind, left me confused and lost. Physical needs though, I understood, so I did what I knew, pretending the rest of the time.

It was being around Mary and seeing her with Anna and Sharon, feeling her warmth as it spilled over into everything she did, that made me ache all the more from what I began to realize were my empty places.

Into Sharon's hair, I whispered, *I love you so much, my lovely*, and I hugged her with all my might.

"I love you, too, Mommy," Sharon answered, returning the hug with the same intensity, absorbing the affection like a dried up sponge.

Then I held her out at arm's length and asked with an unexpected giggle, "How much do you love me?"

Sharon's little arms went outward as far as she could reach, the game we always played, responding instantly to my quick change of mood. "A hundred bags of sugar full," she squealed, her eyes alive with excitement.

We hugged again — but this time it was different. The atmosphere was full of fun and smiles.

She took my hand as we headed into the kitchen together. Another weekend of playing real grown-up house, loving and being adored – roles we lived out as though in a glass house for all the world to see, especially the wealthy Schultzes. They were still keeping watch over my every move, waiting for any slip. There was gossip continuously, and Charity seemed to relish every morsel. Even since Huey had been sent to the reformatory for that unspeakable sex crime, (I had an idea it was some kind of *perversion* but had to look up the word *sodomy*.) his family still watched me. The words of Mr. Simms I repeated often in my head: *Truth crushed to the ground shall rise again.* Yes. *He* believed in me, that I knew. But *why*?

Sharon sat back into her highchair and obediently laid her left hand in her lap, allowing me to tie a dishtowel around her and the chair so she wouldn't forget and eat with her left hand.

As we ate breakfast, I talked to her about why learning to eat nicely would make it easier for her when she grew up and how nutritious food made us feel good and helped us to grow big and strong. As I talked, a part of my mind raced on, as though there were, in essence, two of me: a doing part and a thinking part. Oh, the confusion, and the struggle to keep everything just so. Like a balancing act — striving for the middle of the road, the golden mean of the ancient Greeks I was studying about in my correspondence course. School. *Would I ever get my high school diploma at this rate?* How nice it would have been to go to the Bob Jones' Academy, right on campus with the college students. Just the thought of being there, on campus, excited me. I'd practically memorized Dr. Bob's *Chapel Sayings.* "Get on the right road and you'll come out at the right place." Or "If you learn how to live, you'll never have trouble earning a living." That's why it had hurt so, the Dean's letter saying I was too "worldly" for their school. But even if they had accepted me, and Charity had consented to keep Sharon, I would never have been able to repay Mr. Simms for the tuition. At least the five dollars a month to *American School* I was paying for myself. *Even if! Would I ever be able to repay him as it is?* I thought. Over and over I promised myself that I would — *someday.* The debt piled higher and higher. *It must be over $200 by now, over a month's salary. If I could just be a real secretary like Bonnie, instead of a girl Friday, I might be able to pay it back. And Huey. When he got out would he start the old stuff again in the middle of the night? With the telephone; the squealing wheels; the cops. His family calling, accusing, rubbing it in – my being an outcast divorcee, no place in Christian circles for me. Becoming more of an outsider than ever, no one besides Tony and Sully want to date me or have anything to do with me — no other Christians, that is.* The loneliness. The isolation. The despair. Under the cheerful smiles and happy chatter that got me through every day – just for that paycheck that barely reached, but always did.

Questions, my mind never stopped rattling on, looking for a way out. *But when I found him then I would be safe from stingy demanding bosses, from disapproving women, from men like Daddy who made me feel dirty, like Huey, like Doc, and, oh, please God, not Mr. Simms too.*

As I added up the numbers on the hospital claim forms I had been given, I tried to ignore the telephones that never seemed to stop ringing. "It's not part of your job description to answer the phones," I was told, so I had to let them ring, rattling my already shaky concentration.

Being in a room with other girls all day was a new and unnerving experience for me, having had two years of almost unsupervised freedom at the bank under kind old Mr. Doyle. He had been a ready buffer for any little problem I had encountered: if one of the older ladies was impatient, if one of the men got fresh, or if I was going to be late. He had even arranged for my tonsillectomy after repeated sore throats and earaches had kept me out sick. He looked out for me at work as Mr. Simms did at home. But Bertha White, my new immediate supervisor at Milwaukee Hospital (who had promised I would be making $200 a month – more than the minimum wage of $1 per hour – within six months if I proved myself) did not seem to know or care that I was alive. Unless, of course, I picked up one of the incessantly ringing telephones.

It was common knowledge that Miss White, unmarried, thickly built, and well over thirty, was intent on finding a man. And it appeared, from the attentions that were focused on the big boss, Mr. Perkle (who most of the time sat behind his desk absent-mindedly stroking his red mustache and peering out the window that separated him from the office staff), that it was he upon whom Bertha White had settled her intentions. She found innumerable excuses for which to shower him with her abundant presence.

Mr. Perkle was well over forty and married with children, but none of that appeared to matter to Miss White. Day after day, hour after hour, she would clandestinely pull out a compact to touch up her lipstick and dab her nose with powder, squirt a last minute spray of gardenia fragrance behind her protruding ears, and then give a last little pat to her short, straight, cut-off hair as she gathered up an armful of papers and strode all too casually to his door. He could be heard shouting a "Come in" as she knocked. Her giggles, as the door closed behind her swishing skirts, were all too telltale to pass unnoticed.

Out of earshot of us girls and all the whispering "What do you think of that?" gossip, Miss White could be seen, like a character in a silent movie, bending over her boss's shoulder, holding her hand over her flourishing cleavage, her face flushing pink with laughter at his words.

From the beginning I had watched, unbelieving, trying to stick a pin to my lips and not join in the titter. My Christian faith, I thought, was put to the true test in just such circumstances. Instead, I would smile back at Mr. Perkle whenever I would catch him staring at me. More and more often he stared, and more and more often I quelled the irresistible ringing.

The other girls encouraged me to pick up their phones, saying I had a knack for stalling or soothing ruffled feathers. I took messages most of the time or used the hold button. Either way I felt that I was contributing something, and the day passed much more quickly. The numbers on the stacks of papers had already become dreary and boring. But I needed the money, and the hospital's location, close enough to walk to work, saved me the cost of bus fare. Besides, it had a nice sound to it, working at a hospital — especially one as nice as this. So I was not really prepared for Miss White's angry barrage of accusations, nor for the firing that followed on Friday of my third week of employment.

I did not talk back. I wouldn't. I don't think I could have anyway. It was just impossible to even consider – being fired. A disgrace of the most enormous magnitude. And to be told that it was for not doing my work, for "dilly-dallying on the phone," was more than I could accept so suddenly. *How would I live? Where would I get a job?* I had looked for six months to find this one that didn't require a high school diploma. The head personnel manager was my only recourse.

Mr. Cromwell listened quietly as I spilled it all out: my fears of not being able to feed my child, or pay my rent and baby-sitter. He looked through my file again. When he questioned me about Miss White, I couldn't hold back the tears and told him about the office gossip: about Mr. Perkle. "I just can't figure that out; I never even talked to him. How could she be jealous, like the girls say?"

Then Mr. Cromwell talked to me at length about human nature and how beautiful young women, "like yourself," he said, making me blush, could make someone like Miss White uncomfortable. He would definitely look into the situation about the phones anyway, he said.

"But I never gossiped with the other girls. Never. No matter what they said. I'm a Christian, and I try to live it every minute, with every person I meet," I said, as I reached for a Kleenex he handed me, my tears unstoppable now. Suddenly I decided this was silly, to cry over Miss White, so I stopped crying. Smiling, I said, "No one *ever* answers those phones; I just couldn't believe it."

He did not answer me, but reached for the telephone. "My wife is personnel director at Trostel Tannery. They can always use someone with your dependable record."

I had been sitting on the edge of my seat. As I listened to Mr. Cromwell's end of the conversation, I knew *God* was taking care of me again, and I sat back in my chair.

"You can go right over there now, if you like," he said and handed me a slip of paper. "You did say you can type a little?"

"Yes. Oh, yes. I taught myself," I said, as I turned to leave.

"By the way – this position, during lunch breaks, you'll be learning to run a switchboard – a big one. Trostel's is the biggest tannery in the world, you know. Good luck." His smile broadened as he held out his hand.

I wanted to throw my arms around him and hug him, and laugh, and cry. Instead, I shook his hand and said very calmly, "Thank you. I won't disappoint you."

Down the hall I walked carefully, consciously feeling every step, touching each foot to the floor — for if I didn't, I felt I might just float away.

My typing was not really good enough to impress my new boss. What won him over was my experience at the bank, where I had been in charge of all of the buying of office supplies those last months. I was used to dealing with the ins and outs of the sales reps and their constant come-ons, and I learned quickly who Charlie would cotton to – and to get rid of the others in no time flat. He'd spy them coming down the hall, would groan, and disappear through the nearest door, leaving them to me and my smiling way. As it had at the bank, delivering office supplies gave me excuses to roam freely about the place, meeting and talking to everyone. The few minutes of training, daily, at the large central switchboard, with all its cords and lights, was the most exciting, though, learning all the departments and how to use the loud speaker system that reached far out into the tannery, as well as the Western Union equipment automatically typing out messages from all over the world.

My primary job was in the purchasing department, housed in a small cubicle outside of the large chemical laboratory. As I sat at my desk, I could see the chemists at work in their white coats, looking through their microscopes and mixing things over their Bunsen burners.

Julian Karafotius, a young chemist from Greece, hovered over his work, but would steal a glance my way every so often. I took to stopping by his projects and questioning him at length: What stinks so? Didn't it make him sick to his stomach to have to work in there? I was as curious as a child. Since Julian was a newcomer to this country on a working visa, I thought it only fitting to make him feel welcome. That was how our friendship began.

My enthusiasm about everything seemed to please him. I could see it in his eyes, as they seemed to dance when he'd watch me and listen to me. I would correct his English, so he began to misuse words intentionally, just to get a rise out of me. Our conversations took on depth as I questioned him about his beliefs, wondering exactly what Greek Orthodox meant. I tried to explain about being "born again," so that he would understand I was sincere about my faith. When we began debating creation versus evolution, I knew I was in trouble. I told him that he would have to come to *Highland Fundamental's* weekly Bible Seminar with me, taught by a professor up from Moody Bible Institute in Chicago who would set him straight.

To Mary, who volunteered to baby sit *free, if you'll just go out already*, Julian was a God-send, even if he was ten years my senior. "The girl upstairs (what the other Bagliaccios called me) is finally having a real date," she said, grinning as though she were my coach or something.

It was only the second time I had invited Julian up to my apartment, and I was extremely nervous, remembering all too well that embarrassing encounter with Doc, despite my efforts to forget. I had managed to forestall this event before, after our dates to church or to a movie, by sitting close to the car door as we talked, ready to slide out fast for a quick getaway. But then Julian's mother, visiting from Greece and not speaking any English, needed a haircut, and I offered to cut it.

Mary, thrilled with this opportunity, had baked for the occasion. "He must care for you, Sam, or he wouldn't bring his mother to meet you, so you must make her feel welcome. Serve her some tea." Julian interpreted for us as we ate. Gesturing with our hands, we communicated well. Mrs. Karafotius thanked me over and over and complimented my ability with the scissors. When she pointed to the marimba in the living room, Julian spoke of his violin and being a member of the Milwaukee Symphony. I told him about learning to play the cello in high school. So when he asked to come up again, alone, to hear me play the marimba, I reluctantly agreed.

In his summer shirt sleeves, Julian had loosened his tie and was sitting back comfortably on the two-piece rose love seat. As I walked past him to the marimba, he caught my hand. "Come sit," he said, pulling me down to his side.

It was unexpected, and I began to giggle as my underside got caught straddling the division of the sectional. He pulled me close and tipped my face up to his. He looked strange to me without his glasses, almost cross-eyed with his serious expression, ignoring my giggles. I closed my eyes then and tried to forget my discomfort as he began to kiss me, first on the forehead, then my cheeks, the tip of my nose, my chin, my neck. His fingers pressed into my scalp and then slipped down to my shoulders. I felt his hands as they moved like liquid over my body. I swallowed hard and stopped giggling. My head fell backwards as he held me about the waist, and he kissed me over every inch of my bare neck, his warm mouth sliding over my skin like rain. He kissed me everywhere, except on my mouth. He touched me everywhere, except on my most sacred parts, manipulating every nerve and muscle in my back, bringing to the surface feelings I had never known I possessed. His hands had ignited a tinderbox of impassioned fire beneath the protective cover of this proper Christian girl. Somehow I found the words, "Stop. Please stop," as I tried to gain possession of myself.

But he continued to ignore my protests, putting the warmth of his mouth over my face in a way I had never quite experienced.

My hands had found his richly winding hair, and I was reaching for his lips, but they were covering my skin like warm moist dew. He had somehow taken over, as I could not find his lips. My thoughts were spinning. I had no idea where this would end, for it had never begun for me before. *Not like this.* Suddenly a panic struck at my chest, and I wrenched myself away from his strong grasp, and I ran to the door.

He followed me. "What you do?" he asked with a note of alarm, but his smiling eyes still enveloped me.

I said, "You'll have to go now, I think. Please. Good night. You don't understand. This is not the way Americans kiss. They kiss on the lips... Don't you understand? On the *lips...*" and pointed to them as though he was deaf. But even as I spoke, he was ignoring my words again with the onslaught of his hands and his mouth.

I had begun backing away from him, into my dining room. He stepped close and held my body tightly to him as he crept with me, tipping me backwards, whispering all the time, "This is the

Greek way... the international way... my way," he was saying, as I found my backside flush up against my dining room table, yards from the doorway where I had just said good night.

In the back of my mind I was determined that I would *not* succumb to another. *Never.* But the feelings he had unleashed within me were turning me upside down and backwards. Then he began kissing my eyelids again. Then into my ears, his warm tongue reached for my insides. I had to *stop* this. So I slid back... onto the table — but it did not stop him. He was more possessed than ever. He didn't even notice that my shoes fell off and that I was pulling my stocking feet up under me, inching my way back onto the table. Finally, like a small child, I was on my feet, in the center of the table, and reached for his shoulders. Getting his attention, I said, "Please. Please, listen to me. *Julian. Stop.* I can't stand this... this..."

"Feeling so good?" he interjected. "Oh, you are delicious!"

"Whatever you want to call it. I can't afford to get involved with someone as... as *quick*... as you. I am *not* going to bed with you."

He just looked at me, smiling very devilishly, reaching out with both hands for me again.

To *make* him understand, I spoke with authority. "I will not *let* you get me into bed. Do you understand?"

The tone of my voice must have registered for he dropped his hands to his sides.

Quickly I jumped down onto the floor, took him by his bare elbow above his hairy forearm, and led him to the door. "I'm sorry I have to make you leave like this," I said, trying to keep my voice calm; my giggles, I knew, only teased for more. I opened the door and gently pushed him backwards through it.

With both of his hands, he reached out for me.

I took them both, crossed them, and placed them flat against his chest. At the same time I caught the door with my knee and pushed it closed after him.

Mary was listening as I explained in explicit detail Julian's strange Greek lovemaking, that he never touched my mouth. Not once!

"Oh my God," she was saying, beating her hands upon her large, full breast, "What a man you have landed. *Grab* him, you fool. Can't you see he *cares* for you?"

"I can't... I don't trust myself with him... I never... I'm afraid I'll... I just can't take the chance... I... Don't you see, Mary? If I put myself in a position to do wrong — deliberately – I've already *done* it in my heart?"

But Mary did not see, she did not know about Dr. Bob's principles, "not sacrificing the permanent on the altar of the immediate," or about Ray Malorry and my dream of marrying a preacher. The Greek Julian had touched a hidden part of my being. He had not only made me question my Christian faith with all of his science — the faith that was my rock, my fortress against sin, sin that could lose me my child, my self-respect, my future, my *life* – but this Julian, he had touched my very soul. To sin with him would be with desire and foreknowledge, with my whole being. And surely this was the lust of the flesh of which the Bible spoke, not just acting as a receptacle as I had done in the past. There was the difference. To be *used* carried less responsibility and far less guilt somehow. No, Mary did not understand that I could not ever let Julian into my house again.

It was a hot summer. Mr. Simms had helped me put a window fan in for my expected weekend guests to be able to tolerate the stifling heat. I understood why my rent was so cheap, but the pride I felt as I looked at my nicely polished floor, and the neatly arranged furniture sparsely scattered throughout the large sunny rooms, brought me comfort in times like these when the weight of my adulthood seemed ready to overwhelm me. The responsibility of being the sole breadwinner was not something I even thought of as frightening, but the anxiety inside mushroomed as Sharon grew out of things. New seasons. New styles. New unexpected needs. The fan was a typical example. I could hardly keep up with it all. And then I had only been at the Tannery a couple of weeks when I began hearing rumors about new office changes in the works, a switch over to IBM computers that would eliminate some jobs.

IBM people were in and out doing a job audit. I got wind of it at the switchboard, an island in the center of traffic set apart by a half-wall on three sides. Mrs. Cromwell happened by one day while I sat as relief. At my hiring, I had not been interviewed by the director, but when the attractive, neatly coiffured woman spoke, I knew immediately who she was. Mrs. Cromwell leaned over the narrow wooden counter affair that separated everyone from the switchboard and in a quiet voice said to me, "By the way, I thought you might be interested to hear about your Miss White and Mr. Perkle. At the hospital?"

I nodded, remembering my firing with chagrin.

"They were both put out on their ear. I guess they admitted

carrying on an affair; it seems you girls were right," she winked and patted me on the shoulder.

I felt vindicated and pleasantly flattered at the disclosure, especially by Mrs. Cromwell's manner when she spoke to me – rather secretive and intimate. So I didn't even hesitate to mention the rumors, especially since all Charlie had said was, "I've been working for Trostel twenty-five years; they never did me wrong yet." He'd hidden his face in an order catalogue and refused to say anything more. But the fear of losing another job worried me greatly, so I blurted out my concern.

Mrs. Cromwell's face took on an angular look as her mouth dropped open to speak. Then, as though she thought better of it, she put her finger to her lips and said, "Don't worry; you have my word." She turned and disappeared through the large double doors leading to her carpeted office.

This assurance only created more anxiety for me, now aware that someone that high up was watching me. Some days I would practice my typing ferociously at every spare moment.

Julian knew nothing. His work, primarily with the chemical treatment in the tanning of the leather and testing of new dyes — taking weeks to process – kept him in his lab. He was quite isolated from the general run of business, although very closely connected to the huge warehouse I had visited in the beginning, where the skins were soaked in large stinking vats. Formaldehyde covered the hides to rid them of any remaining flesh before color was added. No females were allowed in this area unless accompanied by a male, not only because the chemicals were dangerous but also our safety, it was feared, might be jeopardized by the black men, wearing hip-high boots, who supervised this stench-filled process. Then there was a huge manufacturing plant, completely separate from the warehouse, where shoes and boots were made from this leather, where many women worked. On payday, I stood in a small secured office behind a barred window and helped to hand out paychecks to this host of employees. Certainly there would continue to be a place for me somewhere, I thought. But my stomach stayed queasy most of the time. Being fired again was never very far out of my mind, in spite of Julian's continual words of encouragement. "A big place like this... and a smart girl like you. No worries."

I saw Julian less and less, believing very strongly in my decision, especially when the mail would come from Ray Malorry. Just the thought of seeing Ray again would make my insides jump – if I could just find a way to get him up here to my apartment when he's in Milwaukee, I thought, so I could cook for him. *A way to a man's heart...* I was thinking, as I prepared for my house guests' arrival any moment.

One last time, I went over everything in my mind. The brownies came out good and chewy, and the tangy spareribs Mary had helped me barbeque were ready to be reheated – they were so much better the next day. My laundry was done and hanging in the basement drying. Everything perfect. I had even put on nylon hose just to please Bonnie.

Sharon's hair had been rolled the night before and was still a little curly. With her rag doll under her arm, she ran squealing to the door. "They're here. Mommy. They're here."

"Just wait," I said calmly, as I walked very deliberately, trying to act indifferent toward the noises coming from the stairs, my stomach in a turmoil as I reached for the doorknob.

Ed Johnston, Bonnie's newly divorced cousin from Illinois, was a tall light-haired young man with searching blue eyes and considerable freckles across the bridge of his nose. He seemed in constant appraisal of me. Bonnie had suggested our meeting, so I invited them for the weekend.

Bonnie had turned out to be my best and only real friend from *Highland Fundamental*, which I attended full time now. She had really fallen for Red, Ray's buddy, in a big way last summer. But nothing ever came of that either, in spite of her attractive hourglass figure. Maybe when she got to Bob Jones for Fall quarter they could pick up where they left off. She was saving every cent to go back, talking endlessly about the men there. "BJU fellahs this and BJU fellahs that... BJU fellahs don't like girls in bare legs. BJU fellahs don't respect you if you kiss on the first date. BJU fellahs follow the six-inch rule." An inch could cinch it for you if you got too close. So I had been proud of myself that I had kept my distance from Ray and refused to be his last fling, before his tying the knot; I had not let him kiss me, even the last night. How I had dreamed of that kiss since, the one I had struggled against, over and over — dreams that kept Ray sweetly alive in my memory. But Ed Johnston was not a BJU boy. He wasn't even a born-again Christian. So I had to be extra careful lest he stumble because of me.

Sharon was standing on one foot in the center of the kitchen, her fingers caught in the hem of her dress from behind, twirling the lacy ruffle as she balanced and twisted on the shiny red and black linoleum. Her audience was larger than usual as she recited *The Lord Is My Shepherd.*[13]

Bonnie and her sister Faye were obviously delighted at hearing a child so young repeating scripture. Enjoying every opportunity to be a *witness* they prodded and clapped until Sharon had sung every song she knew, looking coyly at the two young men sitting quietly in the background. Faye's fiancé, Darrel, was friendly and jovial. Ed, though, had been rather quiet, listening. Bonnie and Faye told me how earnestly they were "praying for his salvation."

Sharon had never been so charming, with her long blonde ponytail and gray eyes, accentuated by the charcoal black eyelashes and brows she got from the Schultzes. *I'll be a sunbeam for Jesus* was on its third go-round. Ed held out some candy to her. She grew quiet and stole a glance at me. A return look was all she needed to whisper politely, "No, thank you."

"It's time for a bath now," I said, disappearing into the bathroom to escape the intensity of his eyes, the disapproval of my parenting that I could read in them. I had been fighting with Mary that whole week, ever since I returned home unexpectedly to find a giant Coke on the dinner table instead of milk. I had emptied Sharon's pocket's filled with candy and gum onto Mary's table, shaking in uncontrollable anger. "I'll find another baby-sitter if you insist on ignoring my rules," I'd told her. My best friend, now, too. So if I could stand up to *that,* I could handle Ed Johnston. *What did I care if he believed me too strict? What did he know, anyway, about raising a child?* I thought, as I turned on the water spigot. How much did this guy really see of his own little girl, after as bitter a divorce as he'd described. I felt very defensive and determined. No one, I told myself, *no one,* is going to tell me how to raise my child.

It was the second day of this weekend visit. I was sitting on my bed brushing Sharon's hair before bed, smiling to myself at the warm feelings Ed's interest in me had begun. He had been so polite and gentlemanly, allowing me to relax and be myself. I could be enthusiastic and talkative when encouraged. It had been a while since I felt that free. Julian had kept me on guard constantly; Ray I thought of only as a ship passing in the night; and Sully and Tony I only cared for as friends. Ed's good looks had intimidated me initially, but his freckles had somehow made me relax. I wanted to smile whenever I caught his gaze. So, impulsively, I whispered into Sharon's ear, "Go give Uncle Ed a

---

[13] Psalms 23, The Bible, King James Version

good-night kiss, and tell him it's from your mommy."

Down she scooted, and before I had time to think about it, Sharon was back with a beaming face. She had not been very far from him that whole day. At the Lake Front and the zoo, he had carried her everywhere.

I was sure Sharon loved not having to share Uncle Ed with her daily playmate, Anna, as she had to with Uncle Mario, Anna's father. Mary told me that every morning our two little girls would drag Mario's cumbersome wooden leg to the side of his bed when he'd yell his staccato commands, "Hey. C'mere. Where's my leg?" before Mary would set the table for them all to eat together. When Sharon and Anna would play house, I would hear them talk about Daddy or Uncle Mario having to leave them and "go to work and earn money."

So Sharon was surprised by Ed's staying all day and night, sleeping on the floor in the other room. When she had asked, was he staying, again, "another night?" he had hugged her and assured her he would be there in the morning when she woke up. "The sooner you go to sleep, the sooner we'll be able to wake up and go to Sunday school," I told her. So Sharon had obeyed in her usual docile way, climbing into her crib. Under her pillow went her clenched fist, to "hide my thumb from my mouth," Sharon said, as I sat down quietly on the floor.

Softly I sang *Blest be-e the tie-ie that binds... our hear-rts in Chri-is-tian love.* It was our nightly ritual. I would sing and then hum until Sharon was still. I looked up to see Ed quietly sliding down next to me on the bare hardwood floor as I leaned back against my bed. He slipped his arm around me and held me. Gently. I continued humming softly to the last note. It was the tenderness with which he held me that melted me, as I turned to look up at him. Then we kissed, softly and with such feeling that my mind raced and my blood rushed to my temples as we held each other, close, for the first time. We sat there in the dark just holding one another, before we had to join the others in the kitchen.

Could he be the one for me? I wondered, as we walked arm and arm through my apartment. I knew he did not profess to be Christian, but he was so earnest about doing everything right — for his daughter, for his customers at his job. And our disastrous young marriages were so similar. My head was spinning from the seriousness of our conversations. He would talk and question and *listen* to me, never turning away from me or from my God. And I believed him when he promised to never use alcohol again –

even though he had admitted using it to numb his terrible hurt for weeks after his divorce. But no one, save Mr. Simms, had ever been so astoundingly honest with me. Still, my desire to have "God's blessing," the only way for a "fruitful" marriage I still believed, tugged at me. Worried at being misled by my physical feelings — Ed's kind of warmth and caring still new to me, frightening me – I held myself in check, waiting, hoping for Faye and Bonnie's prayers for Ed to come true, the prayer that now became mine. Then I would know it was "God's will." In the meantime, I would continue to practice my typing.

Dottie, Bonnie's mother, was very short in stature, and robust. Her cheerful personality seemed to be reflected in the bouncy curls that she fought to keep out of her eyes as she cooked. I had taken the train with Bonnie to Illinois for the weekend. Since Ed rented a room in his aunt's house, I was invited to stay with Bonnie in her old room. Kathleen, Ed's tiny freckle-faced daughter, strode in and out of the kitchen, feeling very much at home with her Aunt Dottie. It was evident the child was the apple of her father's eye, and seeing them together made the love I was already feeling for this new man in my life all the more special. But when, at the dinner table, Ed reached for the salt and poured it unsparingly over Kathleen's food, my mother-ire rose in protest. "What are you doing to that food?" I howled, teasingly. "How do you know she *wants* all that salt?"

"Well, she likes anything I like. Don't you Baby?" he said, tweaking the child on the cheek.

Beaming back at her daddy, she said, "Uh huh," cramming the food into her chubby little mouth.

"It's a useless cause," said Aunt Dottie. "He keeps that kid filled with sweets besides, the whole weekend she's here."

"No," I said in shocked surprise. "Don't you know how *bad* that is for kids?"

"Childhood is the time for pop, chewing gum and candy. Take that away from a kid, and you've taken away the fun of growing up," Ed said. "If you and I get hitched, we're going to tangle on this. I think you are dead wrong in being so strict with that sweet little Sharon."

I smiled, silently registering the *getting hitched* part and decided now was not the time to take on such a disagreement. I would wait. But I knew exactly how much I would budge – not a hair. But then, there were so many if's to this whole affair. *If* he loved me. *If* he "accepted Christ," and *if* I was sure he was really finished drinking. Meeting his old bar buddies, I suddenly felt uneasy, but he reminded me he had been honest with me, even though it had not been too long since he'd hidden for weeks in an alcoholic haze. I'll just have to trust him; *God will show me.*

Because we missed Sunday morning church, we substituted group devotions after the large midday meal. Aunt Dottie read from her frayed worn-out Bible. Bonnie led in prayer, and Ed sat quietly next to me, with his arm around me closely. Kathleen knelt on the floor scribbling in the Bible coloring book Bonnie brought for her. She soon tired, though, and crawled up onto her daddy's lap and fell asleep. After *Amens* were said, and Ed had deposited his sleeping beauty on the couch, he pulled me after him toward the stairs, to his room.

I looked back at Aunt Dottie, who seemed to pay no attention to my whereabouts. "I don't know if I should," I whispered, pulling back from his firm grip.

"Don't be silly. It's my room; we're adults."

"That's not the point. I am a guest in this house."

He put his arms around me at the foot of the stairs and poked me in the tip of my nose as I looked up at him. "Such a prissy one. Can't you just relax? Try, okay?"

Reluctantly, I went with him.

The room was small and decorated in Early American decor which lent a feeling of solitude and peace. Just the sight of the bed, with its handmade quilt, made me tired, but I sat down on the braided rug next to it instead. Ed lay across the bed, face down, letting his long legs dangle over the side, and turned to me. "I'm not so sure I understand all about this religious stuff," he said, reaching for my hand.

"There's nothing to understand," I said. "It's just a matter of faith."

"I wish I had your's, and my Aunt Dottie's. She's been through so much. I don't know how she has raised two girls alone and still remained happy. You'd think she would hate the world."

"It is sort of a miracle, isn't it, when you think of all the rotten stuff that has happened to me, too? Sometimes I get discouraged. But I have to remind myself, it is people, human beings, that fail, not God — *He* never fails."

"Where do you get your faith?"

"Well... faith, or hope, is sort of like air. If you have it, everything is fine. If you don't, well, you sort of shrivel up and die.

"So I'm dead?"

"More like waiting to be born... again, that is." I said in my coquettish voice, reaching for his arm and back and running my hand over his muscular shoulders.

"Well, anytime..." he said, turning over to pull me up into his arms as we kissed. He rolled me over on my back and whispered to me softly about my beauty, inside and out, and how much he cared for me.

I flushed in genuine pleasure, feeling the warmth clear into my abdomen.

We held each other closely, kissing and fondling one another in the most circumspect way for minutes. As time passed, I became conscious of my whereabouts and how this must look. The wetness in my thighs reminded me even more so of my boldness in coming up to a man's bedroom. So I slipped reluctantly out from under him and left him to nap.

The house had that Sunday afternoon quietness that had dominated my childhood. I had hated it and vowed the day would come when Sunday would be my most exciting day. Until then, I was subject to my hostess. Bonnie was curled up reading in the overstuffed chair at the foot of the bed we had shared the night before. It was not the first night we had spent together, although this friendship was a most unusual one compared to those of my youth. Daddy's possessiveness in insisting that I be home to meet him at the door when he arrived from work had limited my play time to the short hours after school. Then Beth was such a brat and only my friend because of our fathers' unique single-parent friendship. It still confused me, Beth and me, and what we'd done as five-year-olds. The tawdry fear of being *that way* I'd had to fight all my life, along with feelings of closeness with any girls, until Bonnie managed to stride right past my fiercely protective barriers. Because of Bonnie's own closeness with her sister and mother, no doubt, and her being a few years older than I, she must have recognized I was tender of footing amongst women from being raised entirely according to Daddy's yardstick for what made little girls *ladies*. Bonnie's following me into the shower that week at Winona Lake, the first experience of seeing another woman alone, in nothing but skin, was not only shocking, but liberating when my most fearful expectations were not met. We had talked about girls' things: shaving, menstruating, douching, things that I had barely broached with Charity before I stopped confiding in her. So that when my feminine needs were calling this moment, I had few misgivings about presenting the problem to my best friend. "Do you have a hot water bottle?" I asked.

"Whatever for? Are you ill?"

"No," I said, suddenly embarrassed. "I have this terrible discharge. Ever since Sharon... It gets worse sometimes. And right now it is... you know... itching. I need a good wash," I said finally.

"Oh," said Bonnie, as though stunned at such a request. "I'll ask my mom. I guess you'll need some vinegar, too?"

"No. I use Lysol. That way you won't have to worry about germs."

"Lysol?" The look on her face was even more puzzled than before. Bonnie disappeared and returned with her mother. Aunt Dottie was visibly distraught. Her hands clasped under the gathers of her frilly Sunday apron. It was Bonnie who finally broke the silence, speaking barely audibly. "Mom thinks you and Ed have... done something... because of your asking for Lysol."

"Oh, my god, no. How could you think such a thing? I just have this terrible discharge, and when it gets bad... irritating, I wash inside and it goes away. I use Lysol very diluted because that is what my ex-mother-in-law told me. She was from the Old Country, you know; she swore by it. Said it disinfects *everything*, kills any germs."

"I guess it *would*," said Aunt Dottie, as she put her hands to her face and heaved a sigh. "I just can't believe such a thing. Why, that went out with the horse and buggy. Granted there are still some horses around, but not the preferred... I'd think it would burn the fire out of you," she blurted out, shaking her head.

Bonnie had left and returned with a large white rubber douche bottle. Not anything like the skinny, finger-thin attachment I had always used from my water bottle. One look at this unfamiliar fat affair and I decided I could not put the awful looking thing inside of me. So I apologized, red faced, for the bother, and Aunt Dottie suggested I just take a warm bath. "Maybe that will ease your problem," she said.

Scooting down under the bubbles Aunt Dottie had provided, I was thinking about how embarrassed they had been at my request. *Somehow I had never learned to be a woman.* It was all so horribly confusing. To even mention *woman's worries* seemed an outrage. That much I had gathered through the years. As a child without a mother, I had been told many things by women in moments of hushed secrecy, things I would usually forget, especially Cousin Myrtle's warnings about *growing together*. It was embarrassing to see Junior in church as he grew up and joined the navy, turning into such a good-looking young man, remembering my four-year-old fear of his being *nasty*. Then

Cousin Essie providing me with more information than I really wanted to hear, about my own part in the course of things sexual. It had almost destroyed my desire to be a wife and mother. But childbirth had all come about with no help from anyone – well almost anyone. I had made it through labor after all those interns passed their index finger beyond my hemorrhoids. What a humiliating experience. Even more so than the day, as a ten-year-old, I had been so bound up with constipation that I had screamed for help on the commode. It had nearly split my rectum by the time Jodi's mother had found the Vaseline and a popsicle stick. We had laughed hysterically together in spite of my pain, but my shame, as I was chided to eat more fruit, had never quite been forgotten. No wonder I hated going to that church where I grew up, where my life was an open book. Everyone knew so much about me. Giggles and laughter were my only protection, so I had joked again during my labor with Sharon, as the numbers of interns turned into dozens. I still thought about kindhearted, aging Dr. Oberman, who had ridden the elevator with me to the delivery room at the end, patting me continuously, assuring me that I would not feel anything. As the nurses had slipped the stockings over my bare icy feet, dropping them into the metal stirrups, I heard his comment just before I slipped into that deep welcomed oblivion, "She's just a baby herself. *What a shame."* Yes, what a shame. That seemed to have summed up my whole life. A shame, I thought, as I let the fluffy perfumed water wash over my small slender frame hoping it would somehow make me more acceptable.

Would I ever learn what to say, or not to say? Would I ever really fit into that mysterious world of women? How sincerely I yearned for that revered place, a fairy princess-like distinction, to be a woman. I looked down at my body and heaved a sigh and pulled the warm wash cloth up over my nipples protruding in shivers. There was just nothing about me that looked anything like a woman. Nothing like Bonnie, with her rounded swaying lofty breasts, her hips smooth and unmarred by pregnancy. I felt of so little value, so cast down in my self-criticism. But my spirits never stayed down too long before the determination that had brought me this far would rise up to my rescue. My spirit seemed to be able to do an about face and would take off like a bird, soaring, pushing me upward and onward, giving me something to grasp, to hang onto, to fight for. *It was happening again.* And as the warmth of the water reached into my brain, reviving me, I thought: to make up for all that was missing – to Sharon, to Ed – I would just

have to be perfect in every *other* way. At least I knew I would try –
every single minute.

C harity was cleaning her glasses with her apron. She spoke
with a touch of amusement in her voice. "He has a bit of a
roaming eye, I would say."

My mouth flew open in astonishment. This exciting new man
in my life had taken me by storm, and I depended on Charity's
jaundiced opinion to settle me, to bring me down to the spitting
earth. But for Charity to conclude something so detrimental about
someone she had only met once, and then only briefly, was even
more prejudicial than her usual callous remarks.

There had been so many moments of cruelty, so many
hurtful, cutting words that had gone down as battle markers to
forever hail the bitter ending to my forlorn and lusterless
childhood. So it should not have surprised me to hear Charity's
cold pronouncement on my new love interest. But it was her *bold
amusement* now, as she spoke of Ed, that prompted me to press
for an explanation.

"What in the world do you mean – roaming eye?"

"Well, you know. He winked at me and gave me the eye,
trying to get me on his good side, I'm sure. Not that I think he
really meant anything by it, but he's got a *salesman's cunning*,
and I'd watch out for him. Too smooth for my blood," she said,
putting her glasses back on, her eyes emanating distrust. "And
just imagine, if he treated *me* this way, what would he do with a
pretty young thing?"

The occasional dreaded visit with my parents had, again, left
me depressed. I had become resigned to my bitter feelings for
Daddy, I have realized since, by relegating them to his wife, but,
at the time, I had no idea I had done this, just that my hatred for
Charity grew with each passing day making me very
uncomfortable. Ed believed that stepmothers were supposed to
be hated, but he had no inkling of the depth of my feeling, its
poison hid beneath my cheerful smile.

A two-dollar room at the Y on his weekend visits was all Ed could
afford on his salesman's commission. He had visions, though, for
the future as he talked of marriage and building a house for us.
The nagging ugliness of the draft hanging over his head had kept
him from being able to make any real plans, reclassifying him to
1-A since his divorce. The draft board's lottery induction system
kept all the eligible young men on pins and needles — chance,

the luck of the draw, and Ed, waiting every day for his number to come up and take him to the battleground of Korea, was no exception. He wrestled with fear, then relief, then anger: a vicious, daily cycle, repeated again, and again.

Ed was insisting that we have a house built before we got married when I told him of the houses Ma Schultz was building – one for each of her children, one of which could have been mine had I stuck it out with Hubert. Despite the warm feelings I still felt for her or no matter how well intentioned, the woman's bribes had not swayed me from my determination to be independent. My Gypsy-like existence in childhood made the thought of a home of my own stir my heart underneath the Christian words I had learned to speak so convincingly, words that applauded spiritual, internal values and denounced superficial, materialistic wants. Responding to my unspoken feelings, Ed was saying, "One of those things I feel strongly about."

"But, it is whether we love each other that matters; the house can wait."

His refusal to entertain such a notion left us at a standstill, so we began talking of other things: my aunts and cousins, and Grandmother Evermardt he'd met at her *Missionary Alliance* church that morning.

"You look like your grandmother, Sam. Your mother must have been beautiful."

"Did you notice all the blue eyes?" I asked, feeling warm inside from his implied compliment and smiling at the mention of my mother, a subject in which I rarely was allowed to indulge; Mama's tragic death had become a closed matter.

"Yes. Where on earth did you get those dark eyes?"

"I think it's the Cherokee, from my father's blue-eyed mother," I said joking, but so proud of that heritage, which Daddy, in his southern bigotry, tried to deny.

"Speaking of eyes," I said, thinking about Daddy and remembering my discussion with Charity. "My stepmother said she thinks you have a roaming eye. Did you wink at her or something?" I giggled.

"I guess I did."

"Well, she thinks if you did this to *her*... to watch you," I said, tipping my head as though looking over the tops of invisible glasses and shaking my finger saucily at him.

He grabbed my finger and pulled me close to him, hugging me. Then lapsing into deep thought, he added, "Your stepmother is telling more on herself, than on me, you know."

"Don't worry about it, I'm not. That's just Charity, always saying something upsetting; I'm used to her," I said.

It was easy to accept Ed's interpretation of Charity's remarks as I tucked away the nagging seed of doubt that she had planted. Suddenly Ray Malorry popped into my mind, and I realized, for some reason not clear to myself, I had never mentioned Ray Malorry to Ed. I had missed Ray's first Sunday morning service – beginning his week of evangelistic meetings I had arranged for him here in Milwaukee – choosing, instead, to take Ed to my grandmother's church that morning. Ed was leaving to go home on the four o'clock train, though, and Ray's Sunday night service, at *Fellowship Baptist*, was just a few nervous hours away.

The first hymn was being sung, the congregation standing, as I entered the service.

> [14] *I stand amazed in the pre-sence*
> *of Je-sus, the Nazarene,*
> *and won-der how he could love me,*
> *a sin-ner, con-demned, un-clean.*

I was just late enough so that my arrival was noticed by the young, blonde preacher who stood to the rear of the platform. He was looking my way, and our eyes met momentarily as I slid into the hardbacked pew. Involuntarily, I smiled. He nodded and kept on singing. He was taller than I remembered. The cut of his clean, fine features, small and narrow boned, struck me anew. But it was his jaw line, pronounced and giving him that set, determined look (similar to Billy Graham's) that had won him this meeting when the men on the church board had seen his picture.

Coming alone, I'd put Sharon to bed in her own crib, and Mary had agreed to run up and check on her for the short time I would be gone. Mary had gotten excited when I mentioned Ray was in town. "Oh, kid, this *is* the end of September. I almost forgot, with this hot love affair you've got going with Ed. First you got no one, then you got them stacked up," she said, poking me in the ribs. "Are you gonna bring him home?" Mary couldn't resist asking.

"I really hadn't thought of that," I lied, and poorly.

"Oh, don't give me that, Sam," Mary said, rolling her eyes, "The way you've been running to that mailbox every day for the last six months. When did *Ed* write you last?" she asked testily.

---

[14] *My Savior's Love* was written by Chas H. Gabriel, 1905

"Never, he always calls, but you never know when he's going to start," I answered quickly, knowing my face turning pink was giving me away.

"Hey, I think you kind of like this Ray. All right, Sam. No need to explain. Hell, I ain't your mother; I'm just your cheering section. Go to it, kid. Just give me a jingle when you get in. Sometimes I don't hear you, you're so damn quiet. That stinker Sharon thumps like a giant. Can't figure out how you can weigh so much more than her and I ain't never heard you yet."

"I guess I'm just light on my feet," I answered her, not fully realizing myself how extremely careful I tried to be. I was thankful for the Bagliaccio's confidence in me, renting to me in the first place. The less they heard or saw of me, though, the better, but Mary missed very little. She seemed, too often, to be able to read things in my face.

I had done well, though, keeping my feelings for Ray hidden – a preacher like I'd dreamed of marrying since my babyhood crush on Pastor Dunham. Remembering the pastor from my childhood – how I'd listen to his every word, cringe every time his fist would hit the pulpit, cry at every sad story he'd tell, and feel like cheering every time he would raise his arms to the heavens and shout to his heavenly father – still brought a lump to my throat. I had heard then about special callings from God. If I ever received one, it was my calling to marry a preacher, to play piano for him, but now it could never be; divorce had destroyed my chances. So, as Ray Malorry stood before the pulpit, reading from the Thompson Chain Reference Bible he had showed me that first week we met – marked in his neat red and blue printing throughout with notes and sermon outlines – I knew nothing would ever come of it, no matter how many letters I wrote or Ray answered, it was just a dream. For a few short minutes, though, I forgot Ed and my tender feelings for him and let myself float into Ray's world of impossibility again, as I had done so many times the past year, making believe I was Ray's woman. I could feel my chest rise and fall. In between snatches of Ray's angry sounding sermon, the air poured out of my lungs, in and out in uneven breaths. Ray spoke loudly, pounding the pulpit, looking at me time and again. Straight into my eyes his blue-eyed stare would pierce my thoughts, making me listen to him as he spoke of his angry God, "His powerful judgment will He bestow upon all who turn their backs on Him. Believe it, my friends," he shouted, as he held his Bible in the air. "It says so in His word." Then, carefully putting the book upon the tilted book rest before him, he bent over the pulpit with bowed head, closed his eyes, and reached his hand straight out in front of him as though reaching out to touch someone, and began praying, "Dear Lord, we come before you as humble servants..."

Ray had borrowed the Pastor's car. As we were parking in front of my house, I was still in stunned disbelief that Ray had actually asked to bring me home.

"It's that cute little Sharon I've been dying to see. Can we wake her up?" he asked, as though reading my thoughts.

"We'll see," I said, as we tiptoed up the creaking stairs together.

Ray saw the marimba and immediately asked me to play. He sat down across the room and picked up a magazine. As he read, I played – remembering that he was reading a magazine the first day I saw him. I didn't think then that I would ever see him again. A week later, when we parted, he was headed home for his wedding. That was surely the last time I would see him. Months later, Bonnie heard through her friends at Bob Jones that Ray's marriage was off. I took a chance and wrote a short letter, asking him if he would be interested in coming to Milwaukee to preach, if I could swing it? And there he sat now, big as life, not a dream, as I played every song I knew while he read every page of that magazine.

When finally I played *Yes, God is Real,* the song Frank Boggs sang our first night together, and Ray still didn't look up from his magazine, I put the sticks away.

"I guess you don't care for marimba music?" I said cheerfully, trying to get a compliment out of him.

"Oh, yes. I was listening. Can you play: *When They Ring Those Golden Bells?"*

That was a strange request, usually sung at funerals, but I played it, making the *bells now ringing* echo like far away bells, rolling all four sticks in harmony as melodiously as I could.

Ray must have liked it for he did look up and smile, and then laid down the magazine. "Where's Sharon?" he asked.

"In here," I pointed, and we tiptoed to the bedroom. I cracked the door so the light's path fell on the crib.

He stood silently, gazing at Sharon as she slept. Turning, he whispered, "Don't wake her up; she's sleeping so soundly."

We walked into the kitchen for a cool drink, "Boy, what a beauty she is. And a blonde, not dark like you. What color are her eyes?"

"They're very light gray. They sort of reflect the color she's wearing. If she wears blue, they look blue."

"Blue? Like mine?"

I nodded, "Uh-huh."

He grinned, showing his chipped tooth. Then his smile faded and his voice changed, "She's just a little younger than Suzie was when we lost her to polio last year."

As we sat together at the kitchen table, Ray told me all about his friend's child dying of bulbar polio, just weeks before the vaccine came out. "She was so full of life. Happy. And within hours, she was dead. That quick," he said, snapping his fingers.

"How terrible. And losing someone suddenly has a way of tearing us apart," I said. "Not so easy to get over."

Ray didn't answer as he sipped his iced tea. I was quiet, remembering the song he had asked me to play and understanding the strangeness of it now. After a while, he asked, "What did you think of my sermon?"

"I like your style," I said, "but I think you are a little negative; you sounded almost angry up there."

"You didn't like my text, then?" he asked, laughing.

"Dead flies in the ointment? It *is* catchy. I never heard that verse before, I must admit. I don't usually read Ecclesiastes," I said a little giggle-y, blushing.

"What didn't you like about it?" he asked.

"Zeroing in on all the sins. I mean, we are already aware of our sins, or *dead flies* as you called them. What we need is a reminder of Christ's love, which we have a tendency to forget. Why torment us with fear? We have enough of *that* already," I said, watching him intently, as I gently pressed the point.

Ray fingered his glass, not looking at me, listening. He said, "Yes. I've been told that before, that I preach a negative gospel."

"And your language from the pulpit. It really shocked me. Poor Sharon wouldn't know what to think. Here her mommy doesn't allow her to use words like *shut up* because it sounds so unkind, and you used it several times in the story you told, even hitting the pulpit for effect. Why, it sounded awful. I wonder if you realize how fierce you sound when you get carried away like that? Your eyes just about pop out of your head. Did you know that?"

He laughed then, shaking his ice cubes.

I got up and refilled his glass.

"Well, I have to tell things in my own way. And that's my way. I'm Irish, you know."

Irish meant nothing to me, except that it was a kind of linen. I only knew Germans and Italians, some Poles and Jews, too, but I smiled anyhow.

"Too much, you think, though, huh?"

"For me, yes. Otherwise, I think you were good. Very interesting to listen to, but I got the feeling tonight, as you pounded on that pulpit, that the kind of God you believe in is angry and unbending."

He was quiet again, staring into his glass.

"I don't know," I said rather thoughtfully, "maybe it was the tone of your voice. I don't know how to explain it. I felt *no love,* that's all I can say. And wasn't that the primary message that Jesus brought to the world? I always thought so. Anyhow, I missed it in your sermon."

His head dropped. He closed his eyes for a moment and then looked back into his glass.

Uh-oh, I've gone too far, I was thinking, even though he'd been the one to ask. From his lack of usual combativeness, I could tell something I'd said had struck a nerve. So I immediately changed the subject and apologized for not making it to his first service that morning. "I've been seeing Ed for two months now," I said. "You remember Bonnie, don't you? Ed's her cousin from Illinois."

"Are you serious about him?" Ray asked, looking me in the eye for the first time.

His look embarrassed me momentarily. "I think so; we have so much in common. The only thing that worries me is that he doesn't profess to be born again, but he's such a good person. He talks of marriage all the time, in fact we can talk about anything – a change from most guys. But he seems to think I take spiritual things *too literally.*

Ray spoke then in a quiet seriousness, quoting Bible verses about the sin of marrying "out of the will of God."

"I know what you're telling me, believe me. I think and pray about this all the time. I haven't really said *yes,* yet. He's worried about the draft. He's 1-A now. How about you? When will you have to go?"

"Never. I have a 4-D classification. Once I was ordained, I'm exempt for life... unless it's all-out war. Then I'd go in as a chaplain."

"Oh," I said, standing up and picking up the glasses. Walking to the sink, I was thinking how lucky he was, remembering how Sully had to leave a prosperous business to go in, and Tony was waiting every day for his number to come up also.

And then, as though reading my mind again, he said, "My dad keeps accusing me of using the ministry to dodge the draft."

I turned to look at him and saw from the strained look on his face that talking about the draft, or his father, had upset him. Deeply into his thoughts, he moved quietly toward the doorway, stopped, turned, and stood with his back to the door, facing me.

I walked over to him to say good night. As I stood there, I felt an impulse to question him, my curiosity getting the best of me. But I tried to disguise my intense interest with a light and airy tone, as though the answer didn't really matter in the least. "By the way," I said, "just what exactly *did* happen with your wedding? I just heard it was off. Do you still go with her, or what?"

"I changed my mind about it," he said in the same matter-of-fact tone, matching mine, folding his arms as he rocked on his heels. "I just decided, especially after my auto accident, that I could serve God better in a single capacity."

"Why? What happened in the accident?"

"Well, I was driving. It was my dad's car. And you know the speed limit in Michigan is seventy-five. I was with my best friend, Mickey. We were driving home from a meeting, and we hit a patch of black ice and the car got wrapped around a tree. I was thrown from the car into a snow bank. When I came to in the snow, I promised God, no matter what, that I'd serve Him the rest of my life if He'd just spare me. But Mickey was pinned in the car: ruptured spleen; busted kidney; you name it. A week later, the day I got out of the hospital for my back – it was broken in three places, but I could walk in the body cast – I went to see Mickey in another hospital. He had been asking for me – if I was okay, to be sure I was alive, I guess, because they said he died right after I left him, before I got off of his ward." Ray stopped talking then and bowed his head, shutting his eyes very tightly as though to hold back the tears, then he continued as before. "I've had an irregular heart beat ever since, and the doctors tell me that it is possible I might have a pinched nerve in my heart from the accident. So to answer your question, that is why I don't want to get married. And no, I'm not going with Jenny anymore. It wouldn't be fair to any girl, not knowing the future of my health. Besides that, if Apostle Paul lived a life apart from marriage in order to serve God better, so can I. Take this meeting, for instance, I wouldn't have been able to take it if I had been married."

"Why not?"

"Do you have any idea how much I get? Why, I couldn't support a wife and a family on what these churches are willing to put out. All I get is the Love Offering, on the last night of services. Sometimes it doesn't even cover my traveling expenses. On the other hand, I couldn't go in with a set fee like is done in *Youth For Christ*. They offered me a job to go with them, you know, but I think they're a bunch of phonies."

"Yeah, I've been thinking the same thing. It seems all they're interested in are numbers and how to get them in."

"It's getting commercial all right. I couldn't believe some of the salaries they get; I just can't agree with their methods."

"What methods? What do you mean?" I asked, enjoying his looking at me. His eyes were darting everywhere unless he was speaking, a disturbing habit Daddy declared conveyed shiftiness. But Ray's eyes would become glued to mine while he spoke, so with my questions, I tried to keep him talking.

"Presetting fees," he said, shoving his hands into his pockets, jiggling his keys, "I don't believe that is the kind of example the disciples set for us," he said, looking firmly into my eyes. "...putting a price on our Christian service. So I have just about accepted the fact that I will never marry."

All this time I had been listening intently, and the seriousness of his story had touched me. I looked up into his intense and determined face and saw the hurt and the pain. I felt the sadness under all of his foolishness, and I wanted to take him into my arms and hold him tenderly, forever. He seemed distant and so alone and in desperate need of some caring, a needy feeling just like I had carried deep within me for as far back as I could remember. Without thinking, I stepped closer to him, reached up, and put my arms around his neck. Suddenly I felt impish, as the marquee of the Black Bomber and Henry Hotsnot flashed through my mind, and all the kisses I had bet and lost. I know my eyes lit up as I looked up at him. "I think I owe you something," I said.

He immediately leaned toward me, gathering me up into his arms and drawing me closely into his slender body. "Yes, you do," he said, his face suddenly alive.

Pulling his head down to mine, when our eyes met, he did not look away. Something tugged at my heart strings as I closed my eyes and reached for his mouth. Our lips touching for the first time was as if we were both feeling the same pent up urgency. For one long moment I let go of something inside of me, losing myself in his arms. At last, I was allowing myself to feel the desire buried so deeply as I held him tenderly in my arms. He was pulling me even closer, tighter into his embrace. My body melted into his as I gave myself over to him, completely. Moving closer, he wrapped himself around me with such a fervor I could never have anticipated or imagined in my wildest dreams. And then his body began to tremble, convulsively. I believed he was crying, so I pulled him in even tighter, our kiss like a flame reaching up and enveloping us both, fusing us into one.

Then suddenly he let go of me and stepped back, away from me. Not looking at me, he whispered a barely audible, "Good night" and let himself out the door directly behind him, without facing me.

Before the door closed, I grabbed it and watched him as he ran down the stairs, his blonde hair picking up the light from the ceiling lamp. I saw the flash of white socks between his dark trousers and cleated wingtip shoes and heard the clicks as he double-stepped all three flights of stairs. I thought he would stop at some point and speak to me, say something, a*nything*. But in his hurry, the look on his face set, he said nothing. He just ran, like his long legs couldn't get him away from me fast enough.

My body was still inflamed with the passion he had stirred within me as I closed the door. *What a strange thing to happen;* I couldn't begin to figure it out. It was the same puzzled confusion I'd felt that last night at Winona Lake. Even though he wore the class ring of his future bride on his pinkie finger all week, that last night he had left it off and acted as though he cared for me. He'd never mentioned his wedding, and I'd never mentioned my circumstances. Consequently, neither of us had any idea what the other one was thinking. It was a guessing game from beginning to end. Oh, how I hated it: the not knowing, the confusion — and here it was again.

Then there was the warring part of me that kept me torn, pulled: one part that felt wanton, bad, with *no morals,* no concern for right or wrong, only loving and being loved. The other part was careful, good, circumspect, desirous of purity and saintliness, virginal, everything I had patterned my life after. Ever since I had fallen for Huey – marring my innocence forever – I'd fought hard to reinstate myself to that realm of decency and honor. But Ray had disturbed my neatly ordered existence. This preacher no less, who preached of sin, hell, and damnation. *What must he think of me now? Of the naked passion I had thrust at him?* His sudden departure must have been his answer. *But what of his trembling?* I wondered, as I stood there, still filled with the intensity of my emotions, remembering my forwardness that surprised even me, and his response to me was oh, so pleasurable. Maybe it was my expressed love for Ed (the suggestion of duplicity?) that had turned him away. I was confused, baffled at the evening's turn of events. He actually *ran* down the stairs away from me, as I had run from him in Winona. *Why, oh, why?*

Questions, with no answers, absorbed my thoughts. Thinking of him, I basked in the pleasure still radiating through my entire being as I got into bed. Then Ed would flash through my mind, and I would dismiss the tinge of guilt wanting to steal my glow.

Comparing the two men in my mind as I wondered off to sleep, I was smiling. With Ed, I felt a strong physical awareness from the tender way in which he held me, his caring for me, talking to me continuously, exciting me to the core as he caressed me. Kissing Ray that evening, I only wanted to reach down inside of him and stop his hurting, to bring to him the love that was so conspicuously missing in his preaching and in his life. How lost and lonely he seemed to be amidst his laughter and dynamic *Irish* storytelling. I sensed his shyness, too, in the impersonal way in which he spoke to me, his eyes darting away from me as I spoke. Oh, to break through those barriers and comfort him! With Ed, I felt comfortable, sure that I would have safety forever, but with Ray, *my* comfort and safety didn't seem to matter – *only his.*

For the rest of the week's meetings, both Ray and I acted as though our giving in to a momentary weakness had never happened. I did not understand any of it. With the mixed messages pulling me one way and then the other, I put the unexplained feelings and events into a cubbyhole of my mind reserved for just such mysteries and dismissed any possibility of his caring for me.

It was easy for me to do this, for Ray seemed more distant than ever as I shook hands with him at the church door each night, saying our courteous farewells, though he held Sharon and took her all over the church the night she, Daddy and Charity went with me. I wished desperately to know why Ray didn't care for me. But I told myself it didn't matter – *loving him, anyhow, would be like grasping for a shadow.*

A week later, I received a half-page letter written on lined, tablet paper thanking me for arranging the Milwaukee meeting, signed the usual, *In Christ, Ray.*

I did not answer his letter, and I told no one of our kiss, save Mr. Simms. To him, I let it all out, though he offered no explanation, only the comfort of his concern.

Holding onto that tiny speck of hope in the far off recesses of my mind – a subconscious wish for Ray, my knight in shining armor, to break down the barriers that kept us apart and declare his love for me, a love which apparently only existed in my dreams – I was withholding a part of myself from Ed. But through this experience I realized, with great relief, that Ed was not in the habit of playing guessing games. Instead, he poured out his feelings for me at every opportunity. Freed from the fairytale expectations I had carried from my childhood, I turned my full attentions to Ed. Finally able to give of myself without reservation, I found that I could love Ed now, even more.

L istening intently to Mrs. Cromwell, I sat rigidly on the edge of my chair. From all the office gossip, I was convinced I had been called in to receive my pink slip. Mrs. Cromwell looked at my records and smiled. She must have sensed my distress as she said, "Relax, Sam, I have a nice surprise for you," and winked. "You know we are being computerized, and some jobs are being eliminated; yours is one of them. Before you get upset, let me explain that you have been chosen to go to keypunch school. It is a two-week course at IBM. Upon successful completion, your pay will jump from... let's see here... from $180 a month to $325. Can you handle that?" she asked. I knew my face radiated my relief even though the figures flew loosely in my head, my concentration was so jumbled. "The course begins next Monday. Hopefully you will have completed the course and be working at your new job by Thanksgiving."

With winter coming, my new raise in pay could not have come too soon, as my finances were a bit pinched. I'd already had to sell my wedding ring set. Though only one third the value, the amount I received covered the cost of the expensive snowsuit I had put on lay-away for Sharon.

The cost of the train fare and the lodgings at the "Y" had stretched Ed's budget also, with his own child support payments, an added strain. He'd skipped last week's visit, but he called now and said he needed to see me, to "discuss something important." He would have to stay at my place to save money. I gave in as I had so much to tell him also.

Mary agreed to keep Sharon downstairs overnight and said, "Sh, don't tell me; I don't know a thing." Then she whispered, "Just tell him not to drop his shoes."

My mind would not let my stomach rest. Surely he was going to ask me to set the date. He seemed so close to it our last weekend together. My excitement grew as we caught up on our news, and I finally told him about keypunch school and my raise in pay.

"I'm so glad to hear that you're going to be all right," he said, a quizzical frown on his face, "because I just can't think about marriage right now, not until I satisfy Uncle Sam."

"Why?" I asked, with a start. "You didn't get your draft notice, did you?"

"Matter-of-fact, I did. That's why I didn't come up last week. I've been trying to figure out what to do. About us," he said, looking away from me, as though searching for words. "There's no way I'm going to tie you down to a commitment for that long – or myself either for that matter."

Suddenly I felt as I used to when I would first take my roller skates off. The ground would seem harder, and everything around me would seem larger than before until I'd gain my new equilibrium.

"What do you mean, tie me down? If I know you want me, I can wait forever, Ed. Don't you know I love you?"

Ed's face took on an angry scowl. It was not what he wanted to hear apparently. He grew quiet and, for the first time, pulled away from me.

Surely he's just upset over receiving his notice, I thought, not believing what he was really telling me.

Then he began talking about his job, being uprooted just when he was getting himself established in his territory. His anger at a draft system that would do this came tumbling out, something, I reminded him, I could do nothing about. His being taken away from Kathleen, without the influence he wanted in her upbringing, he seethed at this disruption of his life. His bitterness seemed to have turned him into someone I hardly knew.

The sounds of dawn, of a car door slamming, a bird chirping, brought me fully awake. The feel of the rough couch on my face as I rolled over reminded me that I had given Ed my bed. I remembered the pain of helplessness that had overcome me the night before, as I silently wept into my pillow. My heart ached for myself and for him, for his distress, and I wanted to right things between us. But I could do nothing except love him, so I quietly slipped into the next room and into bed beside him.

Ed must have been awake, also, as he turned over immediately and took me into his arms. I sobbed then, my heart nearly breaking. "You just can't leave me. Not now, when I'm just beginning to really trust you. I love you so much. Oh, so much," I said.

He held me and kissed away my tears.

We made love then, for the first time, gently, easily, without another word passing between us, as though we'd been married forever. From the depths of my soul, I gave myself to him, loving him, hoping, desperately, to make things right between us, the way we were.

When Ed finally lay asleep beside me, I quietly stole back to the couch. When I awoke in the morning, it was as though our lovemaking had been a dream.

Throughout the day I busied myself with cooking, deep in thought, trying to ignore the turmoil brewing between us. We said little to one another, both lost in our own thoughts, worlds apart.

As we sat down to the evening meal, I helped Sharon into her chair. I slid her chair-tray in while holding her left arm down, to look up into Ed's frown of disapproval. I wondered why, since to teach her good manners, I no longer used the dishtowel to tie it; we'd had some serious words over it. But I said nothing as we ate in silence, except for some small talk with Sharon. Ed picked at the delicious roast beef dinner I'd spent the whole day preparing.

Suddenly, Ed's agitation boiled over, and he slid his chair away from the table, the noise of the wooden legs screeching over the linoleum. "Sam," he said angrily, "this is *it* between us; it *has* to be. I can't have my guts torn out of me this way... and at every mail call, waiting to get a *Dear John* from you."

"But Ed, why does it have to be that way?" I asked in dismay. "Don't you trust me?"

"It has nothing to do with trust, Sam. It has to do with *just being human*, that's all."

My sobs interrupted him, my guilty words poured out of me. "It's because of last night, isn't it? *Isn't it?*" I was crying now. "You're disappointed in me. You think I'm a hypocrite now, don't you? Oh Ed, I'm so sorry if you feel that way. But don't you see how much I love you?" I ran over to him with my arms outstretched.

"Oh, for god's sake, Sam, cut it out," he said, as he turned his back on me and quickly left the room. With his shaving kit in hand, he headed for the bathroom. I cleared the table, going back and forth to the bathroom door, crying, talking, pleading for Ed to listen. I saw no reason for this abrupt change in our relationship. I just couldn't see the necessity of it, *wouldn't* see it.

Ed continued shaving, stopping to stare at me from time to time as though to say something, then thinking better of it, never sharing his thoughts with me.

I had just put away the last dish. My crying was more quiet now, thinking how confident I had become of late since Ed came into my life, loving me, encouraging me constantly. *What was he really saying to me?* In deep thought, trying to decide how to handle this, I happened to look up to see Ed noiselessly slipping through the door, suitcase in hand.

I threw off my apron and ran after him, calling him, but he didn't turn or slow his step as he walked down the stairs. Grabbing Sharon, my coat and purse, and quickly covering my head with a scarf, at Mary's door I called to her, "Please watch Sharon. I'll explain later; I have to catch Ed," and shoved Sharon inside.

As I rounded the corner, I saw Ed boarding the bus. This particular one ran every few minutes. I had no choice but to wait, nervously, for the next one, which trailed almost on the heel of Ed's. All I could hope for was to reach him before he bought his ticket and convince him to stay the night and talk things over. *He couldn't just run out on me like this. It wasn't like him. Why? What had I done?* I had to convince him I loved him. I didn't *have* to have a house...

My bus got caught in traffic just as we reached the train station. Through the front windshield, I could see Ed inside the station at the window, talking to the clerk. The moment the bus stopped, I pushed my way out the door, through the crowd of waiting passengers. The cold fall winds whipped open my coat as I ran.

Just as I went through the door of the terminal, Ed was leaving the window, ticket in hand. He caught a glimpse of me just before he darted through the turnstile leading out onto the train loading platform. I was calling, "Ed. Please, wait, Ed." My sobbing was uncontrollable now. Just beyond my reach, I called his name, again and again. As I reached the turnstile, Ed looked back for one brief moment and then plunged head first into the waiting car.

The ticket agent was saying to me, "Ticket, please, ma'am."

"I don't have a ticket; I just want to talk to a passenger."

"Sorry, ma'am. No one without a ticket allowed beyond this point. Sorry, ma'am."

"What time does that train leave?" I asked, pointing to the car Ed had just boarded.

"In about three minutes, ma'am; the gentleman just made it."

Suddenly conscious of my tear stained face and thrown together appearance, I sadly turned back into the terminal and slumped down into an empty seat. The sound of the train's movement was the sound of death. I held my head in my hands and sought to control the cry that was welling up deep within me, a scream that had been there since forever – the cry of despair, of separation, of rejection, of frightening lonely emptiness. He was gone; it was over. What had he said that I didn't want to hear? *If we still feel this way after my three-year hitch, then we can get together.* If... after my *three-year* hitch... *a forever lifetime.* I knew my crawling into bed with him must have changed things. I didn't know how, but my guilt convinced me it had. *What had I done but love him?* I kept asking myself all the way home. How could I wait *three years* when a ten minute ride home on a bus dragged on like an eternity? – unless I really knew he wanted me, then I could wait *forever.* Oh, but he *did* want me. I knew it. I could *feel* it. I could even see it in his eyes. *Then, why?* Oh, Ed, how could you leave me like this when I know you love me? I kept asking ears that did not hear, over and over I asked... but the silence was like death.

I telephoned, but Ed was never there. I wrote him, in vain. Mary would place the call for me. Upon hearing her voice, his phone went dead.

The very life went out of me. I would be rocking Sharon in front of the TV, and suddenly the tears would pour from my smiling face. "Don't cry, Mommy; please, don't cry," she'd beg, and put her little arms around my neck.

In my new class, I would be in the middle of punching a stack of cards, and as over a dam the tears would explode. My co-workers thought it was my keypunch fumbling that was to blame; a minor problem, it was my heart that was crumbling – *couldn't they see?*

Why Ed walked out of my life, I didn't understand – I only knew that the all enveloping and nurturing love I had received, was suddenly gone – once again. The pain of that small child, long hushed, I was just beginning to feel.

The wind is cold· We are walking away from the cemetery that looks like a park· Daddy is pulling me by the hand, and I am pulling back· I try to look into the big hole for Mama, but Daddy pulls me very hard· I want to stay by the hole, with her; I want to talk to her·

"It's time to go," Daddy says, as I feel the bumpy earth move under my feet, my small weight being dragged along· "Mama's gone to heaven now, to be with Jesus· And

Jesse Woodrow, too," Daddy says·

Mama? And new baby sister? And Jesse? Me too; me go too, Mama, me too· I sniff back the salty tears, but a few slip down my cheeks, my teeth locked shut· The cold wind blows against my face, drying the tears· My ears plug up, and then squeal inside· A pain begins to shoot down in my stomach· Wee-wee my panties? I grab myself and mash my legs together·

Daddy pulls my hand away, picks me up, and locks his arms around me – so tightly I cannot move·

Under the warmth from those arms, down inside me, there is a giant, scared feeling that has no likeness, no name, except – forever!

The turkey dinner was as delicious as I remembered every Sunday at the Simms' table. It was nice being accepted as a member of the family, although Mr. Simms didn't let too many minutes pass by before he managed to get behind Mrs. Simms and mouth to me, "You look pretty today."

I must have blushed, because Mrs. Simms immediately grabbed her chest for her hearing aid controls. Inside I was very upset, but on the outside I managed to remain pleasant and smiling. The invitation for us to spend Thanksgiving, an ordinarily exciting day, with the Simms family, was not what I needed at the moment anyway, even though I knew Mrs. Simms would have a cake for my nineteenth birthday, an event that coincided with the holiday week every year. It was seeing Leona and Marty and having them find out about my losing yet another job that I dreaded. I had two more weeks before the changeover at Trostel would be complete and I would no longer be employed.

Failing keypunch school was not something I'd even considered. The keypunch process was so easy I couldn't figure out why I was getting such an increase in pay – until I spent a few hours at it. My personal life being in turmoil, my natural distract ability aside, didn't help me concentrate on the task. When my new supervisor responded to my plea to give me one more week of training, the pressure on me to succeed was even greater. I could not understand it. When the machines jammed, I could pull them apart, fix them, and put them back into working order, so that the young men assigned to keep our production moving were not always needed. But the monotony of the job, after twenty minutes of punching, turned my mind into a catacomb of activity, followed by a deluge of errors that got worse the longer I punched.

I was frantic, not to mention ashamed, even after it was explained to me that my failure did not mean I was dumb but on the intelligent side. "The higher your IQ, the quicker you'll get bored and make errors on a monotonous job. You need a job that is constantly changing and challenging," my supervisor told me. But none of this really helped pay my rent. So I begged for a chance in the manufacturing plant. It was discouraged, but I insisted I be given a chance before they gave up on me.

After three days lacing boots with leather laces, my bleeding hands brought my personnel supervisor out to my side on the floor. I would have died before I would've quit. He took me gently by the shoulders and led me to the nurse's office. "Didn't I tell you? You're not plant material."

My spirits had never been so low. Hopeless, I tried to keep Ed out of my mind, to keep the tears in check. I answered one ad after another. Finally I found one for Blue Cross Insurance. I'd handled some of their forms at Milwaukee Hospital, so I applied. After I'd filled out the extensive application, I was called into the office of the head of personnel. "I just had to get a look at you," she said, although it wasn't customary. She explained to me that she had never seen, in her many years of personnel work, such a "divergence of scores." I was totally confused then, until she explained. "Your intelligence scores are very, very high, and your skills test out extremely low. It says here that you quit school. Why?"

"To get married. It's a long story. But I'm divorced now. What do you mean, skills?"

"Skills are a reflection of your education," she explained. "Specifically, your math skills that you need to work here. It's a crying shame that a girl with your intelligence was allowed to quit school."

"I'm taking a correspondence course with American School now and..."

"Yes. I see that. I just wanted to encourage you to finish your education. You have such a bright mind; don't let it go to waste. Put school on your agenda, right now, as a number one priority. You must find a way to do it."

This interview was one I would never forget, even though I wasn't hired. For someone that high up to take the time to talk to me left quite an impression. Her words did more to keep me from going crazy than anything anyone has ever said to me before or since. She gave me something to hang onto, to push me forward when my faith in myself would get lost somewhere amongst the harsh realities that faced me every day. So when Leona asked me about my job, I remembered the lady at Blue Cross and held my head up and put a smile on my face. "I'm going to night school now," I said, "taking a couple of secretarial courses, and I've been to the telephone company for testing on all their equipment, since I *did* learn the switchboard at Trostel."

"Switchboard? Can you handle one?" she asked, a little excited.

Yes, I think so. At least the big cord types. The new cordless ones are different, but I seem to be able to figure out machines. I could always fix my sewing machine, and then when the big IBM's would jam, I could figure them out better than keypunch. I always did enjoy dealing with people on the phone, ever since the hospital."

"Oh, Sam. I can't believe it. We've been talking about hiring someone to take over the front desk. That darn phone just drives me crazy. When can you come in for an interview?"

Leona Simms was a beautiful, soft-spoken girl, ten years my senior with long blonde hair and gray eyes, just like my Sharon. Leona would kid me often that anytime I wanted to "get rid of that beautiful kid," she was sure she could talk Marty into letting her quit work. Even though I knew she was teasing, the subject upset me; I was unable to even laugh about it. Leona would notice and poke me and say, "Hey kiddo, lighten up."

Besides being a best friend to me, she made no real demands on me at my job. I was so conscientious she was usually telling me to take it easy. The small six-line switchboard I learned to handle immediately, leaving her time to take dictation and do the books. She could type up a storm, too – my idol, now that Bonnie had gone off to Bob Jones.

I was so thankful for my new job, especially since I received a pay increase from $180 to $225 month. I believed I'd been especially blessed, that *God* had come through again for me. Not only was Milwaukee Glass Works within walking distance of my apartment, Mr. Meinecke, the owner, attended the same Baptist church as Leona and Marty did.

Among my many chores was doing the payroll – from adding up time cards complete to handing out the pay checks – for the fifty employees, most of whom worked in the small shop. Griffith, the office manager, had a desk way off in the corner, but Leona and I worked hand in hand at the large L-shaped front desk.

When she needed copies made of anything, she would send me upstairs to the copy machine. "Ask one of the fellahs up there to show you how it works," she called over her shoulder the first time.

There were two of them, leaning over a huge table with drawings and slide rules and pencils. The younger one looked up and smiled and asked me if he could help. I was nervous. Leona had neglected to tell me there was anyone under fifty years old in the place. Joel Prescott was his name. He had a quiet careful way about him. I figured he was about Leona's age, and I didn't see any wedding ring. I couldn't wait to get back downstairs to ask her if Joel was married.

Leona put her finger up to her lips and said, "Sh," and winked as she shook her head. Pointing to Griffith, she whispered, "Divorced... his nephew." I took that to mean Joel was *hands off* since he was an employee. Mr. Meinecke, in his office just behind us, was very strait-laced. "No fraternizing among employees" was his rule. That was why, if it hadn't been for the icy rain pouring off of me as I walked home that evening, I wouldn't have accepted the lift from Joel. When I reminded Joel of the rules, he said, "Don't worry about it; it's just a ride home." The next day when I told Leona, she put her fingers to her lips again, then covered her ears with her hands. "I don't want to know," she said. Mr. Meinecke didn't like to hear any personal chatting going on in the office anyway, but Leona and I learned to carry on extensive conversations without making a sound. I really loved her. I could share so much with her, like with the older sister I never had. I wanted to tell her about Mr. Simms, too, but I'd never dare. He was her father-in-law and she was family. That would leave me on the outside again, and I was afraid to chance it.

Joel, whose thick sandy hair made you want to stick your hands into it, started to pick me up regularly. He was quickly becoming a good and trusted friend. With his quiet and easy-going manner Joel seemed to sense, by the way I hugged the car door, that I didn't want him to touch me, and I was beginning to like him for that, for letting me be comfortable. But I managed to keep quiet about him to Leona.

Every day, when I got home from work, I'd reach into my mailbox with a wish deep down that there'd be a letter from Ed. *Maybe he's changed his mind,* I'd think, especially when the holidays drew close. It was such a sad time, and I didn't know how I was going to get through it. Sully took me to buy a huge tree. Then Tony came over and helped me decorate it with smooth silver ornaments in different sizes and all blue lights. There is nothing like your very first Christmas tree. Carefully saving for months, I was able to buy all the trimmings. I hung the tinsel one strip at a time, and Tony put the lighted angel on the top while Sharon squealed. We played Christmas carols and ate cheese balls. He always wanted to buy groceries for me but I refused to allow it. "So independent you are," he'd say. "Why can't you let me have a little fun?"

"Because... that way I don't *owe* you anything," I'd say, wishing he would just not push it, it was so embarrassing to have to refuse. But I knew I had to, as much as I could have used the extras; owing Mr. Simms was enough.

It was just a week before Christmas when I got a frantic call from my old friend Muriel. We talked on the phone from time to time. The tone of her voice didn't sound like the Muriel I knew; I couldn't ever remember seeing her cry.

"Oh, Sam, I don't know what to do. I figured you'd give me good advice. Do you remember Johnny Cortez from your class?"

"Yes. I remember." He was so sweet; I couldn't forget. One time we met at the outside entrance at school. He wasn't looking and let the heavy door slam into my head. When Johnny saw it hit me, he grabbed me and hugged me and rubbed my head. His warm caring feelings came through as he apologized over and over for not watching where he was going. I remembered him not only because he was the only Mexican kid in the whole grade school, but because his actions were very unusual for an eighth grade boy.

"Well..." Muriel said, "you're not going to believe this... I'm pregnant."

"Well, you're old enough to get married. I don't understand the problem. Don't you love him?"

"Yes, I love him. Very much, but you know my mom and dad, especially my dad. You know how he hates spics. I just don't know what to do. They won't even care that he has a good job."

"Are you planning to get married?"

"Oh, yes. It's just that I don't know whether to tell my parents first, or get married first and then tell them."

"It seems to me, if you are definitely going to get married, that they might feel a little kinder toward their *son-in-law,* than toward an *ordinary spic on the street,"* I said, laughingly. "I would get married first and let the chips fall..."

"That sounds sensible."

"Maybe *Christmas* would be a good time to tell them," I said,

"They might remember they are *Christians* then."

"That's a thought," she said, dismissing it. She never was one for churchy discussions. "What's going on with Huey? Still in the clink?"

"Yes. Bernice calls me every couple of weeks and screams when I won't let Sharon go with her to see him. I let Sharon go with Mrs. Schultz once, but I rode along in the car. Seeing that place, I decided, never again. I figure that's part of the price you pay when you get put behind bars."

"Amen," she said, teasing, telling me I was preachy.

I laughed. "That sounds more like the Muriel I know," I said.

"When does he get out?" she wanted to know.

"In summer, but Bernice says he's being so good he might get out earlier."

"Figures. He's probably the Queen up there and loving every minute of it. What you gonna do when he gets out, move out of town?" she asked with a snicker.

"I'll cross that bridge when I come to it, get a roommate or something."

Muriel had a way of knowing exactly what was bothering me, sometimes before I knew myself. I tried very hard not to think about Huey getting out. Her call brought it all back, his threats, his phone calls, his following me – that showed up in my dreams at least once a week. As I hung up the phone, I prayed: *Dear God, please help me...*

Christmas eve was the only night of the year when I missed *Holy Ghost* church. It had always been exciting, all of us kids learning a poem and dressing up in our very best to walk up onto the platform, to stand in the dark with colored spot lights on us while we recited. Not only was the whole night exciting for me as a kid, but as I grew up it was fun seeing everyone's relatives again who didn't regularly attend. The church was always jammed packed, people standing in the rear. Part of the curiosity was seeing what everyone else's kids turned out to look like, what brought everyone back. Pure theater in the raw, as was most every church service. Pentecostals knew how to appeal to your emotions; and I'd grown up loving that part of it. But even after both the Simmses and my parents invited me, I refused to go. It was my first year not being there; seeing everyone would just tear me apart when they'd ask me personal questions. Instead, Sharon and I stayed home and watched all the special Christmas shows on TV and had cookies and milk.

Before Sharon went to bed, we opened one present and saved the rest for Santa's coming. Even though I'd never celebrated Santa (one of the Devil's helpers), I wanted her to have everything I didn't have. We hung up our stockings and talked about Saint Nick coming in the night. I was pleased at seeing her go to bed excited. Until she fell asleep, I sang all the Christmas carols I knew.

All alone in the living room, as I was stuffing the stockings, I was thinking that the holidays would all be over soon and I could give up the pretense of being happy, when every bone in my body ached from carrying a river of unspent tears.

I t was an exceptionally lonely January. Because I had little room in my freezer for left overs anyway, I decided to have a few people from church in for dinner, to fix the large turkey Mr. Meinecke had given to each of his employees for Christmas. It turned out even better than I'd expected. Mary gave me her recipe for stuffing and pumpkin pie. Tony and Sully came and Billie Ann with her new husband. I invited Norman Scott, a really handsome guy who hung around with Tony and Sully and who paid a lot of attention to Sharon in church. The big dining room table was full.

It surprised even me that I could put on such a fine dinner for so many. They laughed and talked and ate heartily. After dessert, everyone got up and walked around, acting as though they didn't quite know what to do next. I didn't want them to leave, but I didn't know how to keep them there. Billie Ann helped me clear the table and raved almost enviously about my talent, questioning me about preparing the turkey – a real switch, as she was usually the expert. Table etiquette, though, or being sociable left me strangely lost.

As a child, I was never really taught to socialize, to have friends in; they were considered a nuisance. If I did luck out and have one over, Daddy would embarrass me by reading the Bible. So I avoided that and just never learned how to *be* with anyone. No wonder the excitement of having guests there, in my house, had me scatterbrained, besides the worry that things would go well. Despite being nervous, I did manage to wander in and out of their conversations, but I still felt like an outsider. When everyone left almost immediately after dinner, I felt even more lonely and no closer to being part of their group than when they came.

As I flopped down on the couch from tiredness, I thought about how Tony always compared me to Doris Day. "You've got the class, Sam, just like her – an invisible wall built around you, too, as though you're saying to everyone, *Come only so close…"* I usually took it as a compliment, being set apart, her purity a shining example to follow, but now, as all the excitement of planning and cooking was over and here I sat alone, it suddenly didn't feel so good. Instead, it made me angry. I felt like saying to the whole world, "See if I care if you accept me or not." Never before had I dared to admit such feelings to myself, for fear the *all-knowing God* would punish me.

The tears wouldn't stay back, just as Mary brought Sharon in. "What in the world… Didn't they like the dinner?"

"Yes," I sobbed. "They loved the food; it's *me* they didn't like."

"Oh, pooh. They came, didn't they? You've just got to snap out of this, Sam. Ed is *not* coming back."

As girls do, we were crammed into the car, all talking and laughing at once. After Sunday night church, they had offered me a ride to the bus stop, three blocks away. Margie Morrison, Donny's sixteen-year-old sister, had just said she was getting a driver's license.

"Why?" I asked, "I thought your dad drove you everywhere."

The silence in the car was like a jolt. I was looking right into Margie's eyes when she answered me, "We buried my father last Wednesday."

"No," I said, shocked at my stupid blunder. "I didn't know he was ill."

"He wasn't," she said, her voice wavering. "It was a sudden heart attack. He just had a complete physical the month before. Didn't you see it in the church bulletin?"

"No, I've missed some services lately, I…" but her loss made mine suddenly not worth mentioning. I fought the tears, apologizing again for my not knowing.

Inside my apartment, I threw myself across the bed, thankful that Sharon was spending the night with Anna. The tears that I'd held back for weeks, since starting my new job, came tumbling out. I couldn't understand the overwhelming sorrow that welled up from inside of me. It was as though *I* had lost a parent, not Margie.

When my emotions took over like this, all I could think of doing was to write someone. For some reason that I didn't understand, I decided to write Ray Malorry.

It was unlike any letter I'd written before. Not only did I pour out the heartbreak I'd suffered from Ed's abrupt leaving, and the hurt and embarrassment of that very evening with Margie, I told him, too, about the struggle with my job and the fear of Huey's return, about being ostracized by *Youth For Christ's* trumpet trio and my loneliness, even amongst friends. Then I told him about Wilderness Missions, the new organization comprised mostly of young married couples that *Highland Fundamental* had just started sponsoring, to give the church more of a missionary posture. The Wilderness people were on a crusade to recruit missionaries for their group and had stirred me to rededicate my life to God. I just had not given God enough, I said. The ink in my pen could not keep up with my tears or the words that rushed out onto the paper, words I had no idea I'd written, words I would have never expressed in a more stalwart moment. Finally, in closing, I wrote my favorite Bible verse, "I can do all things through Christ which strengtheneth me." Philippians 4:13.

The letter was signed, *In Christ, Sam.*

Then I wrote another volume of pages to Bonnie at Bob Jones, telling her much the same, only this letter I knew would receive an answer.

S haron and I had walked about seven blocks. Timed, it took exactly twenty-five minutes from our door. Sharon rode in her stroller only because it was so far. She was excited that we were going to look at a *school* for her. The house was huge and had been completely redone inside for a day nursery, supported by the Red Feather agency. Rather than $20, because of my low income, the weekly fee was only $17. I had been paying Mary $20, plus extra for evening hours. The teacher took us through the rooms, showing Sharon her own locker, a table her size, the children's blankets used for their naps all rolled up for the night. The coat hooks were even low enough for Sharon, now three years old, to reach; she was thoroughly ready for "my school."

After the last terrible fight with Mary over candy and Coke, Mary had come upstairs and, in her fury, striped the knickknack shelf she had bought for me off the wall. Stuffing the small china figurines into her pockets, she was taking all her gifts back. I sat there in shocked disbelief as she turned on me in anger, "You ungrateful thing. Don't you know when someone *cares* about you? Look at all the things I've done for you, baby-sitting at the drop of the hat, day or night. Buying you something every time I go to the store, like you were my kid. You think a little candy or

Coke is more important than all of that?" she yelled, waving her hands as she usually did when she talked.

Mary didn't seem to understand it was Sharon's *health* I was concerned with, so I inquired around and found this nice place. It would take much more of my time, a half-hour there, a half-hour back, and then it would take another twenty minutes, at least, to get to work in the other direction, but it was all on foot. I would not have to be dependent on buses or Mary anymore. I could do it; and I did.

Mary was actually relieved when I told her. Extremely apologetic, she hugged me, then brought everything back she had taken and helped me rehang the shelf. "Watch out for us Sicilians; we have bad tempers," she said. "Don't cross one of us; the men use knives," she was laughing. "I'll still baby-sit at night for you, Sam, anytime."

Joel seemed to be around more and more. It was a gradual thing that happened. He was so quiet, always being there when it was cold and I needed a ride, listening when I'd complain about Mary or Mr. Meinecke. He had signed up for a night class also, in January, so we had two evenings together now. He would wait for me and drive me home, so I began asking him up for something hot to drink.

The night it happened we started watching a movie on TV, and he sat next to me on the couch with his arm lightly draped over it. As I got comfortable, it was a natural inclination to rest back into the nook of his arm. Then gradually he began moving his hand over my arm and shoulder. *Oh, the touching; how good it felt.* I wanted to crawl up into a ball inside his embrace and stay there. He was so safe, so caring. Divorced, he told me he had left his wife because of her repeated suicide attempts. He said he just couldn't handle another one, so he'd moved back home. He was lonely, too, I could tell, but he didn't talk much about himself. He just listened and was there, like now, and I couldn't resist his caring, his touching.

It was not a sudden thing, our lovemaking, but rather it seemed to be part of the natural progression of events. Not in any way what you'd call a spur of the moment decision, to let him go all the way. It was more like the expected conclusion to what had been building since the first moment we met. Only Joel had such a slow, relaxed way that it crept up on me without my even realizing it, until I found myself begging him not to stop. So he didn't – not even for a rubber.

When I awoke the next morning, I was surprised at myself. *What got into me?* I had *never* felt such sexual feelings before. When I complained to Joel that night, he just laughed, "You're just growing up, Sam. Don't you know girls don't start to mature sexually until they're nearly twenty? You're just turning into a woman," he said, smiling, holding me, reassuring me. "You're not sinful."

But I was feeling extremely guilty.

Joel was not in the least concerned. He just continued to be there, happy and caring.

The letter, postmarked Porter, Michigan, was thick, written on three-ring, closely lined notebook paper. Ray wrote with a pronounced backhand that was difficult to read at times. He started out by encouraging me in my "striving." Then he told me he had not had a single call since the Milwaukee meeting, which left him "broke." The "love offering" collected that last night, despite the really generous number of large bills filling up the offering plate as it went around the congregation, had shrunk to only $20 by the time it got to him. I began to understand how difficult it was to get started in evangelistic work and why so many young preachers went with *Youth For Christ* until they became known; at least they could count on a definite amount. Ray said he was forced to take a job at the Post Office before Christmas and didn't know what that was going to do to his draft status. He said he hadn't heard about the Wilderness Missions but would ask around. He told me to "keep pressing on" and added, "I knew you were special the first time I laid eyes on you in that ridiculous swimming suit." He signed this letter, *Yours* in Christ, Ray.

When Mr. Simms came to visit, I let him read the letter. He laughed with his deep belly laugh, and with a glowing smile, he said, "Oh-oh, I think my little girl has got a *live* one..." winking at me. "Yes sir-ee, it sounds to me like that kiss did it, Sam. Mark my word, you haven't heard the last from this young man."

"Well, I wouldn't count on it," I said, thinking about Joel *being* there and not having to guess. Mr. Simms knew about Joel and was not too keen on my jeopardizing my job. "We are discreet," I insisted. "I really don't know how I would make it, all the walking I have to do, every little bit helps." But I neglected to tell him we had gotten past the *friends* stage.

Although I felt a great deal of warmth for Joel, Ray's letter, again, made me feel I had wasted my life. These feelings drew me all the more towards the Wilderness Missions, a society of young Christians living on faith, banding together with the sole purpose in life to follow the words of Jesus: "Feed my sheep." Although some of them appeared to be shabbily dressed and could have used haircuts and soap and water, the zeal and fervor with which they approached their mission of the gospel stirred me inside.

Mr. Meinecke listened without interrupting me. Then he said, "Have you really *thought* about this, Sam? I mean, have you weighed every side of this thing? To answer the call of God to the mission field is all well and good, but to give up your job as a test of faith in providing a way of support for your child, literally testing the very foundations of our court system, that is taking quite a risk, my girl."

"But faith is believing something *will be* that is not presently evident. How am I going to let God know that I really *trust* Him, if I don't give up everything?"

"I'm sure you are sincere in your desire to serve God. I don't know about the credibility of this missionary group you are referring to, but that is not really the question. It is the care of your child... *She* is your first responsibility."

"God will take care of my child; He has promised He would – and He's bigger than any court system."

Mr. Meinecke sat back into his chair a bit impatiently. Finally, he said, "Tell you what, Sam. I'm a little busy today, so I'm not going to accept your resignation just yet. I want you to think this over very carefully for a couple of weeks and then come back to me and we'll discuss it, again. All right?"

The only one that I was sure would understand, was Ray. So I wrote him another very long letter, telling him about my decision and Mr. Meinecke's refusal to take me seriously. The fact that my period was late, I was sure, had nothing to do with my decision. I continued to go to the Bible study the Wilderness people had begun. We prayed together for God's will; surely *God* would take care of everything.

Ray's answer was swift in coming. His direct way of speaking came through very strongly in this long letter. He started out by saying he had checked out this new group very thoroughly, and I had been "dealt a deception." He advised me to sever my relationship with them immediately and to thank my boss for his sincere interest in me. "Keep your job. Although you might feel at the moment that this is the way to show your faith in God, it is not" he wrote, "and in time you will see the folly in this line of reasoning. I know you do not want to do <u>anything</u> to risk losing Sharon." The last paragraph of the letter completely surprised me. "I have not been in the position to tell you this in the past, but after much thought and sincere searching of the word and much prayer, I have volunteered for the draft; I passed the physical! I'll be leaving soon for basic training, but before I go, I want to tell you how much I care for you and have always cared for you since the moment I first saw you walking all alone on the beach." It was signed this time, *Love* in Christ, Ray.

A week later Joel took me out to eat at a nice restaurant. I had picked up my roll and was cutting it like a homemade biscuit. He leaned down close to the table and whispered, "Pick up your napkin first, and *break* your bread; don't cut it."

Even though I was glad he was helping me this way, my face grew flushed. Then I asked him, "Well, what do you think? Am I pregnant or not?"

"We'll know tomorrow, but it really doesn't matter; it wouldn't change the way I feel about you."

Knowing how he felt about me would give me one more thing to worry about and I had enough to think about already. *And now Ray's feelings. Oy. What am I going to do?* Trying not to think about Ray until I was certain I was not carrying Joel's child, was becoming confusing. Just the thought of Ray excited me clear to my insides, but I was growing more comfortable in Joel's arms, by the day.

"Do my table manners embarrass you?" I asked him, perkily.

"No, none of these kinds of things are really important once you know them," he said.

Even though the rabbit test came out negative, it was a week too early for the test to be absolute. If we waited another week for the test, the possibility of a false negative could be eliminated, we were told at the medical lab, but I was too impatient. Luckily, it was only a few days later that the test's negative results proved to be correct. I told Mr. Simms about it, since it was now in the past.

"My-my, Sweetheart, you mustn't take such chances. If you are going to engage in such activities, have your young man use a rubber," he said and winked with a mischievous grin. "Of course, it's always better that you *don't* do such things, but if you *must*, it's better to *play it safe.*"

His advice really surprised me. But determined not to go through this torment of waiting again – *playing it safe* would be too deliberate, sinful – his words were forgotten.

Sometimes I would say to Joel, "You're too easy with me. I need someone to be bossier with me."

He would just laugh and go on about the business of being his amiable self, even when he saw the 5 x 7 picture sitting on my dresser signed, *Love in Christ, Ray*. Joel would just look at it and ask me if I'd heard from him lately? I would nod my head, *yes*, and continue my double life — loving Ray from my heart on paper, and Joel with the rest of me.

When Leona told me she was pregnant and would be popping out any day, I got unusually excited and started crocheting a baby sweater set, working on it during lunch hours and every free moment. As I held the finished sweater up one day to examine it, tears suddenly welled up in my eyes. Leona was watching me and asked, "What's this I see? A tear? For goodness sake, why?"

"I really want another baby. Look, Sharon is already three years old. She needs another child to play with so badly."

Leona touched my back with a quick thumbnail rub as she had a habit of doing and said, "You've got to get a husband first, silly."

"I know," I said. "That's the trouble, I wonder if I ever will."

"My goodness girl, you aren't exactly over the hill yet. Only nineteen, why you're barely out of diapers yet. Give yourself time. One of these days Mr. Right will come along. You just need a little more growing up time. That's all you need, just some time."

After a long pause, she asked, "Are you still writing Ray?"

"Yes, but he's in the Army now, stationed at Ft. Leonard Wood."

"Well, Missouri isn't so far."

"I know. Sully used to drive home from there every weekend."

Joel invited me to dinner at the home of a friend who had a very young girlfriend who was in the kitchen preparing steaks.

When I walked in to give her a hand, she put her fingers to her lips and said, "Sh. I never did this in my life, have you?"

I hadn't, neither had I eaten them. We always had beef cooked in gravy; it went farther that way. But I didn't tell her. Instead, I showed her how to broil the steaks (like I'd read in my high school cookbook that Ruby stole from me) to a delicious medium rare.

Joel and his friends had a glass of red wine. After dinner I slow danced for the first time in my life. Oh, it was heaven, being held so close and swaying to the music. He told me over and over that night how proud he was of me. "You really handle yourself well," he said, as he hugged me and swirled me around the room. "You didn't eat too fast, either," he whispered in my ear, as though he was responsible for teaching me to breathe. He was so gentle, I loved being with him, even though he had no Fundamental Christian background whatsoever. His family was Lutheran, but he never refused to attend church whenever I asked him.

Although I still had an interest in spiritual things, and always wanted to do what was right, my enthusiasm for church had cooled considerably since the episode with the Wilderness people. Occasionally I was asked to substitute at the big Hammond organ on Sunday mornings. When I did play, Sharon would sit on the front row all alone, just a few feet beneath me, and look at her books. I was strict with her, telling her she must not speak to *anyone* while she sat alone. Norman Scott loved to carry her around the church after service. She had similar coloring to his, and he could have easily passed for her father. I looked down at Sharon and she was up on her knees, hanging her arms over the seat, giggling at Norman while I was playing. I would have to get the rubber spatula out again, I thought. I used to leave it on the kitchen table, hoping her knowing it was there would prompt good behavior. But I never needed it. Quite a few people were watching her all during the song service, such a beautiful child.

On the way out of church, walking to the bus stop, someone called me. "Sam. Sam. Can you wait a minute?"

I turned around to find Hilda, one of the sisters in whose double wedding I had stood up for as a teenager, was excitedly trying to tell me something. She was a Norwegian blonde with very light skin. Her younger brother was our paper boy on Cherry Lane and my age, so I was asked to stand up with him. Miraculously, Daddy had agreed. "Sam, I was watching little Sharon in church this morning, while you were playing, and I want you to know you have done a remarkable job with her. She is a beautiful child and such a contrast in coloring to yours. More like mine," she added, her pale skin reflecting the flush of her emotions. "You know I've just had another tubal pregnancy, my fourth, and the doctor tells me I dare not get pregnant again, it may be my death next time. I keep trying, and it has weakened me considerably."

"Yes, I know. My girlfriend, Muriel, just had one and nearly died. They don't think she'll be able to get pregnant again either.

She's thinking of adopting. How about you?" I asked her.

"Yes, we thought of it. We went so far as to take in foster children. That was a help, but so painful when you have to give them up finally. And the... the last baby we took died in the night. Crib death, it's called, and I haven't had the heart to do *that* again." Then, with her eyes downcast, she spoke a little shyly, "Sam, I was thinking... today in church... Why don't you let me adopt Sharon? It must be awfully difficult for you, taking care of her."

My ears surely must be deceiving me, I thought, after all I had gone through to keep my child. I was sure my mouth was gaping open, but she kept talking.

"We could give her so much more than you could, Sam. We've done quite well with both of us working. And look, she even looks more like me than her own mother," Hilda said, suddenly chuckling. "Please Sam, please consider it."

The indignation inside me began to rise. Her insult was beyond words, and she was talking like Sharon was a piece of furniture that she could just pick up and move to her house. *What was wrong with her?* Trying to maintain my decorum outside the door of the church, trembling as I spoke, "How dare you suggest that I could possibly give up my child. For *any* reason. Don't you know how hard I've fought to *keep* her? How my every hour of every day is planned around her? And you think that I could give her up," snapping my fingers, "just like that?" My voice got higher and louder, and my cheeks felt hot as I defended what little I had and my right to it, no matter how hard I had to work to keep it. "Why, my child is my very *life*... How *could* you?"

"Oh, I didn't mean... The way it sounded..." She broke into tears, "I just meant..."

Grabbing Sharon and hugging her tightly, I ran to the bus stop. Despite how little I knew about being a mother, I did do my best, and I couldn't even imagine giving up my baby girl.

The bitterly cold March winds off Lake Michigan were whistling through the windows. I threw my coat off, kicked my shoes across the room, and fell across my bed. Like a three-year-old that could not catch her breath, is how I felt; I could not hold back the uncontrollable sobbing. Where the tears came from, I did not know – except that I felt better after it was over.

Joel had brought me home from work and was waiting in the living room. It was our school night, and Mary had just come up for Sharon. I heard Joel say to Mary, "Does she do this often?"

Mary said, "Almost every night."

Joel came in then, pulled me up from the bed, put his arms around me, and held me, quietly. This was something Joel started doing everyday, with few words; he just held me. *How had I managed without him, before his arms?*

The long distance operator was interrupting us for the third time. "Your three minutes are up, sir, please deposit another seventy-five cents if you wish to continue speaking."

As the click of the last coin sounded, I heard Ray say, "Why don't we just get married and save all this money on long distance phone calls?"

"What do you mean? You're rich now working for Uncle Sam?"

"Are you kidding, seventy-eight dollars a month? By the way, that goes up when I get married. I think it's fifteen dollars, but the housing allowance is something around fifty, I think. But that's not considered pay, and you only get that if you live off-post — and then *after* you make Corporal. Speaking of off-post, I get my first weekend pass in three more weeks. How about coming down to see me? — if you don't mind my being just plain Ray, without the Reverend."

"Just a little something to take with you," Mr. Simms said, as he handed me the soft package. It was wrapped in white tissue paper with a pink satin ribbon around it.

When I saw the soft blue negligee slide out of the paper, my stomach began its nervous guilty churning. As I held it up, I could see that he'd spent considerable time in choosing just the right style. The panels crisscrossed and were gathered under the bust-line, an A-shaped piece fit snugly around my waist like a cummerbund, letting more soft gathers fall from that, the back was made the same way. The sight of it left me utterly speechless. I'd never had anything quite so nice. Mr. Simms was saying, "You know the way to a man's heart, don't you?" Then he grinned, a silly look in his eye.

"But I... I... I really wasn't planning..."

"Don't worry," he said with a wink, "You've already got him hooked... but... just in case."

I hugged him then, and this time he held me extra long, which made me so uncomfortable that I pulled away. But he pulled me right back, saying, "I just want one thing from you, a kiss." And as he had done one other time, he reached down and put his lips on mine ever so lightly, and then let me go.

It felt strange, and I didn't look at him again until he was going out the door. Then I said, "Thank you, but I wish you hadn't."

He put his fingers to his lips and said, "Sh," winked, and walked down the stairs.

The train into St. Louis arrived only minutes before the bus left for Fort Leonard Wood, another two hours' ride through the Ozarks into the heart of Missouri.

The ride was long and hot this last weekend in March. The land through which we were traveling was barren, with only an occasional cabin or house trailer on the side of the road and wash lines strung up to a tree. Except for a Cadillac or Buick parked here and there along side one of them, the country seemed godforsaken; I never saw a living soul.

At the large sprawling Fort, the guest house was easy to find with the commuter bus Ray had told me to catch. He would meet me at the Service Club as soon as he could get there. In the meantime, I paid $2 to hold a room and headed for the Club just across the way.

Uniforms of all kinds and butch haircuts were everywhere, and I couldn't help but look for Ed Johnston in every face, on every name tag. Ray shook me out of my concentration when he came dashing towards me and grabbed me around my waist. He bent me backwards and gave me a walloping kiss. His enthusiasm was almost overwhelming as he steered me towards the guest house. "You're not going to stay *there*, tonight, are you? I have plans for us to go into St. Louis and stay at the big hotel." His eyes literally danced as he said *hotel*.

"But I've already paid, I hadn't planned..."

"Nonsense, we'll be in St. Louis in..."

"Two hours," we both said in unison, breaking us into loud laughter as he picked up my luggage, steering me by the arm, but not apologizing for my having to get back on the same bus.

It was while we ate the hot dog, waiting for the bus, that I noticed how thin he was, his new Army butch haircut emphasizing his tiny features. He did not have one ounce of fat on his six-foot frame.

"It looks like you've been out in this hot sun a little bit," I said. His heavy eyebrows had bleached a solid white.

"Shoot yeah, that's all we do here is get suntans," he said and laughed his hearty laugh.

"Well, did you get accepted for CIC yet?" I asked

"So far they haven't told us. But I think I've done well enough on all the tests to qualify."

"Oh?"

"Yeah, I maxed all of them. They're trying to get me to apply for OCS. That's Officer's Candidate School, but I'd rather be a private in the Intelligence Corps than an officer in any other branch, so I'm sticking with CIC. It looks like I'll make it, but the big background investigation will decide it. That takes time. I'll know when my basic training is over in three more weeks. Meantime, I'm careful. They're particular about character. You know, honesty, integrity, and all that good stuff, so they can teach us to lie and steal and pick locks." His laughter could be heard down the block.

The Greyhound bus provided pillows and blankets, a welcomed comfort as the sun began to go down and the chilliness of the evening air set in around us. Ray didn't want a blanket, he said. Instead he snuggled under mine and pulled me over to him, kissing me and kissing me. Since it had gotten dark, and the blanket covered us completely, it was easy to let him, although his sudden ardor surprised me. In the height of one passionate moment, the bus stopped and the overhead lights came on. I got embarrassed, thinking the bus driver was giving us a hint to *cool it*. When this happened the third time, and I scrambled to smooth my hair as the lights came on, I said, red faced, "Maybe we ought to stop snuggling for awhile, till we get the bus driver off our trail."

Ray burst into boisterous laughter. "You think he's onto us, huh?"

"What do *you* think?" I asked, very certain. "Every time we get started good, on go the lights."

"No, Sam. It's railroad crossings he's stopping for. It's a State law. He opens the door, if you'll notice, and when the door opens, the lights automatically go on."

"Oh," I said, relieved we had not been of special interest to the bus driver. I slid back down under the blanket, ready to continue. In between his kissing me, Ray whispered in my ear how much he thought about me, waited for every letter, and couldn't wait to get me into the hotel, but promised we would have separate rooms *for appearances*.

Ray was all business the second we stepped off the bus. He steered me to the lobby and set my night case down. He looked all around to see if anyone appeared to be suspicious and said, "You stay here, Sam, while I go get us two rooms — just in case someone from the Corps is watching me. You never know, they're a sneaky bunch. *Spooks* you know, and they have stressed good character requirements. I don't want to blow it this close to being in."

I sat and watched him walk carefully to the front desk of the Mayfair Hotel to get our rooms. He came sauntering back, looking all around him and speaking out of the corner of his mouth. Just in case someone was "tailing him," he suggested we not walk to the elevator together. He slipped me the key to my room, "I'll see you upstairs," he said with a wide knowing smile as he took off ahead of me.

We shared the elevator with a bellboy; neither one of us spoke. The bellboy got off on another floor; we still didn't speak. A note of excitement was in the air as Ray got off ahead of me, and I followed down the hall quietly, thinking someone *could* be hiding in one of the rooms with a camera, I guess, if you stretched your imagination that far. I reached my room first, and he continued down to the next door.

Undecided just what to do next, I had my nightgown in my hand when a light tap sounded at my door. Through the chain, Ray was whispering, "Open up. *Hurry*, before someone comes."

Inside the room, Ray looked down and noticed I had the negligee in my hand, and a little sheepishly, he asked, "Were you going to put that on?"

"Yes," I said, "until you knocked."

"Oh, well, don't let me stop you," he said, blushing, averting my eyes.

"Really? Are you sure?" I asked, not knowing if he really meant it. He just grinned, but didn't say anything else, so I said, "Well, if you really *want* me to."

"Of course, I want you to. I'll just sit here and read. Go ahead."

Minutes later, when I appeared in the flowing blue gown Mr. Simms had bought me for this very purpose, my guilt and shyness were concealed beneath a racing heart. Ray had slipped out of his uniform and sat in his white T-shirt and Army-issue boxer shorts. He sat in a chair at the little table with the lamp on, thumbing through the Gideon Bible. The bed covers had been pulled back, and I pushed the big fluffy pillows against the headboard and sat back into them, pulling my feet up under the long gown. Ray began reading from the Bible.

There is therefore now no condemnation to them which are

in Christ Jesus, who walk not after the flesh, but after the
Spirit."

The sound of his voice excited me, it didn't matter what the
words were.

*"For the law of the Spirit of life in Christ Jesus hath made me
free from the law of sin and death. For what the law could
not do, in that it was weak through the flesh, God sending
his own Son in the likeness of sinful flesh, and for sin,
condemned sin in the flesh: That the righteousness of the
law might be fulfilled in us, who walk not after the flesh, but
after the spirit."*

My mind began to wander after the third time I heard the
word *flesh*, the Bible's word for *sex*, I believed. A phrase here and
there would catch my attention.

*"For to be carnally minded is death; but to be spiritually
minded is life and peace. Because the carnal mind is enmity
against God:... So they that are in the flesh cannot please
God... Now if any man have not the spirit of Christ, he is
none of his."*

Suddenly, the pulsing in my temples interrupted my
concentration, and I thought: *What am I doing sitting in this bed,
in this getup, while this young man sits across the room in his
underwear, reading admonitions to me from the Bible regarding
the sin he has so eagerly promised me all afternoon we would be
doing later?* The utter contradiction of the moment had me on the
verge of giggles, but the sincerity of Ray's tone as he continued to
read his *favorite chapter,* the eighth book of Romans, kept me
still.

*" For we are saved by hope, but hope that is seen is not
hope; for what a man seeth, why doth he yet hope for? But if
we hope for that we see not, then do we with patience wait
for it."*

Those were the very words Daddy had read over and over,
during his long seven year wait for Charity, just about every night
before he went to bed, like this. *Do you suppose this is Ray's way
of asking me to marry him?* I wondered, but thought it absurd.

Ray kept reading.

> *"And we know that all things work together for good to them*
> *that love God, to them who are the called according to his*
> *purpose. For who he did foreknow, he also did predestinate*
> *to be conformed to the image of his Son... If God be for us,*
> *who can be against us? He that spared not his own Son, but*
> *delivered him up for us all, how shall he not with him also*
> *freely give us all things?... It is Christ that died, yea rather,*
> *that is risen again, who is even at the right hand... Who shall*
> *separate us from the love of Christ? Shall tribulation, or*
> *famine, or nakedness, or peril, or sword?"*

Now I began to listen, for I loved to hear of the love of Christ.
His love, I had always been told, is what took the place of Mama's
love; I had a tendency to wallow in it.

> *As it is written, For thy sake we are killed all the day long;*
> *we are accounted as sheep for the slaughter. Nay, in all*
> *these things we are more than conquerors through him that*
> *loved us. For I am persuaded, that neither death, nor life,*
> *nor angels nor principalities, nor powers, nor things present,*
> *nor things to come, nor height, nor depth, nor any other*
> *creature, shall be able to separate us from the love of God,*
> *which is in Christ Jesus our Lord."*

Ray closed the book and laid it on the table, stood up and
walked towards me. As he reached the bed, I stood up and
reached for him. When our bodies met for the first time
completely, we kissed, full of the passion we had been holding
back all day. He pulled me in closely, tightly, as he had done at
my kitchen door. *Oh, how I love you,* I thought, as I moved into his
warm full embrace. But he began to tremble, again, as he had
done the other time in my kitchen, so I held him closer, and he
grasped me even tighter in his shaking. Suddenly, I felt something
warm against my belly. He pulled away from me in
embarrassment as I looked down at my new beautiful gown,
covered with seminal fluid.

In the bathroom, I quickly rinsed the gown, hung it up to dry,
and put my slip back on to sleep in. Ray was lying face down
across the bed, with his elbow under his head. He would not look
at me even when I assured him no harm had been done, "The
gown will be dry by morning."

Shamefacedly, he reached for me, pulled me into his arms and kissed me again, this time with less enthusiasm. Then he grabbed his clothes and put them on quickly. Over his shoulder, he said, "Good night" and slipped through the door.

Leaving me to sleep alone in the large bed, the night dragged fitfully by, trying to figure Ray out. His uncontrollable passion had left me sad, knowing how embarrassed he must be. It certainly explained his unusual behavior when he ran out of my house that night. Then, as now, he had left me uncomfortably aroused.

At six in the morning I awoke with a start, thinking about the disappointment of the young soldier who had bragged all day of the coming night's adventures, only to be shot down in his impatience. *Surely his sex life would be ruined if I did not right this wrong; he may be afraid to touch a woman again for the rest of his life.* I just had to prove to him he could be a man, so I slipped my coat over my skimpy slip and knocked on Ray's door. He let me in, half-asleep, turned and crawled back into his bed, his back to me. It didn't deter me, I just slid in behind him. The instant I put my arm around him, he turned over and took me in his arms. His eagerness was already showing itself as I slipped my body around him, consummating the love I had felt for him all this time. Afterwards, he held me so tightly, I thought he would cry. I knew I had done the right thing; I sensed it in his sweet shyness.

So as not to endanger his *reputation* by staying too long, or having to admit to myself that I had done what I had just done instead of *fixing things* as I believed, I went back to my room and slept until time for services at the large Baptist church Ray had suggested we attend.

It was a huge church and the Palm Sunday service was beautiful and touching, the most joyful of days in the Christian community. The white-robed choir marched out of the sanctuary carrying the symbolic palms as the congregation rose and followed, the women eyeing each other's hats as the men quickly lit up their smokes on the tall steps outside. Shocked at the sight, I said, "I can't believe they're smoking right in the door of the church"

"Smoking is just a geographical thing, Sam. More of an ethical interpretation and Southerners don't feel the same about it or even an occasional beer. Of course, they don't believe in drinking beer on Sunday, mind you," he said, laughing.

As we left this grand cathedral and walked down the giant flight of cement steps, I suddenly remembered another Palm

Sunday, five years before, when I'd left a similar church service, with similar feelings, following a similar sexual experience, the connection between the two — religion and sex – not yet registering. Although I had felt aroused this time, I had not been a full participant. Still letting myself be used, my feelings locked behind years of piety.

Too, this experience had left me a little less guilty, if only slightly, than my other rendezvous I'd had recently with Joel. But Joel had not read the Bible, he had only told me I was beautiful and that he loved me.

The Chinese food was the first I remembered having, other than the canned chop suey I occasionally had at home. Ray had no problem with conversation. "I've always wanted to have six kids."

"How about that; I've always wanted the same thing."

"And the first little girl I have, I'm going to name her Suzie, after the Suzie we lost. Remember, I told you about her?"

"Yes, I like that name."

"And I have to have a Kelly right off the bat," he continued. "I had this little kid in summer camp while I was a student at Bob Jones, he was the darndest kid to get into trouble that I've ever seen. But cute, boy when he smiled at you, your heart just couldn't stay mad. You just melted."

"For goodness sake, do you know that I had that name picked out if Sharon had been a boy."

"Two out of three's not bad. Huh?" he said, grinning.

Then I heard about Ray's breakup with the waiting bride, Jenny. "I went home and broke up with her. I didn't know if I'd ever see you again, but I knew even if I didn't, I'd met someone that turned my head, so I told Jenny. I'm an honest person, sometimes to my detriment, I'm told, but it would've been dishonest to go through with the wedding. My brother, Rich, broke up with her sister, too."

"You sound like you have a very close family."

"My two brothers and I have always been real close. We're only a year apart, but of course, I'm the best looking."

Shocked at his bragging, I started to speak, but he continued, "My youngest brother, Matt, *thinks* he's the best looking, but he really looks like me. Shorter than me, though, but he's mean, let me tell you. Nobody better mess with him. Never did run from a fight, that kid. Rich is more the one to start the fights and then run, letting you get walloped. But we fixed him once, Matt and I, when I was about nine. He pulled the same thing, got us boys fightin' and then went and called Ma while *he* hid behind a tree. So we got him aside and stuffed beans up his nose."

"Beans?"

"Yeah, you know, *Navy* beans, and I told him my fist would come through his throat if he as much as whimpered to Ma or Dad. Well, at the dinner table that night, the poor kid was sniffin' and his nose was getting puffed and all red, and I was givin' him this glare and had my fist doubled up under the table, and my ma asked him what was botherin' him and he busted out crying. Guess the pain must have been excruciating. Anyhow, before I could even think about my own fist, my old man's was in my face, and I went flyin'. The doctor got the beans out, fortunately, with a tweezers. Guess Rich was lucky... I got it again that night with the barrel staves my dad always used on me. Boy, them hurt. Ooie. My mom never spanked us. She would always tell us, *I'm gonna tell your dad when he comes home.* So we'd go all day in fear of his coming home. Boy, I hated that. I hope you don't think that way. A kid should be tended to that minute, not left in fear all day. You know, I almost hated to see my dad come home most nights, the nights he *did*. He stopped at the beer hall usually, but mostly I didn't care if he ever came home. It upsets me when I think about how she made me feel about him."

Listening to Ray talk and watching him, kept me interested. His large eyes would bug out when he made his point, and his voice boomed so that people all around us would look and listen and sometimes laugh at his overheard stories. He never seemed to run out of things to say, like now. "My mother has the diamond that Jenny wore for a couple years. Do you have any objections to wearing it?"

"Well, I guess not, if I get the *guy* this time."

He laughed and reassured me that he would have his mother mail the ring to me immediately. "So you can just plan to get married as soon as I get out of basic. Marriage isn't allowed before then without special permission, you know. Red tape with the CO and all."

Riding on the train back to Milwaukee, I crocheted furiously to finish the last bootee to Leona's baby's set. My excitement was almost more than I could contain. I wouldn't let myself question the things left unsaid either. Instead, I thought only of the things Ray *did* say and the diamond ring I would be wearing very soon. Then the whole world would know I was engaged.

Mr. Simms listened intently as I told him of the weekend's events in St. Louis. My concern for Ray's impatience was explained away very simply. "The boy no doubt masturbated a lot, probably why he couldn't *hold it*. But don't worry," he said, "you did the right thing by going after him and righting his mistake. A fine young man you've got there. If you handle him just right, he'll make you a fine lover in bed one day," he said, smiling and winking.

Joel continued to bring me home, but he no longer came up to my apartment. He would reach out for me in the car to touch me, but I was keeping myself in check. Now that I was engaged, I wondered if I should even ride with him, but I saw no harm in just talking. When I told him about the ring, he smiled and wished me luck and looked out his side window of the car. I told Leona, also, that Ray had asked me to marry him. Griffith, Joel's uncle, suddenly became very interested in me. It was the first time I suspected that Joel had mentioned me at home. But I couldn't worry about it; I was too happy.

Ray wrote me his first real love letter. It was like a poem, telling me that our union was made in heaven, that "I loved you from the first moment I laid eyes on you in that ridiculous bloomer swim suit." I would be receiving the diamond ring just as soon as his mother got her mail and could send it. He signed his letter for the first time plainly, *Love, Ray*. No *Christ* with it. I got three letters at a time, every day. I couldn't get them answered fast enough. Then suddenly – the mail stopped. I couldn't understand it as I thought I had been prompt in answering each and every one.

A few days later a thick envelope came. Inside was another fat letter addressed to Pvt. Ray Malorry, accompanied by a short note from Ray. It said: *Enclosed is my mother's letter. It will explain why I can't marry you. Ray.*

His mother's letter was biting and stung me to the core. I read it over and over, trying to understand. She called him Everett in the letter, the name he hated:

Easter Sunday 1956
My Dear Son,
It gives me great pain to have to write such a letter to you, my beloved, but I have loved you more than my own life and have spent many hours on my knees searching His word in preparation. My life has not been easy, as you well know, in raising you children in a way pleasing to God, but I have always sought much His guidance in every decision through the years. God's word says, "Bring up a child

in the way he should go and when he is old he will not depart from it," and I have committed all my children unto his care and feel that with this Christian training that I have consistently given you (as well as the fine education at such a fine Christian University, that I have worked hours on my feet nursing in order to pay for), that when you give this matter more thought and hear what I have to tell you, you will not disappoint me in your decision.

Everett, I have personally paid a bitter price for the folly of marrying outside of the will of God. Your father, as much as I know, loves me (as well as anyone), but has fought me in my faith since the day I married him. My mother warned me, but I was headstrong and would not listen, and I have paid dearly for my stubbornness, and I so much yearn for my children to avoid the hurt and anguish I have suffered for my mistake. God says, "In all thy ways acknowledge Him, and He shall direct thy path." And all I am asking is that you commit your way unto Him and let Him lead you in this momentous decision of your young life. I know you have been bitter recently at the inconsistencies of the ministry for which God has called you, and your impatience at awaiting His leading has already tied up your time, unnecessarily, for three years. And had you waited just another week before volunteering for the draft, you would have had three meetings behind you already (as you well know from your mail). "God's ways are not our ways," though, and thank the Lord, we cannot see the future or know His intent or we might falter by the wayside in our human frailty and sinful doubting. So we must trust in His promises. (Read Romans 8, isn't this your favorite chapter?)

When you came to in the snow that day while your friend was already dying, and you gave your life to your Savior for His purpose, it was a commitment not to be taken lightly. And the twelve men of God who signed your ordination paper (that I still have on my wall) put their faith in you to carry out God's will in your life and entrusted you with an awesome responsibility in giving you the power to "marry or bury" even in the eyes of the civil authorities. This responsibility is not to be taken lightly, and although you have given your country first option on your time for the next three years, it can be a time of growing and learning and certainly of great opportunity for testimony as you can live a clean life before all those you serve with, but not by running off half-cocked with a young divorcee that you know next to nothing about. We've talked before about the difficulties of the ministry for a single person and problems surrounding the credibility of this girl's background, besides the questionability of her marital status (you know well there are many who question remarriage for one such as her, even the Catholic church would not condone such a marriage!), and you have a responsibility to uphold the vows you made before man and God at your ordination. And certainly, a girl who would travel a thousand

miles out of her way to crawl into bed with you cannot possibly be the kind of girl God has chosen for you, my son. "Straight is the road, and narrow is the way that leadeth to life, and few there be that find it!"
So, as I close this "epistle," I want you to know that I love you and the welfare of your soul is my utmost concern as I pray daily for God to have his way in your life, and then, and only then, will you find peace that He alone can give. You are always in my prayers.
Love and prayers, Your mother
P.S. I'm sorry to have burst your bubble, Son!

Digesting the letter, I felt the dream I'd carried for two long years slowly fading and being replaced with guilt. We'd talked a lot about his mother, about the hardships she'd suffered at the hands of her drunken husband. Ray said about him, "My father is not an alcoholic; he doesn't go to meetings. He's just a drunk."

It was clear by the letter that his mother believed I'd sexually seduced her son. As I thought about Ray's part in it –I wouldn't have gone to St. Louis if he hadn't invited me – the anger at his meek acceptance of his mother's decision for him irritated me more and more, especially her P.S. at the end, making it clear she expected him to accept her decree. How someone who appeared so strong, sounding so deliberate and determined, would simply give up without a whimper was more than I could understand. It must be that he had changed his mind, I thought. Still, that was a cowardly way to tell me. It didn't seem that I had a chance at any persuasion against such odds. I only had a calendar that said I was late for my period.

Ray did have the courtesy to call me to see if I got the letter and understood. I didn't have much to say, except when he asked if I was sure I wasn't pregnant. "No, I'm not sure yet. It's been a little early to get a rabbit test," I told him.

"Why don't you get it this week, before I get up there. I'll swing by Milwaukee Saturday on my way home. Is that all right?"

"Yes," I said, "That'll be fine." But I was sure I wasn't pregnant. I was always late for my periods, especially under stress. *And how more stressful could things be?* I wondered, hurt, angry, embarrassed. All the things I'd spent my life feeling, I was now going through again in an exaggerated way.

Every day at work I took a few minutes' break, and in the bathroom I did every exercise I knew. Some of the red wine Joel had left in the refrigerator, I warmed and drank it before bed to ease my menstruation into coming. The 8 x 10 color photo of Ray in his uniform sat on my sewing machine in my dining room.

Every time I went past it, I got angrier and angrier. But I told no one, not even Mr. Simms, until I was absolutely certain of where I stood.

Ray arrived late Saturday afternoon and stayed at the Y at my request. He was waiting for Sharon and me when we got home from church Sunday noon. He seemed as friendly as ever, but my cool politeness, as though we had just met, kept him at a distance.

"What's for dinner?" he asked, letting me know he was hungry.

"Chicken," I said. "It's what we always have for Sunday dinner. Do you like it?" I asked.

"Ugh, I *hate* chicken," he said, with an ugly scowl.

"Sorry about that," I said, without a blink of an eye. "Guess you'll have to fill up on other things, because *that's* what we're having."

Ray began laughing loudly, in his boisterous way. "I was just kidding you. Just to see what you'd do. Didn't ruffle you a bit, I see," he said. Then as though in afterthought, he said, "Chicken is my favorite meal. Next to steak, that is."

"That's good," I said, still not wavering. "I never worry about anyone's likes or dislikes at my table. I learned long ago that all food is good and if you don't like it, tough. You'll just have to go without," I said, looking him squarely in the eye.

"Well, I guess you told *me*, huh?"

I gave him a curt smile and went about making my regular Southern fried chicken Grandma Evermardt had taught me to make.

Sharon was sitting in her high chair chewing on a carrot stick. She was hungry and letting me know it. The chicken was ready, and I was in the process of serving it. Sharon's crankiness had gotten Ray's attention, and he came into the kitchen and walked over to her. He bent down and, holding up his large hand, palm out, and in eye-popping fashion, said to her, "Shut up little girl, or I'll give you something to cry *for.*"

Sharon was not used to such a loud voice; even Mr. Simms spoke softly to her. She looked up at him, screwing up her face as she let out an ear piercing howl.

Taking Sharon in my arms then, I hugged her till her tears stopped, while Ray tried to explain that his intentions were to get her to *stop* crying, not *make* her cry. I knew he'd been teasing, that it was his way, but still, the incident was unsettling. Sharon never took her eyes off of him during dinner. I would have given anything to know her thoughts, and the more I watched her and thought about it, the more I prayed for the rabbit test to be negative – especially when Ray disappeared into the living room with the newspaper he'd brought.

After Sharon was down for her nap, I approached Ray, who was hidden behind his paper, and asked him if he would like to talk things out.

From behind his paper, he said, "There is nothing to talk about that I can see, but go ahead; I'm listening."

First Ray's letter from his mother, and then this rejection, his refusal even to look at me when I spoke to him, had torn me up inside. Stretching out across my bed, I couldn't hold the tears back any longer. *How could I get through the next twenty-four hours until the test results came back? What if it was positive? How could I stand it, his ignoring me like he did?*

Suddenly, I felt a touch on my shoulder, and Ray lay down next to me with his arms turning me around. Passionately, he began kissing me... The feel of his tongue inside my mouth, almost gagging me, is what made me shove his arms away.

In rage, I yelled at him, "How dare you think that sex can cure everything, make up for ignoring me and somehow solve everything."

As noiselessly as he appeared at my side, he left me, and went out the door for the Y.

Ray was waiting for me the next day when I arrived home from work. While I dialed the number of the laboratory, Ray was standing there listening. When I repeated "negative," he was out the door almost immediately. He stopped momentarily at the top of the stairs with his duffel bag in hand. He smiled, showing his chipped tooth. I was thinking, *I'll be glad I won't have to feel that jagged tooth cut my tongue anymore."* But I said, "I'm sorry this all happened the way it did, but thank you for coming anyway."

"That's all right. Well... I guess I'll get going." He turned and swung his duffel bag over his shoulder. He was dressed in his dress greens and his flat cap, and I looked at him steadily, without even blinking, as he walked down the stairs, thinking that I would never lay eyes on him again.

As I closed the door, I heaved a great sigh, and said almost aloud, *Thank you, God.*

Joel brought me home from work the next night, and we went out to eat together so I could explain that I was no longer engaged.

Joel didn't say much ever, but he said even less then, only smiled. He came upstairs with me and we watched TV. It appeared that Joel was back in my life again. I had missed his tender caring, but I had not put Ray's pictures away yet; I didn't know why. Joel would look at them as he passed, saying nothing.

The ringing telephone woke me at 6:30 a. m. I knew, because it was Saturday, that it must be Mr. Simms.

"Rise and shine," he was saying over the wire.

He had not called all week, so he was anxious to see me and hear about everything.

We were sitting on the couch, waiting for the coffee to get done. It was a chilly morning, and I had my old blue chenille bathrobe wrapped tightly around me. I was telling him, in detail, all about the events of the past week since I had seen him, about getting the test done and then sending Ray away for wanting sex, when suddenly I was startled at the touch of Mr. Simms large hand inside my robe, tightly clasping one of my small breasts, the ones he had referred to as my *only blemish*. In shock, I pulled his hand away, the hand that had paddled me as *a little tyke*, as he'd called me. "Oh my word, what are you doing?" When I looked into his face, the face of a man whom I'd admired and trusted and who had called me his "little baby-girl, just like my own daughter," I saw that same look of desire I'd seen on others in rare moments. The look startled me. "Have you gone mad?"

He rose abruptly. "I wouldn't get all hot under the collar about this," he said, turning to leave. As though he was dismissing the whole thing, he said, "You don't seem to mind *others* touching you."

My ears burned in humiliation. I thought I was going to literally lose my balance with dizziness as I rose and followed him to the door. My heart was thumping like a galloping horse as I stood there when he said, "It isn't as though you were *untarnished*, my dear; I just wanted a touch."

For a moment I felt like slamming the door, but it was only a moment. Instead, as I had my whole life, I swallowed the pain and the hurt — as I'd already done with all of them, the men, with Ray this very week – and said nothing. I let it all go back inside to a hidden place where pain and anger had their home, leaving behind a terrible empty sadness.

The whole weekend, I slept and cried. Mary assumed I was coming down with the flu and kept Sharon.

With all the rest of them, I managed to explain it away, but

Mr. Simms was different. He *loved* me, or so I believed. He seemed to always be so interested in hearing every little thing about me. Thoughts and feelings I had shared with him that I'd never dared express to another. Girl friends would *tell* the first time someone else came along they liked better; Daddy would punish me for even the hint of wrongdoing, or wrong thinking; Charity had turned my confidences into weapons, much like the little girls in grade school had done, but Mr. Simms I could *trust.* He had never let me down. Most of all, he accepted me, my ignorance, my imperfections. As a child I was his "honey girl" who was "talented" and learned his music. As a young woman I was "beautiful and intelligent," and I trusted his judgment on all things. Because he was a man, I felt awkward with our relationship, true, but I had been loved and taught solely by a man my whole life. Why should that have to change when I felt safe in his care, my innermost secrets treated with love and respect as they always had? But things *did* change. I sensed it as it began happening, but I wrestled with myself, denying the obvious because I felt powerless to sever the ties. The guilt I knew he would extract for such a decision, I was afraid to face. And Mrs. Simms: *What would she think?* Or Leona? It was all too terrible. The despairing thoughts haunted my every waking moment.

When finally I got myself together to go to work Monday morning, my anger had settled into a knot in my stomach, but I forgot it in the feverish trips to the bathroom, upchucking my breakfast; I was sent home with the flu.

After work, Joel came up to visit me. "I was worried about you. They said you left vomiting."

"Yes, and I haven't stopped, I don't think."

Joel came in and sat with me, and I told him about an old friend who was like a father to me... and I cried again, when I told him what had happened. Joel thought maybe my being sick was emotional, since I had no fever and I'd been so distraught. He brought me white soda and crackers, and soon I was feeling almost human. Joel's arms were a welcome haven in this time of storm. And as he began kissing me, he began undressing me, whispering in my ear, "I came prepared, so you won't have to worry anymore." This time he took me to my bed, and as he undressed me piece by piece, he looked at me as if I were a priceless work of art. I felt shy at the touch of his hands on my bare breasts, but his pleasure told me of my beauty, something I never believed I possessed. "The curve of your breasts has the look of a Grecian goddess," he said, as he began to make love to me. Oh, how he loved me, and held me, and caressed me, in ways I had never dared allow before, and brought me to the very pinnacle of the ecstasy that I had always dreamed of, ever since Bernice told me that a woman could. But in a moment of self-consciousness, my naked shyness got in the way, destroying the moment, leaving me, my thighs, longing for more and more of his tenderness.

My body seemed to have taken over the reins and was guiding me, telling me that Joel loved me, and it was safe to love him back. But I didn't know for sure, it was just an intuition. He never really came right out and said it, except that once, before Ray. It wasn't the words "I love you" Joel spoke, but of beauty, and feeling, and caring. But then, I thought of us as only lovers, bound in mutual physical attraction, as I wandered off to sleep in his arms.

It had been a week and a half since Ray left. Every time I walked by the picture of him in uniform, complete with hat and first stripe he'd earned for his completion of eight weeks basic training, I would run to the bathroom and throw up. Finally, I laid the picture face down, believing *it* was making me sick.

"Boy, this sausage is good, and I was so hungry for fried potatoes, and you know I can eat eggs day or night." I rattled on to Joel as he sat and watched me eat this enormous breakfast at midnight, after I had vomited my supper again hours before. Quietly, in his nonchalant way, he suggested, "Your appetite seems a mite suspicious these days, Sam. Craving fried potatoes in the middle of the night?"

At the word *craving,* my lungs took in an extra little breath of air. "What are you saying, Joel"

"Well, it just seems to me, that, well, maybe that test didn't come out quite right. If you were to ask me, I'd swear you were pregnant."

"Oh, my god, no! You don't think…"

"Yes, I think…"

"But it came out negative with you, two months ago."

"But you *weren't* pregnant! They told you at the lab that a negative result really didn't mean much until after the sixth week. Remember?"

"Yes, I remember. Oh, my god." I ran my hands through my hair, pushing it and pulling it the way I always did when I got upset. *What am I going to do?*

Two days later, I stood in my kitchen, my favorite room, looking down at the red and white linoleum, and at the red and white dotted Swiss curtains I'd made on the old treadle machine Muriel's mom had given me. I thought about this home I'd made for Sharon and me, my first home. I loved every inch of it, and the thought of leaving it made me tremendously sad. *What will I do if I really am pregnant*?

Joel was suddenly standing next to me, and without touching me this time, he stood close and looked me in the eyes and said, "Why don't we get married, Sam?"

The shock at his words almost made me stutter. "But... But, wh... what if I'm pregnant?"

"What's the difference? If you are, you are. If you aren't, you aren't; don't even get the test."

My mind suddenly raced to the stories he'd told me of his ex-wife, of finding her in a pool of her own blood, of his subsequent decision to leave her for the last time. "I couldn't help her anymore," he'd said, sadly. This scene in my mind frightened me for some reason, like being afraid to walk near a high ledge for fear you'll fall off, and I wondered if there was something about this kind, gentle, decent man that I didn't know. I had been so fooled by Huey's quietness before it had turned to violence. But instead of voicing my fear, a fear I had squashed and almost forgotten until this very minute when he mentioned marriage, I said, "Oh, I couldn't. I just couldn't."

"Why couldn't you?" he asked gently.

"Well, because, I just couldn't marry one man, carrying another man's baby."

"Why?"

"Well, it wouldn't be fair, that's why. Not to him or to the child. I'll have to tell him and let him decide," I said finally, under my breath, almost to myself.

Before Joel left me that night, he asked me again. "We can get married in three days. We could get our blood tests tomorrow. Think about it," he said again, as I stared into the abyss of the future, not knowing what it held for me. He kissed me behind the ear and squeezed my arm gently as he left me, walking past me out the door.

There was no *thinking* to it, I knew. If the second test came out positive, I would *have* to call Ray, who had one week left of his leave. I would know for sure by Monday.

The phone was ringing on the other end, and I could hear my

heart pounding in my ears. The sound of Mrs. Malorry's soft, honey-sweet voice sent chills to my toes, and I clutched the phone, thinking I would retch right into it. Then Ray was saying, "Hello. Oh, hi Sam, how are you?"

"I'm pregnant; I've been throwing up since you left."

"Did you get another test?"

"Yes, today. It came out positive."

The silence I expected didn't come. Instead, Ray said, "Let me call you back, Sam. Just give me a few minutes."

The next thirty minutes seemed like an eternity. *What if he doesn't come and marry me?* I saw visions of the Schultzes jeering as I walked before them with a big belly, of Huey following behind trying to catch me. I heard the sound of Charity's recriminations. *Oh, God, please hear me and don't make me go through that,* I prayed, as the phone rang. Ray said, "I'll be there on the 10:00 a.m. flight tomorrow morning. I have five days before I have to be to Baltimore for CIC school. There's one hitch, I only have enough money for the ticket to Baltimore from here, so I'll have to change the ticket to come there, but I *have* to be to Baltimore or I'll be AWOL."

How I'd get the money I didn't know, but I said, without hesitation, "Don't worry. I'll get you the ticket somehow."

"I can get a military waiver for the three-day wait for the license, can't I?"

"I think so; I've heard that."

"I'll see you at the airport then?"

"Yes. I'll be there."

The relief I felt was more than I would've believed, almost as much as I'd felt the week before thinking I would *not* see him again. *One surely can't tell about one's feeling in advance,* I thought, humming to myself.

That night, I confided to Mary, "I'm terrified he's not going to show."

"He will. He will. Don't you worry. He's a nice *guy,* Sam. I don't think he'd *lie* to you. I'll keep Sharon for you until this is all over. Don't you worry about it, kid. Now, we have to plan the wedding."

In the end, after Mr. Simms had let me down, it was Mary who kept me going. She gave me a big bear hug and said, "You know something, kid, I'm so *glad* you're normal. I was beginning to really worry about you."

Then she began digging into her linens for a white table cloth.

t was the second day of May, and I awoke with a start to the bright stream of sunlight coming through the tall elm outside my window, telling me that I had overslept. I'd slipped off to sleep the night before, holding an old broken-handled coffee mug half-filled with steaming hot red wine laced with lemon, a folk remedy Grandpa Baumn had told me about *for the miseries.* In the wee hours of the morning, I'd awakened to stare at the moonlit shadows playing on my ceiling, reminding me of the changeableness of each passing moment. The patterns changed even before my eyes as the dawn crept slowly through the blackness, and I drifted back to sleep, trusting in the inevitability of tomorrow.

It was fifteen minutes past my usual arrival time at my desk. I charged out of bed and dialed the phone; Mr. Meinecke answered. My voice got stuck, the morning hoarseness covering up the quivering, "Good morning, Mr. Meinecke. This is Sam. I'm sorry I'm late calling you, but I wanted to be sure you were in, to speak to you personally. I will not be in to work today because I'm getting married."

I hesitated, waiting for him to say something, but the silence was deafening. All I could think of was, *he knows I went to St. Louis,* but I plunged on. "You know the young man in the ministry, the one who talked me out of going with the Wilderness people?"

"Oh, yes. I do recall your mentioning him."

"Well, he's in the Army now, so we're going to get a waiver and get married today, but I was wondering if you would mind if I took off tomorrow, too, under the circumstances?"

"Sam, I... uh..." clearing his throat, "uh... I think that this is as good a time as any to call it quits with us here. You did say your husband-to-be is in the Army, didn't you?"

Why? What had I done? Did he know I was pregnant? Did he know I'd been seeing one of his boys upstairs. Was he angry that I'd broken the rule about not mixing socially with other employees? Had I done a bad job? Was all that helpful, fatherly concern and Christian support a bunch of malarkey, just as with Mr. Simms? Was I going to, in fact, move? Ray had never mentioned my going with him. I'd never even thought...

"Yes," I answered him. "He's in Army Intelligence."

"Then you're no doubt going to be leaving here anyhow before long to be with him, won't you? You see, we've been looking for someone to take shorthand, as Leona's baby is due soon, as you're aware." He cleared his throat again, "We were going to have to make some changes eventually anyhow, so I think this is the best time to do it."

It took a few minutes for the shock of Mr. Meinecke's words to sink in — that he had actually *fired* me. What really hit me immediately was his words, "Then you'll be leaving here, won't you?" Until that moment, the legitimacy of the child I carried was all I'd thought about, but the sting of his rejection, not wanting me to return for *even one day*, made me think he guessed me to be pregnant. The anguish of my shame pressed in on me as I dressed for my wedding day, tears spilling out of my eyes. But the time was flying by, and I had no time to fret over such things if I was to meet Ray's plane.

Because I was nervous, I dressed in my most comfortable outfit, my navy blue wool dress with navy raglan-sleeved coat over it. At the arrival gate, I stood clutching my navy bag and white hat with my white-gloved hands. Searching the crowd for a tall blonde-headed stranger I was about to take as my husband, I had just about given him up in a panic when he came bounding down the runway, putting his fancy billed hat on his head. After he passed the last stewardess, talking to them all as he passed by, he bounded up to me, smiling broadly. He grabbed my elbow and directed me to the baggage area, talking all the while. I'd forgotten how much he talked; it was a relief to hear it today.

"My brother, Matt, said I should show up with a carton of cigarettes in one hand and a six-pack of beer in the other, and you couldn't do a damn thing about it," he said, laughing loudly with his belly laugh.

His words made me wince, as I smiled at the cleverness of his brother. My predicament had been made strikingly clear by this good Samaritan, for the second time that day. A smile, my old standby, was my only recourse from then on. The powerlessness of my situation was not new, but a new twist to an old feeling; I didn't know any other way.

Ray was saying, "My mother asked, *How do you know it's yours?* And I said, *I know it's mine.* My old man spoke up to her — for the first time in my life, I guess – and told her that if it *was* mine, it was my responsibility to come over here and marry you, and so here I am."

Trying to blink back the tears that neared the surface, I smiled. ·

It was becoming easier to be quiet, Ray talked so much about his family. "My brother, Rich, wished me luck and told me one good thing about your being pregnant is that I wouldn't have to worry about rubbers for awhile. They're like taking a bath with your shoes on, he says."

Ray's Irish humor was infecting. It appeared he had taken this marriage in stride and so should I.

As we stood before the Justice of the Peace, we were asked to repeat a simple marriage vow, "Will you, Everett Creston Malorry, take this woman, Samantha Sue Schultz, to be your lawfully wedded wife?"

Ray looked at me with his jagged-tooth smile. "I will," he said.

"And will you, Samantha Sue Schultz, take this man, Everett Creston Malorry, to be your lawfully wedded husband?"

"I will," I said, with my voice trembling.

"And will you promise to have, honor, love each other, until death should so separate you?"

We said, in unison, "I will."

"I, then, pronounce you husband and wife."

The Justice sat down and signed all the documents along with the two other men present as our witnesses. Suddenly Ray grabbed me, pulled off my lacy picture hat and kissed me enthusiastically.

As we walked down the hundreds of courthouse steps, he said, "How did you like the red hair on that Justice?"

"It was red, all right."

"Well, that's the color of my old man's hair. My sister's hair isn't quite so red."

"Your *sister?*" I almost shrieked. "You never told me you had a sister."

"I didn't?" he said, immediately coloring clear to his ears.

"No, how old is she?"

"Oh, she's just a kid. Fifteen, I think," counting on his fingers. "Yes, eight years younger than I am."

The surprise about his sister left me stunned for several blocks as we walked to the bus stop that would take us home to the dinner Mary was preparing for us. I couldn't get over it, as much as he'd talked about his brothers. "What is your sister's name, Ray?" I asked.

"Martha Frances, but we call her Frannie." Then he laughed and added, coloring again, "Or Fanny, when we really want to get her goat. She's a little fat." We had reached the bus stop when he said, "I'd rather not talk about her anymore."

White crepe paper hung across my kitchen and a large white bell hung over the beautifully set table, two extra for the only guests invited: Mr. and Mrs. Simms. I was extremely nervous waiting for them. Mr. Simms had left me in cold rebuke when I asked for a loan of $80 to tide Ray over to his new assignment. "My last paycheck will cover it," I assured him.

Then he had told me, almost begrudgingly, "You can pay me back *all* the money I've spent on you — which comes to about three hundred, roughly."

"I'll surely pay you back, but it will take me awhile," I said, surprised at his sudden change of heart.

"Oh, no hurry. It's just that I want you to be aware of how much I've spent, in case you'd forgotten."

I hung up the phone very hurt, thinking that he must have been grooming me to be his *little sweetheart* all along. Now that he'd found out I not only refused his advances but was actually getting married, he sounded almost angry, rather than happy for me as I had expected. But here we all sat, while I opened my only wedding gift — an electric heating pad.

Mrs. Simms remarked, "Frankly, I just didn't know what to get you, Samantha, you seem to have all the essentials already."

"I'm sure I will get much use out of this," I told her, not realizing how prophetic the gift would turn out to be.

"What did your folks say about you getting married? I see they're not here," she asked, adjusting her hearing aid to hear my soft voice between the booming of the two men that sat beside her.

"We are going over there to see them. I didn't tell them ahead of time; you know how it is with us…"

"Yes, Samantha, I do. That's too bad. Oh well, things will work out one day, mark my word. People have a way of getting softer as they grow older."

G oing up the winding back stairwell to this tiny, upper flat that Daddy and Charity called home, I was embarrassed to have to bring Ray to such a rundown neighborhood, although the house had been recently painted. I was nervous as I knocked on the door. Ray still had on his uniform from our wedding, but they knew him immediately, since they had heard him preach at *Fellowship Baptist*. "I would like you both to meet my husband, Ray Malorry. I think you might remember him," I said, before they had time to speak.

Charity was nervously untying her apron and pulling her hair out of her face from the dinner heat, apologizing for her messy appearance as she went. When she heard the word *husband,* her eyes became large and her mouth flew open. Then she said, "My, you *are* a brave man to hook up with *this* one," squeezing Ray's arm and giving him a knowing look, as though to say, *What I couldn't tell you...*

Daddy seemed to sense the silence Charity's words had brought to the room and immediately walked over to Ray and grabbed his hand, shaking it energetically. "My what a fine preacher, but I see you got caught by Uncle Sam, too, huh? Well, come in. Come in. Samantha did you say you was *married?"*

"Yes, Daddy. We were married today."

"My, you didn't tell us."

Our visit was a short one, even though Charity laughed quite often at Ray's good humor as he told them about being accepted in CIC. As we headed for the door, Charity said to him, "Well, I do believe that Samantha has gone and found someone who can out talk her, and *that's* something."

If I can just keep Charity from finding out about my pregnancy, I thought, as we left. But I'd worry about that down the road.

It was only a few short days before Ray called me long distance from Baltimore and told me to "get yourself on a plane and get out here; I want you here."

While I was busy selling off the furnishings of my entire apartment and setting up a court date to ask permission of the court to take Sharon with me, Huey was suddenly released from the state reformatory. At the court hearing, my attorney told me I had to make sure Huey had at least one visit before I left town.

We were in the Simms living room for that prescribed visit. Huey had not grown any taller, and his added weight made him look even shorter. He had long wide sideburns and a shaggy mustache. He was still as quiet as ever as he sat across from us, Sharon leaning over, looking at him shyly, hanging onto me with one hand. I was coaxing her to go over and say hello to her daddy. She had recently become very shy and had her finger stuck in her mouth as she walked carefully across the room. With her other hand, she was pulling her flared skirt, catching it by the lacy hem and raising it above her head from behind, playing the coy one as she approached the silent man. Just as she was in reach of him, she bent over, showing her ruffled panties, and smiled at him with a tantalizing smile.

Suddenly, he reached out, grabbed her dress, and abruptly pulled it out of her hand. "Don't pull your dress up like that; everyone can see your panties."

Sharon burst into big tears, running from him to hide her face in my lap. She would not budge an inch again.

Huey finally stood up to leave, and as he walked to the door, he commented on what a crybaby she was.

"Well, she *is* just a baby, Huey."

"Yeah. Well, now's the time for her to learn that stuff." He walked out the door, never even turning around to look at his child again or to say goodbye.

A letter finally came from Bonnie. She had started writing it weeks before and kept adding to it, just too busy studying, she said

The last weekend before I left Milwaukee, I attended my last *Youth For Christ* rally. Sitting near the rear, Sully came in and slipped into the seat next to me. He started to put his arm around me, and then he spied my rings. He grabbed my hand and shook it, laughing. "What in the world is this?" When he offered me a ride home, I took it. I had wanted to tell him goodbye anyway and I hoped for a chance to do it in person. He got out of the car to walk me to the door, but I stood at the curb, under the street light, and talked to him. When I told him it was Ray I had married, and that I was pregnant with his child, Sully's answer stunned me. "Why didn't you tell me, Sam? I would've married you in a minute." He put his arms around me then and hugged me and wished me the best of happiness. "Don't take anything from him; just let me know. I'll always be here," he said, as he walked back to his car.

He couldn't have loved me, I thought, almost in tears, realizing what a friend I had in him. I remembered having almost the same conversation with Tony, two days after I was married. The license was in *The Milwaukee Journal*, and Tony, stationed in New York, happened to have bought that particular paper and had excitedly called me long distance. *Where had I been all the time, thinking no one cared for me? First Joel, then Tony, and now Sully.* I felt sad, realizing all of this so late, but I'd made my choice. "The die is cast," Mr. Simms liked saying. My life as Mrs. Ray Malorry had already begun; there was no turning back.

The plane was going into its descent, and the shift in speed sent me into the ladies' room vomiting, despite the Dramamine I'd taken. As I cleaned my face with cool water and redid my makeup, I was pleased at the reflection I saw of a trim figure in a fuchsia red linen box suit, the shade of red in which Daddy always liked to dress me. White angora covered the mandarin collar. I had to admit the color complemented my dark complexion and the dark hair that I had managed to pull straight back off my face into a tight bun. As I looked into the mirror checking my lips I thought, I must have been out of my mind, accepting an invitation to visit Ray's family in Porter on my way to my new home in Baltimore, *alone,* after having only three honeymoon nights together. Going to meet the Malorrys under such circumstances, with only Sharon as my shield, seemed suddenly outrageous to me. But Ray had insisted that his younger brother, Matt, would take good care of us and to not be afraid. "They'll love you once they meet you," he had assured me.

Sharon wore the tiered ruffled dress I'd made her, and lace-trimmed panties and socks. I carried her down the steep stairs from the plane, afraid of what to expect, but my fears subsided when I recognized Matt Malorry instantly. He looked like a miniature copy of Ray. As he came through the gate to take Sharon from me, I was thinking, "*A carton of cigarettes and a six-pack of beer, and I can't do a thing about it, huh?*" But my smile gave no hint of my thoughts as I extended my free hand, cheerfully saying, "Hi. You must be Matt."

He took my hand while hugging me and then reached for Sharon. "God, what a beautiful kid," his affection so genuine, Sharon responded with both arms around his neck. "Hey, my brother better watch out," he said to me over the back of Sharon's head. Then to her he said, "I'm your new uncle Matt, what do you think of that?" returning her hug. Then Sharon kissed him full in the mouth, with no reservation, her eyes literally dancing at his warmth.

He turned to me then and looked me over admiringly as he let out a low whistle, saying, "My brother did it again; he never had an ugly girl in his life." I knew Matt was six months younger than I, but his youth really surprised me, suddenly making me feel ancient as well as forgiving. His eagerness to take care of us and the enthusiasm with which he met Sharon had already put me at ease. I had forgotten that Ray had told me how small he was, so I blurted out, "You look just like your big brother — with his legs sawed off," giggling in relief.

"Hey, I tell everyone, I'd rather be a little shit than a big turd any day of the week," he said, with a cocky air that I would learn to expect from him.

I screamed with laughter and knew immediately I was with a Malorry.

We were only in the house a few minutes when the red-headed Jake, the father I had heard so much about, appeared. I was standing at the kitchen sink sipping a glass of Verner's ginger ale to ease my stomach. The sight of me lit up his face, and he grabbed me with a generous hug and bellowed in my ear, "My, what good taste that son of mine has. Why, you're downright pretty, Sam."

I could see Matt over his shoulder, grinning as he held Sharon. Jake turned around and seeing Sharon, he said, "Lookie here, what have we got?" and he reached out and took Sharon in his arms. She knew very few strangers.

Jake recognized my nervousness as I waited for my new mother-in-law to return from work; we were standing in the kitchen having our drinks. Jake was into his third beer when he drew me close and whispered into my ear, "Don't you worry none about the *old lady* — *her* old lady had to get married at fifteen, so you don't have to fret none. You aren't the first to go through this, and you can be darn sure you won't be the last." He winked with a burst of laughter, and gave me a hug.

Then I remembered Ray saying about his dad, "My dad believes in calling a spade, a spade." I was beginning to see a remarkable resemblance between the man I had just married and this hearty, robust man my little Sharon was already calling Grandpa.

The loud and dramatic, although beautiful, Frannie had taken Sharon over. Her long strawberry hair hung in loose waves down her broad back, and her large blue eyes sparkled as she talked, much like her older brother's. Her resemblance to Ray was remarkable but not as immediately noticeable, her being a girl. Although she was a tall girl, and could carry considerable weight, her small bones accentuated the layer of fat the girl carried about her body. She had obviously been overweight for years, as her muscles were firm. She seemed to be either laughing boisterously or crying in sobs. Either way her presence was seen, heard, and felt at all times, never leaving anyone to question whether she was around. She met Sharon and in a few minutes had taken her to meet all the neighbor children, to the store for chewing gum, and back home again with stories to tell of every little adventure, and repeat every word Sharon had uttered. I had never experienced such attention, and the feeling of warmth already growing inside of me at the sight and sound of my new family was only cemented when Tillie, my new mother-in-law, put her arms around me to welcome me fully to her family, "such as we are."

I had expected reticence or aloofness from Mrs. Malorry,

both from the letter she had written and from her questioning words about the child I carried; they had cut deeply. But in person, she gave no hint of disapproval as she went about the house showing me our bedroom, and the bathroom toiletries we should use as "one of the family."

The middle brother, Rich, "the mischief maker" Ray had called him and the image of his mother with his large brown eyes and dark hair, made my acceptance complete as he warmly hugged and kissed me immediately upon our meeting, and every encounter after that, whether it be on the stairwell or going out the door. The affection that he and Matt both showed us was like we had never before experienced, not even in the Schultz household. Already they were planning to take us up to the cottage to visit Grandma O'Toole. It seemed this family had no reservations – and it was plain, they loved and adored Ray.

As I lay awake long into the night, that last night in Ray's parents' home, feeling very close to the young man I had married only a month before, sleeping in the bed that had been his for most of his life, I was pleased at the warmth in which I had been received. Still a bit shy with the talkative Tillie, I rarely got a chance to finish a sentence before she would interrupt with, "Well, my dear, let me tell you so and so about *that…*" Or, "Mind you, I'm no authority on the subject, but I have reason to believe…" I had always been a good listener, and hearing stories into the night about Everett, Richard, Matthew, and Martha Frances was a most enlightening experience. Tillie also told me about her own beloved father and the consternation with which she was dealing with her aging mother. She told me how Ray evaded responsibility and how she believed he would never have married without being forced to. In fact, she went on to say, "His father had always said the only reason he went into the ministry was to avoid the draft. You see, he would never have had to have served, and I really think that is the reason he volunteered — to prove to his dad otherwise. Of course, Everett has started a lot of things, too, that he left unfinished, like his college education." There was a sneer on her lips and anger was in her large brown eyes as she mentioned this, but her surprising but very Irish use of the "s" word, completely out of character and one I would hear often, struck me in my funny-bone so that I had to bite my lip to keep from giggling. "That little *shit*, why, he has sat around here for two years on and off with that measly little correspondence course for one subject. That's all he had to do to get his degree, and it still sits up there on his dresser." She then laughed aloud, adding,

"But I think he just might finish this Army thing — three years he's signed for." Suddenly the tears began to roll down her cheeks as she declared him to be the subject of her daily prayers. "He's a hard one; God will deal with him, though." And then smiling through her tears, she continued as though tears were not unusual. "I always did say, to get Everett's attention, you have to knock him down first. Maybe that's what God is going to have to do," she said, almost with amusement. A small woman, under five feet, wearing trifocal glasses, when she looked up into my face she had to put her head way back in order to see me through the lowest lens. This made her already large eyes appear even larger, and showed the bulging effect that Ray, without question, had inherited. The woman's conversation never seemed to find an end, but I was eager to learn everything I could about my new family.

When I told her how surprised I had been to hear so late about Frannie, Tillie turned to me in quick defense of her son and then shared with me the bitterness she had felt in finding herself pregnant with the last child, five years younger than Matt.

"I had all I could handle, and their father," she said through pursed lips, "was drunk more than he was sober. Now mind you, he's always supported us, but that is *all*, and what I didn't need was another *baby*." She described the resentment the three boys had felt towards the interference of a "girl" into their play. "I found myself sending her off down the street with a cookie to play with the Mexican family. *There* she was accepted. What was one more child to *them?*" she said, with a touch of sarcasm. "And so she learned to speak Spanish from them and they fed her, and fed her, and fed her. I have to take the blame, I was just too glad to be rid of the problem. By the time she was five years old, she was so fat the boys laughed at her already, and so that is how it went. God forgive me," she said, as again the tears would roll. "If I ever get her raised, it'll be a miracle, because God knows I get no help from Jake. I complained once when he spanked her too hard when she was very tiny, and he's never laid a hand to her since." Again she had her upper lip pursed over her teeth. "But thank God, he has never shirked in disciplining the boys, and they do respect their dad to this day for that, if for nothing else."

Jake seems such an amiable sort, I thought, lying waiting for sleep that would not come. His joviality seemed unending, even when he was sober — in the mornings and the first afternoon I had met him, when he had come straight from work. But I didn't know the hardship this woman suffered, I thought. I could not judge the anger and bitterness that were never very far from the surface, awaiting an outlet to spew forth in either venom or tears. I made a vow to myself, right there in Ray's childhood bed, that I would never stay in such a marriage *for the children*, as Tillie stated many times she had done.

The emotional fuse that was always waiting to be lit when the whole family was together was almost more than I could handle, and I'd left one meal for my bedroom when Matt and his father came up out of their seats at each other over the labor union. Matt didn't like being told what to do by men not his bosses. And his father roared, "You damn well better be glad you got'em, or you'd be making pea shit instead of the decent wages you're making." Matt had come looking for me and told me I'd have to get used to "this Irish family." I was beginning to already, but my warmest feelings of all were for the old lady, Grandma O'Toole. She'd somehow reached me without a lot of words. She showed me the beautiful afghan she had started for Everett, and as we sat and crocheted alone together, she told me what a good choice she thought her grandson had made in a wife. "But I'm sure you'll never hear it from his lips," she said. "In fact, the best way to know what Everett is saying to you is take what he says and just reverse it, and you'll come closer to the truth that way. He's a *funny* one, but I love 'em all, and that one's special to his maw, you know, Sam, being the first. She had such a hard time deliverin' him. She be's so little, and him so big, and then Jake, out on a three day toot, he helped her none on that score." We sat and rocked and chatted over little things as our fingers kept pace with each others'; we both loved anything with a needle.

Having so much to share with my waiting husband the next day, and my excitement at seeing the new apartment Ray had rented, kept my eyes from closing till the wee morning hustle and bustle of the household was heard.

It was very early, and I got up to use the bathroom. As I walked around the corner, I was surprised and embarrassed to find Tillie standing fully nude in front of the bathroom sink, braiding the long dark hair she wore wrapped around her head. I turned abruptly, apologizing for my intrusion. But this middle-aged fleshy woman spoke to me as though nudity was as common as wearing clothes. "I've been up since four a.m. to take my pain shot — I get up early and iron so I'm sure to be wide awake for work at seven, those sleeping pills, they make it hard for me to get going otherwise. Come on ahead; don't mind me."

I had never faced a bare body other than Bonnie's in the

shower — when I'd been likewise bare – in my entire life. Not standing-up-conversation-bare. I did not quite know how to handle it. Visions of Daddy shouting at Charity for running around in her slip passed through my mind. *What would he have done if Charity had taken to doing something like this?* Leaving my mother-in-law's *shamelessness*, I crawled back into bed – that, and my lack of sleep, was making me feel sick.

Hours later, I woke up to the birds' chirping, the sheer curtains blowing in the breeze, and the sunlight in my face. Frannie was looking down at me, holding Sharon and bursting with the latest tale of their morning. "And you better get busy, or you'll miss your plane, and my big brother wouldn't like that." She turned to leave, and just as she was almost out the door, said, "Ma called, she's taking you to the airport. Matt and Rich, neither one, could get off work."

Nervously, I walked through the gate towards the plane that was to take Sharon and me to our new home. My arms were filled with packages, and the diaper bag on my shoulder was weighted down with a whole batch of fried chicken. I turned to my mother-in-law, who had treated me so kindly and had taken Sharon and me into her family. "I really appreciate all you've done for us this week, all the little things you bought for Sharon, and me too. I feel like I just laid around and let you wait on me. I don't know when I've been so tired and took so many naps. I'm really not lazy, believe me, it's just because I'm pregnant."

Tillie took me by the arm and, tilting her head back and looking up at me through her trifocals, she said, "Honey, when you're married to a Malorry, you'll *always* be pregnant."

We laughed and hugged and Sharon took the small package full of gum and licorice that her new grandmother held out to her. "She likes that so much. You don't mind, do you, Sam?"

Feeling my face turn pink and not wanting to be disagreeable in parting, I lied and said, "Oh no, it's all right."

Then Sharon and I got into another big giant bird for our second airplane trip that week.

The plane had settled into the clouds, the seat belt lights had gone off, Sharon had fallen asleep, and I was saying goodbye to the past. I had been too nervous to give it much thought on my very first flight, to Porter. Having that traumatic bridge behind me and only the clouds to look at, my mind let in the crowds of thoughts I'd been keeping out.

My life had been filled with such activity the last weeks, I had very little time for reflection; now I could look back. As I did, I realized I wouldn't miss anything I'd left behind. Saying goodbye to the ugliness, I didn't know then I was throwing away the good with the bad, and that it would take a lifetime to reclaim it. The past seemed filled with nothing but pain and sadness, surely, the future held promise of something different. Truly beginning my life over, with a complete new slate, is what I believed then, but that was before I knew about repression and behavior patterns. Little did I know that the husband I chose and the children I bore would serve to reflect the lost parts of myself, forcing me, eventually, to deal with the emptiness I thought they would fill.

This new humorous way of looking at things... The Malorrys had enthusiasm for every minute of life; laughter seemed to always be one breath away whenever I was with any one of them. They told me, too, how Ray had talked about me from the minute he came home from Winona Lake and broke up with Jenny. Unlike me, they did not seem in the least bit surprised at our marriage. *Would I always be the last one to know?* as Grandma O'Toole suggested I might be? "You'll never hear it from him" she'd said, "but it'll be a deeper love than anyone else will ever give you," I remembered, as I dozed peacefully to the drone of the aircraft.

The pilot woke me, "Ladies and gentlemen, we'll be landing in Baltimore in just twenty minutes..."

Sharon said, "Are we there, are we there, Mommy?"

Combing her pony tail and straightening her anklets, I said, "Yes, Sweetie, we're there."

To keep back the nausea, I took some deep breaths and laid my hand over my tummy. My new baby, a Malorry child, was my ticket to paradise. As the aircraft touched down on the Baltimore runway, I thought, *I hope I'll be worthy.*

◆

CHAPTER TWELVE

A "Christian" Thing: 1957

The camera was all ready, the table set, the aroma of Irish potatoes baking in the oven, near done. Sharon was outdoors riding her trike, and new little Suzie had her face in the blanket, down on the clean, black tile floor, having just scrubbed it on my hands and knees. Suzie was waiting for her Gerber's beets and applesauce to warm up on the stove. That morning, Ray had worn his new cotton cord, wash n' wear suit and his first straw Stetson to work. He looked so cute when he left, I decided right then to get a picture for our album, but mainly to send to his mom. *I'll have to catch him when he comes through the door; otherwise, he'll never stand still for the camera.*

Suzie was hungry and beginning to let the world know it. Only four months old, she had just begun eating vegetables. To establish her feeding schedule close to the family's, so that she would graduate to table food as quickly as possible, was my immediate goal; Gerber's was a mite expensive on an Army corporal's pay. Always a careful planner, but today it seemed to have gone awry. It was after five and still no sign of Ray.

The baby food was stirred and the flame under the pan of water turned off when I saw Ray's car pull into the parking lot. It was a long way out to the front of the apartments, but Ray was always in a hurry; he walked so fast I could rarely keep up with his long legs. Grabbing the camera, I made sure the flash bulb was in tightly. Looking through the lens to focus on the screen door just as Ray, carrying a dry-cleaning bag slung over his shoulder, came through it, I remembered then, he said he would be a minute or two late coming home. He was thoughtful about such things, unlike his father who never got past the corner pub, said Ray, who seemed determined to be different; and he was. Every day was a new experience with him, and I wanted to capture each and every moment to share with my new mom. With our first wedding anniversary just around the corner, Ray was making me so proud, although our new friends and neighbors thought we were old marrieds. Sharon, having just passed her fourth birthday, everyone assumed we had been together all that time. My divorcee status was not something either one of us wanted known. Since Sharon looked so much more like Ray than she did her mommy, and Suzie's early arrival, only eight months following our marriage, was even more shameful, it was easy to let people think what they would. Away from both our primary families, there was no one around who knew. And surely I wasn't about to burst this bubble of happiness by blabbing, *no sir-ee.*

Ray had his hat shoved back to his hair line, so you could see his face. His tie was pulled away from his unbuttoned collar; Georgia was hot in April. Ray was proud to be in civilian clothes, his *undercover uniform* in Army Intelligence. The flash from the camera blinded him for an instant. He was looking down, searching for Suzie, who, by this time, was screaming full throttle; she had a terrible, terrible temper, already!

Ray threw the cleaning down on the couch and walked over to her. "Hey, what is all this fussing about, here youngun," he said in his normally loud voice. "Do you want me to spank your little butt and give you something to *really* cry about?"

The gruffness was obviously overdone and supposed to be funny. But it wasn't, not to me. Ray thought he was a regular Ralph Cramden, the blustery, bossy character Jackie Gleason played on *The Honeymooners,* his favorite TV show. Ray just didn't know that I was a three-year-old at heart who took everything literally. Just the sound of him made my heart take a fast leap. Putting down the camera, I raced Ray to little Suzie and grabbed her up into my arms. "Don't you *ever* lay a hand on this child, not *ever!*" I said, holding my new baby tightly to my breast. By this time my heart was pounding so hard I felt I was in a marathon; tears came tumbling out. Holding Suzie close, I was actually sobbing, as flashes went through my mind of Sharon at only two-weeks old being held over the second-floor banister by her drunken father, Huey, who was threatening to drop her. But of course Ray couldn't have known; I had consciously forgotten myself. Nor was I aware of the new and fierce protectiveness that had begun to mushroom within me that day, despite the rosy glow I was feeling with my new husband.

Ray grinned. He seemed to love getting a rise out of people, *especially me.* "You know I was just kidding," he said.

"No, I didn't know! And *she* surely didn't, from the tone in your voice. Besides, you just don't kid like that, *ever!*"

"Yes, ma'am!" he said in a mocking tone. "Can I hold her now?"

Playing the penitent child eased the encounter somewhat, but it was the gingerly way I relinquished her hold which let him know this child was not a joking matter. It felt as though I loved her so much it hurt inside – so much so that I sometimes almost felt a little guilty, if I really let myself remember how I had succumbed. Finally staying home and being a regular mom, I was able to give this new baby the love and attention that time or energy never allowed for Sharon.

Saturday night was our special TV night together, but Sharon and I had different ideas than Ray on what to watch, who, of course, made the decision: *The Honeymooners* is what we watched. One Saturday night, a little hurt, and since it was *my* TV I had paid for on credit $10 a month before we were married, I said, "We always *used to* watch Perry Como, you know, and I would think you could give in once in awhile."

"Yeah, Daddy," Sharon piped up. "I think you're mean to not let us watch Perry Como."

"Well, when I die, you can put on my gravestone: *Here lies the meanest Daddy that ever lived.*"

"Well, when you die, Daddy, we are going to watch Perry Como!" Sharon answered without a moment's hesitation.

It was with excitement that we were able to move to a *real house*, now that we had our first car (on *my* credit), and I had gotten my first driver's license. Driving to the Commissary and PX on my own was a very special thing, having ridden city buses my entire life.

The house was a pretty little place that had a huge back yard, and a sidewalk in front, so Sharon could skate. It was not far from the Army Post, and just around the corner from the school; Sharon could walk to kindergarten. This place was furnished much nicer, and I took care of it like it was my own.

When we had looked at it the first time, the house was filled with roach and mice droppings all over it. But I cleaned it up quickly, like the German I was, debugged and demoused it. Already I had learned what "draws the little varmints," Daddy called them, pop bottles and bags. The bugs love the glue in the bags and the sugar left in the bottles. "Keeping a house good and clean is the main thing that deters them," I explained to Ray. We never saw a trace of either again.

This house had one furnace vent on the floor of the central hall that joined the two bedrooms, a very large living room, and the kitchen overlooked the yard with roses that bloomed all year.

Finally I had learned to live with the heat and humidity after the Milwaukee cold. Having the luxury of hanging laundry outdoors year 'round kept me in shorts, my legs very tan. We had nice neighbors, too.

The Hutches were in their sixties, retired, and originally from Tennessee. I loved hearing Ms Hutch talk; she sounded so much like my grandma E. and all my southern relatives, many still there. Tennessee had a special accent that I remembered. Dialect is like music. After a person is there, in the South awhile, one learns to be able to tell the difference in sound between the different states. As a child, in the 4th and 5th grades, I had lived right here in Georgia, outside Atlanta. The fact that Sharon would be starting school here come fall, and under the name Malorry, was extra special for me.

Because Ray had started adoption procedures, the school let Sharon use the Malorry name so she wouldn't have to be confused with the change later on; the school was good about that. Divorce was on the rare side in the '50's, especially in the heart of the Bible belt.

The adoption was going fairly well. The lawyer told us it no doubt would not be contested, with Huey's criminal record. Nevertheless, we were required to publish the information in the newspaper to give him a chance to pay up what he owed, never expecting him to respond personally. When the letter came from Huey, giving up his rights in exchange for being free of child-support payments, we were thrilled, although I did worry how Sharon might feel about this, down the road. Sometimes I would wonder if we had done the right thing. At least if Sharon didn't have that letter that gave her up, she might have grown up believing her birth-father cared a little. But, right then, we both were caught up in having a normal family, like everyone else. In all the world, this is what I wanted most, to be ordinary — not continue to stick out like a sore thumb by always being different. The school accepted the explanation until after the waiting period, paperwork, and legal fees were taken care of. Ray seemed to be very sure about wanting to do this, he loved Sharon, at least as much as he loved me, I believed. Ray let people know how he felt. Maybe not to me personally so much, but I was told often how he bragged on us.

With the terrible, fearful beginnings that wrought Sharon's babyhood – the constant moves, police protection, peace warrants, court hearings, my going to work two jobs in order to earn enough at age sixteen to support the two of us, and forcing me to use many different baby sitters – Sharon had missed a full-time mother. But when Suzie came, I *had* the time, the energy, and I showered my new baby with attention every second. Sharon was right beside me, of course, so she wouldn't feel left out.

Our first Christmas together, I spent in the hospital. Hotdogs were Ray's specialty, which he fixed for Sharon, beginning a life-long Christmas Eve tradition. Three days later, I arrived home bringing with me a very special Christmas. Thinking I could outsmart the sibling rivalry bit with Sharon, inside a cardboard box, lined in a soft green satin quilt, was baby Suzie, who was put under the Christmas tree. "See, God sent you a real live baby instead of a doll. Look, she really cries, and wets, and she can love you back," I told Sharon. Having a sister was a dream I had carried in my heart since losing my own little sister while yet a baby myself. Sharon was so excited, especially when she was allowed to hold Suzie, feed her, and push her baby carriage.

My newly formed family made me so proud, and going to Rich Malorry's graduation, at Bob Jones University, would provide the perfect opportunity to show them all off.

Suzie was our very special something, between her mommy and daddy. She started walking when she was eleven months old. That first time, Ray had just come home from working his second job in sales, on a Saturday evening. Sharon and I were sitting on the couch, and he was in the big arm chair across the room. The footstool was in front of it; Suzie was standing up next to it, like she usually did, holding on, when I called her. Suzie started walking over to me then. The instant she reached my safe lap, Ray would call her back. Suzie just giggled in delight, and her walking really took off; no more holding on to anything. She was so proud of herself, too. She would pull a book down off the shelf and stand on it, balancing on one foot. "Look at that smart little thing," Ms Hutch would say, squealing in delight right along with us. Ms Hutch would come for coffee sometimes, but mostly we played Gin Rummy – with Mr. Hutch: the four of us – after the girls were asleep.

When Suzie would wake up with dry diapers, she was put right on the potty. In a couple weeks, she was fully trained. Fearing an accident, when we went to play cards at some friends house and the girls were put to bed, Suzie still had a diaper in her training pants at night for a few months, or to church, but it was a senseless worry.

Suzie gave up the bottle on her own. She would always throw it out of her crib after she emptied it. That last time, when she threw it out, still full, she never got another one. She was drinking out of the *sucky cup* anyway and eating everything else. Suzie seemed to be as healthy as I knew how for her to be. Very short legged, Suzie was cute and funny, and looked like Ray with the same mischievous dance in her large blue eyes. Her hair was golden and she had just enough of it to gather into a rubber band, which held a big hair ribbon on the top of her head. Cameras were kept loaded to catch her mammoth balancing act, or walking under the kitchen table without a bend in her knees, she was so tiny.

Once, when I walked by the bathroom as Suzie was supposed to be sitting on the potty, toilet paper literally covered the floor to her knees, all around her. The instant Suzie saw me, she grabbed the tip of some tissue, bent over, and stuck it between her legs, all while looking me straight in the eye without blinking. Nary a word did I breathe, instead, I quietly left the doorway, and snuck the camera out of the nearby closet. In a minute, I walked by again. Sure enough, Suzie reacted in the same way, and her cute baby trick was captured on film; what a picture!

And more pictures, which I sent proudly to Ray's mom and dad. It was their approval I lived for, I would later realize. They seemed to be crazy about their oldest son, and his family too, when their old stereo, inside a beautiful cabinet, with the latest sound tracks to movies arrived at our door at Christmas, all the way from Porter, Michigan. But it was the *Blackwood Brothers'* albums that seemed to please Ray the most, as he loved country music like his Missouri-born dad.

In short, the Ray Malorrys were a perfect little family, and Suzie had taken us over. Her birth snapped Ray out of a kind of sullenness that, at the time — before we would learn about depressive illness – I attributed to the shame I assumed he carried for our "shot-gun marriage."

It started out innocently enough, just not correcting people's assumptions. But when we began playing bridge with one of our first neighbors, Bill and Nancy Broom, Ray's fabrication of events became so fanciful that I grew more uncomfortable, until finally one day I just blurted out everything to Nancy and confided to her about the lie we had been living. Since Bill and Ray were stationed at the same Army Intel unit and had car pooled together, leveling with her served to ease things considerably for Ray – that, and getting our own car and a set of golf clubs.

Eventually Ray bowled in a league, and pitched softball, bringing his teams to championship. But as tired as he was, he would bounce out of bed in the mornings, whistle while he shaved, and pat me on the behind every chance he got. Despite his lack of verbal declarations of love, he had all the signs of a happy man. This, I attributed mainly to the adorable child we had made together, who seemed to have her daddy's blue eyes and his zany disposition.

It was easy to see how happy I would be at the BJU graduation, not only to be with Rich, but also to see Bonnie, my old friend from Milwaukee, again, now married to one of the professors and living right on Ray's college campus Bonnie had told me so much about.

Rich was always happy, affectionate, and full of silly humor. He would whisper encouragement into my ear whenever Ray would say something unusually unkind. Rich's big brown, puppy-dog eyes lent an innocence to him that, coupled with his humor, managed to soften even the hardest of hearts; he was definitely in my corner. Our friendship had grown considerably the previous summer. During an out-of-state softball championship where Ray was the star pitcher, he had sent us up to his parents, in Michigan, for a vacation. Those weeks up to Grandma O'Toole's cottage, Rich took me everywhere: trout fishing, even roller skating one night. On his way back to school in South Carolina, for fall term, Rich had driven us back to Atlanta. To save money, we had stayed in the same motel room – in twin beds, of course, with Sharon and me in one bed, and Suzie in her car crib between us. We were polite to each other, and I never thought a thing about it being improper. Ray had worked it out so he could play his ball without leaving his wife home alone. Ray was very thoughtful that way, at least that is how I looked at it at the time – until later when he got home and proudly bragged about going to the bar and meeting the WAC... Still, it didn't spoil all the many hours Rich and I had together on that trip, to talk about the crazy mixed up way Ray and I had finally ended up together, after Ray's engagement four long years to someone else. Up until then, I never put worries about other women into conscious thoughts, but underneath there was that feeling of not being sure, ever, besides being on the edge always with Ray's biting, seemingly angry, tongue. This problem would cease, I believed, when he would resolve his feelings for God and the preaching ministry he had left behind. Anyway, up to that point I had not been the object of Ray's verbal sting, but I walked on egg shells. Rich was convinced that turning the other cheek – "Don't *you* give Ray any reason to be mean to you," he'd say – was the best way to deal with the cutting, but always witty, sarcasm.

It was exciting to see both Rich and Bonnie again, but I dreaded Bonnie's judgment. For surely, after adding up our total months of marriage, she would know that we had done it, *the hush-hush thing,* something that certainly a "Bob Jones boy" should *never* do before marriage. Never mind that *it* brought forth a beautiful, healthy, happy baby girl.

"Where do you go to church now?" Bonnie *did* ask.

"Oh, I go to the Protestant chapel, on Post," neglecting to relate how often, or *seldom* I went. Having to face the Sunday morning ritual of pleading for Ray's company, which would end up in hot dispute, but more often into tears of rejection, it became an excuse to stay home. So I attended less and less, and de-emphasized the *I,* hoping Bonnie wouldn't launch into an always appropriate sermon on marrying "out of the will of God," or some such thing. If she did, though, I was ready with all the right words: "God is working in Ray's heart; the Lord will find a way to melt his stubbornness." And of course my favorite stand-by, "All things work together for good..."[15] Believing that, how I believed, is what kept me going. And Rich, intent on assuming the ministry Ray had left behind, was a catalyst for my faith.

Returning to the Fundamentalist Christian environment that had originally brought us together, I began to feel the old prudish scrutiny at work again, or still, and somehow we both seemed to unconsciously shift gears, fighting to hide our exultant pride and excitement bursting within. *Shame on us,* God seemed to say; *shame on us,* Dr. Bob surely would say. Shame seemed to echo through the walls. It sang to us in every hymn, pointed to us in every prayer, and jeered at us in every smile. Secretly, I prayed: *Dear God, what can we do? How can we hide our "sin" when we adore the very breath she breathes?*

Wanting to be the best mother in the world, but only knowing the proper *born-again Christian* way, I felt something very wrong begin to churn away at me inside. But I dismissed it, as I always had, this time chalking it up to the excitement of the momentous occasion.

Sharon captivated her Uncle Rich and her "Aunt" Bonnie. People would often say that Sharon was a "classic," a striking beauty, with her light hair flowing like corn-silk down her back, and her bright, clear, gray eyes framed with black brows and lashes. She could have just stood and smiled, and been adored.

---

[15] The Bible, King James Version, Romans 8:28

But she had such sparkle, under her docile demeanor. "I'm going to be in first grade," Sharon boasted proudly. But she didn't say that it was especially sweet being enrolled as a Malorry, and that when her adoption by Ray would become final very soon, her "daddy" wouldn't have to lie about her name anymore. She carried her little white Bible, and begged to recite the books of the new testament she had just learned. She sang, *I'll be a Sunbeam for Jesus,* while Ray watched, unusually silent, and I unconsciously squirmed at the hypocrisy I was feeling. Otherwise, I was happier than I thought I would surely ever be.

In the middle of summer, a friend of Ray's, a girl from North Carolina, asked to come and stay with us for a few weeks. Leanne was the youngest in her family, a little tyke when Ray spent weekends at her family's place, a short jaunt from the Bob Jones campus. Leanne, just graduated from high school, had turned out tall and beautiful. She was in love with a boy that her well-off daddy didn't seem to think was good enough "for their little girl." Leanne was bound and determined to marry him anyway, but she needed to get away from home to think it through.

The way I was thinking then, I wanted to get some kind of employment to keep up my courage, some temporary vacation relief work for a couple weeks. The job at the switchboard, in a Chevrolet dealership, allowed me to get out of the house and into the public eye, to keep my belief in myself; I needed that. *Having* to go to work before, I didn't want to forget how important that feeling of confidence was, the assurance that I *could* get out there again and make a living if I ever had to. Leanne came in handy that way, and Ms Hutch kept us informed on how good Leanne was with the girls, but also how hateful Sharon was behaving to her little sister, Suzie. Of course, Leanne never said a word, which let the warnings of Ms Hutch fall on deaf ears. *Sharon was a perfect little darlin' that her mommy adored,* and she was special to her daddy, too.

When Ray told Sharon how she was adopted, he had taken exceptional care. Holding her on his lap, he told her that out of all the little girls in the world, she was "picked special." He was so proud too, of the way she looked out for Suzie, "as if she were her mother — instead of just her sister," his father, Jake, had remarked on our last visit. *Ms. Hutch is just an old lady – and a troublemaker sometimes.*

It was just about the nicest summer I could have asked for: a husband who was happy, playing his golf games every Wednesday the Army gave him for PT; having a little extra money to buy some store-bought clothes. My first pair of really honest-to-goodness lizigator heels from Riches cost $42.00, with a purse to match, instead of the $5 shoes at Sears I usually bought. Ray made me get them, and said they would last a lifetime. We had company for dinner sometimes, played cards with Hutches, and Ray's married Army buddy and his wife taught us to play Canasta.

We soon started going to a new church, an excuse to get all dressed up, where we met some old Bob Jones friends of Rays: Hugh and Connie Bradley. Connie loved to sew too, and we started having each other over for dinner, sometimes playing monopoly for hours. The Bradley's had a little girl the same age as Sharon. It worked out very nicely with the kids. Meeting them, I was hoping their going to church would rub off on Ray, although he balked at going and I felt guilty staying home. But we did see to it that our girls got to Sunday School. I felt as if we were the best, most careful parents; "doing the right thing" was very important.

One of our former neighbors, the Whites, had moved to Alabama. They would invite us now and then to drive over, an hour away. They lived in a little country farm house that had water piped into the kitchen, with electricity, but still had an outhouse and slop-buckets under the beds, nighttime. That part of it was no fun, but in a way, it gave us something different to look forward to, to appreciate what we had when we got home. The Whites were real farmers, their food all freshly grown, or killed. We had invited them often, but they could rarely leave the animals. When they finally did come, Ray and I gave up our bedroom. The White's little boy, the same age as Suzie, still slept in the bed with them, as did some country people. It struck me as being unusual, but being born in a small farmhouse myself, still sleeping with Daddy after moving up North well after beginning first grade, my southern beginnings were no different. Wanting the Whites to be comfortable, Ray and I took the living room.

That first night, I was just feeling happy and proud of my family. Sleeping on the couch, I would always remember Ray pulling me down on the floor next to him, and whispering in my ear, "Did you see the doctor today?"

"Yes," I whispered back.

"Is that thing still in you?" Ray asked, biting my ear.

"No, he took it out," I said, snuggling up to him on the hard floor. "I told him you were afraid of hitting it and wouldn't touch me; he said six weeks was long enough to go without sex, said the uterus was tipped back all right now."

We kissed easier then, knowing we could finally *do it*.

By the time we realized we couldn't get to the Delfin cream and the Trojans in our bedroom, for our usual carefulness, I had to stop Ray long enough to talk about it. "Ray, if we do it without using something, it is *that time*, and we planned that for *next* September, remember? This will throw our plans all off." Two pregnancies during the hot summer, and I wanted a nice cool winter one. Besides, Ray's mother had upset me when she declared, "Married to a Malorry you'll *always* be pregnant!" I wanted to prove to her that Ray's wife was more in control of things than that, so she'd know when it happened, this time it wasn't an accident. But Ray was so horny he couldn't have cared if it was the day before yesterday and I was the crack o' dawn, and I so wanted to give him a boy.

Still believing then that praying over things before you did them, no matter what, somehow made them turn out right, in whispers, I prayed and asked God to "Bless us and give us a son, *if you see fit, Lord*," that was the important thing.

Ray usually lost it when the Lord got into it. Guess it was his religious mother or something. But this time he made love like he invented it, right there on the living room floor. I was scared to death someone would get up for the bathroom, sneaking, though, sort of made it feel romantic.

The next day, walking to the mail box, I felt the same familiar tenderness in every bounce of my breasts, so pronounced in my first two pregnancies. That had to be the night Kelly was conceived because the Whites stayed on for two whole weeks. We always teased them that they were responsible for Kelly coming a year early.

It was such a happy time, and proud I had planned the September part. Ray was due to get out of the Army in February, but I never thought much about that part of it. Paying the rent just never seemed to worry me, with Ray around. I knew he would always find a way to work, somewhere. He was very conscientious and I was so proud of him. He had already started talking about reupping, to get that money. The Army would pay him $3,000 in cold cash just to sign on the dotted line for three more years. Hugh Bradley was after Ray to come with *him*, to sell insurance. Hugh was making very good money with a national company. Insurance, insurance, insurance was all we seemed to hear. But Ray was scared to give up the security of the Army, the free hospital care we'd received with Suzie, and, besides, he loved what he was doing, his dream – to be "a spy." He loved it that no one knew he was just a sergeant. The re-up money would give us a houseful of our own furniture for the first time, too, allowing us to move to an unfurnished place, for less rent.

What excitement: A new sewing machine, a second-hand living room set, and with extra beds, we'd be able to entertain when Ray's parents came to visit, come April.

Jake, Ray's alcoholic dad, was in the middle of his only sober year. He'd been hospitalized and had all his blood replaced. Having Jake around, even drinking, was a treat, but seeing him sober, realizing what intelligence, love, and thoughtfulness he had in him, was something special, and it was obvious he loved me. He said, "You can't possibly be pregnant; you just look too good." Sewing all new maternity tops on my first electric Singer, I felt I was blossoming. A favorite one was my own design: white cotton with polk-a-dots of all sizes and colors all over it. My dark Cherokee skin soaked up the Georgia sun so that the bright Orange Frost polish really showed up on my fingers and toes — everyone went barefoot in Georgia! "Why, you look good enough to eat, Sam," Jake said when he grabbed me with his bear hug, patting my full tummy; I even *felt* scrumptious. No nausea to speak of, although I didn't know then that with carrying boys, fewer hormones let you feel so much better, enthusiasm, for every little thing: baking, and eating. June was just around the corner and I was sure it was going to be a boy, *hadn't we asked God for one?* In fact, I was so busy that I didn't notice the subtle change taking place in Ray.

Maybe it was the letter from Rich's new wife, Janine – the second daughter-in-law, and my first rival in the family. Rich had gotten married in September with a big, huge wedding following our last summer vacation, to Michigan. We couldn't afford to stay for it even if Ray really had wanted to. Janine seemed nice, except a little naive – if anyone could possibly be more naive than I was, myself. The first night we all went out together, we were in the car ready to take off, to go out to eat. Ray and Rich suddenly got out of the car and disappeared around the back of the house, into the dark. After a minute, when they came back, Janine kept at Rich. "Where did you go; what were you doing?" Rich kept giving her dumb answers. "We went to see a dog about a horse." We all laughed, but Janine wouldn't give up, insisting. Finally, Rich said, "If you must know, we went to take a leak."

"Outside?" she squealed.

When Rich said, "Yeah, what did you think made Ma's bushes so tall?" the shock of his typical Malorry bluntness sent me into giggles, but Janine burst into tears.

Rich explained later that she was afraid to let him kiss her the first time, because she thought it could get her pregnant. A college student, no less, although only two years the senior, I felt somewhat wiser than my new sister-in-law. Janine and Rich met at school, and Rich was so in love. She was an only child which must have made it doubly hard to have her parents disown her for marrying a Fundamentalist Christian preacher. But she "chose Rich and God," she said. I felt for her circumstances as I had always longed for a family closeness that I never really had, outside of my first in-laws. That's why Ray's family had taken up the slack and had become my whole life, Rich's new wife, now included. We started corresponding then, whenever Janine had time to write.

Rich had gotten a church after graduation; they started right out pastoring. It must have been scary, I couldn't really understand, or the letter from Janine announcing that she had gotten pregnant on her honeymoon; she was due in June also. Her words would be seared into my brain, "We've decided to name him Kelly, and no fair doing pushups to win!"

It was Ray who had chosen the name Kelly, after the little rascal he had at summer camp, in college. "Someday I'm going to have a *Kelly*," Ray would often say, with a twinkle in his eye. When Rich teased, *he* was going to have a Kelly, too, Ray would just dismiss it. But when Janine said that her due date was the 17th and mine was the 20th, it started a slow boil within.

That Rich would do such a thing, since he had always been especially kind and considerate, was what really hurt. As the minister of the family, professing God at every turn, I had put him on a pedestal. But I didn't say much; it wasn't my way. I just made a sure-fire determination that Janine would *not* beat me to the finish, *if it took castor oil...*

It was the 7th of June. Heading down the last stretch, my house was cleaned from top to bottom, floors all done for the month, cabinets, dressers, and closets all neat as a pin. Ray's white shirts were lined up neatly in a row. He wore one for a whole week then, before he started drinking beer to sweat them up, or smoking to turn them black. Clothes for the new little one were all bought or sewed, some saved from Sharon, who was now in third grade, while Suzie was on her occasional happy-time visit to the Post nursery. My suitcase packed, I was ready to have this baby.

The druggist smiled and reached for the sundae dish for my usual fresh peach special. Perched on the stool, more of me hanging off, than on, I held up my hand. "Wait. I'd like that castor oil in root beer," I said.

The pharmacist had been the one to sell me on the idea. "Pregnant women do it all the time. It'll work, if you are ready, but only if you're ready."

"Today, I'm ready," I said, feeling the weight of the baby resting down on my bladder. "The doctor says I've dropped already; I could go anytime. I shouldn't gain too much more either," I said, pinching my fleshy arms.

"It's going to clean you out good," he reminded me, "so you better get home and stay there."

"That's good; I don't want a lot of waiting-around time."

After being in the hospital for hours, the doctor on duty was sitting at my side. "You seem to be especially anxious about something, what is it?" he asked, trying to get to the bottom of why my labor had stopped. By then I was too dilated to send home; I wanted to go ahead and deliver, but my twenty-two-year-old body just wouldn't cooperate. Because I was getting weak and dizzy, I had a needle in my arm giving me glucose. Then is when I told the doctor about the race with my sister-in-law, to delivery.

"I see," was all he said. "Well, we are going to deliver this baby before you get any weaker; I'm going to give you some medication in the glucose."

Only a half hour or so, when the hard pains started, the nurse was close by, watching. I was telling her how quickly I had delivered my last baby, once the pains began like this. "The nurses referred to me as *the quiet one*, so you better get me ready," I told her; but she paid no attention.

Within a short time, the doctor was attending and yelling out instructions: quick this, quick that. I was pushing, and he was cursing, "Stop, goddamn it, pant; didn't they teach you to pant?"

"That was the one thing I never did learn; it always made me dizzy." Then the pains got so bad I *had* to push.

Angrily, the doctor was yelling, "Goddamn it, this is too *fast*. Hold it; hold it. Pant..." Suddenly, I felt the baby slide out of me, while he was cursing. When I heard: *It's a boy,* I forgot all the fuss. "Ray has his Kelly," I said aloud, and promptly passed out.

When I came to in my bed, the nurse was putting in a catheter. "Don't lift your head for the rest of the night," she said. So pleased I was with myself: *My son* was the first grandson in the family; it was only right. Ray, being the oldest and first married, had been the first to make grandparents of Jake and Tillie, even if only by adoption. Sharon was treated as their own; Jake even took her to the pub to show her off, and "my little Suza" (he could never seem to say Suzie) was the cat's pajamas, though Tillie had not as yet recognized the least bit of likeness to any member of her family in this first flesh-and-blood grandchild. Instead, she would bring up the uncanny resemblance between Ray and *that little Sharon*. "If I didn't know better, I'd think Ray had snuck off and been the father. I never saw a child look more like their step-dad." Suzie was another story. It was plain, Tillie would never believe Suzie was Ray's kid. And the hurt went deep for us both, *but this new baby boy would be different.*

When I got home from the hospital with Kelly, I was still not over the ordeal. Fainting for the first time in my life when I tried to stand up, the nurses had kept me quiet, and sometimes would even let me rest right on through feedings, only getting to hold Kelly a few times. He was a beautiful baby with huge dark eyes which darted every which way, as though he wanted to see everything.

There was to be no stairs, doctors' orders. I slept in the living room to be near the kitchen to make formula and wash diapers; Ray could carry me up to the bathroom. Sleeping downstairs, alone, with Kelly beside me in his bassinet, was lonesome, the slant of the couch uncomfortable, and my first night fitful. All of this could have accounted for that terrible, terrible nightmare.

Driving the car alongside a body of water, Suzie was lying next to me on the front seat, just the same as when I was learning to drive with my Sunday School teacher giving me lessons. The car started to go out of control and veer off the road. As the water came rushing into the car, it was pulling us down, down... I was frantic; I just knew Suzie and I were going to drown. All I could think about was getting Suzie out of the car, and safe, but my body was frozen in place; I just couldn't move.

Waking up in a cold sweat, I was terribly frightened. That awful scared feeling, I would never forget, of the dark water slowly overpowering us, and of my utter helplessness.

When I finally got awake enough to overcome the terror, I was very puzzled. Now I had *three* children, *why would I dream about only one, and why was it Suzie, the middle child?* The meaning of it totally escaped me then. *How prophetic would this dream turn out to be, I would later learn!* The ominous feeling never left me, bringing with it questions, questions, tossing around in my brain.

This new baby boy began to preoccupy my every waking moment. Holding Kelly to my hurting, milk-filled breasts those first days, when I put him on my shoulder to burp, instead of cuddling, and sometimes falling asleep like Sharon and Suzie had done, his little head would bounce around as though on a spring. It was as if his little body was on full alert every second; he just couldn't seem to relax. The vague memory of my little brother, Jesse, who died in infancy and who "wasn't right" hovered in the back of my mind, a worry that began to gnaw at me. But I tried to tell myself: *Boys must be different.*

It was Father's Day, Kelly was two weeks old and dressed in his first boy's outfit: blue knit rompers with a billed knit cap to match, which hid the large worrisome protrusion in the back of his head. He was adorable, and his bright eyes were already turning a deep brown, like mine. For the family picture, we all sat on the couch, together. I had on the bright yellow dress with the mushroom buttons dotting my backside that I had on the first night I met Ray. How I had wiggled in church that night. Finally, I had learned that being color blind, yellow was the one color Ray could appreciate.

To celebrate my being able to climb the stairs again, I had planned an outing for the afternoon. Anxious to get Kelly into his pretty crib in our bedroom, where I could be close to my husband, if only physically, for a few hours, I was hoping this was all we needed.

"It's Father's Day," I said. "Can't we go out for a ride and get sloppy Joes?" The Varsity was the only drive-in restaurant then, all the way downtown Atlanta.

Ray wasn't enthused with the idea of going anywhere in the Georgia heat. "*Maverick* is on tonight. You know that's my favorite show! Besides, Father's Day is *my* day."

"It doesn't look like you want to be with us ever, anymore," I said through my tears.

But he didn't move. He just lay on the couch and did his crossword puzzles with the TV going. But I was determined... It was Daddy all over again, having to beg, plead with him for hours, until he finally, unwillingly, *might* give in.

In the car, we had all gotten our food served. I had put my sandwich on the dashboard as I was holding Kelly on my lap with one arm, and holding a chocolate milkshake in the other. Suddenly, Ray turned on the ignition and started the car.

"You're not going to let us finish eating?" I said, bursting into tears.

"I don't want to miss *Maverick*," he said and jammed his foot onto the accelerator.

From the sudden jolt, the milkshake flew all over the ceiling of our nice year-old Chevy and all over Kelly. Ray was cursing, and I was sobbing. Sharon and Suzie were playing invisible in the back seat, not making a sound. *This is your new baby son; what a way to welcome him into this world!* was what I wanted to say. But I was too afraid of pushing him that far again, like that other time; my jaw still ached sometimes. Instead, quietly I wept all the way home – that day, and the next, and the next, in the bathroom I would go to hide the unstoppable tears.

Sometime during those first weeks, after bringing Kelly home, I began to realize Ray had almost stopped talking to me, his laughter gone. It must have begun the day Kelly came that it had all started, I was thinking, that I had done something wrong, that maybe Ray resented this new baby. He would hold him enough, let him lay on his chest while he watched ball games. Sometimes, for hours, they would sleep like that, chest to chest. Or he'd put Kelly on the blanket next to him on the floor. But Ray's sullenness continued, and I blamed it all on myself, for being so headstrong, first in wanting a son in September, then in rushing his birth. Long afterwards, I could hear in my head the doctor's anger during delivery, of his chiding me for my impatience. *Had that too-fast birth hurt Kelly's brain, making his skull protrude so far in the back, before his hair grew over it?* Besides these unspoken worries, I knew he didn't hold right like a baby should, didn't cuddle up to me. I couldn't explain it to anyone, had I tried — something a mother just wouldn't admit to anyone about her baby. *Maybe he'll grow out of whatever it is.*

At six months of age, when Kelly threw his first ball at the Christmas tree and broke half the ornaments I had worked so hard to get on my own that year of my divorce, I was brought to tears, while Ray loudly applauded his son's ambidextrous ability. It was then that I began to think I had made a mistake, that I just didn't know how to raise a son. Ray was just so proud of every little thing Kelly did, no matter how destructive. *How are we ever going to get him raised?* Ray didn't seem to be very understanding of my feelings either -- not really knowing that I had never been allowed to even *speak* to a boy I knew, if I would see one on the street. Daddy's negative opinion about boys, and the behavior of those we had lived with, left me very confused.

Since leaving Aunt Jenny Lou's, upstairs from Grandma, it was at the Nester's house where I first felt a part of a family. The twins, Jan and Ann, were in high school. They loved to do my nails and curl my hair. I was four by then. Carl, their little brother, was a little older than I was. Sometimes he would scare me, telling me, "The Rag Man's gonna get you," and when I'd hear the old man yelling "Rags; rags," coming down the street in his horse drawn wagon, I'd run upstairs into the bedroom closet, and hide, my special place when we played hide and seek. And Carl loved to play chase, even in the house. His mama would yell at us,"Carl, you and Samantha, do not run in this house."

One day, I was running through the kitchen with Carl after me, when Mrs. Nester got really upset, "You're going to make my cake fall," she said, and grabbed me and paddled me. "There now, little lady, you aren't going to get any cake."

Since Daddy's rule was, nobody was supposed to spank me, only him, that night, when he came home, I couldn't wait to tell. "Miz Nester gave me a spanking, and she said now I cain't have any cake." At this, I burst into tears; how I loved cake.

Daddy's eyes started blinking fast. Disappearing into our bedroom, he was emptying our drawers, putting all our things into the car. His bottom lip was jumping when he went to Mrs. Nester to give her money, but she said she just couldn't follow such rules with me being so little. "It's the cake she's crying about, Orin," she said, "Don't you see that?" but Daddy's anger in his eyes made her hush, and take the money.

In the car, my stomach was churning. Daddy was talking fast as he drove, "Aw, it was the best thing, anyway... them girls with their primpin' and wearing all that nail polish."

"But Daddy, it was plain. What's wrong with that?"

"I'll tell you what's wrong with it, it's flirting, that's

what it is, flirting with the devil. Yes, sir, it's
compromising, always in front of the looking glass, all that
hair curling."

His voice trailed off. "Just as well," he was saying
more to himself than to me, as we slowed to a stop in
front of a big, white house that sat close to the street,
this our new home. "Now, Samantha," (Daddy always gave
me last minute instructions) "Listen here, this is the
Coty's house. You remember the Coty boys, don't you?"

My heart just sank. Not *those* boys, I thought,
remembering how the youngest one, Robert, a little older
than I was, had spit at me outside of Sunday School just
the week before.

"Just be nice to Paul, he can't help it he's crippled,"
Daddy was saying. I hadn't seen Robert's teenage brother,
Paul, in a long time; his mother didn't bring him anymore. I
felt so sorry for him.

We were eating breakfast together: me and Robert and
Paul. Always, I was trying to talk to Paul, but he bit his
tongue whenever he tried to talk back to me. Paul's mother
was trying to help him hold the spoon in his bent fingers.
His waggle-y tongue and his drooling made it very hard for
the food to stay in his mouth. Mrs. Coty would sit with us
long enough to get a spoonful in it, and then she'd turn
and go to the sink to continue her dishes. Robert used this
opportunity to throw cereal at me, he was so mean. Even if
Paul was yucky to look at, I knew Jesus loved him; but
Robert was another story; he made my stomach hurt.

Outside, Robert pulled my scarf down, off my head. I
would pull it back up, and he would come from behind and
pull it back down, again. I was trying so hard to be polite in
my new home, even though Robert was holding his nose
shut with his fingers as he danced in and out and around
me, chanting, "Pew. Pew, stinky you. Pew. Pew, stinky
you."

When I was in the bathroom was when Robert did a
really bad thing. After I locked the door, he would wiggle
the doorknob like he was trying to come in. It made it just
too hard for me to go and my stomach hurt worse. But
Mrs. Coty was so busy, she hardly knew there were any kids
around at all. She talked to herself, mostly, or to Jesus

sometimes, but she never seemed to see anything Robert did·

Robert made spit-balls, and with a rubber-band, he would shoot them, first at his brother, and then at me· I just didn't know what to do· No matter what I did, or where I went, Robert was there pestering me in one way or other every minute, indoors or outdoors·

"Shame on you, Robert," I finally said to him, shaming him with my two index fingers, "Ooie, shame on you; God can see you, you know!"

Robert would just laugh, and pull my long curls as he ran around the room holding his nose, saying, "Pew, Pew, stinky you·"

How I hated mean little boys, but I was helpless against them·

Three weeks later, Daddy took me aside and explained that living here had been "temporary," until he could find us another place· I was so grateful that the mass of confusion was soon to be behind me, but the turmoil in my stomach had only just begun·

Since Kelly, *because* of Kelly, it was as if an invisible wall began to spring up between Ray and me. There was no real understanding of the *why?* Ray had been so lively, literally bouncing out of bed in the mornings, not being able to wait to get in the door from work to tell the latest joke or funny story that had happened that day. But *something* had happened; I was not sure exactly what, when, or why? Now it was as though we were worlds apart, when Ray was only inches away. It was like being with Daddy, all over again.

Daddy had deposited Mrs· Kolinski at her front door· She was funny looking because her ankles bulging from dropsy forced her to wear high rubber boots in place of shoes, even in summer· She, like all the other old ladies, adored Daddy· He'd pick one or more up in the car and carry them to church, helping them in and out· Then he'd return them to their old-smelling houses usually with a sweet treat from inside for a thank you· Mrs· Kolinski bragged on what a nice daddy I had and handed me a homemade cookie and an apple·

We were a little ways down the road, and the cookie

looked good· But before I tasted it, I held it to my nose
and sniffed it, when Daddy whisked it out of my hand·

"Give me that," he said and tossed it out the window·
"The birds can have it; no telling what's in it or how long
it has sat there·"

The apple was getting a shine as I rubbed it against my
dress· But Daddy missed nothing· "You can have the apple
after you get home and wash it," he said· Daddy was
careful with me about everything: my baths (he nearly
rubbed the skin off behind my ears), my clothes, my uncut
hair that Mrs Simms had insisted be put into detested
pigtails, my teeth· But my eating he saw to with the
careful, loving diligence he used for Bible reading and praying
– and Bible reading and praying were on my mind, as I faced
another empty "Lord's day·"

I hated Sunday afternoons· We were living at Mr· and
Mrs· Simms house· If Daddy didn't have a headache and wish
to rest – which would mean I had to rest with him and
stay in our small shared bedroom shut away from the rest
of the household – he would probably want to "catch up"
on his Bible reading, in which case I listened· My only hope
was to get him to take me visitin', a southern tradition
Daddy still clung to, though he prided himself that he had
become a Yankee right after I was born· And I definitely was
a Yankee, even though our kin all spoke with that special
gentleness, letting the words slide off their tongues like
sorghum off a biscuit·

"Please Daddy, let's get a hamburger instead of going
home," I suggested, feeling certain if he got into that awful
bedroom I'd never get him out before night church· "Mrs·
Simms is having macaroni and cheese," I said, wrinkling up
my nose· How I hated that yucky stuff· And she fixed it
often since the food rationing from the war had made meat
so scarce· Daddy's extra meat stamps helped a little, but
not near enough· "Look, we're right by that hamburger
place that lets butter melt all over 'em·" I said licking my
lips· Daddy had a soft spot for eating, and it was the only
area in my life where I was allowed to speak my mind· I
didn't have to eat anything I didn't like, ever· To make sure
I got filled up, if it was an especially yucky meal, Daddy
would give me his dessert, while he'd mash butter into

molasses and glob it onto bread· Mrs· Simms got used to that and just kept "Orin's molasses" on the table·

We were just about finished eating hamburgers oozing with the new oleomargarine Hitler and Mussolini's war had brought us, when I proceeded to the next step of changing Daddy's mind· He was looking at the waitress who'd smiled nicely at him, and he was already getting a tract out of his pocket to give her·

"Daddy, couldn't we please go see Uncle Wilbur and Aunt Jenny Lou? Look how long it's been," I said with a puckered lip· "Wonder does she think we got lost, or something?"

"We'll see," he said, not paying much attention· That was his usual answer no matter what it was about, which could mean anything from *No* to *Maybe*, but without some serious begging it would more likely be *No*· He was sorting his tracts that he kept inside a little New Testament in his upper pocket, "where I used to keep my cigarettes," he'd say, patting the bulge in his white shirt· He looked over at the waitress behind the counter and spoke more to himself than to me· "That looks like a nice girl; wonder, does she know the Lord?"

"Are you gonna give her one of the green ones?" I asked, curious· I could tell how bad a sinner he thought someone was by the color tract he picked· The green one said, *What Must I Do To Be Saved?* It had a picture on it of a man on his knees, praying· He usually reserved these for people who smelt of liquor and cigarettes· This girl had on dark red lipstick and bright red fingernail polish "painted up like a Jezebel" so I figured she had a green one coming· But instead he pulled out the thick white one that said, *Where Will You Spend Eternity?* He usually gave that one to nice ladies, shoe clerks, and bus drivers·

He was getting ready to get up to pay the bill and I decided I'd better get him thinking, at least, about where we could go· "Daddy, I wish I could see Maureen and Marilee· I haven't seen them in a long time, not since they moved· Can we? Can we, please?"

Daddy was heading toward the cash register, and I was poking him on the back pocket of his trousers that came just about to my chest· "Please, can we? Please·" I said in the high-pitched whine I used at this particular moment.

He reached behind, grabbed my shoulder and pinched me to Hush, all while speaking to the waitress in his sweet-talk voice. "That was a delicious hamburger," he said and smiled.

"Thank you," she said, reaching for the money he held out to her.

Daddy cleared his throat and reached into his breast pocket and pulled out the tract he'd already chosen. He held it out to her. "Here's a little something for you to read when you're not busy. It's got the name and address of our church stamped on the back of it," he said and turned it over in her hand.

"Well, thank you," she said taking it and smiling down at me.

She was so pretty. I wondered if she came to church, would Daddy drive her home like he did the old ladies? He must have guessed what I was thinking as he steered my shoulders with a firm hold straight to the door, so I couldn't say anything else such as "My daddy don't have no wife." I said that once and got an extra hard pinch with an added angry twist. I was always looking for a wife for Daddy. But I knew it was no use with this girl, not with all that "war paint."

Daddy was fixing the sun visor, and I was up on my knees with my back to the door handle so I could see out. "Daddy, couldn't we just go over to Aunt Jenny Lou's for a minute?" I said in my if-you-love-me-truly pleading voice.

"Well, we'll see," he said and turned the car into a side street that I didn't remember seeing before.

I didn't dare say another word or he might just turn right back the other way and go home. So I watched carefully and noticed all the houses. They were not as nice as the ones on our street; some of them had porches and some didn't. It was early summer and some yards didn't even have grass yet. Others had weeds growing up tall. Mr. Simms kept our grass cut very nicely and up and down the front walk little yellow and black flowers Mrs. Simms would be planting; I liked to watch them work — when they'd let me. Usually they'd tell me to "Run along, now, and play, Samantha Sue." My talking was a "nuisance" when they were busy, and they usually were. So I knew how to be quiet, but I hated it; I had so many questions· Mr· Simms called me *Miss How Come?* Sometimes he'd just give up and say, "If anybody asks you, *How come?* Just tell them you don't know!"

Right then I was trying to be quiet so as not to anger Daddy when he pulled up along side an old, funny-looking house· I looked at it and wondered who lived there· It had been painted bright yellow once, but the paint was dirty and peeling· The large wooden porch looked like it reached all the way around to the back· On it was a rusting, wringer washer, next to which stood an old mattress on end, its ticking covered with circles upon circles of soil and dotted with holes·

"Who lives *here?*' I asked·

"One of God's children," Daddy said as we got out of the car· He instructed me to not touch anything and accept nothing if it was offered·

We followed the sidewalk that led into the back, around the side of the porch· The backyard was filled with litter· Potted plants of every size and shape stood happenstance amongst junk: old cooking utensils, a broken flower vase, and the base of a floor lamp with a bent shade stripped bare· Two small dogs lay sleeping in the sun with their dishes strewn about· A cat was eating heartily out of a small burnt frying pan apparently just put down on the cement walk ahead of us· The dogs, roused, began to bark, and came toward us· I froze and grabbed Daddy's hand· He didn't even slow his step, but instead he waived at them and spoke like he was back on the farm, "Here, now· You git," he said· They both whimpered but settled down to continue their snooze in the sun·

On the porch and barely glancing our way stood a large, stubby-bearded man dressed in a partially buttoned, long underwear shirt· From his dark trousers, button-on suspenders were draped down his sides· He was tending to some washing, wringing out things from a big round wash tub, and I was waiting for Daddy to speak· Instead we kept walking, past a small wiry tree that had some ladies' unmentionables strewn to dry about its branches· Daddy was still holding my hand· I looked around at all the filth and debris as I stepped gingerly, watching where I put my feet·

Daddy stopped, and I looked up· There in front of me was a creature in a wheelchair sitting in the sun, and Daddy was speaking to her· "Well, hello there, Sister Riley· How are you today?"

The woman peered at us from two little specks in the deep-set hollows of her eyes· Her mouth stood open with her tongue quivering, dripping of saliva, just like Paul at our last house· She looked at Daddy and then at me· Her body was small and barely filled the chair· The fingers of her right hand were squeezed together into a contorted fist which shook continuously against her chest· Her left hand lay rigid in her lap clutching the dress she wore, an old feed sack sewn carelessly· Her toes peeked through the holes in her once fuzzy slippers· A look of recognition registered in her eyes· In her effort to respond, the awkward twisting of her tongue distorted the high, tremble-y sound of her words and her pinched up, shaky hand began moving slowly toward me· The movement caught my eye and instinctively I pulled back, hanging on with all my might to Daddy·

He just ignored my fright like he did when I got scared of bees and dogs· Instead, he said, "Sister, God bless you· We came to pray with you today·"

She said something else which Daddy seemed to understand· "Bless the Lord· Be thankful for all things," said Daddy· "The prophet, Job, thanked God for his infirmities· Surely God has a reward for you in heaven, Sister·" I thought he was close to tears·

Suddenly, the man on the porch stopped pouring water into the wash tub· The clothes he had just wrung lay dripping beside him, and water was getting all over his shoes when he turned toward us· The look on his face frightened me beyond words· *He must be the giant at the top of the bean stalk·* I pulled on Daddy's hand, hard· "Let's go, Daddy· Let's go, *please·*"

Daddy gave my hand a sharp, quick squeeze· It was his way of rebuking me quietly unbeknownst to an onlooker· I winced in pain, but I dared not speak again·

Daddy ignored the man staring at us and continued to speak to the woman· "Here are some tracts for you, Sister· Maybe your husband will read them to you·"

As she reached for them, Daddy let go of me and slid

the papers carefully between her paralyzed fingers· She began to speak again, but she stopped when the man took a step in our direction· In an angry voice, the man said, "My wife is well-taken care of and I don't need no busybodies snoopin' 'round·"

Taking a step backwards, Daddy looked over at the man, and spoke in his direction· Daddy's voice was gentle, but firm, "I apologize for any misunderstanding· We are just here to show some concern·"

The man seemed satisfied, and turned back to the dripping clothes·

Daddy took my hand again and tugged at me, pulling me nearer to the woman· When I got closer, I could see she still had a few teeth but her hair was so tangled from lack of care, I was certain I was looking at a witch out of the story books· As we stood next to her, Daddy put my hand on her arm· The skin was warm, but her bones felt so thin I thought they might break· Daddy kept his hand on mine· As she felt our touch, she looked directly into my face and I saw her eyes change· A smile flowed into them, softening those hard specks into pools of warm light· I smiled back at her then, and I was no longer afraid·

As we drove away, Daddy seemed upset· Under his breath he muttered, "Dear God, have mercy· Somehow relieve her of her misery·" Then his voice got angry· "Imagine that big brute *using* that poor soul," he said, shaking his head in disgust making sounds that I knew were bad words if I could only hear them, words that went along with Daddy's lip twitching·

"How can you tell, Daddy?" I ventured, hoping his lip would settle down; the twitching made my stomach hurt·

"Well, she is his *wife*... and some of the ladies of the church have come over to bathe her, and... well, they... well..." Suddenly Daddy stopped short· "But it's not for your young head to worry about," he said quickly· "God will take care of her·"

I didn't know what *his* using *her* meant but I imagined dark and scary cobwebs entangling the both of them and Jesus looking the other way· I got scared for her so I said, "But Daddy, can't anybody *help* her?"

"Mercy, child· She is his *wife* and he can do with her

what he will... no law can stop that·" He was shaking his
head again, saying, "Tsk tsk, it's only the love of God that
makes a man treat a woman right·"

What Daddy was talking about still wasn't clear, but I
felt sad thinking about her, remembering the smile creeping
into her eyes·

Daddy's lip had stopped its nervous habit, and the
quietness in the car was stretching into tomorrow· Finally,
in a timid voice, I asked, "Daddy, can we please stop for a
big double-dipper? You know, where they have chocolate
jimmies?"

It seemed as though he hadn't heard me, that his eyes
were stuck on the road ahead·

"Please, Daddy· Please!" I begged in desperation, trying
to shake him loose· I hated all this quiet; it really scared
me·

Daddy's thinking must have been worrisome from the
sound of his big, tired sigh· It was as though he and God
were all alone in his special world, and I was on the outside
looking in; the flat tone of his voice only counting the
minutes, days, tracts, sinners and sad people, till he'd be
finished·

All I could do now was watch for the street signs,
sounding out their letters in my head – and cross my
fingers·

"We'll see," he finally answered out his window· "We'll
see·"

S ince I had married Ray and left Milwaukee three years
before, it was my girlhood friend, Billie Ann, who, when she
dropped in out of a distant past, thrust a mirror into my
shrouded world. Billie was on my Christmas card list and even
though we had otherwise lost contact, I continued to send a card.
The chilling response stating that her young husband had been
killed in a freak accident more than two years previous left me
embarrassed, and unusually distraught. Sending her an
immediate note of sad apology had kindled a waning friendship,
bringing with it her impromptu visit along with some apprehension.
Ray and I had never had to entertain a personal friend of mine
before, let alone female and single, although we often had Ray's
unmarried buddies over for "a home cooked meal." But Billie's
visit following Kelly's birth, and her intuitive assessment of Ray,

although disturbing, had the effect of shaking me out of a lingering post-partum depression.

It started with Billie's clothes. Despite the fact that she was one of six kids being raised by a single mother, Billie Ann always looked superior. Her taste and style, as well as cost, outdid most in our church set. But nothing in her past wardrobe could compare to the elegance in which she was now dressed as wealthy Big Joe Caglioni's girl, a well-known produce dealer on Milwaukee's North Shore. Billie had only to ask and she was given, she said. But that was not enough; she wanted children. She had yet to become pregnant through two years of marriage. Neither had she conceived during the last year, living with Big Joe. Such a confession was shocking. You would have thought her glad to have avoided the confirmation of her out-of-wedlock living which was a blatant departure from her Fundamentalist Christian upbringing – considering women were still ruled by their mother's dictums. But secretly I envied her nerve, even though, as a teenager, I thought her superficial and frivolous. Billie's reputation then, of being a teaser who lost interest the moment she gained the attention she was seeking, was still decidedly clear in my memory – one of the charmed was my very own father.

It was at summer camp in the Wisconsin north woods and Daddy and his new wife, Charity, had dropped in for a short visit, to check up on me, I believed. Twelve years old, Billie and I were working the dishwashers in the dining hall for our keep. We also shared bunks in one of the worker's cabins. While I posed for a picture for Daddy, Billie was patiently sitting in her black bathing suit on the railing of the log cabin porch above us, in plain view, watching. As I handed Daddy the little Brownie camera, he looked up at Billie, over my head, and smiled in his extra-special way I had seen as a kid when he would give out a gospel tract to a pretty waitress, or cashier. "Billie, why don't you get over here, in the picture," he said to her.

Afterwards, we both walked him to his car where a very pregnant Charity, his bride of one year, was resting. He turned and gave me a hug in return for a goodbye kiss. I knew better than to ask for any spending money. But he would often surprise me, despite their meager finances, with unexpected change – a reward, I assumed, for not asking. So when he pulled out the shiny half-dollar, I was ready to reach for it, when I suddenly realized he was handing it, not to me, but to Billie Ann. Like an unexpected slap in the face, I had to fight to keep back the tears, of embarrassment more than anything, as I waved a feeble goodbye to the disappearing car.

Billie broke the silence. "What a jerk! I don't know why he gave this to *me*; he should have given it to *you*," she said trying to put the money into my hand.

Some things you never forget. Billie Ann was stopping in to visit us in Atlanta, on her way to the islands for a vacation, she said, where she could make some decisions.

The evening of her overnight visit, Ray was stretched out on the couch working a crossword puzzle. It never seemed to occur to either of us that he could *sit* on the couch, and leave room for someone else, instead, he never moved, and offered no apology. But he had worked all day, so I simply got my myself a kitchen chair, with knitting in my lap, as Billie took the padded rocker I usually occupied. Phil Silvers was on TV with his usual dishonest antics, as chief sergeant in charge of pilfering. As many of Ray's favorites, I disliked the Silvers show; the humor simply didn't register. Instead, it made me feel ashamed of *our* service connection.

"What part of the Army are *you* in," Billie ventured.

Ray was so flamboyant with people generally, his joviality, his laughter with his outrageous storytelling, could win over anyone. But now he was unusually reserved; his eyes never left the TV, and he appeared not to have heard her. Ray's lack of response to such an attractive and well dressed female struck me as strange, and certainly not in keeping with his usual behavior. I was sure he would take to her because of the similarity in our looks, dark hair and brown eyes, although Billie still had her girlhood freckles across her nose, under the makeup. But Ray had, in a very short time, already declared us to be "nothing alike." What was more, he seemed annoyed that Billie was even there, almost defensive. In the three years we had been married, our friends had always been his, from work or school. With them, we played canasta, bridge, and even monopoly on occasion, at our respective homes. Kids were put to bed at a reasonable hour, after TV and special snacks. A family picnic was an occasional diversion from the norm, but usually our social life consisted of TV at home and drive-in movies. The care of my children was my primary concern; rarely did I leave them.

Billie was persistent in her questions directed at Ray, "What is your rank?" she asked.

"Do you have a need to know?" he answered sarcastically with his eyes still glued to the TV. Finally, really into the air, he said, "I'm an undercover CIC agent."

"Gosh, you mean I am meeting a real spy? *In person?*"

Billie and I both laughed at the sound of it. But Ray's attention was already back on the TV. Billie looked at me and rolled her eyes.

Embarrassed, I said, "Ray does background investigations. When someone applies for a security clearance for some kind of government job, they run background checks on people. He has to go to their homes and neighbors, and ask questions about character and stuff. You know, find out if they are married to a foreigner, things like that."

"What has that got to do with a person's character?" she asked, a little indignant.

Ray apparently had not missed a word of our conversation despite his lack of responses, as he interjected, "What we're looking for are any reasons that could make a guy turn on his country."

"You mean just because a guy has a wife from, say Italy, for example, does that make him disloyal to his country?" Billie asked.

Ray's attention was back on the TV and apparently did not hear her question. I answered for him. "It's got to do with loyalty, I think."

Watching TV and listening with one ear, Ray did venture an answer. "It just means that if push comes to shove, and he is torn between loyalty to country and loyalty to family, it is figured his family will win. Of course with an *Italian,* there'd be no question!" Ray said in sarcasm, with a burst of laughter.

The contempt in his humor made the air thick with discomfort; Billie's face turned red as she laughed along with him. But it did not deter her interest.

Trying to soften Ray's words, I said, "So if you are married to someone who is not a U.S. citizen, they won't pass you."

At this point, I was hoping Ray would say *something*, during the commercial at least. But his crossword puzzle had taken his attention now, so I continued for him. "That's not the only thing Ray asks about. And just in case he has to interview someone who may outrank him, someone who might not want to give him the information, he wears a suit, not a uniform. This way his rank is never disclosed. In fact, very few of our neighbors even know he's in the Army."

Billie didn't seem to want *my* explanations. Instead she was directing her question to Ray again, to the side of his head anyway.

"Tell me what else you do."

But Ray was laughing his boisterous laugh; something on the Silvers show.

Ray's indifference to one of my friends from my hometown was upsetting, although, in a way, I was secretly relieved.

The next morning Billie was readying her suitcase. When I walked into the room, she was holding up an exquisite lacy nightgown she had apparently worn the night before. Just picturing Ray catching a glimpse of Billie in it rattled me for an instant. But I said, "Oh, how pretty; I don't think I've ever had something that nice."

"But you have three adorable kids; I wish I had them. Although, I wouldn't want your husband; Ray is a real dud."

Speaking in a soft whisper, I said, "I love them all so," Billie's directness bringing me to sudden, silent tears.

Billie immediately saw how deeply her quick words had cut. "Oh, Sam, you're a *good* mother," she said trying to smooth them over. "You take care of all their *physical* needs. But it's like you're not *there* inside." Billie continued to close her suitcase stuffed to capacity with ribbons and lace. She turned and looked at me, and as though she had stumbled onto the solution, Billie said, "Maybe going to work would help."

I had no real inkling of what my friend was trying to tell me, only that the words became etched in my brain that day, and I wished truly to understand. *What have I done or not done? Doesn't she know that every minute of every day is spent in caring for my children? How I love being responsible for them; the accountability gives me an existence. I am somebody, finally. I am the mother I have yearned for since that awful day... My children fill up some of the missing spaces inside of me; and I love the man who has given me the chance to have that. He has given me his name, a home, a life. To have him really and truly love me, besides, is more than anyone could expect. So my prayers come from a humble and begging heart. Maybe someday God will see fit to make it come true. In the mean time, I must do my best to accept whatever comes.* These were the underlying feelings that had allowed my young and seemingly thoughtless husband his indifferent and often caustic way.

Aloud, I said, "I know Ray didn't *mean* to come off so rude. He just *acts* that way sometimes... lately."

"I think something's wrong with him; he doesn't act... *alive*. Does he ever get off that couch?"

"Well, yes, to work every day. And Saturday he plays golf,

when he 's not working his extra job. He bowls, too, in a league, on Post. Then he pitches softball; he takes us to the games."

"Whoopie for you?" she said, twirling her index finger up in the air. "But does he ever *talk* to you, tell you he loves you, stuff like that?"

"No, not really," I said. "I don't think it is his way."

Billie couldn't know how I yearned to hear those words. The silent prayer I carried in my heart was that somehow God would forgive me for my mixed-up past, and *make my husband truly love me, please, God!*

"Well, I think Ray is sick. And if you don't get out of this house, find someone to talk to, you're going to go coo-coo!" she said.

Billie called a cab for the airport. She wouldn't hear of my driving her. The last thing she said was, "Get a job!" and stuck her thumb up for good luck.

Telling Billie Ann the truth would have been unthinkable then, if I had even realized it. Ray didn't want his wife to work anyhow, according to the Biblical way of thinking. Besides, having to leave Sharon so much those first three years of her life gave me a good excuse. Now that I had a husband who supported us, I should never want to leave my children again. But the underlying reason I had never consciously acknowledged, even to myself – *especially* to myself. It was only after our neighbor, Johnny Black, gave us tickets to the Ice Follies, and offered their sixteen-year-old son, Bobby, as free babysitter, that my fears were brought to the surface. Returning from the Follies, as we drove into our driveway, through the front screen door I could see Bobby just coming out of the bathroom. I cringed, *remembering...*

Daddy's warnings about boys, and not letting them fool with me, helped little in my defense; I was only five, and far too small to keep seventeen year-old Marty Simms away. While his mother went to the store, he baby-sat me a few times. He would send me to his room to get his socks, and then chase me to get them, only it was me he was after. I was terrified and exhilarated all at once when he'd grab me, throw me into the air, and catch me by the crotch. He'd carry me, perched on one hand, and parade around the living room. I felt so silly, but I ate up his attentions. While he'd watch out the window for his mother, his hand would wiggle and pinch me and hurt me in my private part. The minute he'd see his mother coming up

*the street with her grocery cart, Marty would drop me like
a hot potato and make a mad dash for the bathroom· Click,
went the lock on the bathroom door before the toilet would
flush·*

*What did Bobby do with you while we were at the Ice
Follies?* I wanted to wake Sharon and ask, but fearing the answer,
instead, I vowed to myself to never use another babysitter.

Until Billie came to visit and made me take a good look at us, I
hadn't realized how out of touch with each other Ray and I had
become. One morning, after Sharon left for school, I swallowed
my fears, and took Suzie and Kelly to the Post day nursery where
grandma *ladies* were in charge, and answered an ad for a front
desk position, in a small company that manufactured ceiling tiles.

My nerves were in their usual place – my stomach. Mr.
Robly was one of those nice southern gentlemen who believed in
treating a woman like a lady, whether she deserved it or not.

"Milwaukee, huh?" he said after reading the application.
"Yes, I can hear a slight accent there, but you don't sound too
bad. That's good. Some of our customers wouldn't like hearing a
Yankee on the other end of the line. You must be one of those
Damn Yankees, then."

I smiled, always the safest thing to do.

Mr. Robly was a talker, too. "You *do* know the difference
between a Yankee and a *Damn* Yankee, don't you?... A Yankee
is a Northerner that comes down here to visit, and then goes
home. A *Damn* Yankee is one who comes down here and likes it,
and stays. The President of our company is one of them."

"Well, I don't expect to stay here long enough for that," I said
with a laugh. Then I remembered, I was hoping he'd hire me
despite being married to a roving military man, so I quickly added,
"We don't expect to be leaving here for at least another year; my
husband is in a special Army school right now. He's learning to be
a polygraph examiner," I said proudly.

"We'll, that'll keep you on your toes, I'd say," he laughed
aloud, and leaned back in his chair. Then he got more serious.
"Do you understand that we have a loudspeaker system that goes
into the warehouse, and occasionally someone that works out
there gets a call, to check stock or something. Have you ever
used one of them?"

"Oh, yes, matter of fact, I was trained on a huge switchboard
that went out into three other buildings."

"Well, then, sounds like you're just the girl we need," said Mr. Robly. "You realize, of course, that we have some customs here in the South that are somewhat different from up there where you come from."

"You mean making Negroes ride in the back of the buses? That kind of thing?"

"Well, yes," he said, leaning on the back legs of his chair again, rocking on them as he talked. "We don't eat together, either. And when you call the warehouse for one of them, their last name is what they're used to."

Job or no job, my dander was up. I wasn't about to let an opportunity go by to tell this *Southerner* just what I thought of his *customs*. "Mr. Robly, I understand how things are down here, but I could never show such disrespect for any human being no matter what color their skin is. I think it's terrible the prejudice of you Southerners, even though my father was one, and I was born in Tennessee myself, but up in Milwaukee..."

"Wa... ait a minute," Mr. Robly said, holding up his hand. The gesture almost tipped him over in his chair, so he sat upright, his face coloring slightly. "I think you are feeling just a little bit self-righteous now. But that stands to reason – you're a Damn Yankee," he said with a grin.

We both smiled.

Then he said, "You see, human beings have a tendency to be prejudicial in their behavior all over the world. It's just one of those sad facts about our species. We are always looking for some way to make us feel better, superior to the next guy, and down here the Nigras are unfortunately the fall guys. But you Yankees are no better than we are. You're just at highfalutin in their regard as we are. Down here, we are just more open about it."

"Well, I don't see how you can say that," I said, a terrific debater in school, and my appetite for mental gymnastics had received little stimulation of late, with Ray. "Why, we sit next to them on the bus, eat with them in restaurants..."

Mr. Robly had a pencil between his teeth. He took it out and was pointing it at me. "Yes, you do. But I'd like to tell you something, you little sweetheart... Yes, we Southerners are guilty of discriminating against the Nigra... but how do you explain them feeding us, tending our children?"

The childhood memory of Lizzy waiting on Mrs. Heath at the Bible School, right here in Georgia, cooking for them as I would watch her in the kitchen. It *was* puzzling, the intimate contact with the maids, caring for the babies, washing hair at the beauty shops...

Mr. Robly interrupted my thoughts. "You see, Sugar, a *Southerner* says to the Nigra, "I don't care how *close* you get, just don't get too *high*. You Yankees say to them, I don't care how *high* you get, just don't get too *close*! So there you have it in a nutshell. We're all just human beings lookin' for someone to look down on, to make us feel better about ourselves."

Part of what he said made sense, when I remembered our high school prom king, a Negro football star, who reigned with a White queen, but it was understood that they would each have respective dates. Thinking about his words, how "highfalutin" I must have sounded — words like *Yankee condescension* came to mind — I was sure I had ruined my chances for the job. It was truly surprising to hear his next words: "When can you start?"

As a front desk PBX Receptionist and Girl Friday, my days were packed and tiring as I'd already done a half-day's work at home, just to get there. The job, though, was very interesting, and gave me the confidence I was somehow lacking, staying at home. Lunch hours had become very special, with Angela, my new friend. Once, she asked me if I was Jewish?

"For goodness sake, why do you ask *that*?"

Blushing, she said, "Aren't *all* Yankees Jewish?"

"Goodness sakes, no. Although I did happen to grow up in a Jewish neighborhood and went to a school that was predominantly Jewish. On their holidays, I was only one of a handful present in class. In fact, in the third grade, the year my dad left me behind while he came here to Georgia, to school, I fell in love with a Jewish boy named Ronnie Oxman. He was blonde and blue-eyed, and he liked me. He would pull my pigtails and then run into the cloak room. I'll never forget that feeling inside to have someone really notice me, *look* at me. He'd pull my bows out and I'd have to retie them over and over, all day long." *Funny how that very first love stays with you, forever.*

"Blonde hair and blue eyes? I thought Jewish people were dark complected?"

"Whatever gave you that idea?" Laughing, I said, "I just don't understand all the stuff that is said about them. Where I come from, everyone's heritage is a special thing. Something to be proud of, your identification. Everyone comes from a different country in Europe, so the first thing you get asked in an interview for a job, is: What kind of name is that? Some kind of human connection, something to talk about. That's why I was happy to get married; I hated my ugly name growing up. It turns out to be a proper English name, but that doesn't help a little kid that has to carry a handle like *Tuckermoore* around. And Samantha Sue, no less!"

"Malorry is a nice name. What nationality is it?"

"It's Irish. And my husband is very proud of it. He says God is Irish. And he knows, because *she* told him!"

Angela burst into laughter. "I bet your husband is fun, huh?"

"Yes, he is, usually." But I neglected to mention what a drag he'd been lately, *since Kelly…*

"I just love hearing you talk, so fast," she said and continued to pump me with questions about *up North* and snow, the Army and all that moving, staying behind, alone, now that Ray had orders for overseas.

Angela's interest in me is a new thing, and the first person, since marrying Ray, who is my friend, only. Having that friendship is so special that I dread the thought of losing it.

I am staring at the small, thin box. Just get over with it, Samantha Sue. It has 14 KARAT GOLD inscribed in the corner of its blue lid. Inside, nestled into a bed of pale orchid velvet, lay one small pearl strung on a delicate gold chain. For one short moment I feel suspended in space, lost, afraid, but somehow in awe. It has something to do with the way the pearl looks under the tightly sealed cellophane. To disturb the perfection, the permanence of which it speaks, seems somehow irreverent.

Flowers· Their scent is everywhere· The room is full of the soft sound of people's whispers· Pastor Cunningham's church folk are milling around· All our Evermardt and Tuckermoore kin are filling up the room: sisters; brothers; nieces; a father; a mother; me· Daddy's arms tighten as we get near the casket· "Give her to me, I'll hold her," someone says· But Daddy shakes his head and pulls me in closer· "Naw, that's all right, I've got her," he says as we make our way through all the people·

We look down at Mama in the grey box· A sweet odor of perfume jars my search· Daddy's chest begins to heave as he lets out a terrible sound, a muffled cry· "I forgot she was so little," he says, sobbing· He blows his nose into the white, folded handkerchief from his inside pocket, the one he always gives me when I cry· Dor… Dor… wake up and make

all this be a dream," he says, bending toward her, reaching
for her hand· "I promise never to take another drink, I
promise· Never·" He cries softly, "Dorie· Dorie·" He hugs
me then so tightly, I feel I could break in two· I put my
pudgy arms around his neck and press my cheek to his,
feeling the wet from his tears·

Inside the pretty box, Mama is sleeping· Her hands are
folded, her hair combed carefully to one side and pushed
into deep, dark waves like she does it with the bright, silver
clips· The orchid, velvet lining of the box lies in soft folds
about her pink dress, the one Daddy bought her "right off
the model·" I search for the baby sister that I haven't seen
yet· Cigarette smoke curls up into my nose; it burns my
eyes as I look around· The people's faces all run together
like flowers in fields flying by the car window· Daddy tells
me to *Hold still·* I look back at Mama, and frown, trying to
understand it all· "The baby, Daddy· Baby Sister, where her
be?"

"She's in there, sleeping at your mama's feet; under
the covers," Daddy says between his sobs, pointing to the
flowers·

Just beyond Mama's hands, I see the red flowers then·
A big, red, bow ribbon almost hides the card with Daddy's
scratchy writing, *My Beloved·* He points to the place where
her feet lie hidden, where baby is – says everyone in
whispers· "But why is her *there*, and not by Mama?" I ask,
a heaviness swelling in my chest·

Daddy's eyes begin blinking, and he says, "Well, the
baby's dead, and all blue, not nice looking, and your mama
wouldn't want anyone to see her like that·"

Sleeping under the dark, can her breathe? And Mama's
eyes, can her see? Suddenly, I twist loose, almost out of
Daddy's arms· He grabs on and holds me· I want to scream
for Mama to open her eyes· Talk to me· Say something·
This is all so funny, not like what I'm used to· I want to
run over to Maureen and Marilee; I beg Daddy to *Let me
down·* But he answers me *No* in a tone that is new, and
final· It reminds me of Grandma's hand over my mouth·

I suck in air in little spurts, matching the thumping in
my chest· Mama not even see me; her not hear me,
neither· I want to scream...

Angela's voice pulls me back to the present, "Aren't you going to open it and put it on?" she asks impatiently.

Her words rescue me from the sinking feeling in my middle for which I have no explanation. "Oh, my gosh. How sweet of y'all to do this," I say, feeling the warmth in my neck as I quickly search my repertoire of appropriate responses. Discomfort at certain moments make me hurry through them. "Y'all shouldn't have done it," I say then in the southern-speak I have learned to wear like a new pair of gloves.

Reluctantly, I pierce the clear wrap, and take the chain out of the notched indentations that holds it in place. Angela quickly reaches to secure the clasp around my neck. "You deserve it," she whispers softly, amidst murmurs of polite agreement. I am sure she means it when she says, "We're going to really miss you."

A farewell lunch from fellow employees is a first for me, a rare group in a job that has truly saved my sanity. The sight of the pearl, so beautiful, so still, pulls a hidden chord inside. It is Angela, though, the special interest she has shown, and having to leave her, that begins anew that old nameless achiness inside.

There was a tap at the front screen door. It was Johnny, our next door neighbor. His wife worked nights and he was home alone in the evenings. Ray had struck up a kind of friendship with him. They would sit on the front porch and smoke, discuss the latest ball scores. Tonight the girls were playing in the front yard, as always, the rule we had so I could clearly see them from the living room; Kelly was in his playpen right at my feet, as I ironed. Ray had invited Johnny into the house. "Well, I got my orders today," said Ray, grinning.

To me, Johnny was an *older man*. Barely twenty-two myself, I felt closer in age to his son, Bobby.

"Where to?" asked Johnny. "To some exotic place, I hope, with a whole lot of pretty girls."

"Hell, no," said Ray. "It's only the pit of the world, they tell me. I have to be in Korea one month from today."

"Oh, I've heard about those slant-eyes... They do it sideways. Even their cu..." Suddenly, Johnny remembered a lady was in the room. He turned to me and winked, a habit he had. He probably flirted with every girl, but it still upset me. Ray didn't understand why I disliked being around him, but I couldn't tell him the truth, so I blamed it on his smoking. Johnny tucked the unlit cigarette he carried above his ear, and spoke directly to me,

"Sounds like you got things set up really good, Sam. You already have a job and a place to keep the kids."

My heart just sank into my stomach. When I was upset, ironing let me work out the anxiety. The thought of being alone, without Ray around to keep this... this... man away, frightened me beyond words. The more I thought about it, the faster I ironed. Before I married Ray, keeping men away had always been my biggest worry. In fact, I would tell a girlfriend who was worried about their husband's cheating, that if he hadn't hit on me, then he was ok, that's how all men seemed to treat me. Finally, now, at least most of the time, they respected my married status and left me alone. But Johnny seemed more daring than most. He was nice and sweet, actually, and extremely attentive, that was the trouble, and he was always around.

The gynecologist was pleased with the return of my figure so soon. "I am on the go all the time," I said, laughing. "How could I possibly stay fat? There just isn't enough minutes in the day anymore." Suddenly, I felt like crying, but I didn't want to break down. Then I told him about the nausea again that had worried me once before, during my divorced period. "It's usually when I am the busiest, running up and down the stairs, cleaning. The nurse at work used to give me some green liquid stuff to take."

"Do you ever sit down, take a smoke break?" he asked.

"Sometimes I have coffee with a neighbor or a friend, but very seldom, I don't have the time. Besides, I don't like coffee, and I don't smoke, either."

"Well, it's a good reason to start," he said. "I think you are running yourself ragged. You know that there are big changes in the family when that third child comes along."

"Oh, is *that* what's wrong with me?"

He could see I was close to tears, so he said, "I'm going to give you some mild tranquilizers to take when you start feeling sick. You shouldn't need them too often," he said. "Break them in half, and start giving yourself some sit-down time."

It was rare that I took the pills; I hated being sleepy. Getting up in the mornings for my family was hard enough most days. But when things got too hectic, when my head would start to swim, as badly as being pregnant, or on a merry-go-round, the pills were there in the medicine cabinet. I was getting more *ordinary* every day.

After marrying Ray, I transferred all my attentions to him and his family. They seemed to welcome me, and appreciate the snapshots of the kids I sent to *Ma and Dad,* sending the most beautiful Mother's Day and Birthday cards, too. Ray didn't seem to really care about cards much, it was always left up to me. Spending our month-long vacations with them, in August, had become a yearly event. The way they treated me left me with such a good feeling, I was certain they wouldn't object to my moving up there, to Michigan. "I'll find a place of my own, of course," I was saying into the phone. Maybe I really was trying to insure that Ray would not forget me on his long year away, ahead.

Ray's youngest brother, Matt, who was six months my junior, was on the other end of the line. "Hell, Sam, you don't want to come up here. Why, Ma would have you and those kids so full of pills."

Remembering the locked satchel when they came to visit, I said quickly, "But, I don't think she will influence me like that, *I'm* not sick."

"You just don't know her. Why don't you stay there and keep your job? There just aren't any jobs up here. What would you do for a year?"

Matt's attitude was very confusing. When he got married recently, he seemed to grow somewhat distant, but Ray was persistent. When he finally reached his dad, Jake Malorry's robust voice, his larger than life personality seemed to fill the air, even over the phone. "You just pack those bags and come on up here. We'd be happy to look out for you. You say you *are* planning to get your own place?"

"Oh, yes. A job, too. I know I'll find something to help out the money situation. We will lose our housing allowance, you know, with Ray gone; he has to have money, too."

"You just come ahead; I know Tillie will agree."

As we got into the car loaded down with our belongings, what a mixture of relief, and yet foreboding, I felt. Leaving there, our first home together, was almost earthshaking. On the expressway that took us due north, I looked back over the city of Atlanta. It had held so much happiness, so many new experiences that I never dreamed could be a part of my life. With Ray's urging and promise to pay for college some day, I *had* finished my high school correspondence course begun five years before, and gotten my diploma. My friend, Connie Bradley, had shared my passion for sewing, which filled every free moment; the girls had the most beautiful clothes – for play, for school, and for Sunday school, where I had to take them by myself almost every Sunday. After we got acquainted with the Bradley's, Ray would attend church occasionally, just to please me, but he continued to resist a regular church oriented life, which was all I really knew. But with his sports, and my sewing, and some friends, we seemed to have established a reasonably normal life. At least our financial future was secured through Ray's re-enlistment, though limited by his noncommissioned status. The decision to make the Army his career was his alone to make; a man *was* head of the family. Now there was no turning back; orders were orders. But this separation thing was something I had not really contemplated. To make matters worse, things had shut down between us personally, even though Ray was not really what you'd call, hateful. At least not since that terrible fight when he slapped me so hard across the face for talking back, but he never even came close to doing it again. Instead, when he was angry, he would get very quiet and shut-away from everything around him. At night, I would lie awake trying to figure out what I'd said, or done. It seemed to have something to do with Kelly's birth, but it would be years before I would be able to put it all together, before we would learn of the affective disorder that ran in Ray's family. And that this disorder was easily triggered by life changing decisions such as he was forced then to make. My being due with a new baby, three months after his Army enlistment would be up, had forced him to commit another three-year hitch to Uncle Sam. (Not until he received his officers commission, later in Korea, would he really feel that this had been the right decision.)

The closer we came to the day of parting, the more his expressed doubt monopolized my every waking thought – his vacant *I don't know* response when I would ask, *Do you love me?* Without words of reassurance from the one who had now become my whole life, facing a year's separation seemed too scary for me to contemplate. But I tried to tell myself that when the day came that Ray *got right with God, our past won't be important.* Didn't God forgive and forget? My mother-in-law seemed to believe it – with his ordination certificate still hanging on her wall. Thinking about her helped. *She* would be there, and she had given me so much love and encouragement often, despite the feelings initially expressed about Suzie's beginnings. My folks rarely even sent a card, but Tillie's long, loving, and happy letters had somehow made up for it. I had reciprocated by crafting personal gifts, to show my appreciation. Yes, I felt as though I had been truly accepted, and moving near them would make everything be all right, Matt's caution only a speck of doubt in the sea of unspeakable fear that transported me.

Little did I know that the world as I saw it and believed it to be would soon begin to crumble, as the Christian certainty upon which my entire life had been built, would slowly disintegrate almost before my very eyes, leaving me in troubling disarray. That childhood feeling of isolation of long ago, of neediness that had been recently hidden away under the superficial happiness of new babies, softball games, and an occasional touching under the sheets, would soon cry out for expression.

Porter, Michigan was a small General Motors town that was either thriving or bust, depending on the auto industry at the moment. The small junior college where I had worked during registration four years before, when Sharon and I had come to stay with Ray's folks while he went ahead to Atlanta to find us a house, wasn't hiring. Only three weeks left before Sharon's school started and Ray would be on his way to Korea, daily we were looking in the papers for a place to live.

Almost September, the cool Midwestern nights had sent me to the sewing machine to make flannel pajamas for all the kids. Kelly, still not walking, was content to play in his playpen as long as he could see me; that is how I had managed to get so much sewing done. Grandma O'Toole had given me a large box of remnants right after we were married that I had mixed and matched, to save money. Working full-time the past months, in Atlanta, the already cut-out pajamas were waiting to be finished. The girls were outdoors, within an earshot, playing with the neighborhood kids, riding their trikes. I was working at the sewing machine trying to keep Kelly entertained, when Jake, Ray's dad, came through the room.

"For goodness sake, what in the world are you doing?" he asked, with a slight tone of a reprimand in his voice that was not like him; usually he was pleasant and complementary.

"I'm sewing warm pajamas. You know we're not used to these chilly nights, here in Michigan," I said, faking a shiver and smiling up at him.

"While Kelly just *sits* there in that playpen, huh? He ought to be out doors, playing, enjoying the sunshine with the other kids," he said.

Stunned, I stopped sewing; I was almost done with the first

pair; I sewed very fast. With a smile, trying to hide the agitation I felt deep inside, I said, "He doesn't seem to mind it, as long as he can *see* me. I can't get anything done chasing him down, you know – even though he is only crawling. Besides, I'm sewing this for *him*."

"Well, that kid doesn't *know* that," Jake shot out over his shoulder as he disappeared up the stairs.

Minutes later, Tillie, came home from work. Her pockets were filled with candy. By this time, like Ray, I was calling her Ma. Sharon and Suzie had come inside, and were sitting on the living room floor, their eyes glued to their favorite Micky Mouse Club. Guiltily, after Jake's comment, I had let Kelly down on the floor while I finished up. Tillie walked past and picked Kelly up. She was hugging and kissing him, saying, "How's Grandma's little boy? You got some kisses for Grandma?"

Kelly lit into a big smile and put his open mouth on hers, banging his already protruding front teeth. His slobber was all over her face, but she wiped it off with her apron without protest, and pulled a piece of candy from her bulging pocket. "Here's a sweet treat for my sweet boy," she said and stuffed it into his little fist as she took him into the living room, and put him down on the floor next to the girls. She turned to me, and said, "I think it's a crying shame this kid isn't walking yet"

"Well, Ma, he's only fouteen months old, and the baby book says some kids are slower than others, not to push them." *My stomach was starting to churn.* "Kelly gets any place he *wants* to, scooting on his belly," I said as nicely as I knew how, trying not to let my irritation show. "So I guess as long as he can do *that*, he isn't interested in walking yet. At least that's how I look at it." How hard I was trying to not push my kids into doing what somebody thinks they *should*, just because *their* kids did it. "Dr. Spock says kids are all individual; we should let them do things at their own pace."

"Hmpf! Well, he's never going to *walk* sitting in that playpen," she said with a derisive laugh.

"In our house, if you remember, we had stairs, just like this," I explained. By now, my stomach was in a total knot. "He's up them in a flash. I'm always afraid he will fall and hurt himself, so I only let him down if I am standing *right there*, watching. He's very quick, you know," I said defensively, fighting back sudden tears.

Reaching into her candy filled pocket, and looking at me over her glasses, through pursed lips, Tillie said, "*I'll* get him to walk! And I bet it's before his dad leaves too, you just watch!"

After giving Sharon and Suzie some candy while they watched TV, Tillie put the bag on top of the refrigerator. Every now and then while she was putzing around in the kitchen, she'd stop, get a piece of candy, and call, "Kelly, where's my sweet baby?"

Kelly would head straight for the kitchen, still on his knees. After awhile, every time Kelly would hear paper rattle, he would turn towards the kitchen. Furious, I was thinking, *I'll be in my own place soon, and all that candy's going to stop.*

It was becoming more and more uncomfortable staying with the Malorrys, although in my mind, I never questioned the decision to move to Michigan. Here, I felt safe from men like sweet-talking Johnny Black, or those like him I'd left behind in Milwaukee. But Tillie and Jake questioning my parenting, upset me, the one thing about which, until now, I had felt reasonably sure. To talk back to either of them was not in my makeup, or to express the anger I was feeling, unthinkable. Ray's leaving was already putting butterflies in my stomach. In the past, creating something new had served me well. *Starting a new home in a new town will, again, be my savior.*

T he place was a large second floor flat above an elderly lady who lived with her adult daughter. Although it was on a busy street, not as nice a neighborhood as the Malorry's was, or as near to the golf course and park, the price was right. It had only two bedrooms, but they were so big, putting the girls beds into bunks and Kelly's crib all in the same room, still left plenty of play area for them and their toys. The hardwood floors creaked when walking across them. The washer was down three flights of stairs in the dark, musty basement. Going down there was frightening, and reminded me of the Simms house at age five, when Daddy, fuming mad, would take me down there to give me a licking. He would look up into the rafters for something to use, to switch me with – for what, I was never really sure – until my arms and legs were striped with welts. Although, once I remembered changing his clock when playing house, so the alarm would ring like grownups. Basements were never a pleasant place for me since, even though this one had a little more light, and enough room to hang a whole weeks wash all through the snowy winter. Throughout my life, I had learned to manage with whatever I had. Already I was figuring out where to hang the cris-cross ruffled curtains that were on their way from Georgia. The Army, for the first time, had provided us with movers, since Ray had been promoted to sergeant. And I kept reminding myself: *This place is only for one year.*

The few days wait for our household goods to be delivered gave us time to spend in Northern Michigan, at Grandma O'Toole's lake cottage, the favorite childhood place which Ray spoke of often.

Driving up in the car, the kids were already worn out from the excitement. Sharon no longer took naps and kept Suzie awake in the car, but Kelly got car-sick. Tillie had a pill for everything though. From the hospital, she brought home oodles of pills left after her patients either died, or were sent home. "Here, give him half of this," she said. In minutes, Kelly was fast asleep, for hours. As a kid, I had never been given even aspirin. This was a whole new experience: first having free medical care in the Army, and now a nurse for a mother-in-law who handed out pills like candy. Matt made no attempt at hiding his disapproval. I wondered why. *Certainly no one as respectable as a nurse could ever be a dope fiend, could they?*

Grandma O'Toole's small cottage was nestled in the pines, set atop a hill that descended down into the water. A boat dock ran next to the boat house, the childhood play setting for the grandkids' many stories.[16] Although Tillie and her mother looked to be two peas in a pod, with only the years to separate them, one prematurely white, and one still very dark headed, I would soon learn how unlike they really were, although they both wore their hair braided and wrapped around their head, with curly bangs to break the forehead part. All of the Malorry kids and their spouses were up at the cottage for the weekend. Out on the porch that overlooked the lake, a game of Hearts was dealt. Grandma hated to lose; when she was behind, everyone teased her of cheating. This last day, Suzie and Sharon were out in the boat with Grandpa Jake, fishing. Grandma Tillie was sitting over on the

---

[16] In fact, Ray told me on our wedding night, after I had been so shocked to hear he had a sister, how "honest" he was, sometimes to his detriment, his pastor had told him. "The only time I ever lied to my old man was about Frannie in the boat house. My dad said to me, *At sixteen, you're too big to be doing that sort of thing.*" Ray said he quickly denied it. Rich and Matt really got beat, but they never squealed on him. "I've been ashamed of that ever since," Ray said. This family secret between the siblings, seemed to me to lay the groundwork for years of ill-treatment of Fran by all three of her brothers. She became their mirror, and it was clear they didn't like what they saw. I knew, but I dared not speak of such private things. Dear Sister, God rest her soul, would pay dearly for her secret with her health, the rest of her life.

swing, reading. Kelly and Rich's little boy, Dickie, a couple weeks younger, were crawling around on the floor, at her feet. Every now and then, she'd talk to them, and hold up a piece of candy from her handy pocket. "Here, see which one of you can come to Grandma the fastest!" she'd say, as they'd scurry on their knees. I tried to ignore this and concentrate on the game, which was difficult at best, my attention being drawn in so many directions at once, being with this Irish family all together. They were here to see their oldest brother, the self-declared king, off to war, and they wanted to show him, they said, that they could beat him at cards. He was an excellent player at everything, but at cards, with his fondness for numbers, he was rarely beaten. The competition between them was unbelievable. In my growing up, I was the family outsider everywhere we lived, and politeness, at least in front of me, never included this kind of loving interaction between siblings. Seeing this for the first time was surprising, and made me feel how strangely different I really was. Still being on the outside of things, I was beginning to realize that marrying Ray didn't seem to change this, but I was content to sit and watch, and listen. Matt and Rich especially liked to tease, even though they were very affectionate with their spontaneous hugs and kisses, a new pleasure I was learning to accept.

The most difficult part of being with this Malorry family was trying to not think or talk about the pending doom which lay head. My decision to move here had not been especially lauded by anyone in the family, except Matt's new wife, Ro, who confided to me one day that she'd been made to feel like an outsider from the beginning "because I'm not Baptist." Jake, of course, appeared to have no use for the church, or Tillie's association with it, and made no effort to hide it. But out of respect for his wife and the raising of her sons, if he was sober, he seemed to say little about it. Since Matt was the only son that didn't go to Bob Jones (which excluded him from having his education paid for by his mother) Ro's religion really didn't bother him at all. Matt and Ray, despite Ray's early attempt at the ministry, seemed to be taking more and more after their dad.

Back in Porter, Ray brought up the subject of his mother. "You know Ma's been calling the shots for a long time. I think it sort of whacked her off that you would go against her and have the farewell party here, but I was kinda proud you did."

Ray's last night, the whole family came over, a welcome houseful. After dessert, they took some pictures. When Ray disappeared for a few minutes, I went looking for him and found him in our bedroom, with his mom. She was in tears. They were speaking softly and hugging, so I discreetly left the room. All evening, I sensed Tillie was on the cool side, and later Ray confirmed it. She and Jake didn't stay too long. Ray walked them out to the car, while Matt stood with me on the upstairs porch, watching. "There goes a real pair," Matt said. "Ray is the one Ma keeps close. You should see the notes they used to write to each other, just like love birds, honest to God. She'd stick notes under his pillow; you wouldn't believe it. She's always had him under her thumb – until *you* came along," he said, grinning, steering me back inside.

After Ray had personally said his farewells to the kids, telling them he would be gone on an airplane when they awoke, we finally got to bed. His taxi would come for him in the wee hours of the morning, but he insisted that he didn't want me getting up with him. "I just want to have one more normal ordinary night at home," he said. We hugged, then, under the covers, and I was hoping, praying for some sign, some word from him that he would miss me. So far he had said nothing, not a word about his leaving. My heart was on the verge of breaking, right there. Then Ray said, "You know Ma came and got me and took me into the bedroom to give me twenty dollars. She knew I wouldn't have much after getting you and the kids set up."

All the emotion that I had kept pent up just exploded. "What do you mean? You didn't *take* it, did you?" All the anger of our very first fight, when he had written a letter to his mom those first days together – when we'd lived on pancakes and hot dogs for a month – boiled up inside. In his letter, he closed it, saying, "I have a quarter in my pocket." Within days, a check for twenty-five dollars came in the mail.

"What do you mean asking your mother for money? It isn't her responsibility to support us; we'll make it on our own. You're just a spoiled brat," I had said in anger. "I *never* had money in my pocket, ever. That kind of problem I thought I left behind with my first mother-in-law, *always* giving us money so Huey could go out and get drunk. This time I'm not even going to let it start. Don't you dare cash it; you just send that check right back to her." Well, we had the biggest fight ever. When Ray picked up the phone, after saying that he was getting a divorce, I just couldn't resist saying, "And who are you calling, *your mommy?*"

That was when he swung around on his heel, and his open hand came across my right jaw. When I grabbed my face, in shock, Ray said, "Oh, come on, it was only my *left* hand."

"You ever touch me again, and it'll be the last time." This sudden flare of anger was never far out of mind whenever we had words, but the money issue seemed forever settled between us, *I thought.* Not asking for help, or taking it from anyone, was something I felt very strongly about, but his mother had never really accepted it. She would stick money in our pockets at every opportunity, even after I had expressly asked her not to do that. But here, the last night with my hubby, Tillie had somehow wedged herself between us with that twenty-dollar bill. Ray said, "I'll leave the money for you to give back to her." But his apology was too late. I was angry; Ray was angry. We were both so upset we could hardly speak, much less say to each other the things that I'd hoped would be said. Matt's words, out on the porch, seemed to tell it all, leaving me full of questions.

Hurt and embarrassed, all I could think of as I lay in my husband's motionless arms those last hours together was that twenty-dollar bill.

One morning a few days later, Tillie came for coffee. We sat at the kitchen table talking, about how much all the little ones had grown since she had seen them last, and about Suzie. "You know, Sam, that first time you brought her to visit us, she was just the homeliest baby one ever laid eyes on, poor child, but you and Ray just thought the sun rose and set in her, so of course we wouldn't dare *say* anything, but she's turning out kinda pretty now."

"Yes," I said. "She looks so much like Fran in all her baby pictures, and screams like her, too," I added, in an attempt to lighten things between us.

Tillie laid her head back, and looked at me through her bifocals, "Suzie looks nothing like anyone in *my* family that I can see," she said with disdain.

It was the tone that cut, and it was all I could do to keep from crying. That was when I pulled the twenty-dollar bill out of my pocket. "Here, Ma, Ray and I want to give you back this money; we don't want it, you know. It really upset us both that you did this. Please take it," I said, and shoved it across the table.

The bill was being pushed back at me as Tillie rose to leave. "I have a right to give my son money if I want to," she said over her shoulder, walking to the door.

Not sneaking it to him in the bedroom, I wanted to say, but instead, I just followed on behind, and slipped the bill into Tillie's pocket before she got to the top of the stairs.

As I followed, the money came floating back at me. Grabbing it, I ran down the stairs with it in my hand. Almost to the bottom of the steps, I caught up with her, grabbed her hand, opened it, and slapped the bill into her palm. Closing her fingers over it, I said as calmly as I could, "Ray's perfectly able to support his family without your help, thank you."

For the second time, Tillie threw the money down on the ground at my feet, turned angrily away, and ran up the street.

"Thank goodness I had enough dignity about myself not to run after her *again,*" I wrote that night in the letter to Ray. "How can a Christian be so inconsiderate of someone else's feelings? It is beginning to seem as though the louder a person's declaration of Godliness is, the meaner they seemed to be."

This is when a huge turning point took place inside my head, my letters to Ray written in large bold script, angry words I had never uttered before in my entire life, to anyone.

Somehow Matt's wife, Ro, just by her mere presence, had allowed me to see the other side of Ray's mother, who was beginning to really act like she had not an ounce of love in her anymore, and certainly not for the Savior she so tearfully and syrupy praised.

Afterwards, relating this incident to Matt, he explained, "Ma is a lost cause, Sam; forget it. When Ray was no longer her *Preacher Boy son,* she only had Rich left to keep her dream alive; she's an *Irish mother,* you know."

Ray said he wrote a long letter to his mom, enclosing twenty dollars, and told her in his candid way, "You can take the ordination certificate down off your wall, Ma. I'm in the Army now, and my wife and family come first."

To Ray, I wrote, "Everything I've believed about God and having a loving Jesus in your heart is beginning to look like it wasn't ever, really true."

The realization that my entire life had been affected by beliefs that I was now doubting – a no-no, to question Daddy would bring severe punishment, to question his Biblical teachings, blasphemy against God, "the unpardonable sin" and would send me to hell – the very thoughts in themselves were strange and disquieting. An "obedient child," Daddy said of me, but I could no longer deny the disappointments, one after another, in my narrow religious world, so that the safety of my inner cocoon was gradually dissolving.

Ray's letters from Korea began coming almost daily. Although short and void of the words I longed to hear, the fact that his family was on his mind began to sink in – until the parade of party photos began to arrive, always with a martini in Ray's hand and a fat cigar in his mouth, surrounded by men in suits and pretty Oriental girls in cocktail dresses. After days and days of crying and writing, trying to get the anger and hurt out at the betrayal I was feeling by his mother, yet another "born again Christian," I wrote him, finally trying to explain what was happening to me, how I was getting a different kind of inner toughness that being divorced so young with a child to rear, had only begun. This new feeling that had come over me was really a complete turnaround, an about face. It became blatantly clear when I wrote, "I'm determined to make our marriage work, even if it means sitting on the bar stool next to you, if that's what you want."

Ray's response was swift, and to the point. "That is what I want!" he said. "Hold that thought until I get home."

The first day I smoked a cigarette at home was in front of Sharon, then seven. Sitting on the couch, proudly I lit up. Sharon was down on her knees, at my lap, gazing up at the not-as-yet-learned-to-inhale smoke as it filled the air. Sharon's eyes grew wide at the sight. "Mommy," she said excitedly, "now you are just like everybody else's mommy."

The storm had left snow piled up in drifts so deep we had to stay in the center of the road. But it was Saturday night, and Penny and Jerry's invitation, to take me to the outskirts of Detroit, a good hour's drive from Porter, was too good to refuse with free babysitting by Penny's bachelor brother. All our kids would be at Penny's house. Married to Jerry, Roanne's brother, Penny had become my newest friend. Just that week I had celebrated my 24th birthday with Matt and Roanne – first time ever inside a nightclub and having my first real drink. Tonight, Penny and Jerry were taking me to my first house party. Finally, I was experiencing *the world*, which, up until now, had been a big, dark satanic secret.

House parties in the Midwest, I was learning, were the social discourse of the day. They were usually held in a recreation room, preferably in the basement away from sleeping kids. It could be a gathering of three or ten couples consisting of bosom buddy neighbors or just down-the-street crazies; girls in their latest "do;" guys donned in a black shirt, white tie, and hair cut in a flattop Hollywood DA, usually sucking on a pipe or cigar. There was

Scotch for the slow-to-crank but steady imbiber, vodka screwdrivers and real-cream grasshoppers for the timid sipper, bourbon for the serious whiskey-in-a-glass drinker – none of which really appealed to me. It mattered little what was in it. What mattered was, I had a drink to carry around. Unconsciously still believing I didn't *really* drink, I was forever losing my glass as I wandered shoeless through the din of smoke, making acquaintances with other guests, so the old sound of Johnny Mathis, and the new of Della Reese, would not go to waste. The razzmatazz of Louis Prima and Keely Smith was a picker-upper when things got too slow, usually directed by the hostess familiar with how to keep the party going. The blue humor of Rusty Warren's *Knockers Up, Girls!* offered a great backdrop for food and coffee, a must before venturing back out into the weather, to go home.

The theme of the evening usually started out with everyone disclosing how much they drank at the last party, inflated to correspond with what they didn't remember, didn't want to remember, or lost track of amongst the drinks, low lights and huggin' to Montavani in stocking feet, roving hands, and (if one was sneaky and the one you came with drunk enough not to miss you) a *dry screw* in the laundry room. It was an *Anything Goes* mandate for the sexual revolution bursting upon us as we danced and drank ourselves senseless.

Wanting to talk to everyone, to experience, to listen, to dance, to be held, touched – oh, to be touched – never in my life had I wanted that more. It was the alcohol, Penny said; it was being alone, without a man, Jerry said. The low lights, the music, the feel of hands touching, the whisper of a breath in my ear, an extra sensual hug in a dark corner, and just enough booze to let me feel that what I wanted, needed, was to go all the way with someone, *anyone who would love me, hold me, take care of me*. But I held myself aloof, careful, strangely proper amidst the sexual undercurrent that permeated the air. Still carrying that Christian good-girl facade that had protected me forever from feeling *anything*... Until one extremely late, and booze filled night, the keeper of our children, the silent caregiver who waited at home for our safe return, broke through that impermeable wall, built solidly as steel by the pain of an eternity of broken promises of love... words, a lifetime of meaningless words read daily from *The Book of Lies* — and believing every single one, with my whole heart and soul — I had forever believed there really was One who cared above all else, the only One who could mend my damaged life; always, I had believed – but now there was no one, *no one*. *Where are you, God?*

Darryl was his name. He was quiet, gentle, some said he wasn't too bright, a little slow, but to the kids he was a father, and sometimes mother, and for me he was the gatekeeper of my psyche who kept the goblins of insanity away. I was terrified for night to come, to be alone, to get up and walk across the floor; the creaky boards would cut through my brain like a ghost in the attic. The nights he would stay, he would lie down in the dark on my bed, on top of the covers, until I was asleep, and then slip soundlessly out the door.

Sleep – never had it been so far away; never had I been so afraid, of what, I did not know, or of what connection Ray's leaving me held in my clouded memories.

Finally, in the frightening confusion, I moved into a small bungalow, with a basement filled with windows; I hoped that would help. The kids each had their own small separate space now, the girls in a finished attic, each with a dormer window for a lot of light. Kelly had his own room, downstairs near mine. Darryl would come and cook, bring his paints, brushes, and canvass. Never had I known about such things, about quiet caring, undemanding giving, just being — that was Darryl. Physically ill as a child, a dead-end kid still finding his way, still living at home with mom and dad, a physical therapist was his dream to be: to touch, to heal, to mend suffering souls. He began with my feet, the pathway to heaven, "to your sexuality," he'd say.

"You mean I *have* such?"

Ray came home from Korea on special leave. Receiving his officer's commission for predicting a bloodless coup, he was now a First Lieutenant. His dad came over alone, to visit his son. To him I would question, tearfully, "What did I do to her, Dad? What did I do?"

"Nothing," he said. "You did nothing."

"But why did she stop loving me?"

"She didn't *stop*," he said. "She never *did* in the first place. She had to behave as though she did, or she would lose her first and favored son — you were only the means to an end. If it had not been you, it would have been whoever Ray chose!"

Never? She never loved me? All a lie? Another lie – but what is one more?

Ray stayed home on leave for three weeks. He'd brought a book with him on how to make love, how to satisfy your woman in bed that he'd read on that long trip home. It was the first time I was happy that without a TV, he had to be reading every minute he was awake. "I never really thought about you, before," he said. "I'm sorry; I'll try. I promise I'll try."

Somehow, he was different. I knew the Oriental girls were more than pictures – I knew. *A wife just knows.* He went back to Soul to finish his Hardship Tour. I went to work full time while Penny took care of all our kids, and Darryl continued taking care of my feet. But my feet were just too cold; it would take years to get to the promised land – forty years it said in the Bible.

That last night at our farewell party to leave Michigan, Darryl told Ray, "You're the only one who will ever reach her. I loved her enough, but it is you she wants; no one else will ever do," he said. "No one else."

Ray said Darryl's eyes were brimming with tears.

The Hardship Tour had lasted thirteen months, and Darryl wasn't even physically eligible for the draft.

◆

CHAPTER THIRTEEN

Civilians: 1976

Following Ray's retirement from the Army, to Tucson, the next three years were filled with many activities. I went to work full time for an educational facility that wrote and provided materials to some Louisiana parishes. Still intent on continuing my education, I took a night course in assertiveness training at University of Arizona, and later, a business course at Pima Junior College – the class that spurred me on to get my Real Estate license. In a raging, but short-lived, seller's market, I worked for a retired Air Force Colonel turned Broker and was moderately successful.

Ray was selling insurance in the afternoon and evenings and he was not very satisfied with his newly retired life. When he finished his Master's in Atlanta, he prepared himself to get a job by buying three very expensive suits and three good pairs of shoes; cheap was not his style. While still in Atlanta, I had quit smoking and Ray was determined to do the same. After a week, he was having a very difficult time of it. I came into the family room to find all his shoe boxes stacked at the door and all his suits in plastic bags hanging over the doorway. I asked him what he was doing?

He said, "I'm leaving."

I said, "Where you going?

"To live on the street, like Kelly."

Laughing, I said, "Then why are you taking all those clothes along?"

"Well, I guess you're right," he said rather sheepishly, and immediately picked all his things up and put them back into his closet. Instead, he decided to take a weekend trip alone, to a golf resort up near Phoenix for a few days. While there, Ray started smoking again, and his leaving, and trying to quit, was forgotten.[17]

Although smoking really made me sick, it had taken me several attempts at quitting myself. One day I said to Dr. Hanks, "I

---

[17] He would eventually be able to quit with the help of the surgeon who gave him a post-operative suggestion after emergency gallbladder surgery, while still under anesthesia, in 1988.

don't think I *can* quit because I am a better person when I am smoking." He laughed right out loud and said, "Now, Sam, you *know* that is not true." Somehow that clicked inside my head. Finding a little book based upon psycho-cybernetics, the psychology of using the subconscious to change habits from the inside, it said if I kept telling myself upon waking and before falling asleep, and anytime in between that I thought of it, that I was *going* to quit, without actually consciously trying, that the day would come when I would not even think about lighting up. After three months of changing my smoking routine, hiding my cigarettes, smoking only alone in the bathroom to take the joy out of it– one day it was just gone. Even though the last page of this booklet showed Sigmund Freud, the father of psychology, in a hospital bed with tubes routing cigarette smoke into his larynx – showing how difficult shaking this nicotine addiction was – never again did I have the desire for a cigarette. Until Sean had run away with some classmates to Las Vegas. While waiting to hear from one of the parents that he was alright, I found myself looking all over for something, moving stuff all over my kitchen counter. Suddenly I realized I was looking for a cigarette, that I had read even though you have quit, and had no physical desire for a cigarette, the muscles have habits as well, and my searching behavior was evident of that. When I realized what was happening, I had to laugh, never to experience such a thing again

Ray's boss invited me to lunch one day. He said he liked to find out what would give Ray incentive to sell, sell, sell. I let it slip that I was really tired of doing all the housework, since I was then working full time myself. Like for instance, Ray never lifted a finger to help with dishes. When it was suggested that I just get up from the table along with him and Sean, and go on in the living and read the paper too. I laughed. "The dishes would rot there on the table, and we'd have ants." But I tried it anyhow. The first time I did it, Ray finished reading the paper, and when he walked back through the kitchen, he said, "My, the dishes are still sitting here." He started picking them up and putting them into the sink, and I started helping him. From then on, he just helped me without my ever saying a word, and has continued to do so, until this day. *Amazing!*

It was one of those times I was sitting in the living room, when Sean came in and sat with me, and started crying. "I just can't do it in school, Mom. I just can't. And the teacher doesn't believe me." This is when I knew I had to do something to get him into a Special Ed program. Even after he was evaluated in a hospital inpatient setting, the high school was dragging their feet. Because he was so proud of my Cherokee heritage, he had marked "Native-American" on his initial application. I decided, being in the South West, if I had to use this to get him into the program, I would.

The day I was invited to the school, I was left in a small cubicle of an office to await an interview. I knew that proving my father's mother was Cherokee would be difficult; she died in 1943 and my father had a hard time getting his social security as the building that housed such information in Tennessee had burned down. I knew it was up to the school to prove me wrong, so I sat and waited. One by one a teacher would stick their head into the small office, and say, *Hi*. Nothing else. Since Sean was a freckled-faced red-headed Irish kid, I assumed they had to get a good look at the mother, and apparently, with my very dark hair, brown eyes, olive complexion and very high cheekbones to boot, I passed with flying colors as Sean was placed into a special class with five other students. A fantastic male teacher, who took a great deal of interest in Sean, told us that Sean was almost a savant, in that a part of his brain was exceptional, while the other part was dismal.[18] "If Sean can ever find something he really loves, he will excel," we were told. It seemed to me that music was that something, although Sean had enjoyed a class in cooking, which he loved also; taking a job in a diner part-time was a way to pursue that interest.

After Kelly had been institutionalized in several hospitals across the country, and I had numerous consultations with social workers handling him, lithium was tried and found successful. Kelly had returned home and was enrolled in Pima J. C., and was working for his room and board in a motel on the other side of town. I was ecstatic, our son was *back*. However, it was evident he had eventually stopped his lithium. For the

---

[18] This in fact turned out to be the actual diagnosis that would be given Sean by the neuropsychologist at New England Medical Center, Tufts U., Boston, in 1983. One side of his brain tested genius while the other side, that understood abstracts, was barely passing, which had created an enormous amount of frustration throughout his entire life, setting him up for substance abuse of one kind or another.

most part, he was not acting out, declaring himself to be all knowing, somehow divine, ranting and raving as he had in the past, so I was hoping he would behave reasonably for a few hours at least. Sharon, who was quite far along in her pregnancy with Candi, was visiting from the D.C. area with her husband, Don, and I invited Kelly over for the day. Kelly and Sharon were out in the pool. Notoriously afraid of water, Sharon was leisurely floating in the pool-chair, and Kelly was playing around in the water, when suddenly the laughter changed to screams. I ran out to find Kelly holding Sharon down under the water with her kicking and splashing. After Sharon caught her breath, she was extremely upset, saying Kelly had tried to drown her. Of course, Kelly denied this, "I was just teasing her," he said. But to me, since he knew very well of her fear of water, this was an indication that Kelly had not settled the past with his older sister.

Later that evening, we all went out to dinner together, after which, we offered to drive Kelly back to where he was living, way on the other side of town. He asked for change to make a telephone call on the pay telephone outside the restaurant.

After dropping Kelly off, and after stopping for ice cream, we drove into our driveway to find a red pickup truck, with out-of-state license plates, parked and loaded down with all our teak furniture we'd brought back from Bangkok. As we went into the house, we could see a young male running from our backyard into the desert with a pillowcase in hand. The house was in shambles: plants dumped, broken glass, all my jewelry spread out on the dresser with the expensive things Ray had bought for me in Bangkok, an emerald princess ring in particular, missing. Sharon was beside herself, terrified that she would miscarry from the upsetting day.

Kelly had been dating the daughter of Ray's boss, and when Ray told him about the incident, it was mentioned that Kelly had been over to their house the day before in what appeared to be the same red truck, the license plates were a dead give-away. When we reported the robbery to the police, a stolen vehicle report had been filed on this truck. Although Kelly denied, at the time, having anything to do with the robbery, we had serious doubts as to his honesty. It would be many years later when Kelly would admit to setting up the robbery: "I owed a fence a lot of money for drugs and wasn't thinking right."

Because Ray had acquired valuable marketing skills in the insurance business, he would soon utilize them, along with his intelligence and security background, in his new field of endeavor: Communications — for a new Army telephone.

We had left Suzie back East to complete her Bachelor's in Psychology at Mercer-Atlanta, after asking Dr. Hanks, still our family psychiatrist, if he thought she would be ok, to leave her behind? He said, "Yes, but don't be surprised if you wake up one morning to find her on your doorstep; she is very dependent." Dr. Hanks didn't believe in "labels" then, so he neglected to inform us of Suzie's serious mental state: already suffering from schizoaffective disorder. *How I wish I had known!*

Suzie brought John, her husband-to-be, an MP getting ready to get out of the military, out for a visit. As soon as Suzie graduated, they were planning their wedding in John's hometown, in Florida. She wanted us there and asked her brothers to be in the wedding party.

Suzie and I found a beautiful wedding gown in one of the Tucson shops. Neither of my marriages did I wear a white dress so Suzie suggested I try it on — and she took a picture. It was such a sweet thing for her to do, and proud that I was still the same size as she was — just a small example of Suzie's life long love-hate feelings for me; I was never quite sure where she was coming from at any one given time. It was later explained to me, this came from the schizophrenia, where there is the "splitting within a single personality of the person's thought content and his or her accompanying emotion"[19] not to be confused with what is mistakenly referred to as split personality, which is an altogether different condition.

Following Suzie's visit, and her setting a wedding date, we started making plans to attend. We had given Kelly our Toyota, on which he began picking up the payments. While drinking, he turned the car over, nearly totaling it. Again, we interceded for him and used my Real Estate's office attorney,[20] who did a plea bargain and got Kelly's fine reduced. When Kelly indicated he wanted to leave for Florida and didn't want the car any longer, we bought the car back from him, giving him enough money for the

---

[19] *Surviving Schizophrenia* A Family Manual, E. Fuller Torrey, M.D.

[20] An aside: This attorney also represented one of the top honcho's in the mafia, Joe Bonanos, who happened to be there that morning. We could see him through an open door in one of the other offices, leaning backwards in his chair straining to see us, nearly tipping himself over — Ray assumed with laughter, to look at me, judging from this man's reputation.

Florida trip. However, his deliberate late arrival, making it impossible for him to be in the wedding party with Sean, struck me as unusual, but I never connected this to his childhood crush on Suzie until much later, when one of his serious girlfriends broke up with him. She disclosed to me the reason: While high and they were having sex, he kept calling her Suzie, which freaked her out, she said.

While there in Florida, Ray applied to a local company who was also interested in developing the same secured telephone system for the Army that his latest company in Tucson was working on. His being hired on the spot generated another move for us. Being civilians was turning out to not be much different than active duty Army, but we were looking forward to being near Suzie again.

Sean, now in 11th grade, was accepted in Florida's Special Ed program. Although he kept a part time job, his drinking and drug use progressed. When Kelly was clean and on his meds, Sean was not, and vice versa. The counselors told me they had a "symbiotic" relationship. I dreaded to pick up a ringing phone, never knowing what I would hear. Sean threatening to "go live with Kelly on the street, or in that barn, wherever my brother is," was a constant threat.

Kelly was spending most of his time in Atlanta, where he had gone to high school. But he would send me tapes of his singing the songs he wrote, and long letters with "lyric's" to the tunes he heard in his head. His desire to be a rock star, had never waned. His psychotic episodes were an expected thing: seventeen times admitted around the country before he was 21. He would come home, skinny, bare chested and in flip-flops, one time even barefooted, and turn himself into the local hospital to detox and get back on lithium. I would buy him a whole wardrobe so he could find a job, and one morning, we'd find the house key on the kitchen table. Gone, again, a losing battle.

Ray had settled in at his new job working with several Ph.D.'s on the new communication system for the Army. Our country was in shock from the taking of the hostages by Iran, and President Carter had made an attempt to rescue them and was using the secured radios Ray's new company was developing. Stress monumental for Ray, when this attempt failed. The first recognizable sign of Ray's PTSD (post traumatic stress disorder) catching up with him since Vietnam, when he found himself in his car parked on the side of the road on the way home from work one day, hours lost. The child psychiatrist Sean was using willingly saw Ray and put him on a heavy dose of his first anti-depressants, several little green pills daily, which were to become a symbol of Ray's outside intervention he would humorously refer to as his "little green men" who had "set up shop between my brain and my skull," he said, keeping watch over his sanity.

Reagan was running against Carter for the presidency and it was common knowledge that they both proclaimed their Christian faith. One day a GOP canvasser knocked at my door and I asked him how he chose between the two of them? He said, "Reagan, of course, because he is more *pliable*." When I asked my dad, then also living in Florida, who he was going to vote for, he said, "When I was poor, with only one shoe to my name and Roosevelt came in, I vowed I would always vote Democratic. So I will have to vote for Carter." But he added quickly with a grin, "I'll pray that Reagan will win."

It seemed that Florida was full of Fundamentalist Christians, especially those in business, even the dentist I went to proclaimed to be of that persuasion, by the literature left in the waiting room. From my personal experience, if someone with whom I was dealing told me they were "born again," I had a tendency to hide my wallet. Oral Roberts had initiated the rich man's philosophy into the evangelical movement, back when I was a girl, which seemed to ignore the teachings of Jesus on this subject.[21] Instead, Oral Roberts taught that if you were really serving God, you would be rewarded financially. (An incentive, I think, to send *him* the "ten percent tithes" off the top, which appears to have been co-opted by TV/radio evangelists since). This new wave of "Christianity" seemed to have turned otherwise honorable people into downright liars and thieves, i.e., Jimmy and Tammy Baker, due, I believe, to our tax-exempt laws regarding religiously affiliated institutions.[22]

---

[21] Jesus said, "It is easier for a camel to go through the eye of a needle, than for a rich man to enter into the kingdom of God." Matthew 19:24, King James Bible

[22] A most recent example if this misuse of the tax law is the "C Street Center" in D.C., (part of *The Fellowship Foundation AKA the Family*, a strongly connected political organization) which is masquerading as a church but is nothing more than a boarding house with cheap rent for influential members of Congress. Joe Hallett, *The Columbus Dispatch*, Feb 23, 2010 blog; Jeff Shallet *The Family*.

Melissa was a beautiful red-head in Sean's school about whom he had become very serious; Suzie was working full time as a waitress and her husband was a new cop on the beat; Sharon had decided to stay at home up in the D.C. area and be a full-time mom with her new baby, Candi, now three years old – her husband, Don, still at the White House.

Kelly had come home and checked himself into the local psychiatric hospital and was going with a new girl who worked there. It was during this stay that he brought her home on a weekend pass, along with Gene, a male nurse who had taken a liking to Kelly. An unusually funny guy, Gene would sit with Ray, in between swimming, and tell stories. It wasn't too far into the weekend that I began to realize that Gene was gay, however Ray had no idea and kept on telling his jokes, mostly slanted to poke fun at his own Irish heritage, and some at the gay community.

After Kelly and his guests had gone back to the hospital that first weekend, I broke it to Ray, who was dumbfounded to learn that Gene was an okay guy. "Had I known ahead of time, I wouldn't have allowed myself to really get to know him" — a real turning point in Ray's life-long feelings toward homosexuals. Here he had spent a better part of his military career as a polygraph examiner rooting out gays, and this personal experience with Gene had taught him a valuable lesson. Kelly's open minded view of the world had forced his father to confront his prejudices in a very subtle but real way. In years to come, we were to have several gay friends as result of this learning experience, which wouldn't have been possible before meeting Gene.

My education was continuing at Eckerd College, majoring in *The Helping Professions*. I was introduced to Clinical Psychology and the many avenues to the subconscious: Fritz Perls and his gestalt therapy; Carl R. Rogers and his humanistic approach to self-actualization (which Dr. Hanks had used with me back in the '60's); Maslow's hierarchy of needs and how a D-responder is so preoccupied with their own needs and agenda, he finds it difficult to even hear what another person is saying, the B-responder is characterized by "just being" – I classified myself in between these two, working at the latter; Rolfing was demonstrated by a Certified Rolfer who used soft tissue manipulation to release stress. Because of my severe headaches I later had several Rolfing sessions, a unique and relaxing experience, actually getting at the emotions from the outside in, rather than the other way around as in most psychotherapy.

Years prior, Dr. Hanks had suggested I look into NLP (Neuro-Linguistic Programing), developed by Bandler and Grinder, *Frogs Into Princes*, who used the teaching tales of Milton H. Erickson, M. D., *My Voice Will Go With You (edited by Sidney Rosen, M. D.)* and his use of psychotherapy and hypnosis. Through therapeutic storytelling we were able to understand how hypnosis works. In the NLP seminars, reframing was demonstrated on how to change negative experiences into positive ones, such as phobias, by using self-hypnosis. Remembering the first time a negative experience happened, one can undo its negative hold upon the subconscious.

NLP taught how individuals interact through respective representational systems, i.e., the five senses: seeing, hearing, touching(feeling) smelling and tasting. Learning how to detect how another person perceives the world through their language can be helpful, not only in day to day interactions, but also in dealing with clients and coworkers. Ray was definitely visually oriented, thus his love for reading and golf, whereas my music background clearly indicated I received communication through hearing, and why Ray's verbal acumen has been the instrument that has kept me so in tune with him, no matter the words; it is the sound of his voice that draws me in. To develop my visual awareness, it was suggested I start transferring what I saw onto canvass, forcing me to *look* at the world around me. Fascinating it was to be aware of another part of myself that had been locked up for so many years. It was inevitable that my subconscious would come through this visual medium and become the catalyst for the therapy I would later receive with Dr. Comas, the psychiatrist who I would meet through Sean's attempted suicide.

The following poem seems to express just one more milestone reached in my emotional evolution.

I Am A Person

I was a mother/I was a wife/but now, I am a person simply alive/My days as a child were a shadow, it seems/I was a child made up of dreams/The world around me went on day by day, but only the future concerned me, but the Past always stayed/When motherhood entered this fantasy world, my dreams became tangible, my future unfurled/ living became centered in my little girl/My days work was anxious/my night filled with tears/the loneliness "mothers" feel — babe's sleep night's sole companion/ Mother, is what I was/I was mother.

I was a wife in between all the others/between laundry and cooking and directing each one, day by day, hour by hour, as I felt I was needed/I generally was there as a wife, unimpeded – as long as my child had not pleaded.

Sometimes, somewhere, among the diversities of four, there arose a great demand in my inner soul/to conquer with love all the short comings I'd done/You see, love conquers a multitude of shortcomings – - a multitude I have, I am/So much love it must take to or'e come all I am, all I have, in my children done.

This love is there, just there, it will never go away/this love is there, in anger, in hurt, in scarcity of spirit and affection/this love is like a teddy bear, it's just there.

My motherhood, the all protecting hour by hour caring part of my life has come to its end – - twenty-seven years of daily, constant caring/I leaned to care for myself while learning to care for my children/I was my own best friend, my mother, I am.

Now I am a person, first, and then a wife/If I do not recognize that I am a person first, I will not survive not being a wife when that day comes/If I am a person first, and then a wife/I can afford to be more generous with who I am as my survival will not depend on the continuance of being a wife, but I will continue to be a person/This person must emerge slowly and strongly and fearlessly/that is what is frightening now.

This new self is emerging with shyness, but with tenderness and love/I am still a mother, nurturing to all who are in need/I am more of a wife as there is more of me to share and care/I love being a wife/I love sharing myself with someone who wants me as well as needs me/

I cannot explain anymore "whys" for my family's behavior – I am tired of trying/Whatever they are for today, I must try to deal with, keeping perspective WHO I AM whether or not I know WHO THEY ARE at the moment.

I am a person first/I am a wife secondly/and the permanence of my motherhood remains as the mirror of how I came to be a person/Perhaps I have been my own mother?

— L. L. Morton, 10 Jan 1980

Through all the new learning taking place, volunteering at a care center for developmentally challenged kids, I was asked to assist in the class of three-year-olds, a true precedent to facing my three-year-old self under hypnosis, with Dr. Comas.

Following Sean's attempted suicide, I became a regular patient of Dr. Comas, who used hypnosis to bring back many memories long repressed and showed me how much my father's sexual ill-treatment of me as a child had influenced my behavior throughout my life. Somehow I had been unconsciously telling men that the only way I could have intimacy was through sex. Even though I had ceased to respond in the old way overtly, I was noticing that when meeting someone with whom I had a real connection, somehow during the conversation, sex was inadvertently brought into the verbal mix. The fact that I was becoming aware of this, was an "encouraging sign," what therapy was all about, in fact, to bring to consciousness underlying tendencies, to which I had been oblivious, for years.

"Overinvestment in your children" was another thing Dr. Comas mentioned regularly, "especially your boys." The poem I had written the year before was evidence that I had already begun to realize this. However, having to deal with Sean, in one residential treatment program or another, made my attempt difficult, and would continue to be for years to come.

Doctor Comas recommended that we put Sean in a two-year program based on behavior modification techniques taught by B. F. Skinner, which neither Ray nor I agreed with.[23] Instead, we chose to work with Sean in the RISK residential program through the State of Florida. This stay had followed Sean's deliberately puncturing his colon while very drunk and needing emergency surgery, another three-month stint in hospital. After RISK's discharge, we accompanied Sean to AA and met with his AA counselors often. We were not only hoping this would help Sean, but Ray and I benefitted from it also. In fact, it was Sean's AA counselor who recommended I "paint" my feelings.

Sean had moved in with Otto, a restauranteur, who ran an exceptionally elegant place we, along with Sean, had frequented. Otto's apparent financial support of Sean appalled me, as it put Sean in an unhealthy situation, but Dr. Comas assured me "it is purely manipulation on Sean's part, making you anxious so you will let him come back home."

---

[23] We were proven correct in our evaluation of Skinner, since he is no longer even recognized in psychology texts. His opinion that we are all born with a clean slate, and that our environment is what fills that in has been disproved by what we have learned about DNA and how the genes we are born with have a great deal to do with who we are and turn out to be, although individual choice as we grow and develop, which NLP likes to stress, is also important, as well as our environment.

Over the holidays, we had a house full: all four kids, to include Kelly, Sharon and Don and their baby girl, Candi; Suzie and her husband who were living in Tampa, near us; Milwaukee house guests from my mother's side of the family, and Daddy and his wife, Charity. Living near the water, relatives were all too eager to visit, but Ray was so out of it from his little green pills, he remembered little of the entire holiday, a typical consequence, I was to learn, which followed such a mental episode.

When Sean was transferred from Dr. Comas to Highland House in North Carolina, after six weeks, I went up to visit him. Sean had been put on lithium, and he was a changed boy. We went to see *Raiders of the Lost Ark*, and Sean sat through the whole movie, paid rapt attention, and we had a delightful time together. Finally, I was finding an answer to Sean's problem through the very medication Dr. Hanks had recommended earlier, even saying that he thought Ray might also benefit from it. (When later I would suggest to the doctor in North Carolina that since Sean was back home, and off his lithium, he didn't seem ready to make changes, his doctor wrote, *"I am sorry to hear that things aren't going well for Sean. From my point of view, what you said about Sean at least not changing until he really wants to, may not be accurate. It seems to me that he suffers from a psychotic illness and that his psychosis is beyond his control much of the time. I believe that there may be an answer for him in medication and in other organic therapies which help the mind function more appropriately."* This evaluation of Sean was clearly contrary to the one Dr. Comas had given, and I took it to heart, and why I was reticent in my dealings with Sean from then on. I had seen, with my own eyes, the difference lithium had made, not only calming his hyperactivity, but Sean's ability to listen and communicate was unbelievably better.)

On the way home from my visit with Sean, I stopped in Atlanta to look up Kelly, where he had gone after leaving the hospital in Florida. I found him living on the outskirts of town, in the end of a friend's barn. Kelly was not present, but his friend showed me his small room. In it was a cot, a throw rug, and a coffee table. The orderliness of this very clean area Kelly was in, struck me as unusual, as his life seemed to be in shambles. It was explained to me later that was how Kelly was dealing with the confusion that went on in his head, by keeping order on the outside to the best of his ability. (Sort of like the reverse of a person whose orderliness is on the inside and is able to operate with a cluttered, piled high desk.) When we later got together, I took Kelly out to lunch and we talked at length. I hated to leave him as I could see he was back into his drug use, but I loved being with him. As I hugged him goodbye, I said, "You are so beautiful, Son."

"That's the first time anyone ever told me that," he said with tears in his eyes.

Now over age twenty-one, his mom was beginning to see the beauty that was her first born son. All the lying and stealing throughout his school years, the running away behavior, the robbery he had set up in Tucson, seemed to fade into the background. A beautiful son was under all that disarray, if we could only get to that part of him that had such potential. I would never stop trying. But it would be years... Meanwhile, Kelly would send tapes home, lyrics to songs he heard in his head, beautiful words that would only confirm what I had said to him that day.

> My name is Kelly Christopher Malorry [pen name: Christopher Zoro]. This is a song called: Sing Me A Song Of Freedom. There's four verses. I wrote it on the highway, hitchhiking. Many times when I'm hitchhiking I get bored, so I'll think of a song to get me by. To make it. And most of my songs are about love, because, as far as I'm concerned, that's the only thing that got me through anything:
> (singing) Sing me a song of freedom, let it whisper through my soul/I ain't got no wife or no children, I ain't under the power of gold/No, no, not me; no, no, not me; no, no-o/
> I don't belong to any organization, I've paid twice my share of dues/Freedom is my point of destination, I've got holes in both my shoes/Ah ha, that's me, ah ha, that's me, ah ha/
> Sing me a song of understanding, so I can better understand/all this delusion people are handling, all the dreams and all their plans/Sing it for me, ah ha; for me, ah ha, for me-e-e/
> Sing me a song of wisdom, to help make clear my mind/I need to kick this syndrome that's making me do time/Sing it for me, ah ha, for me, ah ha, for me-e-e/ [spoken] But most of all...
> [singing, slower rhythm] Sing me a song of tender love and let it pump through all my veins/Loneliness is what I pay for my freedom, and I know I'll never change/Sing it for me, ah ha; for me, ah ha, for me-e/

Kelly has written volumes of words, much of which contains Biblical lingo he learned "when in jail with only a Gideon Bible to read," he says. He especially likes rhyming:

> Devils to Ashes; Angels to Dust/Angels to Love; Devils to Lust/
> Angels to healing; Devils to Pain/Devils to Sun; Angels to Rain/
> Devils to Run; Angels to Fly/Angels know; Devils ask Why?/
> Angels filled; Devils none/It is finished; it is done!

Kelly took piano lessons, as did his siblings, but Sean was the only one who really pursued it. Unfortunately, musicians seem to share a common thread behaviorally: drugs and alcohol. When Sean is sober and taking his meds, he has left his keyboards sit for weeks without touching them, saying, "music makes me want to *use*."

R ay made a point of telling his kids the same thing his father had told him as a teenage driver: "Don't ever let me see any pecker tracks in my car, and if you end up in jail for any reason, I won't lift a finger to get you out." Despite this admonishment from his dad, Sean did end up in jail. I was terrified for him, and even though Ray had said, "Don't go looking for heartache," after several of Sean's pleading calls, I decided I had to visit him. Although his dad had not missed one day of visits with Sean during his three months in hospital following his first suicide attempt, I made the visit to the maximum security facility – alone.

By the time I got into the cell block, I had been refused entrance twice: first to return my handbag to the car trunk, and again, to store my extra keys and metal from the key chain, when the electronic eye beeped me going in.

Finally able to settle down for a conversation with Sean, I looked at him through the heavy glass that was sealed in at the bottom by a few inches of strong, metal mesh. Layered into several thicknesses, it separated the narrow counter between us, forcing us to bend down at a most uncomfortable level to speak. In such a disconcerting posture, I seemed to blurt out whatever came into my head. Not really thinking about where I was, or why, was the best way. I had prepared myself not to cry, but I might throw-up…

"Thanks so much for coming, Mom," Sean said very quietly. "I sure never wanted you to see me in such a place."

"It's been so long since I saw you," I said, wishing for the hug he always gave me. He never passed me in the house that he didn't reach out, it was his way, so like my own father, but he looked and sounded like a small version of *his* father. Such a mixture we all are, I thought, but I said, "You're eating well enough. Or did Otto contribute to all those calories?"

The thought of this situation upset me, so I didn't wait for Sean's answer, instead, I continued the recent telephone conversation we'd had on the subject: "There is no way I am going to believe you have suddenly turned gay," my voice had reached a pitch, "not after all that psychological testing."

Sean's hand shot up. Leaning his head forward and speaking very softly into the mesh that seemed to swallow his words, I only heard, "...friends."

Speaking much louder than I had intended, I said, "No matter what you call it, I call it prostitution."

Sean was waving his hand in front of my bent head, trying to stop my words. The table behind him was filled with men in jailhouse blues, playing cards. The only Caucasian among them had momentarily glanced our way. "Mom... Mom... stop!" Sean was saying. He put his fingers to his lips and rolled his eyes upward, from one side to the other. "Ya wanna get me killed?" he whispered into the mesh.

The look on my youngest son's face I had never seen before; fear was not part of his personality.

"I'm sorry," I said, covering my mouth as I spoke.

"Next time, *think* before you say something," he said. The brittle tone in his voice was so unlike him, his fair Irish skin had begun to turn a bright pink.

Clutching my stomach, new anxiety sent waves of butterflies through my middle. I looked over Sean's head at the men. Even though they were locked in on the other side, they frightened me; there were five of them. The one who had turned especially got my attention. He sat sideways in the chair so that his long legs stretched out the length of the table. His shirt sleeves were rolled up to the shoulder seams exposing tattoos the length of his arms. Over his huge biceps on his right arm, I could make out an eagle; down his forearm, a snake; I tried not to stare. The man looked to be at least in his forties, his closely trimmed hair accentuated its thinning. Clenching and unclenching his jaws made his large ears move. I noticed his right ear was pierced; the ragged empty hole looked grotesque. *Left is right – right is wrong, on the street,* I had heard. All eyes were upon him and the snap-like venom with which he played the cards seemed to reverberate with authority. I tried not to think about the stakes of the game. Sean wasn't kidding, I thought, as my buttocks grew hard in my chair. Bending very close, whispering, I asked, "What about the white guy? Is he..."

Sean raised his hand off the counter just an inch and spread his fingers in a fan-like gesture. His eyebrows shot together into a ferocious frown, his beautiful blue eyes alive with daggers. His lips were pressed together so tightly, they bulged and lost their color.

This unsettling response left me at a loss for words. *What was left to talk about?* Certainly not the rape charge, or the girl in question either. My mind shrugged; what did it matter? My kids never did tell me the whole truth anyway, I was learning, only what would mollify me and stop my questions.

Suddenly, Sean leaned forward and spoke softly, "You're wrong, Mom, with Otto it wasn't..." mouthing the word *prostitution.*

It took a lot of persuasion to get Sean to allow a Public Defender to represent him. He thought at first he could handle it himself. He would await three months for his court hearing.

This was a time of great change, growth within me. It was also a time of social change for the whole country. Even Edith was making great strides standing up to Archie on *All In The Family* a weekly show that was one of our favorites. Phil Donahue and Merv Griffith talk shows were a daily inspiration for me. I had kept a journal for many years I called *My Paper Doctor*. Especially appropriate, as we were anticipating another move, was one particular comment made by an unusually well-spoken woman, Maya Angelo, who wrote, *I Know Why The Caged Bird Sings.* Words she attributed to her grandmother, words of inspiration, paraphrased:

> *Get Steppin'. I am here NOW... all of me... everything I am, was, am not, was not — whatever, HERE I AM. When I leave here, I will take all of me, but I will leave the chair. Give it up! It was good while you sat in it, but leave it behind you. Don't hang on to it. Don't say, "I paid for this chair, it is mine, I won't let anyone else have it." FOOLISHNESS! Give it up! Go, all of you, to the next place, to the NEXT chair. Get Steppin'!*

Being near Suzie, and having such a beautiful home there, it was hard to leave Florida, but as we had so many times before, I knew we would manage to make a new home in the *NEXT* place. The intense therapy with Dr. Comas allowed so many "chunks," as phrased in NLP, to fall away for me to reclaim much of my past, although the anxiety I experienced over my children would never completely cease, I would eventually learn. Drug abuse and mental illness were subjects just being newly addressed publicly. Carol Burnett shocked everyone when she told the world of her teen daughter's addiction, opening up a dialogue on a heretofore unmentionable subject. My search to find answers as to how the unconscionable sexual behavior, perpetuated by my daughters, could have taken place unbeknownst to me, would remain as a life-long emotional burr and drive me to understand.

The many term papers I was doing, I chose to share with Dr. Comas, who encouraged me to continue with my writing outside of school. Leaving me on my own, after such in-depth therapy, was similar to "recovering from major surgery," but I was assured I would continue to "heal."

Through much reading, many of my questions about my religious upbringing had been put to rest. First Mitchner's historical novel, *The Source*: showed me how religion probably came into being; *The Passover Plot: Did Jesus really die on the cross?* by Hugh J. Schonfield, a Jewish scholar who separated fact from fiction in the historical sense, clearly showing how the stories in the Bible were written by men, not "by God." My History of Civilization professor, in Pennsylvania, left me with a clear understanding of how Christianity had managed to survive for so many centuries. The incorporation of the man, Jesus, with the God, Jesus, into its theocracy allowed an identity with the human part, which really is the actual basis of Christian teachings. Learning about the historical man, which Schonfield clearly documents for us, allowed me to continue questioning my early teaching. Since then, knowing that Jesus spoke mostly in symbolic representation, it seems obvious to me that when references were made to himself, our humanity was the intended symbol. And when he spoke of his father, God, the reference was to the soul, or the spiritual, internals. The following is an illustration of such an interpretation:

The Lord's Prayer[24]

A great Jewish teacher once shared, with his closest friends, his personal beliefs and daily expectations for maintaining his own self-esteem, when he said:

OUR FATHER
The caring inner-part of each of us;
WHICH ART IN HEAVEN
Which lives within the soul of each of us;
HALLOWED BE THY NAME.
We acknowledge; especially this part of us that gives us each our own identity and makes us uniquely different even as our own name.
THY KINGDOM COME
May our lives take on constructive paths:

---

[24] Reported and preserved in the King James Version of the Bible: Matthew 6:19-13, paraphrased by L. L. Morton.

our inner-most home be in order;
THY WILL BE DONE
So that our true purpose for living will be exhibited
ON EARTH
In the physical, tangible and visual part of us; our body;
AS IT IS IN HEAVEN
As well as the emotional or innermost part of us; the feeling and nurturing
part that is "felt" by others;
GIVE US THIS DAY OUR DAILY BREAD
May the part of us that is responsible for the upkeep of our physical
existence do its best– just for today!
AND FORGIVE US OUR DEBTS [TRESPASSES, SINS or MISTAKES]
At the same time, we accept that human part of us that makes mistakes
and so sometimes hurts others, as well as ourselves,
AS WE FORGIVE OUR DEBTORS
[THOSE WHO MAKE MISTAKES AGAINST US]
May we also remember that same humanness in others when we become
the recipient of their mistakes.
LEAD US NOT INTO TEMPTATION
Let our judgement and good sense overcome our childish "want to's"–
with strength and perseverance.
BUT DELIVER US FROM EVIL
Let our patience and understanding of life, people and ourselves;
with our strong desire to bring no harm,
win out over obstacles that we might face;
FOR THINE IS THE KINGDOM
For, after all, it is our own life that will be affected
by whatever we choose to do.
AND THE POWER
And we have the strength within us at all times
AND THE GLORY
Sometimes even beyond what would appear natural – as though
possessed of an unusual force.
FOREVER,
And this source of strength is within each of us, on going,
and will never cease, or pass away.
AMEN!
These things I believe, and expect– for me, today!

The interpretation Thomas Harris gives in *I'm OK–You're OK*, the morals chapter, seemed to put the words of Jesus into perspective for me regarding the religious "born-again" experience. When he equates "being struck by grace," a term used by Christian theologians, to "experiencing *I'm OK- You're OK*," it is suggested that at birth we begin to "adapt" to others view of the world to the point of losing ourselves in the process. When Jesus said, *Except a man be born again, he cannot see the kingdom of God,* this "rebirth of which Jesus speaks... is the rebirth of the natural Child. This is possible after the Adult comprehends the NOT OK, which was produced by the adaptive, or civilizing, process. ...Every preprogrammed idea of what God is gets in the way of experiencing God. ...Grace [*I'm OK – You're OK*] strikes us when we are in great pain. ...It strikes us when we feel our separation is deeper than usual, because we violated another life. ..when despair destroys all joy and courage. Sometimes at that moment a wave of light breaks into our darkness, and it is as though a voice were saying: "*You are accepted... Simply accept the fact that you are accepted!* If that happens to us, we experience grace. ...everything is transformed... And nothing is demanded of this experience. ...nothing but acceptance."

In light of this interpretation, I gained a new understanding of the following Biblical passage:

> *WHEN I WAS A CHILD, I SPAKE AS A CHILD*[25]
> *When I was little, with a limited field of experience, my vocabulary was limited to that experience, I understood as a child, my learning was geared to the level of my growth and age, within my limited experience--being only a child, I thought as a child; since my thoughts could only reflect upon what I had up to that point in my life learned and experienced, my thoughts were also limited --being only a child;*
>
> *BUT WHEN I BECAME A MAN, I PUT AWAY CHILDISH THINGS.*
> *But by the time my body grew into a physical adult, my mind --and all that is subject to it in this body of mine-- had gained considerable experience, both in speaking and in my feelings. My vocabulary grew, and my feelings expanded beyond myself toward the whole world. The overabundant concern for myself that I had experienced as a child took on perspective. As an adult I realized that my needs and wants, and my struggle to fulfill them, were no longer the center of the universe, but avenues used to communicate with others, to help each other fulfill each our own needs and wants.*
>
> *FOR NOW WE SEE THROUGH A GLASS, DARKLY;*
> *Now, although I am an adult, there are many things I still do not understand about myself and those around me; but I am beginning to become aware of the importance of my own words, my own*

---

[25] *A letter written by Paul of Tarsus to his friends at Corinth: preserved in the king James version of the Bible (1 Corinthians 13: 11, 12, & 13) and © paraphrased by L. L. Morton©

understanding, and the patterns of my thoughts and how they influence the way that I feel. It is as though I were looking at shadows in a clouded mirror;
        BUT THEN FACE TO FACE:
But one of these days the shadows will become clearer to me, and the images I will see, looking at my own face in the mirror, will be as though I were looking into the face of another human being. Then I will see myself, the real and true me:
        NOW I KNOW IN PART;
Already I am beginning to see outlines of that person who is the real and true me taking shape in the shadows. I am already recognizing some parts of that inner person, and already know parts of that person's feelings. It is like working a puzzle with only one part visible to me at a time;
        BUT THEN SHALL I KNOW EVEN AS ALSO I AM KNOWN.
But someday, as I grow and learn more about myself, I will, I am certain, become fully aware of that whole inner person that is the real and true me who appeared as shadows, in the past, in the clouded mirror. In fact, I believe, from all that I see around me in my adult world, that I will eventually recognize all those shadowy parts; and what I will see will be all the things others already see in me-- the ugly parts as well as the beautiful. Then I will see myself truly -- that inner person that keeps hiding from me it seems, when I am the most needy-- and will understand fully my weaknesses, as well as my strengths. It will be as though I have become acquainted with a brand new person, although-- that person was there all the time waiting for my inner vision to clear up and get into focus.
        AND NOW ABIDETH FAITH, HOPE AND CHARITY, THESE THREE;
Until this fully happens to me, there lives within my field of consciousness a belief that this will eventually truly transpire. Until that time, I will continue to BELIEVE, EXPECT, and ACCEPT whatever comes to me as part of this eventual awareness. All three things are equally important to the fruition of this happening--
        BUT THE GREATEST OF THESE IS CHARITY.
But ACCEPTING whatever comes to me, ACCEPTING all the changes which occur within and without, is the most important thing I can do for that person-- who is me, right now!

My upbringing had closed off my ability to learn, so that I grew up believing I was dumb. My literature books in high school, I had to sneak into the house; the Bible was the only book I was allowed to read, openly. The movie theater, which tempted many of my church friends, I was afraid to enter for fear Jesus would return in the "rapture," and leave me behind, letting me grow up, in essence, outside of my own culture.[26] But finally, in continuing my education with teachers who were very supportive, I was learning that I did have intelligence, eventually passing three Real Estate courses to be licensed in three states. Even though at times, under great stress and heartache, I would wonder how simple it would be to go back to that cocoon where I just "believed." But it was Daddy's devaluing of me through his behavior, creating such hurt and anger, that I *was* able to question his words. Learning to assume responsibility for my own behavior seemed contrary to "believing that no matter what you do, Jesus will forgive you." Personal responsibility seems to have been circumvented, strangely resembling a psychotic state. Choices *do* have consequences, I was learning all too late in life.

When Reagan invaded Granada, the Army personnel had to use private land-lines to report to their Stateside base and call their families. After Ray's interview with Universal Switching Systems(USS), the Boston company that had great interest in building and selling a Roving Secured Telephone(RST) to the Army, USS offered to buy our house and move us. With interest rates above 16%, we were especially thankful. Although we had lived in almost every area of the country, plus Japan and Thailand, New England was a whole new experience for both of us. Going back to "snow country" was a pleasure I was looking forward to. Hot climates were not conducive to cuddling, and I was sure that if we were living back in cooler weather, I would find Ray's arms once again. I hadn't learned as yet that his Vietnam experiences – sleeping with a rifle under his pillow, a machete at his side, and a native interpreter at his feet whose allegiance was never totally certain – had left him so apprehensive that outside of sex our otherwise physical exchanges had grown almost non-existent.

---

[26] The day of Martin Luther King's funeral, I was sent home from work, fearing a race riot in Atlanta. I had to cross over the bridge just above his church; the streets were filled with throngs of people as far as you could see. By the time I got to my house, there wasn't a soul anywhere in sight. At my front door, all of my kids shoes were set out in a row along the top step. The first thought popping into my mind was: *Jesus has come, has taken my kids, and left me behind.* Of course, I had to laugh at myself, but that's how such teachings take hold, in essence – a total programming of the child's psyche. (The kids were all inside, glued to the TV!)

One of the men Ray had worked with in the RST creative stage, in Florida, was already in Boston. It was his influence that persuaded USS that with Ray's Intel background, his having worked on the program since inception out in Tucson when it was just a bunch of diagrams on a blackboard, and his connections inside the military – having been at the Army War College for three years, 300 students per each class, two classes per year, many of whom were now in positions of command and decision making — Ray was their man.

Sean's court appearance on the rape charge was just around the corner. There was little I could do for him even if I had stayed in Florida. Soon after we left, and Sean was finally persuaded to allow a public defender to represent him, the PD had found several witnesses who were at the hotel dance that night. The papers had reported that Sean had taken the girl out on the beach for sex. Sean had apparently made a rude comment about her lack of hygiene after she had disrobed. Angered, she had run into the hotel lobby completely naked, claiming that Sean was trying to rape her. However, the witnesses reported Sean had been so drunk he could hardly stand up to dance, much less pursue the girl sexually. The record showed she had used this accusation on others also, in vain. The case was thrown out, and Sean was released, but the experience left him terrified of ever ending up in such a place again.

In Atlanta, Kelly had been working as a janitor in a mall and was arrested for shoplifting. Incarcerated in the federal penitentiary there, for a two year stretch, with my intercession he was put on lithium and medically supervised throughout his confinement.

Suzie was working and living with her husband in Tampa. She was in a snit, again, this time over her last letter to Sharon, which had been returned – corrected. Suzie's difficulty with reading and writing I believed was due to severe dyslexia, but we would later realize it was a result of the underlying schizophrenia that was building up to crisis proportions.[27] A disorder of the thought processes, it would become more noticeable when the hormonal changes began during pregnancy, complicating her bipolar genetics: a disorder of the mood system,[28] why, we began

---

[27] Schizophrenic writing is referred to as *"word salad."* E. Fuller Torrey, M.D., *Surviving Schizophrenia.*

[28] This combination of the two illnesses, bipolar and schizophrenia, is called: schizoaffective disorder.

to realize, Dr. Hanks had persuaded Suzie to wait until she was at least twenty-five before starting her family.

Suzie's feelings toward both Sharon and me were expressed from time to time in outright rage. Once, in her teens, Suzie had dated a young man upon whom Sharon had a secret crush. Suzie really didn't care that much for him, but she admitted to me she was dating him "just to get back at Sharon." When I addressed this behavior with Dr. Hanks, his response was, "Suzie is what I call pseudo-sadistic. She rather loves to turn the screws at times," much like Ray's mother, I told myself, a trait I would too often forget when dealing with either of them. One of Suzie's latest peeves was she was convinced Sharon was a lesbian, and she didn't want to have anything further to do with her. If a letter came from Sharon, she would throw it back at me and refuse to read it. But it was Suzie's progressive alcohol use that was most disturbing. Our last goodbye-night out to a restaurant with her and John, she only drank mai-tais throughout our dinner.

Sharon had moved in with Val, her neighbor, and had delivered the baby girl she was carrying when she had visited us during Sean's hospitalization. We were to visit Sharon later on in this new living arrangement. Ray, who considered Don a friend, was furious with Val, who had gotten Sharon pregnant despite her still being married to Don. But I was more optimistic. Val was definitely an Italian family man, who had gained custody of his two kids – just one of the excuses Sharon gave for moving in with him – and I had high hopes that Sharon would figure things out, for her own sake and that of the children now in her care.

I n a Boston suburb, in 1982, we were lucky to find a beautiful house in the process of being built. The Real Estate market was so slow, we lucked out and got it on our first offer in time to choose the final decor, i.e., carpeting, paint color, wallpaper, and such. Dealing with the completion of the yard drew quite a surprise when the landscaper came to the door with the shrubs in hand asking for my husband, "to show me where he wants these to be planted." To which, I replied, "My husband is at work, but I can tell you where to place them."

"I don't deal with women," he said, and angrily stomped off.

This story was repeated around the Bridge table by the other girls who had bought from the same builder and had to deal with this same landscaper. Apparently New England was not as progressive as their reputation was propounded to be.

For several years, Ray and I had gone through difficult times, in our personal relationship and with our kids, but underneath all the discord, it seems we never stopped loving each other, both intent on starting anew. Ray was pleased with his new job, and I was ecstatic at being in Boston. Neither Ray nor I were in any way expecting the many changes that lay ahead: Sean came home and began AA in earnest with the intent of being tested by New England Medical Center, Tufts U. after one year of sobriety; following that, Ray himself was put on lithium, which ultimately, after two years, led to his being able to give up alcohol; Kelly was released from the federal facility. Ray declared, "If Kelly comes home, I'm out of here." But I could not refuse Kelly the second chance for a new start – Ray's bark was harsher than his bite. Kelly, instead, accompanied Sean to AA for many months and found a job in another Boston suburb.

Suzie had gotten pregnant with her first, Jo-Marie. She was not able to bury her problems in booze any longer, and was having a hard time of it. One of the notes she sent me was completely irrational, saying, from now on for me to consider her "to be dead; it is easier," she wrote.[29]

Sharon and I spoke from time to time on the phone, but seldom. Through correspondence, I continued taking Eckerd College courses, introducing me to ethics and sociology, showing

---

[29] Until therapy, I had believed Suzie's life-long accusations: "I'm always left out because you and Sharon are buddies" was just a sibling rivalry thing. However, while working full time, back in Atlanta, after being questioned by several co-workers, why I rarely, if ever, mentioned my *second* daughter, the connection was finally made. Through NLP, I learned that my inadvertent and unconscious omission was traced back to that weekend visit to the Bob Jones campus when Suzie's arrival had become the living symbol of my ever increasing joy between Ray and me. Being thrust once again into that old judgmental belief system, at BJU, to which we had been conditioned since childhood, in my guilt and shame, it appears that I began to ever so subtly minimize Suzie's existence – *ever so subtly* – as it was done at the deepest level of consciousness where shame tends to hide. Being so afraid that Sharon would detect my special love for Suzie besides – being the pregnancy that had brought me the man I loved – it became clear to me that I had used one of Freud's defense mechanisms: "reaction formation... that occurs when an anxiety producing impulse is replaced by its opposite in consciousness:" And Sharon's dominant personality seemed to have made it – ever so easy. – Walter Mischel & Harriet Nerlove Mischel, *Eessentials of Psychology*, Second Edition.

me how the "subculture of the Pentecostal religious sect" of my father's, as it was referred to at that time[30] – before the Bush family brought it into the main stream of the political arena[31] – had a real bearing upon my life. The indoctrination against learning, literally glorying in ignorance – unless it is written in the Bible – is the real danger of this form of fundamentalism, as it has now taken up battle against the scientific learnings that is elemental to all that has brought us our advances in medicine, in space, among others, so basic to this age of technology.

Alex Haley's biography of *Malcolm X* showed me that I had a story to tell. I went to a writer's conference at Simmons College, downtown Boston, where I heard the marvelous late John Updike speak. As my education continued, I found a writer's group which was very supportive, consisting of retired Art and English teachers. Two of these beautiful women especially pushed me to continue my education on a full-time basis. Finally accepted at Lesley College, to complete my last year of credit towards my Bachelor of Arts degree, majoring in Writing, I was to gain considerable insight into the underlying causes of sibling sexual abuse: how it is used as a secret weapon to control; that females *can* and *do* sexually abuse boys – the untold story.

---

[30] *The Status Seekers,*Vance Packard,1959, p. 200

[31] Pres. Geo. H.W. Bush chose VP Dan Quayle, 1988, a Pentecostal; subsequently Geo W. Bush chose Attorney General Ashcroft, 2000, a Pentecostal; Senator John McCain chose VP Gov. Sarah Palin, 2008, a Pentecostal; Rep. Michele Bachmann, a presidential candidate for 2012, is a graduate of Oral Roberts Law School. Joe Scarborough, on his Morning Joe TV show, said, "Pat Robertson [a Pentecostal Evangelical] has taken over the Republican Party," MSNBC, Aug 12, 2011. An aside: We were both taught as children in our respective churches that African-Americans were descendants of Ham, the son of Noah, who "did not cover his father's nakedness" when he was drunk. When Noah awoke, and realized what his son, Ham, had done, "he cursed Canaan" (Ham and his descendants) to be "a servant of servants... to his brethren." Do you suppose that the intolerance of Evangelicals for this group of people, President Obama in particular, could stem from their interpretation of this Old Testament Biblical passage - Genesis 9:18-26?

SIGNS OF UNHEALTHY BOUNDARIES

Our thoughts have much bearing on our emotional growth:

Telling all (gossiping) - becoming too vulnerable!
Talking at an intimate level on the first meeting.
Falling in love with a new acquaintance.
Falling in love with anyone who reaches out.
Being overwhelmed by a person - preoccupied.
Acting on first sexual impulse.
Allowing unsafe touches.
Being sexual for partner, not self.
Being sexual with everyone, or no one.
Going against personal values or rights in order to please others.
Allowing yourself to give "negative, put-down statements."
Not noticing when someone else displays inappropriate boundaries.
Not noticing when someone invades your boundaries.
Always giving advice.
Accepting food, gifts, touch, sex that you don't want (or shouldn't).
Touching a person without asking.
Caution: lip kissing.
Taking as much as you can get for the sake of getting.
Giving as much as you can give for the sake of giving.
Not allowing yourself to say "no."
Allowing someone to take as much as they can from you.
Letting others direct your life.
Letting others describe your reality.
Letting others define you.
Believing others can anticipate your needs.
Becoming too intimate with others instead of your spouse.
Expecting others to fill your needs automatically.
Constantly focusing on one person (or couple); never broadening your
horizons.
Falling apart so someone will take care of you.
Self-abuse; sexual and physical abuse; food abuse.

◆

BOOK FOUR

After Therapy

Writing can be a form of psychoanalysis which can allow the discovery of a part of oneself whose existence one had never suspected.

[paraphrased from]
Eric Fromm
Psychoanalysis and Religion

"First comes understanding, then forgiveness. ... Who am I to judge... I'm not God... And wasn't I once a daughter?"

–Kim Chernin
In My Mother's House

"You may give them [your children] your love but not your thoughts for they have their own thoughts. You may house their bodies but not their souls, for their souls dwell in the house of tomorrow, which you cannot visit, not even in your dreams."

— Kahlil Gibran
"On Children," The Prophet

"When we enlarge our view of the world, we deepen our own lives."

— Yo Yo Ma, Cellist

CHAPTER FOURTEEN

A New Friend: 1983

Sitting there in the court room, I was waiting for the judge, for the proceedings to start. Barnes, my attorney, was looking at his notes, and I was thinking about my feet. Why did I wear these darn shoes? I thought, resisting the urge to slip them off. It was always the first thing I did, in the house, in the office, in the car. A quirk I had that always gave me away as to just how comfortable I was in my surroundings. Ray laughed about that little bit of Cherokee in me that always crept out. Getting my shoes off was just a way to gloat and tell everyone I was finally grown up and no longer subject to that rigid world of Daddy's, where I always had to wear shoes. Funny how silly little things out of the past crop up in your mind at a time like this, despite this solemn place and the sad secrets of your life waiting to go on parade…

When I thought about Ray — my mind darting back to that summer of '56, right after we were married – I wanted to giggle· I shocked his curly hair almost straight when I shed my shoes right out in front of Radio City Music Hall·

We had gotten a free ride from Baltimore into New York City for a two-day weekend· I was a few months gone, with Suzie, by then, but opportunities like this didn't come that often — a baby-sitter to leave Sharon with, too· Fresh hayseeds, both of us, and only stationed in Baltimore for that first Army Intelligence school before being sent to God knows where, we had accepted the free ride by Ray's buddy and were let out on some bridge, the same place he'd return to for us the next afternoon at exactly four o'clock· We had only a vague idea where we were headed from the directions, so we started walking, and walking, and walking· Stupidly, I had worn heels· After all, if New York City wasn't the place to look your best, then where was? By the time we got to "Rockerfella Plaza" (my pronunciation: oh, how dumb I was then) I was carrying my shoes· Ray was so

447

embarrassed, he walked a good twenty yards behind me so no one could tell I belonged to him· In my awe at being in such a famous place, I never noticed his embarrassment· Finally, I sat down on one of the benches, wondering what took him so long to join me· Between the blisters on my heels, my aching back, and the constant search for a rest room, I had little thought for my new husband·

We stayed at the once famous, decaying, Times Square Hotel· It was all we could afford· At three in the morning, I woke up to find Ray gone, without a word — just like that first night we met· But I didn't get angry and pout this time, I just went looking for him and found him out on the street sneaking a smoke (what he was doing that first time too, a secret smoker all along)· The sound of the city was like three in the afternoon, everything open for business, so we got a hamburger· We were both amazed that no one seemed to know or care that it was the middle of the night· By the time we got to the bridge that afternoon for our return ride, we had one dime left· I thought we should save the money for the telephone, just in case, but Ray said, "What the hell..." so we spent it for a Coke to share, laughing at what we would do if our ride didn't show up· Young and foolish were we, so long ago...

My left foot was asleep, the tingling jarred me back to the present. The shine of the polished wood in the court room seemed to reflect the pristine image I unconsciously sought to portray. Barnes said we might have a wait, this judge was always late. My shoes were still bothering me; I wanted them off. They never seemed to fit the same way twice — either too big or too small – as if they had a mind of their own, letting my feet know just who was boss. "Skinny goddamn heel," one shoe clerk had said in disgust after he'd bragged he could fit anyone.

The subject of what to wear today for the trial had been alluded to but not really discussed. I wore a lot of black and white. Unquestionably symbolic, Dr. Comas would say, who was always looking for clues. My being closed up to myself, my repression. Maybe that was why I'd chosen to wear the light and dark combination, since I wasn't sure myself which way I felt — good or bad, guilty or not guilty. Neither had I consciously decided which I was. Let the jury decide, I thought. I was tired of trying to figure it all out.

I'd always been so meticulous with my appearance, down to the last detail. At least this I could control, until that recent bout with the anti-depressants when I gained twenty pounds in ten days and then lost it in five. My neck hadn't been the same since, so I practiced holding my head up so the skin wouldn't wrinkle, and wore high necked things; I loved mandarin collars. But for some reason today, I'd chosen to wear a white V-necked blouse under the tailored black suit. "It accentuates your small, fragile frame," Barnes said when he saw me and gave me a thumbs-up sign of approval. I thought the open neckline showed off the beautiful opal pendant Ray gave me, and which I like to wear, even if it did remind me of the one it replaced, the one that disappeared from my drawer next to the earrings. (All along I knew it was one of the kids who took it because of the earrings, a thief would have taken them too; Kelly finally admitted giving it to his girlfriend in 4th grade.) How I'd always loved opals. So did Ray. How many times had I heard, "It'll bring you bad luck if it's not your birth stone," but I'd just laugh. I'd never been one to be superstitious. Bad luck, what? And then the high-pitched voice of the judge cut through my thoughts, beckoning for me, Samantha Sue, "the defendant" to step forward for the oath.

"Will the defendant please rise?"

I shivered as I heard the shrillness of the woman addressing me, wondering how she ever came to be a judge — with her voice. But I reminded myself that it was my life that was on trial here, not hers.

Obediently, I stepped into the witness box. Taking a half-pivot I learned years ago at Christian Dior in Tokyo, I knew I still had the poise and carriage they'd taught me, even though I was a grandmother several times over. "Natural elegance," they'd said. I felt the sadness then, looking over the courtroom, as the controlled rhythm of my breasts rose and fell. Deep breathing, like I'd practiced in my cell block.

I'd asked for internment over a bail bond. For what reason, I wasn't quite sure myself as yet. It was easier for Barnes to see me. And then, at home there was the telephone — and all the questions. Maybe it's penance. And then, too, Barnes thought it *might sway the jury, "seeing a woman of your caliber suffering such indignity." Perhaps. I was tired of looking for answers. What I did seemed the thing I had to do at the time. Just like that night two years ago. And before that… And before that… The doctors called it acting out – anger at Daddy, at Ray. Loving follows anger; all the whipping and the hugging after, why it felt so right; anger and pain, and then sex. When this is all over, I'll understand, after I have time to reflect. Stepping back away from the trees to see the forest, I'll know then whether Ray was the intended victim. Or was my mind playing tricks on me, again? The same original gambit started between me and Daddy? Will it ever end?*

The courtroom was full of spectators, witnesses, and the news services, too. The judge had restricted TV coverage but allowed a press artist from the Boston Globe a seat of distinction on the front row, directly in front of the stand. Behind the young artist sat my latest psychiatrist, Ignatius Comas, MD.

He had agreed to fly up from the Gulf Coast and testify on my behalf, for a fee. If I got off, my insurance might pay for some of it. He knew me so well, and he was famous for his work in the forensic field, but Barnes questioned the advisability of using him. Comas was one of the medical consultants appointed to the special commission set up to look into amending the use of the insanity plea after the Hinckley boy's acquittal.

In view of the final results of this commission's work, Barnes said we had to tread a very fine line to avoid any leanings towards an insanity stance. But I had been a patient of Dr. Comas for some time and he had great insight into my emotional makeup and thought processes. In the end, Barnes had concluded, since Comas had already proven himself to be reliable — enough to gain national recognition – why not build on that reputation already established?

Barnes had seemed impressed and thoroughly satisfied with the interpretation Comas gave of my motives and actions. Barnes said he believed strongly, because of the prosecutor's determination to press for Murder One, attempting to satisfy the New Right emerging in the state, that he had a very good chance of proving that my motive was not to kill anyone but simply to protect myself. And Barnes was depending strongly on the testimony of Comas to prove that, rather than the perpetrator of a crime, I was, indeed, not only the victim, but a victim of long standing.

Seeing Dr. Comas after so many months, as he leaned his

dark bearded head to one side, my heart smiled. And I could hear, in my head, the Hooked On Classics tape I'd taken him. We'd listened to it together in his office. I was nervous about giving it, afraid he'd read something into my motives. But "sometimes a cigar is just a cigar," he'd quoted Freud, so kindly.

Remembering our first meeting, when Sean, then seventeen, was hospitalized following that deliberate overdose of drugs, when the Florida police had taken Sean to the forensic emergency care unit Dr. Comas supervised, I would be forever grateful for his keeping Sean alive through that all-night vigil. Who would have thought then upon our meeting, with his quiet and somber, dark-bearded and almost frightening looking appearance, that his specialty in criminal behavior, which he expertly utilized in dealing with Sean, and which had so impressed Ray (he himself with an advanced degree in criminal justice), was now the very same specialty that was, hopefully, going to aid me in my acquittal on the charge the state was bringing against me: willful and premeditated murder of my husband...

Ray's words came at me sharp, calculated, and with all the ferociousness of a cornered animal· The tears began, as always, down in the inner depth of my soul, welling up behind my eyes, first into my eardrums as I fought, again, to let him know what damage he'd done to me with his always piercing words· Then out of my eyelids the tears ran, burning as they spilled through the contact lenses I wore· How many times had I lived through this same thing and begged for just a touch of tender kindness?

Compassion, Jake, Ray's father, had called it when we were first married, admitting Ray was devoid of it· How greatly relieved Jake had been, he said, that his son was no longer aspiring to make his living as a minister of God· "He just doesn't have the guts for it, the compassion that a person needs in that kind of work·" But never did I associate those words of his father with the cruelty I'd already seen and would someday personally experience from the mouth of my new, young husband·

In the beginning I'd excused Ray's cutting sarcasm because it was always directed at others· Although it made me uncomfortable, I would write it off as a form of insecurity that would eventually cease when I proved to him I loved him; my love would change all that· But now, as I

stood there facing him — after years of laughter and tears,
fighting and giving up, loving and hating – feeling that
violent anger, again, unleashed upon me, now, instead, all
the love and forbearance that I had mustered in the past,
suddenly turned to rage as I felt the literal separation of
my spirit from the hands that hung clenched at my sides.

He flung his words at me, "You are so goddamn smart;
you won't listen to anyone. No one."

"What do you mean?" I cried.

"I keep telling you to go to another doctor and
demand to be treated. Put in a hospital. Whatever it
takes."

"It's not so easy for a woman to demand such things.
Don't you understand? He's just another doctor who
doesn't believe me, that I hurt. They never believe me," I
screamed. My head felt as if a sword were splitting it in
two from the back of my neck to my eyebrows. My
shoulders were one tight spasm of pain that refused to
subside, even when I lay flat on my back in an effort to
relieve the pressure from the pinched nerve – that terrible
flying through the air, whiplash and cracking my coccus,
knocking me out while a houseful of party guests danced the
night away.

"Don't give me that shit, again. Women. They sure as
hell can do a lot of other things, when they want to.
That's just a cop out."

"Then you go call that doctor that didn't even X-ray
me, and hasn't called yet. And you demand to know what
he thinks, and ask him what he's planning to do for this
pain. See what he says."

Ray turned on me suddenly, a look of violence in his
piercing eyes. With all the force and penetration of the
platform speaker that he was, he took a step closer to me,
as though to insure the penetration of every ounce of wrath
that he could muster. Bearing down on me now, and in his
loud stage voice, he yelled at me, "I don't have to call him
because I already know what he would say. He'd tell me to
put her into an insane asylum."

My head surely would explode from the pain. I took a
big, deep breath before I answered him. Calmed, then, by
my surprise, I said almost too quietly, "But why? What

makes you think he would say that?"

"Because... He already told me last week that a pain in the head can make you hurt all over· That's why!" He threw the words at me like daggers, yelling, his large eyes bulging, a look of kill in them·

The rage began somewhere in my recognition that this man no longer valued me — if he ever had· I had no more credibility with him than with any of the others· Even when I had explained to him that the doctor had blatantly lied to him about X-raying me, Ray had come home from the doctor's office questioning ME, accusing ME of lying· Ray somehow believed the doctor over me, taking the other side, just as Daddy always had· And like Daddy, my husband had not wavered in his condemnation of me· The tears were spilling over as my anger rose higher and higher·

I was returning his vengeance now· "I thought all these years that we've lived together, through all the crud and garbage that we've been through — and God knows we've been through enough – I stayed because I believed that the purpose of it all was to face old age together· To have someone there, in your corner· To fight for you· To care for you· To look out for you· To demand for you· To speak for you· Just to be there! But what have I got? No, I have a prosecutor instead· One who sees no value in me, has no interest in my words· You just told me last week that no one listens to you, Sam, like it was a joke! No one ever did listen to me· I don't know why· 'Don't talk while SHE'S here,' I'd hear· 'Don't open the presents in front of HER; how do we get rid of HER?' I could feel them thinking· Even my mother's inquest said she was alone when she fell – like I wasn't there, as if I was a nobody, a nothing, invisible· And you... sometimes you treat me the same way· I stayed with you because of the good part of you — despite your meanness· Somehow, the fun times seemed to overshadow times like these," I said, my voice rising·

"Oh, don't give me that shit! You stay with me because you've nowhere else to go·"

"I have not and you know it," I screamed· "I've always tried to overlook your terrible mean temper, but it's getting harder and harder," I said, my voice cracking· Then, trying to regain my equilibrium, I said softly, "Tell me, Ray,

just for the hell of it, what are some things you like about
me? Is there anything at all?" It was my last speck of
hope, scraped from the bottom of my soul·

"Today..." he answered with unusual cutting sarcasm,
"... there's nothing about you I can STAND·" The sneer on
his face was so pronounced and filled with such disgust that
I felt the very pit of my being had been torn from its
roots and crushed with a devastating blow, leaving a lifeless
quality that once used to be me·

The anger that sprang from within me held only the
need to survive· My rationality was no longer a part of my
being· Instinct took over my hands as I unclenched my fist· I
was standing by the fireplace, so I reached for the only
weapon I allowed in the house, the handmade tomahawk
Sean had made for me in his high
school leather class· I held the
slender instrument in my hand· The
stone was flat and sharpened from
years of corrosion· Painted with red,
white, and yellow Indian-like
markings, red leather strings held
the rock in place, the wooden branch
fit nicely into my small hand· The
stone swung heavily as I picked up
the handle that lay propped on the
hearth· There was no more thought·
There was only rage and a decision
for action· The other time I had
reached such rage was that day in
Bangkok after our guests had excused
themselves from finishing that hand

of bridge and gone home, too uncomfortable with the
violence brewing between us as Ray cursed at me, blaming
me for being so STUPID in my bidding· I picked up a glass
off the bar to empty it, and, as his angry words sunk into
my brain, I let it go flying through the air· Ray looked up
from emptying the ashtrays, to see the shiny streak coming
at him· He reached up to grab it before it could hit him
and it shattered against his wrist· The blood spurted out· I
was remembering that day and feeling the same anger and
rage at his belligerent berating of me, and seeing, again, the

glass flying through the air – but this time it was not the glass· Ray looked away for a slight instant and the turn of the tomahawk spun expertly through the air, as though I'd practiced for centuries· As Ray looked back at me to speak, the weight of the flying stone imbedded its sharp edge into his temple· This time there was no blood to bandage· There was no lieutenant to call to fetch a taxi for the hospital emergency room· There were no lies to be told to the doctor on duty· There was only a silent hump of flesh tumbled over onto the table Ray had been clearing· My aim had been superb, as though out of the eons of generations of Cherokee astuteness, in the survival by our own hand, I still had that instinctual response to an attack on my life – my very existence threatened by the assault of his words·

A sort of calm came over me then, as I looked at what I'd done· I didn't know if it was relief or the feeling of freedom· Then I thought that this must be what death is like – a new beginning? Maybe· I didn't know· I only knew that suddenly, it was all over, and I was overcome with the weariness of a lifetime·

In the court room, I saw Kate Karl. She was the new leader of the largest women's right's movement to spring up nationally in opposition to the New Right. She had kept her word and had not missed a minute of the trial. Her being there, a child of the holocaust, would lend a great deal of credibility to my cause on the stand. She had visited me often in my cell, and we'd had long discussions on the subject of sexuality. It was the first time, since Beth, that I was able to touch a woman's hand without fear, the fear of being a lesbian that had dogged me my whole life. Kate hugged me often, telling me how natural my instincts were. Loving the warmth of her breasts was just wanting Mama who had three babies in a row and never stopped nursing my whole life. Only three years old and never a mama without breasts full of milk, and then she was gone. Kate understood so much. I could tell her anything. More than any doctor I ever had. She was there, rooting for me, easing my horrendous shame with her presence.

My full name was being spoken by a weasel-y little man standing in front of me. The clerk. I was sure he smoked a cigar. He must! What else could he do with a mouth that hideous? His eyes were not pretty either. He kept staring at me coldly. The only things he was missing was a dilapidated felt hat on his head and *a scarf around his neck to look like the doctor who gave me my first pelvic. And like the doctor, his voice was high pitched too. "Samantha Sue Tuckermoore Schlutz Malorry," he said.*

The cumbersome legal name of my youth! It was bad enough I still had to lug it around with me, reminding me daily of Daddy's rigid insistence I use Samantha Sue, never Sam or Sammy – a boy's name. Worldly. Sinful. And the awful Tuckermoore. The humiliating tease of the boys on the school playground still ringing in my ears, shouting after me, Tucker... Fucker... Tuckermoore... Fuck-her-more... That shame had never gone away. So when Schultz, an ordinary and common name, became mine, I had welcomed it. Now, that name was being twisted by the same kind of similarity of sound. Schlutz. Slut. Feeling all the degradation the term brought with it, I remembered Charity calling me that. So I looked the clerk right in the eye, without flinching, and interrupted him, letting my voice get soft as I said, "Not that it matters, but for the record, the name is not Schlutz, but Schultz. You know, like Snooks..." Patronizing in its characterization, but at least it was I who had chosen it. I smiled then, but only with my lips. My dry sense of humor I learned from Daddy. But the little man got the message from my dark eyes.

He cleared his throat, half apologetically. "Slight juxtaposition there," he said, his cheeks coloring, but the sneer came through to me.

I breathed as though in command, his sneer only reminding me of all the pain I had survived. A way of life: pain. A world full of sneering ugly men always striving to be one up on me.

Was it because of my dark beauty, the beauty that I only became aware of so late in life? Or in spite of it? Who could tell about such things?

The ugly little man was continuing, "...resident of Port Hope County, Commonwealth of Massachusetts. Raise your right hand and repeat after me: I, Samantha Sue, do solemnly swear to tell the truth, the whole truth, and nothing but the truth, so help me God."

As I opened my mouth to speak, I looked up to see Kate smiling at me from across the room. It was as though I was speaking to her, "I, Samantha Sue, do solemnly swear to tell the truth, the whole truth, and nothing but the truth, so help me..." and then my voice gave way. My hand came up instantly around my neck. The ache I felt deep in my throat was the same ache I'd always felt in therapy, when I was saying things I'd hidden from myself. And I knew from Daddy's Bible reading, I could never hide from God. He was everywhere... Had been... with me and Beth... me and Daddy... me and Huey... me and Mr. Simms... me and all the terrible others... And then I heard only my throaty whisper breathe the word God. I reached out for the glass of water. But it was not Barnes who held it...

It was Dr. Comas who was sitting across from me, looking intently into my eyes as he had done so often during moments like these. The usual glass of water waited for me on the coffee table between us. I was still holding my neck with my left hand. The whole area of my larynx was aching severely – more than usual. The hot Florida sun was beating into the window behind him and he had pulled the blind. His office struck me that moment as being one big shadow, a blurring of a life of memories poured out in unspeakable anguish, anguish that this unusual doctor had somehow managed to help his patients reverse into a kind of personal triumph. His own bout with cancer in recent years reminded me now that his wrinkled brow contained more than a show of concern, it revealed a mountain of quiet strength as he waited for my next words.

"You just can't imagine how frightening and confusing this has been for me. That's why I took this trip down here especially to see you. Every vivid detail remains in my mind... I've lain awake nights trying to understand it. There's this gnawing pain in my gut when I first come awake, even if it's only a nap in the middle of the day. What's going on with me? Can you figure it out?"

"Tell me about the gnawing pain in your gut," he said imitating me with the same inflection, trying hard to cover up his Latin accent.

"It's the same feeling I've had on and off for years... like I've been a bad girl, and I'm going to get a licking. And since this horrible recurring dream started... It comes back in different parts, some new twist to it every time. That's why I knew going under, here with you, I'd be able to get it all out at once. Make some sense of it. And since this dream started, the pain is there, always, like I really *did* kill my husband, not just dream it. I mean... our fights do happen just like that. You knew about the fight in Bangkok, and the glass I threw, how scary it was. Still, why am I dreaming about murder? And why is it haunting me day and night? It's like I finally got even with my father for killing my mother by killing my husband. But all of it is only in my mind. Does that make sense?"

"Do you think your father really killed your mother?"

With a big sigh I answered, "You've asked me this so many times. I wish I knew what really happened. I know it's somewhere inside this head of mine. I was hoping you could help me remember it. Then it would be settled once and for all."

"Knowing what *really happened* is not the important thing. It is what you *believe* happened that matters."

"You mean, it ain't what you *know* that hurts you. But rather what you know that ain't so, that hurts you?" I said, wanting to giggle, or cry.

"Yes. True," he said, nodding in agreement.

I said, "All I know is that I have this awful feeling inside that my father was somehow responsible for her death. I can't explain it." *Pregnant; Daddy; she died.* I could hear the three-year-old chant in my head that I heard sometimes, waking me up from a sound sleep. *She was pregnant; Daddy did it; she died.* Suddenly, I realized I was shaking my head. *No. No. No. No.* I was just on the edge of grasping it. This happened a lot. I wanted to reach out and grab the idea that danced on the edge of my brain, playing Catch Me If You Can: *Pregnant; Daddy did it; she died.* The chant was there again: *Pregnant; Daddy did it; she died.* But the sound of his words interrupted the thought when he said, "I think you're still dodging the main issue."

"What is that?"

"Your own responsibility in her death."

"Yes, I know you keep telling me that. And it *is* easier to believe my father guilty than myself." When I spoke the last word, *myself,* my voice cracked, and I felt the sadness again that always overwhelmed me when I spoke of Mama. The tears began to well up in my eyes, and I fought the urge to cry. It was such a useless thing, crying was, when what I really wanted to do was scream bloody murder. The words got stuck in my brain. Murder; bloody murder. *I didn't really... Did I? That's absurd. How could I have? I was so little...*

"What are you thinking about?" he asked, bringing me back to the moment. I'd looked away from him, and the large rubber plant at the corner of the room caught my attention. Suddenly I remembered how during one session, while under hypnosis, I had wanted to crawl behind it and hide. As I started to get up, he stopped me and spoke to me as if to a three-year-old — the age I was when my emotions got stuck, when Mama died – and told me to "Sit there now, and tell me about it." I was feeling the same way again, naughty and wanting to run and hide. It was such a guilty feeling. "Tell me about what you are thinking just now," he said again.

"I was thinking about how lucky I am to be alive. I mean, she died, and my brother died, and her baby girl died..."

"And you feel that you didn't deserve to live if they all died?"

"Yes... Yes..." I grabbed my stomach with a tight fist. I could see my mother in the casket and the flowers at her feet covering the baby, and I could hear all the murmuring in the room. *Poor man... Losing three in less than a year... More than one body ought to have to bear, and now having to care for that little one..."* and I remembered feeling so extra... like... in the way. I should've been gone, too, I thought." Suddenly my neck began to twist as it had that first time I'd gone under hypnosis and faced that unknown world of my childhood fears and imaginations, and I began to feel the pain in my neck and my shoulders again like then.

"And perhaps all this happiness you and Ray have finally had, you feel you don't really deserve?"

"Yes, exactly! I feel guilty every time I wake up... It's like I really wish I hadn't."

"What is it you feel like doing when the pain in your head aches so bad... like chopping off your head?"

"Yes, I do say that. Do I really want to die then?"

"I think it's not what you want but what you think you deserve — not to live and certainly not to be happy with your husband. At least he should beat you like her husband did her."

"So that's why I married Huey when I already knew he was mean and cruel, and why, you keep reminding me, I hook Ray into verbally berating me?"

"Something like that... A price you feel you must pay for your life."

Trying to figure this all out in my head, I said, "You mean the victim is really a conspirator of sorts, then, like the sinner, from Shakespeare is it? — the sinner who crieth that he hath been sinned against?"

"Yes. Sometimes," he said, thinking for a moment, then adding, "You seem to like calling yourself a sinner."

Shaking it off, my face grew hot as I persisted. "And my children... I don't deserve them either, do I? Since hers died."

"I think that's how you feel. Why you find yourself rejecting their existence and their happiness from time to time, like you still seem to be rejecting your own."

"Then that must be what my anger at my grandma is all

about — that she lived too. Like we all should share in the guilt in my mind."

I was thinking aloud, "In my mind... In my mind... That dream... I was so poised and self-contained. Untouched by any of it, almost above it all."

"Yes, that's how you've managed so well — to *live above it* — repressing all of it by concerning yourself with *externals* such as your appearance. Clothes, hair... Blaming everything around you for your unhappiness. The shoes. *Externals are always the boss.* The opal bringing you bad luck. You seem always to find something."

"What do you mean? What?"

"Your skinny goddamn heels. Your beauty. It's like saying: Look. I can't help it. I was *born* this way. And, of course, when all else fails, you can always blame God." He waited a minute to let this all sink in. His timing was superb. "And making a joke out of the slur of the clerk when he implied you were a slut — you notice how you tried to have the last word?" Dr. Comas actually chuckled, making his point again about my having to be in charge — even in therapy.

"I guess I'm still protecting myself. Huh? In fear of another Daddy, or sugar-daddy taking me over, limiting me, keeping me a sex object."

"Yes. Ex-*act*-ly," he said, leaning forward in his seat, his eyes bright, "It seems to me you are still wanting to be a *whole* woman." Then his voice turned soft. Gentle. "And recognizing the difference is a start."

It was his tone that struck me. Not only reminding me of the terribly long struggle, but subtly redefining the prize. Suddenly I was tired again. The time loomed forever. *When would it end?* I reached for the glass of water and the court room flashed before my eyes.

"And Barnes, the English lawyer? What of him?"

"I think he's that puritan Victorian inside of you that you keep fighting. The one who not only knows all the rules, but uses them to his own end... all in the name of *right*." Slowly his eyes grew into his square smile that I saw only on very rare occasions.

"The woman judge?... Must be my stepmother, Charity. She's *al*-ways late," I said, giggling. My habitual lightheartedness in the face of pain, though, didn't seem comforting any more.

Still smiling with me, he nodded in agreement.

"Yes," he said, "I believe you expect to be judged rather harshly by the women in your life."

"But Kate. She was a woman... in the court room. What about her?"

"Oh, her... What do *you* think about her?" he asked, sitting back a little casually, clasping his hands over his crossed knee.

I looked up at the large abstract painting on the wall. At the deep, dark, and bright colors on the pale yellow background, the square and odd shapes in mass confusion, thinking it looked like a traffic jam on Madison Avenue from atop the Empire State Building.

"Tell me," he said, leaning forward.

I was still looking at the painting. It was a picture of my life, like the dream — a prison of sorts I had created for myself, being boxed in by the pain – all kinds of innuendos, unending, coming together in one place. "I'm remembering all the women I've been friends with throughout my life. I've been afraid of all of them, fearing them like Beth. And yet, in the dream, I finally met a friend with whom I was not afraid to have intimacy, with whom I felt a closeness, a sharing of even those kinds of sexual fears. *That* was a *friend...*"

He just sat there, listening. Waiting, as he usually did, for the return of my gaze.

Looking at him, I asked, finally, "Do you suppose I will ever find her? *Really?*"

"I tink," he said again with his warm, square smile, "dat *you already have.*"

◆

CHAPTER FIFTEEN

The Win Announcement: 1984

It was a beautiful house full of windows, thirty-six to be exact. Eight hours a day for six months she had sewed on her Singer, soft gold shears hung on stretch rods, to not leave any holes in the precious wood. In this room, she had designed brown, Thai-silk draperies — just a wide piece of cloth tapered at each end, lined with champaign grosgrain. Through clear hoops they hung at the corners. Under the shears, covering the windows, she had ordered custom made, puckered cloth shades with scalloped silk-fringed hems, and silk pull-cords in natural bone color. Never pulled, they were left half-way up throughout the house.

In the center of this room was the oval, brass coffee table, originally used as a servicing tray. On the flat of it, Oriental designs were etched, the edges fluted. On it sat a hand-made ceramic chess set from Kelly's latest love, a blue-eyed beauty he'd met at AA.

The walls of this room were covered with pictures painted in darker days: one huge one, at least five feet wide by four feet tall, during Vietnam sadness. She copied it from a famous print she'd borrowed from her neighbor: Blond haired mother, child on lap holding spoon, an older child at mother's feet peeling an apple. Through the small high windows behind them she had added her own personal touch of far-off mountains. Next to the mother, on the floor, a wicker basket was piled high. The colors in the painting had turned out very dark, gloomy, like her temperament when she was alone, without him, trying to go through every day with her four kids – and those godforsaken nights. On the painting, the sun would catch the highlights of silken hair; this an obvious family of Nordics. Somehow the mother's face turned out to be the face of her oldest child, Sharon, light hair pulled back as she had worn it in high school.

On another wall was the bright, sun-shiny baby reaching for the bluebird up in a tree. Next to it, a large print she bought in Munic, mother and daughter by an American artist. These fit perfectly between two windows.

The back end of this room was enclosed with bay windows. Though them you were looking down a steep drop-off into protected lands, thick with trees and wild flowers shooting up among the rocks where she'd tossed the dead blooms at the end of every summer. In this well of space, the Gulbransen organ – *The President*, named for Nixon, because he had this model in the White House — sat. Her prize. It fit so nicely, the high wide bench backing up to the corner of the windows to give daylight and allow her to see out in all directions: the woods, the dinner guests, while she played — a throne.

Sean had started lessons at age seven, the same age *she* began learning. The baby grand, also a Gulbransen, she got later, ten dollars a month on Army pay. Sean easily switched to that keyboard, his touch later on so like her own, soft, gentle, easy. She had hired the same organ teacher for herself, the one who played with Tommy Dorsey, big fat thumbs that could reach half an octave without moving them. Next to her, he'd sit in a chair and close his eyes. *Play*, he'd say.

So she did... *Monalisa... Blue Moon...* all the oldies. She would look over at him, his eyes still closed, "Now what do you want me to do?"

"Just play, you have such a wonderful touch."

So, while he rested his eyes, she played.

Then, he said, "You don't need to learn anything more, just play."

Her friend, trained as a classical artist in Belgium, would sit and look around this room. Awaiting the artist's critique, instead, she was surprised to hear, "Sam, this room reeks of love; it just reeks."

Having the announcement party *stag* was to be expected. USS was a typical New England company where male chauvinism was the norm, so it was not a surprise. Actually, it wasn't really *stag* as there were a few female engineers sprinkled throughout, but this was how Ray referred to the "Employees Only" get-to-gethers. Winning the Army contract for RST had been a long hard fight. But Ray Malorry loved a fight; his

Irish thrived on it. In fact, his mother used to say, "Ray would fight with Jesus Christ himself." Yes, Sam mused, her dynamic and flamboyant husband would fight anyone, *but only if the trophy was worth it, would he waste his time.* And, in this case, $2.4 bil was one hell of a trophy.

When Ray had called to tell Sam he would be late getting home, that the RST win had finally been announced (only two months late, after Weinberger and mighty Maggie Thatcher had been overruled by Ronnie, or was it Nancy?) Sam fought the nervous jitters wondering whether Ray could handle all the booze she knew would be flowing. Booze always made him *think* horny. She didn't really believe he was screwing around with Denise, his secretary, that would be too obvious. He always said he didn't believe in *playing an away-game at home,* but that sweet southern lassie down in DC, Caro-*line*, was another matter. Ray's call had sent Sam looking for something to keep her busy for the next couple hours.

Ironing used to be her outlet, years ago, before she was liberated by drip-dry shirts and no-press trousers. But the influx of foreign wear into US markets was threatening that liberation, a conspiracy by the male oriented societies. Reading the care labels was a must before purchasing, or the cheapie synthetics would send them all back to pre-'60's laundry maids, she thought, as she sorted the wash she purposely left for just such emergencies, the one thing that relieved her tensions. Washing *anything* seemed to get rid of the clutter and mess in her brain, cleaned out the cobwebs, the disappointments, the fears, that would entangle her thoughts.

This girl, Caro-*line*! She remembered the first time she heard of her. They were sitting at the top of the DC Marriott, having a drink. It was Sam's first time to accompany her husband on a business trip since coming to Boston. He was anxious to get her reaction, he said, to the new bunch of guys that represented USS to the government brass in selling this program. He would be working closely with them, and Sam's opinion always seemed to weigh a great deal. Introduced all around, she was relieved when no eyebrows went up when she ordered a Perier. *Thank God the world was finally catching up!*

Sonny Short, obviously the ring leader, raised her ire when he commented that "Caro-*line* was hoping you'd drive her on home, this evenin', Ray. Why didn't you?" he asked accentuating his Mississippi drawl with pure devilment in his eye. "Didn't think you could h-h-handle all that woman all by your lonesome?"

Ray blushed, but he quickly shot back. "Now, Sonny. I wasn't about to cut into your game. Who knows, I might need you on my side one day!" he said without the slightest change in his voice, looking through the din of smoke straight into the eye of the fat and freckled face of his newest peer.

Sam listened without commenting, maintaining her fixed smile. She thought it Sonny's way of putting Ray on the defensive – in front of his wife. Whoops, a test! But it made Sam angry. And to show it... well, it would have been interpreted as jealousy — another test! "What an ass," she said about him later. "I wouldn't trust that man."

And Ray added, "You're right, I wouldn't either, not any farther than I could p-p-piss in the wind."

Both broke into laughter, but Sam had never forgotten. It's not that she didn't trust her husband, she just wasn't naive to believe that he was any different than any other male on the planet, especially when he was drinking and away from his wife. Once, during a low period, when she was contemplating ending things with Ray, a close friend, who had been married much longer than she had, told her, "Hang on, Dear. No matter who you get, will be no different; trust me. Men are all basically alike. So live, and let live."

Except for the few nite-lites, the place was dark. *Wonder if he'll wake me up?* She mused, half-chuckling to herself. Anytime he came in late, he was never too quiet. Wanting to share every little tidbit and morsel of gossip was part of his Irish heritage; he had a habit of waking her under one pretense or another. He couldn't keep a thing to himself, lucky for her. She loved it, unless she was very tired and wanted to sleep, but tonight Sam was on edge, anxiously awaiting the news of the *Win* announcement.

In the bathroom, Sam could hear him. *Whoops, the scale.* Tripping over it, she could hear the "god dammit" in his sawmill whisper as he lifted the toilet seat and let it fall back against the commode. *Three-sheets-to-the-wind!* Sam had to smile, despite the nervous fear she had been grappling with all day. *Surely that sweet little lassie down in DC couldn't have gotten on a plane since three o'clock? But one could never tell about Caroli-ine!* Ray dropped the toilet seat with another thunderous bang. "God*bless*it" His impatience could've been interpreted almost any way.

The odor of tobacco preceded him as he fell across the moonlit bed and grabbed her arm. "Sam. You asleep?" he asked.

Her sense of the ridiculous usually overcame any agitation. He had a way that got to her. Giggling, she turned over and said, "Well if I was, I wouldn't be *now!*"

"Sorry about that. But I remembered!" he said, pointing his crooked index finger sillily in the semi-darkness. "I didn't want you sitting down in the cold pot again, and screaming in the middle of the night." They laughed, as always. Finding something funny between them was the glue that held them together. "And I'm not drunk, either; I just couldn't see that damn scale."

"Yes, I forgot," she said, giving herself away with her uncontainable giggle.

"You did that on purpose, didn't you?" he said, reaching over her for her shoulder, covering her mouth with his. Reaching past her lips, his tongue was searching, penetrating. She sucked the tip of it. Surprised at his urgency, she gently pushed him back, away. Too sudden, unexpected; news of this momentous day was uppermost in her mind. But involuntarily, she found herself pulling him by the shoulder, kissing his ear. Affection like this was so rare, one of the few occasional benefits of his drinking, Sam soaked it in, and enjoyed it as he slid his tongue over her lips, her eyelids, then took an earlobe between his teeth. Like being pulled between two giant magnets, she squealed like a child, "Tell me; tell me: What happened at the party?"

"Oh, God. You don't want to know. I was in rare form," he said, taking a breath, and unzipping his pants. She could hear them sliding down, onto the floor

"What did you do *now,* Ray?" she asked, a note of trepidation slipping into her voice. "Am I going to be embarrassed?"

"No, no, nothing like that. I just know I felt like screwing for the first time in months, maybe years. God, winning is great!"

"Screwing? What do you mean? Who did you...?"

"Nobody," he said, feeling for her breasts through her slippery gown.

"Who was there?" she ventured. "Was...?"

"Everybody from up here. But somebody was on the phone with DC all night."

"Then you didn't see Sonny? Or any of them?" she asked, just to be certain.

"Hell, no. They couldn't get a flight." He ran his fingernail across her nipple; she felt a gentle jolt deep in her clitoris.

"But I talked to Caroline," he said, sticking his tongue in her ear, twisting it around in a loud swish and slurp. "I told her, *It's a*

damn good thing you aren't here, or I'd screw the shit outta ya."
He laughed aloud into Sam's hair just as he pulled her left breast
out of her gown.

The words set off a small alarm in Sam's head, but she said
nothing. It was *her* breast he was reaching for... She rolled over
into his arms. "Oh, God. You get me going," she said, and
covered his lips with her own.

He grabbed Sam by the fleshy part of the buttocks and
pulled her into him. Slowly he lifted her hips up, up, and in a
circular motion, pressed his body around... up, around, up...
Suddenly he threw her onto her back. On his knees, he reached
for the hem of her gown, and yanked it up to her belly. With the
cool air hitting her, her buttocks squeezed, her hips reached
upward searching for his mouth. She could feel the fullness of her
vulva reaching for its warmth, the softness of his lips – but instead
he surprised her. With one big rush he pulled her legs apart, and
before she could prepare for it, jammed his penis into her. Her
ready wetness was all that kept her from screaming at the thrust.
He was large; he always knew he had to be extra careful with her
— and he usually was. But this time...

With one hand clutching her posterior, the other holding her
head, he gathered her almost savagely up from the bed, into his
arms. "I can't wait," he cried as he furiously pounded his body into
hers. He sounded frantic, crazily groaning obscenities with every
breath. "Fuck me, Baby. Fuck me. Fuck me. I gotta be fucked...
fucked..." he heaved into her ear.

In automatic response, she wrapped her legs around him,
frightened at his onslaught. He had never taken her with such
venom. He always waited, was so careful, afraid he would "hurt"
her, one of his quirks. In rhythm to his cursing breaths, she
moved, tensing in fear, her own passion forgotten, but thankful it
was her he'd chosen. She kept up the pretense, moving
wordlessly, until her silent tears of pain rolled into her hair, onto
the bed. The split of her vagina was quick, the sting of it numbed
by the sharpness of the penetration. In climax, he yelled out and
his voice broke into sobs, "Go. Go. Go, Baby, go! Oh, God."

As quickly and violently as he began, he suddenly and
quietly slid off of her, out of reach. "That was a good one, Babe.
I'm sorry, I couldn't wait," he said in a child's voice.

Trying not to acknowledge the moment, Sam lay there in
shock, listening to his measured breathing, the sound of sleep.
Twenty-eight years of marriage, and he had never taken her with
such unbridled force. *Is this what winning a two-billion-dollar*

contract does, or was it the other?

Long after Ray slept, Sam lay still, like stone. Fear crept into her stomach as she fought the stark reality the blood in the commode had declared, the tearing, the rawness. As his breathing became regular, she wondered if this new aberration was yet another manifestation of his, now *their* family's illness?

In the beginning, after 'Nam, the startle reaction had distanced them – become a wall between them. No more cuddling toward daybreak, when the cool morning air descended and the warmth of each other's arms had, in the past, been so comforting – what Sam had missed those long months during the Korean conflict when he was in Soul, and that traumatic year in Danang, when her safe little world blew apart. Since then, loud noises, or touching him in his sleep, would bring him, springing like a panther tearing out of bed, screaming. Then the nightmares of his mother – always the *bitch* – awaiting to murder him; recounting the plots were chilling. That lapse of consciousness: driving back to work from lunch after what appeared hours, he'd come to on the side of the road, frightened. Then right in the midst of the hottest RST negotiations – the day after they had been given the devastating neurological diagnosis on Sean, one of Ray's secretaries had noticed him in the hall, when he suddenly stopped short, appearing momentarily lost. She'd gone to him, and walked him back to his office. Stress monumental, a precipitating factor. It was Sean's neuro-psychologist who got Ray in with a psychiatrist immediately.

A twelve-member panel of physicians and med-students, from Tufts University School of Medicine, interviewed Ray. His anxiety was relieved first with Xanax, followed by a low dose of lithium, a simple mineral that was found in the water in places like Dallas. The lithium had quieted him, made him "kinder" his golfing buddy said. With the Malorry family history of bipolar illness – *The Happy Disease,* someone referred to it later, their sons in and out of hospitals since puberty, Suzie's latest lashing out anger, and then withdrawal, fearing that the illness she had fought since age seventeen was being triggered anew by her first pregnancy, and Ray's symptoms getting more noticeable every day – Sam knew to expect it, eventually; lithium was inevitable. But this sexually aggressive behavior, sometimes described in the medical research, was altogether new.

Although Sam wanted to understand, it clearly frightened her. But the fear was more for Ray, than for herself. The tear in the flesh would heal, but Ray's vehement emotions seemed to stem from deep within. Classically unaware of his own behavior, *he* clearly didn't understand. Booze and/or caffeine, she had read, wiped out the meds, the controls, and booze had been the stepping stone of his career — first *in* the military, and now marketing it – and he drank coffee all day long. If he *could* manage to quit drinking, how would he survive in this alcohol-driven environment? "With this man," said his doctor, "his job is what keeps him alive." Without it? she wondered, thinking of the future. She shuddered, her own personal needs crying.

Even if a doctor was inclined (which most weren't) to share any new tidbit of research which might enlighten one's way, asking them *How?* or *Why?* seemed fruitless; there were so many differing opinions. In 1984 they were still confusing mood and behavioral disorders with schizophrenia, a biological brain disease. Asking for help from God above was a naivete out of her past, even though turning the other cheek seemed forever a conditioned response. "How to continue?" was what she needed to learn. How to personally function around the members of her family cursed with a mental illness so subtle it was difficult to diagnose, so illusive to be easily deniable, and as unpredictable as fighting a battle in a desert of quicksand. There was no understanding or defending it. And PTSD was such a new thing, hardly even recognized as yet, but a researcher and historian at heart, Sam wore herself out trying. Not giving up until finding answers was Sam's nature. Living with her own debilitating headaches that sometimes put her to bed, an aside. In the meantime, sleep, only sleep, was a blessed retreat – a bridge over troubled waters that would allow her to awake another day, renewed, and for a little while, forget – until some totally new, here-to-fore unimaginable behavior would send her back to her family's inches-thick medical files and volumes of notes, the library, book store – and eventually back to college, once more.

◆

CHAPTER SIXTEEN

Jesus Loves You: 1986

R ay had not changed much these thirty years. He was just as crazy and unpredictable as ever. I think that is what I loved about him, after growing up in a cocoon of commandments. No one else that I've ever met would've even thought of hanging their head over a hotel balcony to moo at a cow, sober and in broad daylight. But that is exactly what Ray was doing just then, our last day in Barbados. We were staying at the Marriott's Sam Lord's Castle and the back balcony of the hotel overlooked an abutting meadow below. The cows grazing in the deep grass had caught Ray's eye, or should I say a particular cow did, a white one with a black face, and the only one that would give him the time of day.

"Could be the old girl herself, spying on me like she always did," Ray had said, when the cow first lifted her head and turned toward us, taking a momentary pause in her chewing. Ray was referring, of course, to his long-departed Irish Grandma O'Toole, who seemed always to know what he had done, where he had done it, and where he'd hidden the evidence. Mooing at her all week, whoever she was, had become a regular ritual since the first day of our second honeymoon, or third honeymoon, or fourth, or maybe even fifth. Who can keep count after so many years?

Our first "second honeymoon" was on our eleventh anniversary in Hawaii for Ray's R & R (Rest and Recuperation) from Vietnam. It was really more like our *first* honeymoon since it took us that long to figure out that sex really could be fun – when we weren't worried about being like everyone else or making babies. Overcoming frigidity and reaching orgasm was a life-long struggle for me. Having dislodged, finally, that psychological block, I was anxious to share my new *whole-woman-self* with my husband. So Hawaii must take its place up there with our children's births or our first puppy. Ray's memorable eloquent phrases he'd picked up the previous six months of that year, living with a bunch of Aussies in Denang, marked the event in my mind forever when he surprised me, yelling at me in the bathroom, "Hey Sam, let's get humping."

I dropped my mascara brush, messing up my eyes royally and came dashing into the bedroom. "I can't believe my ears." I squealed, still undressed while drying off from the shower, enjoying the warm afterglow from such a momentous honeymoon morning. "Not again!" I cried weakly, *literally*.

Thank goodness that, to an Aussie, humping merely meant to hurry. Not that I would have really minded. It had been so very long, besides the three months of Army school prior to Vietnam orders, when we talked of divorce. There were so many ins and outs for us, being separated geographically, or in the same house, emotionally. There are many ways to be apart. Sometimes it takes real work to really *be* together.

It was the therapy that helped me get over being so afraid of sex, afraid of myself. Feelings suddenly seemed excitingly new. As if *I* was brand new, or Ray was. Oh, we'd read those books after his year in Korea, and I was sincerely hoping that it was the reading that had finally taught Ray his part – afraid to think differently since he was gone so much, in spite of a part of me that believed otherwise. It was mostly the therapy for me, though, that had unlocked those feelings – that and the nameless stranger from Savannah, so like the "zip-less fuck" Erica Jong wrote about in *Fear of Flying*. Looking back on all of it now, in the sexually unencumbered 80's with Dr. Ruth, this particular week in Barbados was indeed special to us. We'd both tried other rainbows, forged other seas, but we'd managed to climb our highest mountain together when we reached our thirtieth year in May. (And Ray's mother said it wouldn't last two! *But, then, what do mothers know?*)

To top it all off, I would be celebrating my fiftieth birthday just around the corner come Thanksgiving. It would have to fall right on the holiday this year, giving impetus to Ray's jubilation. He was actually jumping for joy. My being four years his junior had always riled him. Having to pass all those milestones alone: first 30, then 40, then the big 5-oh with me trailing behind. He wanted me up there, right along with him, so I wouldn't give him side glances when that insurance was advertised on TV "If you're fifty or over..." He didn't like me darkening my gray hair either, although I did occasionally just to let him know it was *my* hair. He said he was tired of people thinking he was robbing the cradle, my being so small-boned and tiny-headed. That's the Cherokee in me, I keep telling him, and that one of these days he's going to wake up next to a shriveled up piece of skin, bones and scalp, looking a hundred, overnight.

"Good," he said. "Then I can pass as your house boy."

One just never knows what's going to come out of Ray's mouth. Like this mooing. He hadn't had a drink either since the first day. It was so strong with the local rum, I begged him to leave it off. Surprisingly he had. But the mooing continued.

This last morning, on the way to breakfast, Ray took extra time with his moos. I told him she'd think surely he was courting her – to be careful. But he continued to moo and *beller*, as Daddy would say, and sure enough the old girl stopped her chewing long enough to lift her head way up in the air and let out a whale of a moo. Ray was ecstatic. "I didn't know you had such talent," I told him, knowing our week was now truly complete. The old girl had finally spoken.

The week had started out kind of so-so. We didn't know what to expect, not having been to the West Indies before. But with Honolulu, Japan, and Bangkok behind us, we figured there would be some celebrity floor shows to top off our full days of sightseeing in this island paradise. What a surprise. But surprises never cease when you stay sober, and I had for several years now. The horrendous headaches had forced me to.

The electricity was out all over the island that first day. Not such a big deal to us after living in Thailand. One night while in Bangkok, we had twenty-seven of Ray's enlisted people over for homemade ravioli, my friend Mary's recipe. Chan, our Chinese cook, made it up ahead. When the lights went out, we lit the candles and heated up the ravioli in a roasting pan awkwardly stuck inside the charcoal broiler we'd brought with us from the States. So this showering in the dark did not upset us.

Our extravagant buffet breakfast was catered to by a host of pleasant, very British sounding black waiters – one for each course or utensil, we couldn't decide which – in the huge open air dining hall. It was reminiscent of summer camp: warm summer breezes, cats slithering through our legs and birds chirping, flying overhead, all giving us a sense of our own importance in the universe we sought daily to control. The bright sunshine was a pleasant change from the day before after a warm pelting rain had welcomed us. I knew Ray's insatiable curiosity and that we would have to check out the grounds first. He always has to know exactly where everything is and what everything costs, whether or not he intends to do it or buy it. He's a planner, and an unchartered week of leisurely days lay before us. That he was eager to fill it up only mildly describes his restlessness. I was anxious, of course, to visit the shops. But Ray wanted to check out all the tours available first.

Anything on water was strictly out. Ray always says he can walk a lot farther than he can swim. My shipboard experience, returning from Japan without him on the USS Mitchell with the four kids, cured me. Sean, already hyperactive at age two, had to be harnessed, but Sharon, more beautiful every day and looking more like Ray's daughter than mine, was not so controllable at age twelve with all the goggly-eyed sailors. I thought of putting a sign around her neck saying, "Too Young" or "Jail Bait." Instead, I put her in charge of Kelly, age five and puking at every wave – when he wasn't talking. We couldn't get near Sick Bay because the 3,000 Army GI's picked up in Korea, riding in the ship's hull, had come down with a communal case of "the clap" three days out to sea. They were not allowed up top, though. Suzie, eight then and always my easiest, her hair getting darker every day like mine but her eyes a bright, clear blue like Mama's, stood starry-eyed near the railings, wondering about the fish, the birds, and the people on the islands we neared. With her concern for life in any form, no wonder she fell into hippie ways so easily, a flower child who saw nothing but beauty since birth.

The Captain's dinner, a formal affair to which I was asked to act as honorary hostess, stuck out in my mind. I felt like I was chosen Queen of the Prom. I wore my best outfit, a handmade blue silk suit made at Tokyo's Christian Dior. Suddenly, in the middle of the appetizer, the ship switched the direction of its roll and, luckily, I caught my shrimp cocktail before it hit my lap. Others at the table were not so lucky.

It was on this fourteen-day trip that I was first introduced to island life. On the seventh day, when we passed the international date line and the trip turned into thirteen days, we were given a full day at the beach in Hawaii. It happened to be Sunday, so I dressed all four kids in Sunday clothes (what else?): white shirt and bow ties, short pants for the boys and fancy dresses for the girls. We all had leis around our necks. When we got off the bus at Waikiki, there were sand and palm trees everywhere. I did manage to find the PX at Fort DeRussy, but was shocked to see that bare feet and moo moos were allowed. Later, I took a picture of the kids under a swaying palm tree, an embarrassing moment locked in time as they all looked like they are saying, Mom, how *could* you do this to us? But I shrugged off my ignorance – a common feeling for me through the years, as I had learned so many things the hard way – and pulled off all our shoes and went walking in the sand. If I'd had the money, I would've bought us all new swimming suits just for the day, but Ray had recently made Captain, and I barely made our money stretch as it was. I had another new home to set up, waiting for me. How I managed to stay ignorant of so many things still puzzles me. But growing up in a vacuum, with thoughts for your own immediate welfare so all possessing, keeps you from venturing out beyond those self-imposed limits. Those limits become so comfortable, I guess, that unless you are forced to, you just sit back and let the outside world go by. Looking back at the utter terror I felt at having to face a strange world when I married Ray and left Milwaukee, I was finally able to smile at myself. But even this attitude of being at considerable ease with the world now did not make me want to get on another *Love Boat* or, in this case, the primary excursion boat of Barbados, *The Jolly Roger*.

The caves didn't intrigue me either, although Ray would have gone. I don't like the dark or dampness or what that combination usually grows.

Ray had brought his golf clubs so he set up a tee time for later on in the week. I wanted to rent a car so I could drive him to the course and then go around by myself, but Ray wouldn't have it. He was getting more like Daddy every day – even though he was beginning to look like Mr. Simms with his white curly hair and his voice, deeper every year (something I tried not to think about since I'd paid back all the money and had learned to ignore the sad, sick letters Mr. Simms had written well into his eighties that had followed me around the world).

Ray was convinced I would either wreck the car driving on the left side of the road (even though I'd done it in Japan) or get terribly lost. The latter was more probable. He was not about to tackle driving either. We were in for a bit of walking. The cost of a taxi just to get to the golf course on the other side of the island and back, added onto the incredibly high golf fees, made his day on the links more than a hundred dollars. But with his curiosity, we agreed he must play it regardless. Money was never an object with Ray. *Ma Schultz had taught me well: I managed the money with an iron fist.* But Ray had just about anything he wanted, I saw to it, by shopping sales and discount stores. Ray liked to tell everyone that he had been a King in another life and me his Queen. "Sam however, is still reigning," he'd say. And he loved referring to me as Princess Yes Ma'am.

So, touring the shops, we did, but quickly. The fans were not working, which made the air from the otherwise pleasant warmth of the 80-degree sun absolutely stuffy indoors. There wasn't a great deal to choose from anyway. Our own Faneuil Hall in Boston probably had more selection and better prices. Ray was in luck; we headed for the beach.

Barely were we seated on the lounges enjoying the splashing of the windy waves, and some young fellows trying their best to body surf, when the wind began blowing up the sand so badly we had to leave the beach. *Fate was working in my favor.* I was anxious for the honeymoon to start. I'd just had major surgery six weeks before and this was my coming out party, so to speak.

We were up on the second floor, so we never had to close the sliding glass doors day or night, rain or shine; and on the Atlantic (windward) side of the island we felt the breeze and heard the beat of the surf continuously. We had finally settled things between us. The question always there, under the struggles both real and imagined, whether or not Ray *really* wanted to marry me and I him. Making love, though, had always come about easily enough since Hawaii, except for those few weeks at the beginning of summer after Daddy's postcard.

Things between Ray and I have always been either very good or very bad. However, his going on lithium seemed to ease things. It was my going in and out of extensive therapy that put added stress on us both. Even little changes in my personality could affect the way things were between us. But Ray had ridden the waves, telling me that not knowing what he would come home to on any given day was exactly what kept him coming home. He also knew that the damage to the psyche that had been done to me could not be undone overnight. Years, was more like it. Just when you think you've figured things out and have everything under control, wham, life throws you another spinner. You can either duck it or knock it out of the park. Learning to hit is what therapy is all about.

The spinner came as a postcard in the mail addressed to me in Daddy's large scratchy penmanship. He was going blind from his diabetes, so the sight of his effort moved me. Charity usually did the writing. But I'd had little to do with them for the last few years, since the Freudian therapy when I'd written them in a letter:

"*I'm still having nightmares about that Sunday morning (in the Simms house) at 45 years of age. I don't understand. It doesn't fit with all I believe to be true and caring and loving. It contradicts everything that comes out of Daddy's mouth regarding his love for God and for me... I asked the doctor why all of this had come back, all the feelings of disgust and guilt and unworthiness to be alive that I had put behind me long ago. He said that during extreme stress the underpinnings of the personality come through and all the stress* (with Sean's suicide attempts) *the* (menopausal) *period in my life complicated things even further."*

Charity's unsympathetic answer discounting my pain, although consistent with her past attitude toward me, cut me anew when she wrote:

Dad told me of this incident when we were first married, and, in my opinion, your imagination has really run wild, complicated by the state of mind you are experiencing due to the change of life. Your daddy had been without a wife for years at the time you refer to, and, if you know anything about the anatomy and functions of the male species, I should think you would understand what happened and not put some fantastic setting to it – which is a gross error and figment of your imagination. Shameful to a child – yes, maybe – but you are an adult!?! You are certainly trying once again to possess your dad, controlling, manipulating him, first by your criticism of him – and now by this horrible accusation. And then calling him a hypocrite. What religion has all perfect followers? Jesus came to help the sick in mind and body, not the well. Your dad was a baby Christian at the time you refer to, and babies should be allowed to stumble and fall in order to strengthen the growing process, in order to learn to walk! Can you not allow your daddy to be human? Dad has experienced a divine healing of the emotions, and you are still suffering. But you don't need to! You can receive this divine healing of your inner self and its load of this guilt and shame and (as you put it) "unworthiness to be alive." You don't need to punish yourself this way, as Christ has already taken the guilt of both of you on Himself, and you can find complete freedom in Christ. He is the burden bearer, and that frees you to be forgiving and happy, content to be alive and feeling worthy to be alive! If you really don't want this inner healing, you will go right on having your pity party."

I had told her that her preaching was just like the story Jesus told of the Pharisee who said, "I'm glad that I am not as other men are." So she responded with:

"If your house were on fire and you were inside, unaware of the danger, a 'Pharisee' might stand outside and say, Thank God my house is not on fire. But I would run to you and warn you of the impending catastrophe. That is sharing my feelings, not preaching! What would you and Phil Donahue call me if I failed to warn you and let you perish? Can't you see that it is true love? I really care about you and Ray and your family and your dad! I'm not a Pharisee! Love, Mother.

This was the last time I addressed her as *Mother*. My anger, hidden behind a ton of garbage, finally broke loose.

Dr. Comas was upset with me for bringing the subject up to them. The idea was for me to deal with what happened within me, not by confronting Daddy to make him feel guilty. But my anger had finally gotten the best of me. I got tired of Daddy talking about *God* forgiving him. Finally, one day I said, "I don't care about God, Daddy, what about me? About *my* forgiving you? You didn't do it to God; you did it to me."

Although he'd already asked for my forgiveness at the time, he didn't seem to really understand what serious harm was done to me. The closest he came to recognizing it was in a letter, but even then he sidestepped it:

Sam, if I ever touched you with my hand in a sexual manner, I was temporarily insane at the time. This is true. This is the only way I can describe it. I love you and Ray, and I hope you can leave dead dogs buried forever. You do not need to reply to this unless you wish to on peaceful terms. Love always, Daddy.

These last words told me that he was still dictating to me how I should behave, "on peaceful terms." *Samantha Sue, hush. Don't feel, Samantha Sue.*

Now, again, he was doing the same with the postcard. It had a printed poem on the back, entitled, "Jesus Loves You." It told all the things I'd heard all my life about Jesus caring for me. A sweet poem and he had signed it, Love, Daddy. But the first thought I had, was, *Why couldn't he just have said, I love you Samantha? Why did he have to send this poem?* He *would* have his say about his Jesus' gospel even though I'd already asked him to stop it, to talk in English, not in Biblical quotations. To some degree he had stopped, but he would always find a way to get *the Word* in. It was like having a used car salesman for a father and having him try to hard-sell you a car every time he spoke to you. I tore the postcard up immediately (anger spouted out of me easily these days), and I forgot about it, *I thought...*

The next time Ray and I made love, I could not reach orgasm. I panicked. *What was going on with me?* My sex life seemed to reflect what was going on in my psyche. (Dr. Comas said it was because my life had been built on sex. Charity called Freudians "sinful quacks" and said they were known for interpreting *everything* through sex.) Terrified that I'd had a relapse, I tried everything, afraid I was reverting to the old frigid patterns. We tried different things, music, but nothing worked. Ray knew I was upset about something, but he wasn't sure what, so he suggested we go up to our favorite getaway in Bar Harbor for the 4th of July. (Another Independence Day on the calendar of my subconscious?)

When he got home from work, I was packed and ready to leave. As he started changing clothes, he came over to me and hugged me, telling me he loved me, hinting for a "quickie," a throw back to Army days when he could get home for lunch, our only time alone then, without kids.

My efforts at relaxing, all the things I'd read about to reach orgasm, just wouldn't work, so I resorted to the same thing I had used before: making-believe. It had worked for years before I knew what orgasm was all about, so it would have to work again. Afterwards, I felt so miserable; and I was disgusted with myself. Like I'd been *used* – way back when. But off to Maine we went. *I would think about it later.*

Upon arrival at the hotel we normally stayed in, we were told we mistakenly only had reservations for the following night. So we had to look around for another place to stay. The only thing we could get was a room looking into the afternoon sun. Air-conditioning is not something Maine needs as a rule and not a provision, so the 90-degree heat turned us into fighting tigers. Finally, we rolled up the windows of the car with the cold air-conditioner blowing and drove around town, screaming at each other. Boy, did we fight. Ray let his anger out easily when he was behind the wheel, I'd found. A mean fighter when he was angry: manipulative, consistently trying to make me feel stupid, anxious or guilty. Stupid usually worked, but when he refused to play golf to punish me, that let the guilt loose in my head. We managed to get through the day with the agreement that we would go back home "tomorrow."

When we woke up, our anger had subsided, especially since we believed we were angry at the hotel – not each other. When finally we got into our favorite suite, safe and in comfortable surroundings, I took a hot bath and Ray unpacked. We made love then, and suddenly my orgasm broke through like water bursting through a dam, bringing with it as many tears as Niagara. Sex always surprises me at how different it can be each time, continuing to be pleasurable, besides feeling the relief at being *over* with whatever *it* was.

On the way home, listening to John Denver sing *Sunshine on the water makes me happy* on the car radio, I began thinking about the last few weeks and what could possibly have caused me such a frigid reaction, remembering how awful I'd felt, not being able to experience my part of the beautiful sex we'd come to share. And *that quickie* before we left home – it made me feel almost like a prostitute. A prostitute? Bingo! *An adulterer!* Everything suddenly clicked. As I went back in my mind over everything that had happened recently, to put some sense to it, I remembered the *Jesus Loves You* card Daddy sent me and immediately the story about the woman at the well came to mind. This was always my favorite story in the Bible and the one that had been preached the night I decided to tell Daddy about Huey. If I closed my eyes, I was right back there, in church, hearing the young visiting minister speaking softly into the microphone:

> *"My friend, did you hear what Jesus said? Did you hear the words the man of Galilee spoke to that angry treacherous mob?" His voice was rising in pitch and his throat was rasping as it broke in supplication, this time shouting, "Listen to me my friend, listen to Jesus; He is speaking to you· Listen again to his words·" As he bent over the microphone again, tears were flowing down his cheeks· "Come, my friend, brother, sister, your heart is heavy from carrying this load· You are about to break from the weight of it· Don't worry about all those pointing fingers, my friend· Jesus said, "Woman, I forgive you! Woman, I forgive you·" and he pointed right at me·*

The woman was an adulterer and Jesus loved her *anyhow.* Here Daddy was saying to me, *Jesus Loves You,* but the unwritten, subconscious message I received was, *You are an adulterer, because you enjoy your own body.* Charity had said so many times to me, "A true friend is one who knows *all about you* and still loves you." Even though you are a "slut," I still love you, she seemed to be saying, as Jesus said to the woman at the well, a message I had not heard in years.

In my head anyhow, I always knew that the religious teachings I had internalized had caused me tremendous difficulty: in parenting, in socializing, in accepting life as it was. Instead, I tried continually to make life conform to the way I thought it should be. It was only Ray's patience that got me thus far – besides being my teacher, my connection to the world I'd missed. Suddenly it all fell into place, way down inside of me. Dr. Comas had said, "It's not what you know or understand *intellectually* that will change you, but what you *experience.*" This is "the truth" that sets you free. For the first time I was able to see and feel, to know inside of me where many of my sexual problems came from. And

I only hoped that from this experience they would stay in the past forever, leaving me free to enjoy another honeymoon.

That is why being so relaxed in Barbados brought a real celebration of the most vital part of myself. In between dozing, I allowed those feelings, the ones I'd worked so hard to uncover (but still managed to hide from so easily) to surface again, under the gentleness of the ocean winds that blew over us. We could look out from the bed over the beautiful gardens below us at the ocean beyond. Several couples were in the Jacuzzi. The sound of laughter, mingling with the surf and the sounds from the huge meadow behind us, surrounded us with an aura of contentment. The sadness inside of me that still crept up unexpectedly sometimes was out of mind for the moment.

Tomorrow we would go touring.

And we did go. The ride into Bridgetown was about an hour through very narrow streets. Our bus driver never slowed for oncoming traffic. Had we stuck out our arms, we could almost have touched the sugar cane overhanging the road.

We saw few houses until nearing town. I kept thinking that what I was seeing were the rural areas. Surely we would find some beautiful haciendas. Barbados had won its independence from the Crown some ten years before, and it appeared that when the British left they'd taken the paint with them. The houses were small cubicle affairs, often with shutters for windows. Quite a few tin roofs rusting, and fences, originally attractive, were falling down. With my background in real estate sales, I had expected to find a few fix-ups, but I was stunned at what I saw. The residents we passed, however, seemed to be well dressed and clean and neat. We were told of the many churches on the island and of their strong influence. Thus, the low crime rate. *Certainly people were more important than things here.*

As we passed the statue of the freed slave with the severed chains hanging from his wrists, I thought about how I'd always identified with the plight of the black people. They were much like I was, feeling like I felt. No matter that I was free, it was the inner bondage that enslaved me still – the fear of being different and of the scorn that followed. No matter how long I lived, no matter that the chains were severed, the chains would always be there. Although invisible, I would always feel them, in my striving still to be accepted for who I was or was not — forever feeling the need to apologize for what I somehow should have known, but didn't.

The bus left us at the center of Bridgetown and we had two hours to shop. We sped through the stores feeling as if we'd stepped back into a time warp. Apart from the imports, as there was very little industry on the island, and I saw little to buy other than some beautiful hand crocheted pieces, a very black Barbados babydoll for my collection – blue-eyed with a catching smile and pigtails – and some prints by Jill Walker, the island's artist.

We enjoyed our lunch at a restaurant overlooking the canal. The Creole chicken was especially tasty, and the waitress was an outstanding beauty. She was fine boned and had a Polynesian look, very large and round eyes. She carried herself with impeccable grace, her manner lovely and gracious. Thinking about her as we rode back on the bus, it struck me how different the attitude was here in Barbados toward the natives – as well as their attitude toward us. I couldn't help but marvel at how it felt to be accepted, as well as to be accepting. It was as though the love inside of you that you really wanted to share but were too shy to let go of was allowed to come tumbling out. It was this atmosphere of acceptance throughout the entire week that was setting the stage for another magnificent honeymoon.

Back at the Castle, we walked the grounds again. Neither one of us really liked to wear a bathing suit in public, even though Ray never let me forget the black bloomer suit. We still had a tendency to hide our feelings from each other after thirty years, not wanting to admit how shy we really were. But we both must have felt safe enough there. Maybe it was the milestone we'd just passed, but we comfortably kept our clothes on without any apologies and wore hats for the sun, the peacefulness of the place like the eye of a storm.

Ray played golf, but came back laughing at the lack of upkeep on the course. William, our careful taxi driver, came for us the next day. He was informative and gave us the grand tour. We stopped at the 400-year-old church, the pride of the people, that is still being used for college classes – their 97% literacy rate the highest in the world. We saw the Castle and miles of coastline from the highest point. We ate lunch on the calmer and less windy Caribbean side, passing by some nicer beach homes and deciding we didn't want to retire there. We drove the entire perimeter of the island and were back to the Castle in three hours.

My postcards home read: "Barbados is nice – once." But that was written before it dawned on me what Barbados was all about. It took us at least three days to stop looking for something to do or some place to go. We put our books up and settled back into a chaise enjoying the gorgeous view. We let the warm air flow over our tired bodies like the oiled fingers of a Swedish masseuse, and the sounds of the pulsating surf – the sounds we all left behind inside the womb – soothe our flexed emotions as we enjoyed Barbados and each other.

So it was with a wistful feeling of sadness that I listened to Ray's cow answer back to us that last morning. We laughed on and off through breakfast, sharing his communications' feat with the friends we'd made throughout the week.

Ray left me at the dining hall and went to check out. I walked slowly back to my room knowing a bellboy would be along shortly for our bags.

As I stepped back into the room and out onto the balcony to snap a few last pictures, a lump came into my throat. I felt a sadness grip me like I'd never experienced before. The tears were starting to flow out through my carefully applied mascara. I ran to the bathroom for tissues and found myself looking into the mirror. What a silly thing to cry about! *You're sad you're leaving Barbados?* came the mocking voice within.

Yes. It was sadness at leaving a place we'd begun to love – *or was it a part of ourselves we'd finally begun to love in this quiet, peaceful, do-nothing land?* As I looked into the mirror, I saw beyond my image into the past, all the leavings I'd gone through in my lifetime and all the sadness and tears I'd choked back and never allowed myself to feel. I remembered all the people I'd left; the towns we drove out of and my tears being held in check out of habit – the cars, the buses, the trains, the planes, the ship: *I had never learned to say goodbye.*

Knowing from my therapy that I was overreacting for some deeper reason, I allowed myself to sink below the moment into those feelings. Suddenly I was remembering that last day with Mama. It's like a spot in my memory: a hole in the dark embellished by stories told by others. But now it was me, Samantha Sue, sitting on my little three-legged stool, by the windows that overlooked the parking lot where Daddy was fixing his Model-T Ford. I was being punished – for being stubborn and showing my temper, no doubt. Then I hear Mama call me. I could feel myself climbing up the steep step into her bedroom, the bare hardwood floor so shiny stretching between us.

When Mama called, I remember how slow and shy I was about going to her, as I did when I'd been bad, and she coaxed me to get up on the big high bed. It was like a mountain. My short young legs would hardly reach. She was lying on top of the pale chenille spread that matched her eyes. Her arms were outstretched for me. Mama was crying hard by then; and when I saw it, and felt her horrible sadness (the same as when baby Jesse died), I started to cry with her. She took me into her arms then and hugged me and said, "I love you, my sweet sugar."

I didn't say anything back to her, at least not that I recall. A quiet and obedient child, Daddy said of me. I only remember my tears and letting her hold me and pet me on the head.

The next time I saw Mama was a few days later in the orchid velvet-lined casket as Daddy held me tightly in his arms. We looked down at her together. I asked Daddy where the baby was – a baby sister.

I had a lot more questions, I know. I always did. But Daddy's tears stopped me. And Grandma's words were in my ears –words I'd heard over and over since that day amidst all the confusion of the doctor and ambulance and police; everyone trying to figure out how all of it had happened. "Hush, Samantha Sue, Hush. Can't you see I can't *think* with you hollerin'," Grandma had said while she was calling the doctor on Grandpa's pay telephone? She must've been frantic with me pulling at her skirt trying to find out – *Was the doctor coming? Was it time for the baby?* But I still hear her words, "Hush, Samantha Sue. Hush."

So I hushed. I spent my whole life "hushed" and never said goodbye to Mama. Even though I'd asked for her forgiveness in my therapy many times, I never before thought about saying goodbye. But now, as I stood in front of the mirror, I could not hold back the bottled-up tears. I sobbed like I was sobbing for a lifetime of goodbyes. I put my arms around myself as I had learned in the cradle therapy, and I said, "I love you, Samantha Sue. It's okay to say goodbye to Mama now."

I closed my eyes and felt the warm arms about me, Mama's arms, and it was her words I heard. "I love you, Samantha Sue. Goodbye my darlin' babygirl," I heard her whisper in my ear.

And now, not quite aloud, to that person who, by her absence, had become the focal point of my existence, I was finally saying, "*Goodbye, Mama.*"

A knock came at the door; it was the bellboy for the bags. I quickly dried my tears and let him in. I repaired my makeup hurriedly, as I knew Ray would be right behind him. I didn't want Ray to know I'd been crying, still resorting to that *make-believe face!*

I closed the bathroom door to give me a moment of quietness and thought about how difficult it was for us to settle in and let ourselves enjoy this peaceful place. Maybe we'd both been resisting Barbados because we knew how we hated to say goodbye. (Ray had left for Korea and Vietnam in the middle of the night and refused to allow me to get out of bed. It was awful. He wanted me to feel like he would be back in the morning. His losing his Grandpa O'Toole and Mickey, both his closest friends, and then little Suzie, too, had left their mark.) I heard Ray in the other room just as I opened the bathroom door. At the sound of his reassuring voice, my pulse quickened, and the thought crossed my mind that maybe, just maybe, the fear of death was all about having to say that dreaded little word; *or was it the other way around?*

The bags were carried out, and the bellboy took one last snapshot of us out on the balcony, with the ocean in the distance and the tall palm trees swaying in the wind. He went on ahead of us then. We checked the room, and I picked up my handbag. We took one last look behind us, then slipped out the door. Before Ray closed it he stopped and looked back across the room through the wide-open balcony doors, at the tops of the palms, at the ocean beyond. And in a wee little high voice, as if he were speaking to our youngest baby granddaughter, he said, as he waved his fingers, "Bye-bye, Barbados," and pulled the door to behind us.

As we walked along the back balcony, Ray took my hand – something that had taken years (and a little lithium) – to do on his own. My, how far we each had come together, I thought, as I looked past him at the green expanse of the meadow and the grazing cows. Then, suppressing a giggle, I asked, "Aren't you going to tell the old girl, goodbye?"

His response was instant. "Oh, I already did that this morning. What do you think she was telling me when she mooed back?" he countered with his cat-that-swallowed-the-canary smile, glancing only momentarily in her direction.

Knowing it was Ray's spontaneity that had helped me all this way by allowing the *child* part, the Samantha Sue part of me, to feel safe and loved: the part in which real emotional changes, if they are to last, *must* occur, I squeezed his hand — my own angel, *unaware* — though, one day I would tell him...

But now, to both Barbados and to the continuous underlying feeling of sadness, sometimes overwhelming, that I had lived with for forty-seven years, I was bidding farewell. But to life, and what it still held for me, I was ready to say *Hello.*

◆

CHAPTER SEVENTEEN

The Window Treatment: 1989-1993

To feel like a woman again. That is the real gift our houseguest brought. Even though he was 75, and old enough to be my father, Sark made me conscious of the beat of my heart. It had been awhile since my husband had made me feel this way, before he started leaving off his lithium, unbeknownst to me.

Ray walked into the house one day to find me up a ladder hanging the very wallpaper he had helped choose. In my anger at Sean – for disappointing me in taking the $1,000 I'd put into a joint account to allow him to cash his SSI checks without the enormous fees; selling the California apartment's furnishings I'd paid for, to buy his boat, "so I can dock it free on the shores of Coronado Island," obviously forgetting his promise to, in return, wallpaper this new Boston condo we had just bought – my adrenaline had been spiked. The entire master bedroom suite was in disarray. Hanging at least one strip of each pattern, just to see how it would look, Ray came in furiously objecting, "If I wanted a house with wallpaper in it, I'd go live with my mother," he yelled, as though seeing the pretty cameo rose print for the first time. Ray's sullen behavior had been the tell-tale sign in the past that a depressive episode may be in the offing, the unleashing of that uncontrollable anger, violent in its intensity – an accompanying characteristic.

At first I thought it was Ray's way of letting me know he had no intention of helping; he hated any form of fixing, creative, or otherwise. His expertise usually started with the blow of the hammer, and ended with a telephone call to the nearest repairman. So his reaction was somewhat understandable, but not his cruel disapproval at every cut and corner. At this point, it was too late to halt the project; I was knee-deep in paste and ready-to-hang strips, but it wasn't the wallpaper Ray was avidly protesting, I realized later, rather, it was the changes in his world.

The whole house was in turmoil threatening the stability lithium had provided him since the trip to France, where he had a big hand in supervising the first on-site military war game, testing out the new Roving Secured Telephone, USS, teaming with the

French, was trying to sell the Reagan administration. Being back in that war milieu had triggered the PTSD Ray's latest psychiatrist had just recently pinpointed, along with the underlying cyclothymic disorder.[32] Through the up and down see-saw of mood swings, the lithium provided stability. When that control is threatened, the illness lashes out, not the person.

Besides the fact that he had unexpectantly been relieved as Director and was now reporting to a new boss, Jed Meany, and Ray insisted that his job was no longer that important to him, his doctor had just left the state. Not wanting to break in a new one, Ray was hoping he really didn't need medication anyway, a common misconception with persons who may benefit from the use of lithium,[33] he had, unbeknownst to me, cut his intake back, which sent him spiraling into a dark, hopeless, and humorless mood. When I finally became aware of what was happening, I was frightened, wondering if my lovable husband, as I had come to know him, would ever return, but I finally got him to a new doctor, and he *was* coming back, slowly. This showdown, for all my education on mental illness, and the experience with other family members, had left me hurt, truly scared, and somewhat depressed myself. This man, with whom I had entrusted my life, had suddenly turned the tables on me, but somewhere from within me I gathered strength, and I decided, stubbornly, to show myself I could finish this wallpaper project, without help.

Weeks later, when Ray's new medication finally took effect, he had no recall of his "dip" and proudly showed off my finished decorating handiwork, but before that resolution, when Sark, a new widower, happened to visit, I was caught feeling strange, empty, and quite vulnerable – much like I had felt before I ever met Ray, and often in periods of our early marriage. Maybe that was why entertaining a houseguest, as attentive as Sark, left me with some trepidation.

As he unpacked the car, I was surprised at all the things Sark, who lived in Bar Harbor, Maine, had brought. Besides his

---

[32] Cyclothymic is a non-psychotic disorder characterized by "periods of depression and mania... not of sufficient severity and duration to be included in major affective disorders." Sue; Sue & Sue, *Understanding Abnormal Behavior.*

[33] Lithium carbonate, a true miracle substance is a simple naturally occurring salt found in mineral water and rocks, first discovered in Australia, to calm manic excitement. Ronald R. Fieve, M.D., *Moodswing.*

clothes, he had a large flat box gift-wrapped in blue, a homemade apple pie, many foods for himself, for his vegetarian diet, tons of supplements to fight his cancer all divvied up into tri-daily portions.

The day progressed nicely enough. I was afraid being alone with him would make me uncomfortable, but it didn't. Sark was a real sweetheart, and a gentleman. Very neat and independent, he managed to occupy himself once he was unpacked and settled in. I noticed he got tired easily, and was resting in the living room chair, dozing, until Ray went in and woke him for dinner.

While I was busily engaged with its preparation, Ray pulled the large white ceramic platter out of the box. My first thought was, "What am I going to do with such a large plate?" Then I saw the turkey raised in the center, and thought, "Now I'll have something to put the turkey on — if I ever cook another one, with all my kids gone," but I didn't say it. Instead, I was feeling and admiring it, as Ray turned it over and noticed that it had *Italy 1944* imprinted on the bottom.

"That's something Sam, almost as old as you are."

I looked at Sark, who was looking at us both, studying us.

"Was this something belonging to Frances?"[34] I asked.

He nodded. "Yes, it was. I found it the other day still in the box. I don't know where it came from, or anything about it, but I thought you might like it."

Suddenly I got very excited. "Italy, 1944, I was eight years old that year, the year Roosevelt died, right near the end of the war. I remember it like it was yesterday," I said.

As I looked at the platter again, the turkey registered. My birthday was Thanksgiving week. I had to smile then, awed by the gift, and hugged Sark, thanking him for such a special thing, from his late wife, Frances.

Later at dinner, we talked about our retirement home recently purchased, located on a beautiful golf course in LaQuinta, California, with the mountains behind. After dinner, I dug out the box of family pictures to show Sark, an avid golfer, how pretty it was. Ray was watching a ball game while Sark was looking over my shoulder, at the pictures. In the box, was a big stack of 8 x 10 blow-ups of snapshots I'd sent Ray in Korea, in

---

[34] Frances Sakoian & Louis S. Acker, *The Astrologers Handbook*. Frances was personally honored by JFK at the White House, and was the first astrologist to be accepted to teach astrology as an alternative math course at the JFK University, Martinez, CA in 1970.

1960. In one, I wore a knit dress, another, a new coat with a furry fox over my shoulders. In another, I was standing in a one-piece, white swim suit – in high heels, no less. Another, I wore a floral bikini, and sat with legs outstretched. I looked closely at the pictures, remembering how carefully I had posed for my soldier-husband. Then I looked at my face, and was surprised at what I saw in it, something that I had never seen before. The look reminded me of Julia Roberts in the movie, *Pretty Woman*. Then I realized why that movie had struck me so. I knew something in it reminded me of myself back then, at first I thought it was the fact that we both had brown eyes. I had cried both times when I saw it, in the part where she talks about how she became a prostitute, where she says, *You get so used to people treating you as though you weren't worth much, that you finally end up believing it.* I mentioned the movie, and Sark had seen it too!

I kept looking at the pictures, not wanting to put them down. It was as though I was seeing myself for the first time, that I was *a woman.* How young and fresh, like a beautiful flower, I was then. Such innocence came through, the Julia Roberts look, the way I stood, posing, made me remember how self-conscious I was when the pictures were being taken. How shocked I was at Ray's bringing home so many blow-ups, and hearing that I was "the pin-up of the hooch over there," in the middle of a war. Remembering where I was in my head then, just freshly sprung from my tightly religious past through the terrible fight with my devotedly Baptist mother-in-law — twenty-four years old and rebelling. Just tasting my first drink, and smoking my first cigarette, thinking I was finally *really* grown up now. All those memories flooded over me, as I studied my face in the pictures, almost mesmerized by the look in the dark eyes of that pretty woman of the 50's — when it seemed every man I met tried to get me into bed; I *felt* like a prostitute.

Sark commented that I looked like a movie queen, "but that's how we all looked," I said. We were so innocent, too, like Marilyn Monroe, what grabbed the public about her long after she was dead, their own innocence shouting at them from the screen. *What happened to it? To us? To our beautiful innocence?* I was thinking, as I looked through the pictures of my family as I showed them to Sark, a man growing old without the joy (or pain) of ever being a father, remembering so many days gone by.

Pictures. How they capture your feelings, of happy moments as well as sad or unpleasant ones. Like the Christmas before I quit smoking: I was bone thin, almost gaunt, a cigarette in every photo, what made me decide to give them up, when I saw the pictures and realized what the cigarettes were doing to me. Then there were the kids at different ages. Remembering the happy times: the last Christmas we were all together; the hard times: the drugs and the not speaking for months. The babies. Grandchildren. Feeling anew the fresh pain of having just put our little six-year-old granddaughter, Suzie's oldest, on a plane the week before, after a glorious ten days. Our not having to share her with anyone: No parents, no siblings, just us – Grandma and Grandpa. What a joy to have her all to ourselves.

Parts of myself that I had forgotten existed lately; pictures of each one of our four children. Sharon, her stretch at the White House before she retired to motherhood and had our first granddaughter – now a snappy adolescent giving her mother a taste of her just dessert, sad at our growing apart through the years. Suzie, the most pictures of her, such an attentive daughter. Pregnant now with her third, I wondered, as I looked at her many photos: *Would she look out for me if I got where I couldn't? Would I be able to trust her with my fragile feelings, or would she abuse me as so many children are doing these days?* Then Kelly, where is he now? God knows that kid has seen the hard side of life: hospitals, under bridges, barefoot, hair longer than sin. Poor, poor Kelly, how I love him, *but will he ever know it in all his wanderings, or understand it?* And Sean, our baby, now twenty-seven years old, and struggling desperately to take care of himself on his own, the SSI giving him a sense of independence he never had, living with us. Remembering the past year without him in our lives for the first time, the anger and hurt at having to distance myself from him, forcing myself to let him go, as AA and Alnon teaches. The phone going onto the tape with his pleading forgiveness, for using the money we had provided for emergencies. His calls coming less and less often, the anger going away, leaving behind the hurt and sadness at having a son with whom I could not share myself, because to do so would keep him dependent upon me. I *had* to let him go, and if this was the only way it could be done, then so be it. I had finally accepted it, but looking at the pictures, I suddenly got so homesick to see him, hold him, and love him again, that the tears sprung up without warning. As suddenly as they came, they left, realizing what I had done for us both, was right, but that didn't mean I didn't love him. That mother part of me was still there — in tact – waiting for the right moment when I *could* show him, when he is ready to accept my love without abusing it. Surely that will be soon, I thought to myself.

Ray saw the tears, and said, "It was having Jo-Marie here, being a grandmother, mothering again."

Then is when it happened. It felt as though there was a light trying to break through the darkness, this black shield I had put up to protect me from the pain of the past months, fearing Ray's illness and the loss of that special love, and separating from the child who had taught me who I was. They'd both forced me into dealing with my own codependency, my loving others at the expense of myself. In my anger and hurt, I had shut down my own feelings. Now suddenly, through the crack in the darkness, they were coming back. I felt the love seeping through, pushing, forcing itself into the place that had been left empty.

As I put away the box of memories, a part of me acknowledged the feelings inside, as the other part went on entertaining our newly widowed houseguest, until I lay my head on my pillow that night to sleep...

The turkey plate, and its symbolic messages, suddenly hit me, it being my birthday, and always celebrated at Thanksgiving. I hated sharing my day with the turkey, then my 50th fell right on the holiday, a momentous occasion. Half a century old, and I had survived. I had made it to freedom and dignity. I had patched up a cracked psyche fit for the dumpster, and many missing pieces of it were still coming together, out of nowhere, to find their rightful place, in there somewhere. And Frances, a stroke victim, not being able to speak, had somehow known me, and loved me through all the roadblocks between us. An astrologist, a believer in human behavior based on the science of birthdays and the stars, had left the most apt symbol of my identity, and Sark had unknowingly brought it to me. *Is this karma, or what?* Then the picture blow-ups popped into my thoughts. Suddenly I felt like that girl back then had finally slid into her rightful place, inside of me, somewhere. Click. The woman piece went into place that the mother piece had been hogging — now room for both. The turkey plate brought back all the birthdays when I hated to hear them sing to me — hating myself for surviving, when Mama and they all, didn't. Inside, I felt this beautiful warmth settle into my heart, as though Frances, and Mama, and Grandma, and so, so many others up there, were all looking down on me, applauding, another chunk of hell — repression – chipped away, another foggy memory that became real. The turkey plate. Love for a husband, a child, both thought lost. A 50's smile. *Pretty Woman* — me.

When Ray kissed me good-bye, I said, "Your hair looks so good. I like your beautician."

He smiled. Over the years, I had saved us a bundle, cutting our hair. "Well, at least I have something to do today," he said.

"Oh? What?"

"I have my physical at 10:30."

Ray's salary had tripled in the ten years he had been with the company. Reaching the plateau of required annual physicals, it appeared Ray felt a certain amount of security as he was obviously liked by upper management. Wherever he went, he said he was greeted warmly and had never been refused any trips he deemed necessary to push his products – not until last week when the new regime brought in, to trim the overhead in preparation for a sale down the road, had lowered the boom. Almost wistfully, Ray said he was wishing it was over and done with, so he could go on with his life, "I guess sixty is the magic age."

At first I was stunned beyond belief that he had fallen out of step. He was always on the inside, one of the boys, on first name friendly basis with the big boss – until there came a subtle change amongst his superiors. Ray finally disclosed that on one of his trips to the west coast, with the time change, his meds somehow got off kilter and he "sort of lost it with a senior Army officer" over a disagreement on the internals of the RST system USS was supplying the Army. Ray said he had gotten right up into the guy's face (shouting bug-eyed, no doubt, as he does when he "loses it").[35] The affect of this incident was magnified by Ray's constant

---

[35] This "slip" Ray called it, reminded him of an incident with a Marine General in Vietnam, who appeared to think he was still back in World War II, a story often repeated, regarding Ray's report, of elephants up country, in "I-Corps:"

Ray explained that these large animals brought great bearing on the way Intelligence directed its reconnaissance, as they carried heavy artillery. At the time, Ray flew with the Green Berets, and went into areas less daring troops wouldn't pass. When his report went forward, the response came back from the General's staff: "*The Captain if full of shit; there are no elephants in I-Corps.*" Ray said he decided to prove his point. He went out with his pilot by helicopter, and a jumper was let down by rope into a clearing, to scoop up into an Army pillowcase, a pile of elephant dung; it stunk up the whole area something fierce. Ray got an appointment with the General. In he walked to the General's office, plunked the sack of fresh shit down, right in the middle of the General's

proud banter regarding his membership in the prestigious California golf club, and his eventual retirement there. When Ray took his new immediate boss, Jed Meany, with him on a weekend jaunt from an LA trip, to show off the beauty that had originally enthralled us both: the mountains, the grassy golf green just out our patio door, Jed Meany just sat and stared, saying nothing. *Nothing.* That was the first clue that something had gone awry for Ray, not only with this man,[36] but at USS.

As Ray turned and walked through the door, I was thinking, *He is a good man, but a stubborn one. He learns, but how long it takes. Ve get so soon olt, but yet so late schmart,* I remembered from my German childhood. So late! *Was it too late?*

Since Ray's early grades, he had learned to keep copious notes, as he found his memory to be undependable, thus his notebooks became the talk of the company, as he wrote in them daily. Although Ray said what he did at USS was perfectly legal, it could possibly be construed by some as questionable, consequently, his books became a subject of much curiosity, especially to upper management. When Ray said he heard the rumor: *If the plane goes down, forget the body – get the books,* it amused him to no end, so he kept writing "for job security,"

Ray had always found something to do for a paycheck. When he had first retired from the Army at that ungodly age, we had put everything in storage and packed ourselves up into the two cars, a '73 Caddi pulling a '70 Volkswagen, into which we had put Zsa Zsa and Gigi, the two dogs. The boys in the back of the Caddi, then fourteen and seventeen, fought over every inch of the trip as we headed across country.

We had been lucky to sell the house in the little southwestern suburb of Atlanta. It had become a "transition" neighborhood. White Realtors wouldn't show it to their White

---

desk, and said, "Sir, there are no elephants in I-Corps," turned on his heel, and walked out. The next day the front page of the Army's newspaper, *The Stars & Stripes,* had a picture of elephants decked out in enemy gear, camouflaged with tree limbs. The caption read: *No Elephants.* That General was relieved, finally, after being responsible for several hundred marines being killed while trying to take a hill "hi diddle diddle, right up the middle," a long replaced strategy of war because of its loss of human life.

[36] This man had a reputation for being vindictive; his favorite saying was: *Don't get mad, get even.*

customers and very few of them dealt with "Blacks." It was three months before I finally figured it out and asked to be released from the listing. The Realtor, a son of our good friends and Ray's former retired CO, was only too happy to let go of it. We got the feeling our house was in a twilight zone of never land. Maybe if the Real Estate community ignored it, it would go away, and *the "Black problem"* with it.

That was when we decided the dull mauve-grey trim did nothing for the pretty beige, brick facade. The cathedral ceiling, that rose into the giant pines covering the landscape, was definitely a selling point. Ray and Kelly started painting the trim bright canary yellow on a Friday. By 9:00 that night, we had two offers, back to back, written on the house — both with African-American professionals, each anxious to be the gate crasher in this lily White neighborhood – my first taste of Real Estate sales, that stuck.

One of Ray's old bosses had retired in Arizona and had written in the Christmas card, "Hell, at least there is one place left in the world you can live on your retirement; and there's *room!*" That was what got our attention. So off we went with what was left of our family, and seven-thousand in the bank. For the first time in years, we didn't owe anybody anything; we had the world by the tail. Little did we know then that the tail was fastened to a fire-spitting dragon.

In 1976, seven thousand dollars was a fortune to us – the most we had ever had in one lump sum. Ray had spied a corner lot that was covered with paloverde trees and cactus of every kind, with a builder, whose construction foreman was a tough sounding woman. Our retirement status was accepted, if we could come up with eleven grand in four months, to close. That much we had in cash reserves in insurance policies, but instead, I got a part time job for a dentist.

That was seventeen years ago. Ray was now looking down the tunnel at his 60th birthday. "No male Malorry ever lived that long," he'd always said – but I didn't believe him — until he hit 56 and had that emergency gall bladder surgery. We both thought it was the big one, until the surgeon got there and made the diagnosis. It was enough to make Ray give up cigarettes – after he'd already given up the booze, his doctor said he was a miracle – but the scare made me begin readjusting our lives around his inevitable death, and that's when I decided to secure for Ray the golf club membership.

Ray had never stopped being a Spook of sorts, becoming a hard driving, silver-tongued, industrial marketeer. He said he had few regrets throughout his military career as a polygraph examiner, as his conclusions had only once been overruled -- that by Bobby Kennedy during the Cuban Crisis, when a gay friend needed a security clearance pronto — Ray's character so unquestionably true to the code learned from the barrel staves at his father's knee.

As he looked back over his life, he said he had few moments of regret. And one of them churned away at his gut often, wishing aloud that he could change it somehow.

But there were so many things, subtle things that I'm sure he was only subliminally aware of, that went into the making of that decision five long years ago – during the reorganization, downsizing one large unit into two smaller ones – that was to ultimately put him out to pasture. Ray chose to align himself with, what turned out to be, the wrong side of the house. *How does one know who your friends really are?* Mulling over it, he said it was the cartoon that had gotten to him. When he brought it home, he was shaking his head as he threw it on the table. It was of two large men walking towards a loading aircraft, the larger one carrying a briefcase, the smaller one carrying both suitcases. The picture of the larger man had the name of his present boss – who Ray had traveled with often – penciled in above his head, and over the bag boy was written *Ray*. And then to rub it in, scribbled across the top of the torn out cartoon in big letters was *Congratulations!* At a time of indecision, the negative implications of the jest had hit him right between the eyes "like a softball gone foul." The mental image of this cartoon definitely had a bearing on him, Ray said, when Jed Meany came to him and offered him a "chance to prove himself," at selling a new product. This choice ultimately turned the tide of sentiment against Ray with his former coworkers, but more importantly, with his former boss, who appeared to take that decision as a personal affront. Not having the benefit of company years that Jed Meany had, Ray was to learn, the hard way, that politics would win out over expertise.

Not one to second guess himself, but trying to figure a way out of his predicament had started Ray's abdominal cramps, as firing had done on the helicopter missions he'd run out of Danang, in the 60's. Then, when his aircraft took a hit, his Army boxers took the load, he would tell, embarrassed. Now, he would rush to the Head. He'd been sent rushing so often of late, and sat so long, he found the crapper (he affectionately nicknamed *Claudia*) to be a place where his most profound thinking took place. Being there, he said, did not disturb him terribly as he believed it had no other cause than a nervous colon. It never registered to either of us that it had started soon after he was put on that low level of lithium, back during the field testing of the telephone he had helped sell. But he did worry often of his whereabouts, should his number come up, his 60th birthday growing nearer by the toilet roll. A fatal heart attack *there* could prove even more embarrassing than Rockefeller's. Then there was the matter of finding him – *how long it would take, and who would be the lucky joker.* Sharing this worry with me had no solacing affect when I tried to reassure him that "Surely a janitor would happen by, eventually, if not a USS employee."

Ray had a neat office, everything in it was exceptionally revealing. Symbolic might well be his trips to Claudia, as he kept precious little to himself. Pictures of our family, three granddaughters each by Sharon and Suzie, lined his desk. Kelly and Sean had no children, so they had not yet found a place amongst his bragging. A large picture, beautifully framed, of John Wayne silhouetted against the California mountains, now *his* mountains, covered the wall directly opposite his desk. On the other wall, he'd hung the plaque announcing his membership to the prestigious California golf club. Proud that he had lived long enough to afford a place in the sun, he displayed a picture of our condo on those links. Then there were the games: Toys and trinkets that he had accumulated, which entertained his visitors. He often remarked at how strange spinning a top or twirling a yo-yo in a moment of crisis, relieved some of the tensions. Or how throwing a large dice, covered with trite predictions, jestingly helped sway a vote on a locked decision. The picture framed by a White House photographer, from the days of winning the RST program, stood colorful: Nancy and Ronnie Reagan greeting Maggie Thatcher at the plane (the Brits were RST's biggest competitor) with words printed in over Maggie's head: "I'm so happy to be here Ronnie, in the US." Written over Ronnie with extended hand was, "Welcome Maggie, to the US-S."

Then there was that golf hat he'd worn at the company golf tournament he'd hosted, splashed with bird shit all over the words *DAMN SEAGULLS.* He recalled how it had gotten a bemused chuckle from the crowd as he'd removed it, and tossed it on the ground beside him. Glancing out over the group, suddenly aware of the silence that he had learned to expect when he stepped behind the podium, that silence, which to some would create a dry throat and tightness in the stomach, only had a way of loosening Ray's inane and unpredictable tongue. He was called *The Wild Irishman* and was asked to host the annual event. It didn't seem apparent to Ray that such a quiet moment was a precedent to power, nor that his talent of being at home with an audience of two, or preferably more – learned or inherited from his Missouri-born father – could be his making, or undoing.

When Ray recalled this event to me, I could just see him waving the pile of score cards, when he said, "This has been some impressive golf played here today. You all saw who my partners were: Moses, Jesus, and Jack Nicklaus. Moses got a birdie on the par three, over the water. He dubbed the shot, actually, but somebody pulled the plug in the lake, and his ball rolled all the way, on dry land, right up onto the green for a tap in." Ray said he used the score cards from his foursome that day, and shuffled them as he spoke, to make the story even more real. "And then Jesus got one hell of a drive on the long dogleg par five, over the trees. I thought he damn near drove the green, but his ball hit that tallest tree, 300 yards out. What a cracking sound it made when it bounced off the tree towards the fairway. We all sighed in relief when this big black hawk swoops down, and in mid air, grabs the ball in his mouth, and takes off with it right towards the green. We're all watching in amazement as the bird lets go of the ball, right over the cup – right into the goddamn hole for a hole in one. Well, Jack had not said a word to this point, but you can tell he is getting pissed. I mean, he was birdie, birdie, birdie, eagle, birdie. I mean he was on his game, shooting out of his mind, and this goddamn bird comes out of nowhere... Too much! So he turns to Jesus and says, *Did you come to play golf, or fart around?* So you all know what kind of day I had, as religious as I am." Ray said the crowd booed when he added, "I am *very* religious about golf; I play every Sunday."

Monuments to his good humor, and many friends in days past, *where had they gone?* he would wonder aloud to me, over dinner, remembering, still not comprehending fully what had transpired. Not fired, just sitting there day after day, without a real job or job description, drawing the comfortable salary he had finally acquired. Sitting, with no real goal but to get through just one more day, to retirement. Wondering. Wishing for some kind of change, feeling that his life had somehow been rendered meaningless

On Sunday afternoons, Sharon started calling. She had a daycare business going during the week. Friday nights, she would let her hair down and start "partying." By Sunday, Sharon was beyond coherent conversation. According to her, Val, now her husband, had to get the two younger girls out of the house, bowling, or to a movie. This was when Sharon would call, crying, finally telling me about the disclosure by her oldest girl, Candi, when she turned twelve. Candi said that she had been sexually abused by her older stepbrother (Val's younger child) from age two until nine, that it had even happened on a camping trip while all three kids slept at their parents' feet. This was so shocking to Sharon, it had sent her, for the first time in her life, to a counselor. However, she was not aware of the law that required any report of this sort had to be sent on to the authorities. At this point, it was decided that Candi would move out from her mom's house, and in with Don, her dad, a block away.

Now, the shoe was on the other foot.[37] I understood something of what Sharon was dealing with; I was learning about this uncomfortable subject in my studies at Lesley. *But how could a mother speak honestly about this to the daughter who had been guilty of same?* Even though, thirty years past, Dr. Hanks had discounted such behavior as experimentation, it was clear, sex within families and the damage it had caused in so many lives, had finally been brought out into the open with some very candid talk on the subject. As a result, society was now taking quite a different stance regarding this "sexual play among siblings," and was now labeling it *sexual abuse*.

The relationship between Suzie and I, was the best it had been in some years. With Jo-Marie's visit, a giant trust our daughter had placed in her eldest child, in us, and "in God," she said.

Sean's pleading phone calls went on the telephone tape, for weeks, unanswered, until he finally came home to visit, leaving his boat docked at a free pier off Coronado Island. He had made some sober friends there, but wanted to make things right with us. He

---

[37] There is much evidence that this behavior runs in families. Bradshaw, in his *Bradshaw On: The Family*, calls it a "multi-generational process. Dysfunctional families create dysfunctional individuals who marry other dysfunctional individuals and create new dysfunctional families.

promised, again, he would repay the money he had spent, someday.

Kelly had been absent from us, going on two years. Sean was quite upset at not knowing where his brother was, the longest Kelly had ever gone without being in touch one way or other, either by phone, or mail, with someone in the family. It was all Sean talked about, finding his brother. "I could never do that to you, Mom, not ever," he'd say, tears streaming down his face. "Not ever, Mom."

Meanwhile, Sean got a call that his boat had sunk. He had plugged up a hole in it with a huge rag, he said, that must have come loose in a bad rainstorm, and the boat went down – clear evidence of Sean's lack of abstract reasoning.

Anxious to get his SSI money, go find his brother, and look up the girl he had met, Sean left us with our relationship restored. Within days, Sean did find Kelly in San Diego.

It was the following year that both our sons were together in Fort Meyers, Florida, for Sean's formal wedding held at the water's edge, a memorable occasion captured on video tape – both boys sober, clean and joyful for one entire day.[38]

When Ray's promotion time came around again, and the person writing the evaluation showed him a note in Jed Meany's own handwriting: "Ray talks about California too much," my worries, about Ray's constant references to our beautiful condo, taking several to play golf when business trips could be routed by way of the desert, came to fruition. Being marked down on job performance, at this man's direction, was only the second time in Ray's entire professional life that he had received a bad performance rating against a record of *Outstandings*, always a winner. (The first being from his CO in Bangkok who Ray reported for faulty bookkeeping, and who was forced to retire early; this ER

---

[38] Their sisters were not present, nor were they mentioned. Sean had told me earlier that he'd gone up state to visit Suzie, to introduce his bride to her, but he was so drunk, Suzie wouldn't allow him into her house, near her kids. He said it broke his heart.

was ultimately thrown out at Branch Hqs.) Although, at the time, Ray's giving up alcohol seemed to please those in upper management, being able to function in the afternoons without their former "martini lunches," some others were not so keen on Ray's change. Since Jed Meany was an Irishman who liked his booze, I had a sense that Ray's decision, to drink only Coke with his buddies at the bar "until the 3rd go-round of the same joke was told before hitting the sack," was the beginning of the end for him – but the true beginning for us.

At first Ray said he was impressed with his new boss, who wore three hats. Jed Meany was an engineer, a lawyer, and a bean counter – the latter his most impressive skill, according to Ray. Meany's "golden rule" was: He who has the gold, rules. With this man's smarts, Ray felt they were in the cat bird's seat, until the latest job in the pipeline was heading into completion, which seemed to become a growing concern for Meany. Sometime after Ray had been told in no uncertain terms, to steer clear of the old man, to let him, Meany, do all the talking, Ray's suspicions were sparked when Meany came back from his many trips to the engineering department, stating, "When this system is finished, we are all out of a job." Ray said his Intel antennae shot up like a rocket, fearing Meany was somehow slipping a wrench into the wringer. "He certainly has the smarts to do it," Ray confided to me, "but there isn't a blessed thing I can do about it; I have no proof."

After a week's vacation, Ray said he wasn't the least bit surprised when returning to work to find Meany, who, by the way, just had his sixtieth birthday, no longer with USS. The word was that he had been called into the old man's office, and minutes later, Meany had cleaned out his desk and was gone. Ray came home more dejected than ever; the ground under his feet at USS was changing rapidly.

When, in preparation for unloading the company, an outsider, referred to as *Little Hitler* behind his back, was hired to weed out personnel, and Ray refused to cooperate in providing dirt on his friends, this hire had the effect of a good cathartic on personnel; the stockpile of people diminished without any effort — people transferred, retirees applied for early outs, but others just grew weary worrying how they would be able to survive this man's reign of terror, although Ray had managed to hold onto his salary, thus far, minus the bonus. His new goal was not to gain any increase in pay or position, necessarily, but to try to get relocated out west, in preparation for retirement. He applied for an ideal position, in northern California, just a few hours from our desert condo.

Gradually, Ray was given less and less area of influence, with less and less to do. His trips were infrequent now. The completion of my studies, for the Bachelor's Degree I worked so hard to obtain, was keeping me so busy, I was only minimally aware of what was going on, except that Ray, instead of traveling mid-week regularly, was now home every night for dinner.

First, Ray's traveling money was cut, then, after he was relieved as Director, he was moved from his corner office to a small inner office. When Ray came home and told me his office had then been moved out into the large warehouse, that his secretary had, that morning, been laid off, and that the only other person that remained with him now was his tech man and *he* had been called in and offered another job in another building, I knew I had to do something. This *Window Treatment,* where a man was given less and less to do, less and less responsibility, made to feel valueless, rendered meaningless to his company, to his co-workers, to himself, gradually, so that he slowly dies inside his own skin, was a despicable thing for Ray to be put through, and it accelerated his PTSD in a myriad of new ways.

The week after I finished up with graduation at Lesley, I put an ad in the Boston Globe, advertising our brand new condo we had just moved into. Despite the fact that the Real Estate market was in the dumpster, I got a two-year contract, with a delayed closing, all sewed up in a week. Although the agreement, for the final closing down the road, was at a considerable loss, it was a sale – and we were out from under the huge mortgage.

The day the contract was signed with the lawyers, Ray said he went into the old man's office and told him he had an offer on his house, in the hopes that he would be released to take the job in California. Instead, Ray was offered *The Golden Handshake*, a lump-sum retirement to be effective immediately. Even though it was a bitter disappointment, Ray took the money, gladly. He could now go to his beloved desert home and play golf every day.

As we drove out of the driveway, with movers having just left with all our household goods, the car loaded down for the cross country trip ahead of us, Ray turned to me with tears brimming in his eyes, "Thank you for doing this. If I would have had to stay in that place another week, I would have blown my brains out."

◆

CHAPTER EIGHTEEN

Solutions: 1996

It was the middle of November. The loud thumping knock on the front door jarred my concentration. I was tempted to ignore it, but the insistence sounded vaguely familiar. Sean, bursting with his latest triumph, or defeat – depending on your point of view, had no one else. I was immersed in reading *Primary Colors,* the supposed fictitious expose of the inside workings of Bill Clinton's first successful election bid. In the middle of a delicious bit of sensuous dialogue, I reluctantly put the book down. It was two days after Clinton's reelection, the Republicans having won back congress in midterm. His winning in the first place, and now this supposed fictitious account, penned and sold to the public as *Anonymous,* (later claimed to be the journalist, Joe Klein) was having an alarming impact on me personally, and strangely upon my forty-year marriage. The book not only expressed, through its anecdotal characterizations, the candidate's undisciplined sexual misconduct, it pointedly portrayed, through the writer's eyes, the divided feeling in the country regarding his ability to lead, despite these shortcomings. The undeniable fact that it was women who primarily seemed to be responsible for making this decision was a mystifying paradox. Was it the size of his celebrated vestiges of manhood with which Clinton nuked the Newt by letting the government actually shut down, or was it the "illusion" *Nightline*'s host called Clinton's ability to zero in on a person with miraculously undivided attention, and make them his whole world for whatever few seconds that takes? To connect, to bond, this feeling sought by so many of us females, who spend our lives hanging onto the tail of a similar tiger, waiting for *that one special moment?* Or was it Hillary, the intelligent liberated woman, who is supposed to be freed from these yokes of bondage, who teaches us resigned forgiveness: *If a man says he hasn't ever cheated on his wife – he'll lie about other things?* Whatever! The aura of this highly visible man seemed to insinuate itself into the personal relationship between Ray and me. At first it was a playful thing. Forgetting that I grew up in Wisconsin, the most progressive state in the Union and a closet liberal all along, Ray would often say, "You've turned into a damn *Liberal* since you went to that peace-nik school, in Cambridge." In time, I had learned to respond to his

Republican[39] demonization of that word, by calling it such. But the cuts and jabs got sharper, more vicious, especially when he ridiculed Clinton for not keeping his pants zipped. *That* was when things got really dirty: "You mean like *you* have always done?" Ray's derision had found new impetus through the most despicable term for a career Army man: *Draft dodger.* When Ray pulled this out of the woodwork, with a new neighbor already recognized as a Conservative, I shot back: "The stand Clinton took about the war is really a point in his favor, in my book. If some *other* people would have had the *balls* to stand up for what was right, get out of the Army and take care of his family, instead of waltzing off to a damn foreign country for fifteen months of nonstop booze under the guise of war, maybe our kids wouldn't be so screwed up today!" *Ooh. I shouldn't have said that!* Not only proud of his red-neck bigotries, Ray was a lousy loser.

Sean walked into the room, talking. "I saw my lawyer today; he says I have a case, but even if I win, Social Security could cut me off – in January, or anytime after that, way down the road."

"Yes. And the Republicans now back in congress will surely make it tough. What did the guy... Did you say an attorney? You told me he was a psychologist."

"He is that, and a lawyer too. That's why he would be the best one to help me. But he said I had to pay him $500 up front. He told me to try to get it from y'all, but I told him, forget that."

No reaction from me; I had learned finally not to jump in and offer. It wasn't the money so much, although we really didn't have it to spare, but, *would it give him a crutch for the booze?*

Sean kept talking, "He did say before I left, *I may call you,* whatever that means. I asked him, *What about legal aid?* He said that was better than going in on my own. But they've already decided that I'm not disabled, so there is really a very slim chance..."

I watched his face as he pulled the thoughts out into words, stumbling sometimes with multiple syllables. His ability to talk and talk is what confuses people. He has this "left brain-ness," a concrete, visual attention to things, but the right brain is slow in its abstract abilities, the failure to see around the corner at consequences, and if so – forgets. The memory blanks are

---

[39] George W. Bush was to be the ultimate catalyst in turning Ray completely against the GOP when, in 2003, Bush went into Iraq for reasons "unfounded," Ray believed, also escalating Ray's PTSD – nightmares and startle reaction anew.

random and irregular, sometimes he would remember the days of the week, and other times would miss one of the days, the same with the months of the year. He had learned how to cover up this spotty forgetfulness quite well, however. Collecting SSI and managing to live on it, moving all over the country, settling twice on houseboats docked free in coastal waters outside San Diego and Marina del Rey. For ten years he has been living "the good life," and in *his* mind having the best of everything, able to lie back and tell almost everyone to *Kiss off*. He had an income, security; he didn't have to conform, to "take anyone's shit," he says often. Drinking beer was just one of those freedoms that, more often than not, got out of control. When I told him what Senator Bob Dole had said in one of his speeches, about "the government being a giant enabler to all those substance abusers," Sean just shrugged. "I got my check this month, and they can't cut me off without telling me, and until they do, I'm not going to worry about it." Even after he got his notice of a hearing coming up, he went back to the booze, one more time. He called us from the clinic he had signed into, two days before – "to go on Antabuse; I just can't seem to stay sober lately," he said. He'd only been out two weeks, and besides sobering up, Depakote, the new seizure meds, was seeming to be remarkably affective.

"Sean, how is this Depakote working? You seem like you did that time on lithium, remember? When you were seventeen, at Highland House, that hospital I drove you to, from Florida up to North Carolina?"

"No, I don't really remember, Mom. *How* am I?"

"I can't explain it. It's like you're really *here*."

"I'm *here* because I wanted to share my good news. I went to my second AA meeting. And it's the first time anyone has come up to me, and asked me if I would like help in working the steps. In all the years going to meetings, in and out, all the bull shit, the first time."

"You mean Dirk in Boston never did? I thought he was the best sponsor you ever had."

"No, uh uh. He wasn't that kind. He had problems. Didn't I tell you?"

"You mean about his son being schizophrenic? I knew that."

"No, I mean sexual problems. You know he lived with his wife, separated, in different rooms in the house, and after that he turned gay."

"Oh, did he come *on* to you?"

"No, uh uh. But the fourth step, you know, telling all, I think he did say something about – *If you ever decide to go that route again, let me know."*

"How did that make you feel?"

"I guess it *did* upset me." Sean was taking off his new black boots he had just bought at *Payless* for $19 and proudly threw them on the floor. "I got these jeans at *Walmart's* for $12.50."

"Nice," I said. "It's about time; you needed them."

He was still wearing what I had gotten him in March, when he came home in a hospital gown full of cacti thorns, when his second boat sunk, and his dog drowned. I thought then he had learned his lesson, that booze impaired his ability to take care of himself, but it had only lasted two months.

"Sean, tell me, have you settled all that stuff in your head now? The sex stuff?"

"What do you mean, *settled* it? I don't do that anymore."

"I mean, was it acting out, or anger, or did you decide you are bisexual?"

"Oh, it was acting out, no question. I did it because I was homeless. I just lived with those guys for a place to stay."

"Did you ever figure out how you got like that, decided to use that method? It was like prostituting, you know."

"I don't care what you *call* it, Mom, I don't *do* it anymore," he said a little angrily. Then as an afterthought, he said, "What do you mean, how I *got* that way. How *did* I get that way?"

"It was the way your sisters treated you, I think. You know, the sex."

"How do you know that? Maybe it was Kelly's friend that raped me that summer, when he was hanging out at that shack, the druggie shack in the woods, remember?"

"I never knew about that. I thought it was that weirdo in the woods who offered you the half-dollar for... You told me right in front of Suzie. I can see us still sitting in the dining room, in Carlisle. Why would you tell me something like that, if it wasn't true?"

"It's simple, Mom, Suzie was scared to death I was going to tell you the truth about her, that's why she was sitting there, to be sure of what I told you, and all the times she came to the hospital, too, but it was a lie. I mean, there *was* that weirdo guy who wanted me to suck him off, sure, but it was really Kelly's friend. After that, Kelly got up on the bus, and yelled: *Any of you SOB's want to touch my little brother, will have to deal with me to do it!* On the bus, in front of everyone."

Stunned at hearing this for the first time, I said, "I can't believe I never knew about the rape, or bus incident."

"You didn't know about a lot of things, Mom."

I wanted to talk to Sean more about it, but his mind was on what this doctor had told him. This was now, the other was then, and forgotten.

Sean said, "But this guy today said I looked like I could work, that I should get my life straightened up, stay off the booze, because it was the booze that got my benefits cut off. They don't want to support any more addicts, he says. I have to go at it from the mental illness way, take all my charts, from when I was a kid... before I got into all that... But after meeting this guy at AA tonight, whose gonna be my sponsor, I think I'll apply for that job in LA for a full time Paper Hanger. If they say they need me full time, I'll tell these guys something at the car wash, and I'll be gone. That's good money, like $600 a week. I know I can do it."

It was like this kid lived in a make-believe world, his mind rambling on from one solution to the next. There was no getting through to him.

"You know, Mom, even when I'm sober and working at a job, days I'm home, like when I was married, and she worked – I was lonesome. I have to have balance in my life, you know? Meal times, things to do, friends, things like that."

Were my ears deceiving me, or was he just whistling Dixie, again? All the right words... continuously planning, always talking about what he's *going* do, but never quite getting around to doing any of it – a classic symptom of manic-depressive illness. The illusion that life is just around the bend — *then* I'll make it; *then* I'll be OK. Lithium or Depakote seems to be the only thing that brings them down to the spitting earth, and they won't take it. But *maybe now*...

Sean was back with his dad in the bedroom he sometimes used. The room had a TV in it, and Ray was watching something loud that normally would have grated on my nerves. This noon, I had chided Ray about the ridiculous cleaning job he had done on the garage floor, "Either get your car fixed, or leave it on the street; that nice floor Sean and I put all that work into to paint, will be ruined with that greasy transmission fluid. Just look at it, I don't know if I will ever get it up."

"Well, if the car was there like it *should* be, instead of out on the street, you wouldn't even see it," he said, always trying to get out of being responsible. Like his mother always said, "Ray would never have married had he not been forced into it; he hated the responsibility."

Not a word had passed between us all day. A strained air in the house was unusual for us. It seems to make things much worse than they really are. To find a way to soothe away my anger, my hurt, I read a book, balance my check book, clean something, is how I learned to deal with those hurt feelings. It only takes a few minutes until I am back to feeling okay, putting it behind me. *Ray's mentally ill; I can't start behaving just* like *him,* I tell myself. But today, I just couldn't shake it off. It was the build-up of anger that takes place over prolonged victimization. Anger of this kind can lead one to an explosive end. So late, I was, in realizing the real cause of my anger. It had been misplaced – transferred from my father, for his sexually violating me, to Ray. The devaluation of myself as a female had begun long before Ray; *finally I was understanding.* Something I guess I would fight against for the rest of my life.

Today I just couldn't overlook Ray's belligerent attitude. To get out of this terrible dilemma I was caught in, was to withdraw into my shell of quietness and ignore his very existence. It was a resting place of sorts, inside my head, and had the effect of distancing me from my *stuck feelings* for a time, until I could face my circumstances with a more generous spirit.

My outrage at Ray *now* was really all those women I had swallowed back through the years, which had come out in my dreams in the last month, since Bill Clinton started getting all that press, I realized. Oh, I knew what it was all right, but I just didn't know how to deal with it. And the kids. I couldn't put my finger on it, only a feeling I had that as their father, Ray had imparted his lack of value for me. Besides referring to me at parties as his rent-a-wife to outsiders, those silent funny faces he made behind my back at the dinner table, sticking his tongue out with his thumbs in his ears, while waving his hands at my back to make the kids snicker. One time, catching him in the act, I felt belittled. This was the same kind of ridicule he had grown up with in his mother towards almost everyone who crossed her path.[40] Being made fun

---

[40] When Ray was in puberty and had his first wet dream, he told me he had stuffed his shorts into his bureau drawer, and left for school. When he got home and rode his bike into the driveway, parking next to his mom pulling weeds, she stood up, and grinning, she said, 'Well, Son, did you think you could hide your underwear from your mother?" It embarrassed him terribly. His mother's cruel insensitivity towards this subject was expressed later to me, when she admitted that she had no use for sex, "Never had an orgasm in my life."

On our first visit, shortly after we were married, his mom gave us her

of this way undermines the respect that children inherently feel for their mothers, except for Sean – somehow all that just went over his head. He was the symbol between us of the true affection a family should have for each other.

Sean must have sensed something the minute he walked in. After going back and forth between us, he asked me, "Are you and Dad fighting or something, both in separate rooms, watching different TV's?"

PBS had a documentary on Africa that I had on very softly as I was reading, mainly so Ray wouldn't come in, grab the clicker, and put on one of his westerns. "I was just watching this thing about Africa. You know, Uncle Matt went there for six months, and he loved it. Said it was beautiful."

"I wouldn't want to go there, it's full of *Blacks,*" Sean said, stretching out on the couch.

"I'm so sorry you have this bigotry in you lately. You never were that way before you got married, I don't think."

Just then, Sean went into the kitchen to get a cold drink. Answering his question was safely averted. Already forgetting what it was, he came into the room, asking, "Mom, does it bother you that Sharon, Suzie, and Kelly don't call you much, or come around?"

"Yes, it does," I said looking up from my book.

"How does it make you feel?"

"Very sad."

"I just don't understand it. I know they did all kinds of stuff, but that was then, now is now. We are a *family*. What is *wrong* with them?"

"I'm not sure I really know. I used to think it was the guilt, but

---

bedroom, and she and Dad slept in the rollout bed in the living room. She was still under the covers when we came down for breakfast. Ray sat down on the bed next to her to talk to her, and she reached over and put her arm around his shoulders, and said, right in front of me, "Did you come to Mama to get some titty?"

probably it is the illness. At least that is what I tell myself. Medication seems to be the only way to alleviate this barrier that lies between us. But it is no use; you can see that, so I just wait until I hear, then I answer. That is how it is now."

He was looking down at me with such hurt in his eyes. I could see him as a little kid, crying; they had all moved on and left him behind, alone. "If I couldn't come over and visit you and Dad, I would just go nuts; I just couldn't stand it. Even when I was gone to Florida, all that time, and to Massachusetts, I still had to call you and talk to you. I can't understand them."

Something we did right with him, and this latest thing between Ray and me. *How could we risk damaging this relationship with this child?* This is what kept me hanging in. *For him, Sean; he needs us so; we will be gone soon enough,* I keep telling myself. The major conflict of my life seemed to gel in the form of the major love of my life, a combination of my first husband (my first teenage love), his father, *and my father.*

Daddy chain smoked one cigarette after another, and drank heavily; he was abusive when touting his stubborn will and imposing it upon whomever. Mama found a way to stop taking it — she died. Yes, it was that day that turned all of his wrath upon *me,* his only family still living. *There was no one else.* Oh, he gave up the cigarettes, the liquor, and became a man of the Jesus trade, a born-again. *A new person,* he would say on the street corner, testifying. One who would not do to another woman the same – if God would be so kind as to give him a second, he would often pray tearfully aloud. *What had he done to Mama?*

With his rules, his church, his praying, his Bible ranting, his terrible temper, I never really understood what he was all about. He confused me so much: one minute loving, affectionate, and the next minute – at a wrong word, an accidental flip of my skirt – would lay stripes across my little body. *For what?*

This baffling dualism I thought I had shed as a teenager when I married Huey. But I found out Huey was as two-sided, as unpredictable, who would put flurries of butterflies in my stomach with a look, a gesture. Just the sound of his voice would send me into an anxious maze.

Marrying Ray had finally put all that to rest, *I thought,* until Sean was born.

A physical personification of Ray, this beautiful child was loving, affectionate, and, as Daddy had been, was soft spoken, caring. Sean was full of music too, as I was, as was Huey. As Sean grew into manhood, these emotional giants in my life seemed to fuse into one, so that in time I could not separate them in my mind. This unexplainable hold on my heart tightened. Twisting, turning, it pulled me hither and yon.

Sean especially reminded me of Daddy at the same age when Mama had left us, when Daddy became the center of my life. The same affectionate nature, the stubbornness, the ill-begotten brain, the cruel demanding tongue, the wishy-washy changeableness I had been subjected to minute by minute growing up. Daddy's whippings I could abide, I told myself. But the not knowing when, or what to expect next, that was the terribleness. And it was all repeating itself.

Sean was looking at his 34th birthday just one month away which he shares with his dad – who would be 64. I was trying to prepare myself for the not-yet-to-be believed age of 60. *What to do, where to go with my anger, my pain, my sadness?* To my computer, to write. Taped to the monitor, from Socrates, it says: The solution is inherent in the problem!

Just after Sean started high school, in Tucson, he, along with some classmates, was arrested for breaking into the home of a local judge and stealing some jewelry. Due to the fact that his teachers were regularly begging for some guidance on how to deal with his inability to learn – except in marching band, in which he got all A's – Dr. Miller, the psychiatrist we had also used for Kelly, suggested admitting Sean for extended inpatient evaluation.

Sean had just dismantled their security system, which baffled us, since his IQ tests had shown him to be way below average in aptitude. I could tell Ray was a bit proud, actually. (That was the first time we began to see first hand the confusion Sean must be experiencing, having exceptionally high visual acumen, yet unable to function in a class-room setting because of his inability to process what he heard, which had been pointed out to us by the psychologist who evaluated him in sixth grade, in fact. I was told then to have Sean read aloud, that hearing the words come out of his own mouth would help him to better comprehend.) Ray had just disclosed to Dr. Miller how embarrassing it was to have one of his kids break the law, since he had spent his life's work in law enforcement – the reason behind his choice of Criminal Justice in pursuing his

Masters just completed at Georgia State. Dr. Miller was saying, "Our kids know just how to get to us; how to find the spot where we, as parents, are the most vulnerable. My kids, for instance, would no doubt go nuts!" he said, and we all laughed. Dr. Miller went on to commend us in our parenting, "Sean has an unusually well adjusted personality despite his severe disabilities; you have both done an outstanding job," he told us, giving us hope Dr. Hanks' opinion (back in the '70s) – that Sean would have a prolonged and troubled adolescence, but confident he would "eventually" grow out of it – would come true. "I'm not so sure about Kelly, though," Dr. Hanks had said. "The life expectancy of a drug user is about ten years. If Kelly lives to see his 35th birthday, there is hope that he may gain some insight by then." Pulling no punches, he said, "but it is very iffy."

There were months, and some years, that we didn't have knowledge of Kelly's whereabouts, only an unexpected phone call at Christmas, or a birthday, or Mother's or Father's Day. If Kelly was hospitalized for any length of time, we would get mail then from him, with poems, "songs" he said, to which he heard the music in his head, his dream always of becoming a rock star.

It was clear that Suzie had now succumbed to the illness since the pregnancy of her third and last child, which left a sad schism between us. Her extreme anger, directed at me (just as was Ray's, without medication, and Kelly's, Sharon's, and Sean's when they were using) was most difficult for me to accept. Even though I believed it had something to do with my being the only authority figure in their lives, as Ray was gone so much. When home, he was really just another kid to them (TV, popcorn, parlor games, and billiards was the extent of their interaction), I had been the one to hold our lives together, despite the detours my own personal journey had taken. When Suzie would yell at me, bitterly accusing me of being "buddies" with Sharon, it would take years for me to realize how I had allowed Sharon to hog the spotlight, and why.

Sharon was a pouter· She would clam up when she was angry· Ray used to tease her to make her laugh until she got over it· But it really riled me as she managed to maintain control over the whole household with her silence, her way of getting more attention than her siblings· My stepmother Charity, was also a pouter· When they married, I was hurt by Charity's pouting, as I was so yearning for and needing female love and guidance, and it just wasn't there· The subconscious never forgets· And it finally hit me that my mother was also a pouter· (Daddy wasn't the first one to marry someone the second time who mimicked the first spouse's behavior·) Aunt Jenny Lou said Mama never went to bed without hugging, but she would go to her room and not answer for hours on end· And the day Mama died, the baby may have been saved had she gone in the bedroom earlier to check on her, but she figured her sister "was pouting again·" Aunt Jenny Lou said she didn't know what made her finally open the door, and by then Mama was in a coma, and only lived less than an hour·

I'm learning in therapy, that we are really working out our primary relationships forever, in order to create a different ending· It is easy to see now, why I hung in there with Sharon for so many years, trying to make Mama's ending come out different· Even though Mama's pouting is not what killed her, in my young mind, it was!

Despite all the ups and downs, I never stopped searching, the question always in my mind: "How can I help my children?" This new woman psychiatrist was seeing me for the first time. I was hoping for some answers regarding the mental illness that permeated our family. How was I to deal with it, without being controlling, all the labels that had been applied to someone in my position in AA, in ALNON, by the counselors? I went to her because, at that time, AA just wouldn't recognize that there were any mental illness problems *ever* underlying alcoholism or drug addiction. As I laid out the history briefly of my children, telling her about Sharon's role in her sibling's sexual abuse, she interrupted me: "*Who did Sharon?*"

Her question stopped me in my tracks.

The doctor continued, "Sharon had to learn this from somewhere!"

That night as I tried to get to sleep, I racked my brain trying to remember any inkling of a sign of how Sharon had come to such behavior, which was so clearly directed at me.

When Sean was hanging wallpaper in one of our houses, talking all the time he was working, going from one subject to another, the way he talks continuously when he works, I was half listening, until he said, "All I know, is, if and when I have any kids, I am not going to let them *take baths together!*"

*It is 1954; I am back in Milwaukee· It is dark outside,
and I am late coming home from work· Charity, my stepmother, is already doing the supper dishes· I head upstairs
looking for my baby girl· I think she is in her crib, but when
I pass the bathroom, I hear giggling and water splashing, and
her voice· I find all the kids, Marcie, four, Sharon, then
eighteen months, and Phillip, a year older than Sharon, all
three in the bathtub, playing· My stomach jumps into my
throat as I run downstairs, to Charity, "Together," I shriek·
"You put them all together? As careful as Daddy always was
with me, and nudity·"*

*Charity discounts my worry, "Why, what harm can
come from it? They're just innocent children· It's the
wicked and vile adults who put wrong connotations on
things·"*

*Beneath my acquiescent face, I fight my fears· What
can I say? Working two jobs, saving every penny for my own
apartment at the end of this year's lease, Charity is now
my full-time baby sitter· With nowhere else to go, I am
trying very hard to not rock the boat· A stepmother who is
fourteen years older, I decide I have to trust her· Shouldn't
a daughter be able to trust her mother? I tell my
questioning self; she must know best· Even though I am a
divorced mother, I am still only seventeen· Constantly I run
into huge obstacles, decisions a seventeen-year-old just isn't
equipped to make·*

After Sharon left home, her sexually suggestive greeting cards to
Ray, Father's Day, Birthday's, were so disquieting, Ray would rip
them up instantly, believing Sharon to be an exhibitionist. It
appeared that she was trying to get a rise out of me this way, but
her motivation was lost on me, especially when she would send
me the sexiest negligee' from Victoria's Secret.

On the one visit, by train, Sharon made with her three girls
to see us in Boston, by the time they arrived, Sharon was so
inebriated that she almost fell down the high wooden steps that
brought them from the train platform into our small town. Minutes
later, we were all gathered around the kitchen butcher-block
counter, drinking pop and getting acquainted, when Sharon put
her beautiful arms around me, hugging me, and then kissing me
with open mouth on the lips, a strikingly sensual kiss, telling me
how much she loved me; I was dumbfounded. Her girls, then

fifteen, ten, and six, were obviously embarrassed at their mother's behavior, so I tried to overlook the strange overture. But it reminded me of what Sharon's husband, Val, had commented once about Sharon's feelings towards me, "They just aren't normal."

If therapy is facing the truth about oneself, I wonder if the unconscious message that I unknowingly gave throughout my early life, that, according to Dr. Comas, the only way I knew how to communicate was through sex could have contributed to Sharon's behavior?

During many sleepless nights, I could not help but wonder just how Sharon became so secretively abusive.

Is it any wonder she became the rebellious one against all authority, against what is right, when as a nine-month-old her tiny fingers were spanked for touching the glass tabletop that had become her daily joy to pull herself up on the table's edge, and slap with radiant joy that she had accomplished the impossible· Looking up at me with those joyous baby eyes, thrilled with self beyond all means of expression, I reached down, and instead of praising her, gleefully rejoicing with her that her feat was the grandest this mother could ever hope for, I took her little fingers and gently put them on the wooden edge of the table – off the glass· I had to teach her, didn't I, that glass would break? At the same time stop the dirty finger marks, both equally disastrous to my German· She looked up to this giant of a person, beautiful when approving, but ugly in her disapproval· So the child learned early on to squelch any inclination to express herself unless it pleased Mommy first! So that is how life began for her· A series of moments for which no other purpose existed but to keep that lady beautiful in her life·

The smoke from her cigarette, a thin spiral of silver, curled into the upward air· The child watched, wished, and hungered for more· The white glow of frosty painted fingernails shown in the mirror as they curved themselves around the naked stem of the slender y-shaped crystal· Inside it, the tiny green olive, floating in clear liquid, rolled to the edge of the tipped glass· Vodka barely touched the satiny lips; the narrow tongue slid gently over them, licking

*away the vodka's sting· The child wondered how many tips,
how many licks, would make the drink be gone· She hoped it
would take forever·*

*Moments at ringside, propped on elbows, looking up
from the bed as her mother changed from an everyday
princess into the fairytale queen, were times the child
selfishly savored as her very own· This transformation, the
likes of petals opening in bloom, slowly, before one's very
eyes, was enchantment supreme of which dreams were made·*

*The mother and the child, both children still,
conspiring, intermingling spirits since conception· The fertile
seed had not succumbed to the burning after-wash; old
Country ideas thrust into new puritan times· It was the
early '50's when the two began, before the mother had a
say, but she loved herself in the child, and gave up her
time, her energies, her will· She, the mother, was of
famished breed, unloved, un-nurtured, and wanton, giving
birth just after the proverbial "sweet sixteen·" To the child
she gave, the child took, and the thin spiral of silver
continued to rise from the butt-filled ashtray·*

T hrough the years I have shared the shameful behavior that
went on with my children with several mothers in whom I felt I
could confide. In essence, I was told: *If it was my daughter, I
would never speak to her again.*

Although communication between Sharon and I had been
sparse through the years, when her current husband Val, began
calling me, letting me know that Sharon was drinking heavily and
her behavior worrisome, not really knowing him that well, I
decided to take a trip to DC unannounced, to see with my own
eyes, her condition. After I checked into the Marriott near her
house, I knocked on her door. She was shocked, but did invite me
in. She still had her daycare charges there and appeared sober.
She invited me to stay at her place, on the couch, but I insisted
that the hotel was more comfortable, and I could take her two
younger girls to sleep over and swim, which I did. By Saturday
night, she was very drunk and started calling me and accusing me
of all sorts of things, reminiscent of her birth father, Huey, who
would rant and rave to the top of his lungs for the whole world to
hear. By the end of ten days (I had planned on staying three
weeks) I was ready to head for home. My last night, a Barbra
Streisand special was coming on, the first one she had done in

years.

Sharon (who had a lovely voice and took singing lessons as a child) loved Barbra's music. In Bangkok, we would return after taking someone home from a party, having left Sharon to clean up, only to find her with Barbra's *People* on full blast completely lost in the music. Dancing, swinging her long hair down and around, she would sing to the top of her lungs along with the record. During this concert, Barbra used clips from her movies, therapy scenes, to share her own personal growth through the years, saying: *Women were programmed to believe they would be devastated to live without a man; finally I was able to love myself first.* After the show, it was not surprising to get a call from Sharon, in tears, "I know if Barbra can do it, so can I," she said, and begged forgiveness for all the terrible things she had been saying, that she loved me, "Really, Mom." It was clear; Sharon was in terrible emotional pain. I would find out much later, about Val's brother dying of AIDS, and about his Catholic family's rejection of him, even in death – a sad thing for Sharon to go through.

◆ ◆

CHAPTER NINETEEN

Secrets - 2001

"The hurt and pain is coded in the family secret. Both incest and physically abusive families tend to be dominated by the rules of... the family religion... and often call anything outside [of it] 'secular humanism'....

"Anything psychological is looked upon with suspicion... Hence... guidance is rejected."

—John Bradshaw, *The Family*

In 1997, after a classy golf retirement to the Southern California desert, unfortunately landing in the midst of some really staunch (but bigoted) "born-again" right wingers – when we invited two gay men couples to our regular pool-side potluck suppers who had just moved in on our block, and when they didn't show, the chairs around our table were conveniently removed so that we had to sit alone – we decided we had heard enough of "Praise the Lord" in one breath and "those damn fags" and the N-word in the next. The sun was too much for me anyhow, and the daily golf was beginning to stress Ray's back, both of which pushed us to relocate elsewhere. We ended up in a nice, little sleepy town in Oregon.

It was a hot July, and we were headed down the highway in our new Minnie Winnebago. We hadn't seen our granddaughters in years, so we decided to go into debt for this trip. The whole RV thing came about following Suzie's mental collapse. Suzie was in dire need of medical intervention. Those last years before Ray's final retirement, we had visited Suzie as often as every three months. On the road as marketeer for USS, Boston, his free flier miles allowed us many visits together. That weekend in 1991, three months following the birth of her last baby, when her husband was in tears on the phone, despite being so far away, I was on a plane to Florida in hours. This medical episode, the doctor's called a "psychotic break," left her unable to speak, only groan in fearful sounds for hours until the Haldol shot, the powerful anti-psychotic medication in the ER, kicked in. Her condition, which we could see creeping up through the years —

just seeing the disorganization in her home, cabinets, closets -- had become a full blown case of schizoaffective disorder.

For treatment, rather than go through her Primary Care doctor – for fear of labeling with her insurance company – Suzie found a "cheap doctor," a converted Jew, who introduced her to "the Holy Spirit" as cure-all for her life. This doctor did prescribe Triavil (a combination of anti-depressant and anti-psychotics) but doubt he was informed of the bipolar genetics in her father's family or the schizophrenia in her mother's. Consequently, she was never put on lithium, or similar meds, for continued stability. Instead, she was allowed to go off the medication "until such time as you need it again, no doubt in menopause." Through all of this, her husband had a three-month-old to feed and care for, besides the three and six-year olds. My ability to help was limited as Suzie's life-long anger at me seemed to often boil up unexpectedly between us, but I stayed several weeks, until one angry outburst from her forced me to pack my suitcase. My parting words to her husband were, "You have to make sure Suzie trusts you enough to tell you what is going on in her head, to protect the kids, as her paranoia has greatly increased."

Suzie ultimately split with her husband of twenty-some years and moved upstate, taking her three girls, then ten, thirteen and sixteen. When she enrolled them in a Christian school, we grew very concerned. It wasn't so much that this act was contrary to her neutrally religious upbringing in military protestant chapels throughout the world, it was her declaration of Jesus as her "dance partner" and the one she thanked for a "joyous orgasm," the one she said who was relaying messages to her via the TV: giving her instructions on her CIA "mole" activities on her many trips to Israel; relaying messages to her from her children for any need they might have of her — "the Holy Spirit will tell me" – as well as direct her in obtaining her next husband! Suzie informed us it *wasn't* to be Bill Clinton, for which her father heaved a sigh of relief, but it was possibly Benny Hinn, married also, the Lebanese, white-suited TV healer located there in Florida, who Ray and I both considered to be a Charlatan who preyed on the needy. But who was to question this infatuation? Even when Suzie spent a great deal of money and time to acquire a diploma from one of Hinn's "ministerial" colleges, with some kind of "masters degree in prayer counseling" – which seemed to consist of holing up in her bedroom with her Bible, religious books, and prayer lists on her bed for hours at a time — this new belief in Jesus was obviously substituting for the anti-psychotics she needed. [41]

The last day on her meds, Suzie called me long distance, and said, "I've just come back from a deep depression; it was like being in a dark hole that you cannot get out of." That was the beginning of the long, sad silence between us. The doors completely closed when she sent us a copy of her ordination certificate and invitation to the ceremony. She sent a news letter announcing her "ministry," the guise used by many to get donations. She sent us a typewritten copy of her *Testimony*, declaring her "psychotic break" to be a religious experience and when she got her "calling." I wrote her a note of acknowledgment:

> *Dad said your "calling" was very much like his; he didn't have a job either! Just after high school graduation (he was still only 17 and not very hirable, before fast food) Dad was fired at J. C. Penney's. He was also in the throes of his first true love, Nita, two years his senior and in her second year at BJU. When asked where he received his "call," he said, "In Nita's living room." He also knew that the only way he would get to college after his grandfather died (his Grandpa's wish was for him to be a doctor) was to go to BJU, as his mother paid the bills, and she wouldn't pay for any other college. (Uncle Matt still gripes about the fact that she wouldn't pay for GMI, right there in Michigan!) But Dad got even with his mother when he didn't get his diploma. And despite his ordination exempting him from military duty, he showed his father he was not using it to beat the draft, and volunteered for the Army. Probably the reason your husband is not too clear about your psychotic episode is because it was too frightening; but I remember. It was my first experience with "psychosis." You could only moan and scream terrifying sounds that frightened your children. John never left your side, he held you, and cried, and cried. Maybe the pain is why he chooses to not remember. "Give me the pill; I'll take the pill; just give me the pill," you kept repeating, over and over again until you could no longer speak. In my head, I was frantically planning on how*

---

[41] The view of those treating patients suffering from psychosis: "Some staff members did not feel on safe ground in finding a message from God delusional...because it is endorsed by the myths of our culture.... Some of the delusional and hallucinatory experiences involved encounters with the devil. Many also, "heard" the voice of God and "saw" Christ...believing to be chosen by God for a special mission to save humankind. ...It would seem that an individual's conflict between forces perceived as good and evil is experienced as so overwhelming that it takes on the proportions of a battle between God and the devil." –Harriet Wadeson *Art Psycho-Therapy*

I could convince Dad we had to retire to Florida instead of California, to be near you, to take care of you, your children, so your *husband* could keep his job. Now your illness has become a "religious experience?" Using "God" is a noble way to avoid taking responsibility for your life.

Suzie wrote me only one letter, stating she could no longer share her "ministry" with her parents, but she did send us a postcard on one of her many Benny Hinn trips to Israel, a photo of her riding on the back of an elephant. I hadn't as yet begun to really understand that the "con game" was her acting upon voices in her head.

When finally informing us of her separation with her husband, Suzie had retained custody of her kids. We had no idea of her dire condition that existed at the time, until she called me one morning stating she was "led by the Holy Spirit" to write me but had no address. We received a sprawling, scribbled letter on kindergarten printing paper. She said she wanted to see us and asked for our forgiveness for her "terrible inconsiderate treatment" of us in the past. Right then I knew things were awry in her life. Soon after, she called and asked us to let her come to visit. She was going to California for a "minister's convention," and wanted her brother, Kelly's, address in Los Angeles, "for your birthday gift, Mom." Thanksgiving time, her plan was to get him, rent a car, and drive up the coast, to Oregon.

The day before my birthday, in they walked with a huge red poinsettia plant. As Suzie walked through the door, she said, "Well, Mom, your day is past; *it is my turn now to be beautiful.*"

It was a wonderful unexpected week, having the two middle kids alone, all to ourselves, without any other family.

At the time, Kelly was then working in the drug treatment center in LA he had been residing in as a client and talking about getting a degree in counseling when he finished his two years there. While at home, he mentioned he had blood in his urine regularly, and a pain in his back, by his left kidney. It sounded like either kidney stones, or an infection to me, and he promised he would see the doctor when he got back home.

Kelly's mental stability is what really concerned me, when he had to spend so much time with Suzie, his secret teenage love. Hearing about this from one of his old girlfriends, made me all the more anxious over Kelly's condition. However, it did explain some of his meanness directed at Sean from time to time: Sean was *Suzie's* partner, and Kelly still hated Sharon. In fact, if I would mention Sharon, Kelly might completely ignore it, or say, *Sharon who?* In view of their past history, it was not surprising to hear that after this trip with Suzie, and having so much intimate time together, Kelly left his treatment program. We really had no idea where he was until he returned to treatment the following April, this time to "give up the methamphetamine and booze," and get serious about needed therapy.

Suzie went back home to Florida, and called often, her conversations becoming more incoherent all the time. It was only months later that we were told that her husband had gotten a court order to take their girls, to live with him and his new wife.

Every time I talked with Suzie, I would beg her to come home, and let us help her get on her feet, as none of her teaching jobs seemed to pan out.

It was March of 2001 when we got a call, asking us if our offer was still good, she was ready to get help. Of course we immediately prepaid for a plane ticket, and Suzie arrived safe. She proceeded to get weekly psychological counseling (really the thorough evaluation required for referral to psychiatrist) through our Oregon insurance. Our plan was to get her on SSI as soon as possible. It was apparent to us the schizoaffective disorder needed addressing, professionally.

Having Suzie sit with me day after day, watching movies, crocheting together, talking, was the most enjoyable time I can remember having with her, she was so loving and attentive. We had already accepted the fact that she may be with us the rest of our lives, even though Ray's VA psychiatrist was not pleased with our decision at all: "Adding another stressor to Ray's PTSD and cyclothymic disorder was not wise."

Suzie seemed to be able to control her delusions most of the time, until one morning, when she started talking about her "ministry," disclosing that people called her from all over the world and sent her money.

"Oh, Suzie, you are just a con," I said, without even thinking past my words.

That was when she had a change of heart about seeing the doctor. *If I could have only bit my tongue. I hadn't leaned as yet to accept someone's psychotic delusions without confronting them.* It was that day the appointment with the psychiatrist had come through, and Suzie told her Dad she was *not* going to any doctor, or take any meds. Ray jumped out of his chair and got so angry, shouting, I was afraid he would have a heart attack when he told her she could not stay here under those circumstances; she was violating her agreement when we brought her home. I knew that I could not deal with Ray's mental problems, and have Suzie running about town conning people for "the Lord's work," not to mention the lingering apprehension that I carried, sleeping in an unlocked bedroom, now accelerated, remembering the time she had plunged a butcher knife into her counter top on Thanksgiving day, because I had conversed with her hated mother-in-law over the family dinner; *I was supposed to hate the woman also!* The only way Suzie would ever regain her stability was to be on meds, and only her children had the power to make her want to take them. By midnight that night, we had her to the airport, hours away, for a direct flight back to Florida to be near them.

I t was during this month-long visit with Suzie, that her sister, Sharon, began writing me short, incoherent e-mails. It appeared her drinking had gotten much worse, but she had stopped leaving long inebriated messages on our telephone tape. Instead, she would send these crazy e-mails. Since just the subject of Sharon could get Suzie upset, and she was so fragile already, I had never mentioned any of this to her. At the time we had a small RV, which only could accommodate Ray and me, and that very cramped. Thinking Suzie would be with us indefinitely, we were looking for a larger one, so we could take her with us; in fact she went along on a trial drive, in the one we eventually purchased.

Sharon's e-mails: *I wonder what I am going to wear to Candi's wedding? Candi is really going in for a huge wedding, big time! I don't know how I am going to live through it.*

After several of these kinds of e-mails, when I hadn't responded to her off-hand references, she came right out and said, *You ARE coming to the wedding, aren't you?*

Even though we had not received an invitation from either Sharon or Candi, to this last email, I responded with our regrets. This unleashed a torrent of anger and manipulation, sad tales. Vacillating from one to the other, begging, pleading for us to come "for our first granddaughter's wedding." *Never mind that Candi had barely spoken to us in years.*

We would be in DC for a business trip, and would call Sharon to meet us for lunch; she wouldn't even come to the phone. I would write her, and she never answered. When Ray had a DC trip, he would show up at her house and she would leave him sitting on the couch with the kids watching TV, while she disappeared up the stairs. Finally, we gave up any attempt to visit.

One of the truly sorry mistakes I made was opening my mouth about Sharon's relationship with Don, her ex-, and the new guy, Val, next door. She had moved in with him, to have his baby. She began threatening to get pregnant *again* while still married to Don – no divorce, no new marriage, just babies. Val had two kids, and an ex-wife who was messed up on alcohol and drugs; Sharon had stepped in to *fix* things. She wanted more kids, (Don, didn't, so the story went) and Val appeared to be a terrific father. Sharon wanted him, and she got him, but she wouldn't let Don go. When she mentioned she was planning to have another baby, with Val, I just couldn't keep quiet another minute. One of the few times in her life, I guess, I told her she just couldn't do this, not without getting a divorce, and making a clean break with Don in order to marry the father of her new children. *What about those poor guys, huh? Think about what you are doing to* them, *keeping them on the fence like this. It's just not right!* Her response was, "It's all right, here, Mom; no one thinks a thing about it in DC."

The next time we had dinner in DC with Don, when I told him what I had said to Sharon over the phone, in essence: *Either do it or get off the pot,* his face dropped; he sounded so sad. "I was thinking we could get a condo and grow old together after she has her babies with this guy," he said.

Shocked, would be putting it mildly. Here I thought I was doing Don a favor, but he still loved her, and I had interfered in their lives. The courage it took to speak honestly with my daughter had backfired. While playing Bridge, my friends were saying, "Don't you tell her what she is doing is wrong; how can you keep still? That's what mothers are for!" It turned out, it was *their* lives, and had I not meddled, they might have patched things up, and gotten that condo after all.

But within a month, she had a quickie divorce, and asked me to come to her wedding, in Val's house. (Strangely, she had ceased to mention Ray after she pitched a hissy about his frienship with Don, saying, "If you die, who is going to stand at your grave, Don or me? Ray never called Don again; this was the last time we got to see Candi.) I sent Sharon red roses to go with her long white wedding gown; pictures arrived years later. With a speck of only one ovary left, she got pregnant very soon with her third, and last, baby. That was the end of our speaking for years.

Throughout Sharon's life, I had tried to give her everything that we could afford, to the point that Ray reminded me, when Sharon got into her first apartment, she was only the first of four; what I did for one, I had to be prepared to do for the rest. "So maybe you better put the breaks on," as we were still in the Army, not that well off.

We were so proud of Sharon's choice of a husband, even though Don was nine years her senior, and only seven years younger than I. It was soon after this marriage that Sharon asked to bring her alcoholic girlfriend, one of the President's speech writers, to visit us in Florida. The last time we had been to Sharon's house, for her farewell White House party, this girl was there, drunk, and sprawled all over Ray's lap, right in front of me. Trying to keep Ray away from the booze was hard enough, but when temptation presented itself in the form of a young female, I wasn't about to allow it to happen in my own home. Besides it appeared to me it was just part of the agenda Sharon had been pursuing against me. Having the courage to say *No* to her is what opened up that well of anger she had been keeping bottled up. She had kept it hidden behind a very docile personality as a child. As an adult, she was mostly withdrawn, the times I visited to help her with her new babies. It would be years before I would really understand that anger, forty-five years, in fact, when we hocked ourselves to the hilt, bought this big RV and took off for the east coast and the piney woods of Virginia.

Sharon had divorced Val after a few years of alcohol binges. After Val's brother died of AIDS. Sharon went downhill, and when she would be lucid, she would talk about her love for this sweet gay man who suffered unto death in her arms; there was no one else like him. She said he had taught her how to love. This child had been through so much that I never knew about. All of this was in the back of my mind when she begged for us to come for the wedding. There we were, parked in front of this beautiful Virginia home, on a shady street in Fairfax, plugged into Sharon's garage

Candi was a beautiful girl, poised, articulate, and creative. For her wedding gift, I had crocheted a beautiful white-on-white coverlet in a gorgeous popcorn stitch for her bed; I was proud of it as it took me three months to complete. When we got there, we were invited over to her new condo she and her new hubby-to-be had just bought. On her guest bed, she proudly showed me the orchid afghan (her favorite color) I had made her when she was very little. It surprised me, and to see the beautiful print I found in the art museum in Germany, of the famous Eros dart at a nude pubescent girl.[42] I had framed it and hung it over my bed. On the back I had written, "To Candi, for her 12th birthday" because it reminded me of her so much, the year she left her mother and moved in with her father. (When they visited us in Boston, she mentioned how much she liked it, and was surprised to find her name already on the back of it.)

At the time of that visit, I had gone back to college full time, to learn about this terrible thing that had happened in my family. We were learning about the underlying cause -- the sex, the drugs, the separation, cutting off -- people just didn't know how to cope with the feelings of guilt, anger, and remorse when their own children came along. Sharon now had to deal with the same thing.

After Suzie had little girls of her own, she wrote a letter to Sean begging his forgiveness, in fact, it was the very night before she had the "psychotic break" that she called and read me that letter.

Two nights before the wedding, Sharon had a party for Candi. I was told that all the older women would be there, including the other grandmother and aunts, and I was expected to show, especially since we were parked right out front of the house. The hired entertainer was a male stripper Sharon had found on the Internet. I had never been to one of these things, but I figured if the groom's mother could handle it, so could I. Sharon's house was a tri-level, and I found a spot out of the way inside the front door, on the tri-stairwell landing going up to the top level. The party was being held on the lower level, but I could peek through the railings, and see pretty much what was going on.

The stripper showed up with his buddy. Since they were paid by the hour, they both stripped down to their jocks quite readily. The guests were all sitting around, girls squealing, carrying on at every move and turn, but when the guy asked Candi to lie down on the floor, on her back, I decided to pay attention. He straddled her, with his knees close to her shoulders. He was bare chested, and he had a clear see-through jock-strap affair on over his extended appendage. His erect penis within an inch of Candi's mouth, the girls screaming, I was at this point trying to get the front door open, to get out. Frantically pulling at the stuck door, I think I must've found out what it felt like to be buried alive, as I was turning the lock, banging the doorknob,

---

[42] Girl Defending Herself Against Love, by Wm. Adolphe Bouguereau, 1905.

almost in tears, trying to get the door open – at the same time trying not to make any noise to bring any attention to myself. The only other way out was though the basement, past the guests. I was getting sick to my stomach. Never had I seen something this raw, and here were my other granddaughters in the room, Sharon's youngest only fourteen. While the stripper held his position, he poured champagne from a stem glass slowly into Candi's giggle-y mouth. The whole thing was surreal; I was speechless. Thankfully, the loud, screaming laughter covered for my attempt at invisibility.

The wedding was held in a very expensive old mansion on acres and acres of farm land manicured to perfection, set up outdoors with white lawn chairs despite threatening rain. When I asked what to wear, Sharon said, Candi didn't have any preferences -- just no black, as she thought it was bad luck. Not knowing this, I had brought a gorgeous, very expensive two piece silk tunic coat-dress that had life size roses in every hue, so life-like you'd think you could pluck them right off the dark background. Like new, it had only been worn once. Under it, I had a coral silk blouse that fell in soft folds, a cowl neckline. I had the hope that I could get by without spending any more money. It was extremely well fitting, with knee length straight skirt, and red heels. It had been ages since I had gotten dressed up, but my clothes still fit well. The thimble full of German in my heritage makes practicality my middle name -- if it cost money, I would find a way to scrimp on it, if it was for me. For anyone else, I was generous to a fault. When I asked Sharon what she thought, "It's absolutely beautiful, Mom," she said. "Wear it!" *Was she setting me up?*

When I walked onto the grounds, Candi's aunt, Don's sister, saw me, and turned her movie camera on me, and remarked, "You're wearing black; did Candi see you yet?" I said, "No, but Sharon did and said to wear it; roses say I love you; I hope Candi will recognize that; and it is *silk*. No way could I go out and spend anymore, as much as we spent to get here!"

We were already sitting down on the front row, with Don's family, when Sharon sent for me to come back into the dressing rooms, and see Candi. I took my camera, snapping candid shots. Candi had a frozen smile on her face the whole time, twenty-seven beautiful pictures, one of the three of us, together; Candi was in the middle, leaning against her mom, away from me. This pose should have told me something...

After the ceremony, Ray and I sat down on the porch to wait

our turn, for the pictures with the family. We watched as Sharon stood next to Candi, opposite of her was Don on the other side — divorced, but still held together by this beautiful child. Then Don's family all had several shots. We were patiently waiting just a few feet directly in front of them, in plain sight.

We had overcome all the obstacles that were in our path to get here. At least Sharon could color me faithful, if nothing else, so it was with great surprise that I watched the photographer fold up his camera equipment and disappear. Ray and I looked at each other, wondering, were we going to be photographed *inside?*

When we were called to the dining room for hors d'oeuvres, I pulled Sharon aside, and asked her. "What about *our* pictures?"

She threw up her hands in total ignorance. "I have nothing to do with this wedding; this is all Candi's affair." As she wandered off, she mumbled under her breath, "Maybe I can find out; she probably just forgot."

Forgot her grandparents in the wedding of her life? In one conversation that really stung, Sharon had mentioned how much Candi *loved* her grandparents! *Forgetting she was talking to the other grandmother, was she?* When it was she, Sharon, who had kept us from her children all those years!

Sharon never came back with any word on the photographer. It didn't matter anyhow, as we had watched him head for his van, put his equipment in it, and drive away.

When it hit me, I was devastated and I could not hold back the tears. Only one Kleenex in my little hand bag, I headed for the ladies' room, but to find only flimsy toilet tissue, and slim pickings at that. Back in the dining hall, the tables were all set up in tens, in round tables. I chose one the farthest from the dance floor and the humongous assortment of food being served, buffet style. I was becoming more distraught by the minute. Not seeing the small round table set directly behind us with the wedding cake on it, I was fortunate my back was to it. While the bridal couple fed each other cake, my uncontrollable tears streamed down my face. When Candi walked across the room, to have the first dance with her groom, I saw the likeness of Huey's sister, Bernice, in her gait, her serene shallow beauty that shone like ice from a lavish carving, the same aloof, and sometimes vindictive, personality...

My step-uncle Art — who had grown up with the Schultz boys in church and knew them well — was listening to me explain my ardent views about Sharon being a

Schultz· "*There is no way she is going to turn out like him,*" *I said, on the verge of tears·*

Shaking his head, Uncle Art pointed to two-year-old Sharon, who was engrossed in her play over in the corner· "That kid is a Schultz through and through, and some day you are going to remember my words!"

Candi's gown was magnificent, seed pearls covered the bodice, but every time I looked at her, tears would roll down my face.

After several trips across the hall to the small antique facility they called a ladies room – *authentic, was the word given to the surroundings, maybe Martha Washington used it, do you suppose? At least that is what you were intended to wonder, from the cost of the rental* – my left foot, troubled since birth, was cramping so badly, I could hardly walk. (Being in Oregon, heels were never required; jeans and well-pressed shirts are what my friend told us to wear to *her* wedding. She and her four sisters wore black leotard suits under gold lace overlays, the skirts slit up the sides. Candi was just not with the times – it was clear, *black for weddings was in!)*

The food was delicious and served elegantly. It was obvious that Don had spent a bundle on this wedding. Ray had wondered up to the edge of the floor, to watch Candi dance with her father. Their love affair, between father and daughter, was unparalleled. I felt I knew something of that relationship, only mine was reversed. I lost mine to Daddy's ladylove, and it left me determined to hang onto Ray for dear life, no matter what.

Sharon sat with us and brought her friends; it was the last time we would be together. As we were miles out in the country, I overheard one say she had to leave early, and she agreed to take us back, otherwise I had no idea how I was going to make it through the next hours.

The car was coming around, when Sharon happened to get close enough to see my face. She knew immediately something was very wrong; I could not hide it another minute. The hurt was so great I thought I would collapse from the weight of it. "Mom, is there something wrong?"

Trying to hold back the tears until I was safe in the car, away, I said, "Yes, there is. You can just tell your daughter that no matter what, it was *I* who made her life possible; it was *I* who brought you into the world; it was *I* who got you the job that brought you two together. And one day she will remember this night! What goes around, comes around!"

"But Mom, I think it just slipped her mind; she had so much to think about."

"For two years, she planned this beautiful affair, and you think it *slipped her mind?* You have *got* to be kidding."

The car was waiting, so I started to reach for the door, but not before I turned to Sharon, and said, "But it is a good thing it happened. Now I can quit grieving for something that never was!"

For thirty miles back into town, I couldn't stop the lifetime of tears that flowed out of me. After we got back to the RV, we began to pack. Ray said he never really believed all these years the things I was telling him about Sharon -- *until tonight.* "It is evident that she, or her family, has no regard for either of us," he said. "That was made perfectly clear."

Until daylight, I sobbed continuously. I felt that old pain of so long ago, of that little girl left behind, that loss of love and severe rejection duplicated so many times throughout my life. It felt as though I had died and lost myself. *Would it ever get any easier? Would I never stop feeling it?* I remembered then, Shirley MacLain, in *Out On A Limb*, telling of her good friend, Peter Sellers, who lost his mother in early childhood, and how, despite his successful career, the pain of this loss had never left him.

At seven in the morning we left Virginia for Florida, to visit Suzie's three girls. We cherished every minute of our time together; they were so wonderful to us. At that time, no one knew where Suzie was. When we got ready to part, I said to the oldest, JoMarie, "Well, we couldn't make up for ten years in three days."

She said, "But we tried, Grandma, we tried."

Before Suzie got really sick -- when she was hearing voices to kill us all, or screw the sixteen-year-old neighbor boy -- she had become the joy of our lives. She was so patient, loving, caring, sharing every tidbit of news about each child -- until Sharon's visit, the one and only to our house in Boston, which stopped all communication. If one daughter is speaking to me, the other one isn't. In so doing, I lose them both, as in death. Never did I understand the concept of sibling rivalry, having grown up a lonely child wishing always for my baby sister who was forever gone.

On the long trip across country, the subconscious had time to work. Sharon's most blatant sexual expression yet, which she designed for Candi's bachelorette party, could be ignored no longer. Dr. Miller's words were reverberating in my head as I tried to sort out our children's choices, they're knowing just what button to push. Going into our past, I remembered from my studies that what has the most influence on us in later life, really happens to us in early childhood.

Sharon, having turned three that January; Ray and I married in May. It was July, Ray had left Baltimore and gone ahead to his new assignment in Atlanta, to find us a place to live; Sharon and I were staying with Ray's family in Porter. Sharon's new Auntie Fran, just fifteen, had taken over her new little niece: shopping, to the play ground, for ice cream. When riding back home on the bus one day, sitting on the front seat, no less, getting all kinds of attention by the other passengers, Fran asked Sharon what she was going to do when she got home? Loudly, so the entire bus could hear, Sharon said, "I'm going to go home and fuck my boyfriend."

Fran was red faced, laughing, but truly embarrassed. The house next door seemed to be the gathering place for all the kids in the neighborhood, and on rainy days they played in the garage. Even though, at the time, I believed it to be only a phrase Sharon had heard but did not really comprehend, it had triggered a highly emotional response within, disturbing me greatly. In the '50s, such words were not allowed in movies or on TV. Subsequently, I was determined that my child would not use that awful word again. In the upstairs bedroom, talking very quietly, I explained to her that "there are some words we just don't use, and fuck is one of them; it is a very bad word." Just so Sharon wouldn't forget, I gave her one of the few spankings of her young life, usually I only had to threaten. As my hand came down for each swat, it was as if the rage at every miserable sexual encounter I had experienced in my entire life was coming out through my hand. In fact, it was so intense that Matt, my new brother-in-law, downstairs, chided me for overkill, as Sharon was after all "just a baby." I knew inside of me that he was right, but in strong defense of my actions, never having been allowed to even say darn as a child, I said, "I have to let her know, this is one word that is NOT going to be used in our house!"

My extreme emotional reaction had no context, no

understanding at the time, except that the only person I had ever heard use such words, was Huey, Sharon's birth-father.

Winding up my year's intensive psychotherapy with Dr. Comas, after sending the movers off ahead of us to Boston, in my last session with him, I said, "I think I am afraid to leave here and end this therapy with you."

"It is important to understand your past." Putting his hands together forming a triangle as he spoke, he continued, "I tink that there is a part of you that still hates sex very much and is very much asha-a-a-amed of sex."

Breaking down into tears, I said, "Yes· I believe you are correct, the way I feel when you say it makes me think it must be true· I want to change this so badly, I just don't know..."

Dr· Comas stops me in mid sentence· "You see, I don't tink you are really understanding fully why you act out· You are still in denial· You tink sex is bad, dirty – nasty, even, didn't you say once? Not becoming to a lady· Why, I'm thinking, do you prefer to have sex in the middle of the night? Is it so you can say: It didn't happen; it wasn't me; it was just a dream? Then you can go back to sleep and wake up the virginal lady you are in your head?"

"Like I did with Ed?" I said·

"And your father," he said flatly·

After the stops in Virginia and Florida, we went on to Arizona to see Sean. We found him in terrible shape, his alcoholic condition seriously progressed; we were alarmed. He had just had a terrible bicycle accident, hit by a car going against the traffic, injuring his shoulder. We talked him into coming with us to visit Kelly in LA, where we spent a whole  week together in the new RV, at the water's edge. We tried to persuade Sean to come home with us, to Oregon, but he refused.

We arrived back home on the 10th of September. We were exhausted and went to bed, leaving the unpacking till morning.

CNN was on, as we missed it so much on the road. We were walking through the house with all the belongings in our hands that we had taken on this journey of a lifetime and we were stopped in our tracks. With our arms loaded down, we stood in the kitchen watching the World Trade Center smoking before our eyes. As we tired of holding the shirts, shoes, dishes, dirty laundry, another plane came, and smoke poured out of the other tower. We were transfixed, in shuddering terror.

For a few short weeks our minds were filled with so much sadness and grief, how small in comparison was ours personally. We were still here, and so were our children, no matter in what condition. *As long as there is life, there is still hope!*

Still, I couldn't get through to the *Why*, of Sharon's begging for us to come.

Sometime after the wedding trip, Sharon wrote me stating she had been diagnosed with bipolar disorder also, and was on many meds. *Maybe this would explain her bizarre sexual exploits and her exhibitionistic behavior towards her dad?* Somewhere I read that psychopathic/sociopathic children bury their mothers, because mothers don't believe, and won't let go. From personal experience, I had already seen the change that the right medication can do for bipolar disorder, (which can mimic the manipulative conning, i.e., sociopathic behavior). The change in personality on medication is remarkable, just remarkable – and unbelievable, until you are witness to it, as I have been with my husband, his sister, Fran, and all three of Sharon's siblings. Furthermore, I have found, once stabilized on the right kind of meds, the erratic behavior during those dips are, thankfully, wiped from memory. But having finally accepted the impossibility of real communication between Sharon and me without her getting professional help, I didn't respond to her letter.

It was that December, 2001, by the time Sean came back to Oregon, after being cut off of his SSI. He had traveled all over, hitchhiking, jumping box cars, staying in shelters, working day jobs, doing yard work here and there, until he decided to come back home and try to get himself clean. He started in counseling, went on Zoloft, and began a serious attempt at sobriety. Kelly was still in treatment in LA, getting some therapy himself for the first time in his life. Suzie had found her way into treatment, had gotten her SSI, was on her meds, going to school to obtain her teaching certificate so she could finally teach. Although the communication between Sharon and I had ceased – I decided fifty years was long enough and maybe if I was out of her life, she might be forced to deal with her problems, rather then continue to blame *me* for them — I was feeling so good about my family, that I began preparation to bring Ray's sister, Fran, to Oregon.

Fran had become totally disabled, with rheumatoid arthritis. Her bipolar illness, which really began in her teen years, the same as Suzie's, had become full blown later in life; she had a shunt in her brain for blood clots, bad lungs, congestive heart. Fran's list of medications were a page long, when I finally got her to her new physician.

Sean, Ray, and I met Fran at the airport, and Sean and Fran took to each other immediately; they became bosom buddies. My intent was to find a way for Ray to make amends to his baby sister for all the hardship he, and his two brothers had put on her through the years. The brothers had belittled her, mistreated her, laughed at her... Though now divorced, Fran had married several Mexicans, was fluent in Spanish, and finally adopted a little girl from an orphanage in Mexico. It was plain, Fran found a way to "get even" with her bigoted family, even Rich, the professed Christian who by this time was pastor of an enormous, wealthy Fundamentalist Christian church. I had lost touch with Fran over the years, but on our trip to Virginia, we stopped and visited her in Michigan. Our three days with her were so beautiful, I wanted to bring her to Oregon. She had no family any more in the area, and I felt this was something we could do for her. Ray was not too happy about this at first, but when I decide to do something, he has learned to get out of the way.

In May, 2002, we took Fran down to LA for Kelly's two-year AA anniversary. I took Fran with me in the car, and Ray took Sean in our old El Dorado Sean had fixed up ship-shape as a gift for Kelly. (Yes, Sean was a genius at things he could see and feel.) Fran had never seen the ocean, and we all five stayed in one hotel room together, the boys used the floor. What a wonderful time we had, but I noticed that Kelly was very hyper, anticipating finishing his program, and being given a permanent job on the staff, while he continued to go to UCLA for his counseling degree. By this time, I had learned that major life changes, without meds, could be primary triggers for a psychotic episode.

The counselors through the years had told me the boys had a symbiotic relationship, they fed off of each other, and having been through this so many times before, with both of them, it was not a surprise that two days after we left Kelly, he had left the treatment center following the funeral Wake of an old friend who had been murdered, there he had fallen off big time, and left the area. We heard from him a week later on his drive back to LA from Atlanta, the place where he went to high school, just as Sean would often return to Tucson, where *he* had attended. (Something about the place where each of them had come into puberty had some kind of draw when they were very upset, is all I could figure.) Kelly went into the hospital in LA, and was put on anti-psychotic meds to undo the week he had just spent, off the wagon, but his job was gone and so was the heretofore earned state college education. His life was pretty much in the dumpster again, "not working the steps,"[43] he said, his denial of his mental illness still in tact.

Amidst all of this, Sean had stopped his Zoloft, and moved out.

Three months later, Kelly knocked on our door at dawn, having driven from LA, hardly able to walk. The doctor there called it "a pulled muscle" in his back, but fifteen minutes after he was seen by a doctor here, he was diagnosed with Lambert Eaton Myasthenic Syndrome (L.E.M.S.), a form of MD (muscular dystrophy) and admitted. There they immediately began looking for cancer, the underlying cause of this particular neurological auto-immune condition. After his cancerous left kidney was taken out, he received the full disability which he had applied for several years previously, during one of his "psychotic" hospital admissions in Nashville. Without a new address, Social Security had never notified him. The money he received, that had accrued with SSI, was enough to purchase a trailer, but we had no idea how long he would live to enjoy it.

Through all this, Fran was not getting any better, but Kelly would pick her up and take her to his new church, as he was still able to drive. When Sean was up to it, he would pick Fran up and take her on the bus, pushing her wheelchair all over, to the park, to buy ice cream. And from his high school cooking class, Sean had developed a love for cooking, which he often shared with her.

Sean had been in counseling those six months he was clean, and through this and an attorney, his SSI was eventually reinstated. Strangely enough, Sean's addiction then began to take an ugly turn, as his scrawny underweight, physical appearance

---

[43] The twelve steps of Alcoholic Anonymous (AA).

seemed to indicate he was doing something besides alcohol.

A friend of mine from Boston, a psychologist, was visiting. We were sitting by the pool at the hotel where she was staying, and out of the blue, she said to me, "I don't think you have *really dealt with your father yet!*"

To my new counselor, I said, "What could I possibly not be dealing with?" My father had passed on, and the anger towards him that I felt from time to time, seemed to have subsided. "I was asleep, or if I wasn't, I don't remember it," I said.
    "You don't remember it, or have you blocked it out?"
    "Why would I block it out?"
    "I don't know; because it *felt good?*"
    My face felt as if it was on fire, and I quickly changed the subject. Before I fell asleep that night, since the subconscious never forgets, I used NLP and asked the CEO of my memory to take me back to that happening, as a nine-year-old:

Daddy is on his knees reading his Bible. It was a hot summer night. The high arms of my chair-bed allowed no air flow, so I begged him to let me sleep in his bed, up by the window. Remembering, I found myself falling asleep, when suddenly, I was having that good feeling down there, like with Beth, and I wanted to scream... like I did that time when Ray was out of town, watching the movie, Ordinary  *People – when the kid realizes the guilt he is feeling for his brother's drowning is because he didn't. Now it was that same kind of guilt. NO. NO. The shame of it so overwhelming; to even think such a thing, unimaginable. A blood-curdling scream at that moment could not begin to expel the lifetime of pent up SHAME, TORMENT, and ANGER I was finally allowing myself to feel towards my deceased father, who, when I had approached him on this subject, had told me to: "Leave dead dogs buried forever."*

A s of January - 2006, Kelly was clean and sober, but Sean's ability to hide his using was becoming harder, although while staying at home, he had to be clean, one of our rules. In essence, our home had become his private detox center. With his severe learning disability, ADHD, and underlying depression, he seemed to be unable to stay sober more than a few days at a time, as he refused to take any psycho-medication: "The Ritilin from third grade on messed up my head." Divorced, Sean seemed to have great difficulty with women, had been charged with domestic violence against two wives. For years he cried over the abuse he was dealt by both Sharon and Suzie. He said once he couldn't bear to be around Suzie, because she turned him on. Maybe because he loved her so much, he would rather have believed, for years, that Sharon was the one who sexually used him. When Suzie corrected his memory one Christmas right in front of the whole family, she said, "If it hadn't been you, it would have been a Coke bottle; I was twelve and in puberty, and you were *there!*"[44] Sharon had batted him around and pulled his hair, sticking cigarettes into his mouth at the age of two, which had him addicted by the time he was five, he says. For a long time he shared his brother's hatred for her. *How could I not know?*

Looking back, you remember being the mother. For me, it is very similar to being on a ship in the middle of the ocean, in a storm. When you are there, up in this little city set on the high seas, you don't really fathom where you are, the enormity of it, because in your ceaseless fight to maintain your balance, your digestive juices overwhelming you, when you peer out that little porthole at those white crashing waves, it doesn't even register where you are, and you don't care – you just want it to be over. When you retrace the whole experience, you see it only as a dot in time.

With the schizophrenia being the most prevalent in Suzie's condition, she had finally succumbed to the alcohol after sixteen years sober. (My father had been sober thirty years when he slipped back; he had used *Jesus* also.) Suzie did find her way into treatment, is now sober, and she is on stable meds, working and living close to her beautiful girls, doing so well now. She says she knows she will never take another drink, never, that she *must* take

---

[44] Sean and I went for counseling together for this, learning about the loss of boundaries, and how messed up one can get from childhood abuse.

her meds if she wants to keep her children in her life. We talk on the phone often now.

Kelly is losing strength by the day in his legs and arms. His new church is teaching him how to take care of his body, to be a vegetarian, when, for years, he went days, without eating, sleeping, using drugs. Despite his illness, he is fortunately able to live on his own. The body is a hard task master, it *will* get even with us for our neglect, in time.

My headaches have been diagnosed as simple classic migraine -- simple, they say. It only took thirty years. But at least now there are medications to treat it. It is not my psyche beating me over the head, as many doctors for years tried to make us women believe. Soy is my main trigger, and in our cancer conscious world, soy is put in everything. My doctor says soy is full of hormones. *Do you suppose this is my body's way of still rejecting my being a woman?*

Life has a way of putting in your path just the right things to teach you how to be human, to progress, to become a well-rounded being. When I think about the fact that my dad was so ignorant to think I didn't need more education, it kept me bitter for many years. But somehow that yearning was finally fulfilled, though late in my life; as well as three of my granddaughters have become teachers, and another the valedictorian of her high school.

My true love may not have turned out to be the dream I had as a girl. Had he not been a preacher, someone who knew the Bible inside and out, I wouldn't have trusted him with my life. Instead, he was the window to my mind, my opening to the world around me, and his eventual rejection of his narrow religious upbringing so stalwartly gave me the courage to reject my own. Of course his mother had a big part in that awakening, but she was HIS mother, or I may never have had that confrontation that turned me about face from my "faith driven" life into the open-minded and reflective person I was striving to be. I'm sure it is because of Ray's basic kindness, not always obvious to outsiders, is why we are still together. When I had just received the message that my first husband, Huey, had passed -- seven days after his fifty-sixth birthday from alcoholic cirrhosis -- I was on the phone with Ray. Telling him about it, the tears just burst forth. Immediately, I was sorry for Ray to hear me cry, surprising me after all those years. But Ray's words, "No need to apologize. When you love someone, you don't stop just because you are no longer together," showed me the real man I had married.

One cannot judge another's life, *ever*. One does not know what one would do if put in their shoes. At age seventeen, working at the bank, during break, I was looking through a *True Confessions* magazine left in the lunch room. A coworker noticed, saying, "That's all a bunch of malarkey; I would never do any of the stuff written in there." I turned to her and said, "You're not dead yet, either."

Marriage is a work of the heart. Every single day we are given an opportunity to give of ourselves to someone, if we just open our eyes and look around us. And working at my century old relationship with my husband has been just that, a work of the heart. Every time we got close to separating, we would end up looking into each other's eyes and saying the same thing. We just couldn't walk away from the other one. So we plowed through all the pain, the distrust, the hurtful things, to come out on the other side closer than before. Neither of us is perfect, never were, and we both had much lacking from our parents, but we found a way to accept the other's missing parts and be thankful for the parts that WERE there.

Someone once told me that traditional marriage is like a diamond. In the beginning you are closely aligned as you look to the future. Then you start to separate: he being concerned with his career, and earning a living for the children you want to have; *your* time gets taken with kids, school, and just keeping afloat – until one day, in midlife, you find yourselves each at the furthest width of the diamond.

When the kids leave, you find out that you are a person in your own right, besides being a wife, a mother, a real *me* person. So you go to work, back to college, whatever will let that person feel and grow; he is in the same boat: he's made his mark, he's proven himself, he is *tired*, he just wants to play, to enjoy the fruits of his lifetime of labor. After you veer off from each other into your own worlds, apart from each other, if you are lucky, and can hang in there, the diamond slowly goes back together, and you end up at the end of it, even closer than at the beginning. It's keeping the diamond in your mind, knowing that whatever it takes, it will be worth it all -- at the other end.

"There you are, standing there, loving me, whether or not your should. Somewhere in my wounded childhood, there must have been something good."

◆

AFTER WORDS:

The Perfect Storm–Again?

"We must begin with the realization that we cannot change the past. We must start where we are."
—Thomas A. Harris MD
I'm OK-You're OK

When you love someone, they are forever in your heart.
—L. L. Morton

2011
Dear Sean:

There are many things I wanted to tell you, so many things, but you were gone so suddenly it has taken your dad and me these past five years to deal with the shock. Because you always told me you would never do to us what your brother, Kelly, did, staying away without any contact for months at a time, and you and I have always had such an understanding with each other, that I still do not believe you left willingly. Our counselor always said you and I were joined at the hip, but I think we were really joined at the heart,

and why I have to write you this letter — the last chapter in this story about our family, of which you have been and always will be – a most loving part.

Did you know that even though you were the last one, you were the first of our children that we purposefully tried for? Yes, several months it took us to get pregnant with you.

We were renting a house in a suburb outside of our nation's capital and had some very nice neighbors with whom we became great friends; we played penny-ante poker every Friday night. They teased me that you were going to come out with a penny in your hand saying, "Call you and raise you two." Do you suppose that is where you got your yen for gambling?

When I complained to my doctor that I was tired all the time, he prescribed some pep pills to help me along, Dexedrine, the same as the doctors later would also give you in third grade, only *you* they slowed down.

Those months that I had you in my tummy, I sewed for all the neighbors, making coats and suits; do you suppose that is why you always wanted to use my sewing machine? But I

541

wouldn't let you; what a shame that I was so dumb to think it was sissy for boys to sew. I didn't know then that the greatest tailors in the world were men; you would have been a fine tailor too, with such good hand-eye coordination that you eventually used so well in hanging wallpaper. Dad named you "The Hanging Man" and I made calling cards for you that said:

> *Call the Hanging Man,*
> *and let me hang in your house.*

You were born at Walter Reed Army hospital in the middle of a snow storm, only five pounds two ounces and sixteen inches long, unlike your brother who was twenty-one inches at birth. You were three weeks early, coming into this world on your dad's 30th birthday, just two weeks before Christmas. Dad read Dr. Spock's baby book and learned to actually feed you and change your diapers; he was so happy and loved taking care of you.

Our neighbors helped me to surprise your dad with a pool table for Christmas that year, on which he later taught you and Kelly to shoot so well. Do you remember you boys winning all the billiard trophies at the park in Atlanta that summer? You both learned to run the table and gave your Dad some competition. Dad's eyes are so bad, he doesn't play much anymore.

Your first organ teacher, if you recall, played for Tommy Dorsey's big band, way before your time, and had thumbs so wide they reached down two sets of keys. Then you started piano lessons with my college professor; you really liked him. He told you, as a teenager he played in restaurants for money. That must be what spurred you on to practice so much; you always did like money, and you were good too. For all the nursing homes here, you played for free, just asked enough to pay for Dad's gas to get you there. Learning to play trumpet all on your own, getting all A's in high school marching band, such talent.

Remember the Christmas in Pennsylvania, you were in fourth grade, when you wanted a tool box so bad. When you opened it up and saw all the tools of your very own, to use on your go-cart, you were so happy you bawled big time; our whole family was in tears too.

Gigi and Zsa Zsa: how you loved those dogs, grand dogs of our little Tiisip, in Bangkok. They were just puppies when we got them, by airplane. After Dad got out of the Army, we moved to Tucson; you were a freshman in high school. The first day in our new house you let the dogs out without a leash just as they had been used to at our last house. You wanted them to meet the neighbors barking dogs. They ran across the road ahead of you, ZsaZsa – the biggest and always first – was hit by a truck, dead. Poor Gigi, she never was the same after that, missing her big sister litter-mate; you were very sad. Gigi was so lonesome, we finally asked my friend from work, who had a big furry cat who was lonesome too, to take care of Gigi sometimes. We finally let Gigi stay with her new friend; you thought Gigi needed someone to keep her company, alone all day.

Remember in Bangkok, you were five, when I found some cigarette butts stuffed into the sink overflow drain? I called all four of you kids into that huge bathroom, lined you up, and asked, "Who was it that put these cigarette butts into this drain?" You shot your little hand up, and said, "It wasn't me, Mom. I quit smoking when we left Atlanta." Sharon had put lit cigarettes into your mouth so you wouldn't tattle on *her* smoking, Suzie told me; they pulled your hair too, and why you asked me to cut it off short in a butch to keep them from doing that. Your thick, curly hair was always a joy to cut, how I miss doing that.

Once I even pulled your hair when I got angry – you had left your room a big mess – tears were standing in your eyes, "That's not right, Mom," you said. I apologized and hugged you and we both were bawling; I never did it again. I was so ashamed of myself because I never, ever had to punish you, you were such a good kid, you loved school, and I never had to push you to practice your music. How sorry I have been all these years that you couldn't trust me enough to tell me about your sisters, what they were doing to you and Kelly. It is too horrible to think about, what a burden to have to bear for you boys. The treachery of it is, how much you both loved them despite such ill-treatment.

On Sharon's seventeenth birthday, in Bangkok, we got her the teak vanity she was hoping for. We had it delivered to the upstairs vestibule. She was viewing herself in the full-length mirror, turning this way and that, while Kelly, ten at the time, was sitting with me on the love-seat, admiring her. His whole life he had always drawn such ugly monster pictures with her name at the top; how he hated her, he would say. That day though, he suddenly burst into big tears, all broken up, "I really *do* love her, Mom, I really do." I pulled him close in a big hug, and laughing I said, "Do you think I didn't *know* that?"

Before that, Dad had just come home from Vietnam. Kelly, eight, was gone to the White's Alabama farm, for a visit. Sharon, fifteen, was so late coming home from shopping we thought she had run away. She was apologetic for making us worry. We five were in the living room, hugging, and Sharon said, "Gee, we really have a nice family, don't we? If it wasn't for Kelly, it would be perfect!" Tears were standing in Dad's eyes when he said, "Don't you understand, he's *just* a little boy!"

The estrangement between us, Sharon and I, has really disturbed you. When I sent you away that last Easter morning because you had been drinking all night – when you had come home to spend the day with us and play cards with Kelly – I just couldn't deal with you in that condition. As you walked out of the yard, you turned and yelled back at me, "One of these days, Mom, I'm going to do to you what Sharon has done – and you won't ever see me again."

In the next letter I wrote you, I tried to explain to you that you had it exactly backwards. I tried to make you understand how being married to a drunk, her biological father, Huey, the memories of those awful days with him I just couldn't endure again, with her *or with you*. But, I have learned since, that it was my father's drinking — I believed my whole life had ultimately contributed to my mother's death – that was the subconscious trigger that upset me so much whenever I was subjected to even the smell of booze. I started drinking with Dad so I wouldn't smell it on his breath, in the first place. It was when Dad gave up the booze that our relationship began to grow, before that we were living in each other's shadow desperately grasping at the real person inside which the booze had managed to hide. This is what I wanted you to understand, what possibilities your life held if you would just sober up. You just loved your big sister and hurt from the separation.

When you were ten, she took you to work with her at the White House several days, and gave you errands to run all over. Sharon paid you too, way too much I told her, but she said she wanted you to learn that when you worked hard, you would get rewarded, for you not to forget that. I think you learned it, as you have always worked very hard at everything you've ever undertaken and have done it well.

About Suzie: How it hurt that she didn't even call or send you and your bride a note of congratulations when you had actually been *in* her wedding and everyone knew she had been drinking a ton the whole night before. Such pain love brings, huh?

In Atlanta, you were four, Sharon took you kids to the Post pool and her boyfriends taught you to do a double back-flip off the high dive. After you hit your head, it scared you so you wouldn't go up on it again, but she never told me till years later: she worried that your bump on the head was the cause of your neurological problems later on.

Your fear didn't last long, you water skied off Thailand's Pataya Beach, out in the South China Sea, with Dad, a little dot following on behind. It frightened me to tears, but I was proud of your spunk and determination.

The summer we went to Baltimore, to keep Dad company while he was in the Army school, you loved to swim; and Dad loved to tease. He told you that the way to spell your name was: B.u.m. People around the pool would ask you to spell your name for them; everyone would laugh, you were so little and cute and had no idea what you were saying. I thought of that many times, when we would find you living in the woods, homeless, or we heard you were in a tent by the water down in Corpus Christie, or the day we found your things stashed in that wash in Tucson, before you got your trailer. It scares me hearing about the terrible stuff going on at the Arizona border. You never had too much fear, maybe not enough, you think?

In second grade, do you remember the little girl that wrote you notes in school? With your first curls, I've saved one of them, printed on a torn out scrap of paper:

> *dear sean, your a stink bum*
> *mean and ornry and I hate you.*
> *love, sara.*

And I've saved another note you wrote to me one year, with a dandelion you'd picked, that says:

> *happy anifersry, mom.*

In third grade, in Pennsylvania, when we moved into our newly built house, you wet the bed the first night. I took you right to the doctor and he gave you some little pills, the same kind I took when I was pregnant with you. You never did that again either; the pills calmed you down as well so you could sit still in school.

Do you remember kindergarten, in Bangkok, Thailand? Your teacher would let you sit next to her and would hold your hand so you'd sit still and listen to the story, otherwise you "were a sweet boy," and she was sad when the school asked you not to come back. You finished the year in a "free school" with a nice teacher from India (she had a black dot on her forehead) where you could play in between learning. In first grade, you went back to American School with your brother and sisters.

There, you followed Chan, our Chinese chef, all over. He let you help in the kitchen. Is that what made you like to cook? Grilling steaks for us seemed to bring you such joy.

Later on, you spent most of your time building go-carts. Your friend Joey helped you; his mom made really good cookies. You played baseball at the park; we went to every game. You loved being part of the team.

My how you like to fish. You take after your grandpa Malorry. You never remembered him, he died when you were a little tot; he could fish all day, and he loved to drink beer too, like you. Dad and I used to like beer, but it gave Dad indigestion and made me too sleepy, part of the reasons we quit that, long ago.

Dad was the one got you hooked on beer, I think; he gave you some on your 16th birthday. You were both feeling silly happy, and he raised his beer high up in the air for a toast, and said, "Happy birthday, Son. We share our birthday with the man who invented the electric light bulb. Like Thomas Edison, let's you and me *light up the world!*" I took a picture, but later, when you had so much trouble *not* wanting a beer, I was sorry and ashamed.

When you lost your SSI (you got while in that hospital on the Cape) you started traveling all over the country. I have a map with the routes you took because you called me in every town to let me know you were safe; I always appreciated it. That same year we met you in Salt Lake City, Utah, and we went to an organ concert together in the big Mormon temple. You sat on the bench behind us with your head leaning over, in between us. You and I couldn't keep our tears back at the overpowering, beautiful sound. You loved seeing those mammoth pipes that reached into the heavens and wished you could have played that organ just once, I bet.

We left you behind and went on to meet Dad's two brothers, Matt and Rich and their wives. Too bad you didn't come with us. We got into a nice game of *Oh Hell* in the motel. We had a wonderful time visiting Utah's famous Zion National Park – until the very last five minutes of our week together. Uncle Rich, the Fundamentalist Christian preacher with the huge church, threw an old college notebook of your dad's he had found in their mom's things, clear across the room, and said, "This is what you *used* to believe; what do you believe now?" The first time religion had been mentioned, but Dad was cool: "I don't know, I'll have to read it," he said. (Rich was wrong though, the notes were what the *professor* believed, and Dad knew that to pass a course you had to remember what the professor said in class. And Dad always kept good notes because of his memory blanks, just like yours.) Having enjoyed a very pleasant week, this abrupt and unexpected turn threw Dad into such an angry and emotional tizzy, I had to finish driving the rest of the way home. I guess that's why Dad has always referred to his brother, Rich, as "the trouble maker." Siblings can be so mean, huh?

Just like your brother did to you, that time you called him to introduce him to your latest girl. In their short conversation, Kelly said to her, "My brother is just a girl with a pecker." When you heard that, she said you cried and cried, so long and hard and got so drunk, your eyes rolled back in your head. She was frightened you were OD-ing. It had upset her so much, she called me the next morning. "How can a brother say such cruel things," she said.

In January, 1998, you and Kelly showed up at our new house here in Oregon just after we had moved in. Kelly was high on whatever drugs he was using. I took him to the doctor to bring him down, but it didn't help. With his ranting and raving, we had to ask him to leave. You had told him you thought Mom could get him fixed, but even with the help of the doctor, I couldn't. He was too far gone, his mania had been triggered by the meth again.

You said you hated any of that stuff, even pot. It was illegal and you didn't ever want to get put in jail, afraid that inside you would be murdered. So I was surprised, after you got divorced and she claimed you got rough with her, you chose to do the time rather than go to anger management classes. You said by the time you got out of that class, you were ready to kill someone for sure. Those three months you spent inside, down in California, we visited you and brought Kelly. Remember? He was in treatment by then. You wrote me a letter almost every day and I saved them, with all the many other letters and cards you wrote me since the first day you left home. I get so sad, missing you, when I read all your sweet and loving words.

The last time you were here at home, in April 2006 — after your last gig in town and only two people showed because you scheduled it midweek – when you woke me at two in the morning out of a sound sleep, knocking on my bedroom window and scaring the bejesus out of me, I was very angry as I could hear you and your drunken friend talking and walking around the house, to the back. I told you the next morning that I had the phone in my hand ready to call 911 and if you didn't shape up and stop drinking, I was going to sign for a restraining order; we just couldn't stand it anymore. You called me when you got back to your trailer, the next week, and said, "No restraining order, Mom. I'm your *SON*." You sounded so hurt, but I told you then how it was killing us, Dad, me, and Kelly too, as sick as he was already.

That was when you decided to get sober. You said, "Why I guess I was pushing it too hard; I could see this day was coming." When you said you hated "the depression," I reminded you what that doctor told you when you took your boat out with a case of beer and almost drowned – your dog did and your second boat went down ending you up on Catalina Island in a cactus thicket. Lucky for you, despite pouring rain, the Coast Guard came. While picking the cactus out of your butt, the doctor told you: *The underlying cause of addiction is depression and unless you treat that, it is near impossible to stay sober.*

"Yes, Mom, I know. I saw Patrick Kennedy on Larry King the other night. I'm going to get an appointment, but, until then, can you bring me some of Dad's Zoloft?"

I couldn't do that, Son; a doctor has to prescribe meds for you, you know that, and with your Army disability insurance your Dad got you at age twenty-one, and your SSI covering the rest, you had no excuse not to go.

You told me then about the "bunch of money" you owed, $400; "I need to get some gigs." In fact, you had one scheduled that Friday night. You always did pay your bills, eventually. In fact, you helped us finish the guest house, painting, wallpapering, and building the horseshoe bar out of the original door that was on the garage. You did such beautiful work and paid off all you owed me, one hour at a time. I have a record of every cent, in my budget record book.

Those last weeks, I was so happy to be able to talk to you several times a day. When you said, "It's not your fault, or Dad's, that I am in this fix; you both raised me right – I know what is right to do," I was sure you were on the right road, finally.

Sometimes when you were drunk, you would blame us for all the mixed up problems in your head. How you hated them, you said, even though the meds calmed you down, they made you *think* too much.

When we hadn't heard from you in over a week – every single day we left messages, but you didn't return them – Kelly and I came over to your trailer. As I sat on your bed I had a sinking feeling inside me looking around at all the nice pictures you had of us on your walls, of redheaded Melissa, your first real love: Your place was neat and clean, laundry done and folded in the basket, food in the frig and stuff for sandwiches left out on your counter – I just knew you had left unexpectedly or in a hurry for some reason. Maybe it was on account of the man you told us about threatening to shoot you if you ever got drunk again; you told Kelly that you were down on the floor to talk to him on the phone, hiding. After you had told me you hated the *depression* and was going to the doctor, you told Kelly you hated the *sobriety*. Whatever reason you left us like that, it just broke my heart.

When you were seventeen and ended up back in the hospital, after being in Highland House, up in North Carolina, where they put you on lithium for the first time – remember we watched *Raiders of the Lost Ark* movie together? – I was surprised at how calm you were on lithium. When you came back home, you left it off to go to a party; someone had some "white lightening." You saw a paring knife in the dish drainer, grabbed it, and stuck it into your gut sending you back to emergency, this time for colon surgery. The same doctor, you had before, told me then, "Your son has tried suicide twice already, next time he won't fail." Those words were running through my head when I sat on your bed that day, the week after you went missing in May, 2006.

We couldn't get the police to even go looking through the woods for you since your bike was gone also. You were "forty-three years old and had a right to take off, if you chose," they said. Your last girlfriend, Sheri, the one that had just broke up with you – that sobered you up and made you see that you needed to find someone to help you with your "women's issues" – told us you threatened to ride through those woods to get to the beach, but the police wouldn't even look, said they had no place to start, no traces of you to give them a lead.

Your bartender friend, that gave you rides often, said he met you right in the beginning, and you said you were going to get clean and sober there. "You came to one hole of a town to do that in," he said, to which you replied, "Well, if I can do it *here*, I can do it anywhere."

Other friends you made later on told us you had started hanging around with a bad crowd. Kelly and I saw some of them in the park, bleary-eyed and scary looking. Are they the ones you owed? When you called on the morning of our 50th wedding anniversary, May 2nd, (it was *your* first wedding anniversary too, remember? You had such high hopes, marrying on the same day, for luck) and you asked me to pay your rent, as you had already lost your whole check in one day on the slots, I had to refuse you. I just couldn't keep on supporting your addictions; I had to stop doing that, Son. You know I was right, too, don't you? And you *did* sober up.

In one of your many calls those next days, you told me, "I've found someone to help me with my women's issues." I wanted to ask who it was – and if those "issues" were really about the confusion of your sexuality? But I didn't; I couldn't.

We waited for almost a month, until after your next SSI check would have come, thinking you would show up for sure then, to get your money, but you never came. The bank sent your money back to Social Security, and we got one of Kelly's friends to dismantle your trailer and pull it home; we parked it in front of my bedroom window.

The cigarette smell was so bad inside, I started painting it completely, even the interior of the cabinets and closet, washed the slipcovers and drapes, redid the screens and replaced the broken windows. I even put in a new microwave, and new carpeting in the bathroom. You would've liked the decorative sponge painting of flowers I did in there also, cheerful. A full length mirror on the back of that door made the place look bigger. After I shampooed the carpet, I spot-dyed it to cover the stains from Buttons (losing that sweet dog to old age really hurt you, I know). We tried to get someone to fix the roof so it wouldn't leak, instead we got another new tarp to put over it until we could decide what to do with it. I wanted it to be ready – if and when you came home. Somehow, in all the running back and forth in fixing it up, I had misplaced the door key.

One of the ideas we had was, that you were just waiting until we got the trailer pulled home, as Section 8 had you up on the list for a place soon. (In fact, the availability letter came in July, just as you expected.) We moved all of your things into the guest house, to sort through them and maybe get a clue. Kelly wanted your keyboards, some pretty things you had are reminders when I go out there, the angel pillows. The ceramic angels I brought into the house. You said you believed angels would watch over you and keep you safe. "Don't worry about me, Mom, don't you know I've got nine lives?" When I go out there, the place you made your own, I can still see you in your favorite chair, watching TV. The wallpaper still intact, the cabinets you built, the horseshoe bar you designed in the kitchen, the bookshelves you cut down to fit the windows in my craft room. Everywhere I look, I see you, Son. Without you, it feels so empty now.

Remember how excited you were to have your own trailer and to leave immediately for northern California, where it was cheaper lot rent. Dad and I came down and got your new tag paid for, then left for lunch. Before heading back on the highway, we decided to stop and give you one more hug. When we drove up, unexpectedly, you were already drinking a beer; I just couldn't believe it, after all your promises and everything that had gone down between us. When Kelly said you "hated sobriety," I thought of that day we surprised you in the new trailer we had just helped you buy. I thought when you saved your money, and stayed sober that whole month, you had it licked.

It is too bad that Kelly went so overboard on religion that he couldn't even share a movie, your favorite thing — besides playing cards, that is.

And then the thought of losing your Auntie Frannie, you gave her so much love, pushing her in her wheelchair all over. The day Frannie was released from the hospital into hospice, right here in our town, Dad, Kelly, and I were waiting for her in her new room. When I got home, I called you, and you had just hung up with her; you were bawling big time. You said, "I just can't stand to see her die, Mom, I just can't stand it." That was the Friday before Mother's Day, May 12, 2006.

You called me back later to wish me "Happy Mother's Day Mom, in case I'm not here on Sunday."

I was so used to not prying into your business, that I didn't even question you, "Where are you planning to be?" I could have asked. Maybe I could've talked you out of going wherever that was *or is*. The weeks and months that followed were like living hell, and some days still are. I already got three traffic violations looking at every bicycle or a walker with a backpack.

E-mails, flyers with your pictures, telephone calls, the days were filled up with my searching. We believe you wore the black leather jacket and the shirt we gave you for Christmas, the one you wore in all the pictures with Kelly and Frannie. Nothing else was missing from your things.

By August, three months later, Frannie took a turn for the

worse. Dad was with her several days a week, but I promised to be with her when she passed. He came home in a rush and said to get over there, she was already leaving us. I had just washed my hair, grabbed an old jacket, and ran. It was just days after her 65th birthday when we took her fried chicken livers and pickles to eat; she ate them all too, as sick as she was. There were two hospice nurses in her room overseeing things; Frannie was groaning, gasping for breath, not really lucid any more. After I sang her one of Dad's favorite hymns:

> Peace, peace, wonderful peace, coming down from the
> Father above/Sweep over my spirit forever I pray/
> with fathomless billows of love.[45]

Fran got quiet for a minute and listened. I told her to just let go, "Be a butterfly Frannie." (You know how she loved butterflies, same as you like angels.) I had read the poem to her that I wrote you for your 41st birthday:

> Love is like a butterfly
> It is beautiful and full of life
> It is always in flight, or taking respite
> It is light as a feather with wings of its own
> Different in color, one from another
> Sunshine and movement, all together
> Love is all this, and much, much more
> Free to stay, free to go – unless thoughtless hands
> capture and hold.
> Love is like a butterfly -- it says: Let go!

To Frannie, I said, "Maybe Sean is waiting for you on the other side." She stopped and took a big breath, you could tell she was thinking about this (she kept saying you were in some long-term treatment place getting well, she never wavered from this, no matter hearing that the word on the street was you were dead, shot in the head, murdered; she just wouldn't believe it). I kept her hand in mine until she took her last breath; it was a relief knowing that all her pain was over, finally, after a lifetime of suffering.

As I gathered my things, to leave her quiet body to the nurses, I stuck my hand in my pocket to find the key to your trailer... and when I touched it, I just knew, *knew,* that you were there in that room with us the moment she passed, wherever you

---

[45] Written by Warren D. Cornell & W. George Cooper, 1889.

were, your spirit was there with us; she loved you so; you were so good and kind to her.

That week I called Suzie to tell her about Frannie passing, also bringing her up to date on your missing case. Her first response was, "Wow, Mom, are you on anti-depressants?" No, I said, although I had a RX for some, but hadn't needed them as yet. "I'm doing a lot of crying though," I said. She had been calling us often, the last time she called me was the same day, right after you had called, Mother's Day, and then in June, on Father's Day, she told Dad, "Three years is too long to go without sex." Right then I had the feeling she was getting ready to leave the treatment center, after she had worked so hard on getting her masters degree for teaching. After our conversation in August, she closed out her email, and I called her for her birthday, that Christmas, but she had already left, no forwarding address. All my mail to her has been returned.

After three months working on getting your trailer in good shape, we let Frannie's care-giver and her husband take it in-trade for repairing the front porch that you said you were going to do for us come warm weather; it seemed to be fair. I had to sign the title over with the Power of Attorney we had from the original purchase. Fortunately I had all the papers in my bulging "Sean's File," now two whole file drawers.

We hired a private detective to check out all the rumors. Some said you had been given a bunch of meth to sell and you took off with the money, others said you were too dumb for anybody to trust. They just didn't know how smart you were — when you were sober. Several said you had been trying to hitch a ride to the coast. The PI interviewed a regular at one of the bars, who knew you, and he told the PI, "I doubt he got out though, he was hanging out with a bad crowd. Bodies have been known to be buried in these woods." That town didn't have a very good reputation. As I told you when you would sober up: "Your belligerence when drunk is going to get you killed one of these days."

At first, your last girlfriend, Sheri, was kind to us and kept in touch, and actually seemed to clean up from her meth use for a few months, but she slid back, the PI told us, and said she was afraid of "them," those she turned you on to. *Your angel... of death!*

In the fall of 2008, we were advised to hire an attorney. Maybe in court the police would be forced to tell us something, anything at all that would give us a clue that they wouldn't tell us otherwise. But after 500 hours of investigations, they testified: "We believe your son is deceased." Dad broke down into tears, along with everyone else in the court room, including the judge. Secretly, I think Dad really thought you would turn up one day for your shared birthday with him. He loves you, you know, under all the grumpy teasing or he wouldn't have driven you all over for your gigs or sat for hours playing cards every day you were at home. When you painted the house the previous summer, so drunk most days I was afraid you were going to fall off the ladder, he kept saying, "Leave him alone; he'll be okay." How you did such a professional job, I will never understand. The money we paid you sadly went for naught.

The last time you called, Mother's Day, you played and sang me the song you said you wrote for your latest ex-:

> *You got me wrapped around your finger*
> *like I was some for-ever lover*
> *I'm just tired of being used*
> *tired of being abused*
> *know I'm thinking about me*
> *every time you set me free*
> *now I'm looking into your eyes and what a surprise*
> *You set me free, free to be me*
> *now I'll go though my life*
> *wondering what I'll be*
> *since you set me free.*

"The words are not all that great, but the music is good, could be a hit," you said. You admitted then, "I had a hard time getting over her."

"Yes, I knew that," I said. When you called me the day you decided to marry her, that same night, I woke up out of a sound sleep with a grabbing in my gut, a dark foreboding that if you did this, something terrible would happen; I begged you then not to go through with it, but you just laughed. She proved me correct, she betrayed your trust in a sad way. When I saw a younger picture of her, a spitting image of your sister, Suzie, I realized then what her pull was with you, but I was afraid to tell you. I didn't want to bring all that stuff up, ever; it upset you so. (Suzie wrote you a letter asking for your forgiveness; the night before she had her psychotic break, she called and read it to me over the phone, remember my telling you?) Some months after that last Mother's Day with you, Suzie left her treatment center; she went off her meds and is gone from us now, again, just like your schizophrenic friend here who didn't like taking her meds either. You were so patient and told me I had to learn to "accept people how they were *without meds,* Mom". Yes, you told me that often, that I should even accept you *drunk* if that's what you wanted to be, but I just couldn't.

On Mother's Day, 2007, a year later, after five years without our communicating with Sharon, she called. Kelly was here playing cards; she was crying so hard I could hardly understand her. She said she was sober now, working for three years at the same job, but her daughter, Candi, was now doing to her the same things she had done to us – cutting off and keeping her grandchild away. (I understand Candi now has three.) Life is a circle, huh? I told her about your being missing, and about Suzie, also missing; Sharon soon found Suzie, off her meds, and was shocked to finally be a witness to her sister's serious illness. No matter how sad our life choices turn out to be, they are forever ours alone to make.

Before you played and sang to me that last day, you came back on the phone and said, "You know I love you, Mom," and I said, "Yes, Son, I know you do, and I love you."

Did you leave because I told you I wasn't going to help you anymore? You know I *meant* – help with your addictions. If you were sober, I had already said I'd give you my truck for your gigs and wallpaper hanging, why you had paid off all your DUI fines and was studying for your driver's license.

Were you telling me goodbye, never to return? You did ask Kelly to come get you, but he said he was too weak to drive that far. "Ask Mom. If you mean business about getting sober, she'll come," he told me.

All the times I drove miles to pick you up and bring you home, so many times, but this time you never called. You believed me this time when I had finally said *No.*

You had gotten a telephone company voice mail "so *they* won't bother me," you said. You asked me to call you back and see if it worked, just two days before. I listened to it sometimes a dozen times in a day just to hear your voice once more, even weeks after your phone was disconnected.

Lately, I have visions of you being far-off somewhere, maybe in a warm and beautiful place by the water, you loved boats so much. When you were drunk, you would say you were leaving and going to lie on the beach and drink mai-tais, if I would just keep your trailer and take care of Buttons, remember? Then you'd call the next day and apologize. "I love you, Mom," you'd say, sometimes crying.

When Kelly was missing almost two years and you went looking for him, you would break down in tears talking about it. Over and over you'd say, "I will never do that to you, Mom. Never." And you never did – until now.

You used to say the only way you could quit drinking was to quit smoking also, and the only way you could do that, was to go out into the woods, away from people until you had it licked. We thought maybe that is what you were doing when we found the stop-smoking patch wrappers in the trash you had just gotten from the doctor. With your signed *Release of Information*, I learned that all your tests came out good, *even your HIV*.

We were trying to get a search party together to look for you, but the police said it wasn't safe: "There is pot fields out there patrolled with shotguns." Maybe that is why *they* wouldn't do a search for you, do you think? Besides, so many wild animals live in our Oregon woods: cougars, bears...

After we went to court, and the State declared you to be deceased, we thought having a memorial service for you, at Kelly's church, since they all knew you so well and saw you at your sober best, would help Kelly to stop crying; it was filling up his already weak lungs. It was Easter Sunday, 2009, and he was here for dinner and cards. The program was printed out, and I had chosen the song sung at Grandpa Malorry's funeral. Like you, he was also an alcoholic that couldn't quit. Grandpa loved the song, and would play it and cry, just as I imagine you would, if you heard *it*.

An Evening Prayer
"If I have wounded any soul today
If I have caused one foot to go astray
If I have walked in my own wilful way
Dear Lord, forgive.[46]

---

[46] An Evening Prayer written by C. M. Battersby, 1911.

When Kelly read it, he started bawling big time, and later that night, I think the whole thing sent him over the top, into the manic phase of his illness (and you remember how that was all those years, when he was on meth, pot, and booze). He threatened to go silent for 40 days "in honor of my brother. " He was sobbing, "I've got to go find him, kill him, and bury him," he screamed into the phone. It was this Freudian slip that let me know he was not in his right mind, again. When Aunt Fran passed, she and Dad had decided on no memorial service, and Kelly went apeshit over that decision, having his pastor call me. So I thought maybe being able to say loving words in your memory would ease the pain of missing you.

Kelly was never the same after that. He started smoking and drinking again, went to visit his old friends in LA at the tattoo house, quit his church and those great friends he had throughout his long illness, and he was very distant to us for weeks at a time. Even though his religiosity I recognized clearly as part of his psychosis, and you remember hating to listen to it as well, but the friendship he received from those good church people sustained him through a long, sad illness.

On Good Friday, the next year, I called him and invited him to come for Easter. He called me back this time, and we had a very nice, long conversation. He told me he had stopped going to church "because I think I went a little overboard on it." I burst into laughter, hearing him admit such a thing. He told me his lone-kidney was not going to hold up very long, he was getting weaker and weaker. But he said that after his next treatment on Tuesday, he would try to come over for cards. Dad came home then, and they talked also.

Kelly never made it to his

next treatment. Instead, that following Monday morning, he just didn't wake up, the morning of April 12, 2010.

We had no idea his time was so close. It upset me so, that I went to see his doctor, who told me Kelly's lungs were terribly weak, that when he came for his bi-monthly treatment, even a day late, they were afraid he would expire before they could get the plasma into him for his muscular dystrophy. His doctor had given him Adderall in place of Prednisone, as he didn't know those last months that Kelly had started smoking and drinking again either. Even though I believe smoking hastened Kelly's death, he is free of pain now, as is Frannie, *and maybe you?*

The primary worry about schizoaffective disorder is the possibility of suicide, when the depression sets in. It was evident throughout much of Kelly's writing. The obituary we put into the paper included words of one of his songs written over twenty years ago, in 1989:

> *Seventh Heaven, Yea, it's not far away*
> *I can already hear the children laugh and play*
> *Walls of gold protect us from all our fear*
> *where all is healed and never a tear.*

Son, wherever you are, I miss you, a caring spot of sunshine in my life, the one who showed love in everything you did, in your beautiful music, your sweet cards and letters, your walking-by hugs at every turn, you were eyes for your dad and hands for me, just a plain joy to have around. As you said so often, you were the one kid that was *there* for us, always, always, and why we had made you sole heir in our will. No one could have been better to their parents — *Where are you, Son? I will never stop looking...*

For years I prayed that somehow you would find peace in your life, *somehow, God,* whatever it would take. But I didn't know that the answer to that prayer would take you *from* us, I didn't know, when I prayed... I can only believe Alex Haley of *Roots,* when he quoted his grandmother, who said: **"God doesn't always come when you call, but He is most surely** *always on time.***"**

Forever loving you, Son.
Mom.♥

ACKNOWLEDGMENTS

After my husband came out of one of his low periods of depression, he said to me, "When you write your next book, will you tell how I went crazy?" This is the story about his struggle, about the process of my own emotional awakening, and a family lost in this maze.

The monumental national interest in the Caylee Anthony death case, the shooting of Gabriel Giffords, Jonbonet Ramsey murder, the killings at Columbine, 9-11 bombing, the Fort Hood shooting, and others, tells us that we as a people have an overwhelming desire to understand. By allowing public scrutiny of such cases, we can see ourselves and how we, in our own lives and families, measure up. Although subjects such as this may appall us, sicken us, may even make us want to be judges, jury, and executioner, we are stricken with the innate horror, that – there by the grace of God go I, or worse, one of my loved ones. Only with compassion wrought from an introspective knowing can we as a society reap any benefit from such terrible events. It is because the continuance of our personal growth and freedom depends upon the choices we make, that I feel the need to share, through fictionalized identities, my family's painful story.

Although murder of flesh and blood is a tangible wrong, murder of the spirit is surely as devastating and too often as final. When dealing with the human condition, there are no absolutes. So many different issues need to be examined, weighed, that when all the evidence is in, one still has difficulty making objective determinations. How, too, can one be objective when it is *you, and yours,* when human beings, through both their internal and external environment, grow and change daily so that it is often difficult to recognize the child you reared, much less the person you *thought you were* while doing it? Harsher than all else is self-judgment. If through truth, I can learn to forgive myself, then I can learn to forgive anyone, anything. The light of truth has within it the liberating power of none other.

In preparing this account through a cumulative study I completed at Lesley. I attempted to understand Family, its structure, and to determine if the development of ours had been, in fact, as unusual as it appears to have been. Because of the nature of my own primary orientation, I came to it, I felt, with little knowledge of "normalcy" for comparison. It was through many writers that I learned and found help: Eric Fromm, *The Art of Loving;* Carl R. Rogers, *On Becoming A Person;* Maya Angelou, *I Know Why The Caged Bird Sings;* Alex Haley, *The Biography of Malcolm X;* Thomas A. Harris, MD, *I'm OK-You're OK;* Alice Miller, *The Drama of the Gifted Child;* Virginia Satir, *Peoplemaking;* Erik H. Erikson, *Childhood and Society;* Kay Redfield Jamison, MD, *An Unquiet Mind;* Ronald R. Fieve, MD. *Moodswing;* J. Fuller Torrey, MD, *Surviving Schizophrenia;* Harriet Wadeson, *Art Psycho-Therapy;* Mic Hunter, *Abused Boys: The Neglected Victims of Sexual Abuse;* John Bradshaw: *The Family;* Manuel J. Smith, Ph.D.; *When I say no, I feel guilty;* Kenneth M. Adams, Ph.D., *Silently Seduced: When Parents Make Their Children Partners-Understanding Covert Incest;* Judith Lewis Herman, M.D. (author of *Father-Daughter Incest*) *Trauma and Recovery: The aftermath of violence-from domestic abuse to political terror.* But it has been my ongoing work with my present counselor and friend, Neuropsychologist, Douglas Col, Ph. D., that has especially helped me to develop the understanding, the courage, and the will to undertake this writing.

Credit for the beginning of change in societal attitudes towards mental illness, and much of the maladaptive behavior we now know as attributable to the brain, should be given, among others, to our former first lady, Rosalynn Carter, for her interest in mental health. Without her attempt and determination during her husband's presidential administration – through the National Institute of Mental Health, and still continuing – to bring this sorely lacking archaic field of treatment out of the closet and into the limelight, this gigantic undertaking might not have found voice. The traditionally high standards this nation enjoys in other related areas of science is now being assimilated into this field. We are already being told that as we have entered this new century, when a newborn leaves the hospital he/she has a greater genetic identification than has ever been possible, which will enable him/her to be parented with more sensitivity, and therefore responsibly. The benefit of such information will no doubt help our children and grandchildren with their choices. For those of us whose lives are/and were hampered unwittingly, and often unknowingly, by a cloud of shame and a quagmire of confusion, there *is* understanding and healing.

Why is it that we can feel the pain of others before we can feel our own?

◆◆

To My Children, Yours...

To have loved you more through heaven or hell
Is not to be questioned -- as time does tell.
Your lives were cherished from morning till night,
Yet somehow I missed a most fateful plight.
With this writing, baring my soul -- before the world,
Our history, bold -- I hope you can see, how we came to be.
My sad soul aches for my first born son. From his primary family,
He did run. Our love he sought from the very start;
His humor showed his loving heart.
How sad I feel he fared so ill, his life to keep, by determined will.
We shunned his voice, his loud refrain
Instead of learning whence he came.
Your little brother, his loyalty tall; years of caring -- warts and all.
His way of life was his to call. No more to fear or dread a fall.
Though years are gone, too late the choices
To remedy deeds by illness forced. Forgiveness given,
Love or not, your futures need the past forgot.
Take heed your loved ones, give them your hearts.
What I gave to you -- keep the better parts.
For all of you, your whole lives through,
I loved you, I loved you – is all I knew.
Mom - 2011

◆◆◆

In the interest of accuracy, using memories, family stories, and some supposition, The *Past As Prologue* (Introduction), is an obvious literary invention, as was Chapter Fourteen: *A New Friend*, which is a compilation of thirty years of therapy with several counselors. Without the professional caring of two psychiatrists, Charles H. Hendry, M.D., Clayton, Georgia, and Guillerma W. Cosma, M.D., Clearwater, Florida, and an unusual female therapist, Marcia Burns, Madeira Beach, Florida, this book could not have been written. It was Dr. Hendry who taught me to trust again; Marcia Burns taught me how to embrace a woman: myself. She encouraged me to "paint my feelings" which produced the ultimate catalyst that broke through my severe repression. Dr. Cosma convinced me I could and should write and inspired the therapy scene. Dr. Jean

Hendricks, psychologist and university dean: Mercer-Atlanta, made me believe in my own intellect. My writer's group, Medfield, Massachusetts, taught me to write. But it was the women in this group, especially Sally Adams and Claire Reed, who encouraged me the most, by just loving me.

◆◆◆

BIOGRAPHY

L. L. Morton was born in Obion County, Tennessee, but grew up in Milwaukee, Wisconsin. Although she dropped out of high school in the 50's, in 1971 she and her first child received their diplomas together in Carlisle, Pennsylvania – where she went on to Shippensburg State College. Finally a graduate of Lesley College, Cambridge, Massachusetts (now Lesley University) Morton received her BAL degree in writing at the age of fifty-seven. Her first major literary work was published in 1992 as a fictionalized autobiography under the title, *A Make Believe Face,* now updated and revised as memoir: *First Comes Love: The DeProgramming of An Army Wife*. Her collection of short pieces of mixed genre, *Love 'N' Stuff, was* just released 2011. As a career Army Officer's wife, Morton traveled extensively and lived in both Japan and Thailand. While in Bangkok, she taught English as a second language to the Thais. The mother of four children, the grandmother of six and the great-grandmother of three, Morton presently lives with her husband of over fifty-five years in Southern Oregon.

◆